GREAT EVENTS FROM HISTORY
NORTH AMERICAN SERIES

GREAT EVENTS FROM HISTORY
NORTH AMERICAN SERIES

Revised Edition

Volume 4

1956 – 1996
Indexes

Edited by
FRANK N. MAGILL

Associate Editor
JOHN L. LOOS

Managing Editor, Revised Edition
CHRISTINA J. MOOSE

Salem Press, Inc.
Pasadena, California   Englewood Cliffs, N.J.

Editor in Chief:	Dawn P. Dawson
Managing Editor:	Christina J. Moose
Acquisitions Editor:	Mark Rehn
Manuscript Editor:	Irene Struthers
Research Supervisor:	Jeffry Jensen
Research Assistant:	Irene McDermott
Photograph Editor:	Valerie Krein
Proofreading Supervisor:	Yasmine A. Cordoba
Map Design and Page Layout:	James Hutson
Data Entry:	William Zimmerman

Library of Congress Cataloging-in-Publication Data

Great events from history : North American series / edited by Frank N. Magill ; associate editor, John L. Loos.
   — Rev. ed.
      p.   cm.
   Includes bibliographical references (p.   ) and index.
   ISBN 0-89356-429-X (set). — ISBN 0-89356-433-8 (vol. 4)
   1. North America—History. 2. United States—History. I. Magill, Frank Northen, 1907-   . II. Loos, John L.
E45.G74   1997
970—dc21   96-39165
                                                                                              CIP

First Printing

CONTENTS

LIST OF MAPS

GREAT EVENTS FROM HISTORY
NORTH AMERICAN SERIES

1956 ■ CUBAN REVOLUTION: *a successful attempt to overthrow a corrupt regime institutes land reform, socialism, and a new dictatorship that threatens U.S. interests*

DATE: July 26, 1956-January 8, 1959

LOCALE: Cuba

CATEGORIES: Diplomacy and international relations; Latino American history; Wars, uprisings, and civil unrest

KEY FIGURES:

Fulgencio Batista y Zaldívar (1901-1973), president of Cuba, 1940-1944 and 1952-1959

Fidel Castro (born 1926 or 1927), leader of the Cuban Revolution

Dwight David Eisenhower (1890-1969), president of the United States, 1953-1961

John Fitzgerald Kennedy (1917-1963), president of the United States, 1961-1963

Nikita Sergeyevich Khrushchev (1894-1971), premier of the Soviet Union, 1958-1964

SUMMARY OF EVENT. The Cuban Revolution of 1956-1959, led by Fidel Castro and culminating in the consolidation of the first Communist government in the Western Hemisphere, came as a profound shock to most Americans. Few countries in the world have had their history more closely intertwined with the United States than Cuba. Located ninety miles from the Florida shores, and therefore of great strategic importance to foreign powers, Cuba first aroused U.S. interest at the start of the nineteenth century, when the administration of Thomas Jefferson expressed a desire to buy the island from Spain. The 1898 Spanish-American War, in which the United States intervened on the side of the Cuban rebels, resulted in the occupation of Cuba by the U.S. Army. The U.S. Congress granted Cuba independence in 1902, but the sovereignty of the new Cuban republic was restricted severely by the so-called Platt Amendment to the Cuban Constitution, which guaranteed the United States the right of military intervention and permanent ownership of the Guantanamo Bay naval base. U.S. economic influence in Cuba was protected as well. As a consequence of favorable tariff and customs treaties, U.S. business came to dominate many areas of the Cuban economy, notably the sugar industry, in which Cuba was assigned an annual quota of the U.S. market. This strong North American presence on the island provided the basis for a visceral Cuban nationalism that helps to explain the clash between the Castro revolution and the United States.

Castro's original goals were not explicitly hostile to the U.S. government. When on July 26, 1953, he launched his rebellion to overthrow the dictator Fulgencio Batista, Castro had promised to restore constitutional civilian rule, hold free elections, and respect foreign property in Cuba. Through interviews with the U.S. media, Castro expressed a desire for continued good relations between the two countries. The administration of President Dwight D. Eisenhower, repelled by Batista's repeated violations of human rights, placed an arms embargo on Cuba in 1958, signaling to Castro that the United States would not actively intervene to save the dictatorship.

The triumph of the Cuban Revolution in January, 1959, made it evident, however, that Castro's political and economic program was not compatible with U.S. interests. The execution of several hundred soldiers and policemen who had served Batista and the incarceration of thousands of political supporters of the old regime caused an angry outcry in the U.S. media. Castro's assumption of the premiership of the revolutionary government in February, with near-absolute powers, led the State Department to accuse him of betraying his promise to the Cuban people that he would restore democracy. His appointment of Communist Party members to key ministries seemed to confirm to the U.S. government that Cuba was drifting away from its traditional alliance with the United States. The flight of thousands of Cubans to Florida, and Castro's accusation that the U.S. government was harboring counterrevolutionaries bent on the overthrow of his regime, doomed any chance of reconciliation.

The economic reforms launched by Castro further strained relations with the United States. Laws limiting the size of rural and urban property resulted in the expropriation of United States-owned sugar estates without compensation to their owners. U.S. investments in Cuba's railroad, telephone, telegraph, electricity, and mining sectors were also nationalized. The swank American-owned hotels along Havana's shoreline were turned over to the state. Two years after the revolution, nearly all U.S. property in Cuba, estimated by the State Department at a value of one billion dollars, had passed into the hands of the Cuban government.

Cuban foreign policy underwent a radical shift in the first year of the revolution. The revolutionary government expressed solidarity for rebel forces plotting to oust pro-U.S. regimes in the rest of Latin America, and it sent supplies and Cuban advisers to guerrilla fighters in the Caribbean and Central America. Diplomatic and commercial relations were restored or established with the Soviet Bloc countries and China. The Cuban leader also announced that Cuba no longer felt bound by military treaties signed in the past with the United States and would buy arms and strategic goods from whichever nation would provide them. In June of 1960, the Cuban government seized U.S. petroleum companies that had refused to process Soviet crude oil coming to Cuba. The Eisenhower Administration responded by cutting off the Cuban sugar quota and secretly preparing an invasion of the island by Cuban exiles trained in Guatemala by the Central Intelligence Agency (CIA). That December, Castro gained a pledge from Soviet premier Nikita Khrushchev to support Cuban independence in case of aggression from the United States. On January 2, 1961, Castro called on the United States to reduce the size of its diplomatic mission in Havana, which he accused of espionage activities. The United States broke off diplomatic relations with Cuba the next day and stepped up sabotage and covert aerial bombings of Cuban military facilities.

CASTRO'S CUBAN REVOLUTION

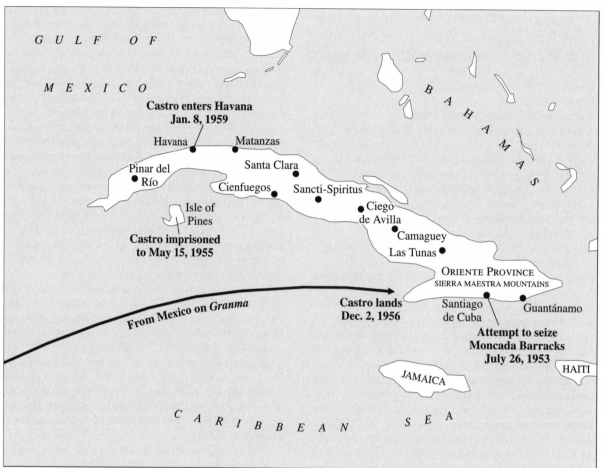

John F. Kennedy was even more committed than Eisenhower had been to reversing the Cuban Revolution and preventing the loss of Cuba to the Soviets. When he took office as president on January 20, 1961, Kennedy substantially altered the nature of the planned exile invasion. Whereas Eisenhower had instructed the CIA to train a small guerrilla army to infiltrate Cuba and harass Castro's military, the Kennedy Administration mobilized a full-scale brigade to land at the Bay of Pigs on the southern end of the island and form the nucleus of a counterrevolutionary government backed by the United States. The invasion, launched in April of 1960, was doomed by bad planning, infighting among the exiles, and the failure of the Cuban people to rise up against Castro as the CIA had predicted. Castro used the defeat of the exile brigade as the occasion for his proclamation of the revolution as socialist. He then signed a treaty with the Soviet Union to protect the island from any future invasion through the installation of Russian nuclear missiles in Cuba. The United States, by attacking Castro, had brought about what it wanted to most avoid: the implantation of a Communist regime and Soviet ally ninety miles from the U.S. mainland.

The Cuban Revolution profoundly altered U.S. foreign policy toward Latin America. The fear of a "second Cuba" appearing in the Western Hemisphere led to the U.S. invasion of the Dominican Republic in 1965 and U.S. covert operations against Marxist regimes in Chile and Nicaragua in the 1970's. The U.S. government also tried to undermine Castro's appeal to the rest of Latin America by channeling massive amounts of economic aid to the region through the Alliance for Progress, launched by Kennedy in 1961. A complicating factor in the U.S. response to the Cuban Revolution was the presence in the United States after 1959 of hundreds of thousands of Cuban refugees who had been granted political asylum. They went on to transform Miami into a thriving financial center linking North and South America, and were hostile to any rapprochement between Washington and Havana, which limited the ability of the United States to offer Castro any incentive to abandon his commitment to socialism.   —*Julio César Pino*

ADDITIONAL READING:

Domínguez, Jorge I. *Cuba: Order and Revolution.* Cambridge, Mass.: The Belknap Press of Harvard University Press, 1978. A Cuban American political scientist examines the breakdown of the Cuban political system after independence and the internal factors that led to revolution.

Mazarr, Michael J. *Semper Fidel: America and Cuba, 1776-1988.* Baltimore, Md.: Nautical & Aviation Publishing Company of America, 1988. Good discussion of Cuba as an issue in U.S. politics.

Morley, Morris H. *Imperial State and Revolution: The United States and Cuba, 1952-1986.* Cambridge, Mass.: Cambridge University Press, 1987. A Marxist analysis of the formulation and implementation of the U.S. effort to reverse the Cuban Revolution. Valuable for its use of U.S. government documents that reveal the covert war against Castro.

Paterson, Thomas J. *Contesting Castro: The United States and the Triumph of the Cuban Revolution.* New York: Oxford University Press, 1994. Discusses how the Eisenhower Administration's early embrace of Batista legitimized Castro's violent anti-Americanism. Presents a strong case that the rift between Cuba and the United States was not inevitable.

Thomas, Hugh. *Cuba: Or, The Pursuit of Freedom.* New York: Harper & Row, 1971. An encyclopedic look at Cuban history from the eighteenth century to the 1960's. Stresses Cuba's continual dependence on foreign patrons as the key to understanding political developments on the island.

Welch, Richard E., Jr. *Response to Revolution: The United States and the Cuban Revolution, 1959-1961.* Chapel Hill: University of North Carolina Press, 1985. Argues that given Castro's radicalism, the Cuban Revolution would have turned socialist regardless of the U.S. response, but that U.S. policy facilitated Castro's decision to align Cuba with the Soviet Union. Valuable treatment of the U.S. media, academia, and the political left in their appraisal of Castro.

SEE ALSO: 1900, Suppression of Yellow Fever; 1903, Platt Amendment; 1933, Good Neighbor Policy; 1961, Bay of Pigs Invasion; 1962, Cuban Missile Crisis; 1980, Mariel Boat Lift; 1980, Miami Riots.

1957 ■ EISENHOWER DOCTRINE: *a bipartisan foreign policy initiative articulates the U.S. effort to combat "international communism" in the Middle East*

DATE: January 5, 1957
LOCALE: Washington, D.C.
CATEGORY: Diplomacy and international relations
KEY FIGURES:

Camille Chamoun (1900-1987), president of Lebanon
John Foster Dulles (1888-1959), U.S. secretary of state
Dwight David Eisenhower (1890-1969), thirty-fourth president of the United States, 1953-1961
Robert M. McClintock (1909-1976), U.S. ambassador to Lebanon
Robert Daniel Murphy (1894-1978), U.S. deputy undersecretary of state

Gamal Abdel Nasser (1918-1970), president of Egypt
James P. Richards (1894-1974), special envoy to the Middle East
Fuad Shehab (1902-1973), commander of the Lebanese army and later president of Lebanon

SUMMARY OF EVENT. In the aftermath of the Suez crisis of October, 1956, which created a power vacuum in the Middle East as a result of Great Britain's and France's invasion of Egypt, the United States government reconsidered its position and policies in the Middle East. Acting through the United Nations, and for once in agreement with the Soviet Union, the United States had brought about the withdrawal of British and French forces from Egypt. The entire episode seemed not only to have weakened Western unity but also to have strengthened the position of the Soviet Union in the Arab countries and that of Gamal Abdel Nasser, the Egyptian president, as the leading spokesman of Arab nationalist feeling. Nasser envisioned himself to be the "voice of the Arabs," and his resisting the West and allying himself increasingly with the Soviet Union caused the United States to fear instability in the oil-rich and strategically located region. The Eisenhower Administration saw a vacuum in the Middle East, which it feared would be filled by Soviet influence. President Dwight D. Eisenhower, therefore, offered a statement of policy, which became known as the Eisenhower Doctrine.

Issued as a message to Congress on January 5, 1957, after consultation with congressional leaders and with Dag Hammarskjöld, the secretary general of the United Nations, the doctrine proposed that the United States fill the vacuum with economic and military aid. Eisenhower asked the new Eighty-fifth Congress to appropriate four hundred million dollars for two years for economic and military assistance to the nations of the Middle East, and to authorize the use of U.S. forces upon the request of any nation in the region threatened by communist aggression. Eisenhower appointed James P. Richards, the recently retired Democratic chair of the House Foreign Affairs Committee, to be his personal envoy to the Middle East. Richards' mission was clear: He was to explain the evils of international communism, solicit support from the region's leaders, and dispense aid to countries that publicly announced their loyalty to the West. Besides the provision of assistance, one purpose of the presidential request to Congress was to give the Soviet Union warning of U.S. intentions to prevent Soviet expansion in the Middle East and to make clear and public the national support for those intentions.

In some respects, the Eisenhower Doctrine followed the precedents of the Truman Doctrine of 1947 and the Formosa Resolution passed by Congress in 1955. It differed, however, from the Truman Doctrine in its application to a particular area; the Truman Doctrine, although occasioned by problems of Greece and Turkey, was a promise of U.S. support for any peoples resisting aggression. Moreover, neither earlier proposal carried the proviso that armed forces be sent only on the request of the other nation.

The House resolution on behalf of the president's request, introduced the same day, was approved by the Foreign Affairs Committee by a vote of 24 to 2 on January 24, and by the entire House on January 31 by a vote of 355 to 61. Senate action was slower. In debates in early March, Senator Richard Russell of Georgia proposed an amendment that would have deleted the military and economic assistance, but the amendment lost. A proposal by Senator J. William Fulbright of Arkansas for a white paper from the State Department detailing U.S. relations with the region also failed. The Senate passed the resolution, with some limiting changes, on March 5, by a vote of 72 to 19; the House accepted the Senate version on March 7, by 350 to 60; the president signed it on March 9, 1957.

The announcement of the doctrine met mixed reactions. The votes in the Congress were probably indicative of general support; they are notable because of the fact that the Democratic Party had majorities in both houses. The public trust in President Eisenhower, so recently reelected, was one factor; the general mood of the Cold War was another. Additionally, the selection of Richards to go to the Middle East as the administration's chief envoy helped solidify bipartisan support for the initiative.

Reactions abroad were less favorable. Denunciations from Moscow and Peking were expected; Prime Minister Jawaharlal Nehru of India thought the dangers of aggression were exaggerated and believed that the interests of peace were not forwarded by the U.S. action. The Arab states, led by Egypt, also reacted unfavorably. A mission led by Richards in the spring of 1957 did not even visit Egypt, Syria, or Jordan. Lebanon, Israel, Iraq, and Iran endorsed the policy, but other Middle Eastern countries, such as Afghanistan and Libya, were lukewarm. Richards was briefly held hostage in Yemen when he refused to award that country enough economic assistance to persuade the small nation to oppose agents of international communism. Lebanon's history and situation explain both its acceptance and its later application of the Eisenhower Doctrine to that country. Alone among the Arab countries, which were overwhelmingly Muslim, Lebanon had a large Christian population; in the absence of accurate statistics, estimates place it near a majority. The ties to Rome of the majority of these (Maronites and other Catholics of non-Latin rites), the U.S. Protestant missionary and educational effort since the early nineteenth century, and the experience of French rule or mandate gave Lebanon a view of the West and a relation to it different from that of the other Arab nations. Independent Lebanon had developed political and social traditions of its own to deal with religious differences. The most notable example was the tradition that the president be a Christian, the prime minister a Muslim. Under the surface, however, religious and regional hostilities were often bitter. These international strains were increased and intensified by Arab feeling inflamed against Israel and by Nasserism—the extreme Arab movement toward unity and belligerence intimately associated with Egypt's leader. The

immediate occasion of trouble in Lebanon was the possibility that President Camille Chamoun intended to have his term extended, contrary to the Lebanese constitution. Opposition forces organized against this move— some religious, some political opponents of Chamoun, some supported by Syrian and Egyptian interests. Civil strife on this issue broke out in May, 1958.

Just as this turmoil in Lebanon seemed to be subsiding, an unexpected crisis erupted in Iraq. On July 14, 1958, a bloody revolution overthrew the pro-Western Iraqi government. President Chamoun appealed to the United States out of fear that the coup in Iraq was the result of a Soviet-Nasserite plot that would soon be reenacted in Lebanon. On July 15, on the orders of President Eisenhower, units of the Sixth Fleet landed United States Marines in Lebanon to preserve order. With the aid of Robert McClintock, the United States ambassador, the U.S. troops were kept in positions where they did not affect the local political situation. Robert Murphy, U.S. deputy undersecretary of state and an experienced diplomat, worked with the differing Lebanese forces to achieve settlement.

Whatever ambition he had entertained, Chamoun now gave up any intention of another term. With some difficulty, the negotiators persuaded General Fuad Shehab to accept the Lebanese presidency, to which he was elected by Lebanon's parliament on July 31. As commander of the army, Shehab had tried to maintain an impartial position, and he was one of the few people acceptable to almost all factions.

The exercise of the Eisenhower Doctrine thus resulted in accommodation. The Marines were withdrawn on October 25, 1958. This diplomatic effort represents the United States' Cold War approach to foreign policy. Egypt's coziness with the Soviet Union and Nasser's vibrant nationalistic rhetoric alarmed the United States and led to Richards' mission and the United States' later presence in Lebanon.

—*George J. Fleming, updated by Joseph Edward Lee*

ADDITIONAL READING:

Ambrose, Stephen. *Eisenhower*. New York: Simon & Schuster, 1984. Part of a two-volume biography of the president's military and political career.

Hooper, Townshend. *The Devil and John Foster Dulles.* Boston: Little, Brown, 1973. A sharp analysis of the Eisenhower Administration's obsession with agents of international communism.

Nutting, Anthony. *Nasser.* New York: Random House, 1972. A good biography of the Egyptian leader who smoothly navigated the waters between the Soviet Union and the United States.

Paterson, Thomas G., et al. *American Foreign Policy: A History.* Lexington, Mass.: McGraw-Hill, 1977. The best general overview of the rationale behind Cold War initiatives such as the Eisenhower Doctrine.

SEE ALSO: 1947, Truman Doctrine; 1952, Eisenhower Is Elected President; 1955, Formosa Resolution; 1973, Arab Oil Embargo and Energy Crisis; 1991, Persian Gulf War.

1957 ■ SOUTHERN CHRISTIAN LEADERSHIP CONFERENCE IS FOUNDED: *birth of a leading force in the nonviolent direct action movement*

DATE: February 14, 1957
LOCALE: Atlanta, Georgia
CATEGORIES: African American history; Civil rights; Organizations and institutions
KEY FIGURES:

Ralph David Abernathy (born 1926), Martin Luther King, Jr.'s closest friend and chief adviser

Eugene "Bull" Connor (1897-1973), Birmingham, Alabama, police chief

Dwight D. Eisenhower (1890-1969), thirty-fourth president of the United States, 1953-1961

Jesse Jackson (born 1941), associate of King

Martin Luther King, Jr. (1929-1968), leader of the SCLC

Rosa Parks (born 1913), seamstress who started the Montgomery bus boycott

Charles Kenzie Steele (1914-1980), minister who called the meeting at which the SCLC was established

Andrew Young (born 1932), King associate and Georgia politician

SUMMARY OF EVENT. The Southern Christian Leadership Conference (SCLC), organized on February 14, 1957, in Atlanta's Ebenezer Baptist Church, quickly became one of the nation's premier civil rights organizations. The SCLC grew out of the 1955-1956 Montgomery bus boycott and the emergence of Martin Luther King, Jr., as the leader of that protest and a new face on the national political scene.

When Rosa Parks, an African American seamstress from Montgomery, Alabama, refused to give up her seat on a bus to a white passenger, her arrest triggered one of the most successful nonviolent protests in the annals of the Civil Rights movement. King, only twenty-six years of age and a new resident of Montgomery, was selected to lead the boycott. King and other protesters created the Montgomery Improvement Association (MIA) to negotiate with the city of Montgomery and determine strategy for the protesters. After more than eleven months, during which protestors walked rather than riding the buses, the MIA and King won a major victory: The Supreme Court affirmed a lower court decision outlawing segregation on Montgomery's buses. King's leadership of the bus boycott transformed him from a local leader into a major national political figure.

Shortly after the Supreme Court's decision, the Reverend Charles Steele of Tallahassee, Florida, called for a conference of civil rights ministers in Atlanta on January 10 and 11, 1957. The ministers established the Southern Leadership Conference on Transportation and Non-violent Integration. Their first project was to ask President Dwight D. Eisenhower to urge compliance with Supreme Court decisions ending segregation in transportation. They also asked Vice President Richard Nixon

to tour the South to monitor compliance with the Court's decision. Neither Eisenhower nor Nixon complied with these requests.

In February, 1957, the organization was called the Southern Negro Leadership Conference; later, the name Southern Christian Leadership Conference was adopted. The name of the organization is important. "Southern" reflected the founders' intention to concentrate their efforts in the states of the old Confederacy. The word "Christian" was added for several reasons. First, most of the SCLC's founders were ministers and wanted the SCLC to be guided by Christian principles. Second and more important, SCLC members hoped that the word "Christian" would make the organization more acceptable in the South and less subject to charges of radicalism.

The SCLC's organizational structure was substantially different from that of the National Association for the Advancement of Colored People (NAACP), the oldest, largest, and most influential civil rights organization of the time. Unlike the NAACP, which had individual memberships—numbering at one time more than half a million—the SCLC used affiliate memberships. The SCLC had as many as 275 affiliates, although in most cases, the affiliates were local Baptist churches. Each affiliate paid twenty-five dollars to SCLC and had the right to send five delegates to the annual convention.

The goal of SCLC was full citizenship and integration for African Americans into American life. Civil disobedience was a key component in achieving its objectives. King urged his supporters to obey just laws, but not unjust laws. According to King, an unjust law is a law out of harmony with moral law or the law of God, a law that the minority, but not the majority, is required to obey, and a law that people have no part in making because they were denied the right to vote.

The SCLC undertook major campaigns in Albany, Georgia (1961-1962), Birmingham, Alabama (1963), St. Augustine, Florida (1964), and Selma, Alabama (1965). These campaigns met with varying degrees of success and criticism. In Albany, the SCLC's activities failed to bring about any real change when their nonviolent protests were met by nonviolent arrests by local police. National attention was focused on Birmingham, Alabama, when Police Chief Eugene "Bull" Connor turned police dogs and fire hoses loose on demonstrators. King was criticized for using children in his marches and for defying a court order not to march. After being arrested, King wrote his famous "Letter from Birmingham Jail," in which he outlined his views on civil disobedience and unjust laws. The Selma campaign was a major success, in that it achieved its objective of forcing Congress to pass the Voting Rights Act of 1965, the most powerful voting rights legislation ever passed. The Selma victory came at a high cost. Many protesters were brutally assaulted during the Selma-to-Montgomery march, and three demonstrators were killed.

Many considered the Selma campaign to be the zenith of the Civil Rights movement and the beginning of the end of the movement. Congress had responded to racial oppression by passing civil rights acts in 1957, 1960, and 1964, as well as the

1965 Voting Rights Act. Many white citizens believed that the federal government was moving too fast in the area of civil rights, and a "white backlash" was becoming a reality.

After Selma, King made two strategic decisions that affected the future of the SCLC. First, he decided to take the Civil Rights movement out of the South and into Chicago. King believed the problem of Northern, urban, poverty-stricken African Americans was the next major battleground. King's campaign to get the Chicago city council to pass an open housing law resulted in violent confrontations with urban whites. King and the SCLC achieved a hollow victory when the Chicago city council made commitments but reneged once King left town.

King became the first prominent civil rights leader to speak out against U.S. involvement in Vietnam. He opposed the U.S. role on moral grounds and also believed that the government was diverting hundreds of millions of dollars away from needed domestic projects. His opposition to the Vietnam War enraged President Lyndon Johnson and made King an outcast at the White House.

The last major demonstration that King directed was the Poor People's Campaign. King wanted to mobilize poor blacks and poor whites to march throughout the South to Washington, D.C., and pressure Congress to pass an Economic Bill of Rights that promised jobs to all Americans, as well as a guaranteed income. Before King was able to start the Poor People's Campaign, he was assassinated on April 4, 1968, in Memphis, Tennessee, where he had gone to speak at a strike of Memphis sanitation workers.

The Reverend Ralph David Abernathy, King's close friend and associate since the Montgomery bus boycott, took over as director of the SCLC and carried out the Poor People's Campaign, although with little success. Other of King's associates in the SCLC launched their own careers in public service. Andrew Young left the SCLC in 1970 to run for elective office. Elected to Congress in 1972 and 1974 from an Atlanta congressional district, he later served as U.S. Ambassador to the United Nations in the administration of President Jimmy Carter. In 1981, Young was elected as Atlanta's mayor. Another King lieutenant, Jesse Jackson, became a national figure with his Rainbow Coalition and his 1984 and 1988 presidential campaigns.

To a great extent, the SCLC was Martin Luther King, Jr., and when King died, the organization's role was diminished. However, the SCLC would go on to sponsor projects, such as Operation Breadbasket, to improve opportunities for African Americans.   —Darryl Paulson

ADDITIONAL READING:

Abernathy, Ralph David. *And the Walls Came Tumbling Down*. New York: Harper & Row, 1989. King's closest friend and trusted adviser provides an insider's view on King and the SCLC.

Branch, Taylor. *Parting the Waters: America in the King Years, 1954-1963*. New York: Simon & Schuster, 1988. Profiles King's first decade on the national political scene.

Fairclough, Adam. *To Redeem the Soul of America: The Southern Christian Leadership Conference and Martin Luther King, Jr.* Athens: University of Georgia Press, 1987. Explains how the SCLC succeeded in spite of limited money and workforce.

Garrow, David. *Bearing the Cross: Martin Luther King, Jr., and the Southern Christian Leadership Conference*. New York: Marrow, 1986. Based on seven hundred interviews and thousands of government documents, this is the most detailed study of King's life to date.

Lewis, David L. *King: A Biography*. Urbana: University of Illinois Press, 1978. A highly readable narrative of King's life and philosophy.

Oates, Steven B. *Let the Trumpets Sound: The Life of Martin Luther King, Jr.* New York: Harper & Row, 1982. A famous historian and biographer brings King's struggle to life.

SEE ALSO: 1909, National Association for the Advancement of Colored People Is Founded; 1942, Congress of Racial Equality Is Founded; 1955, Montgomery Bus Boycott; 1957, Little Rock School Desegregation Crisis; 1960, Civil Rights Act of 1960; 1962, Meredith Registers at "Ole Miss"; 1963, King Delivers His "I Have a Dream" Speech; 1964, Twenty-fourth Amendment; 1964, Civil Rights Act of 1964; 1965, Assassination of Malcolm X; 1965, Voting Rights Act; 1965, Expansion of Affirmative Action; 1967, Long, Hot Summer; 1968, Assassinations of King and Kennedy.

1957 ■ DIEFENBAKER ERA IN CANADA: *the Conservative prime minister ushers in an era of tension with the United States, limiting U.S. imports and rejecting nuclear weapons*

DATE: June 10, 1957-February 5, 1963
LOCALE: Ottawa, Ontario, Canada
CATEGORIES: Canadian history; Government and politics
KEY FIGURES:
John George Diefenbaker (1895-1979), thirteenth prime minister of Canada
Douglas Harkness (born 1903), minister for national defense
Vincent Massey (1887-1967), governor general of Canada during the Diefenbaker era
Lester Bowles Pearson (1897-1972), Liberal Party leader of the opposition during most of Diefenbaker's term

SUMMARY OF EVENT. John George Diefenbaker, a populist lawyer from Prince Albert, Saskatchewan, was chosen as the new leader of the Progressive Conservative Party of Canada at the party's convention in Ottawa, Ontario, on December 14, 1956. At the time, many Canadians were becoming concerned over the increasing control corporations from the United States exercised over Canadian businesses. In the spring of 1956, the minister of trade in the Liberal government, Clarence Decatur Howe, proposed that the Canadian government lend eighty million dollars to Trans-Canada Pipelines Limited, a privately owned company controlled by U.S. financial interests, for the construction of a trans-Canada pipeline. Diefenbaker spoke out against the "bludgeoning" of the Parliament, as the Liberal leadership had severely restricted debate on the pipeline measure, and the sellout of Canadian interests to U.S. big business. During the campaign, Diefenbaker promised he would try to increase the proportion of domestic ownership of Canadian enterprises; shift Canadian imports away from the United States and toward the United Kingdom; and increase the amount of interprovincial trade, shifting from the historic pattern of provinces trading with nearby regions of the United States.

The Liberal Party had governed Canada for the previous twenty-two years, winning five consecutive national elections. During this period, Canada had been prosperous, benefiting from the industrial growth driven by the demands of World War II and the lack of European competition in international markets during the immediate postwar years. By the mid-1950's, European industry was rebuilding, and Canada had more serious competition in the international marketplace. Diefenbaker charged that although the nation had prospered under Liberal leadership, some regions, notably the Atlantic Provinces (Nova Scotia, New Brunswick, Prince Edward Island, and Newfoundland) and the Prairie Provinces (Saskatchewan, Manitoba, and Alberta), had not shared equally in the economic growth.

On June 10, 1957, 6.6 million Canadians voted in a general election that gave Diefenbaker's Progressive Conservatives 38 percent of the vote, and sent 111 Progressive Conservatives to the 265-member House of Commons. Although Progressive Conservatives outnumbered Liberals, who won 106 seats, the former had to make an alliance with smaller parties to assume control of the government. That working majority quickly fell apart, as the Liberals attacked with forecasts of higher unemployment and a worsening economy. On February 1, 1958, Diefenbaker asked Governor General Vincent Massey to dissolve Parliament and call new elections.

Diefenbaker pointed out that Canada's vast natural resources gave it the capacity to play a major role in North America and the world. He appealed for a clear majority, and the Canadian people responded in the March 31, 1958 election, giving the Progressive Conservative Party the largest majority in Canadian history, with 208 of the 265 seats in the House of Commons.

Throughout his term, Diefenbaker took a strong stand on human rights, both at home and abroad. On July 1, 1960, he secured Parliamentary passage of a Bill of Rights. However, this Bill of Rights emphasized the rights of individuals, much to the dismay of French Canadians, who were interested in protection as a distinct cultural group. Support for the Progressive Conservative Party declined in Quebec, the province with the largest French-speaking population.

At the meeting of Commonwealth prime ministers in 1961, Diefenbaker argued that the Commonwealth of Nations should recognize the principle of nondiscrimination on the basis of color or race. His insistence, coupled with similar demands from the prime minister of India, resulted in the withdrawal of South Africa's application for continued membership in the Commonwealth.

Under Diefenbaker, the Canadian economic and social system was redesigned. Diefenbaker's concept of social justice was based on "the principle that public money should be used to relieve distress on the basis of need," establishing the idea that individual Canadians had a right or entitlement to financial help from their fellow citizens. Social welfare payments increased from $885 million in 1957 to $1.97 billion in 1962; by 1960, about 80 percent of the Canadian population was receiving some form of government aid. An extension of Diefenbaker's philosophy of social justice was his belief that Canada should make a particular effort to equalize economic opportunities throughout the country by promoting economic growth in the two poorest regions, the Atlantic provinces and the prairies.

As part of his effort to spread economic growth to the prairie provinces, Diefenbaker entered into negotiations that opened up the large market of communist China to Canadian wheat. At this time, U.S. law prohibited trade with communist China, and Diefenbaker's wheat sales represented a clear foreign policy difference with the United States. At the time, the Atlantic provinces traded mostly with the New England region of the United States. Diefenbaker hoped to encourage more east-west trade between the Canadian provinces. Under Diefenbaker, the economic situation in the Atlantic provinces improved, but the historical pattern of trade with New England did not diminish, and the people in the Atlantic provinces remained significantly poorer than the national average.

Although Diefenbaker had promised to decrease both imports from the United States and foreign control of Canadian corporations, imports from the United States grew faster than imports from the United Kingdom during the Diefenbaker era, and ownership of Canadian enterprises by foreign interests also increased.

After fourteen years of negotiations, the Diefenbaker government concluded an agreement with the United States on how the hydroelectric power potential of the Columbia River would be shared. Signed by Diefenbaker and U.S. president Dwight D. Eisenhower on January 17, 1961, this agreement provided for the construction of three storage dams on the Canadian side of the border, with the initial power production on the U.S. side. The United States agreed to deliver half the electric power back to Canada. However, the Diefenbaker government fell before the Columbia River treaty could come up for debate in Parliament, and a revised agreement was not approved until 1964, after he had left office.

On August 1, 1957, the Diefenbaker government accepted the North American Air Defense Agreement, negotiated in part by the previous Liberal government. This agreement established the North American Air Defense Command, by integrating the air defenses of Canada and the United States under a U.S. commander and a Canadian second-in-command. Part of the plan for North American defense called for the installation of nuclear weapons in Canada: nuclear-tipped Bomarc air-defense missiles to be operated by Canadian forces, nuclear weapons for interceptor aircraft based in Labrador and Newfoundland, and nuclear bombs for U.S. Strategic Air Command bombers based at Goose Bay, Labrador. The United States Atomic Energy Act required that custody of these nuclear weapons remain in U.S. hands, while control over their use could be shared by the two governments.

By 1960, the disarmament movement was gaining support in Canada, and opposition to deployment of nuclear weapons in Canada increased. During President John F. Kennedy's visit to Ottawa in May, 1961, Diefenbaker indicated to the president that he was unwilling to accept the introduction of nuclear weapons onto Canadian soil at that time. When construction of the Bomarc launch sites was completed in 1962, Diefenbaker delayed introduction of the warheads. Relations between the United States and Canada deteriorated as the U.S. Department of State took the unusual step of issuing a press release attacking some of Diefenbaker's public statements on the nuclear weapons controversy. Diefenbaker refused to change his position, prompting Douglas Harkness, Canada's minister for national defense, to resign. This brought about a no-confidence vote in Parliament, leading to the defeat of the Diefenbaker government on February 5, 1963.

Diefenbaker attempted to appeal to Canadian nationalism in his reelection campaign, decrying U.S. interference in the Canadian government's decision on nuclear weapons and saying that his Liberal Party opponent, Lester Pearson, who had endorsed acceptance of nuclear weapons, would make Canada "a decoy duck in a nuclear war." However, Diefenbaker's Progressive Conservative Party was defeated in the 1963 general election, returning only ninety-five members to the House of Commons. —George J. Flynn

ADDITIONAL READING:

Johnston, James. *The Party's Over*. Don Mills, Ont.: Longman Canada, 1971. An inside account of the Diefenbaker years, written by the national director of the Progressive Conservative Party, providing insight into the prime minister's thinking.

Newman, Peter C. *Renegade in Power: The Diefenbaker Years*. Toronto: McClelland and Stewart, 1963. A detailed history of the Diefenbaker era by a journalist who covered Canadian politics.

Robinson, H. Basil. *Diefenbaker's World: A Populist in Foreign Affairs*. Toronto: University of Toronto Press, 1989. An account of Canada's role in foreign affairs, including the controversy over accepting nuclear weapons, during the Diefenbaker era.

Stursberg, Peter. *Diefenbaker: Leadership Gained 1956-1962*. Toronto: University of Toronto Press, 1975. An oral history comprising the recollections of many of Diefenbaker's associates.

SEE ALSO: 1948, St. Laurent Succeeds King; 1952, Massey Becomes Canada's First Native-Born Governor General; 1960, Quebec Sovereignist Movement; 1963, Pearson Becomes Canada's Prime Minister.

1957 ■ LITTLE ROCK SCHOOL DESEGREGATION CRISIS: *in the wake of* Brown v. Board of Education, *attempts to desegregate a public school meet with white protests, leading to a confrontation between state and federal government*

DATE: September 2-25, 1957
LOCALE: Little Rock, Arkansas
CATEGORIES: African American history; Civil rights; Education
KEY FIGURES:

Daisy Bates (born 1920), president of the Arkansas chapter of the National Association for the Advancement of Colored People (NAACP)

Virgil T. Blossom, superintendent of schools in Little Rock

Dwight David Eisenhower (1890-1969), thirty-fourth president of the United States, 1953-1961

Orval E. Faubus (1910-1994), governor of Arkansas

Ernest Green, first African American student to graduate from Central High School

Brooks Hays (1898-1981), representative from Arkansas who attempted to mediate between Eisenhower and Faubus

SUMMARY OF EVENT. The United States Supreme Court, in the case of *Brown v. Board of Education of Topeka, Kansas* (1954), declared racial segregation in tax-supported schools to be unconstitutional. It further ordered that the process of desegregation proceed with "all deliberate speed," under the supervision of the federal courts. In response, the school board of Little Rock prepared, and in May, 1955, adopted, a plan of desegregation. Little Rock had the reputation of being a progressive city in which racial relations were untroubled; the board's proposal was moderate, even minimal. Virgil Blossom, superintendent of Little Rock schools, supported the board's plan. Integration was to be gradual, beginning in 1957 at the senior high school level. The expectation was that one high school would remain all or nearly all white, and one all or nearly all African American, while a few African American students would attend Central High School.

Public opposition to and support of the plan grew in intensity; legal moves to prevent its operation were defeated in the United States District Court in the summer of 1957. Preparations were made for the enrollment of a small number of African American students. These nine pioneers, chosen by the school board because of their excellent grades, were sixteen-year-old Minnie Jean Brown, Ernest Green, and Selma Mothershead; fifteen-year-old Elizabeth Eckford, Jane Hill, and Terrence Roberts; and fourteen-year-old Gloria Ray, Jefferson Thomas, and Carlotta Walls.

On September 2, the day before the opening of school, Governor Orval E. Faubus, declaring that he had knowledge of "imminent danger of riot, tumult and breach of the peace," ordered units of the Arkansas National Guard to Little Rock. None of the nine African American students went to school on

the first day, because of the troops stationed there. All the African American students were to meet the following morning at the home of Daisy Bates, Arkansas NAACP president, to go to school together. However, one student did not have a home telephone and so did not get the message. So, when Elizabeth Eckford attempted to enter Central High School on September 4, the National Guard blocked her while a crowd verbally attacked her. Had it not been for the sudden appear-

A white student at Central High in Little Rock, Arkansas, shouts at fifteen-year-old Elizabeth Eckford, an African American student who stoically walks down a line of National Guardsmen (not visible in the picture) who would not allow her to enter the school. (AP/Wide World Photos)

ance of Grace Lorch, a white woman who shepherded Eckford quickly away from the crowd, there might have been violence against Eckford.

A school board request for delay was refused by the federal judge, who said he was asking the Department of Justice to investigate the obstruction by state authorities. Exchanges between Governor Faubus and President Dwight D. Eisenhower argued their respective legal positions, while the National Guard remained at Central High School. On September 14, the governor met with the president at Newport, Rhode Island, where Eisenhower was vacationing. Each issued a statement of understanding and support for the law, and under court order, Faubus removed the National Guard on September 20. On Monday, September 23, the African American students entered the school. The crowd outside was restrained by city police, but grew in numbers; there were also increasing numbers of threats, with several beatings and incidents of violence. School authorities and police agreed on the withdrawal of the students at noon. On September 24, President Eisenhower ordered units of the 101st Airborne Division to Little Rock after his proclamation ordering the mob to cease and desist was ignored. Under protection of the troopers, the African American students returned to school on September 25.

The paratroopers remained, and the students continued to attend for the 1957-1958 school year. Crowds still gathered in protest, and incidents of shoving, tripping, and name-calling occurred within the school. One of the African American students, Minnie Jean Brown, was suspended and then expelled for retaliating against a white student's taunts. One day in December, Brown dumped a bowl of chili onto the head of a white boy behind her in the cafeteria line who had been verbally assaulting her. Segregationists pleased by her expulsion from school printed and distributed cards reading "One Down, Eight to Go."

The troops withdrew at the end of the school year. One African American student, Ernest Green, was graduated; the rest were promoted. Over the summer of 1958, new legal processes were attempted. The school board asked to have integration steps postponed for two and one-half years. The district court approved, but first the Circuit of Appeals and then the Supreme Court reversed the decision.

In August, the Arkansas legislature passed a group of bills providing for the closing of schools threatened by integration and for local referenda on integration or segregation; allowing state funds to go to private schools in places where public schools were closed to prevent integration; requiring that teachers list organizations to which they belonged; and creating various other measures designed to hamper the work and legal activity of the NAACP. Governor Faubus signed the bills—most of them after the Supreme Court refused to permit postponement of desegregation—and in September, 1958, ordered the closing of Little Rock senior high schools. For the school year 1958-1959, the high schools remained closed. Proposals to lease the public high school buildings to the

newly formed private school associations were enjoined by the courts, but private high schools operated nevertheless, and in this and in other ways, most Little Rock high school students obtained some schooling. Public elementary and junior high schools remained open and segregated.

During 1958, Governor Faubus was elected to a third term as governor, and Congressman Brooks Hays, a self-styled "moderate" who had attempted to bring Faubus and Eisenhower to agreement in their 1957 negotiations, was defeated for reelection by Dale Alford, a segregationist. Increasing support for reopening the schools, however, led to a recall election for the Little Rock school board, in which three segregationists were removed.

The reconstituted school board provided for the reopening of Little Rock high schools in August, 1959, after federal court decisions had declared the closing unconstitutional but had upheld a new Arkansas pupil placement law. Under that law, the school board assigned six African American students to two of the high schools, leaving one high school all white and the other one all African American.

Events in Little Rock, especially the confrontations of September, 1957, attracted national and international attention. Reporters, photographers, and television cameras focused on the Arkansas city. Integrationists and segregationists in the United States, as well as friendly and unfriendly observers abroad, made the situation in Little Rock a test case, not only of educational policy but of racial ideals and practice generally.

—George J. Fleming, updated by Lisa Langenbach

ADDITIONAL READING:

Bates, Daisy. *The Long Shadow of Little Rock: A Memoir.* New York: David McKay, 1962. An eyewitness account of the crisis from the president of the Arkansas NAACP and mentor to the nine African American students enrolled at Central High School.

Blossom, Virgil T. *It Has Happened Here.* New York: Harper and Brothers, 1959. As superintendent of schools in Little Rock during the desegregation crisis, Blossom provides a different eyewitness perspective from that of Bates. Includes details of meetings with citizen groups.

Freyer, Tony. *The Little Rock Crisis: A Constitutional Interpretation.* Westport, Conn.: Greenwood Press, 1984. Details the constitutional questions surrounding the desegregation crisis in Little Rock. Contains much historical and legal information in a readable format.

Record, Wilson, and Jane Cassels Record, eds. *Little Rock, U.S.A.* San Francisco: Chandler, 1960. Excellent collection of documents, editorials, interviews, newspaper accounts, and other materials related to the Little Rock crisis. Arranged in chronological order; very accessible reading.

Wilkinson, J. Harvie, III. *From Brown to Bakke: The Supreme Court and School Integration, 1954-1978.* New York: Oxford University Press. 1979. Chapter 5 details the Little Rock crisis within the context of Southern desegregation.

SEE ALSO: 1954, *Brown v. Board of Education;* 1962, Meredith Registers at "Ole Miss."

1959 ■ ALASKA AND HAWAII GAIN STATE-HOOD: *the United States grows economically with the addition of two Pacific Rim states and new ethnic cultures*

DATE: January 3 and August 21, 1959
LOCALE: Alaska and Hawaii
CATEGORY: Expansion and land acquisition
KEY FIGURES:
Aleksandr Baranov (1747-1819), head of the Russian-American Company in Alaska
John A. Burns (1909-1975), territorial delegate from Hawaii, and governor of Hawaii, 1962-1975
Sanford Dole (1844-1926), president of the Republic of Hawaii, 1894, and governor of the Territory of Hawaii, 1900
Dwight David Eisenhower (1890-1969), thirty-fourth president of the United States, 1953-1961
Ernest H. Gruening (1887-1974), territorial governor of Alaska, U.S. Senator, and champion of Alaska statehood
Kamehameha I (1758?-1819), first Hawaiian monarch to extend reign to all seven islands
Lydia Liliuokalani (1838-1917), last reigning Hawaiian monarch
William Henry Seward (1801-1872), secretary of state who negotiated the purchase of Alaska
Edouard de Stoeckl, Russian minister to the United States

SUMMARY OF EVENT. The admission of Alaska and Hawaii into the Union in 1959 vastly extended the physical boundaries of the United States, adding considerably to U.S. influence throughout the Pacific. Alaska's 586,000 square miles of tundra, mountains, and lakes added an extraordinary wilderness to the lower forty-eight states, as well as rich fishing grounds, oil and gas reserves, and a strategic defense perimeter in both the Eastern and Western Hemispheres. Hawaii, a far-flung archipelago of astonishing tropical beauty, added a predominantly Asian American and Polynesian population and culture to the social fabric of the United States' mainland civilization.

The protracted struggle for admission represented a triumph of tolerance and assimilation over the xenophobic objections of some members of Congress who feared that "racial impurity" would result from granting citizenship to Alaska's Aleuts, Tlingits, and Eskimos, and especially to the Japanese, Chinese, and Filipinos of Hawaii. By granting statehood to Alaska and Hawaii, the United States extended its borders to noncontiguous territories originally peopled by ancient migrations of Asians and Polynesians.

Anthropologists widely concur that people migrated from Asia to Alaska across a land bridge spanning the Bering Strait before the end of the last ice age. Alaska's permanent native settlers comprise four major groups: Eskimos, Aleuts, Athabascans, and northwest coast Indians. The name Alaska comes from an Aleut word meaning "great land."

Western settlement of Alaska began when the Russian czar, Peter the Great, dispatched Vitus Bering, a Danish sea captain, to explore the land east of Siberia. Following Bering's expeditions of 1728 and 1740, Russian fur traders established settlements along Alaska's coast. They conquered the Aleuts, made war on Alaska's Indians, and nearly exterminated the sea otter. In 1799, the Russian American Company, chartered by the czar, curtailed the wholesale slaughter of Alaska's natives while promoting commerce and the spread of the Russian Orthodox Church. Aleksandr Baranov, an early director of the company, established Sitka as the Russian capital of Alaska. Under his firm authority, Sitka became a successful trading center and cosmopolitan town.

Russian interest in Alaska waned in the mid-nineteenth century, however. Fearing an English takeover of Alaska during the Crimean War, Russia attempted to sell Alaska to the United States as early as 1855. Soon after the U.S. Civil War, the Russian diplomat Baron Edouard de Stoeckl went to Washington to negotiate the sale of Alaskan territory. On March 30, 1867, the baron and his U.S. counterpart, Secretary of State William H. Seward, signed a treaty specifying the purchase of Alaska for $7.2 million.

On October 18, 1867, the U.S. flag was hoisted over the Great Land, although Congress paid little attention to the new possession. Seward's now-recognized foresight drew scant praise in his own day. Critics called the treaty "Seward's Folly" and believed that the purchase price—two cents an acre for a vast wilderness—was a worthless investment. Unexplored and largely ignored, Alaska languished as a possession governed variously by the Army, the Navy, and the Treasury Department.

Lacking civil government, Alaskans lived in a virtual state of anarchy. People in Alaska could not own property nor assure their inheritance nor marry. Alaskan delegations journeyed to Washington to request any form of self-government. In 1884, Congress finally passed a law for the governance of Alaska, but it proved woefully inadequate.

The discovery of gold in the Canadian Klondike region in 1898 triggered new interest in Alaska. Before the Klondike strike subsided, a new gold rush began in Nome, Alaska, where eighteen thousand miners converged in a feverish scramble. In 1902, a fresh strike in Fairbanks sparked another rush of "sourdough" prospectors to the Alaskan interior. During this era, miners, adventurers, gamblers, and opportunists of all sorts journeyed to Alaska. Quick fortunes, high prices, and frontier violence made Alaska as rough-and-ready as any region of the Wild West. Few women attempted the trip north; the men who stampeded to Alaska lived an often-undisciplined bachelor existence made tolerable by drink and card playing. The poems of Robert Service and the stories of Jack London celebrated this rugged, pioneer life, making it the stuff of legend.

In 1906, Congress permitted Alaska to send a nonvoting delegate to the House of Representatives. In 1912, the Organic

MODERN UNITED STATES

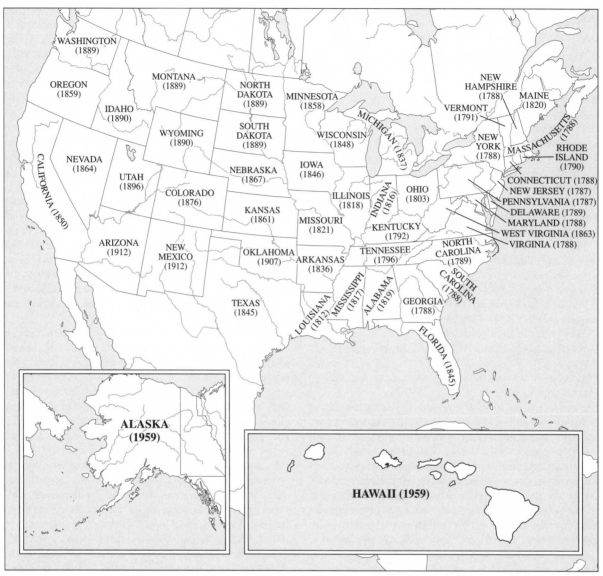

The admission of Hawaii as the fiftieth state completed the modern United States. Current states and their dates of admission to the Union appear above.

Act granted Alaska territorial status under a governor appointed by the president. The bicameral legislature established by the act had no authority to pass laws dealing with excise, game, or fur, however. Congress reserved the right to veto Alaskan legislation.

Alaskans bristled at Washington's distant authoritarian rule and lackluster stewardship. Increasingly, statehood was seen as necessary to enable home rule and to secure voting representation in Congress. On March 30, 1916, Alaskan delegate James Wickersham introduced the first of many statehood bills in Congress. It was referred to committee and died.

Opponents contended that the territory was not ready for

self-rule due to its small, migratory population and its meager resources and revenue base. These perceptions were reinforced when Alaskan salmon packers argued in court that the territorial legislature had no authority to levy taxes on the fishing and mining industries. While the territorial tax was upheld, the opposition of the salmon industry stalled Alaska's halting steps toward self-government.

During the administration of President Franklin D. Roosevelt, Alaskans launched a new movement for statehood in order to rid themselves of the rule-making authority of Roosevelt's Secretary of the Interior, Harold L. Ickes. When Ickes, who had already restricted the private ownership of land in Alaska, proposed an 8 percent tax on gold mines, the Anchorage Pioneer Lodge called for a legislative committee to study statehood. Alaska's territorial governor, Ernest Gruening, whose presidential appointment had been opposed by Ickes, led the chorus advocating statehood.

The statehood movement accelerated during World War II. The military launched a crash buildup of roads, airports, docks, and housing. The strategic Alcan Highway was built by the United States and Canada during 1942-1943. By 1944, both Democrats and Republicans supported statehood for Alaska and Hawaii in their party platforms. Thereafter, the progress and fortunes of Alaska's statehood initiative remained closely linked to Hawaii's own statehood drive, up to the final Senate vote for approval in 1958.

Like Alaska, Hawaii experienced a long association with the United States before attaining statehood. The original settlement of the Hawaiian islands, believed to have occurred between A.D. 400 and 750, was undertaken by accomplished Polynesian navigators who voyaged more than two thousand miles from the Marquesas Islands. During the twelfth century, an exodus of warlike Tahitians arrived and conquered the settled islanders. After the voyages between Tahiti and Hawaii ended, Hawaiian society flourished during a long era of isolation. When the English explorer Captain James Cook arrived at Hawaii in 1778, the population of the islands was estimated to be three hundred thousand, although more recent estimates range as high as seven hundred thousand.

In 1795, a warrior chief named Kamehameha began a campaign of military conquest, leading to the consolidation of all the Hawaiian islands and the establishment of a hereditary monarchy that reigned until 1893. During the reign of Kamehameha I, English and U.S. trading ships began to anchor in Hawaii. Contact with visiting seamen introduced Western diseases to the islands. Syphilis, smallpox, gonorrhea, cholera, and "black plague" took a catastrophic toll; a study commissioned in 1823 reported that the indigenous Hawaiian population had fallen to 140,000.

Western ways also proved fatal to many Hawaiian religious and social customs. Under Kamehameha II, Hawaiian culture succumbed to the inducements of mercantilism and New England Congregationalism. The thirty-year trade in sandalwood to China stripped Hawaiian forests and left many Hawaiians debtors. The *kapu* system of traditional strictures and penalties was abandoned by Hawaiian royalty in 1819. In 1820, the first missionaries arrived from Boston. So thoroughgoing were the conversions wrought by the missionaries that, by the mid-nineteenth century, very little remained of native Hawaiian beliefs. By 1846, during the height of the whaling industry, six hundred ships, of which 90 percent flew the U.S. flag, docked in Hawaiian ports. Two years later, pressure applied by U.S. traders and merchants led Kamehameha III to abolish the traditional feudal land system and permit the private purchase of land in fee.

The emergence of the sugar industry accelerated the U.S. quest for Hawaiian land and cheap immigrant labor. From 1852 until 1930, approximately four hundred thousand foreign men, women, and children—primarily Chinese, Japanese, Okinawan, Korean, Puerto Rican, Portuguese, and Filipino, as well as lesser numbers of northern Europeans—were recruited to Hawaii's sugar and pineapple plantations. A Reciprocity Treaty signed by Hawaii's King David Kalakaua and the United States in 1876 allowed Hawaiian sugar to enter U.S. ports free of customs duties. The sugar industry created fortunes and a new oligarchy in Hawaii. From the sons and daughters of the missionaries came the Doles and Cookes, who would create the Big Five corporations that have continued to control much of Hawaii's land.

During the 1880's, *haole* (non-native) U.S. businessmen, alarmed by the extravagant spending and nativistic inclinations of King Kalakaua, armed and outfitted rifle clubs and demanded a new constitution. With Kalakaua's assent, a new constitution established steep income and property requirements for voters, barred the Japanese and Chinese from voting, and allowed the legislature to override the king's previously absolute veto by a two-thirds vote. Disenfranchised Hawaiians protested this 1887 "Bayonet Constitution." Counterrevolutionary fervor grew.

Following Kalakaua's death, Queen Liliuokalani appointed only trusted Hawaiians to key government posts. When she attempted to draft a new constitution to abolish the restrictions placed upon the monarchy, a haole-organized Committee of Safety, supported by a force of U.S. Marines from the USS *Boston*, seized control of Honolulu on January 16, 1893. The queen was deposed, the monarchy abolished, and a provisional government was organized the next day.

The newly elected U.S. president, Grover Cleveland, denounced the takeover and demanded the restoration of the queen. Cleveland's investigative emissary, John L. Blount, reported that the coup had been accomplished by force with U.S. complicity, contrary to the wishes of an overwhelming Hawaiian majority. When Cleveland rejected a draft Senate treaty for the annexation of Hawaii, the Committee of Safety proceeded to draft a new constitution establishing the Republic of Hawaii. On July 4, 1894, the new republic was proclaimed, with Sanford B. Dole, the son of missionary parents, as president.

After the election of President William McKinley, negotiations for the annexation of Hawaii resumed. On July 7, 1898, an annexation treaty was endorsed by a joint resolution of Congress. On August 12, 1898, the U.S. flag was raised over Honolulu's Executive Building, the former palace of the Hawaiian kingdom. In 1900, passage of the Organic Act established Hawaii's territorial government and conferred citizenship to all Hawaiians. Sanford Dole was appointed governor of the Territory of Hawaii. In his inaugural address, he predicted eventual statehood for Hawaii.

Hawaiian congressional delegate Jonah Kuhio submitted the first bill for statehood in 1919. The *haole* oligarchy of Hawaii was slow to warm to the cause of statehood, however. The Hawaiian Sugar Planters Association was content with existing protective tariffs supporting Hawaiian sugar prices and feared the potential vote of the vast Japanese plantation workforce. When the Jones-Costigan Act of 1934 cut Hawaii's sugar quota to 10 percent, however, the sugar industry threw its support behind a statehood bill in 1935.

In 1935, the territorial legislature created the Hawaii Equal Rights Commission to examine putting the issue of statehood to a plebiscite. That year, Congress conducted its first hearings on Hawaiian statehood. Between 1935 and 1958, twenty congressional hearings on statehood were conducted, gathering testimony from more than a thousand witnesses. In 1940, one year before the Japanese attack on Pearl Harbor, Hawaii's plebiscite voters affirmed their support for statehood by a two-to-one margin.

The outbreak of war in the Pacific lent new potency to the arguments for Alaskan and Hawaiian statehood. Japan's attack on Pearl Harbor in 1941 and invasion of the Aleutian Islands the following year irrefutably established the strategic importance of the United States' Pacific territories. During the war, Alaskans noted, their territory proved nearly as valuable a base for Army and Navy operations as Hawaii had been. Postwar tensions with Russia further underscored Alaska's value as a defense perimeter and early-warning outpost in an age of intercontinental ballistic missiles.

Following World War II, thousands of veterans swelled Alaska's population. In Hawaii, the highly decorated Nisei (second-generation Japanese American) veterans returned home determined to pursue education and political office as full-fledged U.S. citizens. In 1947, the House of Representatives cast its first vote favoring statehood for Hawaii. Meanwhile, Alaskans formed a statehood association, conducted a plebiscite favoring statehood, and rallied national public opinion to their cause. In 1950, the House voted 186 to 146 in favor of Alaska statehood, but the bill foundered in the Senate.

Senate opponents of Hawaii's statehood initiative pointed to the influence of the International Longshoremen's and Warehousemen's Union in island politics and suggested that a Hawaiian delegation would be tantamount to seating "four Soviet agents" in Congress. A secondary and perhaps more insidious objection was the belief that Hawaii's largely Asian population would never assimilate fully into U.S. society.

Following the defeat of a number of statehood planks in Washington, Alaskans held their own constitutional convention in the winter of 1955-1956. Alaska's voters boldly elected two "provisional" senators and a representative to be seated in Congress.

After a succession of Alaska-Hawaii statehood bills were stalled or defeated in Congress, Hawaii delegate John A. Burns devised the "Alaska First" strategy for winning congressional approval. Burns, a protégé of House Speaker Sam Rayburn and Senate Majority Leader Lyndon B. Johnson, had concluded that a joint statehood bill invited too much antago-

nism from detractors of either territory. Convinced that Hawaii's bid would be irresistible once Alaska achieved statehood, Burns's strategy was validated when both houses of Congress supported separate statehood acts in 1958. The principled support of President Dwight D. Eisenhower was also crucial to the winning strategy; Eisenhower won over Republican doubters concerned that both states would elect Democrats to Congress.

Voting in record numbers, Alaskans overwhelmingly ratified their statehood act on August 26, 1958, and on January 3, 1959, Alaska officially became the forty-ninth state to enter the Union. Hawaii's voters endorsed their statehood act in a June, 1959, election by a seventeen-to-one margin. On August 21, 1959, Hawaii officially became the nation's fiftieth state.

The elation felt by the citizens of Alaska and Hawaii was nearly rivaled by the enthusiasm of their fellow U.S. tourists and in-migrants who, borne by the new jet age, rushed to explore and settle in the new states. Federal spending and mounting tourism prompted an economic boom in both states. The discovery of vast North Slope oil reserves in 1969 further hastened development in Alaska. The political life of both states has continued to dwell on themes of local control of land and resources versus environmental protection and the dynamics of boom-and-bust economics versus sustainability. As the drive for statehood demonstrated, determined social mobility and vigorous debate have remained vital to the future of the United States' newest states.

—Rory Flynn

Additional reading:

Cooper, George, and Gavan Daws. *Land and Power in Hawaii.* Honolulu: University of Hawaii Press, 1990. A meticulously cross-referenced study of land-use policies, real estate deals, and Hawaiian politics from 1955 to 1985.

Daws, Gavan. *Shoal of Time: A History of the Hawaiian Islands.* New York: Macmillan, 1968. A scholarly, highly readable general history of Hawaii.

Fuchs, Lawrence H. *Hawaii Pono: An Ethnic and Political History.* Rev. ed. Honolulu: Bess Press, 1992. A superb social history of Hawaii's ethnic groups.

Gruening, Ernest. *The Battle for Alaska Statehood.* College: University of Alaska Press, 1967. A detailed and personal account of Alaska's struggle for statehood.

Lineberry, William P., ed. *The New States: Alaska and Hawaii.* New York: H. W. Wilson, 1963. An excellent collection of essays and reprinted articles on the statehood drives and prospects of Alaska and Hawaii.

Whitehead, John S. *Completing the Union: The Alaska and Hawaii Statehood Movements.* Anchorage: Alaska Historical Commission, 1986. A political review of the Alaskan and Hawaiian statehood movements.

See also: 1728, Russian Voyages to Alaska; 1896, Klondike Gold Rush; 1901, Insular Cases; 1971, Alaska Native Claims Settlement Act; 1974, Construction of the Alaska Pipeline.

1959 ■ St. Lawrence Seaway Opens:
completion of a massive engineering project opens a major trade route between the Great Lakes and the Atlantic Ocean

Date: June 26, 1959

Locale: Upper Midwestern and Northeastern United States and Southeastern Canada (Ontario and Quebec provinces)

Categories: Business and labor; Canadian history; Economics; Science and technology; Transportation

Key figures:

Dollier de Casson, Sulpician who attempted to begin a seaway in the late seventeenth century

Lionel Chevrier (1903-1987), one of Canada's most ardent and influential advocates of the seaway in the twentieth century

Dwight David Eisenhower (1890-1969), thirty-fourth president of the United States, 1953-1961

William Hamilton Merritt (1793-1862), Canadian visionary who joined with friends to dig the Welland Canal

Harry S Truman (1884-1972), thirty-third president of the United States, 1945-1953

Summary of event. The dedication ceremony at the opening of the St. Lawrence Seaway, on June 26, 1959, celebrated an engineering triumph readily comparable with the building of the Suez Canal or the Panama Canal; its long-range effects on the North American heartland region can be compared with those of the Suez Canal on the interior of Egypt. For the first time, the heretofore isolated, landlocked towns and cities of the U.S. and Canadian interiors—Chicago, Duluth, Cleveland, Toledo, Toronto, Fort William, and Port Arthur—became deepwater ports capable of competing favorably with established ocean ports such as Montreal, New York, and Baltimore in the transportation of crude commodities such as grain and iron ore. In fact, the shipping distance between certain northern European ports (for example, Hamburg and Bremerhaven) and an inland U.S. city such as Cleveland was actually shorter than it was between those ports and New York City.

Valuable as the St. Lawrence Seaway has demonstrated itself to be to the upper tier of northeastern states, it may seem strange that it was not constructed much earlier than it was; however, various disagreements, fueled by such matters as Canadian and U.S. nationalism and the smoldering antipathy existing between U.S. states bordering the pre-seaway lakes and rivers, delayed construction until 1954, when the first large-scale building began. It was not only feuds that hurt the seaway's prospects: Everything from the Great Depression to World Wars I and II dampened enthusiasm for the project.

The story of the St. Lawrence Seaway goes as far back as the time of Jacques Cartier, the discoverer of the Grand

Banks fishing grounds. Cartier, who was in the employ of Great Britain, is credited with having had a grandiose vision of sailing ships going far into the North American interior by means of a deepwater passage. At that time, 1536, the necessary technology was not available, so Cartier's recurring dream for the time being was laid to rest. Later, another visionary, Superior Dollier de Casson of the Sulpician Order, hoped to see the day when French ships would sail up the St. Lawrence River to the Great Lakes basin by using a grand canal that he would construct, but his idea came to little. Lionel Chevrier, a historian and member of the Canadian Parliament, noted, "As the explorers were followed by commerce, it became supremely frustrating that it was not possible to load grain at Duluth and sail it to Amsterdam; or load textiles at Liverpool and unload them at Chicago."

Seaway visionaries and advocates such as William Hamilton Merritt, whose friends joined him in the initial dragging and digging of the Welland Canal in the early nineteenth century, kept alive the hope that one day the ocean and lakes would be joined, just as the Welland Canal had joined Lake Ontario and Lake Erie. Perhaps the single most impressive case for a seaway was presented by the example of the successful Erie Canal (built in the early nineteenth century by American-Irish laborers), connecting New York City with the towns and cities of upstate New York. Until the advent of railroads, the Erie Canal was the most efficient purveyor of goods from one place to another. Its operational costs were the lowest to be found, and from the day it opened it made money, so jammed was it by barge traffic.

The St. Lawrence River had been a useful avenue of trade for centuries, supplying Montreal and the small Canadian cities along its banks with durable and crude goods, as well as foodstuffs. Many believed that trade could be enormously expanded by the addition of locks and canals linking the river to the Great Lakes beyond. Aware of the pressing need for more electrical power, people in both the United States and Canada thought that a seaway link with the St. Lawrence River made sense. In 1930, the St. Lawrence Power Development Commission formed the Power Authority of New York State, a precursor of later power authorities; in 1932, a Great Lakes Treaty was brought before the United States Senate, but it was not ratified; and in 1941, an agreement between the United States and Canada was signed. Because of World War II, however, nothing came of this Great Lakes/St. Lawrence Basin agreement.

After the war, President Harry S Truman wanted a seaway, but Congress refused to enact appropriate legislation, in part because of the intense lobbying efforts of East Coast shippers and others who believed that the creation of a seaway would not serve their interests. All the lobbying notwithstanding, great numbers of U.S. citizens had come to the conclusion that a seaway would be in the best interest of the United States, if only because of the vast amount of electricity that would be generated by seaway power stations. By 1950, Ontario and New York had agreed on a plan for the creation of one enormous power station and two large dams on the St. Lawrence River.

With public funds available for the immense task, President Truman, not wanting the Canadians to build a seaway without U.S. participation, was in favor of beginning the project at once. Advocates of the seaway argued that it would not damage the coastal economies, as members of Congress from the East feared. They also argued that the project would be self-supporting and thus a genuine boon for the hard-pressed taxpayer. Nevertheless, the first attempt to garner congressional support failed in a vote on June 18, 1952, and the seaway proposal was sent back to committee. Canadians, dismayed but still determined, went ahead with their own plans to create a seaway, realizing that one thousand miles of it would be within Canada and that the United States ultimately would cooperate, because sizable portions of the seaway would be located in the Northern New York State area. President Dwight D. Eisenhower, recently inaugurated, was at first deeply skeptical about the proposed water route; later, he came to support it, in part because of the persuasive powers of Lionel Chevrier and other prominent Canadian leaders.

In 1953, support for the seaway increased rather dramatically. Not surprisingly, much of that support came from members of Congress from the Midwestern states in the Great Lakes region. More surprising was the enthusiasm of Senator John F. Kennedy of Massachusetts, who argued against the congressional tendency to vote regionally rather than keeping the interests of the nation at large in mind. After many floor battles and behind-the-scenes intrigues, Congress approved the creation of a seaway on May 6, 1954.

From 1954 to 1959, massive public works—on a scale previously unknown even in Suez and Panama—were undertaken by U.S. and Canadian construction teams. The creation of enormous locks, the deepening of the Welland Canal, and the dredging of the channels proceeded without serious difficulties. In June, 1959, the dream of Cartier and Casson became a reality when Queen Elizabeth II presided over the formal opening of the St. Lawrence Seaway.

While the seaway brought prosperity to the urban areas and industries that grew along its path, it had disturbing effects as well. Native American peoples (mainly Mohawks), for example, were devastated. The destruction of the Mohawks' lands and resources was not new. As early as 1834, Mohawk chiefs told Canadian officials that control structures built to channel the flow of the St. Lawrence River near Barnhart Island were destroying important fish-spawning grounds. Environmental degradation in the Mohawk communities of Akwesasne and Kahnawake increased dramatically after the late 1950's, however, when the St. Lawrence Seaway opened up bountiful cheap power. Access to power drew heavy industry that soon turned large segments of this magnificent river into open sewers. The Akwesasne area also had been home to many trappers before construction of the seaway devastated the trapping areas and wetlands. To speed the melting of ice in the spring, the level of the river is raised and dropped very quickly so that air pockets caught in the water will pulverize the ice. The swirling, crushing action of water, ice, and air also floods muskrat and beaver hutches, killing their occupants. The animals drown en masse, destroying the traditional trapping industry in the area.

According to John Mohawk, a professor of American Indian studies at the State University of New York (Buffalo), the seeds of frustration among Mohawks and other Iroquois that gave rise to the Warrior Societies were sown during the 1950's, when the governments of the United States and Canada ignored native protests against construction of the St. Lawrence Seaway. Had the construction of the St. Lawrence Seaway shortly after World War II and subsequent industrialization of the area not destroyed traditional ways of making a living in Mohawk country, gambling and smuggling, with their associated violence and crime, might never have emerged as avenues of economic survival there.

Several decades after its opening, the financial costs and benefits of the St. Lawrence Seaway were debated. Because the project's revenues have never paid its capital costs, the project must be viewed mainly as a government subsidy that aids businesses both in the United States and Canada. In 1955, the Cleveland *Plain Dealer* estimated that the cost of shipping a ton of steel from Cleveland to the U.S. East Coast declined from thirteen dollars to two dollars when the seaway opened. Freight transit through the seaway reached fifty million metric tons per year in the late 1970's, then declined to the point that, in 1994, thirty-eight million metric tons was considered a good year. The United States stopped levying tolls on seaway transit in 1986; in the early 1990's, Canada charged shippers a tonnage rate plus $425 for passage through each of the system's sixteen locks. By 1996, the seaway was facing competition from other modes of transport as well as technological limitations, such as the fact that many newer cargo ships are too large to use its locks.

—John D. Raymer, updated by Bruce E. Johansen

ADDITIONAL READING:

Alfred, Gerald R. *Heeding the Voices of Our Ancestors: Kahnawake Mohawk Politics and the Rise of Native Nationalism.* Toronto: Oxford University Press, 1995. Describes the effect of the St. Lawrence Seaway on the Kahnawake Mohawks.

Hartly, Joseph R. *The Effect of the St. Lawrence Seaway on Grain Movements.* Bloomington: Indiana University School of Business, 1957. Although somewhat dated, this early study of seaway grain shipping offers a discussion of the economic importance of the seaway.

Johansen, Bruce E. *Life and Death in Mohawk Country.* Golden, Colo.: North American Press, 1993. Traces social and political developments among the Mohawks whose lives were affected by the seaway.

Mabee, Carleton. *The Seaway Story.* New York: Macmillan, 1961. One of the most complete accounts of the seaway, tracing its beginnings and building, and discussing its future.

Marine Traffic Control: St. Lawrence River. Ottawa: Queen's Press, 1968. Provides insights into the massive job of supervising barge traffic on the St. Lawrence River section of the seaway.

St. Lawrence Valley Souvenir Company. *The Billion Dollar Story: The International St. Lawrence Seaway and Power Development*. Massena, N.Y.: Author, 1970. Illustrated guide with maps and pictures of construction.

The Seaway in Canada's Transportation: An Economic Analysis. Ottawa: D. William Carr and Associates, 1970. A Canadian perspective on the seaway's past economic performance and its potential.

SEE ALSO: 1825, Erie Canal Opens; 1903, Acquisition of the Panama Canal Zone.

1960 ■ FDA APPROVES THE BIRTH CONTROL PILL: *an oral contraceptive changes both women's lives and larger social structures*

DATE: 1960

LOCALE: United States

CATEGORIES: Health and medicine; Science and technology; Social reform; Women's issues

KEY FIGURES:

Min-Chueh Chang (1908-1991), biologist who helped develop the pill

Robert Latou Dickinson (1861-1950), surgeon and sex researcher who advocated contraception

Carl Djerassi (born 1923), chemist who helped develop progestin

Clarence James Gambel (1894-1966), birth control researcher who advocated educating the indigent about birth control

Kathleen Dexter McCormick (1875-1967), philanthropist who supported contraceptive research

Gregory Goodwin Pincus (1903-1967), biologist considered the father of the birth control pill

Edris Rice-Wray (born 1904), responsible for the day-to-day testing of the pill in Puerto Rico

Margaret Sanger (1879-1966), social activist who campaigned for birth control

SUMMARY OF EVENT. Attempts to prevent conception and the desire to control reproduction have existed in medicine and society for thousands of years. Prior to twentieth century developments in birth control technology, contraception was the primary responsibility of the male. Use of the condom to prevent the spread of syphilis was first described in 1564. By the 1720's, condoms were used for contraception in Europe. Female contraception historically involved various violent gestures, ingestion of potions thought to have magical properties, or the insertion of vaginal plugs and solutions, some with a spermicidal effect. Pessaries and sponges were among the oldest contraceptive devices for use by women. The cervical cap and diaphragm were developed during the nineteenth century as a result of social changes and attitude shifts in England, Germany, and France. Other forces, such as industrialization, urbanization, and the democratization of contraceptive knowledge, resulted in the less privileged gaining knowledge that formerly was only within the reach of the upper class. The European influence spread to the United States, and an effort was mounted to educate the general population about contraception. Pioneers in birth control and women's rights, such as Margaret Sanger, sought to establish a system of clinics where women could obtain reliable birth control devices and information.

Sanger was an ardent crusader for birth control and family planning. Having decided that a foolproof contraceptive was necessary, she arranged a meeting between a friend, biologist and wealthy socialite Katherine Dexter McCormick, and Gregory Pincus, the head of the Worcester Institutes of Experimental Biology. With McCormick's financial backing and Pincus' technical know-how, work began on developing a pill to prevent pregnancy. It was known that the female hormone progesterone could inhibit ovulation during pregnancy, and so it was thought that the same hormone might be used to prevent pregnancy as well. Laboratory studies, conducted under the direction of Min-Chueh Chang, investigated the manipulation of progesterone to inhibit ovulation. In 1937, inhibition of ovulation in rabbits was demonstrated by scientists from the University of Pennsylvania. In 1951, Carl Djerassi and other chemists devised inexpensive ways of producing a synthetic progesterone, called "progestin," in the laboratory, thus clearing the way for the mass-production of the substance that eventually would be used in a contraceptive pill.

Clinical tests were conducted by scientists who had been working with progesterone and progestin to treat female infertility. Hence, the first oral contraceptive was ironically developed in the context of increasing fertility. During the 1950's the contraceptive pill was tested on a wide scale to determine its long-term effects on humans. The population chosen was Puerto Rico, because of a heightened need there for inexpensive contraception as well as legal problems in the United States. In 1956, 221 women volunteered for the first study, which was successful and resulted in minimal side effects. One death from congestive heart failure was deemed not to have been related to the contraceptive pill.

In 1960, the Food and Drug Administration (FDA) approved the oral contraceptive for U.S. distribution. Within two years, more than one million women were using "the pill," as it came to be known. It would have both broad and long-range social, as well as physical, effects on the lives of women—many good, some less desirable. Chief among these was the immediate freedom afforded to women to control their pregnancies: No longer were women at the mercy of unplanned pregnancies, and the likelihood that children would be "unwanted" could now be lessened.

Second, the pill allowed women, and men, to become sexually active with more than one partner, prior to marriage. The "sexual revolution" and changing ideas about premarital chastity followed, leading to a reevaluation of sexual morality and the acceptance or rejection of social and religious values. Options once unavailable to women became realistic, such as postponing marriage until other meaningful life goals were attained. Cohabitation without marriage, once considered indecent and immoral, lost much of its former stigma and became a more accepted way of life. As a result of reproductive freedom and the right to choose when and whether to bear children, women and men began to redraw the boundaries between work and family life. Indeed, the very definition of "family," once considered a unit consisting of a biological mother and a biological father and their children, began to expand to include "blended" families and single-parent families.

Birth control was both a cause and an effect of a number of dramatic changes in society as well. Family size was reduced and life expectancy was increased. At the same time, increased opportunities for marriage and career caused a surge in the workforce; this, in turn, required control of reproduction, liberalization of abortion, and provision of reliable contraceptives. Women who valued childbearing, but in their chosen time frame, began to make the claim that abortion was a woman's right, and one that was integrated into her right to equality. The pill also freed women from unromantic preparations and permitted spontaneity in sexual encounters. Most women were delighted; most men were pleased to be relieved of responsibility for birth control; physicians were relieved of having to counsel patients about problematic contraceptive methods, preferring instead the ease of prescribing a convenient, relatively inexpensive product of scientific research.

Although it initially was regarded as a panacea, the pill's effectiveness depended largely on conscientious use. From the time it was developed, it generated controversy in scientific circles, with the public becoming involved shortly thereafter. The increase in sexual activity and multiple partners spawned by the pill increased the number of sexually transmitted diseases (STDs) in the North American population but, more important, created an expectation among a generation of "baby boomers" and their children that sexual freedom and increased sexual activity was a right of "consenting adults" that had fewer serious consequences (such as pregnancy) than it had had in the past. This freedom had its consequences, giving way, in the 1980's, to a growing concern over STDs, including AIDS, and teenage pregnancies—since the attitudes engendered by the pill were not limited to its users. The pill therefore invited a reexamination of moral proscriptions previously cast aside.

Many people believe that, on balance, the pill's benefits have far outweighed its potential risks and negative social impacts. Proponents point out that the pill poses fewer risks than pregnancy and constitutes an easy, workable method for women to control their own fertility. They argue that the intent of scientists who developed the pill was not to harm women, but to free them, and that STDs are not caused by the pill but by irresponsible behaviors on the part of people. Nevertheless, some feminists see the pill as an outrage perpetrated against women by the predominantly male medical and scientific community. These critics point out that other methods exist to prevent pregnancy and that too few tests were conducted to ascertain the pill's safety. They argue that the pill was released prematurely, proving that the prevailing culture considers women to be expendable commodities, subject to experimentation. Critics believe that the pill's side effects—increased risks for blood clots, breast cancer, pulmonary emboli, heart attack, stroke, hypertension, gall bladder disease, birth defects, benign tumors, and depression—are unacceptable.

Use of the pill and other forms of birth control increased as anxiety about the population explosion, mounting pressures on women trying to combine career and homemaking responsibilities, and a rising resistance to traditional definitions of women's roles became more prevalent. As sex and sexuality became public subjects, the focus of sexual relations evolved from primarily a means for reproduction to a vehicle for emotional intimacy and physical pleasure. The advent of new birth control methods, separating sex and procreation, and questioning traditional authority caused a renewed openness in the discussion of sex.

Studies of fertility control practices in North America reveal that there has been a steady increase in sterilization since the 1970's, because many people see it as a safe alternative to the risks associated with other methods of contraception. While oral contraceptives generally are preferred by women under the age of thirty, voluntary surgical sterilization is the option of choice for many older couples because it is safe, reliable, and permanent. Sophisticated research and technologies, including an oral contraceptive for men, continue to revolutionize the reproductive arena, simultaneously challenging traditional values and creating new opportunities.

—Marcia J. Weiss

ADDITIONAL READING:

Asbell, Bernard. *The Pill: A Biography of the Drug That Changed the World.* New York: Random House, 1995. Readable history of the origins and development of the pill in its social and political context. Discusses the pill's worldwide impact.

Blank, Robert, and Janna C. Merrick. *Human Reproduction, Emerging Technologies, and Conflicting Rights.* Washington, D.C.: Congressional Quarterly, 1995. Examines the complex issues surrounding reproduction from a public policy perspective.

Brown, Philip M. *The Death of Intimacy: Barriers to Meaningful Interpersonal Relationships.* New York: Haworth Press, 1995. A social commentary encompassing psychology, sociology, and feminist theory.

Degler, Carl N. *At Odds: Women and the Family in America from the Revolution to the Present.* New York: Oxford University Press, 1980. Synthesizes the history of women and the history of the family in an effort to resolve the conflict between women's search for equality and their family responsibilities.

Dienes, C. Thomas. *Law, Politics, and Birth Control.* Urbana: University of Illinois Press, 1972. Detailed and well-documented scholarly review of the subject from the latter part of the eighteenth century to the 1970's.

Knight, James W., and Joan C. Callahan. *Preventing Birth: Contemporary Methods and Related Moral Controversies.* Salt Lake City: University of Utah Press, 1989. Political and philosophical aspects of contraception, including the moral debate and social policy concerns surrounding elective abortion.

Linden-Ward, Blanche, and Carol Hurd Green. *American Women in the 1960's: Changing the Future.* New York: Twayne, 1993. Comprehensive interdisciplinary survey of women in the 1960's and the social, literary, artistic, cultural, and political climate of that decade.

McLaren, Angus. *A History of Contraception: From Antiquity to the Present Day.* Cambridge, Mass.: Basil Blackwell, 1990. Traces the concept of fertility control in various cultures.

SEE ALSO: 1973, *Roe v. Wade*; 1978, Pregnancy Discrimination Act; 1981, First AIDS Cases Are Reported; 1988, Family Support Act; 1993, Family and Medical Leave Act.

1960 ■ QUEBEC SOVEREIGNIST MOVEMENT: *sympathies for a separate Quebec begin to grow, leading to the establishment of a new Canadian political party*

DATE: Beginning 1960
LOCALE: Quebec
CATEGORIES: Canadian history; Government and politics; Organizations and institutions
KEY FIGURES:

Charles de Gaulle (1890-1970), president of France
Maurice Duplessis (1890-1959), premier of Quebec, 1936-1939, 1944-1959, and leader of the Union Nationale Party
Georges-Émile Lapalme (1907-1985), cabinet minister whose ideas inspired the Liberal reformist program
Jean Lesage (1912-1980), premier of Quebec, 1960-1966
René Lévesque (1922-1987), Liberal cabinet minister and founder of the Parti Québécois
Jacques Parizeau (born 1930), premier of Quebec, 1994-

SUMMARY OF EVENT. In 1960, Canada's Liberal Party, led by Jean Lesage, won a narrow victory in Quebec's provincial election. Once in power, the Liberals initiated a period of considerable reform and unintentionally unleashed nation-

alist forces that would bring the issue of sovereignty for Quebec to the forefront. For much of the period between 1944 and 1960, this province, where 85 percent of the people spoke French, had been in the grip of Maurice Duplessis and his Union Nationale Party. The Duplessis regime was marked by political corruption and ruthless intimidation of opponents. A powerful combination of political bosses, the Roman Catholic church, and big business successfully suppressed trade unions, radical organizations, and any liberating ideas that challenged the established conservative order. Intellectuals later labeled this era the Great Darkness. Anglo-Canadians and the United States controlled the economy, while most French-speaking Quebecers (Québécois) were relegated to a subservient status within their homeland. While the province became increasingly urban, industrial, and secular, Duplessis still defended the values of a rural, religious, traditional-minded people. In short, Quebec's institutions had become outmoded and no longer conformed to social and economic reality.

Although Georges-Émile Lapalme was the intellectual inspiration behind the Liberal program, it was the pragmatic and energetic Jean Lesage who, as premier, instituted the reforms that were to transform Quebec completely. His cabinet introduced numerous electoral reforms, which included reducing the voting age from twenty-one to eighteen, attacking political corruption and patronage, and providing for better representation of urban areas, previously dramatically underrepresented. Social welfare programs were created, expanded, and better funded, particularly in the crucial areas of health care and old age pensions. The labor code was modernized; many workers were empowered to form trade unions, bargain collectively, and strike under limited conditions. Quebec's educational system, previously dominated by a rigid Catholicism that emphasized classical education, was completely revamped. The government created a modern, secular school system and put in motion plans to create a new University of Quebec and a number of regional colleges. This new educational system was now capable of producing the elites needed to run a modern state, well skilled in the fields of science, technology, and business.

In the crucial economic sector, the state became the engine responsible for economic expansion. Under René Lévesque, minister of hydraulic resources, private power companies were nationalized, creating the giant corporation Hydro-Québec, which provided superior service and reasonable rates to the entire province. The government established the Caisse de Dépôt et Placement, which held government pension funds and provided capital to help Quebec industries. Within the growing public sector, the government systematically inserted an increasing number of French-speaking Quebecers into positions of authority. In all its decisions, the government attempted to ensure that jobs, profits, and raw materials stayed within the province to benefit the people of Quebec rather than foreign interests. Their motto was *Maître chez nous* ("masters of our own house").

The Liberals won reelection easily in 1962 but were upset in the election of 1966; the Union Nationale returned to power, thus ending one of the most dynamic periods in Quebec's history. The Liberal achievement has been labeled the Quiet Revolution, a revolution that was accomplished not by bloody insurrection in the streets, but rather in the confines of government agencies, business offices, and school classrooms. Perhaps the real revolution was a change in values, attitude, and mentality. Quebecers emerged from this period confident, self-assertive, and taking immense pride in their accomplishments. It was inevitable that unleashing such forces would ultimately lead the Québécois to question the constitutional relationship with the rest of Canada, if they were to preserve their French language and unique Québécois culture.

Some, like the radical youth who joined the Front de Libération du Québec, employed violence to achieve Quebec's separation from Canada. The vast majority took the democratic path, like René Lévesque. He had been a popular leader of the Liberal government, an immensely gifted statesman who was both a crafty politician and a profound thinker. Now freed of government responsibility, he came to the conclusion that Quebec must be sovereign in the political sphere, although he desired to retain a close economic association with the rest of Canada. After the Liberal Party rejected his sovereignist ideas at its 1967 conference, Lévesque quit the party in order to found a new movement. Further galvanizing sovereignist sentiment that year was the visit of the French president, Charles de Gaulle, to Quebec. On July 24, in Montreal, de Gaulle issued his famous cry, *Vive le Québec libre!* (Long live a free Quebec!), thereby suggesting that Quebec's sovereignists had a powerful international ally in France.

There already were two small sovereignist parties on the scene, the Rassemblement pour L'Indépendance Nationale (Union for National Independence, or RIN), a left-wing party, and the Ralliement Nationale (National Rally, or RN), which tended to be conservative. Together, these two parties had won almost 9 percent of the vote in the previous election. In November, 1967, Lévesque founded the Mouvement Souveraineté-Association (MSA), committed to promoting political sovereignty for Quebec and economic association with Canada. The RIN and RN began to discuss the prospect of merger with Lévesque's new movement, and within a year they, in effect, merged with the MSA. The larger Quebec trade unions also showed keen interest in this project.

The year 1968 was decisive. In January, Lévesque published his best-selling book, *Option Québec*, which promoted the idea of sovereignty association. In April, the MSA voted to become a provincial political party. The first convention was held in Quebec City from October 11-14, and delegates adopted the name of Parti Québécois (PQ). The party's program was more radical than its leaders would have preferred, giving the PQ a decided left-of-center orientation on social and economic issues and an even more aggressive stance against the Canadian government than PQ's leaders thought

wise. Commentators across Canada were impressed by the quality of the party's debates, and many Anglo-Canadians found René Lévesque a fresh and fascinating figure, honest, passionate, and flamboyant.

The new party generated much enthusiasm and grew quickly. It attracted teachers, students, trade unionists, civil servants, liberal priests, and the new business elites. By the following spring, public opinion polls showed that 26 percent of the electorate would vote for the Parti Québécois. The party was particularly successful with Québécois youth. At its second convention in October, 1969, approximately two-thirds of the delegates were less than thirty-five years of age. The party received a further boost when Jacques Parizeau, a highly respected economist, announced his intention to run as a PQ candidate, thereby legitimizing the party's contention that separation was economically feasible.

Thus, the 1960's saw the emergence of a new Quebec nationalism that differed sharply from that of the past. The old nationalism was defensive and insular, suspicious of the state and the city, believing that both were the enemy of a simple, religious, agrarian folk. This nationalism had valued traditionalism, Catholicism, and even race. It had sprung from feelings of inferiority and a ferocious desire to preserve the past. The new nationalism of the 1960's was confident and assertive. Liberal, secular, and reformist, it revolved more around language and economics than race or religion. It embraced modernity, recognized the crucial importance of a technological society, and viewed the state as a benevolent partner in creating a just and affluent society. This nationalism was to be a prominent feature of the sovereignist movement in the decades to come.

—*David C. Lukowitz*

ADDITIONAL READING:

Behiels, Michael. *Prelude to Quebec's Quiet Revolution: Liberalism Versus Neo-Nationalism 1945-1960*. Montreal: McGill-Queen's University Press, 1985. Examines the intellectual origins of the Quiet Revolution and the separatist, or sovereignist, movement.

Fraser, Graham. *René Lévesque and the Parti Québécois in Power*. Toronto: Macmillan, 1984. Offers a penetrating insight into Lévesque's personality and political style. Although concentrating on the years of power, the early chapters deal with the founding of the PQ.

Gagnon, Alain-G., and Mary Beth Montcalm. *Quebec Beyond the Quiet Revolution*. Scarborough, Ont.: Nelson Canada, 1990. Examines the subsequent impact of the policies, legislation, and trends initiated during the Quiet Revolution.

Gougeon, Gilles. *A History of Quebec Nationalism*. Translated by Louisa Blair, Robert Chodos, and Jane Obertino. Toronto: James Lorimer, 1994. A fascinating series of interviews with seven leading Québécois scholars. Chapter 3 gives an expert analysis of the 1960's by Richard Desrosiers.

Saywell, John. *The Rise of the Parti Québécois, 1967-1976*. Toronto: University of Toronto Press, 1977. Arguably the best introductory account of the party's early years. Written by a leading Canadian historian for a general audience.

Thomson, Dale C. *Jean Lesage and the Quiet Revolution.* Toronto: Macmillan, 1984. The definitive work on the subject, ably researched by a respected Canadian scholar, but chapters on economic development are challenging.

SEE ALSO: 1968, Trudeau Era in Canada; 1969, Canada's Official Languages Act; 1970, October Crisis; 1982, Canada's Constitution Act; 1990, Meech Lake Accord Dies; 1990, Bloc Québécois Forms; 1992, Defeat of the Charlottetown Accord.

1960 ■ U-2 INCIDENT: *the capture of a U.S. spy plane over Russian territory threatens to result in international crisis*

DATE: May 1, 1960
LOCALE: Washington, D.C., Moscow, Sverdlovsk, and Paris
CATEGORY: Diplomacy and international relations
KEY FIGURES:
Dwight David Eisenhower (1890-1969), thirty-fourth president of the United States, 1953-1961
Nikita Sergeyevich Khrushchev (1894-1971), first secretary of the Communist Party of the Soviet Union and premier of the Soviet Union
Francis Gary Powers (1929-1977), pilot of the captured U-2 plane

SUMMARY OF EVENT. In the spring of 1960, the world was basking in a feeling known as "the spirit of Camp David," named after the presidential retreat in Camp David, Maryland, where President Dwight D. Eisenhower had met in September, 1959, with First Secretary of the Communist Party of the Soviet Union Nikita Khrushchev. For the first time since the Potsdam Conference in 1945, the leaders of the two most powerful nations on earth talked face to face. While nothing substantive was accomplished in these conversations, they provided an optimistic ending for Khrushchev's goodwill tour of the United States, and people began to think that the Cold War that had lasted for more than a decade was coming to an end. Now all hopes were placed on the Paris summit conference to be held on May 16, 1960, between Khrushchev, Eisenhower, the British foreign minister, Harold Macmillan, and Charles de Gaulle, president of France.

Such a Big Four summit was long overdue. The problem of a divided Germany, and especially the status of West Berlin, had reemerged to plague world leaders. Germany had been divided into four zones of occupation, each administered by a different member of the Big Four. Berlin, the capital and largest city in Germany, lay deep within the Soviet zone. It, too, was divided into four administrative sectors. The original partition had been intended as a temporary measure, a compromise between Soviet fears of a united, prosperous, and armed German nation and U.S. concerns to build a strong bulwark against communism in Central Europe.

Neither Soviet fears nor U.S. plans had greatly changed in the postwar years, so the uneasy temporary compromise had

simply remained. Between 1947 and 1949, the three Western zones began to merge economically and politically, and on May 8, 1949, they formed themselves into the Federal Republic of Germany, with Bonn as the capital. On October 7, 1949, the Soviet (Eastern) zone became the German Democratic Republic (GDR). The situation in Germany was a frequent point of friction between the Soviet Union and the United States.

In late 1958, the situation had flared up again. The continued U.S. rearming of West Germany excited Soviet fears, especially when some of the more recent supplies included artillery and bombers capable of handling nuclear weapons. The Soviets also considered the proposed integration of West Germany into a close economic union with France, Italy, Belgium, the Netherlands, and Luxembourg (the European Economic Community, or Common Market) to be a threat to their interests. Between November 10 and 27, 1958, therefore, the Soviets made a series of proposals and demands concerning the divided city of Berlin, which essentially gave a six-month deadline to the Western powers to end their occupation of Berlin. The Soviets said that they would turn over administration of their sector to the German Democratic Republic (GDR); that nation would also control the access routes to Berlin. The Western powers would have to leave by that time or turn administration over to a United Nations peacekeeping force. The Western powers, especially the United States, found these terms unacceptable because they did not recognize the GDR as a legal government. They would ignore or force any GDR checkpoints, they said. An attack on the GDR would be considered an attack on the Soviet Union, the Soviets replied. Later, Khrushchev removed the six-month deadline so that the subject could be discussed at Paris.

Ever since his victory over his rivals G. M. Malenkov, N. A. Bulganin, and V. M. Molotov in July of 1957, Khrushchev had been the unchallenged leader of the Soviet Union. As first secretary of the Communist Party and premier of the Soviet Union, he occupied the most powerful positions in the party and state executive hierarchies. Since 1957, he had become one of the strongest advocates of the increased production of consumer goods, opposing the traditional Soviet emphasis on heavy industry and defense spending. One of the most important corollaries of this program was a policy of peaceful coexistence with the West; lowered tensions, he hoped, could allow for a smaller defense budget.

Khrushchev's attitude was highly controversial in the communist world and within the Soviet Union itself. The Chinese communists were especially concerned about the implications of the doctrine of peaceful coexistence. While the Sino-Soviet split was not to emerge into the open until 1962, the issue of rapprochement with the West had already soured relations between the two states. A similar point of view could be heard within the highest circles of the Soviet Communist Party, from the military leaders, who did not trust the West, as well as the advocates of heavy industry, who were unenthusiastic about the whole thrust of Khrushchev's policies. Khrushchev's Camp David initiative, therefore, had been undertaken against heavy internal opposition, but his power was such that he did not have to worry about this opposition as long as his policy was showing visible results. Yet he needed a clear victory at the summit to ensure his domestic political position.

At 8:55 A.M. on May 1, 1960, a U.S. U-2 high-altitude reconnaissance plane was shot down by a Soviet ground-to-air missile near Sverdlovsk, three hundred miles into Soviet territory. The pilot, Francis Gary Powers, did not succeed in destroying the plane, and both he and it fell into Soviet hands. On May 5, Khrushchev reported the incident to the Soviet Union's Supreme Soviet, without mentioning that both the pilot and the plane had been recovered. Later that day, the United States released a story maintaining that the plane was collecting scientific data on the Turkish-Soviet border and had probably strayed across. Two days later, Khrushchev disclosed Powers' capture and confession, exploding the cover story issued by the United States. Khrushchev's statement embarrassed the United States but did not close the door to the summit, as Khrushchev added that he was willing to believe that President Eisenhower had not known of the flight. The United States at first seemed willing to take advantage of this loophole but later vacillated. On May 11, President Eisenhower took responsibility for the U-2 flights, which had been going on since 1956, calling them a "distasteful . . . necessity." Although a moratorium was called on future flights, the United States would not say that it was going to cancel them altogether.

Inside the Soviet Union, the U.S. acknowledgment of responsibility and apparent determination to continue the overflights came as a decisive blow to Khrushchev's policy of peaceful coexistence. On May 10 or 11, Khrushchev apparently was outvoted in a meeting of the Presidium of the Central Committee of the Communist Party and a hard-line stand at the summit was mandated. At the first meeting of the conference later that month, Khrushchev announced that the Soviet Union would not participate unless the United States repudiated the U-2 program and punished those responsible for instituting it. Eisenhower refused, and the much-vaunted summit never took place.

The diplomatic consequences of the collapse of the summit were less than expected. On his way back to the Soviet Union, Khrushchev withdrew his plan to turn over administration to Berlin and its approaches to East Germany. Thus, the Berlin question did not explode—but neither was it settled. Eisenhower's successor, John F. Kennedy, would find this issue to be one of the first diplomatic problems with which he had to deal.

The affair, particularly the failed cover story, somewhat weakened the United States' carefully defined image as a benign force in the Cold War. The Bay of Pigs debacle in Cuba in the following year further tarnished Washington's international reputation. Moscow had its own embarrassments in the early 1960's, particularly during the 1962 Cuban Missile Cri-

sis, which prevented the United States from monopolizing international opprobrium at the height of the Cold War. Although Khrushchev made a point of linking the collapse of the Paris conference to the U.S. violation of Soviet airspace, it is unlikely that any significant resolution of the issues that divided Washington and Moscow could have been achieved in the environment of the early 1960's.

For Khrushchev, the consequences were somewhat more severe. His reverse in the foreign policy arena strengthened his domestic critics. This opposition was expressed in a shake-up in the top leadership of the party, in which some of Khrushchev's most loyal supporters were demoted. Khrushchev's own position was not in danger, but after 1960 he was forced to share more and more power with the other party leaders. For some analysts, the U-2 incident marked the beginning of Khrushchev's decline, which ended in his ouster in 1964.

—Paul Ashin, updated by Steve D. Boilard

ADDITIONAL READING:

Beschloss, Michael R. *MAYDAY: Eisenhower, Khrushchev, and the U-2 Affair*. New York: Harper & Row, 1986. A widely drawn narrative, including details of the principals' personal lives and other tangential details. Especially useful are the appendix, historiographical note, and list of sources. Photographs and illustrations.

Eisenhower, Dwight D. *The White House Years: Waging Peace, 1956-1961*. Garden City, N.Y.: Doubleday, 1965. The second volume of Eisenhower's memoirs, which includes his defense of the United States' handling of the U-2 incident.

LaFeber, Walter. *America, Russia, and the Cold War, 1945-1990*. 6th ed. New York: McGraw-Hill, 1991. An update of LaFeber's classic study of U.S. foreign policy during the Cold War. Chapter 9 covers the years from 1957 to 1972.

Pocock, Chris. "Mayday." In *Dragon Lady: The History of the U-2 Spyplane*. Osceola, Wis.: Motorbooks International, 1989. One chapter discusses the primary facts of the U-2 incident, although it views the entire affair with a focus upon the plane itself.

Powers, Francis Gary, and Curt Gentry. *Operation Overflight: The U-2 Spy Pilot Tells His Story for the First Time*. New York: Holt, Rinehart and Winston, 1970. A somewhat bitter and self-exonerating first-person narrative of Powers' mission, capture, and trial. Highly critical of the reconnaissance program and the United States' handling of the crisis.

Stanglin, Douglas, and Sergei Kuznetsov. "A New Look at the U-2 Spy Case." *U.S. News and World Report* 114, no. 10 (March 15, 1993): 54-55. Summarizes an interview with the Soviet citizens who first found Powers. Not politically significant, but provides additional color to the story of Powers' capture.

Wise, David, and Thomas B. Ross. *The U-2 Affair*. New York: Random House, 1962. Based on interviews with government officials involved in the incident. Written in a breezy, narrative style.

SEE ALSO: 1960, Kennedy Is Elected President; 1961, Bay of Pigs Invasion; 1962, Cuban Missile Crisis.

1960 ■ CIVIL RIGHTS ACT OF 1960:

additional protections for voting rights presage a stronger Voting Rights Act five years later

DATE: May 6, 1960

LOCALE: Washington, D.C.

CATEGORIES: African American history; Civil rights; Laws and acts

KEY FIGURES:

Everett Dirksen (1896-1969), Senate minority leader

James Eastland (1904-1986), chairman of the Senate Judiciary Committee

Dwight David Eisenhower (1890-1969), thirty-fourth president of the United States, 1953-1961

Lyndon Baines Johnson (1908-1973), Senate majority leader

Richard Russell (1897-1971), senator who directed the southern filibuster against the Civil Rights Act

Howard Smith (1883-1976), chairman of the House Rules Committee

SUMMARY OF EVENT. The Fifteenth Amendment to the Constitution, passed in 1870, was designed to protect the right of African Americans to vote. The amendment simply says: "The right of citizens of the United States to vote shall not be denied or abridged by the United States or by any State on account of race, color, or previous condition of servitude." Officials in the Southern states, however, found numerous ways to disfranchise black voters without violating the Fifteenth Amendment, such as the literacy test, poll tax, grandfather clause, and white primary. As a result of these voting barriers, most African Americans were eliminated as voters, in spite of what the Fifteenth Amendment was designed to do.

The civil rights bills of the late 1950's and the 1960's were designed to make the Fifteenth Amendment enforceable. Since the end of Reconstruction, Congress had passed only one civil rights bill, in 1957. The 1957 law sought to empower the federal government to protect voting rights by seeking injunctions against voting rights violations. In reality, the 1957 law was so weak that only a few suits were brought by the Department of Justice against the illegal practices of voting officials. The 1957 Civil Rights Act established the U.S. Commission on Civil Rights, which was given the authority to investigate civil rights abuses. The commission could draw national attention to civil rights problems and recommend legislation to Congress, but it had no enforcement powers. African Americans and civil rights supporters realized that something substantial was needed to protect black voting rights.

In 1959, President Dwight D. Eisenhower introduced a seven-point civil rights program. Three parts of the bill dealt with education and school desegregation, the most significant provision being the attempt to make it a crime to interfere with court-ordered desegregation. The bill requested a two-year extension of the Civil Rights Commission and contained several other provisions to combat economic discrimination. The only section of the law that involved voting rights was the provision that states must preserve voting records for three years. This provision was needed to prove whether there was a pattern or practice of discrimination in voting.

Conspicuously missing from the Eisenhower bill was a request that Congress authorize the attorney general to bring civil proceedings to protect voting rights. This provision, known as Title III, had been the heart of the administration's 1957 Civil Rights Act. Title III would have allowed the federal government to prevent interference with civil rights instead of only being able to punish such interference after the fact. Intense Southern opposition to Title III forced the administration to abandon the provision in the 1957 Civil Rights Act, as Eisenhower believed that Congress was not ready to incorporate Title III in the administration's new bill.

The House judiciary subcommittee, comprising mostly Northern civil rights supporters, strengthened the Eisenhower bill and restored Title III. The full Judiciary Committee, containing many Southern opponents of civil rights, quickly gutted most of the stronger sections passed by the subcommittee. The weakened bill was passed by the Judiciary Committee and forwarded to the important Rules Committee. The Rules Committee, chaired by Howard Smith, a Virginia segregationist, did not act on the bill until civil rights supporters threatened to discharge the bill from the Rules Committee's jurisdiction. The Democratic Study Group, a newly formed organization consisting of liberal Democrats, led the movement to free the bill from the Rules Committee. The Rules Committee finally sent the civil rights bill to the floor of the House for consideration by the entire House.

Southern Democrats led much of the opposition to the bill. Opponents contended that the bill went too far in protecting voting rights and encroached on the rights of states to control the election process. Representative William Colmer, a Democrat from Mississippi, said that "even in the darkest days of Reconstruction, the Congress never went as far as the proponents of this legislation, in this 1960 election year, propose to go." After defeating numerous Southern amendments to weaken an already weak bill, the House voted 311 to 109 to approve the civil rights bill and send it to the Senate.

The United States Senate has often been the burial ground of civil rights laws, especially during the 1940's, 1950's, and 1960's. This was primarily the result of two factors. First, Southern Democrats, by virtue of their seniority, controlled many key committees, including the Judiciary Committee, to which civil rights legislation, by jurisdiction, must be referred. Second, Southern senators were skillful in the use of legislative tactics, such as the filibuster, to kill legislation.

The Eisenhower bill was sent to the Senate Judiciary Committee, chaired by Democratic senator James Eastland of Mississippi. Eastland, a staunch segregationist, refused to act on the bill. Only as a result of a parliamentary maneuver undertaken by Majority Leader Lyndon Johnson and Minority

Leader Everett Dirksen was the bill brought to the floor of the Senate for debate.

Southern senators, led by Democrat Richard Russell of Georgia, organized a filibuster. All Southern senators participated in the filibuster, with the exception of the two senators from Tennessee and the two senators from Texas. Supporters of the civil rights bill attempted to end the lengthy filibuster by invoking cloture, which required two-thirds of the Senate to vote to stop the filibuster. When the cloture vote took place, only forty-two of the one hundred senators voted to stop the filibuster. The civil rights supporters not only failed to get the two-thirds vote required but also failed to muster a simple majority.

The defeat of cloture meant that the Southern Democratic senators had won and could dictate the terms of the final bill. The final, watered-down version of the bill contained little that would protect the voting rights of African Americans. The most significant provision authorized federal judges to appoint federal referees to assist African Americans in registering and voting if a pattern or practice of discrimination was found. The Senate passed the weakened bill by seventy-one to eighteen, and President Eisenhower signed the bill into law on May 6, 1960. The fact that only two other individuals were present when Eisenhower signed the bill into law testifies to its legislative insignificance.

Perhaps the weakness of the 1960 Civil Rights Act was its main legacy. The law proved to be unable to cope with many problems confronting African Americans in the South. Many blacks who attempted to register or vote lost their jobs, were subjected to violence, or were victimized by double standards or outright fraud on the part of voting officials. The impotence of the 1960 Civil Rights Act to deal with these issues, combined with the lack of progress in increasing the number of African American voters in the South, forced Congress to pass the powerful Voting Rights Act in 1965. This legislation would forever transform the political landscape of the South, and its consequences have continued to be felt.

—*Darryl Paulson*

ADDITIONAL READING:

Abernathy, Charles F. *Civil Rights and Constitutional Litigation: Cases and Materials*. 2d ed. St. Paul, Minn.: West, 1992. Somewhat technical, but an interesting approach to the interplay between congressional and judicial sources of civil rights.

Berman, Daniel M. *A Bill Becomes a Law: Congress Enacts Civil Rights Legislation*. New York: Macmillan, 1966. Case study of the passage of the 1960 Civil Rights Act.

Black, Earl, and Merle Black. *The Vital South: How Presidents Are Elected*. Cambridge, Mass.: Harvard University Press, 1992. Examines how presidential politics has changed in the South, primarily as a result of the passage of civil rights laws.

Lawson, Steven F. *In Pursuit of Power: Southern Blacks and Electoral Politics, 1965-1982*. New York: Columbia University Press, 1985. Investigates how civil rights and voting rights laws have impacted Southern politics of blacks and whites.

Tate, Katherine. *From Protest to Politics: The New Black Voters in American Elections*. Cambridge, Mass.: Harvard University Press, 1994. Demonstrates how U.S. politics in the 1990's has been influenced by the policies of prior decades.

Whalen, Charles, and Barbara Whalen. *The Longest Debate: A Legislative History of the 1964 Civil Rights Act*. Washington, D.C.: Seven Locks Press, 1985. A former member of Congress provides an inside view of the politics surrounding the 1964 Civil Rights Act.

SEE ALSO: 1965, Voting Rights Act.

1960 ■ KENNEDY IS ELECTED PRESIDENT: *beginning of a "New Frontier" era in the United States*

DATE: November 8, 1960
LOCALE: United States
CATEGORY: Government and politics
KEY FIGURES:
Lyndon Baines Johnson (1908-1973), Democratic vice presidential candidate
John Fitzgerald Kennedy (1917-1963), Democratic presidential candidate
Henry Cabot Lodge II (1902-1985), Republican vice presidential candidate
Richard Milhous Nixon (1913-1994), Republican presidential candidate
Howard K. Smith (born 1914), moderator of the press panel for the television debates

SUMMARY OF EVENT. In 1960, the American people once again demonstrated their capacity for doing the politically unexpected by electing a Catholic Democrat, John F. Kennedy, to the presidency. A number of factors made this particular election unique, one of which was the shift in party control of the White House during a period of relative prosperity and stability. Seeking to explain this turn of events, political scientists have pointed to the personalities of the candidates, the question of religion, the type of campaign waged by each man, and the voting trends of the previous thirty years. While there is little unanimity as to what was most decisive in creating Kennedy's victory, many scholars argue that the televised debates between the two candidates in September and October, 1960, played a major role.

As with all presidential elections, the story of the 1960 campaign really begins with the quest for nomination. In the case of John F. Kennedy, junior senator from Massachusetts, the quest for the Democratic nomination began in 1956. Failing to take advantage of his senatorial position but concentrating, instead, on his family's past experience in U.S. politics and diplomacy, Kennedy proceeded to obtain as much national exposure as possible and to build a formidable political organization that concentrated on clan-type loyalty and a modern approach to politics. In January, 1960, he announced his candidacy and proceeded to enter the various Democratic primaries. In Kennedy's case, the decision to enter primaries was a political necessity. Many of the major figures in the Eastern wing of the party were skeptical about the Massachusetts senator's national appeal and his ability to capture non-Catholic votes. West Virginia, a predominantly Protestant state, was the perfect spot to test Kennedy's general voter appeal. Through vigorous campaigning and a direct confrontation of the religious issue, he succeeded in winning 60 percent of the vote, eliminating Senator Hubert Humphrey as a rival candidate and finally demonstrating his ability to win support in rural Protestant areas. After this victory, he moved on to capture delegates in Indiana, Nebraska, Maryland, and Oregon. Kennedy won a first ballot nomination in Los Angeles, and surprised many of his Eastern supporters by persuading Lyndon B. Johnson, Senate majority leader and the leading presidential hopeful in the South, to take second place on the ticket. The selection of Johnson energized the New Deal coalition and helped unite the party.

In the Republican camp, the race for the nomination was much less competitive. After New York governor Nelson Rockefeller withdrew in 1959, it appeared clear that Richard M. Nixon, the vice president, was assured of the presidential nomination. After a routine convention, Henry Cabot Lodge

John F. Kennedy, thirty-fifth president of the United States. During an administration cut short by assassination, he oversaw the Cuban Missile Crisis, witnessed the rise of the Civil Rights movement, and challenged the nation to reach the Moon. (Library of Congress)

of Massachusetts, an old Kennedy foe, was selected as Nixon's running mate.

On the whole, the Republican and Democratic platforms were very similar. Both spoke of U.S. responsibility to contain communism, endorsed the economic policies of the Eisenhower regime, took credit for the general national prosperity, and made a commitment to civil rights.

As the national campaign got under way, it appeared that Kennedy faced a difficult task in breaking the Republican hold on the White House. He needed to overcome a number of problems, among which were his youth (he was forty-three years of age) and inexperience, his lack of a national reputation, and his religion. Less controversial today than in 1960, the question of religion haunted the campaign: Americans had never before elected a Roman Catholic to the presidency. Nixon completely ignored the question of religion, but Kennedy was forced to come to grips with it. He was asked to discuss the possible problems of a Catholic's being president on September 11, 1960, at Houston, Texas, before a meeting of Protestant ministers. In this first and last statement on his religion in the campaign, Kennedy emphasized that, if elected, he would make decisions on the basis of the national interest, and he reiterated his belief in the First Amendment. He told the Southern Baptists, "I believe in an America where the separation of church and state is absolute—where no Catholic prelate would tell the president (should he be a Catholic) how to vote. . . ."

As the campaign progressed, Nixon made considerable headway with the issue of experience, while the younger Kennedy attempted to direct the public's attention to the declining prestige of the United States abroad and the complacency at home. The turning point in the campaign for the Democrats came when both candidates appeared on national television for a series of debates. On September 26 and on three evenings in October, the candidates appeared before a panel of newsmen, headed by Howard K. Smith, to answer questions of national importance. The first debate centered on domestic problems, while the following meetings concentrated on questions of foreign policy. Network executives announced that the series had been seen by the largest audience in television history. Following the election, President Kennedy pointed to the television debates as the single most important factor in his victory. The televised image of a calm, self-assured Kennedy and a nervous, ill-at-ease Nixon influenced many of the ninety million people who watched the first televised debates in U.S. history.

Unquestionably, the debates helped Kennedy. On a financial level, the Democrats never could have met the expense required for such national television exposure. More important, however, the debates helped to erase the Republican image of Kennedy as young and inexperienced. Indeed, the well-prepared Kennedy appeared to be articulate, informed, and highly competent. Nixon, for many reasons—including a recent illness and a narrow conception of the function of the debates—did not project well on television. All the subsequent surveys indicated that a decisive number of U.S. voters felt that Kennedy had "won" the debates and that his appearance had influenced their decision to vote for him. After this tremendous boost in prestige, the Kennedy campaign gained momentum.

Before the votes were finally counted, however, the Republicans staged a significant counterattack, which involved lavish use of television spot appearances by Nixon and a hard-hitting endorsement from President Eisenhower, who until the last week before the election had been sitting out the campaign. The final vote tally showed that Kennedy captured 303 electoral votes and 34,227,096 popular votes to Nixon's 219 electoral votes and 34,226,731 popular votes. In popular votes, the election was one of the closest in the nation's history. The Democrats swept to victory on the strength of their backing in urban and industrial areas, the Catholic vote, and the support of labor and African Americans. Nixon, who won a majority in twenty-six states, captured most of the west. Of special significance in Kennedy's victory was his ability to hold most of the Solid South in line through the campaign efforts of Lyndon Johnson.

—George Q. Flynn, updated by Joseph Edward Lee

ADDITIONAL READING:

Nixon, Richard. *Six Crises*. Garden City, N.Y.: Doubleday, 1962. Analyzes the role television played in this, one of Nixon's six crises.

Reeves, Richard. *President Kennedy: Profile of Power*. New York: Simon & Schuster, 1993. A thorough examination of Kennedy as a campaigner and as a president.

Reeves, Thomas. *A Question of Character*. New York: Free Press, 1991. Raises disturbing questions about Kennedy's private life.

Schlesinger, Arthur, Jr. *A Thousand Days*. Boston: Houghton Mifflin, 1965. A Pulitzer Prize-winning chronicle of the brief Kennedy Administration.

Stroter, Gerald S. *Let Us Begin Anew*. New York: Harper-Collins, 1993. A useful history of the Kennedy years.

White, Theodore H. *The Making of the President, 1960*. New York: Atheneum, 1961. A journalist's award-winning day-by-day account of the 1960 campaign.

SEE ALSO: 1952, Eisenhower Is Elected President; 1961, Peace Corps Is Established; 1961, Bay of Pigs Invasion; 1962, Cuban Missile Crisis; 1963, Nuclear Test Ban Treaty; 1963, Assassination of President Kennedy.

1961 ■ PEACE CORPS IS ESTABLISHED:

a volunteer service organization enlists Americans to participate in cross-cultural exchange designed to aid more than ninety countries

DATE: March 1, 1961
LOCALE: United States
CATEGORIES: Diplomacy and international relations; Economics; Government and politics

KEY FIGURES:

Joseph H. Blatchford (born 1934), director of Action, the parent organization of the Peace Corps

John Fitzgerald Kennedy (1917-1963), thirty-fifth president of the United States, 1961-1963

Robert Sargent Shriver, Jr. (born 1915), director of the Peace Corps, 1961-1966

Jack Hood Vaughn (born 1920), director of the Peace Corps, 1966-1969

SUMMARY OF EVENT. The Peace Corps is an agency of the United States government, designed to provide skilled workers in underdeveloped foreign countries. Under its auspices, trained U.S. volunteers serve a minimum of two years as educators, health and environmental professionals, and agriculturalists on foreign soil for modest compensation.

Although the Peace Corps was conceived early in the Kennedy Administration and symbolized the ideals of that era, the project did not originate with John F. Kennedy. Congressional leaders such as Henry Reuss, Richard Neuberger, and Hubert Humphrey had suggested such an organization before Kennedy incorporated the movement into a late-evening election speech delivered at Ann Arbor, Michigan, on October 13, 1960. Pleased with the enthusiastic response the proposal had received during his campaign, the new president issued an executive order on March 1, 1961, creating the Peace Corps. With the passage of the Peace Corps Act on September 22, 1961, the Peace Corps became a permanent agency of the Department of State, with an annual budget of thirty million dollars for fiscal year 1962-1963.

During the first five years of its existence, the Peace Corps was directed by President Kennedy's brother-in-law, Sargent Shriver, who led by example of charismatic energy. He continued in the office under President Lyndon Johnson until January, 1966. While in charge of the Peace Corps, Shriver presided over a period of dramatic and enthusiastic expansion. By the time he left the post, there were more than fourteen thousand volunteers at work in fifty-two countries, and the annual budget had reached more than $110 million. Half the volunteers were in teaching positions, 10 percent were involved in agricultural projects, and the balance were performing a variety of tasks for community development. Most of the volunteers were young, Caucasian, and college-educated. Approximately one in seven asked for termination of the service before the two-year period expired.

Under Shriver's direction, the Peace Corps developed an organizational framework to guarantee its institutional independence. Shriver insisted on separating the activities of the corps from other U.S. foreign aid efforts or intelligence operations, and successfully resisted an attempt to attach the Peace Corps to the Agency for International Development (AID). As director, Shriver gained the title of assistant secretary of state, reporting only to the secretary of state. On the other hand, the Peace Corps remained dependent on congressional budget approval and was subject to a National Advisory Council, composed of prominent citizens and chaired by the vice president of the United States.

The early success of the Peace Corps sparked a number of efforts modeled on it. More than fifteen countries launched aid programs of their own, appealing to the same sense of youthful idealism that motivated the U.S. movement. In 1962, an International Peace Corps Secretariat was established to coordinate those various programs. In the United States, the experience garnered from the Peace Corps was applied to domestic problems, resulting in the creation of Volunteers in Service to America (VISTA) in 1964. VISTA was organized under the Office of Economic Opportunity (OEO), an antipoverty agency also directed by Shriver.

In 1966, President Johnson asked Shriver to devote his time completely to OEO and to head the War on Poverty, and Jack Vaughn became the director of the Peace Corps. During Vaughn's three-year tenure, which coincided with the escalation of the war in Vietnam and an increase in domestic unrest, the number of volunteers began to level off and then to decline. Additionally, the VISTA program and the growing Civil Rights movement in the United States were luring away volunteers. Consequently, many of the original programs were reduced in an attempt to eliminate waste and to produce more tangible results for the host countries. Because there was no upper age limit for application to the Peace Corps, Vaughn also attempted to increase the percentage of older skilled volunteers, but he met with little success.

After 1969, the size of the Peace Corps declined further, although the agency does claim that more than 140,000 persons have served since its inception. Joseph Blatchford, director under President Richard Nixon, continued Vaughn's efforts to draw more experienced volunteers into the corps, particularly those from business and industry. He also reduced the emphasis on the Peace Corps's independence, suggesting it merge with VISTA and other federal volunteer programs.

From the start, the Peace Corps faced persistent criticism. Some congressional critics thought that the expense of the program was far greater than the good produced by it. Others expressed the belief that it was an expensive means of educating middle-class Americans about their less prosperous neighbors. The volunteers themselves shared many of these doubts, as they often were undertrained to deal with situations in which they found themselves or often not needed at all. After 1965, many also began to question their role as a symbol of a U.S. foreign policy with which they could not agree.

The history of the Peace Corps can be viewed as a revealing record of the attempt to channel the idealism evoked by President Kennedy's inaugural address into direct action. However, the enthusiastic rhetoric of its early years contrasts sharply with its more subdued voice since.

—*Courtney B. Ross, updated by Joyce Duncan*

ADDITIONAL READING:

Carey, Robert G. *The Peace Corps*. New York: Frederick A. Praeger, 1970. Presents a balanced survey of the agency's first decade.

Hoopes, Roy. *The Complete Peace Corps Guide*. New York: Dial Press, 1965. A highly enthusiastic, semi-official explanation of the Peace Corps' operation.

Lowther, Kevin, and C. Payne Lucas. *Keeping Kennedy's Promise. The Peace Corps: Unmet Hope of the New Frontier.* Boulder, Colo.: Westview Press, 1978. A lively, historical overview of the Peace Corps, with suggestions for future viability.

Windmiller, Marshall. *The Peace Corps and Pax Americana.* Washington, D.C.: Public Affairs Press, 1970. Attacks the Peace Corps as a front for U.S. expansionism in the Third World.

SEE ALSO: 1960, Kennedy Is Elected President; 1963, King Delivers His "I Have a Dream" Speech; 1964, Berkeley Free Speech Movement.

1961 ■ BAY OF PIGS INVASION: *invasion of Cuba by a CIA-trained guerrilla force results in a crushing defeat*

DATE: April 17-19, 1961

LOCALE: Bay of Pigs, Las Villas province, Cuba

CATEGORIES: Diplomacy and international relations; Wars, uprisings, and civil unrest

KEY FIGURES:

Richard Mervin Bissell (1909-1977), CIA director of operations

José Miró Cardona (1901-1974), leader of the United Revolutionary Front

Fidel Castro (born 1926 or 1927), premier of Cuba

Allen Dulles (1893-1969), director of the CIA

John Fitzgerald Kennedy (1917-1963), thirty-fifth president of the United States, 1961-1963

Adlai Ewing Stevenson (1900-1965), U.S. ambassador to the United Nations

SUMMARY OF EVENT. In 1959, Fidel Castro and his revolutionary forces had overthrown Cuba's government, establishing a revolutionary socialist regime in its place. Lands formerly owned by members of the upper classes and by U.S. companies were seized and redistributed, and many Cubans fled to the United States—primarily Florida—in exile.

In March, 1960, President Dwight D. Eisenhower authorized the Central Intelligence Agency (CIA), headed by Allen Dulles, to train and equip a Cuban exile guerrilla force for the purpose of infiltrating Cuba and joining the anti-Castro underground. With the cooperation of the Guatemalan government, the CIA soon established training camps in that country, and the training of Cuban exile volunteers began. By November, 1960, the CIA operation, under the supervision of Richard Bissell, had changed from the training of guerrillas to the preparation of an invasion force. After that date, guerrilla training ceased, and a small army was trained in conventional assault landing tactics.

Meanwhile, in the Cuban exile community in Miami, Florida, the United Revolutionary Front was formed. Headed by Dr. José Miró Cardona, who would become provisional president of Cuba upon the exiles' return, the group in Miami managed the recruitment of soldiers for the expeditionary force, although the operation was completely directed by the CIA. Volunteers were screened for political acceptability, and leftists were discouraged or rejected. Consequently, the force in training took on a conservative character.

The CIA-directed operation ran into severe problems from the start. Numerous political conflicts that threatened to undermine the entire operation erupted among the exile volunteers. U.S. involvement in the affair was supposed to remain covert, but in Miami the existence of the invasion force and the Guatemalan camps, as well as the CIA direction of the operation, were common knowledge. Increasingly, the American press reported on the preparations in progress for an invasion of Cuba. Castro, premier of Cuba, also knew of the exile army being trained in Guatemala.

In February, 1961, the invasion plans underwent an important change. Originally, the CIA had specified the city of Trinidad as the landing point for the exile force. The newly elected president, John F. Kennedy, decided that the invasion plans could proceed, however, only if U.S. support troops were better camouflaged. The site at Trinidad was judged too risky. In its place, the Bay of Pigs, one hundred miles to the west of Trinidad on the south-central coast of Cuba, was chosen. Trinidad was the better of the two sites for one simple reason: In the event of failure, the invasion force could retreat into the Escambray Mountains with little difficulty. The beaches at the Bay of Pigs, on the other hand, were surrounded by the Zapata swamps. Escape to the mountains some eighty miles to the east would be extremely difficult, if not impossible. In the event that the exiles could not establish a defensible beachhead at the Bay of Pigs, the only realistic retreat possible for them would be in the direction from which they came: to the sea.

By April, 1961, the invasion plans had taken shape. Castro's air force was to be destroyed on the ground by two scheduled air strikes against Cuban air bases. The invasion force of fifteen hundred troops would disembark under the cover of night and acquire the advantage of complete surprise. Meanwhile, paratroopers would be dropped to establish advance positions, from which they could scout approaching Cuban forces and cut off transportation routes. With the skies to themselves, the exile forces initially would be resupplied at the Playa Girón airfield, close to the Bay of Pigs. Simultaneously, a diversionary landing would occur on the eastern coast of Cuba in an attempt to deceive Cuban forces about the exiles' real intentions. The main invasion force then would advance into Matanzas Province with the goal of securing a defensible area of Cuban territory. This accomplished, the leaders of the United Revolutionary Front would be flown to Cuba to establish a provisional government. It was hoped that the local Cuban population might join the invaders in their fight against the Castro regime. With this possibility in mind, the supply ships accompanying the invasion force were to be stocked with arms and ammunition for a force of four thousand.

From the beginning, Operation Pluto, as the invasion plan was called, went badly. On April 15, 1961, eight B-26 bombers, supplied by the United States and disguised as Cuban air force planes, departed from Puerto Cabezas, Nicaragua, and attacked Cuban airfields in an attempt to destroy the Cuban air force. The bombing raid was unsuccessful. Although considerable damage was done to Cuba's small air force, the attack left unharmed two or three T-33 trainer jets, three Sea Furies, and two B-26's.

At the United Nations, Raúl Roa, Cuba's foreign minister, charged that the attack was a prelude to invasion from the United States. Adlai Stevenson, the United States' ambassador to the United Nations, replied that the attacking planes were of Cuban origin. Because one of the planes had landed in Florida after the raid, Stevenson was able to produce photographs showing a B-26 bomber displaying the insignia of the Cuban air force. Stevenson actually believed the Cuban pilots to be defectors from Castro's own forces; he was unaware of the deception. The trick was soon discovered, however, when reporters pointed out certain differences in the nose cones of the Cuban B-26's as compared with the one that had landed in Florida. U.S. complicity in the air strike was apparent, and President Kennedy, at the recommendation of Secretary of State Dean Rusk and Special Assistant for National Security McGeorge Bundy, canceled the second air strike, scheduled for dawn April 17.

In the early-morning hours of Monday, April 17, the invasion force (now named Brigade 2506) began to disembark at two beaches on the Bay of Pigs: Playa Girón and Playa Larga. Contrary to advance intelligence reports that the area was virtually uninhabited and that militia in the area had no communications with Havana, the invaders were spotted almost immediately, and the news of invasion was relayed quickly to Castro's headquarters. Thus, the dangerous night landing was conducted under fire from the very start. The unloading of troops and arms progressed more slowly than planned, and at dawn there were still invasion forces on the ships. The element of surprise had not been achieved, and the force of the undestroyed Cuban planes soon would be felt. Throughout the day on Monday, events continued to go against the invaders.

Cuba's air force, particularly the jets, proved to be the decisive factor in the battle. Two of the exiles' escort ships, the *Rio Escondido* and the *Houston*, were sunk with arms, ammunition, and supplies on board. The exile air force (the Free Cuban Air Squadron), which consisted of sixteen B-26 bombers, lost half of its planes. Flying from Nicaragua, the B-26's carried extra fuel and had no tail guns. Unable to maneuver quickly, they made easy targets for the T-33 jet trainers. At sea, the escort vessels that were not sunk by Cuban planes were forced to withdraw from the invasion area. On the ground, the

President Kennedy examines the combat flag of the Cuban exile force that landed on Giron Beach, Cuba, during an aborted invasion that came to be known as the Bay of Pigs. (National Archives)

invasion forces fought well but were hampered by wet communication equipment and a scarcity of ammunition. Only one of the paratroop drops succeeded. The other failed because the paratroopers were dropped too close to the invasion area and because their heavy equipment was dropped into the swamps, never to be found again during the remainder of the battle.

The Bay of Pigs region was politically one of the worst possible sites for a successful counterrevolution in Cuba. What before 1959 had been an exclusively agricultural zone peopled by woodcutters was being developed by the revolutionary government as a future tourist haven. New roads, markets, and schools had won Castro the support of the populace, and few welcomed the invaders, who represented the middle and upper classes of Havana. Once the invasion foundered, the men of Brigade 2506 could not count on the local inhabitants to give them refuge. The U.S. planners of the invasion, through wishful thinking, had misread the mood of the Cuban people in the spring of 1961. Almost all of those dissatisfied with the revolution had already departed for the United States, and the bombing of Cuban airfields by the exile air force rallied public opinion behind Castro. The national uprising that the CIA was counting on to coincide with the debarkation of the exile force never occurred. The Cuban army and militia remained loyal to the regime, and between April 15 and 17, Castro ordered the arrest of more than one hundred thousand opponents of his government, eliminating

dissident elements in the Catholic church and the Cuban press and destroying the CIA's underground network of agents. With all of these problems at the Bay of Pigs, it probably made no difference in the final result that the diversionary landing on the eastern coast of Cuba never took place.

In Washington, the discouraging news from the Bay of Pigs led President Kennedy to reinstate the second air strike, which earlier had been canceled. The planes of the Free Cuban Air Squadron based in Nicaragua were to strike the San Antonio de los Banos airfield at dawn on Tuesday, April 18. The following morning, six B-26 bombers piloted by Cuban exile pilots were over the designated target, but the bombers were forced to return to Nicaragua without dropping a single bomb because of fog and cloud cover.

On the ground, Castro was moving twenty thousand troops toward the Zapata swamp region as Brigade 2506 was running out of ammunition. Because the Cuban air force still commanded the skies, there was no chance to unload the remaining arms, supplies, and troops aboard the two remaining escort ships at sea.

In the early-morning hours of Wednesday, April 19, President Kennedy authorized an "air-umbrella" at dawn over the invasion area. He gave permission for six unmarked jet fighters from the USS *Essex* in the Caribbean to protect a B-26 attack from Nicaragua and to cover the unloading of the exile escort ships at sea. This final attempt to help the invading forces also proved to be a failure. Probably because of confusion about the difference in time zones between Cuba and Nicaragua, the B-26 bombers from Nicaragua arrived an hour early over Cuba and were shot down by the Cubans; only one escaped. The jets that were to have provided air cover never left the *Essex*.

Later on April 19, 1961, the invasion was crushed. Facing overwhelming opposition and out of ammunition, the leaders destroyed their heavy equipment and ordered a retreat into the swamps. Only a handful of exiles escaped to the sea; the remainder were rounded up by Castro's forces and imprisoned. Of 1,297 brigade members who had come ashore, 1,180 were captured. Cuban losses are difficult to estimate. Although Castro admitted to losing fewer than a hundred men in battle, a more accurate estimate would be 1,250.

—*Charles E. Cottle, updated by Julio César Pino*

ADDITIONAL READING:

Draper, Theodore. "How *Not* to Overthrow Castro." In *Castro's Revolution: Myths and Realities*. New York: Praeger, 1962. Offers a useful post-mortem discussion of how a misunderstanding of the radical nature of Castro's revolution on the part of the United States government led to military failure.

Hunt, Howard. *Give Us This Day*. New Rochelle, N.Y.: Arlington House, 1973. A personal account of why the invasion collapsed by a Central Intelligence Agency officer. A valuable inside look at how the Cuban exile force was trained and how political factions tore it apart before it reached Cuba.

Trumbell, Higgins. *The Perfect Failure: Kennedy, Eisenhower, and the CIA at the Bay of Pigs*. New York: W. W. Norton, 1987. A study of the decision-making process that led to the invasion. Argues that the CIA's success at ousting other leftist regimes during the early years of the Cold War led Kennedy to believe the Castro government would collapse easily.

Welch, Richard E. *Response to Revolution: The United States and the Cuban Revolution, 1959-1961*. Chapel Hill: University of North Carolina Press, 1985. Concludes that Kennedy was not a reluctant warrior but legally and morally responsible for the invasion debacle.

Wyden, Peter. *Bay of Pigs: The Untold Story*. New York: Simon & Schuster, 1979. A narrative history, sometimes hour-by-hour, of how the invasion was planned and fought as seen by the participants in Washington, D.C., Miami, and Havana.

SEE ALSO: 1960, U-2 Incident; 1960, Kennedy Is Elected President; 1962, Cuban Missile Crisis.

1961 ■ FIRST AMERICAN IN SPACE: *Cold War political competition opens a new age of space exploration*

DATE: May 5, 1961
LOCALE: Cape Canaveral, Florida
CATEGORY: Science and technology

KEY FIGURES:

Wernher von Braun (1912-1977), leader of rocket research in Nazi Germany and subsequently the United States' chief missile expert

Dwight David Eisenhower (1890-1969), thirty-fourth president of the United States, 1953-1961

Robert R. Gilruth (born 1913), head of the Space Task Group of Project Mercury

John Herschel Glenn, Jr. (born 1921), the United States' first person to orbit Earth

Virgil Ivan "Gus" Grissom (1926-1967), the United States' second person in space

John Fitzgerald Kennedy (1917-1963), thirty-fifth president of the United States, 1961-1963

Alan Bartlett Shepard, Jr. (born 1923), the United States' first person in space

SUMMARY OF EVENT. United States Navy Commander Alan B. Shepard, Jr., became the first U.S. citizen in space when he successfully piloted the *Freedom 7* spacecraft on May 5, 1961. After a four-hour launch delay, his suborbital flight lasted 15.47 minutes and attained a peak attitude of 116.6 miles, cruising about three hundred miles down the Atlantic Missile Range to a safe splashdown. U.S. national pride and world prestige, badly shaken by a long series of Soviet pioneering triumphs in space, were boosted by *Freedom 7*'s almost flawless performance. Technically, however, Shepard's ride did not equal the orbital mission of Soviet cosmonaut Yuri Gagarin on April 12, 1961. U.S. successes continued to be assessed against a backdrop of Soviet firsts.

The United States might have probed space long before the Soviets, because the principles of multistage rockets were developed by a U.S. physicist, Robert H. Goddard. Goddard's theories largely were ignored in favor of investment in more practical enterprises, such as increased consumer goods. In Nazi Germany, however, Goddard's ideas fired the imagination of a young German rocket scientist, Wernher von Braun, who was responsible for developing the V-1 and V-2 rockets that devastated London during World War II. After the war, von Braun came to the United States, where he became a leader in U.S. rocket research. The Soviet Union, however, made greater strides in this field than did the United States after World War II, hoping to develop rocket technology and reach military parity with U.S. strategic and conventional forces. In 1957, the Soviets orbited the first Earth satellite, Sputnik 1, and followed with other spectacular shots, including launching and recovering live creatures from spacecraft and satellite mapping of the far side of the Moon. In the United States, these milestones created such alarm over the possibility that space would be exploited for Soviet military advantage that the public demanded an accelerated U.S. space program. Both presidents Dwight D. Eisenhower and John F. Kennedy reacted to the outcry.

In 1958, President Eisenhower authorized the creation of the National Aeronautics and Space Administration (NASA) to explore space for peaceful pursuits, and he simultaneously assigned Project Mercury, the U.S. man-in-space program, to NASA for development. NASA immediately appointed a Space Task Group (STG), managed by Robert R. Gilruth, to recruit the first astronauts. From thousands of civilian and military volunteers, seven seasoned military test pilots were finally selected.

Project Mercury received the highest government priority. It was an intense test program that managed to stress pilot safety, even at the expense of launch scheduling. Government and industrial contractors were involved, and a workforce of more than two million people. All component systems were tested thoroughly and paired with duplicate backup systems. Technicians searched meticulously for deficiencies, particularly in unsuccessful test flights. The astronauts were trained extensively on simulators and centrifuges, with all physiological processes monitored. The military provided aeromedical support, because no civilian counterpart existed. Expertise was culled from a variety of federal and private agencies. President Kennedy stated that no astronaut's life would be risked prematurely, even if a delay benefited the Soviets.

Air Force Atlas boosters, the most powerful available, were selected to launch orbital flights; the less powerful Army Redstones, developed by von Braun, were designated for suborbital shots. Smaller solid-propellant rockets, known as Little Joes, were used early in the program for unmanned test shots. Each capsule had to be scaled to mate perfectly with its booster, an engineering challenge that underwent many modifications and improvements. In addition to carrying a finite payload, each capsule had to be equipped with life support and flight operations systems, a form-fitting couch, and duplicate systems that could survive throughout all the critical phases of flight, from launch to splashdown. The Russians already had developed the necessary technology and were launching heavier payloads with boosters larger than the Atlas. As a result, early U.S. tests were often demeaned by the Soviet press, while being followed avidly by a U.S. public that applauded every incremental success.

The program was divided into two phases, Mercury-Redstone (MR) suborbital flights and Mercury-Atlas (MA) orbital flights. Shepard's flight, MR-3, was the first manned shot and followed the success of an unmanned shot and one carrying a small chimpanzee, Ham. The whole world viewed the event, and the world press was represented at Mission Control in Cape Canaveral. MR-3 represented a free world as well as a U.S. initiative that would open space exploration to all nations, not only the militarily aggressive. Such openness contrasted sharply with the secrecy surrounding Soviet launchings.

Shepard arose early on the morning of his flight, dined with other astronauts, underwent a physical examination, and was equipped with biophysical measuring devices before being assisted into his twenty-pound, aluminized, tailor-made, spacesuit. He calmly walked to the launch pad and was strapped into his bell-shaped *Freedom 7* spacecraft. After four annoying holds, he was fired into space and remained in constant radio contact.

In every test, the eighty-three-foot, sixty-six-thousand-pound MR-3 performed nominally. Booster cutoff occurred on schedule, with immediate jettison of the escape tower above the capsule that was designed to blast it free in case of launch problems. Then the clamp ring that secured the booster to the capsule was released, and three small thrusters fired to effect final separation. The automatic stabilization control system maintained proper spacecraft attitude, and Shepard extended the periscope to view Earth below. At this point, he was weightless and, after making a few performance tests, switched to manual control. In one exercise, using a control stick, he maneuvered *Freedom 7* in three separate motions—pitch, roll, and yaw—thus proving that humans could function well under conditions of zero gravity. Since Gagarin had exercised less manual control in his more extensive orbital flight path, Shepard achieved a small milestone for the free world.

Minutes later, Shepard pitched the capsule to the retrofire attitude and activated the retrosequence. This maneuver was not required on a suborbital flight but was used to test the system. After firing, the retropackage was jettisoned, the periscope retracted, and the capsule returned to automatic control. *Freedom 7* descended backward, with its broad heat shield to the astronaut's rear. This phase was critical, because the capsule could disintegrate if the heat shield were not properly positioned to withstand scorching temperatures greater than 1,000° Fahrenheit. As planned, the heat shield slowly burned away as the capsule gently rolled at about ten degrees per second to distribute the heat load evenly. Shepard continued to perform tasks even during peak gravity, when he withstood pressures equivalent to eleven times his body weight. At around thirty thousand feet, the drogue chute, the first of three parachutes, was deployed to stop oscillation and reduce speed. The main braking parachute and recovery antennas were deployed at ten thousand feet. Shepard splashed down in the Atlantic Ocean, three hundred miles south of Cape Canaveral. No leaks inhibited his exit. Shepard crawled into a sling suspended from a hovering aircraft and was welcomed as a hero aboard the carrier USS *Lake Champlain*. He had touched space, a hostile, unknown environment, and had returned safely.

After MR-3, public confidence in the nation's scientific ability surged, as reflected in the significant increase in the price of stock in companies associated with Project Mercury and in the decision of the Kennedy Administration to increase funding of civil and military space ventures. Shortly thereafter, President Kennedy committed NASA to a manned lunar landing goal.

Scientifically, Shepard's performance was of great value. Shepard, like Gagarin, was living proof that humans could survive in space and perform many skilled tasks under varying severe stresses. His excellent postflight condition attested the soundness of the experimental ground training procedure, even though Shepard later recommended elimination or abbreviation of certain procedures. The fact that he needed to use manual override in only one minor instance—when a panel light failed to flash green—demonstrated the vehicle's engineering competence. Since Shepard could rely on primary systems, especially to autopilot *Freedom 7*, he was free to assess more fully the functioning of the telemetry, monitoring, and ballistic trajectory systems, which were then confidently used in subsequent missions. In a sense, Shepard helped qualify Project Mercury as a sound national investment. The pressures of publicity now called for more spectacular missions, which eventually were undertaken in the Mercury-Atlas orbital flights and followed by the Gemini and Apollo programs that fulfilled Kennedy's lunar landing goal.

—*Anne C. Raymer, updated by David G. Fisher*

ADDITIONAL READING:

Emme, Eugene M. *A History of Space Flight.* New York: Holt, Rinehart and Winston, 1965. An examination of Project Mercury from a historical perspective; while the race to the Moon was still under way, its outcome was uncertain at that point.

Hotz, Robert. "MR-3 in Perspective." *Aviation Week* 83 (May 15, 1961): 21. Editorial comments on the significance of *Freedom 7* in the advancement of space flight technology.

Kolcum, Edward. "Mercury-Redstone Procedures Simplified." *Aviation Week* 83 (June 12, 1961): 31-32. Provides details of MR-3 performance in flight, both the spacecraft and the launch vehicle. Pilot performance is also discussed, and comments on public response to the flight of Freedom 7 are given.

Mercury Astronauts. *We Seven.* New York: Simon & Schuster, 1962. Covers all aspects of the Mercury program from the astronauts' perspective. Includes pilots' descriptions of the first several Mercury flights, including MR-3.

Olney, Ross R. *Americans in Space: A History of Manned Space Travel.* New York: Thomas Nelson, 1970. Story of the first NASA manned flights, leading up to the Apollo 11 landing on the Moon. Suitable for younger readers as well as adults.

Shepard, Alan B., and Deke Slayton. *Moon Shot.* Atlanta: Turner Publishing, 1994. Personal account of two astronauts' participation in the early space program.

Swenson, Loyd S., James M. Grimwood, and Charles C. Alexander. *This New Ocean: A History of Project Mercury.* Washington, D.C.: Government Printing Office, 1966. The official technical NASA history of the Mercury program, from inception to completion.

SEE ALSO: 1903, Wright Brothers' First Flight; 1926, Launching of the First Liquid-Fueled Rocket; 1969, Apollo 11 Lands on the Moon; 1977, Spaceflights of Voyagers 1 and 2; 1986, *Challenger* Accident.

1962 ■ REAPPORTIONMENT CASES: *U.S. Supreme Court decisions require election districts to be determined by population*

DATE: March 26, 1962-February 17, 1964
LOCALE: Washington, D.C.
CATEGORIES: Court cases; Government and politics

KEY FIGURES:
Archibald Cox (born 1912), solicitor general of the United States
William Orville Douglas (1898-1980) and
Felix Frankfurter (1882-1965), associate justices of the United States
John M. Harlan (1899-1971), associate justice of the United States and most vocal opponent of mandatory reapportionment
Earl Warren (1891-1974), chief justice of the United States

SUMMARY OF EVENT. Among the many profound changes ushered in by the twentieth century, none has had a more far-reaching effect on U.S. society than urbanization. The United States has not always adjusted to the changes wrought by urbanization. This has been especially true in the area of democratic political representation in the various states. By 1960, there were flagrant examples of malapportionment in the majority of states, both in state legislatures and in delegations to the U.S. House of Representatives. Incumbent state legislatures, dominated by rural elements, had refused to reapportion representation to reflect population shifts accurately; to do so would have strengthened urban areas at the expense of the rural groups in control. Delaware, for example, had not reapportioned its legislature since 1897; Tennessee and Alabama had not done so since 1901. These were only the worst cases. In all but six states, less than 40 percent of the population could elect a majority of the legislature.

State legislatures frequently ignored provisions in their state constitutions that required periodic reapportionment on the basis of the decennial census. Such a situation imperiled the very basis of democracy. Yet the Supreme Court, prior to 1962, had refused to intervene on the grounds that apportionment was a political question and thus outside the jurisdiction of the Court. This dictum had been handed down in the case *Colegrove v. Green* (1946). The resulting malapportionment has been likened to the eighteenth century English "rotten boroughs."

In 1963, the Court finally abandoned its unwillingness to act on the matter of apportionment and took a strong stand in favor of democratic representation in *Baker v. Carr*, a case challenging the apportionment of the Tennessee state legislature. The Tennessee state constitution called for reapportionment every ten years, although none had taken place since 1901. As a result, urban areas were greatly underrepresented in the legislature, while rural areas were overrepresented. Moore County, with a population of 3,454, elected one legislator, while Shelby County (which includes Memphis), with a population of 627,019, elected only three. The inequities were starkly evident.

The federal district court in Tennessee, in which suit had been filed originally, refused to take action on the basis of the precedent established in *Colegrove v. Green.* When the case was appealed to the Supreme Court, however, that body ruled by a six-to-two margin that the Tennessee case was justiciable and returned it to the lower court for a decision. Political reformers finally had realized their aim: The Court, under Chief Justice Earl Warren, had agreed to deal with the problem of equitable apportionment of representation, although it had made no actual decision on the subject. Justices Felix Frankfurter and John Harlan dissented in *Baker v. Carr*, again arguing that apportionment was a political question and therefore not within the Court's jurisdiction.

As a result of *Baker v. Carr*, a spate of litigation and legislation regarding apportionment followed. By the end of 1963, federal suits had been filed in thirty-one states and state suits in nineteen others. During that same period, twenty-six states adopted new legislative apportionment plans. Nevertheless, these plans did not always satisfy political reformers. The plans varied greatly in intent and effect, because the Court had not actually ruled on apportionment and therefore had not established guidelines for the states to follow.

This confusion over the Court's views was partially remedied in March of 1963, when *Gray v. Sanders* struck down Georgia's so-called county unit rule. That rule assigned a certain number of units, or votes, to each county in elections for statewide offices and operated in a manner similar to the federal electoral college. The result of the county unit rule was severe discrimination against voters in the more populous areas. The Court ruled eight to one, Justice Harlan dissenting, that the Georgia system violated the equal protection clause of the Constitution, and Justice William O. Douglas, in writing the majority opinion, used the momentous phrase "one man, one vote." Again, the Court had not ruled directly on the question of apportionment, but it had given a broad hint as to what it expected.

Gray v. Sanders foreshadowed *Wesberry v. Sanders*, a landmark case decided in 1964, in which the Court used the "one man, one vote" principle to void a 1931 Georgia congressional apportionment law. Justice Harlan again dissented, contending that the Court was intruding upon the proper province of Congress. The Court, however, was now clearly committed to guaranteeing equitable apportionment and democratic represented in the United States House of Representatives as well as in state legislatures. Later in 1964, the Court further delineated its standards in six cases involving Alabama, New York, Maryland, Virginia, Delaware, and Colorado.

The cases in Alabama and New York were particularly important because, in addition to rural-urban issues, they also presented strong race issues. As cities such as Birmingham and New York grew after World War I, their most densely populated sections became predominantly African American. Not only was the "one man, one vote" ideal not being met, but racial minorities also were grossly underrepresented. In Alabama, *Reynolds v. Sims* (1964) challenged apportionment policies set up in 1901, when the state constitution was designed to preserve rule by white, conservative Democrats. The New York case of *WMCA v. Lomenzo* received national attention when New York City radio station WMCA decided early in 1961 to begin challenging state apportionment policies outlined in the state constitution of 1894. The Supreme Court ruled in favor of reapportionment in the WMCA case on June 1, 1965; Justice Harlan again dissented.

The effect of these decisions was to create a movement for a remedial constitutional amendment in Congress—a movement that failed, as did a vigorous effort to call a federal constitutional convention to consider apportionment. The Court had served notice that malapportionment would not be tolerated, and in 1967 it reaffirmed its endorsement to the "one man, one vote" principle in *Swan v. Adams*.

—Fredrick J. Dobney, updated by Geralyn Strecker

ADDITIONAL READING:

Ball, Howard. *The Warren Court's Conceptions of Democracy: An Evaluation of the Supreme Court's Apportionment Opinions*. Rutherford, N.J.: Fairleigh Dickinson University Press, 1971. Explores the political dynamics within the Supreme Court and the effects they had on the outcomes of apportionment cases. Particularly interesting are Ball's discussions of Justice Harlan's dissenting opinions.

Cortner, Richard C. *The Apportionment Cases*. Knoxville: University of Tennessee Press, 1970. Explores the genesis and impact of the apportionment cases, paying particular attention to *Baker V. Carr* and *Reynolds v. Sims*.

Graham, Gene. *One Man, One Vote: "Baker v. Carr" and the American Levellers*. Boston: Little, Brown, 1972. Follows the *Baker v. Carr* case from its beginnings, through its effects on other apportionment cases, to its residual impact a decade after the decision.

Lee, Calvin B. T. *One Man, One Vote: WMCA and the Struggle for Equal Representation*. New York: Scribner's, 1967. This in-depth study follows the *WMCA v. Lomenzo* case from the radio station's first decision to fight apportionment in 1961 to the Supreme Court decision on June 1, 1965. Much discussion of the dissenting arguments.

Maveety, Nancy. *Representation and the Burger Years*. Ann Arbor: University of Michigan Press, 1991. Examines the impact of reapportionment after twenty-five years. Particularly examines the post-1965 debate over group rights versus individual rights in regard to representation.

O'Rourke, Timothy G. *The Impact of Reapportionment*. New Brunswick, N.J.: Transaction Books, 1980. Charts the effects of reapportionment on elections in legislative districts in Delaware, Kansas, New Jersey, Oregon, South Dakota, and Tennessee.

SEE ALSO: 1960, Civil Rights Act of 1960; 1964, Twenty-fourth Amendment; 1964, Civil Rights Act of 1964; 1965, Voting Rights Act.

1962 ■ MEREDITH REGISTERS AT "OLE MISS": *the first African American student enrolls at the University of Mississippi*

DATE: October 1, 1962
LOCALE: Oxford, Mississippi
CATEGORIES: African American history; Civil rights; Education

KEY FIGURES:

Ross Robert Barnett (1898-1987), governor of Mississippi
John Fitzgerald Kennedy (1917-1963), thirty-fifth president
of the United States, 1961-1963
Robert Francis Kennedy (1925-1968), U.S. attorney general
James Howard Meredith (born 1933), first African American
to attend the University of Mississippi

SUMMARY OF EVENT. In January, 1961, James H. Meredith, a native Mississippian and an Air Force veteran attending Jackson State College, one of Mississippi's all-black colleges, decided to transfer to the University of Mississippi, affectionately called "Ole Miss." His application was rejected because, Ole Miss officials maintained, Jackson State was not an approved Southern Association Secondary School and because Meredith did not furnish letters of recommendation from University of Mississippi alumni. On May 31, 1961, he filed a lawsuit against the university, charging that he had been denied admission because of his race. In its 114-year history, the University of Mississippi had never admitted an African American student.

A federal district court judge dismissed Meredith's suit, but in June, 1962, a U.S. court of appeals ruled that Meredith had been rejected from Ole Miss "solely because he was a Negro," a ruling based on the *Brown v. Board of Education of Topeka, Kansas* school desegregation case of 1954. The court ordered the university to admit Meredith, and the ruling was upheld by Justice Hugo Black of the United States Supreme Court. On September 13, Mississippi governor Ross Barnett delivered a televised speech and stated, "No school will be integrated in Mississippi while I'm governor." A week later, the board of trustees of Ole Miss appointed Governor Barnett as the university's registrar, and he personally blocked Meredith from registering for courses that same day.

Throughout Meredith's court appeals, the United States Department of Justice had been monitoring the case. Attorney General Robert F. Kennedy, the brother of President John F. Kennedy, made more than a dozen phone calls to Governor Barnett, hoping to persuade him to allow Meredith to matriculate and thereby avoid a confrontation between the state of Mississippi and the federal government. The attorney general had provided Meredith with federal marshals to protect him as he attempted to register.

On September 24, the court of appeals that initially had heard Meredith's case again ordered the Board of Higher Education of Mississippi to allow Meredith to register. The following day, Meredith reported to the registrar's office in the university's Lyceum Building, but again Governor Barnett was there to block his registration. During a phone conversation with Attorney General Kennedy that same day, Barnett declared that he would never agree to allow Meredith to attend the University of Mississippi. When Kennedy reminded Barnett that he was openly defying a court order and could be subject to penalty, Barnett told Kennedy that he would rather spend the rest of his life in prison than allow Meredith to enroll. On September 26, Meredith again tried to register for

courses, and for the third time, Governor Barnett turned him away. Two days later, the court of appeals warned Barnett that if he continued to block Meredith's admission to Ole Miss, the governor would be found in contempt of court, arrested, and fined ten thousand dollars per day. On Saturday, September 29, Governor Barnett appeared at an Ole Miss football game and proudly announced, "I love Mississippi, I love her people, her customs! And I love and respect her heritage. Ask us what we say, it's to hell with Bobby K!"

That evening, President Kennedy called Governor Barnett and told him that the federal government would continue to back Meredith until Ole Miss admitted him. Under direct pressure from the president, Barnett began to reconsider. Finally, he agreed to allow Meredith to register on Sunday, September 30, when, the governor surmised, few students and news reporters would be milling around the campus. On Sunday evening, Meredith arrived at the Lyceum Building protected by three hundred marshals, armed in riot gear and equipped with tear gas.

As Meredith and his escorts approached the campus, a group of twenty-five hundred students and other agitators attempted to block their passage. The crowd began to shout and throw bricks and bottles at the federal marshals, who retaliated with tear gas. Some of the protesters were armed with guns and began firing random shots. One federal marshal was seriously wounded by a bullet in the throat. Two onlookers, Paul Guihard, a French journalist, and Roy Gunter, a jukebox repairman, were shot and killed by rioters.

On Sunday evening, while Mississippians rioted on the Ole Miss campus, President Kennedy addressed the nation on television. The Meredith crisis had captured the country's and news media's attention, and the president attempted to show Mississippians and other U.S. citizens that his administration's commitment to civil rights was serious and unwavering. He reminded his audience that "Americans are free . . . to disagree with the law but not to disobey it. For in a government of laws and not of men, no man, however prominent or powerful, and no mob, however unruly or boisterous, is entitled to defy a court of law." He told Mississippians, "The eyes of the nation and all the world are upon you and upon all of us. And the honor of your university—and state—are in the balance."

The situation at the University of Mississippi was deteriorating. The federal marshals, low on tear gas, requested additional help to control the unruly mob. President Kennedy federalized Mississippi National Guardsmen and ordered them to Oxford. At dawn on Monday morning, the first of five thousand troops began arriving at Oxford to restore order. During the evening's rioting, more than one hundred people were injured and about two hundred were arrested, only twenty-four of whom were Ole Miss students.

On Monday morning, October 1, at 8:30 A.M., Meredith again presented himself at the Lyceum Building to register. He was closely guarded by federal marshals, and National Guardsmen continued patrolling the Ole Miss campus and

James Meredith receives his law degree from Ole Miss, the first African American to be graduated from a Southern university after the Supreme Court's 1954 desegregation ruling in Brown v. Board of Education. (The Associated Publishers, Inc.)

Oxford's streets. Meredith, dressed impeccably in a business suit, registered for classes and began his matriculation at the University of Mississippi. "I am intent on seeing that every citizen has an opportunity of being a first-class citizen," Meredith told a reporter the next day. "I am also intent on seeing that citizens have a right to be something if they work hard enough."

During his tenure at Ole Miss, Meredith was often the target of insults and threats. Federal marshals remained with him during his entire time at the university. On August 18, 1963, Meredith graduated from the University of Mississippi with a bachelor of arts degree in political science. After a year of study in Africa, Meredith enrolled at Columbia University of Law. In 1966, the year before he completed his law degree, Meredith was wounded by a sniper's gunshot during a voter registration march from Tennessee to Mississippi.

As a result of his successful effort to desegregate Ole Miss, Meredith became one of the heroes of the Civil Rights movement. In his "Letter from Birmingham Jail" (1963), Martin Luther King, Jr., states that "One day the South will recognize its real heroes. They will be the James Merediths, courageously and with a majestic sense of purpose facing jeering and hostile mobs and the agonizing loneliness that characterizes the life of the pioneer."

Meredith's victory at the University of Mississippi was a key triumph for the Civil Rights movement during the 1960's.

Within two years, the University of Alabama, the University of Georgia, and other Southern colleges and universities that had prevented African Americans from enrolling were also desegregated, as the era of overt segregation in U.S. institutions of higher learning came to an end.

The Meredith case also convincingly demonstrated that the federal government would use its power to end racial segregation in the South. Despite Governor Barnett's defiance, President Kennedy and his attorney general were able to force the state of Mississippi to comply with a federal court order, signaling that the South would be unable to block the subsequent wave of federal legislation designed to void the region's segregation laws. —*James Tackach*

ADDITIONAL READING:

Barrett, Russell H. *Integration at Ole Miss*. Chicago: Quadrangle Press, 1965. Discusses Meredith's attempt to integrate the University of Mississippi.

Branch, Taylor. "The Fall of Ole Miss." *Parting the Waters: America in the King Years, 1954-1963*. New York: Simon & Schuster, 1988. The crisis at the University of Mississippi is discussed in this chapter of a Pulitzer Prize-winning history of the Civil Rights movement.

Meredith, James H. *Three Years in Mississippi*. Bloomington: Indiana University Press, 1966. Meredith's own story of his years at Ole Miss.

Schlesinger, Arthur M., Jr. *Robert Kennedy and His Times*.

Boston: Houghton Mifflin, 1978. Details Kennedy's involvement in the Meredith case.

Wexler, Sanford. *The Civil Rights Movement: An Eyewitness History.* New York: Facts On File, 1993. This illustrated history of the Civil Rights movement devotes a chapter to Meredith's integration of Ole Miss. Includes a chronology of events and eyewitness testimonies.

SEE ALSO: 1954, *Brown v. Board of Education*; 1955, Montgomery Bus Boycott; 1957, Southern Christian Leadership Conference Is Founded; 1957, Little Rock School Desegregation Crisis.

1962 ■ CUBAN MISSILE CRISIS: *at the height of the Cold War, the United States and the Soviet Union risk nuclear confrontation*

DATE: October 22-28, 1962
LOCALE: Washington, D.C., and Cuba
CATEGORIES: Diplomacy and international relations; Latino American history; Wars, uprisings, and civil unrest
KEY FIGURES:
McGeorge Bundy (born 1919), special assistant to the president
Fidel Castro (born 1926 or 1927), revolutionary leader of Cuba
Anatoly F. Dobrynin (born 1919), Soviet ambassador to the United States
Aleksandr S. Fomin, official at the Soviet embassy in Washington, D.C.
Kenneth B. Keating (born 1900), senator from New York
John Fitzgerald Kennedy (1917-1963), thirty-fifth president of the United States, 1961-1963
Robert Kennedy (1925-1968), U.S. attorney general
Nikita Sergeyevich Khrushchev (1894-1971), premier of the Soviet Union and first secretary of the Communist Party
Robert S. McNamara (born 1916), U.S. secretary of defense
Dean Rusk (1909-1994), U.S. secretary of state
John Scali (born 1918), diplomatic correspondent with the American Broadcasting Company
SUMMARY OF EVENT. When Fidel Castro's revolutionary July 26 Movement assumed power in Cuba in 1959, it marked the end of U.S. political and economic dominance over the island. Ever since the late nineteenth century, the United States, supported by loyal Cuban politicians, had enjoyed control over all Cuba's commerce and industry. Castro, however, refused to adhere to U.S. interests, and as a result, the United States attempted to overthrow Castro's government through the use of covert military operations and an economic blockade.

In 1960, President Dwight Eisenhower and the Central Intelligence Agency (CIA) began organizing and training anti-Castro Cuban exiles for a potential invasion. When President John F. Kennedy entered the White House in 1961, he agreed to continue this program, and in April, more than fourteen hundred commandos landed at the Bay of Pigs. U.S. experts believed that the people would rise up and revolt against Castro during this assault, but Castro easily quashed this rebellion. Afterward, Kennedy hatched several assassination plots against Castro, and he sanctioned the CIA to conduct sabotage raids upon Cuban sugarcane fields, railroad bridges, and oil tanks through Operation Mongoose.

All of these attacks, however, backfired. Threatened with continuous military invasions and the loss of trade, Castro turned toward the Soviet Union for support. He declared himself a Marxist-Leninist in 1961, and, afterward, Soviet influence substantially increased. By 1962, the Soviet Union had stationed several military advisers in Cuba, and Kennedy feared that Communist influence ultimately could undermine U.S. hegemony in Latin America if this relationship continued to grow.

In October, 1962, Senator Kenneth B. Keating of New York startled the United States by alleging that offensive missile bases were under construction in Cuba. Keating did not reveal the source of his information, but a flight by a U.S. U-2 reconnaissance airplane on October 14 substantiated his charges. Long-range nuclear missiles, which had begun arriving in Cuban ports from Russia in September, were being installed at San Cristobal on the western part of the island. An international crisis of potentially catastrophic proportions threatened the safety of the world.

After President Kennedy viewed the satellite photos on October 16, he called his key military and political advisers to the White House. The initial discussion centered on the issue of whether the missiles were fully armed and ready to fire. After concluding that the United States still had time before the Soviets attained nuclear readiness on Cuba, the president and his executive committee (Ex Comm) discussed various options. General Maxwell Taylor of the Joint Chiefs of Staff recommended an immediate air strike. Others, including Secretary of Defense Robert McNamara and McGeorge Bundy, the president's special assistant for national security affairs, suggested that the president resort to diplomacy rather than war.

By Thursday, October 18, a consensus had emerged from the discussions, and the next day, the president indicated that he favored a naval blockade as the first step. He also decided that he would announce his decision to the U.S. people on the evening of Monday, October 22. At 5:00 P.M., he briefed congressional leaders. An hour later, Soviet ambassador Anatoly F. Dobrynin was ushered into the office of Secretary of State Dean Rusk, where he was handed a copy of Kennedy's speech. At 7:00 P.M., the president spoke over nationwide television and radio.

"The purpose of these bases," Kennedy said in a calm but firm voice, "can be none other than to provide a nuclear strike capability against the Western Hemisphere." The Soviet action was "a deliberately provocative and unjustified change in the status quo which cannot be accepted by this country, if our courage and commitments are ever to be trusted again by either friend or foe." The president then outlined the initial steps the United States would take to deal with the situation: a quarantine on offensive military equipment being shipped to Cuba; an assertion that any missile launched from Cuba would be regarded as an attack by the Soviet Union, requiring a total retaliatory response by the United States; emergency meetings of both the Organization of American States and the United Nations to consider this threat to peace; and an appeal to Nikita S. Khrushchev, premier of the Soviet Union, "to abandon this course of world domination, and to join in an historic effort to end the perilous arms race and to transform the history of man." The quarantine was to become effective on October 24 at 10 A.M.

On Wednesday, October 24, the Soviet Union officially rejected the U.S. proclamation of quarantine. Late that day, however, some Soviet ships sailing toward Cuba altered course or stopped in midsea. Yet, a direct confrontation between U.S. and Soviet ships could not long be delayed, as this crisis escalated into an international war of brinkmanship. The American Strategic Air Command went to Defense Condition 2, one step away from actual war; B-52 bombers took off with nuclear arsenals; and soldiers were moved to bases in the southeast and briefed for a potential invasion of Cuba.

The first real thaw in the crisis occurred on Friday afternoon, October 26, when John Scali, diplomatic correspondent of the American Broadcasting Company, received a call from Aleksandr S. Fomin, an official of the Soviet embassy who was also a colonel in the Soviet State Security Committee (KGB) and a personal friend of Khrushchev. At lunch, Fomin proposed a settlement of the crisis and asked Scali if he could find out from contacts in the Department of State if it would be acceptable. The missile bases in Cuba, Fomin said, would be dismantled and the Soviet Union would promise not to ship any more offensive missiles in exchange for a U.S. pledge not to invade Cuba. Scali immediately took this proposal to Rusk, who felt it was legitimate. At the same time, a personal letter from Khrushchev confirmed Fomin's offer, but it also reminded Kennedy that the Soviet Union's actions were simply a response to his provocative measures toward Castro's government.

The next day, the situation deteriorated when Khrushchev seemed to change the proposal markedly when he demanded that the United States abandon its missile bases in Turkey. This angered Kennedy. Despite the fact that the missiles in Turkey were of little strategic value, he felt that U.S. credibility was at stake. Several members of Ex Comm, including U.S. ambassador to the Soviet Union W. Averell Harriman, suggested that this provided Khrushchev with a face-saving alternative. The president and his advisers decided to proceed on the basis of the meetings with Fomin and to ignore Khrushchev's demand, but at the same time, Kennedy sent his brother, Attorney General Robert Kennedy, to meet with Soviet ambassador Dobrynin and secretly agree to remove the missiles

in Turkey if the Cuban crisis were resolved peacefully.

Other news also threatened the peace. The afternoon of October 27, a U.S. U-2 strayed over Soviet air space; it managed to return home safely, but Kennedy feared that the Soviets would view this as the first step in a preemptive strike. On the same day, another U-2 was shot down over Cuba, and as a result, most members of Ex Comm believed that a nuclear exchange was imminent.

On the morning of Sunday, October 28, Moscow radio carried an announcement that had come from Khrushchev: "In order to eliminate as rapidly as possible the conflict which endangers the cause of peace . . . the Soviet Government . . . has given a new order to dismantle the arms which you have described as offensive, and to crate and return them to the Soviet Union." The Cuban missile crisis had passed, and a nuclear holocaust had been averted. The United States removed the missiles from Turkey in 1963, both nations installed a nuclear hotline between Washington, D.C., and Moscow to prevent future misunderstandings over nuclear war, and both nations began to explore talks to curtail the nuclear arms race.

—William M. Tuttle, updated by Robert D. Ubriaco, Jr.

ADDITIONAL READING:

Allison, Graham T. *Essence of Decision: Explaining the Cuban Missile Crisis.* Boston: Little, Brown, 1971. A scholarly study exploring the bureaucratic decision-making process during the crisis. Attempts to explain Kennedy's actions through the use of certain theoretical models.

Blight, James G., and David A. Welch. *On the Brink: Americans and Soviets Reexamine the Cuban Missile Crisis.* New York: Hill & Wang, 1989. Uses key interviews with policymakers, including coverage of the 1987 Cambridge Conference at which key players from both sides reconvened to discuss the crisis. Foreword by McGeorge Bundy.

Dinnerstein, Herbert S. *The Making of a Missile Crisis, October 1962.* Baltimore: The Johns Hopkins University Press, 1976. Provides an exemplary overview of Soviet perceptions.

Kennedy, Robert F. *Thirteen Days: A Memoir of the Cuban Missile Crisis.* New York: W. W. Norton, 1969. The president's brother details the day-to-day activities of the Ex Comm during the crisis.

Nathan, James A., ed. *The Cuban Missile Crisis Revisited.* New York: St. Martin's Press, 1992. Addresses the crisis from the Soviet, U.S., and Cuban perspectives, using several newer archival sources to provide fresh and innovative perspectives on the crisis. A somewhat challenging study.

Paterson, Thomas G., ed. *Kennedy's Quest For Victory: American Foreign Policy, 1961-1963.* New York: Oxford University Press, 1989. Chapter 5 provides a concise overview of the crisis and Kennedy's views on Cuba throughout his presidency.

SEE ALSO: 1956, Cuban Revolution; 1960, U-2 Incident; 1960, Kennedy Is Elected President; 1961, Bay of Pigs Invasion.

1963 ■ GIDEON V. WAINWRIGHT: *the U.S. Supreme Court guarantees the right to legal counsel*

DATE: March 18, 1963
LOCALE: Washington, D.C.
CATEGORIES: Civil rights; Court cases
KEY FIGURES:
Hugo Lafayette Black (1886-1971), associate justice of the United States
William Orville Douglas (1898-1980), associate justice of the United States
Abe Fortas (1910-1982), Gideon's appointed defense counsel
Clarence Earl Gideon, petitioner in the case
Frank Murphy (1890-1949), associate justice of the United States
Earl Warren (1891-1974), chief justice of the United States
SUMMARY OF EVENT. In the 1960's, the Supreme Court effected a virtual revolution in American constitutional rules dealing with criminal procedure. These were part of a series of extensive changes in all phases of constitutional law: First Amendment freedoms, redistricting and reapportionment of electoral districts, and civil rights. Under Chief Justice Earl Warren, the Supreme Court had for some years stressed the protections available to criminal defendants, but in *Mapp v. Ohio* (1962) it issued a major pronouncement on the subject, declaring that evidence seized in violation of the search warrant and reasonable cause provisions of the Fourth Amendment would no longer be admissible in state courts; such evidence had been inadmissible in federal courts since the 1914 ruling in *Weeks v. United States*.

In *Gideon v. Wainwright*, the Court ruled that states are constitutionally required to provide counsel for indigent defendants in trials before state judges, and in a number of subsequent decisions handed down from 1963 through 1966, the Court held that counsel had to be provided at various critical stages of the investigation process. The capstone of the developments in this field was *Miranda v. Arizona* (1966), in which the Court ruled that persons apprehended by the police must be advised of their constitutional rights to remain silent and to have legal counsel at public expense if they are indigent. The testimony of the accused is to be inadmissible in state or federal courts if these admonitions are not given.

In related decisions, the Court has made the following guarantees of the Bill of Rights applicable to the state through the due process clause of the Fourteenth Amendment, and in virtually every instance the result has meant overruling longstanding principles: the Fifth Amendment right to be free from compelled self-incrimination, *Malloy v. Hogan* (1964); the right to a speedy trial, *Klopfer v. North Carolina* (1967); the right to confront opposing witnesses, *Pointer v. Texas* (1965); the right to compulsory process for obtaining witnesses, *Washington v. Texas* (1967); the right to trial by jury, *Duncan v. Louisiana* (1968); and the right to be free from being placed

twice in jeopardy for the same offense, *Benton v. Maryland* (1966).

The Supreme Court had first considered the question of a state's obligation to provide counsel for indigent defendants in 1932. In *Powell v. Alabama* it ruled that states were constitutionally required to provide counsel for such defendants in cases involving capital punishment, but in *Betts v. Brady* (1942) the Court had refused to apply the same requirement to noncapital state cases. A divided Supreme Court had held that there was no general right to court-appointed counsel in state felony cases and that such counsel was available only under "special circumstances." The Court reasoned that to impose such a rule would constitute an excessive encroachment on the prerogatives of the states to manage their own affairs. Justice Hugo Black, with whom Justices William O. Douglas and Frank Murphy concurred, wrote a stirring dissent charging that the Court had no authority to select which provisions of the Bill of Rights it would apply to the states and that the Fourteenth Amendment applied the entire Bill of Rights to the states. Black did not pursue this point, however, but went on to find that even under the "prevailing view of due process" he was convinced that the right to counsel was so fundamental that to deprive a person of counsel constituted a violation of "common and fundamental ideas of fairness and right." In *Adamson v. California* (1946), Black presented a full-scale historical argument in support of his theory that the framers of the Fourteenth Amendment intended to make the entire Bill of Rights apply verbatim to the states. It was most fitting, therefore, that Black should be the author of the court's opinion in *Gideon v. Wainwright*.

Clarence Earl Gideon was a vagrant who was apprehended by the police of Panama City, Florida, and charged with breaking and entering a poolroom with intent to commit a misdemeanor. Gideon was too poor to hire his own defense attorney and therefore requested that the state judge appoint counsel for him. This request was turned down because under Florida law, appointed counsel was available to indigents only in capital cases. Gideon was tried, convicted, and sentenced to five years in prison. He persisted in his efforts to get his convictions overturned, first by the state and then by the federal courts. In January, 1962, he sent his second petition, a crude hand-printed affair, to the Supreme Court, which agreed to review his case. The Court appointed Abe Fortas, who was subsequently to serve on the Supreme Court, to represent Gideon. Fortas was opposed in argument by attorneys for the state of Florida. Only two states sided with Florida; twenty-two other states, recognizing the need for reform but despairing of effecting it through their own processes, filed a brief on behalf of Gideon.

On March 18, 1963, Justice Black delivered the opinion of the Court, which was largely a reiteration of the reasoning in his dissenting opinion in *Adamson v. California*. The individual, and especially the indigent, contended Black, is in greatest need of his constitutional rights when he finds himself in trouble with the law; it is a mockery to construe the Fourteenth Amendment's guarantee of due process so as to deny the indigent legal counsel when it is only through such counsel that he may effectively assert and vindicate his other constitutional rights in trials where the state has formidable advantages in terms of resources and personnel. However, the Supreme Court did not hold that the Constitution requires that individuals are entitled to lawyers able to devote equal time and resources to their cases. *Betts v. Brady*, claimed Black, was an aberration; the Court was now returning to sounder, more venerable precedents.

Three other justices, while concurring in the Court's decision, wrote separate opinions. The fact that these concurring opinions were written in *Gideon v. Wainwright* did not weaken the effect of the Court's ruling: States were constitutionally required to provide legal counsel for criminal defendants who were too poor to secure an attorney. The ruling was also a reflection of the Supreme Court's growing solicitude for the constitutional rights of disadvantaged persons. Gideon was retried in the same Florida Circuit Court in which he had earlier been convicted. He was represented by qualified counsel, which he had selected himself. At this trial, Gideon was acquitted by a jury.

The securing of the right to counsel for all defendants opened the floodgates in the review courts across the United States. In some jurisdictions, the rate of appeals reached as high as 90 percent of all convictions. An overloaded review system caused an increase in the workload for state and federal judges, as well as extended periods of litigation that eroded the belief that a conviction for a crime is final. The decision in *Gideon v. Wainright* also opened the door to subsequent decisions involving not only the rights to counsel under the Sixth Amendment but also protection against self-incrimination under the Fifth Amendment. *Morrissey v. Brewer* (1972) provided the right to counsel at parole board revocation hearings, and *Gagnon v. Scarpelli* (1973) guaranteed that right at probation revocation hearings. —*James J. Bolner, updated by Janice G. Rienerth*

ADDITIONAL READING:

Bennett, Fred W. "Toward Eliminating Bargain Basement Justice: Providing Indigent Defendants with Expert Services and an Adequate Defense." *Law and Contemporary Problems* 58, no. 1 (Winter, 1995): 95-138. An extensive discussion of court cases dealing with aspects of the right to counsel.

Cushman, Robert F., ed. *Cases in Civil Liberties.* New York: Appleton-Century-Crofts, 1968. A collection of Supreme Court opinions on civil liberties. Functions as a sourcebook on the rights of the criminal defendant.

Gest, Ted. "One Poor Man's Legacy." *U.S. News and World Report* 114, no. 11 (March 22, 1993): 19. Rehearses the history of the case and the impact of the decision.

Hermann, Robert, E. Single, and J. Boston. *Counsel for the Poor.* Lexington, Mass.: Lexington Books, 1977. Distills the findings of a large-scale research project on criminal defense in urban America.

Lewis, Anthony. *Gideon's Trumpet.* New York: Random House, 1964. This case study delineates important judicial processes relevant to the making of policy in constitutional areas.

Mueller, Jean W., and W. B. Schamel. "The Bill of Rights—

Due Process and Rights of the Accused: Clarence Earl Gideon's Petition in *Forma Pauperes.*" *Social Education* 54, no. 7 (November/December, 1990): 421-424. A discussion of the right-to-counsel cases. Includes teaching activities and a copy of Gideon's petition.

Uelmen, Gerald F. "2001—A Train Ride: A Guided Tour of the Sixth Amendment Right to Counsel." *Law and Contemporary Problems* 58, no. 1 (Winter, 1995): 13-29. An examination of landmark cases. Points out that the courts have had trouble distinguishing between denial of counsel and provision of inadequate counsel.

SEE ALSO: 1868, Fourteenth Amendment.

1963 ■ PEARSON BECOMES CANADA'S PRIME MINISTER: *Conservatives are ousted by a new Liberal Party administration*

DATE: April 22, 1963
LOCALE: Ottawa, Canada
CATEGORIES: Canadian history; Government and politics
KEY FIGURES:
John Diefenbaker (1895-1979), Conservative prime minister of Canada, 1957-1963
John Fitzgerald Kennedy (1917-1963), thirty-fifth president of the United States, 1961-1963
Lester Pearson (1897-1972), Liberal prime minister of Canada, 1963-1968
Louis St. Laurent (1882-1973), Liberal prime minister of Canada, 1948-1957
Pierre Elliott Trudeau (born 1919), Liberal prime minister of Canada, 1968-1979 and 1980-1984

SUMMARY OF EVENT. Before he was elected head of the Canadian Liberal Party, in the summer of 1957, Lester Pearson had achieved great prominence as an important Canadian diplomat. From 1928 until 1957, he occupied increasingly important positions in the Canadian diplomatic service. During World War II, he represented Canada at numerous international conferences. Prime Minister William Lyon Mackenzie King appointed Pearson as the Canadian ambassador to the United States in 1944. Pearson earned the respect of both Canadian and U.S. political leaders and played a major role in the 1945 San Francisco conference that created the United Nations. In September, 1948, Prime Minister Louis St. Laurent appointed Pearson as minister for external affairs, a position he held for nine years. From 1952 to 1953, he also served as the president of the General Assembly of the United Nations. In 1956, he helped to avoid a major international crisis by persuading French and British officials to end their invasion of Egypt, which had been provoked by President Gamal Abdel Nasser's decision to nationalize the Suez Canal. For his efforts, Pearson was awarded the Nobel Peace Prize in 1957. He was the first Canadian to receive this prestigious honor.

Canadian political traditions required cabinet members to

serve in the House of Commons. For this reason, Pearson ran for, and was elected to, Parliament in 1949. He represented the Ontario district of Algoma East (near Sault Ste. Marie) until his retirement from politics in 1968. Although Pearson was a greatly admired diplomat, no one knew how skillful he would be as a politician.

In the June, 1957, election, the Conservatives, under the leadership of John Diefenbaker, won more seats than the Liberals. However, two relatively minor parties—Social Credit, from Quebec, and the Cooperative Commonwealth Federation (later called the New Democrats)—prevented the Conservatives from obtaining an absolute majority. Former prime minister St. Laurent soon resigned as the head of the Liberals, and Lester Pearson succeeded him.

In 1958, the Conservatives won a resounding majority in the federal parliament with 206 seats, while the Liberals won in only 49 districts. Most Canadians felt that Pearson was a singularly ineffective politician, but they badly underestimated his tenacity. John Diefenbaker made a series of major political blunders: alienating French-speaking Canadians by failing to appoint Quebecers to any important cabinet positions, opposing increased U.S. investments in the Canadian economy, and especially refusing to support the United States immediately during the Cuban Missile Crisis of October, 1962. His needless alienation of President John F. Kennedy increased tensions between the Canadian and U.S. governments and persuaded many Canadians that Diefenbaker's actions were harming their economy.

In the June, 1962, elections, the Conservatives won 116 seats, the Liberals 97, and two minor parties 49. Unlike Diefenbaker, Pearson understood that a Canadian prime minister could govern effectively only by recognizing the aspirations and rights of both French- and English-speaking Canadians. In a December, 1962, speech in the House of Commons, Pearson argued that the fair treatment of French-speaking Canadians was essential for maintaining national unity. This speech was singularly effective, both in Quebec and in the English-speaking provinces. The thirty Quebec members of Parliament from the Social Credit Party, on whom Diefenbaker had relied for support, increasingly sided with the Liberals.

After the Cuban Missile Crisis, more people in Canada and the United States came to believe that indecisiveness might provoke another war. When Diefenbaker exacerbated an already bad situation by refusing, in January, 1963, to accept nuclear weapons from the United States in order to defend Canada against a possible air attack from the Soviet Union, his own defense minister, Douglas Harkness, resigned in protest. Sensing that the Conservatives were in disarray, Pearson, with the support of the Social Credit and New Democratic Parties, asked the House of Commons for a vote of no confidence in the leadership of John Diefenbaker. This motion was approved by a margin of 142 to 111 on February 4, 1963. For only the second time since the creation of the Canadian Confederation in 1867, a prime minister had lost a vote of no confidence. This vote dissolved the House of Commons, and new parliamentary elections were held on April 8, 1963. Although the

Liberals won 125 seats in the House of Commons to the Conservatives' 95, the Liberals were still four votes short of an absolute majority. With the support of the Social Credit and New Democratic Parties, Pearson was able to form a new government and became Canada's fourteenth prime minister on April 22, 1963.

During the parliamentary campaign of 1963, Pearson had promised Canadians that he would accomplish a great deal in his first sixty days in office. He had spoken of "sixty days of decision," and he realized that decisive action had to be taken if the Liberals were to remain in power for long. Within three weeks after becoming prime minister, Pearson flew to the United States to meet with President Kennedy, and relations between the U.S. and Canadian governments improved significantly. This helped encourage additional U.S. investments in the Canadian economy.

Pearson improved the status of senior citizens by persuading the House of Commons to approve a national pension plan. He appointed a Royal Commission on Bilingualism and Biculturalism, which proposed many laws designed to protect the linguistic and cultural rights of all Canadians. French speakers from Quebec were made to feel once again that they were equal partners with English-speaking Canadians.

Pearson's most lasting contribution to Canadian unity was his proposal, in 1964, to create a purely Canadian flag with a maple leaf, the traditional symbol of Canada. Until then, the Canadian flag had contained a Union Jack and was called the Red Ensign. This proposal was highly controversial, especially with veterans who had fought in the two world wars under the old flag. Recognizing the sensitivity of the issue, Pearson first made his proposal at a veterans' meeting. He argued persuasively that the Canadian flag should not contain either British or French symbols but should, rather, represent the unity of this diverse country. Pearson understood that French-speaking Canadians found it difficult to feel an emotional bond for a flag that reminded them of the British flag. After much acrimonious debate in the House of Commons, and even a filibuster orchestrated by Diefenbaker, the Liberals voted closure and the new flag was approved. The new maple leaf design was presented to the Canadian people in a ceremony on Parliament Hill on February 15, 1965. Despite all the controversy, Canadians from all ten provinces and the two territories came to feel great pride in their new national flag.

In the November, 1965, election, Pearson's Liberal Party once again won more seats than the Conservatives, but they still lacked an absolute majority. However, Pearson remained as Canada's prime minister until April, 1968, when he was succeeded by his minister of justice, Pierre Elliott Trudeau. The Liberal Party remained in power until 1979.

—Edmund J. Campion

ADDITIONAL READING:

Bothwell, Robert, Ian Drummond, and John English. *Canada Since 1945: Power, Politics, and Provincialism*, Rev. ed. Toronto: University of Toronto Press, 1989. Contains a good summary of the political, economic, and social changes in

Canada between the end of World War II and the late 1980's.

Hutchison, Bruce. *Macdonald to Pearson: The Prime Ministers of Canada*. Don Mills, Ont.: Longmans, 1967. Contains excellent short biographies of the prime ministers of Canada, from John A. Macdonald to Lester Pearson.

Kent, Tom. *A Public Purpose: An Experience of Liberal Opposition and Canadian Government*. Kingston, Ont.: McGill-Queen's University Press, 1988. A reliable history of Lester Pearson's service as the opposition leader from 1957 to 1963 and as prime minister from 1963 to 1968.

Pearson, Lester B. *Memoirs*. 3 vols. Toronto: University of Toronto Press, 1972-1975. A thoughtful, well-written autobiography, begun after Pearson's retirement as prime minister in 1968 and completed shortly before his death in 1972.

Thoradarson, Vruce. *Lester Pearson: Diplomat and Politician*. Toronto: Oxford University Press, 1974. A sympathetic, well-documented biography. Contains a well-annotated bibliography of important studies on Pearson's career in diplomacy and politics.

SEE ALSO: 1957, Diefenbaker Era in Canada; 1960, Quebec Sovereignist Movement; 1968, Trudeau Era in Canada.

1963 ▪ EQUAL PAY ACT: *the federal government acknowledges that women's work is as valuable as men's*

DATE: June 10, 1963
LOCALE: Washington, D.C.
CATEGORIES: Civil rights; Laws and acts; Women's issues
KEY FIGURES:
Charles Goodell (1926-1987), Republican representative from New York
Edith Green (1910-1987), Democratic representative from Oregon
Pat McNamara (1894-1966), Democratic senator from Michigan
Esther Peterson (born 1906), director of the Women's Bureau in the Kennedy Administration
Eleanor Roosevelt (1884-1962), chair, President's Commission on the Status of Women

SUMMARY OF EVENT. The Equal Pay Act of 1963—the first federal legislation designed to promote equal employment opportunity for women—began its development as a national policy during the Kennedy Administration. On December 14, 1961, President John F. Kennedy signed Executive Order 10980, establishing the President's Commission on the Status of Women (PCSW). From 1961 to 1963, the PCSW investigated women's position in U.S. society and drew up an agenda of reforms. Kennedy delegated responsibility for women's affairs to Esther Peterson, a labor unionist who supported labor legislation and opposed the Equal Rights Amendment. Peterson's appointment as director of the Women's Bureau and assistant secretary of the Department of Labor in charge of

women's affairs made her the highest-ranking woman in the administration. At Peterson's bidding, Kennedy appointed former first lady Eleanor Roosevelt as chair of the PCSW. The PCSW legitimized discussion of government policy for women, and at its first meeting it endorsed equal pay legislation. Securing passage of the Equal Pay Act (EPA), however, fell primarily to Peterson.

Previously, the Women's Bureau had secured clauses requiring equal pay in some of the regulatory orders issued by the War Labor Boards during World Wars I and II, and in various National Recovery Administration codes during the New Deal in the 1930's. The first federal legislation relating specifically to equal pay was introduced in 1945, in partial acknowledgment of women's contribution to the war effort. The Women's Equal Pay Bill did not pass, nor did any of the 104 similar bills introduced from the Seventy-ninth to the Eighty-seventh Congresses. The business community objected, while a general feeling persisted that the problem was neither widespread nor urgent.

The Equal Pay Act of 1963 was the first legislative recognition of federal responsibility toward working women. It required employers subject to the Fair Labor Standards Act of 1938 (FLSA) to pay equal wages for equal work, regardless of the sex of the worker. The bill (S 1409) was similar to equal pay proposals that had come before Congress to no avail since 1945. In 1946, a women's equal pay bill passed the Senate, but it failed in the House. In 1952, the Women's Bureau brought together a coalition of women's organizations, trade unions, employer associations, and civic groups to organize the National Committee for Equal Pay, which lobbied for a bill. By 1953, only fifteen states had passed equal pay laws, nine having done so after 1946. Although equal pay bills were introduced in every session of Congress, no hearing had been held since 1950. A study of 510 union contracts in 1956 showed that 195 (38 percent) had equal pay clauses. By 1962, twenty states had enacted equal pay laws, virtually all in the North.

Peterson's strategy for passing an equal pay bill involved gathering data proving a need for the bill and refuting arguments against it, then using that information to educate Congress. She had persuaded Secretary of Labor Arthur Goldberg to approve a bill prohibiting wage differentials because of sex, which was introduced early in 1962. An employer in commerce would be forbidden to "discriminate . . . on the basis of sex by paying wages to any employee at a rate less than the rate he pays to any employee of the opposite sex for work of comparable character on jobs the performance of which requires comparable skills." There was one exception: unequal wages paid "pursuant to a seniority or merit increase system which does not discriminate on the basis of sex."

The bill raised the question of whether the principle of nondiscrimination would apply to "equal" work or to "comparable" work, and its coverage concerned many businesses and manufacturers engaged in interstate or foreign commerce, or which produced goods for commerce. The act was amended, however: "Comparable" was changed to "equal," and "equal work" was defined as jobs of "equal skill, effort, and responsibility and . . . performed under similar working conditions." In effect, the courts came to interpret the law to mean virtually identical work. For example, a female social worker who could show that she was paid less for the same work done by a male social worker could win a case under the Equal Pay Act. However, if she were paid less than a male legal aid lawyer whose job was rated equally with hers in their employer's job evaluation plan, she would have no recourse.

Most of the opposition to the bill came from business and manufacturing interests. They argued that federal legislation was unnecessary, since market forces, backed by state equal pay laws, were already correcting inequities in pay. Another, contradictory, argument was that women had to be paid less because their higher turnover and absentee rates made them more costly to employ. By extension, opponents argued, an equal pay law might cause employers to cease hiring women altogether, or force employers to segregate jobs still further so that men and women would not be doing the same work.

The legislative history of the EPA was a steady retreat from the Department of Labor positions on comparable work and coverage. The first major concession occurred in the House Committee on Labor, which limited coverage by exempting employers with fewer than twenty-five employees. On the House floor, equal work replaced the comparable work standard. Coverage was further limited to single plants or establishments, making it legal for a firm with several plants to pay a higher rate to a man in plant A than to a woman in plant B doing the same work. The Senate insisted that EPA be part of FLSA, accept the same coverage (exempting women in agriculture, hotels, restaurants, laundries, smaller retail establishments, and administrative and managerial positions), and combine enforcement in the Wage and Hour Division of the Labor Department.

In the end, the House bill resembled the Senate's version. Representative Charles Goodell (Republican, New York) had proposed making the Equal Pay Act an amendment to the FLSA. Representative Edith Green (Democrat, Oregon), who sat on the House Committee on Education and Labor, which held hearings on the bill, incorporated Goodell's idea into her own bill. Senator Pat McNamara (Democrat, Michigan) presented a similar bill to the Senate. On May 23, 1963, the House adopted its own bill, and on May 28, the Senate went along. Kennedy signed the bill on June 10.   —*Richard K. Caputo*

ADDITIONAL READING:

Bergmann, Barbara R. *The Economic Emergence of Women*. New York: Basic Books, 1985. Explores the origins and consequences of the transformation of women from housewives to wage earners; discusses past and present policy options addressing equal employment opportunity for women. Notes, bibliography, index.

Bernstein, Irving. *Promises Kept: John F. Kennedy's New Frontier*. New York: Oxford University Press, 1991. Examines congressional hearings on, and the impact and significance of, the Equal Pay Act of 1963 in the broader context of the Kennedy Administration's domestic policy agenda. Notes and index.

Caputo, Richard K. *Welfare and Freedom American Style II: The Role of the Federal Government, 1941-1980*. Vol. 2. *Federal Responses to People in Need*. Lanham, Md.: University Press of America, 1994. Discusses the legislative history of the Equal Pay Act of 1963 in the context of government's role in promoting equal opportunity for women. Notes, bibliography, index.

Evans, Sara M., and Barbara J. Nelson. *Wage Justice: Comparable Worth and the Paradox of Technocratic Reform*. Chicago: University of Chicago Press, 1989. Places the idea of equal pay for work of comparable worth within the broader context of the history of wage discrimination policy. Shows how this concept has, at times, been attached to managerial agendas having little to do with remedying past discrimination. Appendices, notes, index.

Graham, Hugh Davis. *The Civil Rights Era: Origins and Development of National Policy, 1960-1972*. New York: Oxford University Press, 1990. Shows the influence of the Civil Rights movement on federal antidiscrimination policies affecting women. Notes, bibliography, index.

Murphy, Thomas E. "Female Wage Discrimination: A Study of the Equal Pay Act, 1963-1970." *Cincinnati Law Review* 39 (Fall, 1970): 615-649. Examines the congressional debates, provisions, and initial impact of the Equal Pay Act throughout the 1960's.

Zelman, Patricia G. *Women, Work, and National Policy: The Kennedy-Johnson Years*. Ann Arbor, Mich.: UMI Research Press, 1982. Concisely examines the formative years of national policies affecting women's employment opportunities. Appendices, notes, index.

SEE ALSO: 1938, Fair Labor Standards Act; 1941, 6.6 Million Women Enter the U.S. Labor Force; 1975, Equal Credit Opportunity Act.

1963 ■ ABINGTON SCHOOL DISTRICT V. SCHEMPP: *a landmark Supreme Court ruling addresses the issue of Bible reading in the public schools*

DATE: June 17, 1963
LOCALE: Washington, D.C.
CATEGORIES: Court cases; Education; Religion
KEY FIGURES:
Thomas Campbell Clark (1899-1977), Supreme Court associate justice and author of the majority opinion in the case
Madalyn Murray (born 1919) and
William Murray (born 1946), plaintiffs and residents of Maryland
Edward Schempp and
Sidney Schempp, plaintiffs and residents of Abington Township, Pennsylvania
Potter Stewart (1915-1985), Supreme Court associate justice and author of the dissenting opinion
Earl Warren (1891-1974), chief justice of the United States

SUMMARY OF EVENT. Like the Progressive Era and the New Deal, the 1960's in the United States have assumed the stature of an important, almost classic, age of reform and liberalism. Civil rights legislation, the Great Society programs, and antiwar protests were all symptomatic of a general quest for greater justice. Unlike earlier episodes of reform, however, the changes of the 1960's often were introduced almost in defiance of popular opinion. Although liberal measures often resulted from, and received the support of, vocal and active groups, just as often they did not reflect the goals of the "average" citizen, nor was there the kind of massive endorsement of reform that Franklin Roosevelt had enjoyed in 1936. One of the prime examples of these unpopular reforms was the Supreme Court's ruling regarding prayer and Bible reading in the public schools.

The issue of Bible reading in public schools reached the Supreme Court in 1963, in two cases emanating from the adjoining states of Pennsylvania and Maryland. Pennsylvania law required that ten verses from the Bible be read without comment at the beginning of each public school day. Although participation in the exercises was voluntary, Edward and Sidney Schempp and their children, Roger and Donna, members of a Unitarian church, filed suit in the federal district court for the Eastern District of Pennsylvania to enjoin the state's superintendent of public instruction from continuing to conduct religious recitations in public schools. At Abington Senior High School, which Roger and Donna Schempp attended, the religious exercises were broadcast into classrooms through the intercommunication system and consisted of a student reading ten verses of the Bible of his or her choosing, followed by students standing in class and repeating the Lord's Prayer in unison.

The Maryland case originated in Baltimore, where, since 1905, religious exercises had been held in the public schools and included a reading from the Bible or the recitation of the Lord's Prayer. Madalyn Murray and her son, William, both professed atheists, filed suit to force the cancellation of the religious exercises in Baltimore schools.

The majority opinion in *Abington School District v. Schempp* was written by Associate Justice Tom Clark. One year earlier, the Supreme Court, in *Engel v. Vitale*, had struck down the New York Board of Regents' prayer ("Almighty God, we acknowledge our dependence upon Thee; we beg Thy blessings upon us, our parents, our teachers, and our country") as a violation of the establishment clause of the First Amendment, which had been made applicable to the states through the due process clause of the Fourteenth Amendment. Clark now did the same for the recitation of biblical passages and the Lord's Prayer. In his opinion, he pointed out that the Court had firmly rejected the argument that the establishment clause prohibited only governmental preference of one religion over another. An examination of the precedents demonstrated conclusively that the First Amendment was designed to forbid all laws respecting the establishment of a religion. Justice Clark denied that the Court's decision would establish a religion of secularism. He noted that nothing in the opinion precluded the

study of the Bible in the public schools in its literary or historical context. "The place of religion," he wrote in conclusion, "in our society is an exalted one, achieved through a long tradition of reliance on the home, the church, and the inviolable citadel of the individual heart and mind. We have come to recognize through bitter experience that it is not within the power of government to invade that citadel, whether its purpose or effect be to aid or oppose, to advance or retard. In the relationship between man and religion, the State is firmly committed to a position of neutrality."

Although the Court's eight-to-one decision provoked widespread disappointment and anger, it was not unexpected. For nearly twenty years, a series of eight rulings by the Supreme Court gradually had removed the practice of religious activities from state-supported schools. After World War II, a growing number of freethinkers, Jews, and liberal Protestants had resisted the assumption of most local and school authorities that society was, or should be, based on the teachings of the New Testament. Most states permitted or encouraged a variety of religious exercises in the schools, ranging from Bible classes to the recitation of prayer. Increasingly, these practices were challenged in the courts. In the New Jersey case of *Everson v. Board of Education* (1947), the Supreme Court had defended the use of state funds to bus children to parochial schools but warned that a wall of separation between church and state must be maintained. A year later, in *McCollum v. Board of Education*, the Court banned a program of religious instruction from the schools of Champaign, Illinois. The justices' chief objection to the Champaign system was that religious teachers were actually brought into the schools, thus involving the state too closely with religion and pressuring dissenting students into conformity with the majority. In 1953, however, the Supreme Court approved a released-time program whereby students could apply to leave schools early in order to attend religious classes at their churches or synagogues.

While the Supreme Court's opposition to classroom instruction in religion enjoyed widespread support and sympathy, even among churches, the question of school prayers and Bible reading was more delicate. Most people agreed with Justice William O. Douglas' observations that Americans were a religious people; it seemed right and natural that the school day should begin with some recognition of the general belief in God. To prohibit any sort of observance in schools was tantamount, many argued, to state opposition to religion. There were widespread protests after the Supreme Court ruled in *Engel v. Vitale*, and a hostile reaction to the Court's decision in *Abington School District*. Most people tended to agree with dissenting Justice Potter Stewart, who wrote that he could not see "how an official religion is established by letting those who want to say a prayer say it." At the same time, most religious and educational leaders expressed relief that the Court had finally laid down clear limitations for the schools to follow and had placed responsibility for religion firmly in the hands of families and churches.

Since 1963 and *Abington School District*, the Supreme Court's construction of the establishment clause has been erratic and, at times, confusing. The Court's record has reflected a profound philosophical division between those justices who favored an almost complete separation of church and state and those who advocated an accommodation with religion. In *Lemon v. Kurtzman* (1971), the Court, under Chief Justice Warren Burger, established a three-pronged test to determine the constitutionality of state laws providing various forms of support for religious schools. The test required that the statute must have a secular legislative purpose, its principal effect must be one that neither advances nor inhibits religion, and it must not foster an "excess government entanglement with religion."

In 1973, in *Committee for Public Education and Religious Liberty v. Nyquist*, direct state financial aid to religious elementary and secondary schools was held to offend the establishment clause. The Court went on to allow therapeutic and remedial services performed by public school employees off the premises of religious institutions, and diagnostic services (such has hearing and speech testing) when performed by public school employees at religious schools. In *Wallace v. Jaffree* (1985), the Court struck down an Alabama statute that required teachers to announce a period of silence for meditation and that allowed them to state that the period could be used for voluntary prayer. However, it permitted Pawtucket, Rhode Island, to erect a Christian symbol of the Nativity, a crèche, in front of its city hall during the Christmas season, and in 1995 the Court required the venerable state-supported University of Virginia, founded by Thomas Jefferson, to fund an avowedly religious student newspaper.

—*Richard H. Sander, updated by David L. Sterling*

ADDITIONAL READING:

Boles, Donald E. *The Bible, Religion, and the Public Schools*. Ames: Iowa State University Press, 1965. Covers a wide array of material on the historical, legal, and cultural background of the *Abington School District* decision.

Duker, Sam. *The Public School and Religion: The Legal Context*. New York: Harper & Row, 1966. Discusses the major court rulings concerning religion in the schools, providing lengthy excerpts from court opinions.

Levy, Leonard W. *The Establishment Clause: Religion and the First Amendment*. New York: Macmillan, 1986. Analyzes the origins of the establishment clause and critiques the Supreme Court decisions pertaining to its construction.

Lytle, Clifford M. *The Warren Court and Its Critics*. Tucson: University of Arizona Press, 1968. Traces the reaction of Congress, interest groups, and the general public to the major rulings of the Warren Court; tries to explain the lasting hostility to the Court.

Sizer, Theodore R., ed. *Religion and Public Education*. Boston: Houghton Mifflin, 1967. Contains a wide selection of provocative essays; some are partisan, others are exclusively analytical.

Sullivan, Winnifred Fallers. *Paying the Words Extra: Religious Discourse in the Supreme Court of the United States*. Cambridge, Mass.: Harvard University Press, 1994. Examines the religious viewpoints of Justices Warren Burger, Sandra

Day O'Connor, and William Brennan as illustrated in their opinions in the Christmas crèche case.

SEE ALSO: 1954, *Brown v. Board of Education*; 1962, Reapportionment Cases; 1963, *Gideon v. Wainwright*; 1965, *Griswold v. Connecticut*.

1963 ■ KING DELIVERS HIS "I HAVE A DREAM" SPEECH: *a great African American civil rights leader articulates his vision for a color-blind America*

DATE: August 28, 1963
LOCALE: Washington, D.C.
CATEGORIES: African American history; Civil rights; Cultural and intellectual history; Social reform
KEY FIGURES:
Martin Luther King, Jr. (1929-1968), head of the Southern Christian Leadership Conference
Asa Philip Randolph (1889-1979), labor leader and director of the March on Washington
Bayard Rustin (1910-1987), civil rights activist and an organizer of the March on Washington

SUMMARY OF EVENT. The Reverend Dr. Martin Luther King, Jr.'s "I Have a Dream" speech is the most famous moment of the March on Washington, on August 28, 1963. In a year during which the Civil Rights movement had met with both success (in the fight to take steps to desegregate department stores in Birmingham, Alabama) and tragedy (the murder of Medgar Evers, a leader of the National Association for the Advancement of Colored People, or NAACP), King's speech was an unmitigated success.

The spring and summer of 1963 was one of the most important times of the Civil Rights movement. On June 12, NAACP leader Medgar Evers was assassinated; white supremacist Byron de la Beckwith would not be found guilty of his murder for nearly thirty years. In April, 1963, protest against discrimination in the downtown department stores of Birmingham, Alabama, culminated in protests on April 4. King's arrest during these demonstrations and the media coverage of police violence against the demonstrators catapulted both the movement and King, the leader of the Southern Christian Leadership Conference (SCLC), into the national spotlight to an even greater degree than before. The boycotts and mass marches eventually provided sufficient pressure that white leaders promised to desegregate the stores' facilities, hire African Americans to work in the stores, and establish a biracial committee for ongoing talks concerning racial problems.

These gains were achieved at a price, however: King was jailed briefly; police brutality occurred against protestors; and arrested protesters filled Birmingham's jails. Nevertheless, the filled jails negatively affected the capacity of police to arrest and hold demonstrators, which was exactly what King and other civil rights leaders had hoped; news coverage of police brutality outraged many citizens; and, while jailed, King wrote his "Letter from Birmingham Jail," a document that delineated the need for and goals of the direct action campaigns of the Civil Rights movement. The acclaim that met this document foreshadowed the reaction to his speech at the March on Washington two months later.

The purpose of the March on Washington was not merely to make an emotional plea on behalf of African Americans; its

Martin Luther King, Jr., delivers his "I Have a Dream" speech during the Poor People's March on Washington, D.C., in 1963; the Washington monument is visible in the background. (AP/Wide World Photos)

primary purpose was to expose the American public to the economic basis of racial inequality. Thus, the focus of the march was the need to increase jobs and economic opportunities for African Americans, in order for them to realize racial equality. These especially were the goals of the leaders of the March on Washington, A. Philip Randolph, labor leader and organizer of the Brotherhood of Sleeping Car Porters, and civil rights activist Bayard Rustin, one of the earliest planners of the event. In fact, the full title of the event was "The March on Washington for Jobs and Freedom." The march, therefore, had a set of important goals: more jobs, a higher minimum wage, support for President John F. Kennedy's antidiscrimination legislation, and arousing the conscience of the United States to the plight of African Americans. King's speech was especially important on this last point, for the "I Have a Dream" section of the speech was an eloquent plea for a society based on racial harmony. Nevertheless, while King's speech is best remembered for his vision of racial equality, its true import lies in the fact that the renown accorded the speech helped advance the multifaceted goals of the march, thus helping to pave the way for the Civil Rights Act of 1964.

The passage in which King reiterates, "I have a dream," should be understood in the overall context of the talk. Although King started by reading from his prepared text, he disregarded this text about halfway through the speech and incorporated a theme he had used in some previous speeches: "I have a dream." This theme introduced into the speech two of the main tenets of the SCLC: interracial cooperation and social equality. King's eloquent vision of a future without racial divisions captured the emotions of many viewers and, later, readers of the speech. In fact, the emotional power of that section of King's remarks sometimes blurs the memory of other, equally important aspects of his speech.

King's speech has become widely known as a masterpiece of rhetoric and argumentation. One rhetorical device that King used to great effect is repetition. The most obvious example is the repetition of the phrase "I have a dream" to detail different aspects of King's vision of racial harmony, but there are other, equally important examples. In the opening section of the speech, King reiterated the phrase "one hundred years later" to emphasize that one hundred years after the Emancipation Proclamation, African Americans still had not achieved equality. Immediately after the "I have a dream" section, King repeated the phrase that it is "with this faith" in his dream that he and other people could hope to transform American society. These examples demonstrate King's consciousness of the use of rhetoric to produce the emotional impact of the speech.

Perhaps one of the most important rhetorical strategies of King's speech is his reference to the principles voiced by the Founding Fathers in his appeal for racial equality. This strategy was especially important in light of the fact that the government (including the Federal Bureau of Investigation and the Justice Department) was concerned that the Civil Rights movement might discredit the United States abroad. Hence, it was perceptive of King to imply in the speech that he

was not undermining the United States but asking the country to do justice to the principles that were asserted to be the bedrock of the U.S. political and societal character. King stated, for example, that his dream was "deeply rooted in the American dream," and that he dreamt of a day when Americans "will be able to sing with new meaning 'My country 'tis of thee, sweet land of liberty, of thee I sing.' " King then immediately used the words of that song to delineate the different areas of the country where he hoped the United States would soon let freedom ring for all its citizens. He referred to the Declaration of Independence and the Constitution as being a "promissory note" to all citizens, which those at the march now were claiming as their inheritance. The speech gained power from King's stressing that he was asking the United States to live up to its principles and thus to fulfill the greatness of its pronounced creed.

King's speech became not only one of the most publicized events of the Civil Rights movement but also one of the most highly regarded speeches in U.S. history. Although much of the acclaim rests on the emotionally powerful "I have a dream" section of the speech, the entire speech is a masterpiece of rhetoric and argument. One of the most essential aspects of the speech was at the end, when King stated that on the day "when we let freedom ring" the United States will only be speeding up the day—not arriving at it—when "all of God's children, black men and white men, Jews and Gentiles, Protestants and Catholics, will be able to join hands and sing in the words of the old Negro spiritual, 'Free at last! Free at last! Thank God Almighty, we are free at last!' " This stands as the lingering, haunting challenge of Martin Luther King's speech at the March on Washington.　　　　　*—Jane Davis*

ADDITIONAL READING:

Baldwin, James. "The Dangerous Road Before Martin Luther King." In *The Price of the Ticket*. New York: St. Martin's Press, 1985. Detailed consideration of the difficulties facing King as a moral leader and a major African American leader.

Fairclough, Adam. *Martin Luther King, Jr.* Athens: University of Georgia Press, 1990. Concise biography focuses on the major protests in which King was involved.

Garrow, David J. *Bearing the Cross: Martin Luther King, Jr., and the Southern Christian Leadership Conference*. New York: Vintage Books, 1986. Detailed, Pulitzer Prize-winning biography of King that examines the strategies of civil rights protests and conflicts between various civil rights groups. Invaluable for showing the strategies of many important protests.

McPhee, Penelope, and Flip Schulke. *King Remembered*. New York: Pocket Books, 1986. Concise, introductory biography of King that focuses on his philosophy as a leader of a nonviolent movement. Contains more than a hundred photographs, many never before published.

Oates, Stephen B. *Let the Trumpet Sound: The Life of Martin Luther King, Jr.* New York: Harper & Row, 1982. Detailed account of King's leadership of the Civil Rights movement; contains extensive passages from his speeches and writings.

SEE ALSO: 1955, Montgomery Bus Boycott; 1957, Southern Christian Leadership Conference Is Founded; 1957, Little Rock School Desegregation Crisis; 1960, Civil Rights Act of 1960; 1962, Meredith Registers at "Ole Miss"; 1964, Civil Rights Act of 1964; 1965, Watts Riot; 1965, Expansion of Affirmative Action; 1967, Long, Hot Summer; 1968, Assassinations of King and Kennedy.

1963 ■ NUCLEAR TEST BAN TREATY: *a major step in prohibiting the testing of nuclear weapons is ratified*

DATE: September 24, 1963
LOCALE: Washington, D.C., Geneva, and Moscow
CATEGORY: Diplomacy and international relations
KEY FIGURES:

Leonid Ilich Brezhnev (1906-1982), general secretary of the Communist Party, 1964-1982

Alec Douglas-Home (1903-1995), foreign secretary of Great Britain

Andrei A. Gromyko (1909-1989), foreign minister of the Soviet Union

William Averell Harriman (1891-1986), principal U.S. negotiator of the treaty

John Fitzgerald Kennedy (1917-1963), thirty-fifth president of the United States, 1961-1963

Nikita Sergeyevich Khrushchev (1894-1971), general secretary of the Communist Party, 1953-1964

Harold Macmillan (1894-1986), prime minister of Great Britain

Richard Milhous Nixon (1913-1994), thirty-seventh president of the United States, 1969-1974

Dean Rusk (1909-1994), U.S. secretary of state

SUMMARY OF EVENT. The story of the 1963 Nuclear Test Ban Treaty has its origins in the last year of World War II. On July 16, 1945, the United States for the first time exploded an atomic bomb, at Alamogordo, New Mexico. On August 6 and 9, the United States dropped the only atomic bombs ever used in wartime—on the Japanese cities of Hiroshima and Nagasaki. The end of the war came very shortly thereafter, but so did the realization that the United States had developed the most dreadful weapon ever devised by humans. Thus, from the end of World War II, people and governments began to seek a way to outlaw or control this newly developed power. Contributing greatly to the urgency of these efforts was the development of a so-called Cold War, an ideological struggle for power and influence that aligned the Soviet Union against its former wartime allies in the West, which were led by the United States. Although the Cold War was not a physical conflict, it was dangerous because of the possibility that the tension, hostility, suspicion, and fears that it generated could evolve into a shooting war. If that occurred and nuclear weapons were used, it would, some contended, destroy civilization.

Despite strenuous efforts, particularly by the United States government and its allies, nothing in the area of nuclear arms control was achieved for several years. During that period, nuclear weapons were developed further, becoming more sophisticated and destructive. The need for controls became more and more urgent.

The initial proposals for controlling nuclear energy came from the United States, Canada, and Great Britain. On November 15, 1945, a Three Power Declaration called on the United Nations to establish a commission to deal with issues of atomic energy. The following month, foreign ministers from the United States, Great Britain, and the Soviet Union met in Moscow and endorsed the creation of a United Nations Atomic Energy Commission.

On June 14, 1946, the United States delegation presented to the first meeting of the U.N. Atomic Energy Commission the Baruch Plan, named after its drafter, Bernard Baruch. The Baruch Plan called for the creation of an International Atomic Development Authority that would supervise all atomic development and see to it that the manufacture of all atomic weapons would cease and that all existing bombs would be disposed of. Soviet rejection of this proposal became clear a few days later, when Deputy Foreign Minister Andrei Gromyko offered an alternative proposal that called for a voluntary commitment to destroy existing bombs and not produce any others. The Soviet proposal called for control to come after disarmament, while the U.S. delegation proposed that controls be established first. This fundamental difference would complicate all subsequent negotiations for disarmament and arms control.

For several years thereafter, discussions continued in various United Nations committees and subcommittees without any agreement being recorded. A deadlock between the U.S. and Soviet positions constantly blocked progress. In September, 1949, the Soviet Union joined the United States as a nuclear power, by successfully exploding an atomic bomb. Following this, no significant new proposals in the area of nuclear arms control emerged for several years. Instead, each side reacted to the other's advances in nuclear technology. In October, 1952, the British exploded their first bomb; in November of the same year, the United States successfully tested its first hydrogen bomb; and in August, 1953, the Soviet Union exploded its first hydrogen bomb. While work proceeded on the peaceful uses of atomic energy, the United States and the Soviet Union embarked on a nuclear arms race that continued virtually without interruption for years, even after the two superpowers had achieved a capacity for overkill.

Efforts to find some means of controlling, limiting, or even eliminating nuclear weapons continued, but fundamental differences between the two sides plagued the negotiations, and no agreements emerged. Nevertheless, the pressure of world opinion to find some way to reduce the threat of nuclear conflict mounted. On March 1, 1954, a U.S. nuclear test conducted in Bikini Atoll in the Pacific Ocean produced worldwide reaction, because of the extent of the radioactive fallout. Protests came from the Japanese government and others. On

April 2, the prime minister of India, Jawaharlal Nehru, proposed a halt to further nuclear testing. In the U.N. General Assembly, Burma soon called for an end to all further testing. A year later, in the General Assembly, both India and the Soviet Union proposed a test ban without supervision or inspection, on the grounds that no significant testing could go on undetected anyway. The Western powers balked, arguing against any proposal that did not entail effective inspection and verification. No agreements were concluded.

The year 1955 brought some relaxation in the relations between the United States and the Soviet Union, partly because of the so-called Spirit of Geneva that emerged from the Geneva Summit Conference in July of that year. This spirit did not produce any immediate progress in disarmament or arms control, but it did improve the atmosphere in which negotiations could proceed. In April, 1958, Soviet Premier Nikita Khrushchev wrote to President Dwight D. Eisenhower that the Soviet Union had decided unilaterally to halt its testing, and he called on the Western powers to do the same. Testing continued by both sides until October, but the Soviets, the United States, and Great Britain agreed to begin a new round of meetings in Geneva on October 31, 1958, aimed at a nuclear test ban treaty. Testing would be suspended for the next year. This voluntary moratorium on testing went into effect on November 3, 1958, and lasted until broken by the Soviet Union in September, 1961. In the meantime, France had joined the nuclear circle by exploding a bomb on February 13, 1960.

The Geneva meetings, properly called the Conference on the Discontinuance of Nuclear Weapon Tests, began on schedule at the end of October, 1958, and lasted for several years. In March, 1962, the work of the conference was transferred to a subcommittee of the Eighteen Nation Disarmament Conference. At first, there was some real progress, and agreement on a number of articles of a draft treaty was achieved. In May, 1960, following the much-publicized U-2 incident, the proposed Paris Summit Conference collapsed, and East-West tensions mounted again. The Soviet position hardened: The Soviets insisted that a test ban be considered as part of a larger treaty for general and complete disarmament. That relations had deteriorated drastically was evidenced by the Soviet announcement on August 30, 1961, that the Soviets intended to resume nuclear testing, which it did two days later. The United States and Great Britain responded on September 3 with a proposal for a ban on all atmospheric testing without international supervision; when no positive reply came from the Soviet Union, the United States resumed underground tests. On October 30, the Soviet Union exploded the largest bomb ever tested. Immediately, there were new outcries in the United Nations demanding an end to nuclear testing. The General Assembly adopted two resolutions to this effect, including one submitted by the United States and Great Britain.

The next major push for a test ban came from the Eighteen Nation Disarmament Conference in March, 1962. At that time, a joint resolution from the eight nonaligned nations in attendance proposed a test ban agreement to be supervised by an international committee of experts that could conduct on-site investigations of unusual seismic disturbances at the invitation of the nation on whose territory the event occurred. The Soviet Union accepted the resolution as a basis for further discussion, but the Western powers accepted it as only one of the bases of discussion. The resolution was, in the Western view, too vague as to whether the on-site inspections would be mandatory or optional.

The issue of international inspection and verification continued to stand in the way of agreement between the Soviet Union and the United States. However, efforts to find a common ground did not cease. In August, the United States and Great Britain submitted jointly two proposals to the Test Ban Sub-Committee of the Eighteen Nation Disarmament Conference. One provided for a comprehensive test ban with an unspecified quota of on-site inspections; the other provided for a partial test ban with underground testing not included and with no international control of verification required. The Soviet delegation, while informally expressing interest, officially rejected both proposals. The potential for continued negotiations lifted hopes for an eventual agreement, but such hopes were shattered by the Cuban Missile Crisis in October.

The Cuban crisis marked another turning point in Soviet-U.S. relations. For the first time, the prospect of a nuclear confrontation became very real and frightening. As a result, talks between U.S. and Soviet negotiators resumed, and the leaders of the Soviet Union and the United States, Premier Khrushchev and President John F. Kennedy, became increasingly involved in the formulation of policies and strategy. Kennedy was especially anxious to persuade the Soviets of the United States' sincere desire to reach some kind of agreement that would both ease the tensions and curtail the dangers from radioactive contamination of the environment. Discussion through the winter months of 1962-1963 indicated clearly that the principal obstacle to agreement was the issue of on-site inspection of unexplained seismic disturbances. Parts of the Soviet Union experience numerous earthquakes each year, which produce seismic effects similar to those of low-yield underground nuclear tests. The United States, therefore, insisted that a comprehensive test ban treaty must permit at least eight to ten on-site inspections to verify the causes of such occurrences. The most that the Soviet Council of Ministers would agree to was three inspections a year. By the spring of 1963, it appeared that another impasse had been reached.

President Kennedy was determined, however, not to miss any opportunity for agreement, and there were indications that Khrushchev was not averse to some kind of compromise. Consequently, on April 24, 1963, Kennedy and British prime minister Harold Macmillan issued a public appeal to Khrushchev to resume negotiations for a test ban treaty, to be conducted in Moscow by high-level representatives of the three powers. By June 9, Khrushchev had sent word to Washington, D.C., and London of his willingness to host the resumed talks in the Soviet capital. The following day, when Kennedy delivered the commencement address at American University, he not only announced the resumption of talks in Moscow but also declared that the United States had decided, as a sign of its sincere concern for peace, to bring to a halt its nuclear testing in the atmosphere. Such tests, he declared, would never be resumed unless other powers continued their own testing.

Kennedy's speech had the desired effect on Khrushchev. On July 2, in a speech delivered in East Berlin, Khrushchev responded by announcing that the Soviet Union was ready to agree to a limited or partial test ban treaty. On July 15, 1963, a U.S. delegation led by Averell Harriman, a British delegation led by Lord Laisham, and a Soviet delegation led by Foreign Minister Andrei Gromyko sat down in Moscow. In the next ten days, they hammered out the final treaty, which they initialed on July 25. On August 5, the Treaty Banning Nuclear Weapon Tests in the Atmosphere, in Outer Space, and Under Water was formally signed in Moscow by U.S. secretary of state Dean Rusk, British foreign secretary Alec Douglas-Home, and Gromyko. On September 24, by a vote of eighty to nineteen, it was ratified by the U.S. Senate.

The treaty as finally signed was concise and clearly stated, consisting of only five articles. The first article contained the statement of intent—that the signatories agreed to cease all nuclear testing in the atmosphere, in outer space, and under water, and also underground, in the event that such tests caused radioactive debris to fall outside the territory of the testing nation. The second article concerned the procedure for amending the treaty; the third invited the adherence of other nations; the fourth defined the treaty's duration as unlimited; and the fifth pertained to the depositing of the treaty, in both English and Russian, with the governments concerned.

Kennedy and Khrushchev each considered this treaty a significant achievement that could pave the way for other agreements and contribute to a reduction in international tension. It was hoped that the Western powers could persuade France to sign the treaty, while the Soviet Union urged the Chinese Communists to adhere as well. Such hopes were unfulfilled: The French were determined to develop their nuclear capacity independently, and the Chinese were soon to become the fifth nuclear power, by exploding an atomic bomb on October, 1964. However, more than a hundred other nations subsequently added their pledges to those of the United States, Great Britain, and the Soviet Union. A major first step had been taken toward creating a more peaceful world, as the treaty demonstrated that confrontation need not be the prevailing characteristic of East-West relations.

Subsequently, both China and France acceded to the treaty. Negotiations continued throughout the Cold War to end underground nuclear tests, which were permitted under the original treaty. A step in that direction was made on July 3, 1974, when Richard Nixon and Leonid Brezhnev signed the Threshold Test Ban Treaty in Moscow. This treaty prohibited nuclear weapons tests that had a yield exceeding 150 kilotons.

Serious efforts to prohibit all nuclear weapons tests had to await the end of the Cold War, in 1990. In December, 1994, the U.N. General Assembly resolved that adoption of a Compre-hensive Nuclear Test Ban Treaty should be a priority objective. The issues that had to be resolved were whether to permit a limited number of underground tests, what methods of verification would be used, and whether the International Atomic Energy Agency should be the implementing organization. These issues were debated by the Conference on Disarmament, a thirty-eight-member disarmament body created by the United Nations.   *—Tyler Deierhoi, updated by Joseph L. Nogee*

ADDITIONAL READING:

Blacker, Coit D., and Gloria Duffy, eds. *International Arms Control: Issues and Agreements.* Stanford, Calif.: Stanford University Press, 1984. A balanced analysis of arms control negotiations. Contains the complete texts of the major arms control agreements.

Bloomfield, Lincoln P., W. C. Clemens, Jr., and Franklyn Griffiths. *Khrushchev and the Arms Race: Soviet Interests in Arms Control and Disarmament, 1954-1964.* Boston: MIT Press, 1966. A scholarly examination of the formulation and implementation of Soviet arms control and disarmament policies during the Khrushchev years. Concludes that Khrushchev's policies aimed at achieving real, although limited, agreements with the West.

Bundy, McGeorge. *Danger and Survival, Choices About the Bomb in the First Fifty Years.* New York: Random House, 1988. A comprehensive, balanced history that explains the many complex factors that determined U.S. atomic energy policy. Written by a scholar who participated in government policy making in the 1960's.

Carnesale, Albert, and Richard N. Haass, eds. *Superpower Arms Control, Setting the Record Straight.* Cambridge, Mass.: Ballinger, 1987. Examining eight arms control agreements, each essay rigorously follows a common framework designed to explore ten hypotheses regarding popular beliefs about arms control. The findings are original and persuasive.

Dean, Arthur H. *Test Ban and Disarmament: The Path of Negotiations.* New York: Harper & Row, 1966. A diplomat involved in arms control negotiations for the United States, Dean gives an authoritative account of the diplomacy of the test ban treaty.

Epstein, William. *The Last Chance: Nuclear Proliferation and Arms Control.* New York: Free Press, 1976. Discusses the diplomacy surrounding efforts to control the buildup and spread of nuclear weapons. Focuses primarily on the Non-Proliferation Treaty but treats the 1963 treaty as an important building block on the road to nuclear arms control.

Mandelbaum, Michael, ed. *The Other Side of the Table: The Soviet Approach to Arms Control.* New York: Council on Foreign Relations Press, 1990. Five authors examine the intricacies of Soviet policy on several issues of arms control, including the nuclear test ban, SALT I, and the intermediate-range nuclear forces (INF) agreement. Particularly useful because it contrasts the Soviet approach to arms control with that of the United States.

SEE ALSO: 1942, Manhattan Project; 1945, Atomic Bombing of Japan; 1952, Hydrogen Bomb Is Detonated; 1979,

SALT II Is Signed; 1991, Bush Announces Nuclear Arms Reductions; 1993, START II Is Signed.

1963 ■ ASSASSINATION OF PRESIDENT KENNEDY: *after only two years in office, a charismatic world leader is slain, leaving a nation stunned*

DATE: November 22, 1963
LOCALE: Dallas, Texas
CATEGORY: Government and politics
KEY FIGURES:

John Bowden Connally (1917-1993), governor of Texas
Claudia Alta Taylor "Lady Bird" Johnson (born 1912), Lyndon Johnson's wife and later First Lady
Lyndon Baines Johnson (1908-1973), vice president of the United States
Jacqueline Lee Bouvier Kennedy (1929-1994), wife of the president of the United States
John Fitzgerald Kennedy (1917-1963), thirty-fifth president of the United States, 1961-1963
Lee Harvey Oswald (1939-1963), employee, Texas School Book Depository, and assassin of President Kennedy
Jack Ruby (Jacob Rubenstein, 1911-1967), Dallas nightclub operator
Ralph Webster Yarborough (1903-1996), U.S. senator from Texas

SUMMARY OF EVENT. At approximately 12:30 P.M. Central Standard Time on November 22, 1963, President John Fitzgerald Kennedy was shot in Dallas, Texas. At the time, President Kennedy and his party, consisting of wife Jacqueline, Vice President Lyndon B. Johnson and Mrs. Johnson, Senator Ralph Yarborough, and Texas governor John B. Connally and Mrs. Connally, were traveling in a motorcade from Love Field to the Dallas Trade Mart, where the president was to make an address as part of a fund-raising drive for the national Democratic Party. The stricken president was rushed to Parkland Hospital, where he was pronounced dead within the hour. Two hours after the shooting, Lyndon B. Johnson was sworn in as the thirty-sixth president of the United States. Johnson immediately left Dallas for Washington, D.C., on board *Air Force One* with the corpse of the murdered president. Within a matter of minutes after the plane landed at Andrews Air Force Base near Washington, D.C., Johnson appeared on television and made his first public statement as president to the people of the United States.

Certainly, a statement from the new president was needed. The nation appeared panic-stricken; every newscast and many rumors heightened the suspense and fear. Never before had so great a tragedy been covered so completely by the communications media. Forty minutes after the assassination, Walter Cronkite, a noted news commentator for the Columbia Broadcasting System, reached all that network's affiliated stations with a news flash: "The president has been shot." The business of the entire nation ground to a halt. Defense Secretary Robert S. McNamara hastily summoned the Joint Chiefs of Staff to an emergency meeting. The panic was heightened by a breakdown of the Washington telephone system. Senator Edward Kennedy, the murdered president's brother, was unable to place a call to Parkland Hospital. In Dallas, there was difficulty with the police radio network. A series of documentable but lamentable events confused the search for the assassin and added to public fears. Americans felt such a deep personal loss over the assassination of the young president that they seemed unable to carry on any but the most routine of daily affairs, pending the last services and interment in Arlington National Cemetery. To many, especially the young, the fallen president rapidly became a folk hero.

Lee Harvey Oswald, who had once renounced his U.S. citizenship to become a Russian national, on Thursday, November 21, had carefully examined his Mannlicher-Carcano rifle and placed it in a specially made bag before departing for work at the Texas School Book Depository. On the morning of the murder, he took his gun in this bag to the sixth floor of the depository and arranged boxes against the window so that he would have a "dead-fall" shot on occupants in cars approaching and leaving the highway below. Earlier, while serving in the U.S. Marine Corps, Oswald had qualified as expert with the M-1 rifle. Oswald knew that the Kennedy motorcade would have to turn just in front of the depository before heading down toward the underpasses. It was on the sixth floor of the depository that witnesses saw the marksman and the gun. The evidence bears out the fact that Oswald left the depository within three minutes after the shooting and boarded a bus, from which he soon disembarked to enter a taxicab. Soon after the shooting, the Dallas police radioed a description of the suspected assassin to all members of the police force and placed them on alert. Oswald, who had gone to his room and secured a .38-caliber pistol, shortly was approached by police officer J. D. Tippit. He shot Tippit and ran to the Texas Theatre, where at 2:50 P.M., police arrested him. On Saturday, November 23, Oswald was formally charged with the murder of the president. Immediately after the arrest, J. Edgar Hoover, director of the Federal Bureau of Investigation, urged that Oswald be secretly transferred out of the Dallas jail. This advice was ignored. On Sunday morning, plans to transfer Oswald to the county jail were completed. While the move was being made, Jack Ruby, a Dallas nightclub operator, shot Oswald. An audience of millions saw the shooting because the television networks had been permitted to cover the transfer. This third murder in less than two days served to confuse forever the reasons for the assassination and the positive identification of the killer. Again, the nation recoiled in horror. Hastily, the mythmakers began to follow their craft, weaving Ruby in the fabric of their story.

Events at Dallas shocked the world. Part of the national crisis resulted from the fact that Presidential Press Secretary Pierre Salinger, in company with Secretary of State Dean Rusk and Presidential Adviser McGeorge Bundy, had been sent to Honolulu to conduct a Vietnam council of war. The day before the assassination of the president, joined by five other cabinet members, Salinger and Rusk left Honolulu about noon on Friday, November 22, headed for Japan. When the radio news reached them, the party turned in mid-Pacific and came back to Washington, arriving on Saturday, November 23.

The state funeral began when the coffin of the president was taken to the White House. The following day the casket was taken to the Capitol, where hundreds of thousands of silent mourners filed by, many of them in tears. More than ninety million Americans watched the television broadcast of the funeral procession from Capitol Hill to the graveside in Arlington National Cemetery.

Kennedy had gone to Dallas because of the factional split in the Democratic Party in Texas. One wing of the split was headed jointly by Vice President Johnson and his supporter, Governor Connally; the other unit was led by Senator Ralph Yarborough. Because of the uninspired leadership of several extremely wealthy Texans, Dallas had become renowned as a center for right-wing conservative and reactionary politics, despite the fact that most of its citizens were considered law-abiding and peaceful. Prior to the assassination, some political visitors had been verbally abused, and one reportedly struck by a woman zealot. The Kennedy motorcade participants all remembered the adverse political slogans that appeared as the president passed. Fearing this sort of atmosphere, many close associates of the president had warned him against going to Dallas.

Political necessity prevailed, because presidential aides feared that the small margin by which the Kennedy-Johnson ticket had carried Texas in 1960 had been dissipated by Kennedy's advocacy of liberal measures, including a civil rights program. National polls also showed the president's popularity to be at its lowest point. His economic and social programs, known as the New Frontier, were stalled in Congress. The U.S. public had not forgotten the Bay of Pigs incident, which had placed the president and the nation in a poor light internationally. The president decided to go to Dallas and actually used some of his political clout to force Governor Connally and Senator Yarborough to ride in the same motorcade with him. For the first time since the loss of her baby in August, Mrs. Kennedy had agreed to accompany her husband on a political trip. Her wit, charm, and great popularity enhanced the president's visit. Evidently, the president achieved considerable success in arousing Democratic leaders, for prior to his visit to Dallas, he had been greeted by large and friendly crowds at Houston, San Antonio, and Fort Worth. Everyone in the presidential party appeared pleased when they left Fort Worth for Dallas. Hopes soared that the Democratic Party in Texas would be reunited because of Kennedy's visit. Then came the trip from Love Field, Dallas, that had been scheduled to terminate at the Trade Mart. The route had been published in the newspapers, and Oswald perfected his plans on the basis of that route.

One week after the assassination, President Johnson appointed a commission to gather all the facts about the event. This commission, chaired by Chief Justice Earl Warren, became known as the Warren Commission. Six other distinguished public figures served on the commission with Warren. Beginning in February, 1964, the commission held hearings, gathering fifteen volumes of testimony and depositions and eleven volumes of exhibits. In late September, 1964, the commission reported to the president its conclusion that President Kennedy had been assassinated by Oswald and that there had been no conspiracy.

The Warren Commission Report did not still the cries of those who believed that the assassination could not have been perpetrated by a paranoid loner. Soon, some respectable writers began to attack the commission's conclusions; those anxious to capitalize on the murder had begun feeding the public half-truths and juggled facts in numerous volumes ranging from the fanciful to the absurd. In New Orleans, District Attorney Jim Garrison began a vendetta against a wealthy businessman named Clay Shaw. Shaw was a former president of the International Trade Mart and a man noted prominently for his work in restoration of New Orleans' historic French Quarter. In December, 1966, Garrison began to question Shaw about his alleged role in the Kennedy assassination. Garrison later obtained an indictment against Shaw, accusing him of planning Kennedy's assassination. Garrison's investigation went nowhere and eventually fell apart. Nevertheless, director Oliver Stone would later base his 1991 film *JFK* in part on Garrison's investigation.

A large number of books also came to market during this period, each with its own version of a conspiracy theory. The first of these, *Whitewash* (1966) by Harold Weisberg, was a direct attack on the Warren Commission Report. It was soon followed by *Rush to Judgment* (1966), by Mark Lane, a prominent New York attorney. Lane was to write a series of books accusing numerous agencies in the government of taking part in a conspiracy. Despite little real evidence for his theories, he remained a popular speaker on the subject for many years.

The U.S. government itself often provided impetus to conspiracy theories with its own confusion. In 1975, it was revealed that the Central Intelligence Agency had attempted to assassinate Cuban dictator Fidel Castro in the 1960's. The Warren Commission (and perhaps even Kennedy himself) had never been aware of these activities; it was a short jump to the question of what other information the CIA had withheld. As a result, a new investigative committee was established in September, 1976, with congressman Thomas Downing, a devotee of the conspiracy theories, as its chairman. Downing eventually was replaced by Louis Stokes of Ohio, and in December, 1978, the commission reported that it could find nothing substantially inaccurate in the Warren Commission Report. Before the 1978 report was released, two acoustics experts, analyzing a dictabelt recording of the actual assassination, argued they could hear an additional shot being fired from the front of the motorcade. Although the analysis was shown to be inaccurate, it clouded the issue still further.

Despite the loose charges, no significant evidence indicating a conspiracy has ever been established, and most thoughtful persons have accepted the findings of the Warren Commission that Lee Harvey Oswald, acting alone, assassinated President Kennedy. Nearly all the conspiracy theories were put to rest in *Case Closed* (1993), by Gerald Posner. Posner's analysis of all aspects of the case clearly indicates that Oswald alone was guilty.   —*Bennett H. Wall, updated by Richard Adler*

ADDITIONAL READING:

Bishop, Jim. *The Day Kennedy Was Shot*. New York: Funk & Wagnalls, 1968. An hour-by-hour account of the fateful day in Dallas.

Donovan, Robert J. *The Warren Commission Report on the Assassination of John F. Kennedy*. New York: Popular Library, 1964. A synopsis of the twenty-six-volume report on the assassination.

Lane, Mark. *Plausible Denial*. New York: Thunder's Mouth Press, 1991. Accuses the CIA of a role in the assassination.

Manchester, William. *The Death of a President*. New York: Harper & Row, 1967. A well-researched account of the trip to Dallas, written by one of the president's closest friends.

Posner, Gerald. *Case Closed*. New York: Doubleday, 1993. Accurately debunks the conspiracy theories. Must reading for anyone interested in the details of Kennedy's murder.

SEE ALSO: 1960, Kennedy Is Elected President; 1965, Assassination of Malcolm X; 1968, Assassinations of King and Kennedy.

1964 ■ TWENTY-FOURTH AMENDMENT: *state and federal governments are forbidden to impose poll taxes as a qualification for voting*

DATE: January 23, 1964
LOCALE: United States
CATEGORIES: Civil rights; Government and politics
KEY FIGURES:
Virginia Durr and
Joseph Gelders, co-leaders of the National Committee to Abolish the Poll Tax
Lee Geyer (1888-1941), Democratic congressman from California and founder of the National Committee to Abolish the Poll Tax
Spessard Holland (1892-1971), Democratic senator from Florida and sponsor of Twenty-fourth Amendment
Claude Pepper (1900-1989), Democratic senator from Florida and sponsor of legislation to ban the poll tax
Harry S Truman (1884-1972), thirty-third president of the United States, 1945-1953
SUMMARY OF EVENT. Poll taxes, or the payment of a fee in order to vote, originated after the Revolutionary War as a

means of expanding the electorate. At the end of the eighteenth century, the right to vote was restricted to white, male property owners. The poll tax became a substitute for the property qualification and allowed more men the right to vote.

It was not until after the Civil War that the poll tax was used by Southern states to prevent voting by African Americans and poor whites. Florida was the first Southern state to adopt the poll tax, in 1889, and other Southern states quickly followed. The poll tax, in conjunction with other voting barriers such as white primaries and literacy tests, was effective in eliminating most blacks from the voter registration lists, as well as many poor whites.

Most states imposed a tax of between one and two dollars, and the tax was cumulative. Voters had to pay the tax every year, not just the year they wanted to vote. In Alabama, the tax could accumulate for twenty-four years. Many states gave exemptions for the aged, disabled, or veterans. The veterans' exemption angered many women, who were limited by law from serving in the military and, therefore, had to pay the tax. As a result, many women led the opposition to the poll tax.

Another unique feature of the poll tax was that it frequently had to be paid six months to a year before the election. A person who forgot to pay on time could not vote. Most states also required voters to keep poll tax receipts. Even if blacks and poor whites paid the tax, they had to retain receipts for several years to prove they had paid.

On its surface, the poll tax appeared to be nondiscriminatory. Everyone had to pay the tax, whether black or white, and the fee was the same for both races. The fact that several non-Southern states with small minority populations used the poll tax allowed Southern politicians to argue that the tax was fair and constitutional. The evidence is clear, however, that Southern states that adopted the poll tax did so for one overriding reason—to eliminate African American voters.

Poll taxes had several consequences. First, they were successful in eliminating most black voters and many poor white voters, both of whom were perceived to be threats to the elite dominant political organizations in the South. Second, poll taxes had a corrupting effect on elections, as candidates and party organizations would frequently try to buy elections by paying the poll taxes of their supporters. Finally, the waiver of poll taxes for veterans clearly discriminated against women, who were restricted by law and tradition from military service.

A serious effort to abolish the poll tax began in the 1930's and was given impetus by President Harry S Truman's Commission on Civil Rights in 1948. The commission's report, *To Secure These Rights*, served as the basis for Truman's ten-point civil rights program. One of those points was the abolition of the poll tax. Truman introduced legislation to abolish the poll tax, but Congress failed to act on the administration's request.

Many Southern states eliminated the poll tax on their own because of the corruption associated with the tax, because the Great Depression of the 1930's had made poll tax payments impossible for millions of potential voters, and because there were more effective methods of preventing African Americans from registering and voting. On the national level, the effort to eliminate the poll tax was led by the National Committee to Abolish the Poll Tax (NCAPT), headed by Democratic congressman Lee Geyer of California. When Geyer died in 1941, the leadership of NCAPT was assumed by Joseph Gelders and Virginia Durr.

The NCAPT and poll tax opponents pursued two approaches in their quest to ban poll taxes. They first concentrated on trying to persuade Congress to abolish the tax. Beginning in 1939, legislation to repeal the poll tax was introduced in every session of Congress. Durr was able to persuade Senator Claude Pepper of Florida to introduce poll tax repeal legislation in Congress. On five occasions, the House of Representatives passed legislation banning poll taxes, but on each occasion, the bill was defeated in the Senate as a result of filibusters by Southern senators. Supporters of a poll tax ban realized the legislative approach was not practicable, and many questioned whether it was constitutional, since it involved Congress in regulating how states conducted their elections.

A second approach to eliminating the poll tax was through a constitutional amendment. Advocated by Senator Spessard Holland of Florida, who believed that poll taxes could be prohibited only by constitutional amendment, several efforts were made to persuade Congress to propose such an amendment. As late as 1958, Frederic Ogden, a leading scholar on poll taxes, concluded that "Since only five states now have a voter poll tax, the Constitution will not be amended for this purpose." Ogden's prediction proved incorrect. In 1962, Congress proposed a constitutional ban on the poll tax and, within two years, the necessary thirty-eight states had ratified the Twenty-fourth Amendment.

At the time the Twenty-fourth Amendment was ratified in 1964, only Alabama, Arkansas, Mississippi, Texas, and Virginia used poll taxes in state and local elections. Arkansas abandoned its state and local poll taxes after passage of the Twenty-fourth Amendment. The view of the four remaining states was that the Twenty-fourth Amendment banned poll taxes only in federal elections and not in state and local races.

In 1965, the U.S. House of Representatives passed a poll tax ban in state elections as part of the 1965 voting rights bill. The Senate failed to support the ban, and the final version of the Voting Rights Act of 1965 merely said the poll tax "denied or abridged" the constitutional right to vote. The Justice Department was encouraged to pursue litigation to end poll taxes in the remaining jurisdictions.

African Americans in Virginia brought suit against that state's $1.50 annual poll tax as a requirement for voting in state and local elections. The U.S. district court, citing the 1937 case *Breedlove v. Suttles*, dismissed the claim. In *Breedlove*, the U.S. Supreme Court held that, except where constrained by the Constitution, the states may impose whatever conditions on the suffrage that they deem appropriate. On appeal, a six-to-three majority overruled *Breedlove* and held

that the requirement to pay a fee in order to vote violated the Constitution.

Although the plaintiffs were African American, the ruling was based on economic discrimination rather than racial discrimination. "To introduce wealth or payment of a fee as a measure of a voter's qualifications," wrote Justice William Douglas in the majority opinion, "is to introduce a capricious or irrelevant factor." In the view of the court's majority, voter qualifications had no relationship to wealth. The three dissenters believed that a fairly applied poll tax could be a reasonable basis for the right to vote.   *—Darryl Paulson*

ADDITIONAL READING:

Black, Earl, and Merle Black. *Politics and Society in the South*. Cambridge, Mass.: Harvard University Press, 1987. Examines the interrelationship between Southern culture and Southern politics.

Garrow, David. *Protest at Selma: Martin Luther King, Jr., and the Voting Rights Act of 1965*. New Haven, Conn.: Yale University Press, 1978. Demonstrates how a political interest group pressured Congress to pass a major voting rights bill.

Lawson, Steven F. *Black Ballots: Voting Rights in the South, 1944-1969*. New York: Columbia University Press, 1990. Discusses major impediments to black voting, including the poll tax, in chapter 4.

Ogden, Frederic. *The Poll Tax in the South*. University: University of Alabama Press, 1958. Still the best single account of the history of the poll tax and efforts to abolish it.

SEE ALSO: 1960, Civil Rights Act of 1960; 1962, Reapportionment Cases; 1964, Civil Rights Act of 1964; 1965, Voting Rights Act; 1970, U.S. Voting Age Is Lowered to Eighteen.

1964 ■ CIVIL RIGHTS ACT OF 1964: *responding to a vigorous activist movement, Congress passes the most far-reaching civil rights legislation since Reconstruction*

DATE: July 2, 1964

LOCALE: Washington, D.C.

CATEGORIES: African American history; Civil rights; Laws and acts

KEY FIGURES:

Everett McKinley Dirksen (1896-1969), minority leader in the Senate

Hubert Horatio Humphrey (1911-1978), senator, later vice president

Lyndon Baines Johnson (1908-1973), thirty-sixth president of the United States, 1963-1969

John Fitzgerald Kennedy (1917-1963), thirty-fifth president of the United States, 1961-1963

Martin Luther King, Jr. (1929-1968), first president of the Southern Christian Leadership Conference

Malcolm X (Malcolm Little, 1925-1965), African American leader

Rosa Parks (born 1913), African American civil rights activist

SUMMARY OF EVENT. The road to the passage of the Civil Rights Act of 1964 was long and tortuous. In June, 1963, President John F. Kennedy had addressed the nation and appealed to the American people to cooperate to meet the crisis in race relations. On June 19, he urged Congress to enact an omnibus bill to meet the demands of African Americans for racial equality. The bill he proposed included titles dealing with public accommodations, employment, federally assisted programs, and education.

The bill was reported by the House committee in November, just two days before the assassination of President Kennedy (November 22, 1963) in Dallas. As the stunned nation recovered, there was an outpouring of emotion for the late president. President Lyndon Johnson addressed the Congress and urged it to honor President Kennedy's memory with the passage of the omnibus civil rights bill. Johnson, who had been viewed as a part of the conservative establishment opposed to civil rights when he was Senate majority leader, now became its most vigorous champion. Whether this transformation came from a change in conscience, a change in position, or a desire to be seen as a national leader cannot be known, but Johnson made a firm commitment to civil rights in his state of the union address. He challenged this Congress to become known as the one that had done more for civil rights than any in one hundred years.

Martin Luther King, Jr., who had been at the forefront of a decade of struggle by African Americans for equality, gave his support to President Johnson at the time. However, he announced plans to resume demonstrations, which had been suspended since the assassination of President Kennedy, to make it clear to Congress and the country that the time to pass a civil rights bill had come. Together with the lobbying of civil rights groups and the efforts of activists and leaders, in cooperation with labor and religious leaders, King's actions forced the passage of the bill in the House. Despite the favorable action in the House, success in the Senate was difficult because of a filibuster. Senator Hubert H. Humphrey, who was a coordinator for the civil rights effort in the Senate, worked to gain the cooperation of Senator Everett M. Dirksen, the Senate minority leader. After compromise language was worked out with Senator Dirksen, a bipartisan vote ended the filibuster, and the Civil Rights Act of 1964 was passed on July 2.

The passage of the 1964 Civil Rights Act was largely in response to protests and demonstrations initiated by civil rights activists and African American leaders. In the 1950's, African Americans had mobilized a social movement, which spanned several decades, to eradicate the social injustices they faced throughout the United States. The mass effort to end legal segregation in public accommodations in the South had been sparked by Rosa Parks, an African American woman who, in 1955, had disobeyed the law by refusing to relinquish her seat to a white man on a crowded bus in Montgomery,

Alabama. The subsequent Montgomery bus boycott heralded a new Civil Rights movement, which ended the Jim Crow laws that had forbidden African Americans from using the same public accommodations—transportation, hotels, restaurants, schools, and other public facilities—along with whites. Leaders such as Malcolm X—who encouraged African Americans to challenge unfair practices and laws by teaching black nationalism and racial pride—also played a major role in the passage of the 1964 Civil Rights Act.

The act contained provisions designed to eliminate discrimination in areas other than public accommodations, such as voting, employment, federally funded programs, and education. Although laws had been passed in 1957 and 1960 to eliminate voting discrimination, unfairly administered literacy tests were still used to discriminate against African Americans. The 1964 act prohibited local officials from applying different standards to African Americans and whites when literacy tests were administered in federal elections. Completion of the sixth grade in an English-language school created a presumption of literacy.

Voting was viewed as a local issue, and there was general concern by those who opposed the Civil Rights Act that it would permit undue intervention of the federal government into local affairs. This argument was significant in determining the authority of the attorney general to bring suits concerning voting discrimination. The issue was resolved by providing that the attorney general could bring action if it were determined that a pattern of discrimination existed to prevent citizens from voting. This limited the possible federal intervention in local affairs, because litigation could not be initiated for an isolated incident of discrimination against one citizen. The act provided for a three-judge federal district court to hear cases of voter discrimination, which then could be appealed directly to the Supreme Court. One problem with the 1957 and 1960 acts had been the great length of time required to bring suit and process an appeal. The voting provisions of the 1964 act brought little change, and a major voting rights bill was passed the following year.

The results of the public accommodations provisions of the 1964 act were more impressive. Hotels, restaurants, service stations, places of amusement, and government-owned public facilities were forbidden to discriminate because of race, color, religion, or national origin. Although the attorney general could intervene only in cases of general public importance, discriminatory practices in public accommodations changed dramatically, and in a short time, the rigid separation of the races in places of public accommodation ended.

Ending discrimination in public accommodations proved to be much easier than desegregating schools or eliminating employment discrimination. The U.S. Supreme Court had decided in 1954 in *Brown v. Board of Education* that maintaining separate schools for African Americans and whites was unconstitutional, because African Americans were being deprived of their right to equal protection, as guaranteed by the Fourteenth Amendment. The Court held that in the sphere of public education, the doctrine of separate but equal was impracticable and that school desegregation should occur with all deliberate speed. However, schools were slow to comply with the Court's decision. A strong stand by Congress was important, because the courts had borne the entire burden of school desegregation, and they were vulnerable to the charge of usurping the power of Congress to make law. In cases of school discrimination, the attorney general was given greater latitude in bringing suits than in other civil rights areas, having only to determine that a complaint was valid and that the complainant was unable to maintain a suit before court action could be initiated. Although the attorney general's power in this area was more extensive than in other civil rights matters, Congress made clear that the goal was *desegregation* only; the 1964 act did not give any official or court the power to order racial *balance*.

Guidelines issued by the Office of Education were important in reducing segregation in schools. These guidelines also stipulated that there could be no discrimination in programs funded by the federal government. Because the federal government funds a great variety of programs, such as housing and urban development, the potential for this provision as a weapon against discrimination is great.

Preventing discrimination in employment was another major goal of the Civil Rights Act. Employers were forbidden to discriminate on the basis of race, color, religion, national origin, and (unlike the other parts of the 1964 act) sex. The act covers employers' practices in hiring, paying, promoting, and dismissing employees; referral by employment agencies; and trade unions' admission of members. Employers with as few as twenty-five employees ultimately would be covered, but this figure would be reached over three years. Employers were required to keep records, which have been useful in determining practices of discrimination.

An Equal Employment Opportunity Commission was established but, until a 1972 amendment, did not have power to bring suit against an employer. The commission could only try to persuade the employer; if that failed, the case could be referred to the attorney general with a recommendation that a suit be instituted. The attorney general had the power to bring suit not only upon the recommendation of the Equal Employment Opportunity Commission but also if there was a pattern or practice of discrimination. If a suit were brought and there was a finding of discrimination, the court had a wide range of remedies: It could enjoin the employer from further discriminatory practice, order reinstatement of an employee with back pay, or order the hiring of an employee. However, the act specifically stated that an employer is not required to grant preferential treatment because of an imbalance in the races of employees.

The act, at that time revolutionary in its coverage, would nevertheless encounter obstacles to its effectiveness. These limitations included the large caseloads of enforcement agencies, such as the Equal Employment Opportunity Commission, delaying timely investigations; the great length of time required to litigate cases; difficulty in retaining attorneys; the high costs of litigation; problems in identifying coworkers willing to be witnesses; and reverse discrimination lawsuits arguing that employer policies to ensure the civil rights of protected classes violate the civil rights of others. Many of these conditions would hinder the effectiveness of the 1964 Civil Rights Act, its provisions, and enforcement agencies. Thus, although the 1964 Civil Rights Act has remained the foundation of a series of civil rights acts passed since the 1960's, the goal of equal opportunity for all citizens of the United States has continued to be a worthwhile and necessary pursuit.   —*Doris F. Pierce, updated by K. Sue Jewell*

ADDITIONAL READING:

Abraham, Henry J. *Freedom and the Court: Civil Rights and Liberties in the United States*. New York: Oxford University Press, 1967. Focuses on civil rights and liberties in the United States.

Bell, Derrick. *Faces at the Bottom of the Well: The Permanence of Racism*. New York: Basic Books, 1992. Employs literary models in addressing how African Americans experience injustice in the judicial system.

_____. *Race, Racism and American Law*. 2d ed. Boston, Mass.: Little, Brown, 1977. A comprehensive analysis of U.S. law that reveals how racial inequality is integrated into the legislative and judicial systems.

Harvey, James C. *Black Civil Rights During the Johnson Administration*. Jackson: University and College Press of Mississippi, 1973. An analysis of the political influences and compromises at the birth of the civil rights laws of the Johnson Administration.

Jewell, K. Sue. *From Mammy to Miss America and Beyond: Cultural Images and the Shaping of U.S. Social Policy*. New York: Routledge, 1993. Discusses how institutional policies and practices in the United States contribute to social inequality for African Americans in general, and African American women in particular.

_____. *Survival of the Black Family: The Institutional Impact of U.S. Social Policy*. New York: Praeger, 1988. Examines how societal institutions, including the legal system, affect the stability of the African American family.

Schwartz, Bernard, ed. *Civil Rights*. Vol. 2 in *Statutory History of the United States*. New York: Chelsea House, 1970. Contains the actual texts of the acts together with debates and commentaries.

SEE ALSO: 1866, Civil Rights Act of 1866; 1868, Fourteenth Amendment; 1954, *Brown v. Board of Education*; 1955, Montgomery Bus Boycott; 1957, Southern Christian Leadership Conference Is Founded; 1957, Little Rock School Desegregation Crisis; 1960, Civil Rights Act of 1960; 1962, Meredith Registers at "Ole Miss"; 1963, King Delivers His "I Have a Dream" Speech; 1965, Voting Rights Act; 1972, Equal Employment Opportunity Act; 1977, Canada's Human Rights Act; 1978, *Regents of the University of California v. Bakke*; 1988, Civil Rights Restoration Act; 1991, Civil Rights Act of 1991.

1964 ■ Vietnam War: *U.S. involvement in a costly, prolonged, and ultimately futile war has a profound impact on Americans' social and political attitudes, as well as U.S. foreign policy*

Date: August 2, 1964-January 23, 1973
Locale: Indochina
Category: Wars, uprisings, and civil unrest
Key figures:

Ho Chi Minh (Nguyen That Thanh, 1890-1969), communist leader of the Viet Minh opposition to French colonialism in Indochina and subsequently head of state in North Vietnam

Lyndon Baines Johnson (1908-1973), thirty-sixth president of the United States, 1963-1969

John Fitzgerald Kennedy (1917-1963), thirty-fifth president of the United States, 1961-1963

Henry A. Kissinger (born 1923), Nixon's foreign policy adviser, responsible for negotiations ending the Vietnam War

Robert Strange McNamara (born 1916), secretary of defense under Presidents Kennedy and Johnson and an influential adviser on Vietnam

Richard Milhous Nixon (1913-1994), thirty-seventh president of the United States, 1969-1974

Ngo Dinh Diem (1901-1963), president of South Vietnam

William Westmoreland (born 1914), primary military commander of U.S. forces in Vietnam, 1964-1968, and leading architect of the large-scale ground war

Vo Nguyen Giap (born 1912?), military leader of the Viet Minh war against France and later of the North Vietnamese Army against the United States

Summary of event. Early in 1954, representatives of nineteen nations gathered in Geneva with hopes of settling a revolutionary war that had been plaguing French Indochina since 1946. Before a truce could be concluded, Vo Nguyen Giap's insurrectionary guerrilla army overran a vital French outpost at Dien Bien Phu. France had gambled its hopes on the staying power of this one garrison; when it fell, French power in Indochina fell with it. By the middle of the year, the Geneva Accords had ratified France's withdrawal from Southeast Asia and divided French Indochina into Laos, Cambodia, and a Vietnam divided at the seventeenth parallel. The communist-oriented Viet Minh revolutionary forces, led by Ho Chi Minh, controlled the northern half of the country, while the remnants of the French colonial regime, now headed by Ngo Dinh Diem, controlled the southern part.

Aside from France, the country most interested in the fate of Vietnam and Southeast Asia was the United States. Since the inception of this colonial war, U.S. money and materiel had found their way into the Asian jungles in support of the counterrevolutionary French Union Forces. At the conclusion of the French phase of the war, U.S. aid to Indochina totaled billions of dollars.

Prevailing assumptions about the character of the communist threat among foreign policy experts during the mid-1950's emphasized the unanimity of communism and its single-minded expansionism. When the defeat at Dien Bien Phu signaled the failure of France to hold the line against the communist advance in Southeast Asia, these precepts dictated that the United States throw itself into the breach. When considering the implications of the Geneva Accords, the National Security Council believed they were a disaster that foretold the collapse of all Southeast Asia. The United States embarked upon a political, economic, and military aid program to the government of South Vietnam. Thus, by the end of 1954, the United States government began a limited gamble that it could protect the sovereignty of South Vietnam.

The U.S. effort in Southeast Asia from 1954 to 1964 was a measured one, characterized by a steady increase in power and influence. For several years following the Geneva Accords, politico-military opposition to Diem was quiescent; in 1959, the United States still had only a few hundred military advisers, well within the number allowed by the Geneva peace agreement. However, the United States and South Vietnam rejected the Geneva Accords' proposal for nationwide elections and reunification of the country in 1956, fearing that would lead to the takeover of the entire country by Ho Chi Minh, the popular leader of the movement that had won independence from France. By the end of the decade, as political attempts to overthrow Diem and reunify the nation failed, and as Diem jailed or executed tens of thousands of political opponents, fighting between the remnants of the Viet Minh in the South and the Diem government increased dramatically. Terrorism and assassination increased apace with renewed government campaigns to end political resistance. By 1960, open military actions became the norm, and the insurgents announced the formation of the National Liberation Front (NLF), a clandestine political group informally known as the Viet Cong.

Between 1960 and 1964, the U.S. presence in South Vietnam became more pronounced. Advisers to President John F. Kennedy were sanguine about the ability of South Vietnam to withstand the increasing pressure of the Viet Cong. Although repeatedly urged from all sides to embark on a large-scale military intervention, Kennedy refrained from giving in to such suggestions. Nevertheless, at the end of 1963, there were more than seventeen thousand U.S. "advisers" in South Vietnam, and Kennedy's years in the presidency were marked by a pronounced expansion of the U.S. commitment of military, economic, and political support for South Vietnam.

In 1963, the Kennedy Administration, believing that corruption and dictatorial policies would prevent Diem from ever garnering the support of the people of South Vietnam, supported a military coup that led to Diem's assassination. A few weeks later, Kennedy himself was assassinated in Dallas. The problem of what to do about Vietnam was in the hands of

VIETNAM WAR, 1954-1975

(1) France falls, 1954. (2) Tet Offensive, January, 1968. (3) Cambodian invasion, April-May, 1970. (4) Sihanouk falls, April, 1970. (5) Laotian incursion, February, 1971. (6) Areas of U.S. bombing, 1972. (7) Mining of Haiphong Harbor, May, 1972. (8) Lon Nol falls, April, 1975. (9) North Vietnamese offensive, spring, 1975. (10) South Vietnam surrenders, April 20, 1975.

Kennedy's successor, Lyndon Johnson. Despite increasing U.S. support and the removal of Diem, the South Vietnamese government continued to lose ground in the war.

Full-scale U.S. military involvement was occasioned in August, 1964, when Johnson informed Congress that North Vietnam recently had made a naval assault on U.S. warships in the Gulf of Tonkin. The resolution that Congress passed in response gave Johnson a free hand to conduct a presidential war, although it would later turn out that the administration had lied to the press and the public about the so-called Tonkin Gulf incident. The United States responded to the Tonkin Gulf incident with bombing raids against selected sites in North Vietnam. Then, as Viet Cong attacks against the South Vietnamese government continued, an attack on U.S. military advisers at Pleiku, in February, 1965, provided the opportunity to commence Rolling Thunder, a steady air war against the North. In March, 1965, the first U.S. combat troops were authorized, initially to protect U.S. air bases, but soon they were involved in offensive search-and-destroy maneuvers against Viet Cong and North Vietnamese troops. By the end of 1965, there were nearly two hundred thousand U.S. combat troops in South Vietnam; within two years, the number had grown to more than half a million. Under commander William Westmoreland, the United States took primary control over the ground war in the South. Each step of U.S. escalation was more than matched by the opposition, however, so that despite massive bombing and growing U.S. casualties, the position of the South Vietnamese government remained precarious and the strength of the enemy seemed undiminished.

Domestic discontent over U.S. involvement in what many considered to be an Asian civil war began as early as 1964, but the spectacle of U.S. bombers over North Vietnam and U.S. casualties on the ground encouraged the formation of more groups in the United States demanding peace. The protraction of an undeclared war in a part of the world where the United States had little obvious interest also contributed to a growing public disapproval of the Johnson Administration's war policies. The initial strength of the antiwar movement derived from college campuses, but as the war continued, greater numbers of the citizenry advocated a general withdrawal. In addition, many people who were not vehemently against the war disapproved of the manner in which the United States was conducting the war. When these critics charged the successive administrations with simply reacting to North Vietnamese moves as they were made, they showed an appreciation of the fact that U.S. intelligence had consistently underrated the ability of the Viet Cong and North Vietnamese to resist the U.S. military machine.

The most telling demonstration of this fact occurred on January 30, 1968, when the Viet Cong launched an offensive against all the urban areas of South Vietnam. Embarrassingly, the U.S. embassy in Saigon was assaulted by a Viet Cong suicide squad. It has since been acknowledged that the Tet Offensive (so called because it was launched on the eve of Tet, the lunar New Year) was of major importance in changing the war policy of the government and encouraging renewed efforts to negotiate the United States out of a war it could not win. Partly because of the implications of the Tet Offensive and partly because of increased antiwar activity, President Johnson announced he would not seek reelection in 1968. The field was thrown open to candidates who identified themselves as much by their positions on the war as by political party. The several candidates advocated a spectrum of solutions, which ranged from an immediate withdrawal to a negotiated peace. The election of Richard Nixon in 1968 seemed a mandate for negotiation, but Nixon continued Johnson's peace and war efforts for five more years, with some changes in emphasis but little apparent success.

On January 23, 1973, the United States and North Vietnam concluded a peace agreement that called for a U.S. troop withdrawal, an exchange of prisoners, and a cease-fire throughout a devastated Indochina. This agreement was hardly the "peace with honor" that Nixon proclaimed. At best, it provided a decent interval between the U.S. withdrawal and the collapse of South Vietnam. Almost immediately after the withdrawal of U.S. troops, fighting began anew. President Nixon, bogged down in the Watergate scandal, resigned in 1974; in any case, he was not in a position to provide the assistance he secretly had promised the South Vietnamese in order to get their support of the treaty. A spring, 1975, North Vietnamese offensive, planned to last several years, met surprisingly little resistance from South Vietnam, and in April, 1975, Saigon was overrun and Vietnam reunified under the control of the North Vietnamese government. Cambodia and Laos, which had been drawn into the conflict, also came under the control of communist revolutionaries.

The effects of the Vietnam War on U.S. society lasted long after the war ended. It was the longest and least successful war in U.S. history. More than fifty-five thousand U.S. troops died in combat in Vietnam. Long after the war ended, its aftermath plagued U.S. society. A long-running controversy over the possibility that U.S. prisoners of war had been left in Southeast Asia would continue to simmer more than twenty years after the withdrawal. Large numbers of veterans continued to suffer from general post-traumatic stress syndrome, and specifically from massive exposure to Agent Orange, a chemical defoliant widely used in South Vietnam. The appropriate "lessons" of the Vietnam War continued to be hotly debated, and there was probably no more consensus on Vietnam in the 1990's than there was in the midst of the fighting and protests.

Slowly, however, the animosities began to fade. "The Wall," the official Vietnam memorial in Washington, D.C., was a stunningly successful commemoration of those who fought and died in Southeast Asia. Finally, after decades of continued hostility, in the summer of 1995 the U.S. resumed full economic and diplomatic relations with the government of Vietnam. —*Emory M. Thomas, updated by Kent Blaser*

ADDITIONAL READING:

Hayslip, Le Ly. *When Heaven and Earth Changed Places: A Vietnamese Woman's Journey from War to Peace*. New York:

Plume, 1990. The perspective of a Vietnamese woman who was involved with the Viet Cong, and later married an American and emigrated to the United States.

Karnow, Stanley. *Vietnam: A History*. New York: Viking Press, 1983. An excellent comprehensive survey of the Vietnam War. Closely coordinated with the television documentary *Vietnam: A Television History*.

McNamara, Robert S. *In Retrospect: The Tragedy and Lessons of Vietnam*. New York: Times Books, 1995. Long-awaited assessment of the Vietnam War by one of the most influential policymakers of the United States' involvement.

Sheehan, Neil. *A Bright Shining Lie: John Paul Vann and America in Vietnam*. New York: Random House, 1988. Massive study by one of the war's leading journalists, focusing on the war from the perspective of an influential grass-roots-level military and civilian adviser involved in Vietnam.

SEE ALSO: 1964, Berkeley Free Speech Movement; 1964, Johnson Is Elected President; 1967, Long, Hot Summer; 1968, Tet Offensive; 1968, Nixon Is Elected President; 1970, United States Invades Cambodia; 1973, U.S. Troops Leave Vietnam; 1995, United States Recognizes Vietnam.

1964 ■ BERKELEY FREE SPEECH MOVEMENT: *students at the University of California launch a decade of student activism, protest, and social change*

DATE: Beginning September 14, 1964
LOCALE: Berkeley, California
CATEGORIES: Civil rights; Cultural and intellectual history; Education
KEY FIGURES:
Bettina Aptheker (born 1944), student leader of the movement
Edmund G. "Pat" Brown (1905-1996), governor of California
Clark Kerr (born 1911), president of the University of California
Mario Savio (1942?-1996), principal student leader of the Free Speech movement
Katherine Toule, dean of students at the University of California, Berkeley
Jack Weinberg (born 1939?), former Berkeley student, whose arrest helped to focus discontent
SUMMARY OF EVENT. In the fall of 1964, after a September 14 ban on all political activities—from leafletting to soliciting funds—at the edge of the University of California (UC), Berkeley, campus, student activists launched a protest that soon spread campuswide. The Free Speech movement, as the students proclaimed themselves, signaled an end to silence and conformity at the nation's colleges and universities, announcing a new era of social protest, political questioning, and unrest.

UC Berkeley's administration had long feared radicalism. The original ban against political activities on the campus dated back to the 1930's. Students then moved their information tables to the area just outside campus, where they existed without university interference until the fall of 1964. In the 1950's, during the McCarthy era, UC Berkeley's administration limited political speech on campus. Even presidential candidate Adlai Stevenson was subject to the ban, addressing students from his convertible parked at the corner of Bancroft and Telegraph Avenues, just off campus. In 1957, students gave the university a target for their fear of radicals by forming SLATE, a student political party that demanded a cooperative bookstore and an end to compulsory participation in Reserve Officers' Training Corps (ROTC) classes. Most significant, SLATE rejected anti-communism. In 1961, the chancellor banned SLATE from campus, effectively disenfranchising many graduate students and contributing further to a sense of disaffection.

The paternalistic attitude toward the student body clashed with its changing composition. By the early 1960's, the baby-boom generation had arrived on campus, expanding student enrollment to twenty-five thousand and reducing the ratio of tenured faculty to students. Graduate students represented a larger proportion of the students and did more of the teaching. These older students chafed the most under campus regulations. In addition, UC Berkeley had recently constructed its first high-rise dormitories, breaking the fraternity system's conservative hold over campus life. More students also lived off campus in apartments, reflecting their greater independence and sense of individual responsibility.

Politically, the Civil Rights movement had touched Berkeley students by 1964. Few could ignore the racial division within the city of Berkeley itself. The Berkeley chapter of the Congress of Racial Equality (CORE) recruited students to protest job discrimination at local employers. That fall, dedicated student volunteers returned from Freedom Summer activities in the Deep South, determined to sign up new civil rights workers and raise funds. The ragtag assemblage of activists and their political tables at the entrance to campus provoked concern on the part of the administration with the university's public image.

On September 14, Dean Katherine Toule informed the students of the prohibition on political activity at the campus edge, although she personally opposed it. She listened to student complaints but lacked the power to revoke the ruling. Campus police arrested five students for violating the regulations. Four hundred students responded by signing statements claiming equal guilt and demanding equal punishment. Student activists demanded not just a return of the right to set up tables at the edge of campus, but the end to any regulation of political activity on campus. They based their demands on the constitutional right of free speech.

On October 1, to call attention to their demands, students set up political tables directly in front of the administration building. When the police arrested activist Jack Weinberg, students began a spontaneous sit-in, surrounding and immobilizing the police car for thirty-two hours. During the sit-in, students removed their shoes, climbed on top of the police car, and spoke to the crowd. Never before had campus administrators witnessed such defiance. Students, heady with a sense of power, mobilized. A core group of activists, including Mario Savio, Bettina Aptheker, and Jack Weinberg, worked on strategies to involve non-activist students. Clark Kerr, president of the University of California, attempted to divide the coalition of students, only further cementing student solidarity. Savio's rhetoric transformed the issue into one of student freedom and autonomy, to which students across the political spectrum could respond. Meanwhile, administrators continued to meet in committee to determine the proper punishment for students who had originally violated the ban. They pressed for the suspension of Savio, the magnetic student orator and leader. The administration's dogged attempt to end and punish campus dissent only egged students on, attracting more to the free speech cause throughout the fall.

On December 2, a group of more than eight hundred students occupied the administration building overnight. When Governor Edmund G. "Pat" Brown dispatched police to arrest students, the movement proclaimed a weeklong strike. The crackdown worked to undermine administrative authority, pushing faculty to take a stand for the students' right of free expression. The Academic Senate met and voted in favor of the students, 824 to 115. The events of December prompted the regents to intervene. On December 18, they enacted new rules that opened the campus to political activity. The students had won their demand for free speech.

The Free Speech movement attracted so many college students because "free speech" echoed U.S. values of liberalism and democracy. Students objected to the hypocrisy they saw on campus and in society as a whole—the clash between reality and U.S. ideals of equality. Protest took some students at Berkeley and nationwide in a radical direction as the decade progressed. With the increased militancy came an identification with the international student movement in Europe. At the protest at Columbia University in 1968, this tendency came to its fullest fruition. The targets and goals of student protest had extended to questions of life in the twentieth century, opposition to the Vietnam War, and the place of the university in the larger community, far exceeding the earlier question of peaceful disobedience in the face of unjust laws.

The Free Speech movement meant the death of *in loco parentis* (the concept that an institution of higher learning should supervise students' lives in place of their parents) at UC Berkeley, and this principle began to crumble on campuses across the country. Students chafed against curfews, parietals, and other regulation of their lives. Educated, informed students demanded autonomy.

Youths in the United States, and Europe as well, rejected twenty years of postwar liberal consensus. Incorporating the tactics they learned in the Civil Rights movement—the sit-in,

passive resistance, mass demonstrations, and strikes—students questioned the status quo and sought to ameliorate social conditions. The protests at UC Berkeley highlighted the issue of bureaucratic impersonality in conflict with individual autonomy that undergirded the later protests of the 1960's. The rejection of bureaucratic conformity came to full flower in the counterculture. Mario Savio presaged those developments when he proclaimed, "We must construct our own community of protest to take back our self-government."

The Free Speech movement, the first and most successful student protest of the 1960's, showed young people that they could fight bureaucracy and gain power to change laws and regulations. By the summer of 1970, students across the country had challenged the internal structure of their universities and sought to connect their campuses to larger social issues. The war in Vietnam and faculty war research imbued these protests with particular immediacy. The massive demonstrations at Yale on behalf of the Black Panthers, the student deaths at the hands of Ohio National Guardsmen at Kent State University, and disturbances on such traditionally quiet Southern campuses as the University of South Carolina attested to this new force in American life.

The divisions beneath the surface at the beginning of the decade were glaring by the decade's end. The violence of, and in response to, student protests in the late 1960's convinced many Americans that the nation was on the verge of crumbling, paving the way for a reassertion of a politics of law and order by the "silent majority." Nevertheless, campus life in the United States has not returned to the orderly and isolated ways that university officials had sought to preserve in 1964.

—Jessica Weiss

ADDITIONAL READING:

Breines, Wini. *Community and Organization in the New Left, 1962-1968: The Great Refusal.* New York: Praeger, 1982. A history of the new left, focusing on how ideals of participatory democracy undermined attempts to organize effectively.

Farber, David. *The Age of Great Dreams: America in the 1960's.* New York: Hill & Wang, 1994. A synthetic account of the tumultuous decade, outlining the decline of liberalism, student radicalism, and the silent majority's resurgence.

Kitchell Films in association with P.O.V. *Berkeley in the Sixties.* San Francisco: California Newsreel, 1990. A videotape documentary history of campus protest, from the House Un-American Activities Committee hearings to People's Park. Includes interviews with key participants.

Rorabaugh, W. J. *Berkeley at War: The 1960's.* New York: Oxford University Press, 1989. A multidimensional history of Berkeley, both town and gown, in the 1960's.

University of California. Academic Senate. Select Committee on Education. *Education at Berkeley.* Berkeley: University of California Press, 1968. One of the earliest attempts to define the problems facing U.S. higher education in the 1960's.

SEE ALSO: 1967, Long, Hot Summer; 1968, Chicago Riots; 1970, Kent State Massacre; 1970, U.S. Voting Age Is Lowered to Eighteen.

1964 ■ JOHNSON IS ELECTED PRESIDENT:
Johnson's election marks the rise of the Great Society programs and escalation of the Vietnam War

DATE: November 3, 1964
LOCALE: United States
CATEGORY: Government and politics
KEY FIGURES:

Barry Morris Goldwater (born 1909), senator from Arizona and Republican presidential nominee

Hubert Horatio Humphrey (1911-1978), senator from Minnesota and Democratic vice presidential nominee

Lyndon Baines Johnson (1908-1973), thirty-sixth president of the United States, 1963-1969

William Edward Miller (1914-1983), representative from New York and Republican vice presidential nominee

Nelson Aldrich Rockefeller (1908-1979), governor of New York and leading contender for the Republican nomination

SUMMARY OF EVENT. On November 22, 1963, at approximately 12:30 P.M. Central Standard Time, as the motorcade of President John Fitzgerald Kennedy passed the Texas School Book Depository Building, shots rang out that brought an abrupt end to the tenure of the young leader and catapulted Lyndon Baines Johnson into the nation's highest office. The fifty-five-year-old Johnson had accepted the vice presidential nomination in 1960 to the surprise of his friends, who thought that he would not give up his powerful position as Senate majority leader. Johnson gave up his Senate seat and helped the Democratic ticket to win a very narrow victory in 1960.

As the new president, Johnson compiled an outstanding legislative record in the year after Kennedy's assassination. Most of the dead president's programs were enacted under the shrewd leadership of Johnson, and the new leader added legislation of his own. By the summer of 1964, Johnson had an impressive list of accomplishments to present to the voters. There was little doubt that he would be nominated by his own party.

The Republican situation was less certain. The early favorites for the Republican nomination—Senator Barry M. Goldwater of Arizona and Governor Nelson A. Rockefeller of New York—were upset in the New Hampshire primary by write-in candidate Henry Cabot Lodge II, ambassador to South Vietnam. Goldwater was hurt by his statements favoring voluntary participation in Social Security and the granting to NATO commanders of the right to use nuclear weapons at their discretion. Rockefeller was damaged politically by his divorce and subsequent remarriage.

The Lodge boom stalled when Rockefeller won the Oregon primary, and the contest again boiled down to a choice between Goldwater and Rockefeller in the California primary. Goldwater needed to prove his voter appeal with a victory, and when he won by a narrow margin, his nomination was virtually assured.

The Republican convention, meeting in San Francisco in mid-July, was dominated from beginning to end by the Goldwater forces. A last-minute Stop Goldwater movement, led by Pennsylvania governor William W. Scranton, failed dismally. The conservative wing of the Republican Party had finally achieved control, and it had no intention of settling for half-measures. A conservative party platform called for limited, frugal, and efficient government, with an end to deficit spending and a reduction in taxation. It also called for a dynamic strategy aimed at victory abroad.

In keeping with the no-compromise temper of the conservatives, Goldwater selected Representative William E. Miller of New York, a little-known conservative, as his running mate. Goldwater was determined to offer "a choice, not an echo"—a chance for voters to repudiate the New Deal policies that had dominated U.S. politics since 1933. In accepting the Republican nomination, Goldwater made the most widely quoted statement of the campaign—a statement that Democrats would use against him: ". . . extremism in the defense of liberty is no

Lyndon Baines Johnson, thirty-sixth president of the United States. His ambitious goals to create the Great Society saw fruition in much social legislation, notably the Civil Rights Act of 1964, but fell victim to the nation's Vietnam War commitments and the rising protests of Americans at home. (Library of Congress)

vice . . . moderation in the pursuit of justice is no virtue." To many U.S. voters, this statement linked Goldwater irrevocably with the extremists he refused to disavow.

Meeting in late August, the Democratic National Convention in Atlantic City, New Jersey, was anticlimactic. Lyndon Johnson controlled the convention completely and, although some sympathy existed for naming Robert F. Kennedy the vice presidential nominee, Johnson chose Minnesota senator Hubert H. Humphrey, a longtime liberal. The Democratic platform endorsed Johnson's Great Society programs. It also condemned both right-wing and left-wing extremists, in an obvious slap at Goldwater.

The campaign itself lacked drama. The question was not whether Johnson would win but by how much. As international tensions increased, so did Johnson's margin of victory. With the Soviet Union's ouster of Premier Nikita Khrushchev on October 15 and China's detonation of its first nuclear device on October 16, Johnson's election was assured. The American people were uneasy about international affairs in the nuclear age, and they feared Goldwater's extreme conservatism. On November 3, 1964, Johnson received the largest popular vote ever given a presidential candidate up to that time; he swamped Goldwater forty-three million votes to twenty-seven million. The electoral vote was 486 to 52, with Goldwater carrying only five Deep South states and his native Arizona. The Democratic sweep extended to every level. The Democrats gained thirty-eight seats in the House, two in the Senate, and more than five hundred in state legislatures around the country. The Republican conservatives had had their day, with dismal results.

Given this resounding popular mandate, Johnson set forth the goals of the Great Society in his state of the union message in January, 1965. The Great Society—a term first used by Johnson at the University of Michigan in May, 1964—was to include medical care for the aged, a war on poverty, an end to pollution, solutions to urban and housing problems, and—the keystone of the Great Society—educational opportunities for all. Johnson's legislative successes in his promised program would be exceptional,˙ but the Great Society would founder on foreign shores as an unpopular war in Southeast Asia dissipated the energies of domestic reform. Faced with the choice of "guns or butter," U.S. citizens increasingly became disillusioned with both costly social activism and foreign intervention.

—*Fredrick J. Dobney, updated by Joseph Edward Lee*

ADDITIONAL READING:

Chafe, William H. *The Unfinished Journey*. Oxford, England: Oxford University Press, 1995. An early post-Cold War examination of the tumultuous period following World War II.

Dallek, Robert. *Lone Star Rising*. Oxford, England: Oxford University Press, 1991. A revealing portrait of Lyndon Johnson's political rise.

Gettleman, Marvin E., ed. *The Great Society Reader*. New York: McGraw-Hill, 1976. A documentary treatment of Johnson's domestic policies.

Johnson, Lyndon B. *The Vantage Point*. New York: Holt, Rinehart, 1971. The former president explains his hopes for the Great Society and his motivation for expanding the Vietnam War.

Patterson, James F. *America's Struggle Against Poverty, 1900-1980*. New York: W. W. Norton, 1981. Traces the nation's century-long effort to eradicate poverty.

White, Theodore H. *The Making of the President, 1964*. New York: Atheneum, 1965. A journalist chronicles Johnson's landslide victory over Goldwater.

SEE ALSO: 1963, Assassination of President Kennedy; 1964, Civil Rights Act of 1964; 1964, Vietnam War; 1965, Voting Rights Act; 1965, Expansion of Affirmative Action; 1967, Long, Hot Summer; 1968, Tet Offensive; 1968, Fair Housing Act; 1968, Nixon Is Elected President.

1965 ■ ASSASSINATION OF MALCOLM X: *bullets fell a militant and inspiring spokesman for African American rights*

DATE: February 21, 1965
LOCALE: Harlem, New York City
CATEGORIES: African American history; Civil rights
KEY FIGURES:
Elijah Muhammad (1897-1975), leader of the Nation of Islam
Malcolm X (Malcolm Little, 1925-1965), spokesman for the Nation of Islam
Marcus Mosiah Garvey (1887-1940), early African American nationalist and leader of the Universal Negro Improvement Association
Talmadge Hayer,
Norman 3X Butler, and
Thomas 15X Johnson, convicted assassins of Malcolm X

SUMMARY OF EVENT. Perhaps no twentieth century African American leader better expressed the anger and frustrations of urban African Americans than Malcolm X. During the 1960's Civil Rights movement, Malcolm X, the national spokesman of a black separatist Muslim sect known as the Nation of Islam, articulated in militant language the effects of the nation's historical pattern of racism against African Americans and the social consequences the country faced if significant change did not occur. Before his assassination in 1965, Malcolm X had come to symbolize the disenchantment of African American ghetto residents, a group who were disillusioned about the benefits of racial integration and becoming increasingly impatient with the dominant nonviolent philosophy of the Civil Rights movement.

Malcolm X was born Malcolm Little on May 19, 1925, in Omaha, Nebraska, to Louise Norton Little and J. Early Little. His father, a Baptist preacher, worked as an organizer for the Universal Negro Improvement Association, the black nationalist organization led by Marcus Garvey. In his later life, Malcolm too, would consider himself a black nationalist. In

Nation of Islam leader and civil rights activist Malcolm X was controversial for the militant stance he took to advance the cause of equality for African Americans. Like John F. Kennedy, Martin Luther King, Jr., and Robert Kennedy, he fell victim to an assassin's bullet in the growing violence of the turbulent 1960's. (Library of Congress)

1931, Malcolm's father died mysteriously in East Lansing, Michigan, where the family had relocated. Thereafter, Malcolm's life was marked by a series of crises.

The impoverished family, now comprising Malcolm, his mother, and six siblings, was soon separated: Malcolm's mother was committed to a mental hospital and no longer influenced his development. Malcolm was placed in a foster home and began to get into trouble as he grew older. Hoping to change the direction of the troubled teen's life, Ella, an older half sister, brought him to live with her in Boston, Massachusetts. Although he possessed a good mind, he did not find school rewarding and dropped out to work at odd jobs. An attraction to street life overcame his interest in legitimate employment, however, and he gradually gravitated toward hustling, drugs, and petty crime.

For a time, Malcolm loved the culture of urban street life and seemed to flourish in it. In the 1940's, he wore the zoot suit and wide hat popular among young African American and Hispanic hipsters and patronized the night spots in Boston's Roxbury and New York's Harlem ghettoes. The seedy side of this life proved to be his downfall. His graduation to the more serious crime of burglary eventually landed him in prison, and at twenty years of age, he began serving six years of a ten-year sentence in Massachusetts' Charlestown and Norfolk penitentiaries.

Initially, Malcolm was hardly a model prisoner. In many ways, however, prison proved to be his redemption, for it was in prison that Malcolm converted to a version of Islam that changed his life. Largely through the efforts of his sisters and brothers, who visited him regularly, Malcolm was introduced to the ideas and philosophy of a little-known Muslim sect, the Nation of Islam, headed by Elijah Muhammad. Gradually, Malcolm abandoned his aggressive behavior, adopted Muslim prayer and life practices, and enmeshed himself in the teachings of Muhammad.

Malcolm absorbed the Muslim interpretation of the history of races, an interpretation that explained how and why white people came to be regarded as "devils" and the oppressors of black people throughout the world. Based on Muhammad's teaching, Malcolm's own life experiences, and wide reading in history, politics, and economics, Malcolm came to understand how central the role of white people had been in causing the lowly conditions of African Americans. Muhammad could not have found another adherent with a wider breadth of knowledge about black and white race relations than Malcolm. Their attraction to each other and Malcolm's commitment to spreading Muhammad's message placed Malcolm in an ideal position for elevation to a more visible role in the Islamic organization.

Shortly after his parole in 1952, Malcolm was appointed minister of Temple No. 7 in Harlem by the Muslim leader. Articulate and intellectually gifted, Malcolm undertook his duties with a passion and energy unmatched by his peers. He increased the membership in his own temple and traveled throughout the country organizing new mosques. By 1959, the sect could boast of forty-nine temples nationwide and more than forty thousand members. In six years, temple estab-

lishment increased nearly tenfold, and Malcolm almost single-handedly accounted for this.

By 1960, Malcolm clearly had emerged as the second most influential man in the Nation of Islam, and was the national spokesman for Elijah Muhammad. Malcolm was heard on the radio and seen on national television. Converts and sympathizers read about his views through the columns of the newspaper that he established, *Muhammad Speaks*, and in other African American urban newspapers for which he regularly wrote. In his Harlem street meetings, he railed against police brutality, and he quelled potentially explosive confrontations between African Americans and law enforcement officials. He continued to "fish" on the ghetto streets for new converts, appealing to them with a mastery of oratory that condemned white racism and the failure of liberal black and white leaders to address the real needs of the African American community. In no uncertain terms, he told listeners that African American men sought to present and defend themselves as men, violently if necessary. Change would occur in the United States, he said, either by the ballot or by the bullet.

In the span of a few short years, Malcolm's name was as familiar as that of Martin Luther King, Jr. Malcolm's national notoriety and influence sparked rivalry and jealousy within the ranks of the Nation of Islam, however. Even Elijah Muhammad, who had warned Malcolm of potential internal dangers from becoming too powerful, grew envious of his national prominence. Rival factions looked for ways to bring him down.

The opportunity occurred in December, 1963, following President John F. Kennedy's assassination, when Malcolm violated Muhammad's order for Muslims to remain silent about the murder. In an interview, Malcolm equated the president's death to "chickens coming home to roost," an impolitic remark that provided the excuse for Muhammad to punish him. Discredited and officially silenced for ninety days, Malcolm's influence within the Nation of Islam waned precipitously.

Unable to forge an effective reconciliation with Muhammad and increasingly determined to speak more broadly for African Americans independent of Nation of Islam constraints, Malcolm left the organization in early 1964 to form his own group, Muslim Mosque, Inc. A pilgrimage to Mecca, the Hajj, and subsequent travel to Africa expanded his understanding about the true nature of Islam, validated his status as an international personality, and helped him to define new agendas in his fight for black people worldwide. A new Malcolm with a new Islamic name, El-Hajj Malik El-Shabazz, hoped to accomplish his agenda through a more politically oriented organization of his making, the Organization of Afro-American Unity.

Malcolm remained a marked man, however, and was unable to escape the vilification of enemies in the Nation of Islam. Privately and publicly, they denounced him as a traitor to Elijah Muhammad and placed him under surveillance. From many quarters, those threatened by Malcolm's mass appeal and influence called for violent retribution. In February, 1964, he and his family escaped death from a bomb that destroyed their home.

Malcolm's pleas for peace with the Nation of Islam could not stave off another attempt on his life. On February 21, 1965, while speaking before a crowd of several hundred followers in Harlem's Audubon Ballroom, Malcolm was felled by a fusillade of bullets. In March, 1966, a racially mixed jury found three men—Talmadge Hayer, Norman 3X Butler, and Thomas 15X Johnson—guilty of first-degree murder in Malcolm's death. Despite their conviction, conspiracy theories about Malcolm's death have remained, including theories implicating non-Muslims and even the federal government.

For many African Americans who regarded him as their champion, Malcolm's death was a devastating psychological blow. For those who felt disfranchised, lost in an uncaring system tainted by the historical effects of racism, Malcolm's death silenced a voice that articulated their anger, frustrations, and aspirations. The urban ghetto had forged his life and he understood its victims; they understood him, too, and drew from his aggressive spirit. Malcolm's loss also had meaning for whites, as it stilled a voice that effectively raised whites' consciousness about their role in the plight of African Americans. In the harshest of language and the fiercest of manners, Malcolm had sought to ensure white accountability for past deeds and to encourage remedies.　　*—Robert L. Jenkins*

ADDITIONAL READING:

Breitman, George, Herman Porter, and Baxter Smith. *The Assassination of Malcolm X*. New York: Pathfinder Press, 1976. Investigates the authors' claim of a cover-up regarding Malcolm's death. Includes firsthand coverage of the trial of the murderers.

Evanzz, Karl. *The Judas Factor: The Plot to Kill Malcolm X*. New York: Thunder's Mouth Press, 1992. A detailed, documented account revealing the author's theory that the intelligence community was involved in Malcolm's death.

Friedly, Michael. *Malcolm X, the Assassination*. New York: Carroll & Graf, 1992. Explores the various conspiracy theories advanced about Malcolm's murder. Gives extensive coverage of his relationship with Elijah Muhammad.

Karim, Benjamin, with Peter Skutches and David Gallen. *Remembering Malcolm*. New York, Carroll & Graf, 1992. An account of Malcolm's life by an assistant minister who served under him.

Perry, Bruce. *Malcolm: The Life of a Man Who Changed Black America*. Barrytown, N.Y.: Station Hill, 1991. Revises earlier images of Malcolm's life and public career, presenting a man whose childhood was burdened with hardship and violence and who was driven by the need for acceptance by the society he condemned as racist.

Strickland, William. *Malcolm X, Make It Plain*. New York: Viking, 1994. A popular biography of Malcolm, based on interviews and research originally conducted for a Public Broadcasting Service documentary.

SEE ALSO: 1930, Nation of Islam Is Founded; 1955, Montgomery Bus Boycott; 1957, Southern Christian Leadership Conference Is Founded; 1957, Little Rock School Desegregation Crisis; 1960, Civil Rights Act of 1960; 1962, Meredith Registers at "Ole Miss"; 1963, King Delivers His "I Have a Dream" Speech; 1964, Civil Rights Act of 1964; 1965, Watts Riot; 1965, Expansion of Affirmative Action; 1967, Long, Hot Summer; 1968, Assassinations of King and Kennedy.

1965 ■ GRISWOLD V. CONNECTICUT: *the U.S. Supreme Court strikes down a state ban on the use of contraceptives, affirming the constitutional right of privacy*

DATE: June 7, 1965
LOCALE: Washington, D.C.
CATEGORIES: Civil rights; Court cases; Women's issues
KEY FIGURES:
Hugo L. Black (1886-1971),
William O. Douglas (1898-1980),
Arthur J. Goldberg (1908-1990),
John Marshall Harlan (1899-1971), and
Potter Stewart (1915-1985), U.S. Supreme Court justices
Estelle Griswold (1900-1981), appellant in the case
Margaret Sanger (1879-1966), feminist and birth control activist

SUMMARY OF EVENT. In this, one of the most important cases decided in the twentieth century, privacy was established as a right guaranteed by the United States Constitution. The decision was important for several reasons, not the least of which was that the word "privacy" appears nowhere in the Constitution, including the Bill of Rights. Use of the term to connote personal seclusion from unsanctioned intrusion developed largely after the Constitution was written, in conjunction with the emergence of a more urban society. Not until the end of the nineteenth century did scholars begin exploring the need for legal recognition of such a right. Although cases were brought on this issue throughout the first half of the twentieth century, courts refused to recognize that a right of privacy existed.

Beginning in the 1960's, however, a major reversal took place. Circumstances leading to this development involved efforts to repeal a Connecticut law criminalizing both use of and encouragement to use birth control devices. The law had been written in 1879 when, compliant with Victorian attitudes generally, similar statutes were being enacted throughout the United States. As part of her crusade on behalf of women, Margaret Sanger spoke in opposition to the Connecticut law and was joined by others such as Katherine Houghton Hepburn, Katherine Beech Day, and Josephine Bennett. Together they founded what was eventually called the Connecticut Planned Parenthood League.

In the late 1950's, officers of the league, joined by married women whose health conditions required that they bear no more children, challenged the 1879 law. After losing in the Connecticut courts, they appealed the case to the U.S. Supreme Court in 1961. A majority of the high court, however, dismissed the case on procedural grounds, leaving the state law in place. Four years later, the statute was challenged again when Estelle Griswold, executive director of the league, was convicted for violating it. With the aid of professors from the Yale Law School, arguments were assembled, an appeal commenced, and, once more, the nation's highest court was approached on the matter. Reversing its earlier position, the Court voted by a seven-to-two majority to strike the Connecticut statute down. Justice William O. Douglas, who delivered the majority opinion, justified the ruling on grounds that the law was a violation of the right of privacy. Beyond the personal victory for Griswold and her associates, the case is significant because of the methods Douglas used to locate this newfound right.

Douglas first acknowledged that there were no specific references in the Constitution to either privacy or intimate relations between husbands and wives—the subject matter of the case. He pointed out, however, that on previous occasions the Supreme Court had identified other rights also not present in the document, such as the rights to freely associate with others, to study and pursue a profession of one's choice, and to educate one's children in schools of one's own choosing. These rights, he said, were derived from guarantees that were in the Constitution, such as the First Amendment. So it was with privacy, he argued. It was a "penumbra," an "emanation" from other protections already in the federal Bill of Rights.

Those provisions Douglas cited as implying a right of privacy were the First Amendment, with its guarantees of freedom of expression; the Third Amendment's prohibition against quartering soldiers in private homes in peacetime; the Fourth Amendment's right of people "to be secure in their persons, houses, papers, and effects, against unreasonable searches and seizures"; the Fifth Amendment's protection against self-incrimination; and the Ninth Amendment's declaration that other rights, beyond those specifically enumerated, belonged to U.S. citizens and were not to be denied. All of these, said Douglas, created "zones of privacy" that the court was obliged to protect.

Of the six justices who joined Douglas in the decision, some wrote important concurring opinions. Justice Arthur Goldberg devoted considerable space to the Ninth Amendment. He pointed out that it was a provision authored by James Madison to counter fears that the Bill of Rights excluded and overlooked other important protections. The right of privacy, Goldberg contended, was an instance of the kind contemplated by Madison and the Founders. Justice John Marshall Harlan's opinion was also important. He and Douglas had vigorously opposed dismissal of the case dealing with the Connecticut law when it first came before the court in 1961. Now, agreeing with Douglas' judgment, he returned to the argument he had made at the earlier hearing. Rather than resorting to "emanations" from existing rights as Douglas had done, however, Harlan believed the better way was to vest a right of privacy in the word "liberty" as it appears in the due process clause of the Fourteenth Amendment. Because this clause is binding on the

states, by saying that it carried a guarantee of privacy, it could be used to invalidate the Connecticut law.

The two dissenters in the case, Hugo L. Black and Potter Stewart, objected to the decision on grounds that would be repeated many times in criticisms of *Griswold*. By relying on "penumbras" and "emanations," the majority, Black and Stewart felt, undertook a return to natural law arguments of the past. This invited excessive subjectivity into the decision-making process, such that the Constitution, accordion-like, would diminish and expand depending on what ideas were fashionable at a given time. Only by reading its provisions literally could the Court avoid what a later commentator described as playing "charades with the Constitution."

Criticisms notwithstanding, the right of privacy survived and was soon given even broader applications. In 1966, the year following the *Griswold* decision, Congress passed the Freedom of Information Act; it became law on July 4, 1967, providing citizens with greater access to government records concerning themselves. The Privacy Act of 1974, a companion law to the 1966 enactment, prohibited government disclosure of information about citizens that might violate their privacy interests. In this law, Congress echoed *Griswold* by explicitly stating that "the right to privacy is a personal and fundamental right protected by the Constitution of the United States." Subsequent amendments to this act have extended its effect, especially in connection with the government's enormous collections of computer and databank information.

The Supreme Court also extended application of the *Griswold* principle to other areas. The best-known example occurred in the 1973 case of *Roe v. Wade*, in which abortion within the first trimester was affirmed as a right of privacy belonging to pregnant women. The right was also used in a Wisconsin case to buttress the freedom of individuals to marry. On the other hand, the Court was unwilling to allow use of privacy rights as a basis for disallowing state antisodomy statutes. Neither has it been willing to link the right of privacy to arguments for a right to die. Coerced urinalysis as part of a government agency's drug screening program was upheld over the protests of employees who contended it violated their privacy rights, as were regulations governing haircut styles for police officers.

Despite the Supreme Court's reservations in certain areas, the right of privacy has been firmly established as a fundamental protection guaranteed by the United States Constitution. For this reason, *Griswold v. Connecticut* is a significant milestone in the development of U.S. constitutional law.

—B. Carmon Hardy

ADDITIONAL READING:

Dixon, Robert G., Jr., ed. *The Right of Privacy: A Symposium on the Implications of "Griswold v. Connecticut."* New York: Da Capo Press, 1971. Contains critical analyses of the decision, including one by Thomas I. Emerson, counsel for Griswold. Includes, as a supplement, a complete transcript of the case.

Epstein, Lee, and Thomas G. Walker. *Constitutional Law for a Changing America: Rights, Liberties, and Justice.* 2d ed.

Washington, D.C.: Congressional Quarterly Press, 1995. An excellent college-level treatment of *Griswold* and cases related to it in the contexts of public policy and judicial process appears on pages 267-327.

Friendly, Fred W., and Martha J. H. Elliott. *The Constitution: That Delicate Balance.* New York: Random House, 1984. Readable overviews on both *Griswold* and *Roe v. Wade.* Helpful background information on individuals involved in the cases.

Murphy, Paul L., ed. *The Right to Privacy and the Ninth Amendment.* 2 vols. New York: Garland Publishing, 1990. Articles from law journals providing a variety of scholarly perspectives on *Griswold* and related cases.

Westin, Alan F. *Privacy and Freedom.* New York: Atheneum, 1968. Excellent survey of the intrusions on personal privacy in the United States in the twentieth century and the reasons for legal protection against them.

SEE ALSO: 1960, FDA Approves the Birth Control Pill; 1967, Freedom of Information Act; 1973, *Roe v. Wade.*

1965 ■ VOTING RIGHTS ACT: *prohibition of the denial of voting rights on the basis of race or color also protects language minorities*

DATE: August 6, 1965
LOCALE: Washington, D.C.
CATEGORIES: African American history; Civil rights; Native American history
KEY FIGURES:
Lyndon Baines Johnson (1908-1973), thirty-sixth president of the United States, 1963-1969
Martin Luther King, Jr. (1929-1968), leader of the Southern Christian Leadership Conference
John Lewis (born 1940), leader of the Student Nonviolent Coordinating Committee
SUMMARY OF EVENT. In 1863, President Abraham Lincoln signed the Emancipation Proclamation, which announced an end to slavery. After the Civil War, Congress passed the Reconstruction Act of 1867, which had an immediate impact on the national political body through the election of African Americans by the newly freed citizens. In 1870, the states ratified the Fifteenth Amendment to the United States Constitution, prohibiting the denial of voting rights on the basis of race, color, or previous conditions of servitude. Two enforcement acts, called the Ku Klux Klan Acts or Force Acts, were passed in 1870 and 1871 to give federal authorities extensive powers to enforce the Fourteenth and Fifteenth Amendments, respectively.

African American legislators were elected in every Southern state. In South Carolina, where African Americans were in the majority, the majority of legislators were African Americans. At the national level, twenty African Americans served in the House of Representatives and three served in the Senate between 1869 and 1899.

This brief experiment in participatory democracy was quickly aborted, however. State legislatures had the authority to determine the criteria governing the boundaries of voting districts and the qualifications required for citizens to vote. Court decisions permitted Southern states to rewrite their constitutions to exclude African Americans by methods such as literacy tests, good character tests, and poll taxes. Other methods included the intimidation of potential black voters, corruption and fraud at the ballot box, Supreme Court decisions invalidating the various enforcement statutes, and the complicity of federal authorities in failing to protect African Americans who attempted to vote. By 1900, the constitutional mandate of the Fifteenth Amendment effectively had been nullified. In 1940, approximately 3 percent of African Americans of voting age in the South were registered to vote, which was about the same proportion it had been forty years earlier. By 1964, the percentage had increased to only 43.3.

These illegal methods of disfranchisement were perpetrated by corrupt officials and members of white supremacist groups such as the Ku Klux Klan (established in 1866), but just as often, minority voters were disfranchised through legal methods devised by white legislators to ensure that the strength of minority voters would be diluted. Racial gerrymandering— creating voting districts in which whites are the majority— ensured that the proportion of minorities within a district would be too small to elect a minority candidate. Alternatively, at-large elections—in which candidates are voted on by the entire city rather than only by voters in their districts—were used to enhance the chances that white candidates would receive a majority of votes across several districts in each of which black voters were the majority. A majority-runoff requirement mandated that a candidate in the primary election must win a majority of the votes or run in a second election against the candidate who received the second highest number of votes. Therefore, if a minority candidate received the highest number of votes but less than half, and two or more white candidates split the white votes, in the two-candidate runoff the white candidate was likely to receive most of the white votes and gain a majority.

The Civil Rights movement, characterized by peaceful protests and violent urban riots, forced the states and the nation to begin to correct their inequitable treatment of minorities. In the early 1960's, the Southern Christian Leadership Conference, led by Dr. Martin Luther King, Jr., and the Student Nonviolent Coordinating Committee, led by John Lewis, organized a voting rights campaign in Selma, Alabama, to force the nation to confront de facto disenfranchisement of African American voters.

It was against this background that the Voting Rights Act of 1965, which has been hailed as one of the most important civil rights statutes in U.S. history, was passed. It prohibited all practices that denied or abridged the right to vote on grounds of race or color. The act requires that any proposed electoral changes in jurisdictions covered by the act be submitted for approval to the U.S. attorney general (or, for the District of Columbia, to the Federal District Court). Such changes include any voting qualification or prerequisite to voting, or standard, practice, or procedure with respect to voting. Many of the standards, practices, and procedures described above, which had the effect of minimizing minority voting strength, became unlawful.

A pervasive practice to minimize the voting strength of members of non-English-speaking minority groups was the English-only election requirement. In 1975, the Voting Rights Act was extended to cover minorities whose primary language was not English. This provision requires that special assistance—such as information and ballots in the language of the applicable minority group, as well as oral assistance—be available in jurisdictions with large populations of citizens who do not speak English. The voting strength of language-minority groups, such as Latinos, Asian Americans, and Alaskan Natives, has increased significantly as a result of these provisions.

In the 1980's, minority political participation was threatened by a politically conservative Supreme Court. In 1982, the Supreme Court ruling in *Bolden v. United States* diminished the power of the Voting Rights Act by changing the fundamental legal principle underlying the act. Prior to this decision, any practice, procedure, or rule that had the *effect* of limiting the minority vote, regardless of the *intent*, was deemed unlawful or in violation of the act. The Supreme Court changed this standard by ruling that, to prevail under the Voting Rights Act, plaintiffs must show that the racially discriminatory impact of the contested violation was intended by the legislature. If allowed to stand, this interpretation would have made it practically impossible to challenge practices that minimized minority voting power. However, in 1982, Congress extended the Voting Rights Act again, this time explicitly rejecting the intent standard by declaring that only effects are to be considered in determining whether minority voting rights have been violated.

Although the effectiveness of the Voting Rights Act has been threatened by such rulings, statistics on elected minority officials since 1965 attest to the positive impact of the law. Between 1971 and 1991, the number of African American elected officials increased 510 percent, from 1,469 to 7,480. The number of black congressional representatives increased from 17 in 1981 to 39 in 1993, a 230 percent increase; for Hispanics, the number increased from 6 to 17 in the same period, a 285 percent increase. These dramatic increases were attributed to redistricting—which created more districts in which minorities constituted a numerical majority within the districts—as well as changes in other rules that previously had restricted the minority vote.

In 1995, however, a conservative majority of the Supreme Court ruled in *Miller v. Johnson* that a district is unconstitutional if race is the predominant factor in drawing the district. In 1996, the Supreme Court's decisions in *Bush v. Vera* and *Shaw v. Hunt* continued this trend by ruling that minority

districts in Texas and North Carolina were unconstitutional because they were drawn with race as the major factor. The effect of these Supreme Court decisions was to nullify the intent of the Voting Rights Act. —*Richard Hudson*

ADDITIONAL READING:

Berry, Mary Frances, and John Blassingame. *Long Memory: The Black Experience in America*. New York: Oxford University Press, 1982. Chapter 3 analyzes the impact of African American voting on Southern politics during Reconstruction.

Davidson, Chandler, and Bernard Grofman, eds. *Quiet Revolution in the South: The Impact of the Voting Rights Act, 1965-1990*. Princeton, N.J.: Princeton University Press, 1994. A collection of critical studies of the significance of the Voting Rights Act in changing the political scene in the United States.

Garrow, David J. *Protest at Selma*. New Haven, Conn.: Yale University Press, 1978. A detailed analysis of the importance of the Selma voting rights campaign to the passing of the Voting Rights Act.

Joint Center for Political and Economic Studies. *Black Elected Officials: A National Roster, 1991*. 20th ed. Washington, D.C.: Author, 1992. An annual report detailing the election of African American officials at all levels of government.

U.S. Commission on Civil Rights. *The Voting Rights Act: Unfulfilled Goals*. Washington, D.C.: Government Printing Office, 1981. Examines the progress and problems associated with minority voting since 1965.

SEE ALSO: 1866, Rise of the Ku Klux Klan; 1866, Civil Rights Act of 1866; 1868, Fourteenth Amendment; 1883, Civil Rights Cases; 1917, Canadian Women Gain the Vote; 1920, U.S. Women Gain the Vote; 1960, Civil Rights Act of 1960; 1964, Civil Rights Act of 1964; 1970, U.S. Voting Age Is Lowered to Eighteen.

1965 ■ WATTS RIOT: *violence in south Los Angeles raises concerns among nonviolent civil rights activists and underscores the need among African Americans and ethnic minorities for basic social reform*

DATE: August 11-17, 1965

LOCALE: Los Angeles, California

CATEGORIES: African American history; Wars, uprisings, and civil unrest

SUMMARY OF EVENT. The outbreak of racial violence on August 11, 1965, shattered the summer calm of Los Angeles, California, and eroded the elation felt by many people when President Lyndon Baines Johnson had signed the 1965 Voting Rights Act into law only five days earlier. Official investigations confirmed that the causes of the upheaval were deeply rooted in the conditions of ghetto life in the sprawling metropolis. In less immediate terms, however, the upsurge of anarchistic energy stemmed from the existence of intolerable tensions in relations between whites and blacks within U.S. society.

The Watts area of Los Angeles provided a perfect setting for racial conflict. The neighborhood had long been the center of African American life in the city. As a result, Watts offered its inhabitants full exposure to the hazards of ghetto existence. More than 30 percent of the workforce was unemployed. Approximately 14 percent of the population was functionally illiterate. The black residents of Watts faced serious barriers in their pursuit of better housing, more remunerative jobs, and improved education. Separated from white society, Watts was a storehouse of combustible material on the southeast side of Los Angeles.

A minor clash between police and African American residents caused the explosion that ripped through Watts. Along the edge of the ghetto, on the night of August 11, a California Highway Patrol officer arrested two young African Americans for reckless driving. While the officer administered a sobriety test, a hostile crowd gathered. The confrontation led to more arrests. Finally, the police departed amid a hail of rocks thrown by irate blacks. Rumors of police brutality spread through

Watts. In the hours before midnight, a full-scale riot developed. Automobiles traveling through the ghetto were pelted with rocks and bottles. Police moved back into the area at 11:00 P.M., but flurries of violence continued throughout the night.

After a day filled with tension, the rioters returned to the streets on the night of August 12. Commercial buildings were set ablaze, and firemen who responded to the alarms were greeted with rocks and gunfire. California state officials received reports that estimated the number of rioters at eight thousand. The police were unable to prevent widespread burning and looting.

The upheaval reached its climax on the night of August 13. Crowds of angry African Americans surged through Watts. Arsonists began the systematic destruction of whole city blocks in the ghetto. Police and firemen faced added peril from snipers who took up positions in the ruins. At its height, the riot encompassed an area of more than fifty blocks.

In the early hours of August 14, law enforcement officers began to regain control of the streets. At the request of city officials, National Guard troops joined the Los Angeles Police

National Guardsmen patrol the Watts district of Los Angeles after burnings and lootings destroyed much of the area during some of the worst race riots in U.S. history. (AP/Wide World Photos)

Department in battling the rioters. Ultimately, nearly fourteen thousand members of the National Guard entered the fray. Burning and looting continued sporadically, but the presence of fully armed soldiers in large numbers gradually restored quiet to the riot-torn area. A dusk-to-dawn curfew went into effect on Saturday night, August 14. Three days later the curfew was lifted, and most of the National Guard troops left the city. Amid the rubble, the people of Watts returned to their everyday concerns. The six days of rioting had wreaked widespread destruction on the African American neighborhood. Thirty-four deaths were reported, and police made more than three thousand arrests. Property damage reached the forty-million-dollar mark, as 288 businesses and private buildings and 14 public buildings were damaged and/or looted, and 1 public and 207 private buildings were destroyed.

Yet the most significant harm caused by the riot was beyond specific assessment. In the realm of race relations, the outbreak of violence exacerbated tensions between blacks and whites throughout the United States. Watts became the first chapter in a history of race riots that included upheavals in Detroit, Michigan, and Newark, New Jersey, in 1967, and Washington, D.C., in 1968.

Faced with repeated outbreaks of violence, the Civil Rights movement, with its emphasis on civil disobedience and interracial cooperation, suffered a significant setback in the short run. Beginning with the explosion at Watts, U.S. race relations entered a new, more ominous phase. The riot did not, however, mean the end of nonviolent direct action or the total reversal of the multiracial cooperation that had brought important legal victories for desegregation in the United States. The history of civil rights reform after 1965 was marked by a growing realization that the socioeconomic conditions in which African Americans, Mexican Americans, and other minorities lived could not be ignored in the quest for social justice and personal fulfillment for all U.S. citizens. The last major effort by civil rights leader Dr. Martin Luther King, Jr.—who visited Watts at the time of the rioting and asked the insurgents to change their motto from "Burn, baby, burn" to "Build, baby, build"—was a Poor People's Campaign that was implemented two months after his assassination on April 4, 1968.

—John G. Clark, updated by Thomas R. Peake

ADDITIONAL READING:

Fogelson, Robert. *The Fragmented Metropolis: Los Angeles, 1850-1930*. Cambridge, Mass.: Harvard University Press, 1967. An authoritative study in urban history that sets the background for Watts in the growing isolation of social subgroups and growing economic disparities.

Governor's Commission on the Los Angeles Riots. *Violence in the City: An End or a Beginning?* Los Angeles: Author, 1965. Focuses on the details and location of damage, with useful maps. Attributes the disorder to the lack of basic means to encourage hope, especially schools, job training, effective local leadership, and responsive governments.

O'Neill, William L. *Coming Apart: An Informal History of America in the 1960's*. Chicago: Quadrangle Books, 1971. An early effort to place Watts and other events of the 1960's in historical context, including discussion of the increasing economic isolation of minorities.

Peake, Thomas R. *Keeping the Dream Alive: A History of the Southern Christian Leadership Conference from King to the Nineteen-Eighties*. New York: Peter Lang, 1987. A comprehensive history of the SCLC, which includes extensive material on the urban riots and post-1965 efforts to deal with social problems in large city ghettos.

Sears, David O., and John B. McConahay. *The Politics of Violence: The New Urban Blacks and the Watts Riot*. Boston: Houghton Mifflin, 1973. A scholarly study that reviews the history of the crisis, the views and actions of urban blacks, and official reactions. The implications of Watts for racial identity—of African Americans and other racial and ethnic communities—are analyzed in depth.

Watts Writers' Workshop. *From the Ashes: Voices of Watts*. Edited and with an introduction by Budd Schulberg. New York: New American Library, 1967. Writings by residents of Watts during the time of the 1965 riots and their aftermath, showing their frustrations as well as their hopes for better answers to social, personal, and economic problems.

SEE ALSO: 1943, Urban Race Riots; 1963, King Delivers His "I Have a Dream" Speech; 1964, Berkeley Free Speech Movement; 1965, Voting Rights Act; 1967, Long, Hot Summer; 1968, Chicago Riots; 1980, Miami Riots; 1992, Los Angeles Riots.

1965 ■ DELANO GRAPE STRIKE: *success of the strike brings gains in farmworkers' rights*

DATE: September 8, 1965-July 29, 1970
LOCALE: Delano, California
CATEGORIES: Business and labor; Latino American history; Wars, uprisings, and civil unrest
KEY FIGURES:
César Chávez (1927-1993), leader of NFWA
Joseph Di Giorgio, one of California's largest grape growers
Delores Huerta (born 1930), major organizer of the Delano Grape Strike
Larry Itliong (1913-1976), Filipino organizer and activist in AWOC

SUMMARY OF EVENT. Delano, California, a small grape vineyard community of about eleven thousand in the southern San Joaquin Valley, was the scene of a historic farmworkers' strike. The strike began on September 8, 1965, when farmworkers walked off the fields protesting low wages and poor working conditions; it ended on July 29, 1970. This strike was coordinated by César Chávez and the National Farm Workers Association (NFWA). Half the world's table grapes were produced in the Delano area, which thus attracted thousands of vineyard workers.

The seeds of the Delano strike emerged on September 30, 1962, when Chávez and a few hundred workers met and founded NFWA. Workers began to formulate their agenda. Incentives were provided to encourage members to remain in the union. NFWA member benefits included a co-op store, a gas station, and a service center. By mid-1965, the union had twelve hundred members.

NFWA became involved in striking against Delano vineyards when Larry Itliong, a Filipino organizer, and another union, the Agricultural Workers Organizing Committee (AWOC), called a strike against grape growers in the Delano area. AWOC, founded in 1959 by the AFL-CIO, convinced a large group of farmworkers to walk out of the vineyards. Between six hundred and eight hundred mostly Filipino workers demanded the right to bargain with their employers for fair wages and just working conditions. Many strikers were aware of better wages, having worked in California's Coachella Valley, where the grape harvest is earlier than in Delano. Workers were paid $1.40 an hour in Coachella; Delano growers were unwilling to pay more than $1.25 an hour.

AWOC asked NFWA to join their strike, and five days later, after much deliberation, NFWA members voted unanimously to join the strike, which had spread to nine ranches and involved two thousand workers. The strike meeting was called on Mexican Independence Day, symbolically linking their struggle to the one 145 years past. Al Green, leader of AWOC, did not like NFWA's proposition for a joint strike. NFWA called its own strike against the area's thirty other major grape growers. Chávez sent letters and telegrams to the growers, offering to negotiate contracts setting minimum pay at $1.40 per hour and specifying several other conditions of work.

AWOC concentrated demonstrations within the Delano area. Small picket groups demonstrated in front of vineyards and packing sheds. NFWA used other tactics, such as marches, fasts, and the grape boycott. In fall, 1965, Chávez visited several campuses, where rallies were held to garner student support. This effort resulted in hundreds of volunteers and supporters from the students and faculty. Their inclusion helped publicize the movement beyond the Delano area.

A feud between NFWA and the International Brotherhood of Teamsters, which began competing with NFWA for union membership, threatened the success of the strike. NFWA was being undercut by the Teamsters, who were making deals with local growers. This feud was settled temporarily in 1966, when the two groups merged to become the United Farm Workers Organizing Committee (UFWOC). Chávez became director and Itliong became associate director.

The Delano Grape Strike was waged primarily against a group of growers who refused to recognize or deal with NFWA. One of the tactics used to encourage the growers to negotiate a contract was fasting, which Chávez and others used on several occasions. One of Chávez's fasts lasted from February 15 to March 10, 1968. The march was another useful tactic. A 1966 march (the Pilgrimage), went from Delano to Sacramento, the California state capital. This well-publicized march ended with

a large rally at the Capitol Building on Easter Sunday. The United States, Mexican, and Philippine flags, along with a banner of Our Lady of Guadalupe, flew at the front of this march, which began March 16. Hats with the union's red hatbands displaying the black eagle and *huelga* (strike) flags were well represented among those gathered at the capital. The national director of organizing for the AFL-CIO, Bill Kircher, marched with the farmworkers. This resulted in a period of lasting cooperation and support between Chávez and the leaders of the AFL-CIO. Union members throughout the United States and Canada voiced support for the farmworkers.

Calling the boycott against grape growers proved to be the most effective tactic. The boycott succeeded in reaching the middle class in the United States. In addition, Chávez was a charismatic leader, which blended well with the excellent press coverage of the boycott activities. Chávez stressed nonviolence as the union's guiding principle. Following the Civil Rights movement, in which Martin Luther King, Jr., had espoused nonviolence as a technique for peaceful protest, this tactic was viewed as acceptable by large segments of the U.S. population. Nationwide focus on the farmworkers' movement compelled farmworkers to visit major cities in the United States and Canada seeking support for the grape boycott. Usually churches, unions, or universities provided venues for farmworker presentations.

The boycott originally was directed against the Di Giorgio Corporation, whose Sierra Vista Ranch covered forty-four hundred acres, and Schenley Industries, whose product lines, S&W Fine Foods and Treesweet juices, were nationally known. Consumers were urged to stop buying these brand names. Schenley became the first winery to settle a contract. Several small wineries run by Catholic religious orders also settled with a contract. Most of the growers in the Delano area were 1920's immigrants from southern and eastern Europe. John Giumarra, Jr., spoke proudly of how his family came from Sicily and built the largest of the vineyard operations, a twelve-hundred-acre complex that grossed $5.5 to $7.5 million annually. Their cultural backgrounds were of economic struggle to success, where workers needed little beyond what the patrons granted them. This background left most of the growers with little tolerance for farmworker demands.

The Giumarra Vineyards became the target of a nationwide boycott in the spring of 1967. Consumers could identify Giumarra grapes, because they arrived at the store in clearly labeled boxes. By late summer, 1967, Giumarra, feeling negative effects of the boycott, counterattacked. He persuaded other Delano growers to allow the use of their labels on Giumarra grape boxes. This was designed to prevent consumers from identifying Giumarra grapes in the market.

In January, 1968, the union expanded its boycott to include all table grapes. In October the focus shifted from the products themselves to their outlets. Stores that handled table grapes were faced with mounting pressure, as farmworker union members and supporters began distributing leaflets at stores and publicizing stores that handled the grapes. The boycott was bolstered by picketing at large stores. The boycott grew, and consumers increasingly refused to buy grapes. By 1969, more than seventeen million U.S. consumers had stopped buying grapes. Growers began to feel the financial impact of these tactics and slowly began the move toward granting union demands. This boycott was a major factor in achieving acceptance of the union, collective bargaining, and the signing of contracts. In 1970, 140 grape growers signed contracts with the UFWOC as a result of the Delano Grape Strike. This was a major victory for the farmworkers, but not the end of the struggle. The 1970's and 1980's were punctuated by numerous protests between growers and farmworkers. In 1984, Chávez was compelled to call another strike. Despite these setbacks, the Delano strike remains one of the most important events in the struggle for farmworker rights.   *—Gregory Freeland*

ADDITIONAL READING:

Dunne, John Gregory. *Delano: The Story of the California Grape Strike.* Rev. ed. New York: Farrar, Straus & Giroux, 1971. A clear, concise history of the Delano strike.

Fusco, Paul, and George Horowitz. *"La Causa": The California Grape Strike.* New York: Macmillan, 1970. Very useful to anyone seeking the causes and effects of the farmworkers' strike.

Jenkins, Craig. *The Politics of Insurgency: The Farmworker Movement in the 1960's.* New York: Columbia University Press, 1985. Excellent analysis of the strategies and consequences of the farmworker movement.

Levy, Jacques. *César Chávez: Autobiography of "La Causa."* New York: W. W. Norton, 1975. A well-researched and detailed account covering Chávez's life and work.

Rodriquez, Consuelo. *César Chávez.* New York: Chelsea House, 1991. A brief but informative book that captures Chávez's activities after 1970.

SEE ALSO: 1930's, Mass Deportations of Mexicans; 1942, Bracero Program; 1954, Operation Wetback; 1965, Immigration and Nationality Act; 1972, United Farm Workers Joins with AFL-CIO; 1986, Immigration Reform and Control Act.

1965 ■ EXPANSION OF AFFIRMATIVE ACTION: *Executive Order 11246 requires nondiscriminatory employment practices, including proactive efforts to hire minorities and women, in businesses holding federal contracts*

DATE: Beginning September 24, 1965
LOCALE: Washington, D.C.
CATEGORIES: African American history; Business and labor; Civil rights; Education; Social reform
KEY FIGURES:
James Earl "Jimmy" Carter, Jr. (born 1934), thirty-ninth president of the United States, 1977-1981

Dwight David Eisenhower (1890-1969), thirty-fourth president of the United States, 1953-1961
Lyndon Baines Johnson (1908-1973), thirty-sixth president of the United States, 1963-1969
John Fitzgerald Kennedy (1917-1963), thirty-fifth president of the United States, 1961-1963
Richard Milhous Nixon (1913-1994), thirty-seventh president of the United States, 1969-1974
Franklin Delano Roosevelt (1882-1945), thirty-second president of the United States, 1933-1945
Harry S Truman (1884-1972), thirty-third president of the United States, 1945-1953

SUMMARY OF EVENT. Affirmative action, as developed through executive orders, has a long history, beginning with defense contractors in World War II. President Lyndon Johnson's executive order of 1965 was an important milestone, best understood as an expansion of an evolving governmental commitment to nondiscrimination, which enjoyed bipartisan support until the 1980's. In the mid-1990's, affirmative action would become a lightning rod for discontent over class, race, ethnic, and gender differences in the United States in a time of shrinking economic and educational opportunities.

The term itself has many definitions. Some see affirmative action as merely a way to produce nondiscrimination and equal employment opportunity. Others characterize it as preferential treatment or quota hiring: choosing people solely because of a race or gender identity, with little or no reference to their qualifications or actual disadvantage. Affirmative action can refer to recruitment efforts at colleges and training for apprenticeships, government mandates that a percentage of contracts or radio licenses go to minorities, voluntary efforts on the part of employers to diversify the workforce, or court-ordered remedies for proven cases of unlawful discrimination.

All the preceding examples of affirmative action have been subjected to judicial scrutiny by the U.S. Supreme Court to see if they violate the Fourteenth Amendment's constitutional guarantee of the equal protection of the laws. Those who seek a definitive answer to the legal status of affirmative action are often frustrated and confused. The Court has spoken with many voices on the subject and changed its position over time. Perhaps even more confusing is the public debate over affirmative action, which often fails to articulate carefully which of the many incarnations of affirmative action is being debated, but instead lumps them all together.

The development of affirmative action through executive orders has its origins in the conviction of Franklin D. Roosevelt's administration that companies receiving federal government defense contracts should open their doors to nonwhite workers. The idea was that government money should not be spent to discriminate against people because of race, color, religion, or national origin, specifically, by closing jobs to African American workers. President Dwight D. Eisenhower extended the purpose beyond ensuring that racism not hinder national defense to a more general commitment to equal employment opportunity. Eisenhower's Government

Contracts Committee, chaired by then-vice president Richard Nixon, recommended that government overcome private employers' indifference by requiring them to take positive steps to ensure nondiscrimination. It was President John F. Kennedy, in 1961, who mandated that government contractors have an equal employment opportunity clause in all contracts, that they implement affirmative action, and that the ultimate sanction for noncompliance would be loss of the contract.

President Lyndon Johnson continued the bipartisan support for nondiscrimination in government contracts when he issued Executive Order 11246, on September 24, 1965. The executive order stated:

> It is the policy of the Government of the United States to provide equal opportunity in Federal employment for all qualified persons, to prohibit discrimination in employment because of race, creed, color, or national origin, and to promote the full realization of equal employment opportunity through a positive continuing program in each executive department and agency. The policy of equal opportunity applies to every aspect of Federal employment policy and practice.

The second part of the executive order prohibited federal contractors and subcontractors from discriminating and required them to take "affirmative action." Johnson moved responsibility for the program from the Office of the President to the Department of Labor. In 1967, Johnson added sex to the list of prohibited categories of discrimination. In 1975, when the executive order program was extended to disabled and Vietnam War veterans, the office was renamed the Office of Federal Contract Compliance Programs (OFCCP). President Jimmy Carter later consolidated governmental efforts in the OFCCP and stepped up enforcement.

Regulations issued in 1968 and modified in 1970 defined affirmative action as "specific and result-oriented procedures designed to achieve prompt and full utilization of minorities and women at all levels and in all segments of the contractor's workforce where deficiencies exist." All contractors who employed fifty or more employees and had a contract worth more than fifty thousand dollars were forbidden to discriminate and were required to develop an affirmative action plan. Not only were contractors required to monitor and report on the composition of their workforces, but they also were to identify problem areas and develop goals and timetables to rectify them. The most important feature was the utilization analysis. Employers were to compare the composition of their workforces to the composition of the relevant labor market. Say, for example, a contractor employed only white men as carpenters and needed to hire more carpenters. An analysis of the number of qualified carpenters in the contractor's labor market (for example, within a 50-mile radius) might reveal that 25 percent were African American, 10 percent Hispanic, and 3 percent women. According to the regulations, the employer would be required to develop goals and timetables to hire more African American, Hispanic, and female carpenters to close that gap.

Critics of the program argued that it was unfair to infer discrimination from underutilization, and that the setting of goals and timetables led employers to hire people according to quotas rather than qualifications, which was unfair to those passed over for jobs. Although the executive order program required considerable reporting on the part of employers, it was rare for companies to lose their contracts because they failed to diversify their workforces.

After President Ronald Reagan was elected in 1980, his administration sought to weaken, if not dismantle, the OFCCP. The Reagan Administration challenged many types of affirmative action in court, urging the Supreme Court to move away from positions the Court had taken in the 1970's. In *Regents of the University of California v. Bakke* (1978), the Supreme Court had held that state medical schools could not set aside a fixed number of places for students of color, although they could take race into account in seeking a diverse group of students. In *Fullilove v. Klutznick* (1980), the Supreme Court held that after Congress had made a finding of widespread discrimination in contracting, it could legislate to set aside a fixed number of contracts for minority-owned companies. Judicially ordered affirmative action as a remedy to a judicial finding of illegal discrimination, as well as affirmative action that did not disrupt the legitimate expectations of whites, was more likely to be upheld by the Court as constitutional. For example, the Court was more likely to uphold affirmative action in education or training programs, than to permit employers to ignore seniority in laying off workers to protect newly hired minorities.

The administrations of Reagan and George Bush argued against affirmative action in court. They urged that only identifiable victims, rather than classes, be allowed to receive remedies for findings of discrimination, that all race-based policies should receive the strictest scrutiny, and that employers and governments be allowed to adopt policies only to remedy their own prior discrimination rather than to attempt to ameliorate more diffuse societal inequalities. The Reagan and Bush appointees to the Supreme Court were much more dubious of the constitutionality of many forms of affirmative action that had been endorsed by their predecessors.

The justices could not agree on the standard of scrutiny for race-based policies that sought to ameliorate the present effects of past discrimination. Some believed such policies should receive a moderate level of scrutiny. In particular, if a state entity had made a determination of prior discrimination (such as Congress in *Fullilove*), the Court should defer to its judgment. Other justices believed that any policy that used race as a criterion—whether in setting aside medical school places, contracts, or apprenticeships—should receive the same strict scrutiny that the Court used in policies that discriminated against people of color. In *City of Richmond v. Croson* (1989), a Court majority took this position and struck down Richmond's requirement that city contractors set aside 30 percent of their business for minority-owned subcontractors. A bare majority of a badly divided Court also concluded that there was no proof that the city had discriminated against minorities, although they held few contracts.

In *Adarand Constructors, Inc., v. Pena* (1995), the Court reaffirmed its rejection of the position that so-called benign discrimination should receive lower scrutiny than malevolent discrimination, and that only people of color who were disadvantaged by race-based policies could challenge them, but not whites. *Adarand*'s requirement that all affirmative action programs be narrowly tailored to achieve compelling state interests (in other words, be subject to strict scrutiny by the Court) has called into question whether the executive order program's requirement of affirmative action would be considered constitutional by the mid-1990's Supreme Court. The Court left the issue of applying its new standard to that program to another day. President Bill Clinton reviewed governmental affirmative action programs and concluded that they were valuable, yet by 1996, several presidential candidates were advocating immediate repeal of the executive order program, and its future remained uncertain.   —*Sally J. Kenney*

ADDITIONAL READING:

Annals of the American Academy of Political and Social Science 523 (September, 1992). Special issue, "Affirmative Action Revisited." Includes essays by many of the leading public voices, debating different sides of the issue.

Badgett, M. V. Lee, Andrew F. Brimmer, Cecilia A. Conrad, and Heidi Hartmann. *Economic Perspectives on Affirmative Action*. Washington, D.C.: Joint Center for Political and Economic Studies, 1995. Comprehensive summary of economic studies evaluating the effectiveness of affirmative action.

Burstein, Paul. "Affirmative Action, Jobs, and American Democracy: What Has Happened to the Quest for Equal Opportunity?" *Law and Society Review* 26, no. 4 (1992): 901-922. A broad overview of the issue by a leading expert in discrimination law. Useful bibliography.

Leonard, Jonathan. "The Federal Anti-Bias Effort." In *Essays on the Economics of Discrimination*, edited by Emily P. Hoffman. Kalamazoo, Mich.: W. E. Upjohn Institute, 1991. A broad overview of affirmative action history and law, and an assessment of studies on the issue. Written by a scholar who has conducted numerous studies measuring the effectiveness of affirmative action programs.

U.S. Congress. House. Committee on Education and Labor. *A Report by the Majority Staff on the Investigation of the Civil Rights Enforcement Activities of the Office of Federal Contract Compliance Programs*. 100th Congress, 1st session, 1987. This comprehensive staff report includes a lengthy history of the executive order program, an in-depth analysis of how the controversy over affirmative action has affected the OFCCP, an assessment of the agency's ability to carry out its mission, and a case study of enforcement actions against Los Alamos National Laboratories. An appendix contains all the relevant orders, memoranda, and regulations.

U.S. Congress. Senate. Committee on Labor and Human Resources. *Committee Analysis of Executive Order 11246 (Affirmative Action Program)*. 97th Congress, 2d session, 1982. A detailed, comprehensive legal and political history of the executive order program.

SEE ALSO: 1941, Executive Order 8802; 1960, Civil Rights Act of 1960; 1962, Meredith Registers at "Ole Miss"; 1964, Civil Rights Act of 1964; 1972, Equal Employment Opportunity Act; 1978, *Regents of the University of California v. Bakke.*

1965 ■ IMMIGRATION AND NATIONALITY ACT: *new legislation significantly alters the composition of immigrants entering the United States by breaking previous policies of restricting non-European admissions*

DATE: October 3, 1965
LOCALE: Liberty Island
CATEGORIES: Immigration; Laws and acts
KEY FIGURES:
Lyndon Baines Johnson (1908-1973), thirty-sixth president of the United States, 1963-1969
John Fitzgerald Kennedy (1917-1963), thirty-fifth president of the United States, 1961-1963

SUMMARY OF EVENT. The Immigration and Nationality Act of 1965 was a major event in U.S. immigration history because it allowed non-Europeans to enter the United States on an equitable basis with Europeans. Before the 1965 legislation, U.S. immigration policies favored northern and western Europeans. Starting with the colonial period, the people entering North America came predominantly from western and northern Europe, and were dominated by the British and Germans. Restrictions were not imposed until the Chinese Exclusion Act of 1882 started a process of legislating discriminatory restrictions against certain nationalities. The various laws were brought together in the Immigration Act of 1917, which initiated the Asiatic Barred Zone and the literacy test—both features designed to prohibit Asians and persons from southern and eastern Europe from immigrating.

After World War II, the Immigration and Nationality (McCarran-Walter) Act of 1952 codified the legislation that had developed haphazardly over the past century. Although it liberalized some areas, it was discriminatory in that quotas were allotted according to national origins. This resulted in western and northern European nations receiving no less than 85 percent of the total allotment.

With the election of John F. Kennedy in 1960, circumstances for meaningful immigration reform came into being: Kennedy believed that immigration was a source of national strength, the Civil Rights movement had promoted an ideology to eliminate racist policies, and the U.S. position during the Cold War necessitated that immigration policies be just. Thus, Kennedy had Abba Schwartz, an expert on refugee and immigration matters, develop a plan to revise immigration policy.

In July of 1963, Kennedy sent his proposal for immigration reform to Congress. His recommendations had three major provisions: the quota system should be phased out over a five-year period; no natives of any one country should receive more than 10 percent of the newly authorized quota numbers; and a seven-person immigration board should be set up to advise the president. Kennedy also advocated that family reunification remain a priority; the Asiatic Barred Zone be eliminated; and nonquota status be granted to residents of Jamaica, Trinidad, and Tobago, as it was to other Western Hemisphere residents. Last, the preference structure was to be altered to liberalize requirements for skilled people.

After the assassination of President Kennedy, President Lyndon Baines Johnson took up the cause of immigration. Although immigration was not a major issue during the 1964 campaign, both sides had courted diverse ethnic communities, whose will now had to be considered. The Democratic Party's landslide victory gave Johnson a strong mandate for his Great Society programs, of which immigration reform was a component. Secretary of State Dean Rusk argued the need for immigration reform to bolster U.S. foreign policy. Rusk, Attorney General Robert Kennedy, and others criticized the current system for being discriminatory and argued that the proposed changes would be economically advantageous to the United States. Senator Edward Kennedy held hearings and concluded that "all recognized the unworkability of the national origins quota system."

Outside Congress, ethnic, voluntary, and religious organizations lobbied and provided testimony before Congress. They echoed the administration's arguments about discrimination. A few Southerners in Congress argued that the national origins concept was not discriminatory—it was a mirror reflecting the U.S. population, so those who would best assimilate into U.S. society would enter. However, the focus of the congressional debate was on how to alter the national origins system, not on whether it should be changed. The most disputed provisions concerned on whether emphasis should be on needed skills, family reunification, or limits set on Western Hemisphere immigration. Family unification prevailed.

In a ceremony on Liberty Island, President Johnson signed the Immigration and Nationality Act of 1965, saying, "This bill . . . is not a revolutionary bill. It does not affect the lives of millions. It will not reshape the structure of our daily lives, or really add importantly to our wealth or our power." Johnson's statement was a gross underrepresentation of a significant turning point in U.S. immigration history. This bill provided equal opportunity for Asians, Africans, Latinos, and the highly skilled and educated to enter the United States.

The new law replaced the national origins system with hemispheric caps, 170,000 from the Old World and 120,000 from the New. Spouses, unmarried minor children, and parents of U.S. citizens were exempt from numerical quotas. Preferences were granted first to unmarried adult children of U.S. citizens (20 percent); next, to spouses and unmarried adult children of permanent resident aliens (20 percent). Profession-als, scientists, and artists of exceptional ability were awarded third preference (10 percent) but required certification from the U.S. Department of Labor. Married children of U.S. citizens had fourth preference (10 percent). Next were those brothers and sisters of U.S. citizens who were older than twenty-one years of age (24 percent), followed by skilled and unskilled workers in occupations for which labor was in short supply (10 percent). Refugees from communist or communist-dominated countries or the Middle East were seventh (6 percent). Nonpreference status was assigned to anyone not eligible under any of the above categories; there have been more preference applicants than can be accommodated, so nonpreference status has not been used.

The law had unexpected consequences. The framers of the legislation expected that the Old World slots would be filled by Europeans. They assumed that family reunification would favor Europeans, because they dominated the U.S. population. However, those from Europe who wanted to come were in the lower preference categories, while well-trained Asians had been coming to the United States since 1943 and were well qualified for preference positions. Once they, or anyone else, became a permanent resident, a whole group of people became eligible to enter the country under the third preference category. After a five-year wait—the residential requirement for citizenship—more persons became eligible under the second preference category. As a result, many immigrants were directly or indirectly responsible for twenty-five to fifty new immigrants.

The law set forth a global ceiling of 290,000, but actual totals ranged from 398,089 in 1977 to 904,292 in 1993. Refugees and those exempt from numerical limitations were the two major categories that caused these variations. The refugee count had varied according to situations such as that of the "boat people" from Cuba in 1981. In 1991, refugees and asylees totaled 139,079; in 1993, they totaled 127,343. Persons in nonpreference categories increased from 113,083 in 1976 to 255,059 in 1993. Total immigration for 1991 was 827,167 and for 1993 was 904,292—well above the global ceiling.

The Immigration and Nationality Act of 1965 enabled some of the most able medical, scientific, engineering, skilled, and other professional talent to enter the United States. The medical profession illustrates this trend. In the ten years after the enactment of the 1965 act, seventy-five thousand foreign physicians entered the United States. By 1974, immigrant physicians made up one-fifth of the total number of physicians and one-third of the interns and residents in the United States. Each immigrant doctor represented more than a million dollars in education costs. In addition, they often took positions in the inner-city and rural areas, which prevented the collapse of the delivery of medical services to those locations.

Immigration itself is selective, in that it is usually the most innovative and self-motivated who move. Thus, even among the unskilled, the United States has over the years gained a largely productive workforce from its immigrants.

—Arthur W. Helweg

ADDITIONAL READING:

Daniels, Roger. *Coming to America: A History of Immigration and Ethnicity in American Life*. New York: HarperCollins, 1990. A good general history of U.S. immigration. Analyzes the causes and consequences of the Immigration and Nationality Act of 1965.

Glazer, Nathan, ed. *Clamor at the Gates: The New American Immigration*. San Francisco: ICS Press, 1985. A superb evaluation of the "new immigration" that resulted from the Immigration and Nationality Act of 1965.

_____. *Ethnic Dilemmas 1964-1982*. Cambridge, Mass.: Harvard University Press, 1983. Although not specifically stated, this is an analysis of the ethnic situation created, in part, by the Immigration and Nationality Act of 1965.

Helweg, Arthur W., and Usha M. Helweg. *An Immigrant Success Story: East Indians in America*. Philadelphia: University of Pennsylvania Press, 1990. An ethnographic presentation of one community categorized as part of the "new immigration," the highly educated professional and technical people who became substantially more prominent as a result of the Immigration and Nationality Act of 1965.

Papademetriou, Demetrios G., and Mark J. Miller, eds. *The Unavoidable Issue: U.S. Immigration Policy in the 1980's*. Philadelphia: Institute for the Study of Human Issues, 1983. High-quality articles assessing U.S. immigration policy from various foreign, domestic, and international perspectives, concerning social, demographic, economic, refugee, and illegal immigration.

Reimers, David M. *Still the Golden Door: The Third World Comes to America*. 2d ed. New York: Columbia University Press, 1992. A detailed historical study of the significant political and social events and personages leading to and implementing the passage of the Immigration and Nationality Act of 1965.

SEE ALSO: 1882, Chinese Exclusion Act; 1917, Immigration Act of 1917; 1924, Immigration Act of 1924; 1943, Magnuson Act; 1952, McCarran-Walter Act; 1986, Immigration Reform and Control Act.

1966 ■ National Organization for Women Is Founded: *birth of a major force in women's rights in the latter twentieth century*

DATE: June, 1966
LOCALE: Washington, D.C.
CATEGORIES: Organizations and institutions; Women's issues
KEY FIGURES:
Kathryn Clarenbach (1920-1994), head of the Wisconsin Commission on the Status of Women
Betty Friedan (born 1921), feminist leader and author of *The Feminine Mystique*

SUMMARY OF EVENT. The National Organization for Women (NOW) was founded in June, 1966, by a group of twenty-eight women attending the Third National Conference of Commissions on the Status of Women, in Washington, D.C. A few participants at the conference had concluded that the status of women in the United States would be improved not by continuing to meet in this conventional, conservative series of conferences, but by dramatic and direct action. Such action, they thought, would best be effected through a separate civil rights organization dedicated to achieving the full equality for women that they had hoped would come about with the passage of the Civil Rights Act of 1964, which had included a ban on discrimination on the basis of sex.

Kathryn Clarenbach, head of the Wisconsin Commission on the Status of Women, was chosen as the first coordinator of NOW, and Betty Friedan, author of *The Feminine Mystique* (1963), was elected president of the organization. Its stated purpose was "To take action to bring women into full participation in the mainstream of American society *now*, assuming all the privileges and responsibilities thereof in fully equal partnership with men."

NOW's first separate conference, held in Washington, D.C., in late October, 1966, confirmed Friedan as president, and elected Richard Graham, former Equal Employment Opportunity commissioner, as vice president, and Caroline Davis of the United Auto Workers as secretary-treasurer. Men who are interested in furthering women's rights have from the beginning been welcome to belong to NOW—it is the National Organization *for* Women, rather than *of* women. Task forces were set up to address the problems of women in such areas as employment, education, religion, poverty, law, and politics, and the image of women in the media. Internal committees to handle such tasks as public relations and membership also were formed.

When Friedan stepped down as president in 1970, to be succeeded by Aileen Hernandez, NOW had about six thousand members in chapters in all of the states. In 1995, the organization had grown to half a million members in more than a thousand chapters. However, NOW has not escaped controversy—it has been accused of being an organization of and for white, middle-class women, and an organization that is hostile to homemakers and traditional women. These are images that it has taken pains to dispel, but they have remained problems for NOW as a group.

During and after the suffrage movement, women active in women's rights issues disagreed on agendas and methods. It has been no different since. Those who are dedicated to women's rights have disagreed on whether protective legislation is necessary for or detrimental to women. Women have been divided on the advisability of an equal rights amendment (ERA) to the U.S. Constitution. The history of the women's movement has always included controversy about whether to further the cause through confrontation or by working through the system. NOW has worked on both fronts.

NOW has continued to work for its original goal of full

equality for women in equal partnership with men, and it has continued to focus on reproductive rights; equal opportunity and pay in the workplace; recognition that because poverty is largely a women's problem, a safety net for the poor is imperative; the importance of education for women; and rights for homosexuals of both sexes. NOW was active in the unsuccessful battle for the ERA and has been active in campaigns for state ERAs. It has continued to sponsor marches and rallies, many in the nation's capital, in support of reproductive and economic rights, and its officers have remained vocal in these areas. Many of NOW's founding members were also founders of the Women's Political Caucus, which was created in 1971 with the goal of involving women in politics. The NOW Political Action Committee (PAC) was created to raise money in support of women candidates for public office who support the agenda for which NOW works. In this effort, the NOW PAC raises money for selected women and campaigns against candidates who oppose a feminist agenda. In 1992, NOW formed Our New Party, a political party designed to recruit members to work toward a more humane world. NOW also publishes the *NOW Times*, a periodical that reviews political activities of interest to feminists and urges members to participate in planned future activities.

NOW has pressed for such legal reforms as Title IX of the Education Amendments of 1972 and has campaigned actively in this regard for the removal of sex bias in school textbooks. It has filed petitions with the Federal Communications Commission challenging the license renewal of television stations that it believes have distorted news coverage of women's issues and perpetuated condescending daytime programming and commercials. It worked ardently for the adoption of the proposed ERA, and has swayed some elections through its efforts to help elect to office advocates of women's rights. Some of NOW's legal and legislative battles have been more successful than others in reaching their stated goals, but each has brought to the fore some aspect of society that should be examined. —*Margaret S. Schoon, updated by Erika E. Pilver*

ADDITIONAL READING:

Carabillo, Toni, June Bundy Csida, and Judith Meuli. *Feminist Chronicles, 1953-1993*. Los Angeles: Women's Graphic, 1993. Presents a chronological history of U.S. feminism in the latter half of the twentieth century. Bibliographical references and index.

Cohen, Marcia. *The Sisterhood: The True Story of the Women Who Changed the World*. New York: Simon & Schuster, 1988. Focuses on Betty Friedan, Gloria Steinem, Germaine Greer, and Kate Millett in telling of the quiet birth of NOW in the 1960's, its triumphs in the 1970's, and its troubled legacy in the 1980's.

Friedan, Betty. *The Feminine Mystique*. New York: W. W. Norton, 1983. A twentieth-anniversary edition of the book that is considered to have been the impetus for the modern women's movement. Bibliographical references and index.

_____. *The Second Stage*. New York: Summit Books, 1981. Further thoughts on feminism from one of its modern-day leaders.

Ireland, Patricia. "The State of NOW: A Presidential (and Personal) Report." *Ms. Magazine* 3, no. 1 (July/August, 1992): 24. Discusses NOW's achievements relating to child care, abortion, lesbian rights, and the ERA in the previous two decades.

Morgan, Robin, ed. *Sisterhood Is Powerful: An Anthology of Writings from the Women's Liberation Movement*. New York, Random House, 1970. A mixture of viewpoints from the more and the less radical elements in the women's movement. Bibliography.

SEE ALSO: 1964, Civil Rights Act of 1964; 1965, *Griswold v. Connecticut*; 1970's, Rise of Women's Role in the Military; 1973, *Roe v. Wade*; 1978, Pregnancy Discrimination Act; 1982, Defeat of the Equal Rights Amendment.

1967 ■ LONG, HOT SUMMER: *race riots plague major cities across the United States*

DATE: April-August, 1967
LOCALE: Newark, Detroit, and other major U.S. cities
CATEGORIES: African American history; Civil rights; Economics
KEY FIGURES:
Jerome Cavanagh (1928-1979), mayor of Detroit
Lyndon Baines Johnson (1908-1973), thirty-sixth president of the United States, 1963-1969
Otto Kerner (1908-1976), governor of Illinois
George Romney (1907-1995), governor of Michigan

SUMMARY OF EVENT. From Omaha, Nebraska, in April, to Washington, D.C., in August, during the summer of 1967, race riots wracked nearly 150 U.S. cities. The most severe of these civil disorders were the July riots in Newark, New Jersey—which left twenty-seven dead (most of whom were African Americans), more than eleven hundred injured, and fifteen million dollars in property damage—and in Detroit, Michigan. In the wake of the Detroit riot, President Lyndon B. Johnson established a National Advisory Commission on Civil Disorders, with Governor Otto Kerner of Illinois as its chairman. Other members included New York mayor John V. Lindsay, vice chairman; Senator Edward Brooke of Massachusetts; Senator Fred R. Harris of Oklahoma; Congressman James C. Corman of California; Congressman William M. McCullough of Ohio; Roy Wilkens of the National Association for the Advancement of Colored People (NAACP); the president of the Steelworkers' Union, I. W. Abel; the chairman of Litton Industries, Charles B. (Tex) Thornton; Kentucky commerce commissioner Katherine Graham Peden; and Atlanta police chief Herbert Jenkins. The Kerner Commission was charged with investigating the origins of the disorders, the best methods of control, and the role of state, local, and federal authorities in handling them. They issued their report on March 1, 1968.

At first glance, Detroit was a curious place for such a violent explosion. Many African Americans commanded high wages in the automobile factories and high positions in the liberal United Auto Workers Union. Of Detroit's 550,000 African Americans, 40 percent owned or were buying their homes. Community leaders, both white and black, had long made a civics lesson of the city's bloody race riot of 1943, which had left thirty-four dead and moved President Franklin Roosevelt to send in federal troops. Detroit's mayor, Jerome Cavanagh, had been elected with the support of the African American community.

A trivial police incident provided the spark that ignited the Detroit ghetto. On July 23, a routine 4:00 A.M. raid of a speakeasy on a run-down street resulted in knots of African American onlookers taunting the police. Soon, a brick crashed through the window of a police cruiser. The police could have pulled out completely or responded with force to break up the crowds, but they did neither. They dispatched cruisers, but did nothing further. Mobs gathered and started fires; then looting began. As the fires spread, so did the looting, until it assumed a carnival atmosphere. Youngsters and adults raced from stores with their arms full of groceries, bottles of liquor, or jewelry; others filled their cars with appliances. Both the mayor and the governor seemed paralyzed. Given the fires and the stiflingly hot weather, Mayor Cavanagh ordered more swimming pools opened; Governor George Romney suggested seeding rain clouds above the ghetto. Neither police nor peacemakers could stop the riot.

By midnight on July 24, President Johnson, emphasizing that his action came at the specific request of Governor Romney, used the authority of a 1795 law authorizing the president to use troops to put down an insurrection and announced that he was sending in federal troops to quell the disturbance. The trained, combat-hardened paratroopers quickly brought order to the eastern sector of the ghetto. The fighting then shifted back to the western sector, where ill-trained and jittery National Guardsmen combined with police to represent authority. Finally, the riot burned itself out.

A subsequent investigation by a team of reporters from the *Detroit Free Press* into the forty-three riot-related deaths (all but eight of them African Americans) found that most official reports about these deaths had been fabricated. Three blacks had been riddled as they sat in a car. A deaf man was killed because he could not hear a warning. A child was gunned down while holding a broom.

In order to head off congressional committees, Johnson moved quickly to get his own in operation. Within forty-two hours, the Kerner Commission was working in Washington, D.C. The president asked the commission to "guide the country through a thicket of tension, conflicting evidence, and extreme opinions." Chairman Otto Kerner described it as an attempt to probe into the soul of the United States. The commission operated under two premises: that the nation must ensure the safety of its people, and that it must identify the root causes of racial disorder.

The commission found that, although every civil disorder evolved from a complex set of circumstances, certain generalizations characterized the rioting and the rioters. The stereotype of race riots involving angry, poor blacks attacking affluent whites was not accurate. The 1967 riots were racial, but not interracial. African Americans rose up against the property and authority of white America, not against white people. The typical rioter was an unmarried black man between fifteen and twenty-four years of age, a native of the city, underemployed, resentful of white stereotypes about blacks, and generally better informed about politics than those blacks not involved in the rioting. The commission described a central trend in a causal chain of "discrimination, prejudice, disadvantaged conditions, intense and pervasive grievances, a series of tension-heightening incidents, all culminating in the eruption of disorder at the hands of youthful, politically aware activists. . . ."

The commission also identified a process that the riots followed. African American ghettos harbored many people with deep resentments about living conditions and police practices. A series of incidents, sometimes beginning with an event as minor as a routine traffic stop, caused mounting tension. A final precipitating incident usually happened after a hot day, on an evening when many people were on the street. Violence led to more violence and efforts at control by the authorities. Frustration exploded.

The frustration had long historical roots. The commission noted that the historical pattern of black-white relations had been pervasive discrimination and segregation, resulting in white flight from the inner cities and the establishment of black ghettos. Most African Americans had been denied a share in the material benefits of the United States and had suffered indignity, disrespect, and lack of acceptance by white Americans. Many young African Americans felt alienated by these circumstances and flocked to the banner of Black Power.

The commission concluded that the nation was rapidly moving toward two separate societies, one white and one black, separate and unequal. It warned about the possibility of sustained violence in the nation's cities and the loss of the democratic ideals of dignity, freedom, and equality of opportunity. It called for an expanded commitment to national action in order to open opportunities for all, to remove the frustration and powerlessness felt by minority communities, and to increase communication among races and thus end stereotypes and hostility.

The need for action was dramatized by a December, 1967, memo to President Johnson from his pollsters. A public opinion survey in the aftermath of the riots showed a sharp polarization in white and black attitudes. Of whites, 45 percent blamed the riots on outside agitators with communist backing. Only 7 percent of African Americans saw it that way; 93 percent blamed general frustration. Two-thirds of the African Americans polled felt that the police had contributed to the riots, whereas only one-sixth of whites polled acknowledged police brutality. Johnson felt betrayed by what he called the "crazy riots," which threatened to ruin everything he had tried to accomplish in civil rights. He never endorsed the Kerner Report, and elected officials failed to move on a campaign of national action to redress black grievances. —*Brian G. Tobin*

ADDITIONAL READING:

"An American Tragedy, 1967—Detroit." *Newsweek* (August 7, 1967): 18-33. This article details events of the riot.

The Encyclopedia Britannica's Annals of America. Vol. 18, 1961-1968, pp. 651-653. Summarizes the Kerner Commission's report.

Goodwin, Richard N. *Remembering America: A Voice from the Sixties.* Boston: Little, Brown, 1988. A former Johnson speechwriter puts the riots in the context of the times.

Kearns, Doris. *Lyndon Johnson and the American Dream.* New York: Harper & Row, 1976. Provides insight into the inner workings of the Johnson Administration.

Serrin, William. "The Crucible." *Columbia Journalism Review*, January/February, 1991, 39-42. A journalist shares his firsthand account of the Detroit riot.

SEE ALSO: 1943, Urban Race Riots; 1965, Watts Riot; 1968, Chicago Riots; 1970, Kent State Massacre; 1980, Miami Riots; 1992, Los Angeles Riots.

1967 ■ FREEDOM OF INFORMATION ACT: the U.S. government affirms the right of access to federal records other than classified or personal information

DATE: July 4, 1967
LOCALE: Washington, D.C.
CATEGORIES: Civil rights; Laws and acts
SUMMARY OF EVENT. The participation of citizens in the democratic process is one of the most important factors in making a democracy work. This participation is effective, however, only if citizens have access to information about the way their government works. In the words of former president James Madison, "a popular government without popular information or the means of acquiring it, is but a Prologue to a Farce or a Tragedy; or, perhaps both." This connection between information and participation in the process of government is the basis for the Freedom of Information Act (FOIA).

The First Amendment to the U.S. Constitution addresses the right of the people to assemble and to express themselves, but it does not guarantee specific rights to gather information concerning the government. Throughout the history of the United States, various federal, state, and local governments have attempted to enact laws restricting access to government information. Sometimes these agencies have acted in the public interest, such as attempting to protect the privacy of citizens or to guard sensitive defense information. Other times, however, restrictions have been used to cover up illegal activity or hide major bureaucratic mistakes.

Journalists were the driving force behind the Freedom of Information Act. In 1954, one of the premier journalism or-

ganizations in the United States, Sigma Delta Chi (later known as the Society of Professional Journalists), began to push for the adoption of a bill that would guarantee access to government records at the state level. Although this access would be available to all citizens, it would be particularly helpful to journalists, since their daily job involves the collection and dissemination of information. Within three years, nearly half the states in the country had open-record laws. Today, all states have some form of laws ensuring, in varying degrees, access to government records.

In 1966, Congress amended Section 3 of the Administrative Procedure Act of 1946 to incorporate the Freedom of Information Act. The act made certain specific government records open to inspection, access, and use. It became law on July 4, 1967. The act includes limitations on the type of information that can be requested. It applies only to offices and departments of the executive branch of the federal government, such as the Defense Department, and independent federal regulatory agencies, such as the Environmental Protection Agency. The act does not apply to the legislative or judicial branches of the government. The records that are covered include documents, computer tapes, photographs, and other tangible forms of data. Requests are honored only for data in existing forms; the government is not required to generate new lists or records in response to an FOIA request, and one cannot request access to a person—for example, through an interview—through the FOIA.

The Freedom of Information Act was based on the premise that, in a society whose government is the people, government records are, by definition, open to public inspection, unless an agency can give specific reasons why the records should be kept from the general public. The original act included nine exemptions that the government could use to block FOIA requests. A government agency could refuse a request if the information involved national security; the internal personnel rules and practices of an agency; material specifically exempted from public exposure by other statutes; trade secrets or certain commercial or financial information collected by the government from individuals or companies; interagency and intra-agency material involving internal decision-making processes (commonly called the "executive privilege" exemption); personal information files, such as medical records; investigatory information used in law enforcement; financial institution regulation information; or oil and gas exploration data, such as geological and geophysical data.

While these exemptions may appear to be sharply defined, considerable debate has developed over the scope of each category. For example, if a key federal official is suddenly fired from his or her job, a journalist might make an FOIA request to determine the reasons. A federal official could respond by citing the second or sixth exemption to keep the journalist from getting the information. In another example, the president of the United States might make an extremely controversial decision, and a reporter could make an FOIA request to see the same information that the president used, to determine whether the information supported the decision. The president might cite the executive privilege exemption to deny the request.

Such decisions frequently are challenged in court. Since the passage of the act, the courts have generally supported the rights of the person making the request, strengthening the law and placing the burden on the government to prove why information cannot be released. Cases such as *Wellford v. Hardin* (1970) and *Department of the Air Force v. Rose* (1976) demonstrate that the growing body of legal decisions argues for disclosure rather than secrecy, and frequently limits the use of the exemptions to block FOIA requests.

Not all cases are decided in favor of the FOIA, however. In 1973, an FOIA case was appealed all the way to the Supreme Court, and the court sided with the government in its attempt to block the request. Congresswoman Patsy Mink, along with thirty-two other members of Congress, had asked President Richard Nixon to immediately release information on underground nuclear testing, and the request had been denied based on national defense and intra-agency activity grounds. The Washington, D.C., Court of Appeals ruled that secret and nonsecret parts of the documents in question could be separated by a judge in privacy, so that the congresswoman could get some of the information. In *Environmental Protection Agency v. Mink*, however, the Supreme Court disagreed when it ruled that the president's executive order to keep documents secret was sufficient to block the FOIA request.

Although members of the press were instrumental in the development of the Freedom of Information Act, anyone can make a request: members of the general public, corporations, foreign nationals, academicians, or representatives of state or local governments. According to a 1984 congressional review of the FOIA process, between 15 and 20 percent of the FOIA requests made to government agencies were made by journalists. The types of people making requests change from department to department: More than half the requests to the Drug Enforcement Administration, for example, come from prisoners in federal jails.

An agency has up to thirty days from the date of the request to either provide the information or deny the request and explain the reason for the denial. The timeliness of the information can be extremely important for reporters trying to meet deadlines or attorneys building a case. Many federal agencies started with excellent compliance records when the act first became law, accepting as many as 98 percent of the requests and fulfilling nearly all of them within the specified time. As more people have started to use the FOIA, however, compliance has become more difficult. The Federal Bureau of Investigation, for example, developed such an extensive backlog of requests that it can take as long as a year to get information.

In 1986, Congress amended the act to allow agencies to charge fees for requests. These fees are based on three factors: the agency's policy, the actions taken to fulfill the request, and the status of the person making the request. Fees vary from agency to agency. The actions taken to fulfill the request include finding, reviewing, and duplicating the documents. Commercial sources making requests pay for all three actions, while journalists or academicians making requests pay only for duplication costs. Fees may be waived on a case-by-case basis. —*Edward J. Lordan*

ADDITIONAL READING:

Adler, Allan. *Using the Freedom of Information Act: A Step by Step Guide*. Washington, D.C.: American Civil Liberties Union Foundation, 1990. A pamphlet informing citizens how to make use of the law to obtain information contained in FBI and other government records.

Holsinger, Ralph L. *Media Law*. 2d ed. New York: McGraw-Hill, 1991. Chapters 7 and 8 address the Freedom of Information Act.

Tedford, Thomas L. *Freedom of Speech in the United States*. 2d ed. New York: McGraw-Hill, 1993. A history of free-speech rights in the United States.

U.S. Congress. House. *Citizen's Guide to the Freedom of Information Act*. Chicago: Commerce Clearing House, 1987. An introduction to the Freedom of Information Act and the Privacy Act of 1974. Explains the process for making a request.

U.S. Department of Justice. Attorney General's Advocacy Institute. *The Freedom of Information Act for Attorneys and Access Professionals*. Washington, D.C.: Government Printing Office, 1989. Includes bibliographic references.

_____. U.S. General Services Administration. *Your Right to Federal Records: Questions and Answers on the Freedom of Information Act and the Privacy Act*. Washington, D.C.: Government Printing Office, 1984. The government's guide to using the law.

Weaver, Maureen, ed. *The Freedom of Information Act: Why It's Important and How to Use It*. Washington, D.C.: Campaign for Political Rights, in cooperation with the Center for National Security Studies, 1982. A handy pamphlet containing practical information.

SEE ALSO: 1965, *Griswold v. Connecticut*.

1968 ■ BILINGUAL EDUCATION ACT: *in the face of a changing U.S. populace, legislation authorizes bilingual education studies*

DATE: January 2, 1968
LOCALE: Washington, D.C.
CATEGORIES: Asian American history; Education; Latino American history; Laws and acts
KEY FIGURES:
George Edward Brown, Jr. (born 1920) and
Edward Ross Roybal (born 1916), representatives from California
James Haas Scheuer (born 1920), representative from New York
Ralph Webster Yarborough (1903-1996), senator from Texas

SUMMARY OF EVENT. When the Declaration of Independence was written in 1776, English was not the only language spoken in the thirteen colonies. Twenty percent of the colonists were non-English-speaking Europeans, including Dutch, French, and German settlers, while twenty percent spoke African languages, and a variety of languages were spoken by the indigenous peoples. During the early nineteenth century, the United States occupied the Louisiana territory, absorbing French speakers. Later in the century, more Europeans arrived, especially from Germany. Spanish-speaking territories, as well as Alaska, Guam, Hawaii, and the eastern part of Samoa, were incorporated into the United States, mostly by conquest. Bilingual constitutions were written by the new states of California and New Mexico, preserving certain language rights of Spanish speakers. Nevertheless, English was the principal language of commerce and government throughout most of the United States.

Languages other than English continued to be spoken at home. In the nineteenth century, the state of Ohio permitted each public school district the option of allowing instruction in German, fearing that otherwise, parents would withdraw their children and send them to private schools. During World War I, however, the tide turned against instruction in German and other foreign languages, and various laws were passed to restrict instruction to English.

After World War I, English-only schooling statutes were challenged successfully in the courts, notably in *Meyer v. Nebraska* (1923) and *Farrington v. Tokushige* (1927). During World War II, Japanese-language schools closed voluntarily in Hawaii, but Chinese who wanted their children to attend private language schools in Hawaii had to await a favorable ruling in *Mo Hock Ke Lok Po v. Steinback* (1949), the first Supreme Court case to affirm the value of cultural diversity, when the government's need of foreign-language experts was cited in support of instruction in languages other than English.

Bilingual education was thrust into the forefront of public attention in the 1960's, when Dade County, Florida, announced a successful experiment with a bilingual program for newly arrived Cuban refugees, most of whom were non-English Proficient (NEP) or limited-English Proficient (LEP). Citing Title VI of the Civil Rights Act of 1964, which prohibits discrimination in school districts receiving federal funds, Mexican advocacy groups supported the concept of bilingual instruction as a programmatic remedy for unequal educational attainments by Mexican Americans. The advocacy groups argued that without the ability to speak English, Mexican Americans could participate in neither the economic nor the political mainstream of the country.

Responding to pressure from his constituents, Texas senator Ralph W. Yarborough championed the cause of bilingual education by introducing a bill in early 1967 that sought to assist schools with a high percentage of low-income Hispanics. In the House of Representatives, the bill ultimately gained forty-nine cosponsors, notably George E. Brown, Jr., and Edward R. Roybal of California and James H. Scheuer of New York. As the bill received bipartisan support, attention broadened to consider the plight of LEP/NEP students of American Indian, Asian, French Canadian, French Creole, and Portuguese ancestries. During the debate, statistics were presented showing that 11 percent of U.S. residents had a mother tongue other than English, and three million school-age children spoke a language other than English, 1.75 million of whom spoke Spanish.

Public hearings on the proposed legislation were held in Los Angeles, New York City, and three cities in Texas (Corpus Christi, Edinburg, and San Antonio). In addition to Hispanic advocacy groups, support for the bill came from the National Education Association. Since professional educators had no consensus on which teaching strategy worked best in boosting achievement levels for LEP and NEP students, they lobbied Congress to provide funding for research.

Congress passed the Bilingual Education Act of 1968 as an amendment to the Elementary and Secondary Education Act of 1965. Four hundred million dollars was authorized to be spent for research from 1968 to 1973, although much less actually was appropriated. Funds were to be used to remedy LEP/NEP problems in languages other than English spoken by a substantial number of students.

On January 21, 1974, the Supreme Court ruled in *Lau v. Nichols* that failure to use special methods to enable language-minority students to enter mainstream English classes was impermissible. The court, however, refused to rule on what pedagogical method would be best for mainstreaming LEP and NEP students into English-only classes, leaving the choice of method to local school districts.

Subsequent to *Lau*, Congress held hearings to assess the impact, which was determined to affect five million schoolchildren. One result was the Equal Educational Opportunities Act in 1974, a provision of which requires "appropriate action to overcome language barriers that impede equal participation." A second statute was the Bilingual Education Act of 1974, which provided federal funds to finance efforts at compliance with *Lau* for all affected students, not just for low-income students. In 1978, when the law was extended, objections to experiments in bilingual education mounted, and Congress restricted funding to educational projects in which no more than 40 percent of the students were native English speakers.

Several alternative methods of language instruction were studied. Submersion, which entailed placing LEP/NEP students into English-only classes on a sink-or-swim basis, was the method outlawed by *Lau*. Teaching English to Students of Other Languages (TESOL) was designed to remove LEP/NEP students from the mainstream to take special instruction in English. Immersion involved employing bilingual instructors who could teach in either language. Transitional bilingual education, the most popular program, involved fast-track English instruction aimed at rapid mainstreaming. Bilingual maintenance programs were designed to enable LEP/NEP students to retain language proficiency in the native language while learning English. Bilingual/bicultural programs went beyond bilingual maintenance to provide instruction in aspects of both the root and U.S. cultures. Culturally pluralistic programs, as adopted later at Texas border towns, were designed to integrate LEP/NEP and English-speaking students into multilingual/multicultural classrooms, so that both majority and minority children could learn together.

When objective studies demonstrated that the various bilingual instructional programs did not improve achievement levels for Mexican Americans, Congress passed new legislation, providing funds for capacity building, that is, to train teachers from language minority groups and to develop instructional materials for use in the classroom. The first such law, the Bilingual Education Amendments of 1981, was followed by the Bilingual Education Improvement Act of 1983, and the Bilingual Education Acts of 1984 and 1988.

During the eight years that Ronald Reagan was president, civil rights compliance reviews on language and other forms of educational discrimination decreased by 90 percent. In 1991, after Congress held hearings on the matter, the U.S. Department of Education's Office for Civil Rights set equal educational opportunities for national-origin minority and Native American students as its top priority. Although the battle to recognize Spanish and other languages as legitimate languages of instruction succeeded in the 1960's and 1970's, efforts to abolish bilingual education gained momentum in the 1980's and 1990's.   —*Michael Haas*

ADDITIONAL READING:

Bull, Barry L., Royal T. Fruehling, and Virgie Chattergy. *The Ethics of Multicultural and Bilingual Education.* New York: Columbia University Press, 1992. Contrasts how liberal, democratic, and communitarian approaches to education relate to bilingual and multicultural education.

Moran, Rachel F. "Of Democracy, Devaluation, and Bilingual Education." *Creighton Law Review* 26 (February, 1993): 255-319. Contrasts special-interest bargaining and bureaucratic rule-making methods for dealing with needs for bilingual education. Gives a brief explication of provisions of the Bilingual Education Act of 1968 and subsequent related statutes.

Porter, Rosalie P. *Forked Tongue: The Politics of Bilingual Education.* New York: Basic Books, 1990. An indictment of efforts to deliver bilingual education.

Rossell, Christine H., and J. Michael Ross. "The Social Science Evidence on Bilingual Education." *Journal of Law & Education* 15 (Fall, 1986): 385-419. Reviews scientific evidence concerning alternative methods for teaching English to limited-English-speaking and non-English-speaking students. Appendices list methodologically sound and methodologically flawed studies.

Wagner, Stephen T. "The Historical Background of Bilingualism and Biculturalism in the United States." In *The New Bilingualism: An American Dilemma*, edited by Martin Ridge. Los Angeles: University of Southern California Press, 1981. Lead essay in a symposium that discusses pros and cons of bilingualism in many facets of U.S. society.

SEE ALSO: 1828, Webster's *American Dictionary of the English Language*; 1982, *Plyler v. Doe.*

1968 ■ Tet Offensive: *a series of Viet Cong attacks against South Vietnam turns public opinion against the war*

DATE: January 30-March 31, 1968
LOCALE: Vietnam
CATEGORY: Wars, uprisings, and civil unrest
KEY FIGURES:
Clark McAdams Clifford (born 1906), U.S. secretary of defense
Lyndon Baines Johnson (1908-1973), thirty-sixth president of the United States, 1963-1969
Dean Rusk (1909-1994), U.S. secretary of state
William Childs Westmoreland (born 1914), commander of Military Assistance Command in Vietnam
Earle Gilmore Wheeler (1908-1975), chief of the Joint Chiefs of Staff

SUMMARY OF EVENT. On the night of January 30, 1968, Viet Cong and North Vietnamese military units began a surprise offensive throughout Vietnam. They attacked thirty-nine of South Vietnam's forty-four provincial capitals, five of its six autonomous cities, and at least seventy-one of the 245 district towns. A Viet Cong unit even penetrated the grounds of the U.S. Embassy in Saigon before being killed in a furious gun fight. All over Vietnam, cities that previously had been immune to the war were attacked, occupied, and in some cases nearly destroyed, as U.S. and Vietnamese troops moved in to liberate them. The war had been going on since 1946, but there had never been fighting like this. Two months later, on March 31, 1968, President Lyndon Johnson addressed the American people on television to announce that in the pursuit of peace, he was ordering a partial halt to the bombing of North Vietnam, and that he would neither seek nor accept the Democratic presidential nomination.

The United States had been supporting the Saigon government of South Vietnam since Vietnam was divided in 1954. The military situation had been steadily deteriorating during those years, and in July, 1965, President Johnson made a fateful decision. Henceforth, U.S. troops not only would be used in a defensive capacity to protect U.S. airfields but also would go on the offensive. U.S. military units would carry the fight to the enemy in what became known as search-and-destroy missions. The new policy, strongly backed by Secretary of State Dean Rusk and General Earle Wheeler, chief of the Joint Chiefs of Staff, was to defeat the enemy. This aggressive policy required more U.S. troops. In June, 1965, there were fewer than sixty thousand U.S. troops in Vietnam. By the year's end, that number had grown to 184,300. A year later, it had moved to 385,300; by the end of 1967, nearly a half million U.S. troops were stationed in Vietnam. The war had been Americanized.

This strategy led to increased U.S. casualties, but it did not lead to an end of the war. As U.S. troops continued to die and peace was not in sight, public support for the war began to decline. To stop this trend, President Johnson orchestrated a series of optimistic statements by key civilian and military leaders late in 1967. The American people were assured that progress was being made, that there was "light at the end of the tunnel."

Meanwhile, the United States continued its strategy of making the price of war so high that the North Vietnamese would have to give up. Search-and-destroy missions and U.S. bombing of North Vietnam continued. However, there was a limit to the military effort the United States would make in Vietnam: Bombing of North Vietnam would stop short of provoking a confrontation with China or Russia. U.S. troops would be limited to a number that would not require total mobilization of the U.S. economy, something the U.S. people would not tolerate. Although a limited war, this was not a small military effort. A half million troops had been sent; four hundred thousand air attack sorties per year had dropped 1.2 million tons of bombs. The enemy had lost two hundred thousand killed and the United States twenty thousand of its own. That was the situation when Vietnam prepared to celebrate the lunar new year of Tet.

Tet was the most important holiday in Vietnam, a time for rejoicing and traveling to see friends and relatives. It was not a time for war but a time for truce. Yet in Saigon, General Westmoreland, commander of U.S. forces in Vietnam, knew something was going to happen. The enemy had been building up its forces, and captured documents indicated an offensive of some kind. That the offensive came on Tet was a surprise. That it was so large and well coordinated was a shock.

Precisely what the North Vietnamese sought to gain from the Tet Offensive is not clear. The captured documents indicated that they thought large areas could be seized through popular uprisings against the South Vietnamese government and the defection of whole units of the South Vietnamese army. In addition to these military goals, there were psychological victories to be won. A forceful attack would discourage the United States and show the people of South Vietnam that neither their own government nor the United States could protect them.

Militarily, the North Vietnamese lost. Although they were able to capture several cities and to hold out in the old imperial city of Hue for more than three weeks, in the end they held no city and there was no popular uprising or large-scale defection. In fact, the South Vietnamese rallied to the defense of their country to a far greater extent than they yielded to the enemy forces. Psychologically, however, Tet was a North Vietnamese victory. They had demonstrated that there was no "light at the end of the tunnel." All the U.S. bombing and search-and-destroy missions had not prevented North Vietnam from attacking virtually any place in South Vietnam. It was not important whether Hanoi had won any military victories in the battles that were fought during the Tet Offensive. What was

important to U.S. officials and the American people was that little had been accomplished during two and a half years of major U.S. fighting, and too much remained to be accomplished before peace would be at hand.

Tet reinforced the U.S. public's dissatisfaction with the war. Perpetuation of the U.S. policy would result in more deaths, greater economic sacrifice at home, destruction of countless South Vietnamese towns, and the extension of human suffering over ever larger areas of Vietnam. Even then, there was no assurance of victory. North Vietnam had promised a long war, and the Tet Offensive showed that the price would be high. The American people gradually concluded they did not want to pay that price.

Within official Washington, the Tet Offensive sparked a major debate. Military leaders concluded that Hanoi had been defeated and urged the president to take advantage of this victory and expand the war. Within the Defense Department, however, a growing number of civilian officials, among them Secretary of Defense Clark Clifford, doubted the wisdom of escalation or even continuation of the way the war was being fought. Their analyses showed that no progress had been made since the summer of 1965. They advised the president that the policy of confronting the enemy on the field of battle had failed. It was time to pull back and provide a shield behind which the South Vietnamese army would rebuild with U.S. arms. Thus rebuilt, South Vietnam would fight its own war. Lyndon Johnson rejected escalation and reluctantly accepted this policy of Vietnamization. Peace was still a long way off, but the course of U.S. withdrawal had been charted.

—Jonathan G. Utley, updated by Edward J. Rielly

ADDITIONAL READING:

Braestrup, Peter. *Big Story.* Abridged ed. New Haven, Conn.: Yale University Press, 1983. Examines the reporting of the Tet Offensive.

Davidson, Phillip B. *Vietnam at War: The History 1946-1975.* Novato, Calif.: Presidio Press, 1988. Presents a comprehensive history of the Vietnam War from a military perspective.

Esper, George. *The Eyewitness History of the Vietnam War, 1961-1975.* New York: Ballantine Books, 1983. A chronological overview of the war with eyewitness accounts and some of the war's most famous photographs. Includes a chapter on the Tet Offensive.

Moss, George Donelson. *Vietnam: An American Ordeal.* Englewood Cliffs, N.J.: Prentice-Hall, 1990. One of the most thorough analyses of the Vietnam War.

Oberdorfer, Don. *Tet! The Turning Point of the Vietnam War.* 2d ed. New York: Da Capo Press, 1984. A landmark account of the Tet Offensive, essential for anyone studying this portion of the war.

Westmoreland, William C. *A Soldier Reports.* Garden City, N.Y.: Doubleday, 1976. An important account by a general who was in charge of the U.S. military effort in Vietnam.

SEE ALSO: 1964, Vietnam War; 1964, Berkeley Free Speech Movement; 1964, Johnson Is Elected President; 1967,

Long, Hot Summer; 1968, Nixon Is Elected President; 1970's, Rise of Women's Role in the Military; 1973, U.S. Troops Leave Vietnam; 1995, United States Recognizes Vietnam.

1968 ■ Assassinations of King and Kennedy: *following the assassination of President John F. Kennedy only five years before, the slayings of his brother and the leader of the Civil Rights movement elevate all three as martyrs to the cause of reform*

Date: April 4 and June 4, 1968
Locale: Memphis, Tennessee, and Los Angeles, California
Categories: African American history; Civil rights; Government and politics
Key figures:
Robert Francis Kennedy (1925-1968), brother of President John F. Kennedy, senator from New York, and Democratic presidential candidate
Martin Luther King, Jr. (1929-1968), African American civil rights leader
James Earl Ray (born 1928), escaped convict and convicted assassin of King
Sirhan Bishara Sirhan (born 1944), unemployed Jordanian American and convicted assassin of Kennedy

Summary of event. In the first half of 1968, Martin Luther King, Jr., and Robert F. Kennedy, two prominent Americans whose careers had been identified with demands for social change and dreams of building a better world through nonviolent reform, were shot to death in separate attacks. Although there is no evidence to suggest that the murders resulted from a common plot, their close proximity in time and the similarity of the victims' political viewpoints linked them together in many minds.

King had returned to Memphis, Tennessee, in early April, 1968, to aid the efforts of striking sanitation workers, after earlier marches had failed and King's image as an effective leader had been caricatured in some press accounts. Already tired and increasingly depressed, King worried about the possibility that critics might argue that he could not keep order in the planned Poor People's Campaign in Washington, D.C., that was scheduled to begin in late April. Against the advice of some of his close colleagues, King interrupted his work on the Poor People's March to try again to vindicate both the nonviolent method of reform in Memphis and his own leadership image. For more than a decade, King had led the Southern Christian Leadership Conference (SCLC) and was, for many people, the quintessential symbol and spokesman for nonviolence. By the spring of 1968, however, King had lost some of his mystique, as the relatively simpler issues of voting rights and access to public facilities were superseded by more costly

and divisive social and economic problems, accompanied by the deepening U.S. involvement in the Vietnam War.

King had lost his close alliance with President Lyndon Johnson because of his opposition to the president's Vietnam policy. King also faced challenges from younger, more militant African American leaders, for whom King's philosophy of passive resistance seemed too slow.

On the evening of April 4, King walked onto the balcony of his Memphis motel and was struck down by a bullet, fired from a building across the street. He died almost instantly. Initial attempts to identify and apprehend the killer failed, and while fires and riots raged in several cities in protest of King's death, an intensive search began, spreading eventually to Canada and Great Britain. On June 8, British immigration officials arrested an escaped U.S. convict traveling under the name of Roman George Sneyd and returned him to the United States to stand trial for the murder of King. The prisoner, whose real name was James Earl Ray, pleaded guilty to the charge in March, 1969, and was sentenced to ninety-nine years in

Martin Luther King, Jr., during a press conference in May, 1963. Baptist minister, founder of the Southern Christian Leadership Conference, tireless social activist, and winner of the 1964 Nobel Peace Prize, King sought advances in civil rights for all by means of nonviolent direct action. Ironically, he would fall to an assassin's bullet. (Library of Congress)

prison. Later, Ray changed his position, claimed innocence, and wrote a book entitled *Who Killed Martin Luther King?* (1992), with a foreword by the Reverend Jesse Jackson that cautiously endorsed Ray's conspiracy argument.

Four days before Ray's arrest, Senator Robert F. Kennedy of New York had completed his campaign in the California Democratic presidential primary. On the evening of June 4, he waited at a Los Angeles hotel for election returns, which showed him to have defeated Senator Eugene McCarthy, the winner of the Oregon primary in May. After a short victory speech to his supporters in the Ambassador Hotel, Kennedy was leaving the building through the kitchen when a single gunman approached him suddenly and fired several times from close range. After more than a day of unconsciousness, Kennedy died early on the morning of June 6.

Both assassinations received extensive coverage in the national and international press, where much speculation was centered on the assassins' motives and on the possibilities of conspiracies involving persons still at large. Less effort was made to assess the significance of the men's deaths for the movements and ideas with which they were identified. However, certain immediate repercussions were evident.

One of the most important results was that Kennedy's death drastically altered the presidential campaign of 1968. When President Johnson had declared, in March of that year, that he would not run for reelection, the Democratic nomination became a three-way contest among Kennedy, McCarthy, and Vice President Hubert Humphrey, who had not entered the primaries but could count on the support of many party leaders still loyal to Johnson. Kennedy's California victory had boosted his delegate count and strengthened his hope that McCarthy eventually would shift support to him, because both men shared a common opposition to the administration's war policy on Vietnam. As it was, McCarthy's campaign stagnated after June, and some of Kennedy's supporters withdrew from the campaign in bitterness. The convention nominated Humphrey amid riots that evinced a divided Democratic Party and led to a narrow Republican victory in November. Whether Kennedy could have gained the nomination, much less the presidency, must remain a moot question. Yet the fact remains that he was the only opponent of the war whose political appeal had spread beyond the middle- and upper-income groups who provided McCarthy's strength. Kennedy's removal greatly damaged the chances of a Democratic repudiation of the Johnson war policy.

The immediate aftermath of King's death was marked by serious urban rioting in several cities, and somewhat later, by the granting of a substantial number of the strikers' demands in Memphis. More difficult to appraise is the place that his martyrdom earned for him and for his ideas in the Civil Rights movement. At a time when his influence was threatened by men such as Rap Brown and Huey Newton, King was killed in a way that served to restore his prestige among many African Americans. Under the leadership of King's longtime assistant Ralph David Abernathy, the SCLC continued to play a leading

role in the Civil Rights movement after King's death. On the other hand, some African Americans, finding in King's death a confirmation of the futility of passive resistance, turned instead to more militant tactics.

Unlike the earlier assassination of John F. Kennedy, the deaths of King and Robert Kennedy did not lead to the passage of any significant legislation that they had promoted. Despite repeated calls for enactment of strict gun control laws, little was done in this area of concern, beyond a testimony to the truth of the contention that the control of violence posed one of the major problems for U.S. society in the late 1960's. It would be difficult indeed for anyone in sympathy with Martin Luther King, Jr., and Robert Kennedy to find any consolation in their deaths. Nevertheless, in death, both King and Kennedy remained inspiring symbols, even martyrs, to many people who supported their causes. It is significant that the SCLC, which King helped to found and which he led for eleven years as its president, continued under presidents Ralph Abernathy and Joseph E. Lowery to keep the vision of a nonviolent society central to their organizational and personal goals.

—*Courtney B. Ross, updated by Thomas R. Peake*

ADDITIONAL READING:

Frank, Gerold. *An American Death: The True Story of the Assassination of Dr. Martin Luther King, Jr.* Garden City, N.Y.: Doubleday, 1972. A well-documented analysis of King's assassination that argues that Ray acted alone.

Huie, William Bradford. *He Slew the Dreamer: My Search for the Truth About James Earl Ray and the Murder of Martin Luther King.* New York: Delacorte Press, 1970. Based on a long series of letters between Huie and James Earl Ray, rejects Ray's contention that King was the victim of a conspiracy and that Ray had been framed for the murder. Presents Ray as an insecure, small-time criminal who hungered for recognition.

Kaiser, Robert Blair. *RFK Must Die: The History of the Robert Kennedy Assassination and Its Aftermath.* New York: E. P. Dutton, 1970. A journalist's account, based on his direct access to Sirhan as a special investigator for the defense team. Explores Sirhan's motives and leaves open the question of a conspiracy.

Koch, Thilo. *Fighters for a New World.* New York: G. P. Putnam's Sons, 1969. An illustrated tribute to John Kennedy, Robert Kennedy, and Martin Luther King, Jr., by a German journalist. Interesting as an example of how the three reformers were linked together in the minds of many foreign observers.

McKnight, Gerald D. "The 1968 Memphis Sanitation Strike and the FBI: A Case Study in Urban Surveillance." *South Atlantic Quarterly* 83, no. 2 (1984): 138-156. A detailed analysis of the difficulties, mistakes, and complexity of FBI surveillance of the Memphis labor strike that led to King's assassination.

Meyer, Philip. "Aftermath of Martyrdom: Negro Militancy and Martin Luther King." *Public Opinion Quarterly* 33, no. 2 (1969): 160-173. A scholarly study of the impact of King's assassination upon African American attitudes, focusing on increased racial nationalism, disillusionment with government policies, growing support of black political candidates, and increased militancy in some segments of African American society.

Ray, James Earl. *Who Killed Martin Luther King: The True Story by the Alleged Assassin.* Washington, D.C.: National Press Books, 1992. An apparently self-serving account by the convicted assassin of Martin Luther King. Argues that Ray did not commit the murder but was a scapegoat. Makes no specific charges, but strongly implies that the FBI and other official agencies were somehow involved.

Turner, William W., and Jonn G. Christian. *The Assassination of Robert F. Kennedy: A Searching Look at the Conspiracy and Cover-Up, 1968-1978.* New York: Random House, 1978. An intriguing account, written in part to convince the Carter Administration to reopen the Kennedy case. Turner, a former FBI agent and journalist, and Christian, an ABC broadcast newsman, argue that Sirhan did not act alone but with the help of anti-Kennedy government officials and possibly even FBI agents.

United Press International Staff. *Assassination: Robert F. Kennedy, 1925-1968.* New York: Cowler Press, 1969. A compilation of wire service reports of Kennedy's assassination. Its main value lies in following the events closely as details became available.

SEE ALSO: 1963, King Delivers His "I Have a Dream" Speech; 1963, Assassination of President Kennedy; 1965, Assassination of Malcolm X.

1968 ■ INDIAN CIVIL RIGHTS ACT: *a controversial but important measure is designed to guarantee Indians living under tribal governments the same rights as those of other U.S. citizens*

DATE: April 11, 1968
LOCALE: Washington, D.C.
CATEGORIES: Civil rights; Laws and acts; Native American history
KEY FIGURES:
Samuel James Ervin, Jr. (1896-1985), North Carolina senator who proposed bringing tribal governments under the framework of the Constitution
Benjamin Reifel (born 1906), South Dakota congressman and member of the Rosebud Sioux tribe

SUMMARY OF EVENT. A significant but controversial piece of legislation designed to guarantee the rights of individual American Indians came about in special Indian titles of the Civil Rights Act signed into law on April 11, 1968. The existence of tribal governments and tribal courts had raised the issue of protection of the individual rights of American Indians living in a tribal context. Tribal governments have been considered to be inherently sovereign, because they predate the

Constitution and do not derive their power to exist or to govern from either federal or state governments. Federal recognition or regulation of tribes does not make them part of the United States government or guarantee constitutional protection for tribal members. An 1896 Supreme Court case, *Talton v. Mayes*, determined that the Bill of Rights of the Constitution does not apply to tribes, because tribes derive and retain their sovereignty from their aboriginal self-governing status. The Indian Citizenship Act of 1924, which gave American Indians dual citizenship in their tribes and the United States, did not make the Bill of Rights applicable to situations involving tribal government.

There was little interest in the lack of individual rights for American Indians living a tribal existence until the 1960's, when national attention turned to civil rights. When the United States Senate began to investigate civil rights abuses throughout the nation, some attention was directed at tribal governments. In 1961, the Senate held hearings on civil rights issues on reservations, and investigators heard many examples of infringement on individual liberties and the lack of any way to redress grievances. Contributing to the problem was the fact that tribal societies emphasized the good of the group and were inclined to consider the good of the people as a whole more important than the preservation of individual rights.

An 1886 Supreme Court decision in *United States v. Kagama* determined that Congress has authority to govern the internal affairs of tribes and to make laws that directly affect American Indians. Therefore, Congress could impose restrictions on tribal governments and move toward granting greater individual protections to American Indians living on reservations.

In 1968, when civil rights legislation was proposed to remedy the unequal protection of some groups in the United States, Senator Sam Ervin of North Carolina proposed bringing tribal governments under the constitutional framework of the United States. After a good deal of political maneuvering, Congressman Ben Reifel of South Dakota, a member of the Rosebud Sioux tribe, rallied support for the bill, and Public Law 90-284, the Indian Civil Rights Act, became law. This act was a set of special titles within the Civil Rights Act. It was intended to protect the rights of individual American Indians; however, it was controversial for its emphasis on individuals rather than the tribal group. The act was intended to preserve tribal autonomy while protecting the rights of individual tribal members. Largely as a result of tribal protests that the full Bill of Rights would severely upset traditional governing practices, a blanket imposition of the Bill of Rights on tribal governments was replaced by a more selective and specific list of individual rights that were to be protected. Those parts of the Bill of Rights that seemed to infringe on the special character of tribal government were omitted.

The Indian Civil Rights Act prohibits tribal governments from interfering with freedom of speech, religion, press, assembly, and petition for redress of grievances. It specifically authorizes a writ of habeas corpus for anyone detained by the tribe, and it grants due process. This bill also protects the right of privacy against search and seizure, using language identical to that of the Bill of Rights. The Indian Civil Rights Act does not guarantee persons free counsel in criminal proceedings nor the right of indictment by grand jury.

In addition to protecting individual freedoms, the Indian Civil Rights Act contains some provisions that impact tribal governments directly. The Indian Civil Rights Act permits tribal governments to establish an official tribal religion in order to allow the continuation of the quasi theocracies that form the basis of government in some American Indian communities. However, the act does require that individual freedom of religion be protected. The secretary of the interior is charged with the responsibility of drawing up codes of justice to be used in courts trying American Indian offenders. Assault resulting in serious bodily injury was added to the offenses on reservations that are subject to federal jurisdiction under the Major Crimes Act. In an important victory for tribal autonomy, Section 7 of Public Law 83-280 was repealed. Public Law 83-280, passed by Congress in 1953 in an attempt to abridge the rights of tribal courts, had given states the authority to extend civil and criminal jurisdiction over reservations. The passage of the Indian Civil Rights Act authorized the retrocession of jurisdiction already assumed by a state. A provision in the bill guaranteed the automatic approval of tribal contracts if the secretary of the interior did not act on a tribal request within ninety days.

The Indian Civil Rights Act was controversial when it was proposed and has remained so. Many American Indians view it as an attempt to impose non-Indian values on tribal societies and regard it as a violation of tribal sovereignty, because Congress unilaterally imposed the bill on tribal governments and people. This raised many questions regarding the meaning of "consent." Tribes do not seek to be protected from misuse of power, but there are questions about both the legality and cultural implications of the Indian Civil Rights Act. The fact that Congress intended to bring tribal governments more within the constitutional framework of the United States caused a good deal of controversy. Tribes have questioned the legality of permitting Congress, which basically represents states, to have a direct role in the formulation and passage of a law for tribes. No mechanism was afforded for tribes to accept or reject this legislation, although tribal cultures and customs are directly impacted by this law because it emphasizes individualism. Many tribal leaders feel the Indian Civil Rights Act restricts tribes in the exercise of their inherent sovereignty.

Since passage of the bill, numerous individual challenges to tribal authority have been litigated in federal courts, and many court decisions have favored the individual and weakened the concept of tribal sovereignty. More recent court decisions have tended to use tribal customs and traditions in interpreting the act. A landmark decision, *Santa Clara Pueblo v. Martinez*, supported a tribe's right to extend membership only to the children of male tribal members, as this was in keeping with tribal custom. The court ruled that it did not violate laws against sexual discrimination, because the Indian Civil Rights Act had a dual purpose of protecting individual rights as well as tribal autonomy.　　　　—*Carole A. Barrett*

ADDITIONAL READING:

Deloria, Vine, Jr., ed. *American Indian Policy in the Twentieth Century*. Norman: University of Oklahoma Press, 1985. Several essays deal with the impact of the Indian Civil Rights Act on American Indian tribal governments. Also explores larger constitutional issues and tribal governments.

Deloria, Vine, Jr., and Clifford M. Lytle. *The Nations Within: The Past and Future of American Indian Sovereignty*. New York: Pantheon Books, 1984. An important discussion of the impact of legal and legislative measures on tribal autonomy and self-rule.

Olson, James S., and Raymond Wilson. *Native Americans in the Twentieth Century*. Chicago: University of Illinois Press, 1984. Examines the Indian Civil Rights Act and its assault on tribal sovereignty. Discusses numerous contemporary issues in a historical context.

Prucha, Francis Paul. *The Great Father: The United States Government and the American Indians*. Lincoln: University of Nebraska Press, 1984. Examines the relationship of the federal government and tribal governments from the formation of the United States to the 1980's. Explores the Indian Civil Rights Act in this context.

Wunder, John R. *"Retained by the People": A History of American Indians and the Bill of the Rights*. New York: Oxford University Press, 1994. Chronicles the history of the relationship between American Indians and the Bill of Rights. Presents a detailed assessment of the 1968 Indian Civil Rights Act.

SEE ALSO: 1924, Indian Citizenship Act; 1934, Indian Reorganization Act; 1953, Termination Resolution; 1969, Alcatraz Occupation; 1971, Alaska Native Claims Settlement Act; 1972, Trail of Broken Treaties; 1973, Wounded Knee Occupation; 1978, American Indian Religious Freedom Act; 1988, Indian Gaming Regulatory Act.

1968 ■ FAIR HOUSING ACT: *legislation that prohibits discrimination in housing helps to break racial enclaves in residential neighborhoods, promoting upward mobility for minorities*

DATE: April 11, 1968

LOCALE: Washington, D.C.

CATEGORIES: African American history; Civil rights; Laws and acts

KEY FIGURES:

Edward William Brooke (born 1919), Republican senator from Massachusetts and cosponsor of the Fair Housing Act

Everett McKinley Dirksen (1896-1969), Republican senator from Illinois

Lyndon Baines Johnson (1908-1973), thirty-sixth president of the United States, 1963-1969

Walter Frederick Mondale (born 1928), Democratic senator from Minnesota and cosponsor of the Fair Housing Act

SUMMARY OF EVENT. The Civil Rights Act of 1866 provided that all citizens should have the same rights "to inherit, purchase, lease, sell, hold, and convey real and personal property," but the law was never enforced. Instead, such federal agencies as the Farmers Home Administration, the Federal Housing Administration, and the Veterans Administration financially supported segregated housing until 1962, when President John F. Kennedy issued Executive Order 11063 to stop the practice.

California passed a general nondiscrimination law in 1959 and an explicit fair housing law in 1963. In 1964, voters enacted Proposition 14, an initiative to repeal the 1963 statute and the applicability of the 1959 law to housing. When a landlord in Santa Ana refused to rent to an African American in 1963, the latter sued, thus challenging Proposition 14. The California Supreme Court, which heard the case in 1966, ruled that Proposition 14 was contrary to the Fourteenth Amendment to the U.S. Constitution, because it was not neutral on the matter of housing discrimination; instead, based on the context in which it was adopted, Proposition 14 served to legitimate and promote discrimination. On appeal, the U.S. Supreme Court let the California Supreme Court decision stand in *Reitman v. Mulkey* (1967).

President Lyndon B. Johnson had hoped to include housing discrimination as a provision in the comprehensive Civil Rights Act of 1964, but he demurred when Southern senators threatened to block the nomination of Robert Weaver as the first African American cabinet appointee. After 1964, Southern members of Congress were adamantly opposed to any expansion of civil rights. Although Johnson urged passage of a federal law against housing discrimination in requests to Congress in 1966 and 1967, there was no mention of the idea during his State of the Union address in 1968. Liberal members of Congress pressed the issue regardless, and Southern senators responded by threatening a filibuster. This threat emboldened Senators Edward W. Brooke and Walter F. Mondale, a moderate Republican and a liberal Democrat, to cosponsor fair housing legislation, but they needed the support of conservative midwestern Republicans to break a filibuster. Illinois Republican senator Everett Dirksen arranged a compromise whereby housing discrimination would be declared illegal, but federal enforcement power would be minimal.

In the wake of *Reitman v. Mulkey*, the assassination of Martin Luther King, Jr., on April 4, 1968, and subsequent urban riots, Congress established fair housing as a national priority on April 10 by adopting Titles VIII and IX of the Civil Rights Act of 1968, also known as the Fair Housing Act or Open Housing Act. Signed by Johnson on the following day, the law originally prohibited discrimination in housing on the basis of race, color, religion, or national origin. In 1974, an amendment expanded the coverage to include sex (gender)

discrimination; in 1988, the law was extended to protect persons with disabilities and families with children younger than eighteen years of age.

Title VIII prohibits discrimination in the sale or rental of dwellings, in the financing of housing, in advertising, in the use of a multiple listing service, and in practices that "otherwise make unavailable or deny" housing, a phrase that some courts have interpreted to outlaw exclusionary zoning, mortgage redlining, and racial steering. Blockbusting, the practice of inducing a white homeowner to sell to a minority buyer in order to frighten others on the block to sell their houses at a loss, is also prohibited. It is not necessary to show intent in order to prove discrimination; policies, practices, and procedures that have the effect of excluding minorities, women, handicapped persons, and children are illegal, unless otherwise deemed reasonable. Title VIII, as amended in 1988, covers persons who believe that they are adversely affected by a discriminatory policy, practice, or procedure, even before they incur damages.

The law applies to about 80 percent of all housing in the United States. One exception to the statute is a single-family house sold or rented without the use of a broker and without discriminatory advertising, when the owner owns no more than three such houses and sells only one house in a two-year period. Neither does the statute apply to a four-unit dwelling if the owner lives in one of the units, the so-called Mrs.-Murphy's-rooming-house exception. Dwellings owned by private clubs or religious organizations that rent to their own members on a noncommercial basis are also exempt.

Enforcement of the statute was left to the secretary of the Department of Housing and Urban Development (HUD). Complaints originally had to be filed within 180 days of the offending act, but in 1988, this period was amended to one year. HUD has estimated that there are about two million instances of housing discrimination each year, although formal complaints have averaged only forty thousand per year. The U.S. attorney general can bring a civil suit against a flagrant violator of the law.

According to the law, HUD automatically refers complaints to local agencies that administer "substantially equivalent" fair housing laws. HUD can act if the local agencies fail to do so, but initially was expected only to use conference, conciliation, and persuasion to bring about voluntary compliance. The Fair Housing Amendments Act of 1988 authorized an administrative law tribunal to hear cases that cannot be settled by persuasion. The administrative law judges have the power to issue cease and desist orders to offending parties.

HUD has used "testers" to show discrimination. For example, a team of blacks and whites might arrange to have an African American apply for a rental; if turned down, the black tester would contact a white tester to ascertain whether the landlord were willing to rent to a white instead. That testers have standing to sue was established by the U.S. Supreme Court in *Havens v. Coleman* (1982).

Under the administrative law procedure, penalties are up to

ten thousand dollars for the first offense, twenty-five thousand dollars for the second offense, and fifty thousand dollars for each offense thereafter. Attorneys' fees and court costs can be recovered by the prevailing party. In 1988, civil penalties in a suit filed by the U.S. attorney general were established as up to fifty thousand dollars for the first offense and one hundred thousand dollars for each offense thereafter.

Title IX of the law prohibits intimidation or attempted injury of anyone filing a housing discrimination complaint. A violator can be assessed a criminal penalty of one thousand dollars and/or sentenced to one year in jail. If a complainant is actually injured, the penalty can increase to ten thousand dollars and/or ten years of imprisonment. If a complainant is killed, the penalty is life imprisonment.

Under the laws of some states, a complainant filing with a state agency must waive the right to pursue a remedy under federal law. In 1965, a couple sought to purchase a home in a St. Louis suburban housing development, only to be told by the realtor that the home was not available because one of the spouses was African American. Invoking the Civil Rights Act of 1866, the couple sued the real estate developer, and the case went to the Supreme Court. In *Jones v. Mayer* (1968), the Court decided that the Civil Rights Act of 1866 did permit a remedy against housing discrimination by private parties.

The effect of the 1968 Fair Housing Act, however, has been minimal. Without a larger supply of affordable housing, many African Americans in particular have nowhere to move in order to enjoy integrated housing. Federal subsidies for low-cost housing, under such legislation as the Housing and Urban Development Act of 1968 and the Housing and Community Development Act of 1974, have declined significantly since the 1980's. Conscientious private developers are confronted with the text of a law that aims to provide integrated housing but proscribes achieving integration by establishing quotas to ensure a mixed racial composition among those who seek to buy or rent dwelling units.

—*Michael Haas*

ADDITIONAL READING:

Kushner, James A. *Fair Housing: Discrimination in Real Estate, Community Development, and Revitalization.* Colorado Springs: McGraw-Hill, 1983. A compendium of all legislation and litigation. Supplements issued annually.

Metcalf, George R. *Fair Housing Comes of Age.* New York: Greenwood Press, 1988. A comprehensive evaluation of the precedent, purposes, and problems of enacting, implementing, and enforcing fair housing legislation.

Schwemm, Robert G., ed. *The Fair Housing Act After Twenty Years.* New Haven, Conn.: Yale Law School, 1989. Proceedings of a conference held at Yale Law School in March, 1988, involving twenty-two recognized authorities, who evaluated the political and social impediments to achieving nondiscrimination in housing.

SEE ALSO: 1954, *Brown v. Board of Education*; 1955, Montgomery Bus Boycott; 1957, Little Rock School Desegregation Crisis; 1964, Civil Rights Act of 1964; 1988, Civil Rights Restoration Act.

1968 ■ TRUDEAU ERA IN CANADA:
Trudeau's administration inaugurates a period of dramatic changes in the nation's constitutional structure

DATE: June 25, 1968-June 30, 1984
LOCALE: Canada
CATEGORIES: Canadian history; Government and politics
KEY FIGURES:
René Lévesque (1922-1987), leader of the Parti Québécois and premier of Quebec
Jean Marchand (born 1918), trade union leader, federal cabinet minister, and speaker of the Canadian Senate
Gérard Pelletier (born 1919), secretary of state for external affairs, Canadian ambassador to France, and permanent representative to the United Nations
Pierre Elliott Trudeau (born 1919), prime minister of Canada, 1968-1979 and 1980-1984

SUMMARY OF EVENT. Pierre Elliott Trudeau, one of modern Canada's most remarkable leaders, was born in Montreal on October 18, 1919. The son of a millionaire, he grew up speaking English and French with equal facility. Trudeau attended the prestigious Collège Jean-de-Brébeuf, received his law degree from the University of Montreal in 1943, and did further study at Harvard University, the École des Sciences Politiques de Paris, and the London School of Economics. From 1949 to 1951, he worked with the Privy Council Office in Ottawa, Ontario, then returned to teach law at the University of Montreal.

Trudeau quickly established a reputation as a man keenly interested in civil liberties and workers' rights. In particular, he fought against the oppressive regime of Maurice Duplessis, the long-serving Quebec premier who held the province in a tight political grip. Trudeau also questioned the insular values and innate conservatism of French Canadian society. To this end, he cofounded the *Cité libre* in 1961, a lively journal in which some of the most talented and progressive French Canadians of the time debated the future of their society. It was during this period that the two guiding principles of Trudeau's career emerged: He passionately believed in the freedom of the individual, and he wanted to counter the rising tide of Quebec sovereignism. Trudeau maintained that if Canadian federalism could be rejuvenated, if it could show itself capable of allowing the French language and Québécois culture to flourish within the Canadian state, then sovereignist sentiments could be quashed.

In 1965, along with two close colleagues, Jean Marchand and Gérard Pelletier, Trudeau entered federal politics as a Liberal. All three were elected that year, and in 1967, Trudeau was appointed minister of justice and attorney general. He piloted legislation through the House of Commons that liberalized existing laws concerning divorce, homosexuality, and abortion. In 1968, he was chosen leader of the Liberal Party

The charismatic Pierre Elliott Trudeau served as Canada's prime minister from 1968 until (with a brief interruption) 1984. Among his chief goals during his administration was tolerance for a multicultural and multilingual nation to the end of maintaining a united Canada. (AP/Wide World Photos)

and won a stunning electoral victory. During his lengthy career, he would stand in five general elections and serve as prime minister from 1968 to 1979, and again from 1980 to 1984.

His extraordinary personality contrasted sharply with that of most Canadian politicians. He was charismatic, flamboyant, projecting a youthful, playboy image; on his serious side, Trudeau was an intellectual, widely read in the classics and possessing razor-sharp debating and analytical skills. Loyal and affectionate to friends, he could also be dismissive toward his enemies. Shortly after the election of 1968, he set about his main task: to fight Quebec sovereignism while simultaneously transforming Canada into a bilingual country. The Official Languages Act (1969) mandated that the federal government offer services across Canada in French and English in order to make Quebecers feel that all of Canada was their homeland, not simply Quebec province, but this policy was misunderstood and bitterly resented in western Canada. In October, 1970, the Front de Libération du Québec, a terrorist organization dedicated to achieving an independent Quebec, kidnapped the British trade commissioner and the provincial minister of labor. Trudeau pressed the Quebec government to act firmly, sent the Canadian army into Quebec, and proclaimed the War Measures Act, which suspended many civil liberties. The episode became known as the October Crisis, and for his actions Trudeau was criticized vigorously by civil libertarians.

Opinion polls, however, revealed his measures to be immensely popular.

Like many other Western leaders during the 1970's, Trudeau seemed unable to cope with devastating inflation and high unemployment. Moreover, the election of a sovereignist party in Quebec in 1976 suggested that his policies had failed to contain the rise of Quebec nationalism. His Liberal Party lost the 1979 election, and Trudeau announced his retirement from politics, but fate intervened. The new Conservative government was unexpectedly defeated in a Commons vote, and new elections were called for in 1980. Because there was too little time to settle the leadership issue within the Liberal Party, Trudeau was asked to lead the party once again. That he did, winning a clear majority.

Now began the most important work of Trudeau's career: securing for Canada a new constitution, creating a federal Charter of Rights and Freedoms, and defeating the sovereignist movement in Quebec. In 1980, Quebec held a referendum on the issue of separation from Canada. Initially, prospects looked good for the sovereignists, but Trudeau threw himself and the resources of the federal government into the antisovereignist movement. The result was that the sovereignists lost the referendum by a decisive margin of three to two.

Trudeau then set about to give Canada a new constitution. He envisioned Canada as a politically mature country that should eliminate its constitutional dependence upon Great

Britain. The centerpiece of the new constitution was a Charter of Rights and Freedoms, establishing individual rights for all Canadians as well as collective rights for certain minority groups. While Trudeau's interest in civil liberties was genuine, it was equally true that he viewed the new charter as a means of increasing the prestige and power of the federal government, especially the Supreme Court of Canada, at the expense of provincial autonomy. Initially, opposition to the new constitution and charter was strong, not only from Quebec but from most provinces as well. Provincial premiers feared the centralizing trends of the federal government and the loss of regional and provincial powers. Through skillful negotiating, which included all sides resorting to political trickery, unkept promises, and backroom deals, Trudeau managed to obtain the assent of all provinces to accept the new constitution, with the important exception of Quebec. In these negotiations, Trudeau was able to outwit his nemesis, René Lévesque, the sovereignist premier of Quebec. The new Constitution Act was signed into law by the Queen of England, Elizabeth II, at an elaborate ceremony held in Ottawa on April 17, 1982.

Foreign policy never engaged Trudeau as domestic events did, but he did try in an unsystematic way to make Canada more independent of the United States and to project a more forceful image for Canada on the international stage. The Foreign Investment Review Agency (1973) and National Energy Program (1980) were attempts to prevent foreign domination of Canada's economy. Trudeau's government recognized the communist People's Republic of China, improved trade with communist regimes, reduced the number of Canadian soldiers serving in the North Atlantic Treaty Organization, and supported a North-South dialogue on removing the vast disparity of wealth between the two areas. In 1983 and 1984, Trudeau went on a series of peace missions to a number of countries in the hope of reducing Cold War tensions, but despite much publicity, he achieved little. He often was accused of lacking consistency in foreign policy, ignoring the advice of diplomatic experts, and acting as a dilettante.

Despite his achievements in the constitutional realm, he still was bedeviled by economic problems; the western provinces continued to remain disaffected by his federalist policies, especially on energy issues; and he had largely alienated the powerful province of Quebec by forcing an unpopular constitution upon it. Feeling his major work was done, he resigned from office on June 30, 1984. This move spared him from the electoral debacle to come, when in September of that year the Liberal Party went down to its worst-ever electoral defeat—a disaster largely crafted by Trudeau himself. His retirement generally has been tranquil, save for his aggressive and successful opposition to the Meech Lake Accord (1987-1990), which would have amended the constitution in favor of Quebec. Despite all Trudeau's efforts to promote federalism and Canadian unity, Canada would witness an explosion of regional and provincial resentment against federal centralization in the years to come. —David C. Lukowitz

ADDITIONAL READING:

Clarkson, Stephen, and Christina McCall. *Trudeau and Our Times.* 2 vols. Toronto: McClelland and Stewart, 1990-1994. Scholarly, entertaining, and balanced, this is arguably the finest study of the Trudeau era.

Granatstein, J. L., and Robert Bothwell. *Pirouette: Pierre Trudeau and Canadian Foreign Policy.* Toronto: University of Toronto Press, 1990. This well-documented study by two able scholars claims that Trudeau's foreign policy tended to lack commitment and consistency, resulting in few substantive accomplishments.

Laforest, Guy. *Trudeau and the End of a Canadian Dream.* Translated by Paul Leduc Browne and Michelle Weinroth. Montreal: McGill-Queens University Press, 1995. Argues persuasively that Trudeau's confrontational policies shattered any possible accommodation between Quebec nationalism and Canadian federalism.

Trudeau, Pierre. *Federalism and the French Canadians.* New York: St. Martin's Press, 1968. A collection of speeches and articles by Trudeau on the relationship between Quebec and the federal government.

_____. *Memoirs.* Toronto: McClelland and Stewart, 1993. Relatively brief and superficial, with little additional information about major events in Trudeau's career but with excellent photographs.

SEE ALSO: 1963, Pearson Becomes Canada's Prime Minister; 1969, Canada's Official Languages Act; 1970, October Crisis; 1978, Canada's Immigration Act of 1976; 1979, Clark Is Elected Canada's Prime Minister; 1982, Canada's Constitution Act; 1984, Mulroney Era in Canada.

1968 ■ CHICAGO RIOTS: *police and protesters clash outside a hotel housing the Democratic National Convention*

DATE: August 25-30, 1968
LOCALE: Chicago, Illinois
CATEGORIES: Government and politics; Organizations and institutions; Wars, uprisings, and civil unrest
KEY FIGURES:
Richard J. Daley (1902-1976), mayor of Chicago
Rennie Davis (born 1941),
David Dellinger (born 1915),
John Froines (born 1939),
Tom Hayden (born 1939),
Abbie Hoffman (1936-1989),
Jerry Rubin (1938-1994), and
Lee Weiner, political activists known as the Chicago Seven, tried on charges of incitement to riot
Julius Hoffman (1895-1983), federal district judge who presided over the trial of the Chicago Seven
Hubert Horatio Humphrey (1911-1978), U.S. vice president and Democratic presidential candidate

William Kunstler (1919-1995), attorney who defended the Chicago Seven

Eugene McCarthy (born 1916), Democratic presidential candidate who ran on an antiwar platform

Richard Milhous Nixon (1913-1994), Republican presidential candidate

Bobby Seale (born 1936), Black Panther Party founder arrested in the Chicago riots but tried separately from the Chicago Seven

SUMMARY OF EVENT. During the Democratic National Convention in August of 1968, activists from all over the United States arrived in Chicago to protest President Lyndon Johnson's policy in Vietnam. The demonstrators slept in public parks and openly challenged the authority of police officers. The Walker Commission, appointed to investigate the cause of the violence that erupted, found that "most of those intending to join the major demonstrations scheduled during convention week did not plan to enter the convention, did not plan aggressive acts of physical provocation against the authorities, and did not plan to use rallies of demonstrators to stage an assault against any person, institution, or place of business. But while it is clear that most of the protesters in Chicago had no intention of initiating violence, this is not to say that they did not expect it to develop."

Mayor Richard Daley of Chicago had openly sought the Democratic convention as a means of bestowing prestige on his city. Beset by rioting earlier in the year, Chicago's image would benefit from endorsement by the party. Daley promised security above all else, and the party accepted. Daley and his supporters controlled the security apparatus of the city as well as most of its infrastructure, and they intended to maintain security at all costs, for the people of the city and for the convention. The demands of the security forces placed restrictions on the movements of reporters and television technicians, fostering tension that was further complicated by an unresolved communication workers' strike.

Police and demonstrators skirmished during the week of the convention. Many young people converged on the Michigan Avenue area, some planning to protest, others simply watching. Amid the turmoil of convention week, young people in tie-dyed clothing slept in public parks, bathed only occasionally, shaved infrequently, and in the process added a new ingredient to an already tense Chicago. In such a confusing environment, it was difficult for older middle-class people and the police to differentiate between spectators and instigators, or between serious protest and playful publicity stunts. One group mocked the police, whom they called "pigs," by nominating an actual barnyard pig, Pigasus, for the presidency—a move guaranteed to arouse emotions. The pig was promptly arrested, demonstrating that the police, at least, saw no humor in the nomination.

Aside from Pigasus, the immediate issues of contention between the protesters and the police concerned trespassing, crowd movement control, fire safety, and traffic flow. Each side feared the other, and in the crowded streets of Chicago

epithets were hurled, an unidentified person threw a rock, and police began moving aggressively to subdue the crowd on Sunday, August 25. Using clubs and tear gas, the police attacked the crowd indiscriminately at first. Protesters continued their demonstrations on Monday and Tuesday. On Wednesday, David Dellinger, leader of the National Mobilization Committee to End the War in Vietnam, followed through on his threat to march his supporters from Lincoln Park to the convention site. The protesters selected routes that carried them across private property, providing city officials with a convenient reason for rejecting the request for a parade permit.

That Wednesday, August 28, news reports and rumors circulating on the street gave protesters and onlookers the impression that Hubert Humphrey and the convention had conspired to silence any dissent on Vietnam policy. The crowd grew restless, and in the late afternoon, a National Guard commander, fearing Dellinger's threats of confrontation, ordered the use of tear gas to disperse the protesters. Dellinger's forces converged on the site by sunset, carrying megaphones and portable public address systems to direct the amorphous crowd. Police apparently charged the demonstrators from a side street and violently dispersed them, attacking protesters and bystanders with equal force. Television and newspaper reporters were singled out for special attention and received violent beatings.

Within two hours, pictures of the confrontation were on network television. The news media presented the story as an unprovoked attack on peaceful protesters. Believing most Chicagoans supported his position, Daley defended the actions of the police and denounced the demonstrators as outside agitators bent on embarrassing the political system. Some members of the Democratic Party called for a forum to examine the protests and the police response. Furious that fellow Democrats would even discuss the matter on the convention floor, Daley exploded in anger, hurling anti-Semitic expletives at Senator Abraham Ribicoff of Connecticut when Ribicoff questioned his motives.

The following night, as the business of the convention was concluded, police continued their tense watch over the city. From the Hilton Hotel, an unidentified person or persons threw objects—allegedly beer cans, ashtrays, even ball bearings—down onto the police. Police, evidently acting without explicit orders, stormed the hotel where the convention was winding down and attempted to round up supporters of antiwar candidate Eugene McCarthy, who had just lost the nomination to the incumbent vice president, Humphrey. Finding the students playing bridge, officers arrested several for "threatening a sit-in." McCarthy, who had taken great pains to make sure that those connected with his campaign had stayed out of the fracas, stepped in to protect his supporters, many of whom were college students, and the police retreated.

After the riots, Humphrey found himself having to defend Johnson's domestic and foreign policies, policies that many associated with the collapse of law and order evident in the riots themselves. Republican candidate Richard Nixon's campaign staff capitalized on this by creating television commercials that openly accused Humphrey of being unconcerned about, or incompetent to handle, the increasingly tense domestic situation. Nixon won the election by appealing to the law-and-order vote.

As a result of the riots, seven sociopolitical activists were tried in federal district court on charges of conspiracy and incitement to riot. These activists—Jerry Rubin, Abbie Hoffman, David Dellinger, Rennie Davis, Tom Hayden, Lee Weiner, and John Froines—became known as the Chicago Seven. An eighth, Bobby Seale, was tried separately. During the trial of the Chicago Seven, Judge Julius Hoffman ignored defense objections, frequently refused to allow the defendants and their attorneys to pursue their defense strategy, and repeatedly ridiculed one defense lawyer's surname. Judge Hoffman's openly confrontational approach was aggravated by the defendants' outspoken disregard for matters of judicial etiquette; they interrupted the formality of the proceedings with frequent jokes and occasional profanity. During his trial, Seale was placed on the stand while bound and gagged, and was jailed for contempt of court.

All of the Chicago Seven were acquitted on federal conspiracy charges. Five were convicted of incitement to riot and sentenced to five years in prison. All seven were sentenced by Judge Hoffman on various contempt-of-court citations; the contempt sentences ranged from six months to slightly more than four years, with attorney William Kunstler singled out for harsh treatment. The trial polarized American society, with many youth seeing their lifestyle on trial and many adults seeing their society under attack.   —*Stephen Wallace Taylor*

ADDITIONAL READING:

Elzy, Martin I. "Illinois Viewed from the Johnson White House." *Journal of the Illinois State Historical Society* 74, no. 1 (Spring, 1981): 2-16. Places the riots in the context of the president's dependent political relationship with Illinois politicians. Offers little discussion of the riots' aftermath.

Farber, David. "'Welcome to Chicago.'" *Chicago History* 17, nos. 1/2 (Spring/Summer, 1988): 62-77. Contrasts the localism of Daley and his people with the national focus of the protesters and the media. Biased in favor of Daley, but provides useful insight into the mayor's motives.

Leinwohl, Stef. "August 1968." *Chicago History* 17, nos. 1/2 (Spring/Summer, 1988): 78-105. Brief memoirs of a professional photographer who covered the protests, accompanied by an excellent and vivid photo essay. Generally sympathetic to protesters and somewhat antipathetic to police.

Levine, Mark L., et al. *Tales of Hoffman*. New York: Bantam, 1970. Selections from the twenty-two-hundred-page transcript of the trial of the Chicago Seven are assembled here, with no claim of objectivity. The pseudonarrative framework ably demonstrates the confrontational atmosphere of the trial.

Walker, Daniel. *Rights in Conflict*. New York: Signet Books, 1968. An official report to the National Commission on the Causes and Prevention of Violence, which places a large share of the blame for the riots on Mayor Daley.

White, Theodore H. *The Making of the President, 1968.*

New York: Pocket Books, 1970. An exceptionally detailed and balanced first-person description of the election campaign of 1968. Chapter 9 includes a substantial description of the riots and their impact.

SEE ALSO: 1943, Urban Race Riots; 1963, King Delivers His "I Have a Dream" Speech; 1964, Vietnam War; 1964, Berkeley Free Speech Movement; 1965, Voting Rights Act; 1965, Watts Riot; 1967, Long, Hot Summer; 1980, Miami Riots; 1992, Los Angeles Riots.

1968 ■ NIXON IS ELECTED PRESIDENT: *the "silent majority's" election of a Republican repudiates Johnson's policies in Vietnam and marks the start of the most controversial presidency in U.S. history*

DATE: November 5, 1968
LOCALE: United States
CATEGORY: Government and politics
KEY FIGURES:

Spiro Theodore Agnew (1918-1996), Republican vice presidential candidate

Hubert Horatio Humphrey (1911-1978), Democratic presidential candidate

Curtis E. Lemay (1906-1990), American Independent Party vice presidential candidate

Eugene Joseph McCarthy (born 1916), Democratic presidential candidate

Edmund Sixtus Muskie (1914-1996), Democratic vice presidential candidate

Richard Milhous Nixon (1913-1994), Republican presidential candidate and thirty-seventh president of the United States, 1969-1974

Nelson Aldrich Rockefeller (1908-1979), Republican presidential candidate

George Corley Wallace (born 1919), American Independent Party presidential candidate

SUMMARY OF EVENT. The tone of the office of the presidency was established from its beginning. The primary qualities embodied in the office included all the synonyms of the word "integrity," plus dignity, humanitarianism, leadership in war and peace, and an authoritative approach to domestic problems. This list of attributes is the mark left by the first man to hold the office, George Washington. Outstanding leaders succeeded Washington—John Adams, Thomas Jefferson, Abraham Lincoln—to enhance and solidify the image of the office. Theodore Roosevelt rescued the presidency from the doldrums, and through it helped to solidify the position of the United States as a world power. Woodrow Wilson elevated the leadership aspects of the office still further; Franklin D. Roosevelt took charge at a time of national dismay and despair and through the force of his leadership brought the country through its most trying times since the Civil War.

The 1960's brought another crisis to the nation, which tested the presidency of Lyndon Baines Johnson. As a result of the social unrest sparked by the war in Vietnam, the nation's racial problems, and the ambitious government programs of Johnson's Great Society, the president's political base had collapsed by the beginning of 1968, and the Tet Offensive in Vietnam forced Johnson to withdraw as a candidate for reelection in March, 1968. Elected only four years before by the highest percentage of the popular vote in history, Johnson had become the focus for dissatisfaction and disappointment across the spectrum of U.S. politics.

The political vacuum created by Johnson's decision not to run for reelection soon was filled by a number of eager aspirants. Chief among them were Hubert Humphrey, the incumbent vice president; Robert Kennedy, the heir to "Camelot" and his slain brother, John F. Kennedy; and Eugene McCarthy, a Minnesota senator and bitter enemy of the administration's Vietnam War policy, often credited with being the man who

Revered by some, reviled by others, and ultimately a victim to his own drive to retain the presidency at any cost, Richard Nixon oversaw significant foreign policy advances—bringing the Vietnam War to a close, negotiating rapprochement with communist China, and achieving détente with the Soviet Union—as well as social legislation such as the Twenty-sixth Amendment, granting eighteen-year-olds the vote, and the Equal Employment Opportunity Act. His fatal flaw resided in an inability to understand the deeply felt idealism and resentments of many of his constituents, and ultimately his failure to defer to the limitations of law. (Library of Congress)

"dethroned" President Johnson. The Republican possibilities to run against them were George Romney, who fell early in the campaign, partly because of an unfortunate public reply to a question on Vietnam; Richard Nixon, the former vice president who had lost to Kennedy in 1960; and Nelson Rockefeller, governor of New York and a perennial candidate, who dropped out of the race for the nomination, then reentered when it was too late. Offstage stood Alabama governor George Wallace, a right-winger who was gathering strength from opponents of racial integration, widespread crime and violence, and big government.

Issues were abundant in 1968, but the prime ones—after the violent conflict over the Vietnam War—were civil rights and the attendant integration, poverty, and welfare pressures; riots and revolutions in cities and on campuses; extreme political and ideological polarization; a credibility gap at the highest levels; a not-inconsequential generation gap; and crime in the streets.

The Republican convention was held at Miami Beach in early August. It seemed a foregone conclusion that the nomination belonged to Nixon, yet there were diehards. Rockefeller, who earlier had hoped to package Romney as the "Republican with a future," had himself been inclined to run but had withdrawn his name on March 21, 1968. Five weeks later, he reconsidered and became a serious candidate. Waging a vigorous campaign that was aimed at the young, African Americans, and those Republicans who yearned for new leadership, Rockefeller made a gallant effort, but to no avail. A more serious challenge to Nixon came from the governor of California, Ronald Reagan, but Nixon, with the help of his Southern allies, retained control of the nomination. At Miami Beach, the first ballot gave Nixon 692 votes, Rockefeller 277; no one else was close. Nixon selected as his running mate Spiro Agnew, the governor of Maryland—a surprising choice to many—and the ticket was set.

The strife and controversy attendant upon the Democratic convention at Chicago late in August did little to reassure the average U.S. voter that all was well or soon would be. Robert Kennedy had fallen to an assassin's bullet in June, and McCarthy had no real professional base. It was left for Humphrey to inherit the nomination after an abortive effort of Southern delegates to offer Johnson (who did not even attend the convention) as a candidate to succeed himself, and a proposed effort to draft Edward Kennedy, which failed to materialize. Rioting in the streets by antiwar demonstrators and Chicago police added to the impression of disarray among the Democrats.

There was little similarity between the ways in which the two presidential campaigns were run. Nixon's was extremely well financed, and there were virtually no limits on his expenditures. On the other hand, the Democrats were poorly financed, which severely handicapped Humphrey in his efforts. It has been suggested by some political pundits that given two more weeks and another few million dollars, Humphrey might well have overtaken Nixon. In the late polls, the Democratic candidate was gaining on Nixon and closing the gap fast. A late peace initiative in Vietnam by Lyndon Johnson contributed to the Humphrey surge in late October and early November. Nixon used back-channel diplomacy with South Vietnam to dilute the effect of Johnson's peace offensive.

During the fall, Nixon campaigned relatively little, believing firmly that with the nomination he had won the election. Reporters often complained of Nixon's aloofness, claiming that he acted as though he were already president. Such strategy was no doubt based on Nixon's belief that in the minds of most voters, his opponent was "Johnson's man" and thus doomed regardless of what he might do. Furthermore, Nixon had made special efforts to court the South, and he counted on that fact and on the popularity of Wallace to cut deeply into an important block of Humphrey's natural territory.

The election was closer than many experts expected. When the votes were counted, Nixon had 31,770,237 popular votes to 31,270,552 for Humphrey and 9,906,141 for Wallace. In the all-important electoral votes, however, Nixon won handily, 302 to 191 for Humphrey and 45 for Wallace. Although the issues were many, none seemed as clear-cut as "Johnson's War." Humphrey was stuck with it; Nixon promised to end it. Despite the numerous domestic problems, especially the race question, the war situation was the big issue, and Nixon represented a change in the status quo. Many presidential elections hinge on minor issues or even personalities, but the election of 1968 revolved around a deep schism in the body politic. The continued flow of U.S. blood in distant lands, where citizens had no emotional ties and no national commitment, was intolerable. A change of command in Washington, D.C., seemed the only hope—and the message was delivered at the polls on November 5, 1968.

The administration that this election brought to power was to end in disgrace in the Watergate scandal of 1973-1974. Although Nixon did achieve the end of direct U.S. military involvement in Vietnam, the United States failed to secure the "peace with honor" that Nixon had promised in the 1968 campaign. The most enduring result of the election was to open a prolonged period of Republican dominance in national politics, based on the electoral coalition that Nixon had forged in 1968.   —*Frank N. Magill, updated by Lewis L. Gould*

ADDITIONAL READING:

Ambrose, Stephen. *Nixon: The Triumph of a Politician, 1962-1972*. New York: Simon & Schuster, 1989. A clear, readable treatment of the campaign, from the point of view of the winner.

Carter, Dan T. *The Politics of Rage: George Wallace, the Origins of the New Conservatism, and the Transformation of American Politics*. New York: Simon & Schuster, 1995. Examines the effect that Wallace's candidacy had on the Nixon campaign and the outcome of the election.

Chester, Lewis, Godfrey Hodgson, and Bruce Page. *An American Melodrama: The Presidential Campaign of 1968*. New York: Viking Press, 1969. The best of the contemporaneous accounts of the election. Fascinating for its insights into U.S. politics from a British perspective.

Farber, David. *Chicago '68*. Chicago: University of Chicago Press, 1988. A thorough and thoughtful examination of the controversial Democratic National Convention in 1968 and the violence that occurred in the streets outside the convention hall.

Gould, Lewis L. *1968: The Election That Changed America*. Chicago: Ivan Dee, 1993. Argues that the race issue had a greater impact in the minds of the voters in 1968 than did the war in Vietnam.

Kaiser, Charles. *1968 in America*. New York: Weidenfeld & Nicolson, 1988. Strong on the cultural and social setting of the turbulent events of 1968.

SEE ALSO: 1964, Vietnam War; 1970, United States Invades Cambodia; 1971, Devaluation of the Dollar; 1972, Rapprochement with China; 1972, Watergate Affair; 1973, U.S. Troops Leave Vietnam; 1973, Détente with the Soviet Union; 1974, Nixon Resigns.

1969 ■ STONEWALL INN RIOTS: *police harassment of patrons of a homosexual bar results in confrontations that mark the beginning of the Gay Rights movement*

DATE: June 28-July 2, 1969
LOCALE: New York City
CATEGORY: Civil rights

SUMMARY OF EVENT. The Stonewall Inn was located on Christopher Street in Greenwich Village, the heart of New York City's homosexual community in 1969. Primarily a gay bar, it was frequented by persons from all segments of what was then called "gay" culture—drag queens, transvestites, and clean-cut, chino-clad college students—with patrons ranging in age from their teens to their forties. To refer to the Stonewall Inn as a "bar," however, is inaccurate. It had only two sinks, in which glasses were dipped throughout the evening, to be used over and over by different patrons, and ice was continually purchased from a neighboring grocery store. The drinks were continually watered down, and bouncers routinely made their way through the clientele to ensure that patrons were buying drinks. Such was the state of the gay bar scene in 1969, even in relatively liberal New York.

Like so many gay bars of the time, the Stonewall Inn was owned and operated by reputed Mafia figures who saw the opportunity to garner an immense profit from homosexuals, because prohibitions against same-sex dancing and dress codes mandating proper female and male attire were subject to enforcement by the New York Police Department's vice squad. It was an established fact that the Stonewall Inn's owners were paying bribes to the local police—as did many establishments that catered to homosexuals—to prevent police enforcement of existing vice laws. Thus, in spite of watered-down drinks, poor sanitation, and the ever-present possibility of arrest (which could lead to disclosure of a patron's homosexuality), places like the Stonewall Inn offered at least a venue in which gays could be themselves. Police payoffs notwithstanding, the neighborhood constabulary would often visit clubs like the Stonewall Inn to make arrests for liquor violations such as underage drinking or to harass the clientele as a way of reminding negligent bar owners not to be tardy with bribe money.

In the early-morning hours of June 28, 1969, a detail of eight New York City police officers under the command of Seymour Pine raided the Stonewall Inn. The raid was typical of previous raids that had been conducted there: employees, transvestites, and underage patrons were singled out and detained by police, arrested, and escorted to a waiting patrol wagon. Those arrested typically offered little resistance; those detained would be taken to the local precinct, given a court appearance date, and released soon after posting a personal recognizance bond.

The area around the Stonewall Inn was a well-known "cruising" area for homosexuals, often attracting fairly large crowds. That was certainly true on June 28: Many gays had taken to the streets to vent their grief at the death of Judy Garland, an entertainer venerated by the gay community. While being led to the wagon by the police, amid a growing crowd of onlookers as well as patrons escaping the police bust, many of the more flamboyant homosexuals struck poses and flaunted their attire, drawing whistles and applause from the crowd—in effect, egging the crowd on. Some people in the crowd (variously estimated at between four hundred and one thousand) started throwing coins at the police—symbolically mocking police corruption—and hurling insults and curses while the officers attempted to place those arrested in the patrol wagon. While there is no consensus concerning the event that precipitated the riot, virtually all observers agree that coins and insults soon gave way to bottles, bricks, garbage cans, and dog feces, and the police retaliated with their fists and billy clubs.

When a brick broke the glass window at the front of the Stonewall Inn, police began retreating into the bar, drawing their guns and nervously awaiting the next action by members of the crowd. Someone sprayed lighter fluid through the front door, followed by a lit match, which started a small fire. The police quickly used a fire hose within the premises to extinguish the fire and to spray the increasingly hostile crowd as a means of dispersing it. Fearing that events were getting out of hand, Pine placed a call for help.

Help arrived in the form of the Tactical Patrol Force (TPF), which—armed with tear gas, batons, and face shields—walked in a wedge formation to clear the streets and quell the escalating disturbance. The crowd continued to shout insults and hurl objects at the police, often circling back behind their formation as means of escaping arrest. In response, the TPF broke ranks, indiscriminately clubbing onlookers and rioters alike. Some two hours after the initial arrival of the police, at 3:35 A.M., relative calm was restored, and the police emergency signal was canceled. In the wake of this initial foray, thirteen people (seven of them Stonewall employees) were arrested on a variety of charges, and four policemen, as well as an undetermined number in the crowd, were hurt.

The calm proved to be short-lived. Emboldened by the fact that homosexuals actually had fought back against police harassment, large numbers of people returned to the Stonewall Inn (which was closed due to the damage inflicted), and bottle-throwing and police retaliation continued for four days. Disturbances similar to those of the first night took place on July 2. Homosexuals carried leaflets and placards calling for an end to police harassment, gay bars that would be legal and free of Mafia control, and recognition of "gay power."

The latter demand is especially significant. While a number of gay organizations had pursued antidiscrimination legislation in the 1950's and 1960's, most of them were mainstream groups working for piecemeal change within establishment politics. After the Stonewall Inn riots, more activist gay rights organizations arose, such as the Gay Liberation Front and the Gay Activist Alliance. Drawing on the experiences, ideology, and tactics of the Civil Rights, antiwar, and women's movements, the movement for equality for homosexuals became more confrontational in its efforts to secure rights for all members of the gay community in the wake of the Stonewall Inn riots. Empowered by the events that transpired at the Stonewall Inn in the early morning hours of June 28, 1969, gay organizations began to work to secure basic human rights for homosexuals, eradicte homophobia, obtain funds for AIDS research and testing, and promote positive self-concepts for gay men and women.

—*Craig M. Eckert*

ADDITIONAL READING:

Cruikshank, Margaret. *The Gay and Lesbian Liberation Movement*. New York: Routledge, Chapman & Hall, 1992. Provides a brief overview of the Stonewall Inn riots and a first-person narrative of how the incident launched a more activist and determined gay rights movement.

Duberman, Martin. *Stonewall*. New York: Dutton, 1993. One of the definitive accounts of the riots, describing the personal, social, and political climate against which the riot is best understood and providing a detailed account of the riots. Outstanding bibliography, especially of many primarily gay periodicals.

Goldstein, Richard. "The Coming Crisis of Gay Rights." *The Village Voice* 39, no. 26 (June 28, 1994): 25-29. Thoughtful and provocative essay on the legacy of Stonewall, the status of the gay movement in the 1990's, and the need for an alliance of gays and feminists to promote individuality.

_____. "Stonewall Riots." *New York Magazine* 26, no. 16 (April 19, 1993): 120-122. Brief general overview of the riots and their legacy.

Marcus, Eric. *Making History: The Struggle for Gay and Lesbian Equal Rights, 1945-1990—An Oral History*. New York: HarperCollins, 1992. Part 3 contains vignettes of seven gay men and women describing what their lives were like during this period and how Stonewall affected them.

1969 ■ CANADA'S OFFICIAL LANGUAGES ACT: *the foundation of Canada's multi-language policy encourages the growth of a multicultural society*

DATE: July 9, 1969
LOCALE: Ottawa
CATEGORIES: Canadian history; Laws and acts
KEY FIGURES:
Lester B. Pearson (1897-1972) and
Pierre Elliott Trudeau (born 1919), Canadian prime
ministers and architects of the Official Languages Act

SUMMARY OF EVENT. The implementation of the Official Languages Act of 1969 was a crucial element of Prime Minister Pierre Elliott Trudeau's policy of maintaining a united Canada. It also was a major step in developing a policy enabling French, English, and immigrant and aboriginal communities to maintain their ethnicities and languages. To maintain national unity while promoting cultural diversity, Canada assumed that a workable language policy was crucial. Canada was unique, in that it attempted to implement a language policy designed to influence language usage in ways to serve the interests of the Canadian people—a mutable policy developed without establishing linguistic territoriality. The Official Languages Act of 1969 become the foundation to this process.

The language issue in Canada was not new. The conflict between the two major colonizing powers in North America, the French and the English, set the stage for ongoing contention. When the French territory was ceded to the British, the French were allowed to practice their Roman Catholic religion, and the French language continued to assert itself. Since then, a two-language and two-culture policy has been in effect. The Constitutional Act of 1791 divided the colony of Quebec into two units, Upper Canada and Lower Canada, where the majority of the Parliamentarians were Francophones. Although challenged in practice, administratively and legislatively, the French language remained vigorous. The Constitution of 1867, from which Canada claims its origins, institutionalized the use of French in the Quebec legislature and in some federal and Quebec courts. The constitution seemed to enable the French language and culture to spread. In addition to the right to use French in Quebec, Francophones were led to believe that as French settlers moved west, they would find adequate guarantees of linguistic rights elsewhere. Also, the French viewed the constitution as an agreement between two "founding people."

The next fifty years proved disastrous for the use of French. In 1890, Manitoba abrogated the use of French (which was not restored until 1985); Ontario abolished French schools in 1912; and limitations were imposed on instruction in French in other provinces. Francophones became increasingly confined to Quebec, with Montreal becoming an Anglophone area. It was the high birth rate of the French in Quebec that compensated for the large French emigration from Quebec to the United States and English-speaking immigrants flocking into Montreal. In spite of accommodations to have French presence in the courts, military, and other official bodies, it was clear that English was ascending over French or any other language. As a result of the majority rule principle and the decline of French language usage, the two peoples became cut off from each other—the French had to separate themselves or they would, under majority rule, lose to the English and become extinct.

By the 1960's, the language issue required serious attention. The French language was in rapid decline outside Quebec and, although less rapidly, inside the province as well. Within Quebec, the birthrate of the French had declined to one of the lowest in the world. It was becoming apparent that English was not only the language of North America but also the international language. Even Francophones were learning and using English.

This situation resulted in civil unrest and a movement to have Quebec separate from Canada. In 1963, Prime Minister Lester Pearson created the Royal Commission on Bilingualism and Biculturalism (the B & B Commission) to examine the relationship between English and French Canada. More specifically, the commission was asked to review and assess Canadian language policy. The primary concern was to promote a federal-provincial response to the crisis in English-French relations. The commission also had to consider the increasing number of Canadians who had no inborn allegiance to either French or English.

In its report, the commission rejected territorial solutions. It found, however, that the use of French had fallen behind English, for example, in public service, to a politically and socially unacceptable level. It urged that a new charter, founded on the concept of "equal partnership," be implemented at both the federal and provincial levels. It was in response to the commission's recommendations that the Official Languages Act of 1969 was created.

The B & B Commission endorsed the value of linguistic diversity as an "inestimable enrichment that Canadians cannot afford to lose. . . . Linguistic variety is unquestionably an advantage and its beneficial effects on the country are priceless." What happened eventually was the establishment of the "official languages," English and French, and the "heritage languages," recognized languages of other ethnic communities. Initially, the issue of heritage languages was not supported, but after pressure from other communities, three types of heritage programs were in place by the 1990's: instruction incorporated into the school curriculum, instruction in the school system but afterhours, and instruction that used school resources but was not part of the school program.

In the meantime, Canadian nationalism was rising, especially against U.S. policies concerning Vietnam. Outside economic and cultural influence on Canada was resented, especially in 1971, when Canada's economic dependency on the United States was made manifest—the United States could not buy enough of Canada's products, and Europe provided no help. In Quebec, the decline of French was becoming a prominent issue. In Montreal, riots promoting Quebec's nationalism became endemic. One particular disturbance was in 1968, when rioting had broken out at the Saint-Jean Baptiste Day parade, and Trudeau coolly faced a bottle-throwing crowd. The maintenance of a united Canada was a central issue for Trudeau. Dismissing the "two nations" vision of Canada, he argued that Canada must be a truly federal state with equality for all provinces, yet also a homeland for both French and English culture. The Official Languages Act became the key to this policy.

The Official Languages Act of 1969 was supported by the opposition as well as the party in power. Based on the findings of the B & B Commission, the act named French and English as the official languages and guaranteed official-language minorities in the country certain basic rights in dealing with the federal government and its various agencies. It was, however, the Francophone minority outside Quebec that needed such guarantees. The act also set forth a number of measures to provide the Francophone community with the same guarantees outside Quebec that the English enjoyed within Quebec. Parliament's intention was to place French on an equal footing with English as far as the federal government was concerned. The federal government improved its capacity to deal with Canadians in the official language of their choice and to allow public servants to use either language at work, in certain areas. Some provinces, such as Ontario and New Brunswick, provided government services in both languages and tried to implement their own language policies, particularly in regard to minority and second-language education.

As a result of the act, a commissioner of official languages was created and appointed—a linguistics ombudsman to report annually on the progress of implementing various provisions of the act. However, the commissioner had to devote much time to persuading Canadians that the reforms were necessary and just.

The act created a great deal of controversy. Some Anglophones complained that the act forced French on them. The act was also criticized for giving French a position it no longer merited, especially in areas where speakers of languages other than English outnumbered Francophones. In spite of the controversy, principles of the Official Languages Act were incorporated into the 1982 Canadian Constitution through its Canadian Charter of Rights and Freedoms. The British Parliament renounced any future legislative role in amending the Constitution, and on April 17, 1982, Queen Elizabeth II proclaimed the Constitution effective. Quebec, headed by René Lévesque of the Parti Québécois, did not agree to the Constitution and refused to sign it, charging that it did not go far enough in protecting Quebec's unique place in Canada.

—*Arthur W. Helweg*

ADDITIONAL READING:

Bourhis, Richard Y., ed. *Conflict and Language Planning in Quebec*. Clevedon, Avon, England: Multilingual Matters, 1984. Analyzes the internal policy implications of the language issue for the province of Quebec.

Driedger, Leo. *The Ethnic Factor: Identity in Diversity*. New York: McGraw-Hill Ryerson, 1989. Includes an outstanding chapter on the language issue for Canada.

Fleras, Augie, and Jean Leonard Elliott. *Multiculturalism in Canada: The Challenge to Diversity*. Scarborough, Ont.: Nelson Canada, 1992. Good analysis of the language issue within the multicultural policy of Canada.

Wardhaugh, Ronald. *Language and Nationhood: The Canadian Experience*. Vancouver, B.C.: New Star Books, 1983. A classic, often-cited work delineating the language issue for Canada.

SEE ALSO: 1968, Trudeau Era in Canada; 1970, October Crisis; 1977, Canada's Human Rights Act; 1978, Canada's Immigration Act of 1976.

1969 ■ APOLLO 11 LANDS ON THE MOON: *the first persons to communicate with Earth from the Moon achieve a technological, political, and social victory, reminding the world's peoples of their essential union*

DATE: July 20, 1969
LOCALE: Earth's Moon
CATEGORY: Science and technology
KEY FIGURES:

Edwin E. "Buzz" Aldrin, Jr. (born 1930), U.S. Air Force, lunar module pilot on Apollo 11

Neil Alden Armstrong (born 1930), civilian astronaut and commander of Apollo 11

Wernher von Braun (1912-1977), designer of the Saturn 5 launch vehicle

Michael A. Collins (born 1930), U.S. Air Force, command module pilot on Apollo 11

Kurt H. Debus (born 1908), director of the Kennedy Space Center

Robert R. Gilruth, director of the Manned Spacecraft Center, Houston

John Fitzgerald Kennedy (1917-1963), thirty-fifth president of the United States, 1961-1963

Christopher C. Kraft, Jr., director of flight operations, Mission Control, Houston

Richard Milhous Nixon (1913-1994), thirty-seventh president of the United States, 1969-1974

Rocco A. Petrone (born 1926), director of launch operations at Kennedy Space Center

SUMMARY OF EVENT. On July 20, 1969, hundreds of millions of people all over the planet watched a television broadcast sent live from the Moon. They saw Apollo 11 commander

Neil A. Armstrong climb slowly down the ladder of his lunar landing vehicle and step cautiously onto the lunar surface. Mounted on the lunar module *Eagle* was a plaque inscribed with the words:

Here men from the planet Earth first set foot upon the Moon. July 1969 A.D. We came in peace for all mankind.

This first lunar landing was the climax of an intense thirteen-year competition between the Soviet Union and the United States in space exploration. The space race, as it came to be called, began on October 4, 1957, when the Soviets launched Sputnik 1, the world's first artificial Earth satellite. Its roots could be traced back much further, however. As early as the 1920's, individual scientists and engineers—such as the Russian Konstantin Tsiolkovsky, the German Hermann Oberth, the American Robert Goddard, and Frenchman Robert Esnault-Pelterie—for the most part unaware of one another's work, had laid the theoretical and mathematical foundations for space exploration by means of high-powered rockets.

During the 1920's and 1930's, small groups of enthusiasts had formed organizations such as the German Society for Space Travel (Verein für Raumschiffahrt), the British Interplanetary Society, the Group for the Study of Reactive Motion (GIRD) in the Soviet Union, and the American Rocket Society, to discuss the problems of space exploration and conduct experiments with primitive rockets. None of these organizations, however, had sufficient funds to conduct the type of research necessary to tackle the basic problems of spaceflight, and by the end of the 1930's, rocket research in most countries was almost at a standstill.

The exception was Germany, where, in 1932, the army had become interested in the military possibilities of rockets and had established a rocket research group in the Army Weapons Office. Under the direction of Colonel Walter Dornberger, a German army engineer, and Wernher von Braun, a visionary young scientist, this group, endowed with relatively generous financial support, succeeded in developing a sophisticated series of rockets culminating in the famous A-4, or V-2, that the Germans used to bombard England during the final year of World War II. The V-2 had a range of almost two hundred miles, could attain an altitude of more than one hundred miles, and could deliver to target a payload of slightly more than a ton.

After the war, both the United States and the Soviet Union secured large numbers of V-2 rockets and shipped them back to their home countries for study and experimentation. Most of the German research and planning staff, including von Braun, eventually went to the Americans and were relocated to the United States to help in rocket research. During the latter half of the 1940's, these men, together with U.S. scientists, continued their program of rocket research, first at the White Sands Proving Grounds in New Mexico and later at the U.S. Army's Redstone Arsenal at Huntsville, Alabama.

In February, 1949, a U.S. high-altitude rocket, the WAC-Corporal, was fitted to a V-2 booster, creating the first multi-stage launch vehicle. This rocket achieved a new altitude record of 250 miles. By 1953, U.S. rocket scientists had developed an even more powerful rocket called Redstone. The U.S. government was little interested in space exploration during the early 1950's, however. Charles E. Wilson, then secretary of defense, complacently remarked to some reporters, "I've got enough problems here on Earth." Nevertheless, in July, 1955, President Dwight Eisenhower announced that the United States would put a small artificial satellite into orbit as part of U.S. activities in the International Geophysical Year (1957-1958). This satellite, dubbed Vanguard, was tentatively scheduled to be placed in orbit in 1958 and was designed to carry a small payload about the size of a grapefruit.

On October 4, 1957, the Soviet Union reported that Sputnik 1, a 184-pound sphere with a transmitter, was in a stable orbit about the Earth. News of the Soviet achievement caused consternation, fear, and dismay throughout U.S. society and government. To most people in the United States, the Sputnik scare seemed to suggest that the United States had fallen behind the Russians, not only in the development of rockets and satellites but also in science and technology generally. When on November 3, 1957, the Soviets orbited Sputnik 2, a satellite weighing more than a thousand pounds and carrying a dog (Laika), public concern increased.

The Navy's crash program to put Vanguard into orbit was dealt an embarrassing setback on December 6, 1957, when a Vanguard rocket exploded immediately after ignition, enveloping the launch pad in a fireball and dropping the satellite to the ground, its transmitter still functioning. After the Navy's failure, the Army was given permission to allow their frustrated German rocket scientists to proceed to attempt a satellite launch, using a Jupiter-C rocket, a modified Redstone, and the Explorer satellite. The United States achieved its first success in placing an artificial satellite, Explorer 1, into orbit on January 31, 1958. Vanguard eventually placed satellites in orbit, the first success coming in March, 1958.

With the space race now in full gear, President Eisenhower, in October, 1958, decided to consolidate all nonmilitary space programs under the general authority of a civilian agency approved by Congress—the National Aeronautics and Space Administration (NASA). This was an outgrowth of the old National Advisory Committee on Aeronautics (NACA), but with a greatly increased staff and budget. Space became a national priority of the highest order.

Almost from the beginning, it was apparent that Soviet space research was directed toward development of a manned spaceflight capability. Sputnik 2's canine passenger had been connected to biomedical sensors to monitor the dog's health in weightlessness and under exposure to cosmic radiation. In 1960, the Russians successfully launched and recovered a pair of dogs in Sputnik 5.

The United States shaped its space program to emphasize manned spaceflight development with the authorization of Project Mercury and the selection of seven astronauts in 1959. On April 12, 1961, Soviet Army colonel Yuri A. Gagarin was

Astronaut Edwin "Buzz" Aldrin stands on the Moon in this photo, taken by astronaut Neil Armstrong, in which the Lunar Module, Armstrong, and the U.S. flag can be seen reflected in Aldrin's face mask. The Moon landing marked the achievement of a goal set less than a decade earlier by President Kennedy. (AP/Wide World Photos)

launched from the Baikonur cosmodrome (Tyuratam) in Vostok 1, completing one orbit about Earth and returning to the Soviet Union. NASA succeeded in placing the first U.S. citizen, Commander Alan B. Shepard, in space for fifteen minutes on May 5, 1961, with a suborbital launching of the Mercury-Redstone booster. The new president, John F. Kennedy, speaking on May 25, stated his belief

> that this nation should commit itself to achieving the goal, before this decade is out, of landing a man on the Moon and returning him safely to the Earth. No single space project in this period will be more impressive to mankind, or more important for the long-range exploration of space; and none will be so difficult or expensive to accomplish.

Five more successful Russian Vostok flights were completed in 1962-1963; five more American Mercury astronauts flew in space, four of them in orbit, the first being John H. Glenn, Jr., on February 20, 1962. A brief pair of Russian Voskhod flights in 1964 and 1965 were followed by the tremendously successful American Gemini series, in which pairs of NASA astronauts accomplished spacewalking, rendezvous and docking, long-duration spaceflights, and controlled reentries during ten manned missions flown in 1965 and 1966. During the Gemini missions, the groundwork for the Apollo lunar mission was laid.

Gemini was to be followed immediately by initial flights of the Apollo three-person spacecraft. During a dress rehearsal on January 27, 1967, astronauts Virgil I. "Gus" Grissom, Edward H. White, and Roger B. Chaffee perished inside the Apollo 1 command module when a fire broke out while the capsule was pressurized with highly flammable pure oxygen. NASA's plans for a lunar landing were placed on hold. Ironically, the first flight of the Soviet spacecraft that was to have played a major role in the Soviets' own lunar program, Soyuz 1, ended in tragedy in April, 1967, when Vladimir Komarov crashed to Earth inside the Soviet Union when his spacecraft, tumbling out of control, failed to deploy its parachute properly.

On November 4, 1967, von Braun was successful in launching the first Saturn 5 moon rocket on the unmanned testflight of Apollo 4. After a twenty-month accident investigation and redesign of the Apollo spacecraft, Apollo 7, the first manned Apollo mission, was launched on October 11, 1968. The Soviets returned to flight operations with the joint Soyuz 3/2 manned/unmanned flight at roughly the same time. Apollo 8 was launched on December 21, 1968, to orbit the Moon during the Christmas holidays. Apollos 9 and 10 performed dress rehearsals using the entire Apollo spacecraft in Earth orbit and lunar orbit in February and May, 1969, respectively.

The crew assigned to attempt the first lunar landing mission comprised Neil A. Armstrong, Edwin E. Aldrin, and Michael A. Collins. Apollo 11 was launched on July 16, entering lunar orbit on July 19. Armstrong and Aldrin safely landed their lunar module, *Eagle*, on the Sea of Tranquillity on July 20. Approximately six hours after the landing, Armstrong opened *Eagle*'s hatch and carefully descended to the Moon's surface down a ladder. Making his final step onto the Moon's surface, he declared, "That's one small step for man, one giant leap for mankind."

Collins remained in orbit in the command module, *Columbia*, during the thirty-one hours that *Eagle* rested on the Moon. During an extravehicular activity lasting a little more than two hours, Armstrong and Aldrin stood up the U.S. flag, deployed scientific equipment, and collected rock and soil samples. Four days later, with President Richard Nixon in attendance on the recovery carrier USS *Hornet*, Apollo 11 splashed down in the Pacific Ocean, bringing the first samples from the Moon back to Earth for study.

There could be no doubt that the United States had recovered the prestige it had lost in the wake of Sputnik in 1957. Although NASA had beaten the Russians to the Moon, the broader implications of the space race remained unclear. The Moon shots of 1969 and the early 1970's marked a high point of public interest in and commitment to human space travel; the first images of Earth from the Moon, broadcast worldwide over television, reminded people at the height of the Cold War that no divisive political borders are visible from space. As NASA entered the 1970's, the form and direction of future manned space exploration remained undecided, soon to be subsumed by the space shuttle program.

—Ronald N. Spector, updated by David G. Fisher

ADDITIONAL READING:

Aldrin, Buzz, and Malcolm McConnell. *Men from Earth.* New York: Bantam Books, 1989. A personal account of one participant in the Apollo 11 journey.

Armstrong, Neil, with Gene Farmer, and Dora Jane Hamblin. *First on the Moon: A Voyage with Neil Armstrong, Michael Collins, and Edwin E. Aldrin, Jr.* Boston: Little, Brown, 1970. The story of Apollo 11, complete with NASA public address announcements interspersed throughout the text in proper chronological sequence from pre-launch to post-splashdown. Excellent reference.

Brooks, Courtney G., James M. Grimwood, and Lloyd S. Swenson, Jr. *Chariots for Apollo: A History of Manned Lunar Spacecraft.* Washington, D.C.: National Aeronautics and Space Administration, Scientific and Technical Information Branch, 1979. A technical and engineering history of the development and flight of the Apollo lunar spacecraft.

Chaikin, Andrew. *A Man on the Moon: The Voyages of the Apollo Astronauts.* New York: Viking, 1994. Masterful, enjoyable presentation of all Apollo lunar flights from the perspectives of the crews that flew them and the flight control teams that directed them.

Collins, Michael. *Carrying the Fire: An Astronaut's Journeys.* New York: Ballantine Books, 1974. Describes the author's participation in the NASA space program, emphasizing his two flights in space, Gemini 10 and Apollo 11.

_____. *Liftoff: The Story of America's Adventure in Space.* New York: Grove Press, 1988. A personal account of one of the participants in the Apollo 11 journey.

Lewis, Richard S. *Appointment on the Moon*. New York: Ballantine Books, 1969. A nontechnical history of the space program from the V-2 to Apollo 11. Discusses efforts in the Soviet Union as well as in the United States.

Murray, Charles, and Catherine Bly Cox. *Apollo: The Race to the Moon*. New York: Simon & Schuster, 1989. Thorough flight history of the Apollo missions; multiple perspectives. Essential for the spaceflight enthusiast.

Riabchikov, Evgeny. *Russians in Space*. Edited by Nikolai P. Kamanin. Translated by Guy Daniels. Moscow: Novosti Press Agency Publishing House, 1971. A reasonably straightforward presentation of Soviet manned spaceflight activity, from Gagarin's Vostok 1 orbital flight (1961) to the tragedy of the Soyuz 11/Salyut 1 space station (1971).

Shepard, Alan B., and Deke Slayton. *Moon Shot: The Inside Story of America's Race to the Moon*. Atlanta: Turner Books, 1994. The inside story of the early Astronaut Office, told by two of the original Mercury astronauts. An excellent companion video is also available.

SEE ALSO: 1961, First American in Space; 1977, Spaceflights of Voyagers 1 and 2; 1986, *Challenger* Accident; 1993, Astronauts Repair the Hubble Space Telescope.

1969 ■ ALCATRAZ OCCUPATION: *the takeover of the former prison highlights the grievances of both urban and reservation Indians*

DATE: November 20, 1969-June 11, 1971
LOCALE: Alcatraz Island, San Francisco Bay, California
CATEGORIES: Government and politics; Native American history; Wars, uprisings, and civil unrest
KEY FIGURES:
Tim Findley, reporter for the *San Francisco Chronicle*
Adam Nordwall, also known as *Adam Fortunate Eagle*, a Chippewa-Crow and one of the leaders at Alcatraz
Richard Oakes, a Mohawk, one of the leaders at Alcatraz
Robert Robertson, federal negotiator at Alcatraz
John Trudell, a Lakota who was an announcer for Radio Free Alcatraz

SUMMARY OF EVENT. Eighty-nine Native Americans landed on Alcatraz Island in San Francisco Bay during the early, brisk morning hours of November 20, 1969. Calling themselves Indians of All Tribes, the group declared that the island belonged to them by the provisions of the Treaty of Fort Laramie of 1868, which allowed American Indians to claim abandoned federal property that had once been tribal land. The occupation lasted for nineteen months and symbolized American Indian protests against the federal government.

Prehistoric tribes regarded Alcatraz Island as a landmark and a refuge for waterfowl. The Spaniards garrisoned the island; later, after the United States acquired California, Alcatraz became a military prison and had American Indians among its inmates. Indeed, after the Modoc War in the 1870's, two young Modocs were sentenced to Alcatraz rather than hanged. Later, other American Indians, including Paiutes and Chiricahua Apaches, were incarcerated at the prison. In 1933, the army relinquished control to the Federal Bureau of Prisons. Thirty years later, Alcatraz closed.

During the turbulent 1960's, Native Americans joined other discontented minorities protesting against injustices. American Indians demanded self-determination, better housing, better medical care, more jobs and educational opportunities, and recognition of treaty obligations. Urban Indians were especially upset, because federal relocation policies had promised them employment in large cities once they left their reservations; instead, they found themselves alienated and destitute. Broken promises and delays in attaining these objectives fueled an activism among urban and rural Indian people. The abandoned island became an opportunity to expose and redress their grievances.

On March 9, 1964, five Sioux, dressed in full regalia and led by a descendant of Crazy Horse, claimed the island under the terms of the 1868 treaty. They occupied the island for only four hours and left it under threat of arrest. This brief encounter became a harbinger of American Indian unrest and foreshadowed a more concentrated, large-scale occupation.

Upset with the loss of their Indian Center, which had been destroyed by fire, and by proposals to sell Alcatraz to commercial developers, young, educated tribe members joined with other American Indians to plan the second occupation. On November 9, 1969, under the leadership of Richard Oakes and Adam Nordwall (also known as Adam Fortunate Eagle), fourteen Native Americans landed on the island and held it for nineteen hours. Before their forced expulsion, the tribe members recounted their grievances and claimed the island on behalf of Indians of All Tribes. They offered to purchase the island for twenty-four dollars' worth of beads and cloth, the same price early Dutch colonists had paid natives for Manhattan Island.

On November 20, 1969, eighty-nine American Indians from a number of tribes took over the island for a third time. A much more organized and prepared group, they held the island for nineteen months. During their stay, they elected a council that assigned such daily operational duties as security, laundry, cooking, and sanitation to individuals. Instead of dumping waste into San Francisco Bay, which had been the policy in the past, the American Indians devised a type of septic tank to avoid polluting the environment. They established a preschool and day care center and offered classes in Indian beadwork, leathercraft, and woodworking. A noted tribal artist taught art to the children, while others provided them with music and dance instruction. American history classes, from an American Indian point of view, were also part of the curriculum. Emotional and financial support for their cause grew, as well-known actors, writers, and others became involved. The population of the island fluctuated, ranging up to about one thousand.

One week after the occupation had begun, American Indian

unity was expressed in a special Thanksgiving Day ceremony on November 27. Several hundred American Indians attended and participated in ceremonies that included pipe-smoking, singing, and dancing—all of which symbolized spiritual renewal. Ironically, just as natives had provided the Pilgrims with food during the first Thanksgiving, white owners of a California restaurant furnished much of the food for this unique celebration.

Two individuals who played prominent roles in publicizing the occupation were Tim Findley and John Trudell. Findley, a non-Indian reporter for the *San Francisco Chronicle* whose beat was demonstrations and protests, covered all three occupations, served as the media liaison for the tribe members, and generally sympathized with them. His reports garnered widespread support for the American Indians' demands and may have convinced federal officials to modify their position from insisting that the tribe members should leave the island to agreeing to hold formal negotiations. Trudell, a Lakota, broadcast thirty-minute programs nightly from Alcatraz on Radio Free Alcatraz, which was picked up by Berkeley's KPFA. He often focused his reports on the need for American Indians to establish a cultural and educational center on the island. During the occupation, Trudell's wife, Lou, gave birth to a boy, whom they named Wovoka, after the famous prophet and founder of the Ghost Dance religion.

The Indians met with federal negotiators, including Robert Robertson of the National Council on Indian Opportunity, and demanded recognition of their ownership of Alcatraz and establishment of an educational and cultural center for Native American studies. The Indians wanted Alcatraz to become a haven of traditional instruction regarding such matters as spirituality, healing ceremonies, and native customs. Federal negotiators rejected these demands. Their counteroffers included renaming the island after a nearby tribe, providing appropriations to build a park that included a museum and trading post, and building monuments that honored Native Americans. The Indians rejected these proposals, feeling that these offers did not meet their demand for self-determination.

The Indians' frustration with the government's refusal to meet their demands, coupled with internal friction among the occupants, weakened their will. The tragic death of one of Oakes's daughters, who fell down three flights of stairs at Alcatraz, shocked the American Indian community. Overcome by the loss of his daughter and unable to deal with tribal factionalism, a grief-stricken Oakes left the island. Shortages of water, fuel, and food, waning support from non-Indians, and tribe members' having to leave the island for various reasons further diminished American Indian resolve. On June 11, 1971, U.S. marshals landed and removed the remaining fifteen American Indians in less than thirty minutes, without incident. Nevertheless, the occupation of Alcatraz had focused attention on tribal grievances, both on and off the reservation, and had demonstrated a resurgence of Native American pride and the need for self-determination.

—*Sharon K. Wilson and Raymond Wilson*

ADDITIONAL READING:

Fortunate Eagle, Adam (Adam Nordwall). *Alcatraz! Alcatraz!: The Indian Occupation of 1969-1971*. Berkeley, Calif.: Heyday Books, 1992. A personal account of the occupation by one of the Native American leaders at Alcatraz.

Johnson, Troy R., ed. *Alcatraz: Indian Land Forever*. Los Angeles: American Indian Studies Center, University of California, Los Angeles, 1994. Poetry and political statements written by American Indians during the Alcatraz occupation.

_____, ed. *You Are on Indian Land!: Alcatraz Island, 1969-1971*. Los Angeles: American Indian Studies Center, University of California, Los Angeles, 1995. Contains 152 photographs that depict the varied emotions of the Native American occupants at Alcatraz.

Mankiller, Wilma, and Michael Wallis. *Mankiller: A Chief and Her People*. New York: St. Martin's Press, 1993. A sound overview and evaluation of the occupation.

Nagel, Joane, and Troy Johnson, eds. "Special Edition: Alcatraz Revisited: The Twenty-fifth Anniversary of the Occupation, 1969-1971." *American Indian Culture and Research Journal* 18, no. 4 (1994): 1-320. Los Angeles: American Indian Studies Center, University of California, Los Angeles. Seventeen articles on Alcatraz, most of which were written by participants at the event.

SEE ALSO: 1924, Indian Citizenship Act; 1934, Indian Reorganization Act; 1953, Termination Resolution; 1971, Alaska Native Claims Settlement Act; 1972, Trail of Broken Treaties; 1973, Wounded Knee Occupation; 1978, American Indian Religious Freedom Act; 1988, Indian Gaming Regulatory Act.

1970's ■ RISE OF WOMEN'S ROLE IN THE MILITARY: *expansion of women's roles in the U.S. military contributes to a broader acceptance of women in traditionally male roles throughout American society*

DATE: 1970's
LOCALE: United States
CATEGORY: Women's issues
KEY FIGURES:
Mildred Caroon Bailey (born 1919), director of the Women's Auxiliary Corps (WAC)
Harold Brown (born 1927), U.S. secretary of defense
Thomas S. Gates, Jr. (born 1906), chairman of the All-Volunteer Force Commission
Jeanne M. Holm (born 1921), director of Women in the Air Force (WAF)
Robin L. Quigley (born 1947), director of Women Accepted for Volunteer Emergency Service (WAVES), the women's branch of the Navy
Edith Nourse Rogers (1881-1960), representative from Massachusetts who introduced legislation into Congress to create WAC

Jeanette I. Sustad (1922-1978), director of the Women
Marines

SUMMARY OF EVENT. Instances of women's involvement
with the U.S. armed forces go back to the Revolutionary War,
in which many women worked as nurses and a few even saw
combat by disguising themselves as men. Women served in
similar roles in the Civil War. By the early twentieth century,
however, women were beginning to serve more integral roles.
In 1941, Edith Nourse Rogers, a member of Congress and a
champion of military service by women, introduced a bill to
create a Women's Army Auxiliary Corps (WAAC), later the
Women's Auxiliary Corps. The bill passed, and with the U.S.
entry into World War II, women's auxiliaries were added to all
the branches of the military.

Although many women served with distinction during
World War II, they were not integrated into the all-male military force. Various stated objections, including women's pre-
sumed physical limitations and emotional dispositions, concerns about fraternization between the sexes, and traditional
beliefs that women should be shielded from the business of
war and violence, weighed against integration. By and large,
the U.S. military remained an all-male preserve. Even the
passage of the Women's Armed Services Integration Act in
1948, which provided for the peacetime military service of
women within the four branches of the U.S. military, did not
lead to significant integration of women within the armed
forces. For two decades, the proportion of women in the military would not approach even the 2 percent ceiling imposed by
the 1948 act. Various other restrictions on the assignment and
promotion of women kept their numbers small.

By the beginning of the 1970's, two developments were
converging to promote the fuller integration of women into
the military. As U.S. involvement in the Vietnam conflict began to wind down, the Nixon Administration was looking for
a way to end the military draft and institute an all-volunteer
force (AVF). Responding to Nixon's request, a Central All-
Volunteer Task Force within the Department of Defense put
forward two suggestions for ensuring that enough personnel could be recruited to sustain an AVF: offer recruits a range
of benefits, including higher pay and better working conditions, and make wider use of women for certain noncom-
bat tasks. The government's desire to expand its recruitment
base for an AVF coincided with the expansion of a nationwide campaign for women's rights, most visibly under the
rubric of a proposed Equal Rights Amendment to the Constitution. The combination of these two developments paved the
way for a significant widening of opportunities for women to
serve in the military.

Despite the task force's recommendations and mounting
pressure from women's groups and other organizations, military leaders were slow to pursue actively increased participation by women in the armed forces. In 1972, a congressional
special subcommittee released a report that criticized the Department of Defense for alleged tokenism in the recruitment
and promotion of women. This prompted the AVF task force to

establish a target of doubling, over five years, the proportion
of women in all services except the Marine Corps, whose
combat-intensive mission presumably justified only a 40 percent increase. The results were promising. By 1977, the combined number of women in the armed forces had surpassed the
task force's targets.

The integration of women into the military in the mid-
1970's was the subject of various official and quasi-official
studies. In particular, effects on troop readiness, discipline,
morale, and overall effectiveness were studied. By most accounts, the net impact of women was positive. Female recruits
tended to be better educated and better disciplined than male
recruits. They tended to adapt well to the military environment. Overall, the all-volunteer military, utilizing a significant
proportion of women, was judged to be an effective and sus-
tainable force. Various political leaders, including Presidents
Nixon, Gerald Ford, and Jimmy Carter (all of whom, by virtue
of being president, were also commanders in chief) supported
the integration of women to sustain the AVF.

Women's integration into the military in the 1970's set a
broad range of precedents. One such precedent concerned the
integration of women officers. Although women had served as
officers in the military since World War II, their promotion
opportunities were severely limited, due largely to the practice
of keeping promotion lists segregated by sex. This practice
slowed in the 1970's and by 1981, had been entirely eliminated. The early 1970's saw the first promotions of women to
the rank of brigadier general (WAC director Elizabeth P. Hois-
ington and chief of the Army Nurse Corps Anna Mae Hays).
Women also became integrated into all Reserve Officers Training Corps (ROTC) programs by the end of the decade, and the
U.S. Congress required that the service academies be integrated in 1976. Women began to receive weapons training.
Gender-based affirmative action programs helped increase the
proportion of women in traditionally male roles, such as helicopter piloting and electronics.

Nevertheless, opposition to the full integration of women
remained within the military branches and within parts of the
civilian population. In a 1976 report, the Army claimed that
the use of large numbers of women was not economical, because they lost time as a result of pregnancy, child care needs,
and other factors. However, the exclusion of women on such
grounds could not be justified by experience and data.

The question of women in the military gradually shifted
to the issue of combat assignments. Although by the mid-
1970's few questioned whether women could fill various administrative and support positions, there remained a pervasive sense that women should be excluded from combat roles.
Such views rested on two arguments: that women were incapable, physically or otherwise, of battlefield combat; and
that it was morally wrong to subject women, as potential
mothers and the "weaker" sex, to the dangers and horrors
of battle. Significant numbers of men and women, civilian
and military, shared these beliefs.

The legacy of the integration of women in the 1970's was

strongly in evidence in the mid-1990's, when about 10 percent of the U.S. military comprised women, from the enlisted ranks to generals commanding major military installations. Nevertheless, the continuing restrictions on women in combat positions, instances of sexual harassment such as that which occurred at the 1991 Tailhook convention, and the still-low proportion of women in relation to their numbers in society suggested that significant obstacles still stood in the way of the integration goals of the 1970's.   —*Steve D. Boilard*

ADDITIONAL READING:

Binkin, Martin, and Shirley J. Bach. *Women and the Military*. Washington, D.C.: Brookings Institution, 1977. Argues that gender restrictions in the military unfairly deny access for women and unnecessarily weaken the pool of qualified recruits. Makes a strong case on the basis of economics. Includes appendix assessing the experiences of foreign countries with integrated militaries.

Blacksmith, E. A., ed. *Women in the Military*. New York: Wilson, 1992. Presents a variety of viewpoints on the integration of women in the military. The collection's primary focus is on the question of women in combat. Bibliography.

Holm, Jeanne. *Women in the Military: An Unfinished Revolution*. Rev. ed. Novato, Calif.: Presidio Press, 1992. Provides a thorough account of the integration of women into the U.S. military, from the founding of the country through the Persian Gulf War. Bibliography and appendices.

Mitchell, Brian. *Weak Link: The Feminization of the American Military*. Washington, D.C.: Regnery Gateway, 1989. A critical account of women's integration into the U.S. military. Argues that U.S. military strength is diluted by the physical limitations and psychoemotional disposition of its women.

Stiehm, Judith Hicks. *Bring Me Men and Women: Mandated Change at the U.S. Air Force Academy*. Berkeley: University of California Press, 1981. An assessment of the 1975 requirement that women be admitted to the national service academies, as seen in the Air Force.

SEE ALSO: 1941, 6.6 Million Women Enter the U.S. Labor Force; 1960, FDA Approves the Birth Control Pill; 1963, Equal Pay Act; 1965, Expansion of Affirmative Action; 1966, National Organization for Women Is Founded; 1972, Equal Employment Opportunity Act; 1975, Equal Credit Opportunity Act; 1978, Pregnancy Discrimination Act; 1982, Defeat of the Equal Rights Amendment; 1988, Family Support Act; 1992, Tailhook Scandal; 1993, Family and Medical Leave Act.

1970 ■ UNITED STATES INVADES CAMBODIA:

an abortive effort to hasten the end of U.S. involvement in Vietnam plunges Cambodia into two decades of civil war

DATE: April 29-June, 1970
LOCALE: Cambodia, adjacent to the border with Vietnam
CATEGORY: Wars, uprisings, and civil unrest

KEY FIGURES:
Creighton Williams Abrams (1914-1975), commander of U.S. military forces in Vietnam
Henry Alfred Kissinger (born 1923), assistant to the president for national security affairs, 1969-1973; United States secretary of state
Lon Nol (1913-1985), Cambodian chief of state, 1970-1975
Richard Milhous Nixon (1913-1994), thirty-seventh president of the United States, 1969-1974
Norodom Sihanouk (born 1922), Cambodian monarch deposed in 1970 and restored to the throne in 1993

SUMMARY OF EVENT. In 1968, when Richard M. Nixon was voted into office on the basis of his promise to bring peace to Vietnam, Cambodia was at peace. Its ruler, Prince Norodom Sihanouk, had successfully maneuvered to keep his country separate from the Vietnam War by allowing the North Vietnamese to use border provinces both as sanctuaries and to channel supplies destined for South Vietnam through Cambodian territory. For Sihanouk, the decision to aid the Vietnamese communists in this manner was one of expediency rather than sympathy. In his eyes, the choices were few; he must either help the communists or accept "American imperialism."

According to the Nixon doctrine, in the future the United States would provide material support to troops of countries resisting communist aggression but refrain from sending U.S. personnel to the battlefield. The key to Nixon's plan for ending the war was "Vietnamization," a program calling for the gradual extrication of U.S. troops and their replacement by Vietnamese. In essence, it was a solution to the U.S. problem of disengaging from the war rather than a solution to the war. In the same way, the prospect of invading Cambodia was viewed only as a means to ease disengagement. That it would actually widen the war and introduce a previously neutral country to the conflict were possibilities that remained secondary considerations.

In April, 1964, U.S. planes, flying from bases in Thailand, strafed two Cambodian villages. Sihanouk soon severed diplomatic relations with the United States. Subsequent border forays by the South Vietnamese army into Cambodia, coordinated with U.S. military advisers, also had little effect on stopping the flow of support from North Vietnam to South Vietnam.

The U.S. military leadership had, for some time, sought permission to invade Cambodia. President Nixon's immediate predecessor, Lyndon B. Johnson, had rejected several requests on the grounds that the impact of such an invasion on the course of the war would be negligible. In February of 1969, however, less than a month after Nixon assumed office, General Creighton W. Abrams, commander of U.S. forces in Vietnam, requested that B-52 bombers be used against sanctuaries and supply routes. Nixon, in concurrence with his national security adviser, Henry A. Kissinger, agreed, and in March, 1969, the bombing of Cambodia began. As the U.S. Constitution specifically holds that only Congress can decide to wage war, this act to widen the war almost certainly was illegal. To prevent the issue of legality from arising, however, Nixon ordered that the bombing be kept secret. To prevent a news leak, he even bypassed the ordinary military chain of command, failing to notify the Pentagon. The domestic outcry over the bombing forced him to order a halt. In this manner, without the knowledge of Congress or the American people, Cambodia was introduced to the war one year prior to the U.S. invasion.

Although the bombing in itself achieved limited success in interdicting North Vietnamese supply routes and storage areas, it killed more Cambodians than North Vietnamese, had a significant impact on the Cambodian political situation, and was primarily responsible for initiating a series of events that would impact Cambodia's future for years. First, it pushed the communists out of the border sanctuary areas and deeper into Cambodia. This irritated rightist elements in Sihanouk's government who, already dissatisfied with his permissiveness in allowing Vietnamese communists access to Cambodian territory, became even more so as they witnessed the communists usurp still more. Sihanouk, aware of the discord, took measures to allay it. He reopened diplomatic relations with the United States. He informed Washington that he would not object to some attacks on Vietnamese sanctuaries inside Cambodia, but he never agreed to indiscriminate bombing. By not protesting the B-52 raids, which he strongly opposed, he felt he was making a significant concession to these same rightist elements who supported them. Fearing eventual annexation by Vietnam, rightist General Lon Nol, Cambodian armed forces commander, ordered all Vietnamese to leave the country, and anti-Vietnamese demonstrations were organized in Phnom Penh and the provinces along the Vietnamese border.

In March, 1970, as tensions continued to mount within his government, Sihanouk departed Phnom Penh on a diplomatic mission to Moscow and Peking. Again, motivated by the need to settle the unrest among his ministers, he intended to urge both governments to restrain the North Vietnamese from encroaching further into Cambodian territory. However, he had failed to assess accurately how far the crisis in his capital had actually advanced. While still in Moscow, he learned he had been deposed by his pro-U.S. defense minister, Lon Nol. Although there is no evidence that the United States or any other foreign power promoted the coup, it precipitated crucial policy changes on both sides of the Vietnam War. The struggling Cambodian communist movement Khmer Rouge, which previously had been judged by Hanoi to be too small to be effective, was suddenly thrust by Sihanouk's downfall into a position from which it could make a serious attempt at gaining power. As a result, Vietnamese assistance increased dramatically, and the Khmer Rouge received the support it needed eventually to achieve power. For those among the U.S. leadership who supported an invasion plan, Sihanouk's downfall was a fortuitous event, since he alone among Cambodia's leaders had remained strongly

opposed. With his removal, all Cambodian opposition to an invasion attempt ended.

On April 29-30, 1970, an invasion was mounted with thirty thousand U.S. and South Vietnamese troops crossing into Cambodia. Secrecy had so pervaded the operation's planning that no one in Cambodia, including the United States mission and least of all Lon Nol, learned of it until after it occurred. Although Nixon spoke of the invasion as a decisive victory, the military regarded it as having attained a temporary advantage at best. While uncovering enormous stores of supplies, it encountered few enemy troops. In effect, military planners had failed to take into account the communists' move westward under the impact of the bombing. Thus, while temporarily disrupting the communists' logistics, the invasion made little impact on their long-term conduct of the war. Pentagon estimates suggested that North Vietnamese plans for an offensive had been set back by no more than a year; in keeping with this assessment, the North Vietnamese, within two months of the withdrawal of United States invasion forces, had reestablished their supply trails and sanctuaries.

Within the United States, the effect of the invasion was devastating. The antiwar movement reacted with intensified demonstrations and student strikes. The death of four students at Kent State University as the result of a confrontation between National Guardsmen and protesters enraged the nation. The extent of the reaction engendered by the invasion surprised President Nixon. Although he defended his action to the American people, his arguments appeared flimsy and misrepresentative. Claiming that the United States had for five years respected Cambodian neutrality, he neglected to mention the bombing. Declaring that the invasion was intended to destroy the headquarters for the entire communist military operation in South Vietnam, he ignored overwhelming evidence offered by the military proving that no such target existed. Depicting the invasion as a necessary step taken against the North Vietnamese to preclude the possibility of attack on U.S. troops withdrawing from the war, he hid the fact that during the course of negotiations for peace, the North Vietnamese had already offered to refrain from such attacks once a withdrawal date was determined. Finally, asserting that his decision was crucial to the maintenance of U.S. prestige abroad, Nixon contradicted evidence indicating a substantial fall in U.S. prestige following the invasion. Both internationally and domestically, the feeling prevailed that the president had succeeded only in expanding an already wearisome war.

For Cambodia, the invasion completed the destruction of a tenuous neutrality already severely damaged for more than a year by the bombing campaign. It precipitated an internal war that had not existed before U.S. forces crossed the border and that subsequently enveloped Cambodia in a prolonged conflict between United States-supported anti-communist forces and Vietnam-supported Khmer Rouge insurgents, thereby subjecting the country to still further devastation and eventual communist rule.

In this way, the fate of Cambodia was decided. U.S. policy-makers, interested only in exploiting Cambodia's territory as an adjunct to the Vietnam War, held the welfare of Cambodians and their land in small regard. President Nixon made this clear when in December, 1970, he stated that the Cambodians were "tying down forty thousand North Vietnamese regulars [in Cambodia and] if those North Vietnamese weren't in Cambodia they'd be over killing Americans." The Cambodians were thus reduced to acting as surrogate U.S. targets for North Vietnamese guns. The tragedy of the U.S. invasion was that so much was suffered for so little reason.

Cambodia was but a sideshow for Nixon, who failed to take either the subtleties of Indochina or the domestic antiwar movement into account. Sihanouk's assessment of policymakers in Washington was, in characteristic hyperbole, that "They demoralized America, they lost all of Indochina to the communists, and they created the Khmer Rouge."

When U.S. and Vietnamese troops withdrew from Cambodia, civil war ensued. The Khmer Rouge, which came to power in 1975, soon attacked Vietnam to regain lost territory. Hanoi counterattacked in 1978, pushing the Khmer Rouge to the border with Thailand by 1979. In 1989, Vietnamese troops withdrew, and in 1993, the United Nations held elections, resulting in an elected parliament, which restored Sihanouk as king of Cambodia.

—Ronald J. Cima, updated by Michael Haas

ADDITIONAL READING:

Caldwell, Malcolm, and Lek Tan. *Cambodia in the Southeast Asian War.* New York: Monthly Review Press, 1973. A review of contemporary Cambodian history, critical of the U.S. role.

Gordon, Bernard K., with Kathryn Young. "The Khmer Republic: That Was the Cambodia That Was." *Asian Survey* 2 (January, 1971): 26-40. Prophetically asserts that the U.S. invasion, by bringing Vietnamese into Cambodia, unleashed a Cambodian-Vietnamese enmity that would be difficult to resolve.

Grant, Jonathon S., et al. *Cambodia: The Widening War in Indochina.* New York: Washington Square Press, 1971. Essays by Asian scholars opposed to the war.

Kissinger, Henry S. *Years of Upheaval.* London: Weidenfeld & Nicolson, 1982. Chapter 8, on Indochina, attempts to explain Kissinger's motives and refute his critics.

Shawcross, William. *Sideshow: Nixon, Kissinger and the Destruction of Cambodia.* New York: Simon & Schuster, 1979. A thorough account of the way in which U.S. policy upset the delicate balance that held Cambodia together.

Sihanouk, Norodom. *My War with the CIA.* London: Penguin Books, 1973. Blames problems in Cambodia in the 1960's and 1970's on the Central Intelligence Agency.

SEE ALSO: 1964, Vietnam War; 1964, Berkeley Free Speech Movement; 1964, Johnson Is Elected President; 1967, Long, Hot Summer; 1968, Tet Offensive; 1968, Nixon Is Elected President; 1973, U.S. Troops Leave Vietnam; 1995, United States Recognizes Vietnam.

1970 ■ KENT STATE MASSACRE: *authorities react violently to student protesters, killing four and wounding nine others*

DATE: May 4, 1970
LOCALE: Kent State University, Kent, Ohio
CATEGORIES: Civil rights; Wars, uprisings, and civil unrest
KEY FIGURES:
Allison Krause (1951-1970),
Jeffrey Miller (1950-1970),
Sandra Scheuer (1950-1970), and
William Schroeder (1951-1970), students killed by Ohio National Guardsmen at Kent State University

SUMMARY OF EVENT. The tragic events that unfolded at Kent State University on May 4, 1970, emphatically signaled the end of a turbulent decade of antiwar protest that characterized many college and university campuses during the 1960's. The primary factor that sparked the Kent State demonstrations was President Richard Nixon's decision to expand the Vietnam War by authorizing a brief military incursion into Cambodia.

Nixon's momentous decision was made public on Thursday, April 30, 1970. The president's seemingly contradictory course of action—to end the war by expanding the war—created domestic problems. Student protest over the Cambodian incursion came quickly. Within days, some form of protest had occurred at almost two-thirds of the colleges and universities in the United States. Most of the demonstrations were peaceful; however, at more than one hundred universities, protests turned violent and disorderly.

At Kent State, a brief, peaceful protest rally was held on the commons—a field near dormitories and major pedestrian walkways—at noon on Friday. The first serious disorder started on Friday evening, near the Kent State campus. At approximately 11:00 P.M., students barricaded a street on which several bars were located. A bonfire was started in the street, and students began to harass passing motorists. Initially, city police did not interfere. As complaints mounted, the city police decided to close the bars, hoping that students would retreat to the campus. Instead, angry patrons left the bars and began to congregate in the streets. Soon, antiwar chants were raised, and some students hurled rocks and bottles at the police as well as at fellow students. Some in the crowd of about twelve hundred people broke store and office windows. The police chased the crowd toward the campus and, at about 2:00 A.M., finally dispersed it with tear gas. Sixty arrests were made, and the damage to businesses in downtown Kent was estimated to be in excess of thirty thousand dollars.

All day Saturday, the Kent State campus was relatively calm. However, local merchants in downtown Kent claimed that they received numerous threats. At about 8:00 P.M., a crowd began to congregate on the commons, and within an hour, more than one thousand students were present. People began to throw rocks at the Reserve Officers' Training Corps (ROTC) facility, which was located adjacent to the commons.

After several windows were broken out, a fire was started inside the facility. At 9:00 P.M., the fire department arrived. The fire department's arrival was greeted by thrown rocks and numerous attempts to puncture fire hoses. The fire trucks retreated under this barrage, and at 9:30 P.M., campus police dispersed the crowd with tear gas. Shortly thereafter, the Ohio National Guard arrived on the commons under orders to protect the ROTC facility. At this point, however, they could do little more than watch the ROTC facility burn. Once the crowd had been dispersed from the commons, there were no further incidents on Saturday night.

On Sunday morning, the governor of Ohio arrived at Kent State. After a brief tour and inspection of the ruins of the ROTC facility, the governor denounced the student protestors in strong and inflammatory terms. The university president met briefly with the governor; at 4:00 P.M., the university issued orders prohibiting all forms of demonstration, peaceful or otherwise.

On Sunday evening, a few hundred students marched toward the center of downtown Kent. Members of the National Guard stopped the students before they could leave campus. The students next sat down in the street and asked to meet with the university president and the mayor of Kent. After approximately ninety minutes, guard members informed the students that they were in violation of a curfew, and tear gas was used to scatter students who refused to leave. The remainder of Sunday night was punctuated by the noise of helicopters and the flash of searchlights.

On Monday morning, May 10, students returned to classes, and it seemed as if the university might return to normal. At about 11:45 A.M., a crowd that eventually grew to three thousand students began to gather on the commons. Although no organized protest or demonstration was attempted, some two hundred students began to taunt the guard members who were posted around the remnants of the ROTC facility. The students were informed they were in violation of Sunday's order prohibiting demonstrations. Tear gas was then used to disperse the crowd.

One group of students descended a shallow hill that led to a nearby football practice field. They were followed by about seventy National Guard troops wearing gas masks. Other students remained in the general area of the commons. The National Guard troops essentially marched themselves onto a field that was enclosed on three sides—they could not go any farther. Students began to throw rocks and chunks of dirt at the troops, who responded by firing tear gas canisters. Soon students were throwing the canisters back at the guard members. After tossing tear gas canisters back and forth, the National Guard regrouped, knelt, and leveled their weapons at the students. Students responded with taunts and the chant, "Shoot, shoot, shoot." Abruptly, the troops marched off the field and back up the shallow hill. When they reached the top, at 12:24 P.M., about two dozen members of the guard turned around and began firing at the crowd of students below them. The firing lasted for thirteen seconds, and when it was

over, four students—Jeffrey Miller, Allison Krause, William Schroeder, and Sandra Scheuer—were dead or dying, and nine others suffered wounds of varying degrees of severity.

Once the firing stopped, some students began to cluster around the dying and wounded. Others began to group together and move slowly toward the National Guard. The troops who had fired were immediately ordered from the area, and the remaining troops assumed a formation in order to advance against the crowd. For a brief moment, it looked as if another clash was about to occur. Several faculty members moved between students and the National Guard. Faculty members pleaded with students to remain calm or leave the area, and with the guard officers not to advance against the remaining students. There was a standoff until ambulances started to arrive. After the dead and injured were removed, the size of the crowd diminished. Shortly thereafter, Kent State University was closed by order of its president for the remainder of the semester, and a new wave of protest and demonstrations swept college and university campuses throughout the United States.
                                                —*Ernest G. Rigney, Jr.*

ADDITIONAL READING:

Davies, Peter. *The Truth About Kent State*. New York: Farrar, Straus & Giroux, 1973. Davies' controversial book uses many photographs to support his contention that the shootings at Kent State were the result of a conspiracy on the part of certain guard members.

Gordon, William A. *The Fourth of May*. New York: Prometheus Books, 1990. Presents a wealth of information about the shootings at Kent State and the numerous hearings and court cases that followed in their aftermath. Based on material gathered through use of Freedom of Information requests made to the Federal Bureau of Investigation.

Michener, James A. *Kent State*. New York: Random House, 1971. While Michener did not have all the facts at hand when he wrote this account of the shootings, his evocative writing skills enable him to convincingly describe and effectively convey what it must have felt like to be a student at Kent State in the spring of 1970.

Miller, David L. "Individuals and Riots." In *Introduction to Collective Behavior*. Illinois: Waveland Press, 1987. Using a social science perspective, offers a succinct description of events as well as several explanations of why especially violent demonstrations occurred at Kent State University.

President's Commission on Campus Unrest. *The Report of the President's Commission on Campus Unrest*. New York: Avon Books, 1971. This report, published in October, 1970, is considered the official version of what happened at Kent State. Based on FBI investigations, commission staff work, and hearings held at Kent State, at Jackson State, and in Washington, D.C.

SEE ALSO: 1964, Vietnam War; 1964, Berkeley Free Speech Movement; 1967, Long, Hot Summer; 1968, Assassinations of King and Kennedy; 1968, Chicago Riots; 1970, United States Invades Cambodia; 1970, U.S. Voting Age Is Lowered to Eighteen.

1970 ■ OCTOBER CRISIS: *responding to terrorism and kidnapping in Quebec, the Canadian federal government suspends civil liberties*

DATE: October 16, 1970
LOCALE: Quebec
CATEGORIES: Canadian history; Civil rights; Wars, uprisings, and civil unrest
KEY FIGURES:
Robert Bourassa (born 1933), premier of Quebec
James Cross (born 1921), British trade commissioner in Montreal
Jean Drapeau (born 1916), mayor of Montreal
Pierre Laporte (1921-1970), Quebec's minister of labor and immigration
Gérard Pelletier (born 1919), Canadian secretary of state for external affairs
Pierre Trudeau (born 1919), prime minister of Canada
John Turner (born 1929), Canadian minister of justice
SUMMARY OF EVENT. The October Crisis of 1970 was a tragic period in Quebec's history, marked by kidnapping, murder, and the suspension of civil liberties. It followed a decade of profound change and intellectual turbulence, not simply in the province of Quebec but throughout the world. Decolonization was in vogue, wars of liberation were being fought in several countries, and youth were questioning the values of their parents and the capitalist system. During the 1960's, Quebec society, once rural and religious, had undergone rapid transformation and was well on the way to becoming a modern, secular, progressive society. Increasingly self-confident and assertive French-speaking Quebecers (Québécois) were no longer willing to accept passively the Anglo-Canadian domination of previous centuries. In addition, they feared for the future of the French language and Québécois culture. This led many to join the ranks of the so-called separatist, or sovereignist, movement, which advocated political sovereignty or even outright independence for Quebec.

While these sovereignists followed a democratic path, others were not so patient. The Front de Libération du Québec (FLQ) was an underground revolutionary movement dedicated to creating a socialist, independent Quebec. Officially founded in 1963, it was composed primarily of French Canadian youth, often college or university students, willing to accept political violence as a means to liberate Quebec and destroy capitalism. They drew intellectual inspiration from the popular left-wing cult figures of this epoch, including Herbert Marcuse, Karl Marx, Mao Zedong, and Ernesto "Che" Guevara. They were also deeply influenced by recent historical events, especially the successful wars of national liberation that had been waged in Algeria and Cuba. The FLQ perceived itself as part of a worldwide movement fighting for liberation and decolonization, which included such groups as the Weath-

ermen and Black Panthers in the United States, the Palestine Liberation Organization in the Middle East, Roman Catholics in Northern Ireland, and the Viet Cong engaged in bitter conflict with the United States in Vietnam.

The FLQ never had a large membership; it was limited, at any one time, to perhaps fewer than one hundred activists. Nor was it highly organized: There was no mastermind or central committee that operated on a strict hierarchical basis. The FLQ was composed of cells, each one knowing little or nothing about the other, which made it difficult for police to penetrate. Five or ten young zealots would form a cell and then commit acts of violence or publish revolutionary tracts under the FLQ banner.

The FLQ began operations in 1963, planting bombs in post office boxes located in the affluent English-speaking section of Westmount in Montreal. Eventually, other targets were selected, including armories, federal buildings, the provincial Department of Labor building, and the Montreal Stock Exchange, at which a particularly bloody bombing in 1969 injured twenty-five people. FLQ members also robbed banks for funds and stole explosives from construction sites. Occasionally, the police were successful in destroying cells, but there were always new ones to take their place. It was estimated that the FLQ was responsible for some two hundred bombings, seven deaths, dozens wounded, and millions of dollars in property damage between 1963 and 1970. Although their propaganda was crude and unsophisticated, it resonated with many Québécois who could understand the forces that propelled young people to lash out against the injustices of society.

This violence, at first directed mainly against property, took a deadly turn in 1970. On October 5, one cell kidnapped the British trade commissioner in Montreal, James Cross. The kidnappers' ransom demands included receiving $500,000 in gold, the release of twenty-three political prisoners, and broadcasting the FLQ manifesto. The federal and provincial authorities allowed the broadcast but rejected the other demands, although they did offer to fly the kidnappers out of the country if they released their hostage. On October 10, another FLQ cell kidnapped Pierre Laporte, the provincial minister of labor and immigration.

The immediate result was confusion and chaos. In Montreal, Mayor Jean Drapeau believed his city was close to panic. Police forces throughout Quebec appeared stymied and incapable of protecting property or individuals. No one knew if this was the work of a few individuals or whether the province was facing the prospect of a large, well-organized left-wing insurrection. Quebec's premier, Robert Bourassa, was inexperienced, only thirty-seven years of age, and in office for only five months. His cabinet was divided as to whether to negotiate with the kidnappers or take a tough line. Police pushed for more legal powers to combat terrorism, while Laporte's friends and wife pressed the cabinet to negotiate.

The federal government in Ottawa was in no mood for compromise. The Canadian prime minister, Pierre Trudeau, a Quebecer, was pushing authorities in Quebec to take a stiff line, and John Turner, the federal minister of justice, feared an erosion of will on the part of the Quebec government. Gérard Pelletier, the Canadian secretary of state for external affairs, privately was alarmed at what he thought was too much sympathy for the FLQ on the part of many students, intellectuals, and sovereignists within Quebec. Eventually, the Quebec government formally requested that the Canadian Army be sent into the province and that the War Measures Act be invoked. On October 12, the Army moved into Quebec in order to guard public buildings and protect government officials, and on October 16, the War Measures Act was proclaimed. Public opinion polls showed that Canadians and Quebecers overwhelmingly approved of these federal actions.

Nevertheless, implementation of the War Measures Act eventually caused much controversy. This act permitted the government to suspend normal civil liberties and empowered authorities to use a variety of weapons—including censorship, arrest, detention, deportation, and control of transportation—to fight a state of apprehended insurrection. Many civil libertarians believed this proclamation was heavy-handed and unnecessary. Even Trudeau, who advocated a tough stance, was not enthusiastic about using this legal tool, but he deferred to the judgment of authorities on the scene in Quebec. More than 465 people were detained, but no charges were filed and most of those arrested were innocent of any criminal wrongdoing. It appears that the authorities considered almost anyone who was a sovereignist or embraced left-wing views to be a potential insurrectionist. Civil libertarians later pointed out that when the kidnappers were apprehended, it was due to routine police work and not to the special legal powers granted to the authorities.

On October 18, Pierre Laporte was found dead in the trunk of an automobile, having been strangled by his captors the previous day. Eventually, all the police work began to yield dividends. In early December, the police located the hideout at which James Cross was detained. After negotiations, Cross was released unharmed and the kidnappers allowed to fly to Cuba. Later that month, police finally apprehended the men responsible for the kidnapping and death of Pierre Laporte. Paul Rose and Francis Simard were found guilty of murder and sentenced to life imprisonment, although neither served more than twelve years before being paroled. In January, 1971, the Army withdrew from Quebec, although the state of emergency legislation remained in effect until April 30, 1971.

After these events, the Front de Libération du Québec went into a period of steep decline. The organization had completely alienated public opinion in Quebec, including leftists and sovereignists. Moreover, the increasing popularity of the Parti Québécois, founded in 1968 to fight for sovereignty, was convincing many people that there was a viable alternative to violence and revolution. The memory of the October Crisis remained firmly imprinted upon the Québécois psyche, one of the darkest moments in their modern history.

—David C. Lukowitz

ADDITIONAL READING:

Daniels, Dan, ed. *Quebec, Canada and the October Crisis*. Montreal: Black Rose Books, 1973. A collection of the revolutionary literature of the period, including documents, pamphlets, and poetry. Normally available only in French, but here translated into English.

Fournier, Louis. *F.L.Q.: The Anatomy of an Underground Movement*. Translated by Edward Baxter. Toronto: NC Press, 1984. A detailed, sympathetic account of the organization, placing it and the October Crisis within the context of national and global events.

Pelletier, Gérard. *The October Crisis*. Translated by Joyce Marshall. Montreal: McClelland and Stewart, 1971. The Canadian secretary of state at the time justifies his agonizing decision to support the use of the War Measures Act.

Rotstein, Abraham, ed. *Power Corrupted: The October Crisis and the Repression of Quebec*. Toronto: New Press, 1971. Essays by Anglo-Canadians highly critical of the suppression of civil liberties in Quebec.

Stewart, James. *The FLQ: Seven Years of Terrorism*. Richmond Hill: Simon & Schuster, 1970. A brief, readable introduction to the subject, recreating the atmosphere of those dangerous, turbulent times. Extensive collection of photographs.

Trudeau, Pierre Elliott. *Memoirs*. Toronto: McClelland and Stewart, 1993. The Canadian prime minister justifies his actions in a relatively brief section dealing with the events of 1970, but leaves many questions unanswered.

SEE ALSO: 1960, Quebec Sovereignist Movement; 1968, Trudeau Era in Canada; 1969, Canada's Official Languages Act; 1982, Canada's Constitution Act; 1990, Bloc Québécois Forms; 1992, Defeat of the Charlottetown Accord.

1971 ■ SWANN V. CHARLOTTE-MECKLENBERG BOARD OF EDUCATION:
the Supreme Court rules that busing is a constitutional means of achieving public school desegregation

DATE: April 20, 1971

LOCALE: Washington, D.C.

CATEGORIES: African American history; Civil rights; Court cases; Education

KEY FIGURES:

Warren E. Burger (1907-1995), chief justice of the United States and author of the majority opinion in the case

Julius L. Chambers (born 1936), chief attorney for James E. Swann

J. Braxton Craven, federal district court judge who originally ruled in favor of the board of education

John A. Finger (born 1920), court-appointed expert

Benjamin S. Horack, attorney for the Charlotte-Mecklenberg Board of Education

James B. McMillan (born 1907), federal district court judge
for the Western District of North Carolina

James M. Nabrit, attorney for James E. Swann

James E. Swann, plaintiff

William J. Waggoner, attorney for the Charlotte-Mecklenburg
Board of Education

SUMMARY OF EVENT. The original catalyst for this case was
the plan of the school board of Charlotte, Mecklenburg
County, North Carolina, to close some African American
schools, create attendance zones for most of the schools in the
district, and allow a "freedom-of-choice" provision under
which students could transfer to any school in the district,
provided that they could furnish their own transportation and
the school was not already filled to capacity. The litigation
began on January 19, 1965, when eleven African American
families, including Vera and Darius Swann and their son
James, were convinced by attorney Julius L. Chambers to sue
the district for relief. The plaintiffs challenged the plan on the
premise that the closing of the African American schools
would place the burden of desegregation on the African
American students, and that the other features would only
perpetuate segregation.

In 1965, federal district court judge J. Braxton Craven
rejected the plaintiff's challenge and approved the school
board's plan. A year later, the Court of Appeals for the Fourth
Circuit affirmed Craven's ruling. At this point, Chambers
opted not to appeal to the Supreme Court, because he feared
that the Court would only affirm the lower rulings under the
precedents established at that time.

After the Supreme Court's ruling in *Green v. County School
Board of New Kent County, Virginia* in 1968, however, Chambers decided to petition for further relief. In *Green*, the justices
ruled that freedom-of-choice plans did not aid in the process of
desegregation, and that other methods must be used to comply
with *Brown v. Board of Education* (1954). On September 6,
1968, the *Swann* plaintiffs filed a motion for further relief in
the federal district court in Charlotte. The motion came before
Judge James B. McMillan. Both parties agreed that the school
system fell short of achieving the unitary status required by
Green. Two plans were submitted, one by the school board and
the other by a court-appointed expert from Rhode Island College, Dr. John Finger.

Judge McMillan essentially accepted the Finger plan,
which required more desegregation than the school board was
willing to accept. The board plan would have closed seven
schools and reassigned the students involved. Attendance
zones were to be restructured to achieve greater racial balance,
but the existing grade structures were left intact. Furthermore,
the board plan would modify the free transfer plan into an
optional majority-to-minority transfer system (students in a
racial majority in one school could transfer to another where
they would be in the minority).

Under the board plan, African American students would be
reassigned to nine of the ten high schools in the district,
thereby producing in each an African American population of

between 17 and 36 percent. The tenth high school would have
an African American population of 2 percent. The junior high
schools would be rezoned so that all but one would have from
none to 38 percent African Americans. One junior high school
would have an African American population of 90 percent.
Attendance at the elementary schools, however, still would be
based primarily on the neighborhood concept. More than half
the African American children at this level would remain in
schools that were between 86 and 100 percent black.

The Finger plan used the board zoning plan for high
schools, with one modification. Three hundred additional African American students would be transported to the nearly
all-white Independence High School. This plan dealt similarly
with the junior high schools. Nine satellite zones would be
created, and inner-city African American students would be
assigned to nine outlying, predominantly white junior high
schools. As was typically the case, the biggest controversy
concerned the elementary school students. Rather than simply
relying on zoning, Finger proposed that pairing and grouping
techniques be used as well, with the result that all elementary
schools would have a black student proportion that would
range from 9 to 38 percent. Pairing occurs when two schools,
one predominantly white and one predominantly black, are
combined by either sending half the students in one school to
the other for all grades or by sending all the children to one
school for certain grades and then to the other school for the
remaining grade levels. Bus transportation would be used for
the affected students. After the district court's busing order,
McMillan was hanged in effigy. Crowds demonstrated at the
courthouse, in front of the judge's house, and at the *Charlotte
Observer*, a newspaper that had supported busing. McMillan
and his family received threatening phone calls, his law office
was fire-bombed by an arsonist, his car was dynamited, and
his home was vandalized.

The Charlotte-Mecklenburg Board of Education appealed
McMillan's busing order to the Fourth Circuit Court of Appeals. The appellate court vacated McMillan's order respecting elementary schools, and affirmed his ruling only on the
secondary school plans. This time, because of the *Green* case,
Chambers appealed the decision to the Supreme Court.

By the time the Supreme Court ruled on *Swann* in 1971,
Earl Warren had retired as Chief Justice, and President Richard
Nixon (who had publicly condemned forced busing) had filled
Earl Warren's seat with Warren Burger in 1969. *Swann v.
Charlotte-Mecklenburg Board of Education* dealt with the
constitutionality of several different techniques to achieve desegregation. In writing the unanimous decision, Burger admitted that the Court had not, as of that time, provided federal
district courts with comprehensive guidelines for implementing its 1954 landmark case, *Brown v. Board of Education of
Topeka, Kansas*. He declared:

> Understandably, in an area of evolving remedies, those courts
> had to improvise and experiment without detailed or specific
> guidelines. This Court . . . appropriately dealt with the large

constitutional principles; other federal courts had to grapple with the flinty, intractable realities of day-to-day implementation of those constitutional commands. Their efforts, of necessity, embraced a process of "trial and error," and our effort to formulate guidelines must take into account their experience.

In accepting the Finger plan, the justices ruled that federal district courts could decree as tools of desegregation the following: reasonable bus transportation, reasonable grouping of noncontiguous zones, the reasonable movement toward the elimination of one-race schools, and the use of mathematical ratios of blacks and whites in the schools as a starting point toward racial desegregation. Thus, the nation's highest tribunal had ruled that school districts could transport students in an effort to implement different techniques for the purpose of desegregating their schools. —*Brian L. Fife*

ADDITIONAL READING:

Barrows, Frank. "School Busing: Charlotte, N.C." *The Atlantic* 230, no. 5 (1972): 17-22. Assesses the school desegregation plan's impact on the citizens of Mecklenburg County during its implementation.

Fiss, Owen. "The Charlotte-Mecklenburg Case—Its Significance for Northern School Desegregation." *University of Chicago Law Review* 38 (1971): 697-709. Argues that the *Swann* ruling was not relegated to Southern school systems, and that districts in the North would be affected as well.

Gaillard, Frye. *The Dream Long Deferred.* Chapel Hill: University of North Carolina Press, 1988. Gaillard, a reporter for the *Charlotte Observer*, documents the desegregation process in the Charlotte-Mecklenburg school district.

Goldstein, Robert D. "A *Swann* Song for Remedies: Equitable Relief in the Burger Court." *Harvard Civil Rights-Civil Liberties Law Review* 13 (1978): 1-80. Surveys three principles that the Supreme Court has applied in its review of injunctions against state officers.

Schwartz, Bernard. *Swann's Way: The School Busing Case and the Supreme Court.* New York: Oxford University Press, 1986. In interviewing members of the Supreme Court and other principal personages, Schwartz provides an inside account of the Court's decision making in *Swann*.

SEE ALSO: 1954, *Brown v. Board of Education*; 1957, Little Rock School Desegregation Crisis; 1962, Meredith Registers at "Ole Miss."

1971 ■ U.S. VOTING AGE IS LOWERED TO EIGHTEEN: *young voters become a powerful new political force*

DATE: June 30, 1971
LOCALE: United States
CATEGORIES: Civil rights; Laws and acts
KEY FIGURES:
Dwight David Eisenhower (1890-1969), thirty-fourth
    president of the United States, 1953-1961
Edward Moore Kennedy (born 1932), senator from
    Massachusetts and cosponsor of the amendment
Richard Milhous Nixon (1913-1994), thirty-seventh
    president of the United States, 1969-1974
Jennings Randolph, senator from West Virginia

SUMMARY OF EVENT. In the United States, most colonies adopted the English practice specifying twenty-one years of age as the minimum voting age. A lower age was allowed only for men voting on militia officers. A uniform lowering of the voting age was debated as early as the New York Constitutional Convention of 1897. By 1942, when the U.S. Congress discussed it in relation to lowering the draft age to eighteen years of age, the notion had acquired significant public support. Between 1925 and 1964, nearly sixty proposals had been introduced in Congress.

The argument most often advanced for lowering the voting age—and the principal argument during the first period (1941 to 1952) of the thirty-year movement—was youth's forced military participation. In 1942, the Selective Service and Training Act lowered the draft age to eighteen years. Between fall, 1942, and October, 1944, several joint resolutions were introduced in Congress to lower the voting age by amending the Constitution, and forty resolutions were introduced in thirty states. The 1944 Democratic National Convention included voting age as a plank in the party platform, and the issue was the 1943-1944 national school debate topic. Interest escalated; from 1945 to 1952, nearly one hundred bills were introduced in the legislatures of more than forty states.

President Dwight D. Eisenhower endorsed the measure in his January, 1954, state of the union message. In 1956, he again urged a constitutional amendment. During this period, youth's military service was still a major argument. In Senate debate on the issue, in April, 1943, it was argued that because the nation had interrupted the careers and jeopardized the lives of eighteen-year-olds, it should honor their sacrifices by extending them the vote. Senator Hubert Humphrey argued that the measure would get youth to participate in politics at a point when they were interested in and enthusiastic about government, lessen voter apathy, and broaden the base of democracy by adding a large number of voters.

Several widely varying arguments against lowering the voting age were advanced in 1953: Youth younger than twenty-one years of age did not have the wisdom and experience to evaluate political issues and would espouse the views of their parents; youth should obtain both schooling and experience before exercising the vote, rather than learning from the experience of voting; the parallel between military service and voting is false, because soldiers need only uncritical obedience and physical, not intellectual, maturity; youth do not have enough knowledge of the country's history and are susceptible to the appeal of radicalism; since the U.S. government is representative, the voice of youth could be heard through their elders, who elect legislators; and the argument "old enough to fight, old enough to vote" does not enfranchise women and suggests that those too old to fight should lose the right to vote.

During the second phase of the movement (1953 to 1960), arguments generally related to youths' cognizance of their political place in society. In 1954, a quiz was conducted by the American Institute of Public Opinion. On seven questions testing basic political knowledge, persons between eighteen and twenty-one years of age did much better than adults.

In 1967, Senator Jennings Randolph of West Virginia introduced his eighth joint resolution for a constitutional amendment to lower the voting age to eighteen years; his first had been in 1942. That same year, more than one hundred measures were introduced in thirty-six state legislatures, and a Gallup poll showed support at an all-time high: 64 percent of adults and youth. In 1968, President Lyndon Johnson proposed that Congress submit a constitutional amendment for ratification by the states—the second such proposal from a president. Richard Nixon, in his 1968 campaign for president, promised youth "a piece of the action." Late that same year, a youth movement called Let Us Vote (LUV) was founded by Dennis Warren, a student at the University of the Pacific in Stockton, California. In six weeks, the sophisticated, widely publicized campaign expanded to more than three thousand high schools and four hundred colleges in all states. The Youth Franchise Coalition (of which LUV was a member) was organized on February 5, 1969. It used the multiple strategies of working through state legislation, a constitutional amendment, and separate campaigns mounted by member organizations. In 1968, the Republican Party called for state action to lower the voting age, while the Democratic platform endorsed a constitutional amendment. In April, 1969, a survey found that 93 percent of U.S. representatives favored the cause, as well as most federal and state senators. In this final phase of the movement, youth's strategy of active insistence on being enfranchised was making a difference.

Additional rationales for the measure surfaced during this period. Those who defended the existing age restrictions, it was argued, should prove that eighteen-year-olds, as a group, lacked the knowledge and maturity to vote responsibly and that allowing them to vote would damage the system of responsible government. Others argued that the real objective of the states should not be to limit the vote to those best informed but to see that all voters were reasonably well informed. Statistics and surveys showed that, as a result of improvements in education and mass communication, eighteen-year-olds were at least as well informed as twenty-one-year-olds had been when that minimum age was established. Voting rights cases had argued that all who have a stake in an election should be allowed to vote. This point added relevance to the "old enough to fight, old enough to vote" rhetoric. Men between eighteen and twenty years of age were the most vulnerable to conscription and to career disruption, injury, and death in wars; and elections arguably have an impact on war and peace.

On March 11, 1970, Senate Majority Leader Mike Mansfield introduced Amendment 545 to the Voting Rights Act of 1965. The amendment, cosponsored by Senator Edward Kennedy, would lower the voting age to eighteen years in all elections. Kennedy's support was buttressed by the opinions of several esteemed constitutional lawyers—in particular, Archibald Cox, whose 1966 article in the *Harvard Law Review* suggested a statutory amendment, as opposed to the cumbersome constitutional amendment process.

The bill passed, and President Nixon signed PL 91-285 into law on June 22, 1970. A test case against the law was filed in district court that same day. In 1970, seventeen states, three jurisdictions, and the U.S. Supreme Court assessed youth's suitability for the vote. On December 21, 1970, the latter upheld PL 91-285 in respect to presidential and congressional elections, but found it unconstitutional for state and local elections. Nevertheless, on January 1, 1971, millions of youth gained the right to vote in national elections when they turned eighteen years of age.

On January 25, 1971, Senator Jennings Randolph introduced a joint resolution to amend the Constitution to allow eighteen-year-olds to vote. On March 10, the Senate passed the resolution unanimously. The House passed it on March 23, by a vote of four hundred to nineteen. In eight days, ten states had ratified the amendment. On June 30, 1971, Ohio became the thirty-sixth state to ratify the amendment; thus the Twenty-sixth Amendment to the U.S. Constitution became law.

In the 1972 election, the voting patterns of eighteen- to twenty-year-olds were similar to those of twenty-one to twenty-four-year-olds. Since then, persons between the ages of eighteen and twenty years have voted less than any other age group. In 1972, 48.3 percent reported that they voted in the presidential election. By 1988, the rate had dropped to 33.2 percent. It rose slightly, to 38.5 percent, in 1992.   —*Glenn Ellen Starr*

ADDITIONAL READING:

"Congress and the Voting-Age Controversy." *Congressional Digest* 49 (March 15-April 15, 1970): 130-160. Similar in format and information to the 1954 *Congressional Digest* article cited below. Updates the information on congressional and state actions. Reprints lengthy, detailed testimony from Senator Edward Kennedy.

Cultice, Wendell W. *Youth's Battle for the Ballot: A History of Voting Age in America.* New York: Greenwood Press, 1992. Detailed analysis, dividing the effort into four periods and examining the role of various constituencies during each. Selective bibliography of sources, 1941-1991.

Johnson, Julia E., comp. *Lowering the Voting Age.* New York: H. W. Wilson, 1944. Anthology reprinting discussions and arguments for and against the measure, including newspaper and magazine articles, journal articles, pamphlets, books, and excerpts from congressional hearings.

"The Question of Lowering the Voting Age to Eighteen." *Congressional Digest* 33, no. 3 (March, 1954): 67-95. Provides background information on the origin of the twenty-one-year-old voting age, constitutional references to voting age, states' rights, and the voting age in other countries. Includes statements from congresspersons and others.

Roth, Robert. "A Rapid Change of Sentiment." *Annals of the American Academy of Political and Social Science* 397

(September, 1971): 83-87. Explains the rapid dissolution of resistance to lowering the voting age and speculates on the political impact the voting patterns of new young voters might have.

SEE ALSO: 1868, Fourteenth Amendment; 1920, U.S. Women Gain the Vote; 1965, Voting Rights Act.

1971 ■ DEVALUATION OF THE DOLLAR: *in the face of mounting balance-of-payments deficits, President Nixon suspends the gold standard and issues wage and price controls*

DATE: August 15, 1971
LOCALE: United States
CATEGORIES: Business and labor; Economics
KEY FIGURES:
Arthur Burns (1904-1987), chair of the Federal Reserve Board
Richard Milhous Nixon (1913-1994), thirty-seventh president of the United States, 1969-1974
Karl Schiller (1911-1994), West German economics minister
Pierre-Paul Schweitzer (1912-1994), managing director of the International Monetary Fund

SUMMARY OF EVENT. During the Great Depression in the 1930's and the political unrest and tumult generated by World War II, foreign exchange rates were uncertain and highly unstable. The leading nations of the world, with the exception of Soviet Russia, met in July, 1944, at Bretton Woods, New Hampshire, to address the problems of foreign exchange. An agreement intended to stabilize international exchange was reached. This agreement, known as the Bretton Woods agreement, established international standards for official foreign exchange. By this agreement, the U.S. dollar became the key currency for international exchange. The dollar was a dominant world currency utilized as a standard for trade between many countries and as a reserve to "back" the currencies of many underdeveloped countries. The underdeveloped countries in Africa, Asia, Europe, and Latin America were anxious for American capital in order to expand their industrial development, while capitalists in the industrially developed nations, who were reluctant to risk ventures in foreign currencies, were seeking the stability of an international order. It was largely expected that the dollar would emerge as *the* international currency.

The major accomplishment of the Bretton Woods conference was to define parities of currencies for international exchange and finance. These parities were defined not only in terms of gold but simultaneously in terms of the American dollar, pegged at the equivalent of one thirty-fifth ounce of gold per dollar. Official changes in the parity value of any currency were permissible under the agreement as a method of dealing with a disequilibrium in a nation's balance of pay-

ments. The World Bank and the International Monetary Fund (IMF) were also established by the Bretton Woods agreement as measures supportive of international monetary stability. It was this established order that governed international finance and exchange until August 15, 1971, when President Richard M. Nixon of the United States suspended the agreement.

A series of events and building pressures led to the collapse of the Bretton Woods agreement and to international monetary reform. By the 1950's and through the 1960's, the European community experienced balance-of-payments surpluses, while the United States' balance of payments ran an average deficit of $1.5 billion per year. This chronic deficit situation for the United States was not alarming in view of the large amounts of dollars involved in foreign exchange. Even to the more pessimistic critics, the role of the dollar as a worldwide reserve currency for a growing world economy appeared successful.

By 1965, however, the United States' balance-of-payments deficit began to increase, and the increases in the deficit quickly escalated. It was apparent that the United States' foreign exchange deficit was a major problem. In early 1971, a large movement of funds from the United States to Europe began to create difficulties in maintaining parity between the dollar and other currencies. In March and April of 1971, overt speculation in foreign exchange markets became newsworthy to the extent that by May 4, 1971, the German *Bundesbank* had absorbed a capital inflow of one billion dollars in one day and, after forty minutes of trading on May 5, had absorbed another billion dollars and had then suspended support of the American dollar. By July, 1971, the United States' reserves deficit had soared to more than eleven billion dollars and the official U.S. gold stock had fallen to nearly ten billion dollars. A congressional subcommittee called for a general realignment of exchange rates, and President Nixon responded on Sunday, August 15, by announcing a major new program that included a ninety-day freeze on wages and prices, new tax measures, a temporary surcharge on imports, and the suspension of the conversion of dollars into gold. This action ended the twenty-seven-year formal role of the U.S. dollar as the world reserve currency.

Many factors contributed to the United States' balance-of-payments problem and the eventual demise of the Bretton Woods agreement. American military expenditures and generous aid programs continued after World War II. The expensive Cold War programs, including the Korean conflict, the Vietnam War, and the U.S. participation in the North Atlantic Treaty Organization (NATO), contributed to an expanding volume of American dollars abroad. Funding the Vietnam conflict through extended debt rather than taxation contributed unanticipated pressures on the United States' balance of payments.

In addition, increasing productivity in other countries brought about significant problems for the United States' balance of payments. Remarkable increases in productivity in Western European countries and Japan dramatically changed the position of the United States in world trade. These countries were increasingly able to produce for themselves and to rely less on goods from the United States. With increasing productivity, these countries were able to compete effectively with the United States in international markets and even to capture significant shares of markets within the United States. The Western European countries were most anxious to advocate changes in the international monetary order, with Karl Schiller, West Germany's economics minister, among the most articulate and outspoken advocates of establishing floating exchange rates.

The development of the European Common Market strengthened the competitive position of the European economies and presented the opportunity for a more unified front in the international financial scene. Pierre-Paul Schweitzer, director of the International Monetary Fund, was a leading spokesman for the European communities and encouraged a continuation of the convertibility of dollars into gold. The increasing productivity in European economies was creating attractive opportunities for American investors, and the European community did not favor any additional impediments to this important flow of capital.

Domestic inflation in the United States and a growing lack of trust in the dollar were also contributing factors to the balance-of-payments problem. In the early 1960's, the European economies were rapidly approaching full employment. European wage and other money costs were rising at a faster pace than those in America. As the sluggish American economy approached full employment in the mid-1960's, however, this situation changed to the point that money costs in the United States grew at rates comparable to those in the European economies. The financial advantages were obliterated and the chronic deficits in the balance of payments became alarmingly apparent. A general apprehension that the U.S. dollar would depreciate in value relative to other currencies became prevalent. Many individuals and governments attempted to liquidate holdings of U.S dollars in favor of gold, thereby contributing to an escalated "gold drain" for the United States in the late 1960's.

Generally, a country may attempt to adjust to a persistent balance-of-payments deficit through internal deflation, through a devaluation in its exchange rate, or through restrictive controls on trade, investment, and exchange. The United States had instituted a series of programs throughout the 1960's that attempted to control investment abroad. In 1963, the interest equalization tax attempted to reduce the flow of dollars to foreign countries. In 1965, the voluntary restraint program was designed to limit direct investments abroad. In 1968, mandatory investment controls were instituted by the U.S. government. "Swap agreements" were made between the Federal Reserve System and the central banks of Europe, and bonds were issued by the U.S. Treasury that were payable in dollars or in a specific foreign currency. These programs were not successful in reducing the balance-of-payments deficit, but they did lessen the drain of gold from the United States and impacted the speculation on the dollar in international exchange markets.

By mid-1971, the U.S. deficit had become more acute. In one week, more than four billion dollars moved into foreign reserves in spite of the view that the dollar was overvalued and would be depreciated. Arthur Burns, chair of the Federal Reserve Board, reported to the Joint Economic Committee on the failure to deal with domestic inflation and the deficit in payments, recommending stringent action. As a result, Nixon made his August 15 announcement of the suspension of gold convertibility of dollars as part of the plan to deal with inflation and the chronic deficit of payments. By this action, the order established by the Bretton Woods agreement was ended. Nixon's move, in effect a devaluation of the dollar, was officially confirmed in the international Smithsonian agreement of December 18, 1971.

Despite the preliminary support occasioned by this agreement, exchange markets found great difficulty in achieving stability. Devaluation had been expected to help reverse the deficit but did not consistently do so. Internationally, the floating exchange rates bogged down trade for a number of months; world currency became more stable as the focus shifted from gold and the dollar to other currencies. Domestically, wage and price controls promised short-term success, but in the long term such controls bent to pressures for wage and price increases, and the problems of unemployment and inflation returned.

—Jonathan M. Furdek

ADDITIONAL READING:

American Enterprise Institute for Public Policy Research. *International Monetary Problems*. Washington, D.C.: Author, 1972. Proceedings of a conference which considered the issues of international monetary reform.

Miller, Robert LeRoy, and Raburn M. Williams. *The New Economics of Richard Nixon: Freezes, Floats, and Fiscal Policy*. San Francisco: Canfield Press, 1972. A critical analysis of Nixon's program, with appendices printing Nixon's August 15 announcement and executive orders.

Mundell, Robert A., and Alexander K. Swoboda, eds. *Monetary Problems of the International Economy*. Chicago: University of Chicago Press, 1969. An account of a September, 1966, conference in Chicago which brought together experts in the field of international finance to debate the theoretical issues surrounding monetary reform.

Sobel, Lester A., ed. *Inflation and the Nixon Administration*. 2 vols. New York: Facts On File, 1974-1975. Presents major economic events in chronological order, allowing the reader to review facts with minimal interpretation by the editors.

Solomon, Robert. *The International Monetary System, 1945-1976: An Insider's View*. New York: Harper & Row, 1977. Provides insights into the international financial situation through the author's association with the Federal Reserve and through interviews with key participants.

Triffin, Robert. *Out International Monetary System: Yesterday, Today, and Tomorrow*. New York: Random House, 1968. Provides historical background to the forces affecting the international monetary system.

Weber, Arnold Robert. *In Pursuit of Price Stability: The*

Wage-Price Freeze of 1971. Washington, D.C.: Brookings Institution, 1973. An explanation of why and how the freeze was implemented from the point of view of an administrator of the program.

SEE ALSO: 1943, Inflation and Labor Unrest; 1968, Nixon Is Elected President; 1973, Arab Oil Embargo and Energy Crisis.

1971 ■ ATTICA STATE PRISON RIOTS:
inmates revolt against inhumane prison conditions, resulting in the most deadly prison riot in U.S. history

DATE: September 9-13, 1971
LOCALE: Attica State Prison, New York
CATEGORIES: Civil rights; Wars, uprisings, and civil unrest
KEY FIGURES:
Roger Champen (born 1933), Attica inmate and spokesman during the riot
Arthur Eve (born 1933), New York State assemblyman and an observer
Vincent R. Mancusi, superintendent of Attica state prison
Russell G. Oswald (born 1908), New York's commissioner of correctional services
Nelson A. Rockefeller (1908-1979), governor of New York
Herman Schwartz (born 1931), professor of law, State University of New York, Buffalo, and an observer
Bobby Seale (born 1936), chairman of the Black Panther Party and an observer
Tom Wicker (born 1926), associate editor of *The New York Times* and an observer

SUMMARY OF EVENT. By the summer of 1971, tension among inmates, guards, and administrators in the New York State prison system had reached a feverish pitch. U.S. penal practice generally was modeled on a system of authoritarian restraint, by which inmates were incarcerated but not trained, and small prison staffs maintained control by bargaining with key inmates. This led to a prison subculture virtually ignored by administrators, including a regular system of rackets and enforced homosexuality, in which violence was the only means of maintaining one's precarious social position. Shrinking state budgets prevented officials from correcting what they acknowledged to be serious problems: understaffed prisons, overcrowding, lack of educational opportunities, censorship, bad food, and decaying facilities. In an unprecedented ruling in 1970, two federal judges had demanded that New York change the disciplinary rules in its prisons. Compliance was slow, however, and had affected prisoners little by the following year. In the summer and fall of 1970, a series of riots and strikes erupted in prisons in New York City, Attica, Napanoch, and Auburn. Although the uprisings ended peaceably, the underlying grievances were not adequately addressed and tensions remained high.

Russell Oswald was a reformer who had taken over as state prison commissioner in December, 1970. Sensing that abuses were particularly acute at Attica, where a prison and budget designed for 1,600 inmates was being used to care for 2,250 men, he complained to Governor Nelson Rockefeller. As if to reinforce Oswald's argument, in the spring of 1971, four hundred inmates went on strike against low shop wages. Although the strike was suppressed, Attica inmates were determined to be heard.

Oswald received many letters from Attica inmates, recounting abuses and complaining about Superintendent Vincent Mancusi's methods. The Attica Liberation Faction petitioned the commissioner, demanding twenty-seven changes to improve the "brutal and dehumanized conditions" at Attica. Eleven inmates sent petitions to federal courts in Buffalo, arguing that they had been treated illegally. Although many prisoners belonged to what traditionally had been competing ethnically based groups—the Black Panthers, Black Muslims, and Puerto Rican Young Lords—the August 21 shooting of the idolized activist George Jackson in San Quentin prison had brought many of them together. The morning after Jackson's death, more than eight hundred Attica inmates came to the dining hall but did not eat breakfast, as a demonstration of inmate organization and solidarity. Lawyers who visited the prison warned officials and the media that the situation in Attica was approaching a flashpoint, with Mancusi losing control. Mancusi cracked down with increased cell checks and more rigid discipline, but neither he nor Oswald dealt substantively with inmate demands.

Tensions escalated on September 8, when officers had difficulty removing two scuffling inmates from a recreation yard. Later that evening, as the two inmates were being taken to solitary confinement, officers were assaulted verbally and one was pelted with a full can of soup. The next morning, as officials attempted to return the guilty inmate to his cell, a lieutenant was attacked by prisoners in a hallway. At 9:00 A.M., the company of prisoners poured down the hall toward Times Square, the main intersection controlling access to all prison blocks. There a faulty gate gave way, enabling prisoners to gain strategic control of all four prison blocks. Frantic prisoners, long frustrated in their attempts to have their grievances heard, turned baseball bats, pipes, hatchets, chains, and hammers into weapons to be used against prison guards, who were outnumbered twenty to one. Using a forklift, the prisoners battered their way into the metal shop and set fire to the chapel, schoolhouse, and other buildings. One officer was killed in this initial phase of the uprising.

After nearly an hour and a half, more than twelve hundred inmates had gathered in the recreation yard of D-block with forty-three hostages, several of whom were later released for medical reasons. Roger Champen, a respected inmate, quickly took control of the situation, issuing orders to organize mattresses, food, and water. Other inmates also spoke, convincing ethnic factions to put aside differences for the common goal of prison reform. By noon, however, five hundred troopers, correctional offices, and deputies had arrived outside the prison, expecting the worst.

Overshadowing Mancusi, Oswald arrived around 2:00 P.M. to begin negotiations, allowing two activists to pass through inspection and into D-yard. Two observers, law professor Herman Schwartz and state assemblyman Arthur Eve, immediately were handed a list of demands, including total amnesty, transportation to a nonimperialistic country, federal jurisdiction, and observation by a select group of media and ethnic representatives. After twenty-five minutes, during which they tried to convince inmates that transportation out of the country and federal jurisdiction were unrealistic, Eve and Schwartz left the yard. Later that afternoon, Oswald himself hesitantly entered the yard and was presented with five demands and fourteen Practical Proposals, including more prisoner rights, minimum wages, true religious freedom, uncensored communication, and more out-of-cell time.

By the afternoon of Friday, September 10, many of the thirty-six observers had arrived. The negotiating team numbered almost thirty when it entered D-yard. Having talked with inmate leaders and taken votes on individual points, observers came out in the early morning of September 11 with a clearer view of prisoner demands.

Saturday brought some hope, as Wyoming County district attorney Louis James issued a statement indicating that indiscriminate prosecutions would not be carried out against rebellious inmates. After further negotiations, a document containing twenty-eight "proposals acceptable to Commissioner Oswald" was agreed upon by observers. After observer Bobby Seale, chairman of the Black Panther Party, refused to endorse the twenty-eight proposals, inmates rejected the document and observers once again left the yard.

The light rain of Sunday morning foreshadowed an unproductive day. The committee of observers tried to get Governor Rockefeller to reinforce personally what were still perceived as hollow government promises. They also hoped his presence would deter the hundreds of armed troopers and correctional officers who were anxiously preparing for the attack, which was already being planned. Despite the pleas of observers, however, Rockefeller refused to come.

On Monday, September 13, Oswald released his final ultimatum to the prisoners, giving them one hour to surrender. Despite the sight of blindfolded hostages with knives held to their throats, after inmates rejected the twenty-eight proposals, Oswald ordered the attack. At 9:43 A.M., power to the prison was shut off, two helicopters swept D-yard with tear gas and pepper gas, and troopers armed with gas masks and guns raided the yard. By 9:52 A.M., the firing stopped, and by 10:30 A.M., D- and C-blocks were cleared and secured.

Although forty-three people were killed in the Attica uprising, the press was quick to praise the government attack, taking at face value the rumor that many of the hostages had had their throats slit by inmates. Later autopsies and investigations proved that only one officer had died at the hands of inmates, from wounds received on September 9, while ten

hostages and twenty-nine inmates were killed by the rifle fire of officials on the morning of September 13. Since that time, it generally has been accepted that the carnage of Attica could have been prevented by patient firmness in negotiation. In the quarter-century following the Attica riots, there were no comparable confrontations in which unrestricted armed attacks led to considerable loss of life.   *—John Powell*

ADDITIONAL READING:

Badillo, Herman, and Milton Haynes. *A Bill of No Rights: Attica and the American Prison System*. New York: Outerbridge and Lazard, 1972. An account by a principal observer, who urges drastic reform of the U.S. prison system.

Five Days at Attica. Rochester, N.Y.: *Democrat* and *Chronicle*, 1971. Accessible reprints of contemporary articles from September 10 to September 14.

New York State Special Commission on Attica. *Attica: The Official Report of the New York State Special Commission on Attica*. New York: Praeger, 1972. Commissioned by the courts, this authoritative investigation determined that misunderstandings and abuses could lead to another Attica. Illustrations and seven appendixes.

Oswald, Russell G. *Attica: My Story*. New York: Doubleday, 1972. Defense of the state's use of force against Attica prisoners.

Wicker, Tom. *A Time to Die: The Attica Prison Revolt*. 1975. Reprint. Lincoln: University of Nebraska Press, 1994. A thoroughly researched account by one of the principal participants. Concludes that the Attica "massacre" was principally the fault of callous procedures of the state of New York.

1971 ■ ALASKA NATIVE CLAIMS SETTLEMENT ACT: *Native Alaskans receive compensation in return for relinquishing their claims to lands they historically occupied*

DATE: December 18, 1971
LOCALE: Washington, D.C.
CATEGORIES: Laws and acts; Native American history
KEY FIGURES:
Walter J. Hickel (born 1919), secretary of the interior. 1961-1969
Richard Milhous Nixon (1913-1994), thirty-seventh president of the United States, 1969-1974
Stewart L. Udall (born 1920), secretary of the interior, 1969-1970

SUMMARY OF EVENT. The Alaska Native Claims Settlement Act (ANCSA) was signed into law by President Richard M. Nixon on December 18, 1971. It represented the culmination of a long struggle over native land claims that was compounded by the immediate need to construct a pipeline to carry oil from Prudhoe Bay to Valdez through lands claimed by Native Alaskans. The ANCSA granted forty-four million acres of land and $962.5 million to Native Alaskans in exchange for the relinquishment of their claims to the remaining nine-tenths

The Alaska Native Claims Settlement Act provided for an equitable distribution of funds among the three primary native groups of the region, Aleuts, Inuits, and Eskimos, such as this Eskimo family of the Kuskokwim River region. The measure transformed Alaskan native economies from subsistence-level hunting and fishing economies to business-for-profit economies. The difficult transition from life on reservations to membership in native corporations nevertheless gave Native Alaskans influence in state politics that they had never before enjoyed. (Library of Congress)

of the land in Alaska. The law provided for an equitable distribution of funds among the three primary native groups (the Aleuts, Inuits, and Eskimos) and allowed first village corporations and then the regional native corporations, formed by the ANCSA, to select their lands. The Alaska Federation of Natives, speaking for the Alaskan native groups, accepted the settlement by a vote of 511 to 56, despite concerns about how it would affect traditional native patterns of hunting and fishing.

Land claims had long been a disputed issue between Native Alaskans and the U.S. government. A Supreme Court ruling in 1955 declared that the Fifth Amendment to the Constitution did not protect native land rights. When Alaska became the forty-ninth state of the Union in 1959, it was granted the right to select 103.3 million acres of land over the next twenty-five years without any acknowledgment of claims by Native Alaskans. Between 1959 and 1969, the state claimed nineteen

million acres. By comparison, Native Alaskans owned only five hundred acres and had restricted title to another fifteen thousand acres. Since the state claimed nearly 28 percent of Alaskan territory, fears arose that there would be little valuable land remaining to satisfy native claims, and native opposition to state land claims intensified.

Some Native Alaskans believed that proposed use of their lands by the state or federal government would violate traditional rights enjoyed by the native inhabitants. The Atomic Energy Commission, for example, sought to use Cape Thompson as a nuclear testing site; it was situated near an Eskimo village, with a population of three hundred, at Point Hope and the ancestral lands the villagers used for hunting. Another issue under dispute was the proposed Rampart Dam, a hydroelectric project that was to be built on the Yukon River in the north-central region of the state. Opponents of the dam argued that it would damage wildlife breeding grounds, displace twelve hundred natives from seven small villages, and endanger the livelihood of five thousand to six thousand others who depended on salmon in that area. Finally, the state was beginning to legislate hunting restrictions on state-owned land, which natives believed would threaten their traditional way of life. In the early 1960's, native groups began to take action to protect their interests. Between 1961 and 1968, Alaskan natives filed claims protesting the state's use of 337 million acres of Alaskan territory.

In 1960, Native Alaskans constituted roughly 20 percent of the Alaskan population. For those living in native communities or villages, life consisted of subsistence hunting and fishing, which necessitated access to large amounts of land. Many were seasonally employed and lived in poverty. Seventy percent had less than an elementary education, and only ten percent had received a secondary education. Owing to disease, alcoholism, and impoverished conditions, the life span of Native Alaskans was about thirty-five years of age, half the national average. Many Native Alaskans believed that existing laws, rather than protecting them, stripped them of rights to lands that they claimed. They generally did not consider either the state or the federal government to be supportive of their concerns.

Two other groups who entered the contest over land claims were developers and environmentalists. Developers desired the construction of more fisheries and canneries, as well as highways and industries that would enable Alaska's natural resources to be fully developed. Environmentalists sought protection of certain lands as parks, natural wilderness areas, and wildlife refuges. By 1966, land disputes had become so hotly contested that Secretary of the Interior Stewart Udall ordered a freeze on all transfers of land claimed by the natives until a mutually acceptable agreement could be reached.

Following the discovery at Prudhoe Bay, on the North Slope of Alaska, of one of the largest oil fields ever found, the federal government proposed that a pipeline be constructed across the state to transport the oil to Valdez, a city easily accessible for loading petroleum because of its position as a year-round ice-free port on Prince William Sound. The proposed route of the eight-hundred-mile Trans-Alaska Pipeline included twenty miles of land that was claimed by Native Alaskans, who feared that construction of the pipeline would likely lead to other infringements of their land claims. By this time, however, the Alaska Native Brotherhood and the Alaska Federation of Natives, among other native groups, were well organized to press for their interests. It became evident that the land issue would have to be resolved before the pipeline was built.

Walter Hickel, Udall's successor as secretary of the interior, extended the land-freeze in 1970. A federal restraining order halted the project until a settlement could be reached. Because developers and oil companies were anxious to get the project under way, pressure was applied to settle the issue quickly. Other interested parties anticipated benefits from the construction of the pipeline, which promised lower petroleum prices to the federal government, revenue to the state, land preservation

to environmentalists, and previously denied rights to natives, particularly title to land that they believed was theirs. British Petroleum, one of the interested parties, agreed to lobby for a bill that would protect native land interests. A joint Senate-House conference committee drew up the final bill, which gained widespread support. It passed Congress and was signed into law by Nixon on December 18, 1971.

The ANCSA resolved the long-standing dispute regarding native rights to land in Alaska. Native land claims were extinguished in return for title to forty-four million acres that included mineral rights, as well as $962.5 million in additional compensation. Twelve regional corporations were established between 1972 and 1974 (to which a thirteenth was added for natives not living in Alaska) in order to manage the funds and organize land selection. Every Alaskan native became a member of a regional corporation, in which he or she was given one hundred shares of stock. In addition, about 220 village corporations were formed to oversee the distribution of land at the local level. Native reservations were abolished, and sixteen million acres of land were set aside for selection by the village corporations.

The village corporations were allowed to select their land over a three-year period and the regional corporations over four years. Beneficiaries of the land claims were required to be one-quarter native Alaskan (either Inuit, Aleut, or Eskimo) and had to be born on or before December 18, 1971. While the land selection involved a lengthy process, native corporations eventually selected 102 million acres instead of the allotted 44 million. For twenty years after the passage of the act, Native Alaskans were not permitted to sell their stock to non-natives, and their undeveloped land was not to be taxed. In 1987, Congress passed the "1991 amendments," which preserved the tax-exemption benefits on undeveloped lands indefinitely and allowed new stock to be issued to Native Alaskans born after December 18, 1971.

The ANCSA was, in many respects, a watershed in the history of Native Alaskans that promised to change their way of life permanently. The act began the transformation of Alaskan native cultures from a subsistence economy based on traditional hunting and fishing patterns to one based on ownership of modern business-for-profit ventures. Many Native Alaskans embarked on a difficult transition from life on reservations to membership in native corporations that undertook a variety of commercial enterprises. These corporations invested in banking, hotels, fisheries, real estate, and mineral exploration. Some were successful and some were not. Nevertheless, the acquisition of land and income gave Native Alaskans a position of influence in state politics that they had never had before.

—*Anne-Marie E. Ferngren*

ADDITIONAL READING:

Anders, Gary C. "Social and Economic Consequences of Federal Indian Policy." *Economic Development and Cultural Change* 37, no. 2 (January, 1989): 285-303. Includes discussion of the effects of the ANCSA on the Alaskan Natives.

Arnold, Robert D., et al. *Alaska Native Land Claims.* Anchorage: Alaska Native Foundation, 1978. A comprehensive discussion of the act and its significance.

Berger, Thomas R. *Village Journey: The Report of the Alaska Native Review Commission*. New York: Hill & Wang, 1985. A critical account of the effects of the ANCSA on Native Alaskans.

Berry, Mary Clay. *The Alaska Pipeline: The Politics of Oil and Native Land Claims*. Bloomington: Indiana University Press, 1975. Describes the influence of the construction of the pipeline on the passage of the ANCSA.

Case, David S. *Alaska Natives and American Laws*. Fairbanks: University of Alaska Press, 1984. A detailed description of the historical interaction of Native Alaskans and U.S. law.

Flanders, Nicholas E. "The ANCSA Amendments of 1987 and Land Management in Alaska." *The Polar Record* 25, no. 155 (October, 1989): 315-322. Discusses the modifications of the ANCSA by the 1991 Amendments.

Strohmeyer, John. *Extreme Conditions: Big Oil and the Transformation of Alaska*. New York: Simon & Schuster, 1993. Illustrates the impact of the petroleum industry and law on native peoples.

SEE ALSO: 1974, Construction of the Alaska Pipeline.

1972 ■ UNITED FARM WORKERS JOINS WITH AFL-CIO: *the AFL-CIO formally recognizes the farmworkers as a union, marking the rise of a major organization fighting for workers' rights*

DATE: 1972
LOCALE: Salinas Valley, California
CATEGORIES: Business and labor; Latino American history
KEY FIGURES:
Bud Antle, a major lettuce grower in the Salinas Valley
César Chávez (1927-1993), leader of the United Farm Workers of America
Bill Grami, official of the Western Conference of Teamsters
SUMMARY OF EVENT. The success of strikes and worker organization during the 1960's in the San Joaquin Valley in Delano, California, inspired farmworkers to organize in the Salinas and Santa Maria Valleys, where 70 percent of the United States' head lettuce was grown. Many of the nation's strawberries, broccoli, cauliflower, tomatoes, carrots, artichokes, celery, garlic, and other vegetables are also grown in this area. In 1970, after 140 grape growers signed contracts with the United Farm Workers Organizing Committee (UFWOC), lettuce growers were faced with demands for union recognition of elections, in which the UFWOC appeared to be the certain winner. Growers had to choose between signing the agreement and facing the same type of farmworker strategies that had proved successful in Delano. Growers elected to bypass the elections and negotiate with the Teamsters Union. This strategy, utilized successfully in 1961 by one of Salinas' largest lettuce growers, Bud Antle, when he signed a contract with the Teamsters,

allowed growers to avoid the more stringent demands by the Agricultural Workers Organizing Committee (AWOC). A 1972 agreement between the farmworkers and the American Federation of Labor-Congress of Industrial Organizations (AFL-CIO) provided members of UFWOC with official recognition and a crucial ally in their struggles with the Teamsters.

By 1970, California field-workers were organized and threatening strikes and boycotts. This created an unstable flow of produce handled by truck drivers, cannery workers, and other Teamster members. At this point, Teamster officials wanted representation rights that would allow them to control the field-workers. Since the 1930's, the Teamsters had had jurisdiction over those field-workers who drove trucks, operated field conveyors, and pulled shed trailers with tractors. The Teamsters were aware that UFWOC would protest any moves in this direction as a violation of the 1967 jurisdictional agreement made in Delano with UFWOC. The result would likely be demands for elections, and a vote in favor of UFWOC would demonstrate that the Teamsters did not represent the field-workers.

July, 1970, is a crucial date in the escalation of conflict between growers and the UFWOC. Several vegetable growers approached Western Conference of Teamsters official Bill Grami during new contract negotiations with Teamster truck drivers. The growers wanted Teamsters to expand their representation to include field-workers. When truckers called a strike, the Teamsters found a reason for expanding representation to include field-workers when they decided to remain off work until contracts were also granted to field-workers. Grami responded that Teamsters had received numerous informal requests from field-workers for Teamster representation.

Following grower ratification of a new truckers' contract, they also agreed that the Western Conference of Teamsters would be allowed and encouraged to recruit farmworkers. Shortly thereafter, nearly all of the 170 growers in the area announced that they had signed Teamster agreements. Under terms of the agreement between the Teamsters and growers, workers would be required to join the Teamsters and pay $1.25 a week in dues. The agreement included pay raises of ten to fifteen cents an hour and minimal health and welfare benefits. The union hiring hall, utilized by farmworkers to staff the fields, was eliminated by the agreement giving growers freedom to hire workers.

The grower-Teamster agreement came one day after UFWOC leader César Chávez announced an organizing drive aimed at the vegetable fields. Chávez reacted to the grower agreement and marched into Salinas with several hundred farmworkers and an AFL-CIO contingent headed by organizing director Bill Kircher. One grower was picketed after firing 250 workers for not joining the Teamsters. UFWOC also began preparing legal action and a nationwide lettuce boycott.

Teamsters at the national level favored conciliatory action. The Auto Workers Union, a close ally of UFWOC, pressured national Teamsters leaders to help resolve the conflict. The Western Conference of Teamsters was asked to arrange a treaty with UFWOC, with assistance from the bishops' committee, which had been instrumental in the vineyard settlement. This settlement reallocated jurisdiction over fieldworkers to UFWOC and stipulated that the growers who had recently signed Teamster contracts could switch to UFWOC. However, growers refused to give up Teamster contracts, and Grami claimed that the treaty bound both unions to honor the growers' wishes. After two weeks of attempts by UFWOC and the bishops' committee to get the growers to relent, a strike was called. Hundreds of UFWOC members and supporters picketed in front of targeted farms around Salinas and held outdoor rallies highlighted by emotional speeches. Growers countered by going to court for a restraining order against picketing, while the Monterey County Board of Supervisors in Salinas adopted an antinoise ordinance that prohibited UFWOC from using any voice-amplifying equipment. Despite dozens of arrests, pickets ignored these orders.

The California Supreme Court overturned rulings by the Monterey County Superior Court and ruled that there could be one informational picket at each of twenty-two of the Salinas Valley farms that constituted the strikers' prime targets. UFWOC was refused the right to call a boycott against any of the 170 growers holding Teamster contracts. UFWOC ignored the ruling and called a boycott that focused on food markets in sixty-four U.S. cities. This boycott was difficult, because lettuce is a staple and growers waged a strong counterattack. Antle, for example, persuaded another Superior Court judge that UFWOC's actions against his firm violated the state's Jurisdictional Strike Act and UFWOC's treaty with the Teamsters. In a favorable ruling for the growers, Judge Gordon Campbell ordered the arrest of Chávez. This event intensified support for UFWOC and Chávez. More than two thousand UFWOC members and supporters, including Ethel Kennedy and Coretta Scott King, accompanied Chávez to the jailhouse. They initiated prayer vigils and highly publicized demonstrations. Three days before Christmas, the judge ordered the release of Chávez.

The boycott continued into the early months of 1971, while national Teamster leaders and a bishops' committee continued unsuccessful attempts to persuade growers to sign UFWOC contracts. The greatest conflict was over the hiring hall, which was a crucial method for granting the union the authority promised by the vineyard contracts. Growers did not like the workers sent out by the halls, complaining that dispatchers sent out older workers, whose seniority gave them priority, rather than the faster young workers requested by the growers.

AFL-CIO leaders agreed in 1972 to grant Chávez a charter that formally recognized the Organizing Committee as a union. UFWOC became a full-fledged affiliate of the AFL-CIO and was renamed the United Farm Workers of America (UFW). This gave the organization official standing, a role in AFL-CIO decisions and operations, and a sense of stability. This agreement did not abate the conflict between the grower-Teamster coalition and the UFW. In January, 1973, the Teamsters went after the UFW's grape contracts. Teamster organizers went through the fields to get signatures on petitions asking the growers to sign up with their union. Nine hours after the UFW

contract expired, Teamster and grower representatives announced they had negotiated contracts covering virtually all of the Coachella Valley's vineyards. The Teamsters would eliminate the union hiring hall through the contracts and sign agreements with labor contractors to help supply workers.

The conflict between farmworkers and growers increased during the early 1970's. This period was characterized by increasingly violent strikes among Teamsters and UFW supporters. California's efforts at legislating a solution to the conflict were largely unsuccessful. The UFW was able to survive in part because of their formal agreement with the AFL-CIO, which continued to support them with financing and staff. From 1975 to 1980, more than five hundred elections were held in the fields of California, the majority won by the UFW. Finally, in March, 1977, Chávez and the Teamsters president Frank Fitzsimmons agreed that UFW would represent all farmworkers.   —*Gregory Freeland*

ADDITIONAL READING:

Edid, Maralyn. *Farm Labor Organizing: Trends and Prospects.* Ithaca, N.Y.: ILR Press. 1994. A brief examination of farmworker labor organizing that discusses the farmworkers' situation in the 1980's and early 1990's.

Fuller, Varden, and John Mamer. "Constraints on California Farm Worker Unionization." *Industrial Relations* 17 (May, 1978): 143-155. Includes an examination of policies of resistance to farmworker organizing.

Meister, Dick, and Anne Loftis. *A Long Time Coming: The Struggle to Unionize America's Farm Workers.* New York: Macmillan, 1977. A clear, concise discussion of the farmworkers' movement and negotiations between workers, Teamsters, and growers.

Segur, W. H., and Varden Fuller. "California's Farm Labor Elections: An Analysis of the Initial Results." *Monthly Labor Review* 99 (December): 25-30. A useful analysis of voting patterns in crucial farmworker elections.

Taylor, Ronald. *Chávez and the Farm Workers.* Boston: Beacon Press, 1975. A clear description of César Chávez and the movement for farmworker rights.

SEE ALSO: 1930's, Mass Deportations of Mexicans; 1942, Bracero Program; 1954, Operation Wetback; 1965, Delano Grape Strike; 1965, Immigration and Nationality Act; 1986, Immigration Reform and Control Act.

1972 ■ RAPPROCHEMENT WITH CHINA: *after two decades of Cold War, détente between the United States and the People's Republic of China signals a more pragmatic approach to U.S. interests*

DATE: February 21, 1972
LOCALE: Beijing, China
CATEGORIES: Diplomacy and international relations; Government and politics

Key figures:

Henry Alfred Kissinger (born 1923), special assistant for national security affairs to President Nixon, 1969-1973, and secretary of state, 1973-1977

Richard Milhous Nixon (1913-1994), thirty-seventh president of the United States, 1969-1974

Mao Zedong (1893-1976), chairman of the Chinese Communist Party and effective ruler of China

Zhou Enlai (1898-1976), Mao's lieutenant and premier of China

Summary of event. In the eyes of the world, the harmony that emerged between the People's Republic of China and the United States in 1972 came with stunning swiftness. For the prior generation, the two countries had been the deadliest of enemies: Americans had regarded Chinese communism as even more hateful than Russian and maintained an almost belligerent defense of Taiwan; mainland China was filled with attacks against the "paper tiger" of U.S. capitalism. In less than a year, all of this changed—or even reversed course. A U.S. table tennis team touring Japan received and accepted an invitation to visit the People's Republic of China in April, 1971. Three months later, Henry Kissinger was in Beijing, acting as a special emissary from the president and arranging for United States leaders to make a state visit to China. In February, 1972, the actual visit occurred in a welcoming, almost effusive atmosphere. Ten months was very little time for so dramatic a realignment of national friendships, but the way had been prepared by years of developments.

Rapprochement between China and the United States followed a slow change in the logic of world affairs. In the early 1960's, the setting of foreign policies was established and straightforward. The United States and the Soviet Union represented two opposite societies and dominated the rest of the world through overwhelming military and economic strength. World maps showed a wide swath of red stretching from central Europe to Southeast Asia: the communist "monolith," under the leadership of the Soviet Union. Western Europe, North America, and Japan were closely coordinated in their opposition to further communist gains, and the poor nations of the Southern Hemisphere were still largely subservient to Western guidance. Almost all important diplomacy was geared to the Cold War struggle between these two spheres of power.

Over the decade that followed, the two opposing sides each loosened somewhat, and the unquestioned power of their leaders gradually slipped. As the free countries of Europe's Common Market recovered and identified their interests more closely, the economic and political leadership of the United States declined noticeably. Japan developed from a junior partner of the United States to a rival economic power. U.S. interventions in Cuba, in the Dominican Republic, and above all in Vietnam caused widespread resentment against such free use of military might and encouraged the appearance of Third World nations that opposed the influence of U.S. capitalism. By 1970, the United States had less influence in the world than at any time since World War II.

Soviet influence had declined even further. The postwar spread of communism had slowed considerably by the mid-1950's. Underdeveloped countries tended to be as wary of the Soviet Union as they were of the United States, and the ruthless Soviet suppression of Czechoslovakia in 1968 testified to the restiveness of the communist satellites in Eastern Europe. Finally, there was the problem of China. As it had prospered and stabilized after long decades of revolution, the People's Republic showed signs of marking its own course. Soviet aid and technology were welcomed, but party chairman Mao Zedong and Premier Zhou Enlai insisted on freedom from Soviet influence. Chinese communism became very different from that prevailing in the Soviet Union; there was a greater emphasis on the social and mental life of the people, and less concern with immediate industrial growth. Soviet attempts to apply pressure only estranged the two countries; a border dispute was revived, and each nation began to view the other as a dangerous ideological opponent.

By 1966 or 1967, these changes were pushing China and the United States toward mutual recognition. The People's Republic was dangerously isolated; the economic trade and diplomatic prestige afforded by closer relations with the United States were clearly needed. The United States, for its part, could use China as a counterweight against the Soviet Union, as a buttress to the alliance with Japan (which sought trade with China), and as a bolster to its darkened image as a friend of the Third World. Richard M. Nixon, writing in the prestigious journal *Foreign Affairs*, in October, 1967, admitted as much: The fight against communism, he argued, must accommodate itself to a more realistic approach. Other problems hindered any thawing of relations, however. The Vietnam War was raging, and both China and the United States feared clashes between their troops. Ideological anger in the two countries was still very great, and a liberal president such as Lyndon Johnson would be especially susceptible to charges of pro-communism if he risked an approach to the People's Republic. At the same time, the Chinese were passing through the upheaval of the Cultural Revolution, turning the nation inward and very much away from cooperation with capitalist nations.

Within a few years, all of these barriers had disappeared. President Nixon's formidable reputation as an anticommunist could survive détente. Within a few months of taking office, he sent out feelers to China and received encouraging responses. The Cultural Revolution wound down in 1969, and a sobered Beijing sought to solidify its international position. By 1971, when a gradually withdrawing United States did not support a South Vietnamese invasion of Laos, the Chinese were satisfied that they had nothing to fear from the United States. Invitations soon followed.

Both the Nixon entourage and their Chinese hosts set modest goals for the February visit, and these were easily achieved. The two countries agreed to extend diplomatic, economic, and cultural ties, and arranged for further visits of U.S. leaders to China. More important than specific exchanges, however, were the symbolic acts of friendship: the handshakes, discussions,

President Nixon shakes hands with the chairman of the Chinese Communist Party, Mao Zedong. Détente between the United States and China, formerly bitter enemies, marked a new, pragmatic approach to U.S. foreign policy. (National Archives/Nixon Project)

toasts, and the famous photograph of Mao and Nixon chatting together. The visit was surrounded with a certain aura of wonder, as both sides found they could like those who had so recently been deadly enemies. U.S. journalists and diplomats expressed surprise at the serene order of Chinese society; the Chinese were eager to share ideas with people from the United States. Both sides were pleased that friendship came so easily.

Subsequent years witnessed a growth and widening of U.S.-Chinese cooperation, although there were no major diplomatic achievements. The chief obstacle to full relations was the existence of Nationalist China, and on this issue the two nations agreed to disagree. China sent gymnasts, students, scientists, and table tennis players to the United States, both to perform and to observe. Thousands of U.S. citizens went to China and came away impressed. Boeing negotiated the sale of several jets to the People's Republic, and the United States government arranged for large shipments of wheat and corn. Ideological tensions remained and showed no sign of going away, but this only made the achievement and implications of Sino-American détente all the more impressive. The rapprochement between the United States and China survived several leadership changes in both countries, as well as various geopolitical events. After years of an ideologically charged Cold War, the world seemed to be moving away from the war of ideas.

Then came the collapse of the Soviet bloc and the discrediting of communism in Eastern Europe in 1989. In the 1990's, the Soviet Union was only a Cold War memory, and China stood as one of the few countries still committed to communism, and certainly the most important. Without the geostrategic necessity afforded by the logic of the Cold War, Washington's relationship with China was suddenly subjected to reevaluation. Latent misgivings about Sino-American rapprochement returned to the surface. Alleged human rights violations in China, most dramatically illustrated at Tiananmen Square, reinvigorated the old Taiwan lobby. However, years of growing trade relations between the United States and the People's Republic, including Washington's granting of most favored nation status to Beijing, militated against a break in Sino-U.S. relations. The need for political stability in Central Asia also bolstered the case for normalized relations with China. As the end of the twentieth century drew near, relations between the leader of global anticommunism and the world's largest communist country remained stable.

—*Richard H. Sander, updated by Steve D. Boilard*

ADDITIONAL READING:

Chiang, Hsiang-tse. "From Hostility to Reconciliation." In *The United States and China*. Chicago: University of Chicago Press, 1988. Offers a Chinese perspective on Sino-U.S. relations. Although the book covers the period from 1783 until 1978, this chapter focuses on the time from the 1950's through the 1970's. Somewhat anti-American in tone.

Cohen, Warren I. "Rapprochement—At Last." In *America's Response to China: A History of Sino-American Relations*. 3d ed. New York: Columbia University Press, 1990. Written in easy, narrative style, with a strong focus on international factors, particularly the role of the Soviet Union. Somewhat pessimistic about prospects for U.S.-Chinese relations in the 1990's. Bibliographic essay.

Garson, Robert A. "From Cultural Revolution to the Beijing Summit, 1966-1972." In *The United States and China Since 1949: A Troubled Affair*. London: Pinter, 1994. A focused historical narrative on the emergence of rapprochement.

Garver, John W. *China's Decision for Rapprochement with the United States, 1968-1971*. Boulder, Colo.: Westview Press, 1982. Explains China's rapprochement decision in terms of the international system, Chinese internal political dynamics, and individual personalities. Includes data on China's relative military strength, economic and trade position, and internal political makeup. A thorough, focused account.

Schaller, Michael. "The Long Journey: Sino-American Détente." In *The United States and China in the Twentieth Century*. 2d ed. New York: Oxford University Press, 1990. Analyzes U.S.-Chinese relations during the Nixon years. Photos and suggested additional readings.

Stoessinger, John G. "The Winding Road to Reality." In *Nations at Dawn: China, Russia, and America*. 6th ed. New York: McGraw-Hill, 1994. A brief account of Sino-American détente under Nixon and Kissinger, and its legacy into the early 1990's.

United States Foreign Policy, 1972. Washington, D.C.: Government Printing Office, 1973. The government's official report on foreign affairs in 1972, including rapprochement with China.

SEE ALSO: 1950, Korean War; 1955, Formosa Resolution; 1973, Détente with the Soviet Union; 1979, United States and China Establish Full Diplomatic Relations.

1972 ■ EQUAL EMPLOYMENT OPPORTUNITY ACT: *landmark legislation helps redress historic discrimination against women and minorities in hiring and promotion*

DATE: March 13, 1972
LOCALE: Washington, D.C.
CATEGORIES: African American history; Civil rights; Women's issues
KEY FIGURES:

William Brown III (born 1928), chairman of the Equal Employment Opportunity Commission
Alan Cranston (born 1914), Democratic senator from California
Samuel J. Ervin (1896-1985), Democratic senator from North Carolina
John F. Kennedy (1917-1963), thirty-fifth president of the United States, 1961-1963
Richard Milhous Nixon (1913-1994), thirty-seventh president of the United States, 1969-1974

SUMMARY OF EVENT. The Equal Employment Opportunity Act of 1972 was an omnibus bill appended to Title VII of the Civil Rights Act, which had been enacted on July 2, 1964, to meet a need for federal legislation dealing with job discrimination on the basis of "race, color, religion, sex or national origin." The 1964 act was charged to enforce the constitutional right to vote, to protect constitutional rights in public facilities and public education, to prevent discrimination in federally assisted programs, and to establish an Equal Employment Opportunity Commission (EEOC). Title VII did not, however, give comprehensive jurisdiction to the EEOC.

A series of laws and executive orders has built up over the years to add to the momentum against discrimination in all areas of American life. With enactment of the Fourteenth and Fifteenth Amendments, the Civil Rights Acts of 1866 and 1875, and a series of laws passed in the mid- and late 1880's, the government and the president, in theory at least, gained sufficient authority to eradicate racial discrimination, including employment bias. No president, however, used his constitutional power in this regard. With the peaking of the Civil Rights movement in the early 1960's, the pace of progress toward equal opportunity accelerated. President John F. Kennedy's Executive Order 10925 established the Committee on Equal Employment Opportunity, the predecessor of the EEOC. Numerous other executive orders by succeeding presidents followed, each chipping away at discrimination in employment.

The first modern federal legislation to deal specifically with employment discrimination, however, was the Equal Pay Act of 1963. As a result of this act, more than $37.5 million was subsequently found to be due to 91,661 employees, almost all of them women, for the years between 1963 and 1972. Then followed the momentous Civil Rights Act of 1964, which contained the provision for equal employment opportunity that would be expanded with the 1972 law.

The push for the Equal Employment Opportunity Act was a natural result of many forces in the early 1970's: The economic disparity between white men, on one hand, and minorities and women, one the other, had become more apparent and disturbing. Women and minorities were generally last hired and first fired, with little chance for promotion. Yet, one-third of the U.S. workforce were women. Although most women worked in order to support themselves and their families, many people still considered their employment to be expendable and marginal. This was especially true for poor women, minority women, and female heads of households. Female college graduates earned only slightly more per year than the average white man with an eighth-grade education. In the 1960's, female-headed households were largely black women with one thousand dollars less than their white counterparts in annual median income. The median annual income for white women in 1971 was slightly more than five thousand dollars, and for non-white women, four thousand dollars. Blacks in general suffered more from lower salary and lower job security and benefits because, in part, they either were discouraged or, in many cases, were not permitted to join labor or professional unions. In 1972, some 88 percent of unionists—about 15 million—were white, while only 2.1 million were from minority groups.

Another motivation to push for the EEO Act was unemployment. In 1971, the general unemployment rate was close to 6 percent as compared to 3.4 percent as recently as 1969. Rates of joblessness were highest among the veterans returning from Vietnam (12.4 percent), and in cities with high minority populations such as Jersey City (9 to 11.9 percent) and Detroit (6 to 8.9 percent). The U.S. Department of Labor reported in 1972 that one-fifth of all wage and salary earners were unionized and males outnumbered females four to one.

The unemployment issue had plagued government and business ever since Congress passed the Employment Act of 1946, which declared, among other things, that it was federal policy to promote "maximum employment."

On March 13, 1972, the EEO Act was passed by Congress, and on March 24, it was signed into law by President Richard Nixon. Primary responsibility for eliminating employment discrimination was entrusted to the Equal Employment Opportunity Commission (EEOC). Congress increased EEOC's authority dramatically by giving it power to issue cease-and-desist orders, to receive and investigate charges, and to engage in mediation and conciliation regarding discriminatory practices. Jurisdiction of the EEOC was extended to cover all companies and unions of fifteen or more employees, private educational institutions, and state and local governments. The EEOC found broad patterns of discrimination. It resolved most of them and referred unresolved cases to the attorney general, who had authority to file federal lawsuits.

Affirmative action became one means to promote equal employment opportunity. It was a controversial measure from the start. Opponents of affirmative action viewed it as preferential treatment or "reverse discrimination," often invoking the decision in *Griggs v. Duke Power Company* (1971), in which the Supreme Court noted that Congress did not intend to prefer the less qualified over the better qualified simply because of minority origin. Proponents of affirmative action believed that when properly implemented, the policy did not do away with competition but, rather, leveled the playing field to create equal *opportunity* for jobs in hiring, on-the-job treatment, and firing policies. Affirmative action, according to proponents, meant a conscious effort to root out all types of inequality of employment opportunity, such as unrealistic job requirements, non-job-related selection instruments and procedures, insufficient opportunity for upward mobility, and inadequate publicity about job openings.

The U.S. Civil Service Commission provided technical assistance to state and local governments in developing affirmative action plans and provided training manuals for the purpose. The thrust of EEO guidelines, however, was that gender, racial, ethnic, national origin, or religious status alone should be avoided as an employment consideration. Women and minorities had taken the lead in getting the EEO proposal through Congress, thus making EEO a women's and minority issue.

The EEO Act dealt with areas where discrimination had been blatant, such as hiring and promotion by small businesses and by police and fire departments, as well as admission to local unions such as branches of the longshoremen in the Northeast and Southeast. Discrimination in some areas was so blatant that the federal appeals courts actually had to order hiring of minorities to rectify the situation. For example, after the passage of the EEO, Minneapolis hired its first minority-group fireman in twenty-five years.

The EEO Act also dealt with various forms of discrimination against women, such as denying employment because there were no toilet facilities for women. The act required that women receive equal opportunities for sick leave, vacation, insurance, and pensions. It also became illegal to refuse to hire or to dismiss an unmarried mother as long as unwed fathers were holding jobs. Newspaper classified sections were no longer permitted to segregate help-wanted listings under male and female headings. Only a few jobs, such as that of actor, could be proved to have a *bona fide* occupational qualification on the basis of sex.

Opposition forces focused on the confusion created by the passage of the EEO Act. Many of the existing labor laws protecting women and minorities seemed to become invalid in the context of the act. For example, the classic prohibition on work that would require a woman to lift more than a specified maximum weight could not stand. Qualification for employment would have to be based on ability to meet physical demands, regardless of gender. Banning women from certain jobs because of the possibility of pregnancy appeared to be impermissible. Leaves or special arrangements for the rearing of children would have to be available to the father, if the couple decided he was to take over domestic duties. In fact, "Men's Lib" became a new trend in the 1970's. Women's campaigns for full equality prompted men to reassess their own situation. The result was that "liberation" was becoming an issue for both men and women.

Men began moving into jobs once reserved for women, seeking alimony from wives, and demanding paternity leaves. The Supreme Court ruled that airlines could not limit flight attendant jobs to women, and most airlines began hiring some male stewards. AT&T had filled 25 percent of its clerical positions and 10 percent of its telephone operator positions with men by 1974. More men enrolled in nursing schools.

On the other hand, by the time the EEO was enacted in 1972, 31 percent of families were headed by black women—the fastest-growing type of family. One decade later, in 1982, this figure had grown to 45 percent as compared to 14 percent for the white families headed by women in the same year.

The EEO Act worked in tandem with or initiated investigations into other areas of discrimination, such as education. For example, by the late 1960's, more than a decade after the Court struck down "separate but equal" laws, more than 75 percent of the school districts in the South remained segregated. This meant markedly disproportionate employment opportunities for blacks.

Armed with its new authority, field investigators, and two hundred newly hired lawyers, the EEOC was able to respond effectively to complaints of discrimination. Within a few weeks of assuming its new, authoritative position, the EEOC had filed suits against many big companies. The actionable charges of sex discrimination surged from 2,003 cases in 1967 to 10,436 by June of 1972. Sex discrimination cases, in only three years from 1970 through 1972, increased by nearly 300 percent. By June 30, 1972, however, only 22 percent of cases involved sex discrimination and 58 percent racial and ethnic discrimination, with 11 percent involving national origin and 2.5 percent religious discrimination. In 1972, the EEOC forced employers to give raises to some twenty-nine thousand workers, mainly women, after finding violations of the law. The total underpayment of wages amounted to about fourteen million dollars.

Much of the business sector objected to the EEOC's efforts, contending that the new law would permit employees to file class-action suits without the employer's being given fair notice of the identity of its accusers. Such criticism protested that as many as eight different laws gave employees an unfair advantage in pressing charges. Nevertheless, companies—including many large corporations that did work for the government—were forced to change their employment policies to comply, and the composition of the workforce began to change. The Equal Employment Opportunity Act, along with subsequent follow-on legislation, opened the door for many women, African Americans, and ethnic minorities to rise out of poverty and begin a movement toward middle- and upper-middle-class status that later would begin to change the power structure in the United States. —*Chogollah Maroufi*

ADDITIONAL READING:

Blumrosen, Alfred. *Modern Law: The Law Transmission System and Equal Employment Opportunity.* Madison: University of Wisconsin Press, 1993. Statistical and historical account of discrimination in employment; considerable discussion of the Equal Employment Opportunity Act of 1972 and its aftermath.

Equal Employment Opportunity Act of 1972. Washington, D.C.: Government Printing Office, 1972. The actual text of the Equal Employment Opportunity Act, which became law on March 13, 1972.

Libeau, Vera A. *Minority and Female Membership in Referral Unions, 1974.* Washington, D.C.: Equal Employment Opportunity Commission, 1977. Considers the special problems of women in trade unions and how they deal with job discrimination.

National Committee on Pay Equity. *Recommendation to EEOC.* Washington, D.C.: Government Printing Office, 1983. Specific proposals made to the EEOC regarding the question of equal pay for equal work.

Sedmak, Nancy J. *Primer on Equal Employment Opportunity.* 6th ed. Washington, D.C.: Bureau of National Affairs, 1994. Basic information regarding the identification of discrimination in employment and related legal remedies, explained in understandable language.

Twomey, David. *Equal Employment Opportunity Law.* 2d ed. Cincinnati: South-Western Publishing Co., 1990. An illuminating discussion of legislation concerning discrimination in employment, with considerable attention to the Equal Employment Opportunity Act of 1972.

SEE ALSO: 1946, Employment Act; 1963, Equal Pay Act; 1965, Expansion of Affirmative Action; 1975, Equal Credit Opportunity Act.

1972 ■ WATERGATE AFFAIR: *criminal activities on the part of the White House and the chief of state degrade the office of president*

DATE: June 17, 1972-August 9, 1974
LOCALE: United States
CATEGORY: Government and politics
KEY FIGURES:

Archibald Cox (born 1912), former U.S. solicitor general and special prosecutor, fired during the Saturday Night Massacre

John W. Dean III (born 1938), White House counsel

John Ehrlichman (born 1925), presidential assistant for domestic affairs

Samuel J. Ervin, Jr. (1896-1985), chair of the Senate select committee investigating Watergate

Harry "Bob" Haldeman (1926-1993), White House chief of staff

E. Howard Hunt, Jr. (born 1918), White House consultant, one of the Watergate Seven indicted for the break-in

Leon Jaworski (1905-1982), Watergate special prosecutor

Richard Kleindienst, U.S. attorney general

G. Gordon Liddy (born 1930), lawyer for Nixon's campaign committee, one of the Watergate Seven indicted for the break-in

Jeb Stuart Magruder (born 1934), official of Nixon's campaign committee

James W. McCord, Jr. (born 1918), official of Nixon's campaign committee, one of the Watergate Seven indicted for the break-in

John Mitchell (1913-1988), former U.S. attorney general and Nixon's 1972 campaign manager

Richard Milhous Nixon (1913-1994), thirty-seventh president of the United States, 1969-1974

Charles "Bebe" Rebozo (born 1912), friend of Nixon who kept a $100,000 contribution to Nixon's campaign for three years

Elliot L. Richardson (born 1920), U.S. attorney general following Kleindienst who resigned during the Saturday Night Massacre

William Ruckelshaus (born 1934), deputy attorney general who was fired during the Saturday Night Massacre

Harry L. Sears, former New Jersey Senate majority leader, indicted in connection with illegal campaign contributions

John J. Sirica (1904-1992), U.S. federal district judge for the District of Columbia

Maurice H. Stans (born 1908), former commerce secretary and head of Nixon's campaign finance committee

Robert L. Vesco (born 1935), financier indicted for making illegal contributions to Nixon's campaign

SUMMARY OF EVENT. On June 17, 1972, five men were arrested during a bungled break-in at the Democratic campaign headquarters at the Watergate hotel-apartment complex in Washington, D.C. Their action was later found to be at the behest of the Committee to Reelect the President, and to involve major figures in the administration of Richard Nixon in the conspiracy and in the subsequent attempted cover-up. When in 1974 definitive proof was made public of Richard Nixon's involvement in the cover-up of the break-in, if not the break-in itself, he became the first president in American history to resign from office.

Nixon had risen politically during the first few years of the Cold War, in a period of concerted anti-communism that dominated U.S. politics after 1945. He had used unfair attacks on Jerry Voorhis and Helen Gehagen Douglas to win seats, respectively, in the house and senate of California, beating both opponents by accusing them of being "soft on communism." As a member of the House Un-American Activities Committee, Nixon had gained national prominence by accusing Alger Hiss of communist sympathies (accusations never fully proven). The 1948 Hiss case propelled Nixon into the vice presidency under Dwight Eisenhower for two terms (1953-1961). Nominated by the Republicans for the presidency in

1960, Nixon lost an extremely close election to John F. Kennedy. He then proceeded to lose in a 1962 bid for the governorship of California. He made a comeback in 1968 to capture the Republican slot for the presidency. With the Democrats deeply divided over America's involvement in Vietnam, epitomized by violence outside the Democratic national convention, Nixon captured the presidency in 1968.

Nixon's first term was marked by a foreign policy aimed at scaling down American involvement in Vietnam while bombing the North Vietnamese into negotiations to end the war there. Détente with the Soviet Union and attempted solutions to problems in the Middle East, coupled with rapprochement with the People's Republic of China (communist China), marked the achievements of Nixon and his secretary of state, Henry Kissinger, in foreign affairs.

Domestic politics under Nixon were clearly related to the Watergate break-in and cover-up. Elected on a "law and order" platform in the turbulent years of the late 1960's, Nixon's domestic policies hinted at repression, real and threatened. When secret bombing missions against Viet Cong supply routes in Cambodia were disclosed in the press in May, 1969, the president, believing these leaks to be subversive, authorized seventeen wiretaps on newsmen and his own White House aides for "national security" purposes. In July, 1970, Nixon approved the Huston Plan, which called for a major expansion of intelligence-gathering within the United States. He reversed his public support for this controversial plan a few days after its adoption, yet events clearly indicated that this administration was intent on destroying the influence of domestic opponents to the regime. The Justice Department under Attorney General John Mitchell stepped up surveillance of the growing antiwar movement, as did the Central Intelligence Agency (CIA) in a clear departure from its mandated purposes. Antiwar demonstrators faced increased arrests and detention, along with disruption and spying by paid informants and government operatives. Nixon, Mitchell, and the others were in the process of eliminating domestic "security threats" through repressive moves.

In the 1972 presidential campaign, Nixon faced Democratic nominee Senator George McGovern, who stood to the left of many in his own party. For the Nixon team, the Democratic campaign fell under the rubric of "security threat." The Watergate break-in, which would ultimately topple Nixon, occurred during a campaign that the president was virtually assured of winning. McGovern had alienated substantial numbers of moderate Democrats with his liberal views, and his ideological isolation brought defeat as sure as the defeat of ultraconservative ideologue Barry Goldwater in 1964. Thus, the break-in was totally unnecessary, since the reelection of Nixon seemed assured. Ironically, the very "law-and-order" issue Nixon used so effectively against his enemies over the years of his public service would become the basis of an effective campaign to remove him from office.

On June 20, 1972, Nixon reacted to the arrests in a telephone conversation with Mitchell. There is no record of what was said, because the call was not taped by Nixon's now-fabled recording system. That same day, Nixon discussed the burglary with White House Chief of Staff H. R. Haldeman in a conversation recorded by the president but later found to have an 18.5-minute gap, an erasure Nixon blamed on mechanical failure; the contents of that key discussion were lost. Later attempts to explain how this gap occurred were neither proven nor accepted by the courts. On June 23, 1972, Nixon and Haldeman held a recorded conversation in which Nixon and Haldeman agreed to order the CIA (against its legally mandated activities) to impede an investigation of the break-in by the Federal Bureau of Investigation (FBI). This event alone pointed the finger back to the White House as at least a co-conspirator in the cover-up of the events at the Watergate complex. This use of the CIA was a clear obstruction of justice by the Nixon White House. On September 15, 1972, Hunt, Liddy, and the five burglars were indicted. The linkage with the president and his highest advisers to the Watergate affair was not yet clear. As a consequence of this lack of public knowledge of Nixon's involvement, he won the November, 1972, election with a very convincing plurality of votes. In

January, 1973, the seven men directly involved in the burglary were convicted.

But the Watergate affair refused to go away. February, 1973, saw the U.S. Senate establish a select committee under the chairmanship of Democrat from North Carolina Sam Ervin to investigate the break-in. Ervin was a good choice, as he had a well-deserved reputation for being both a constitutional expert and a staunch defender of the separation of powers between the executive and the legislative branches of government. Also in that month, the president and his counsel, John Dean III, made arrangements to cover up the involvement of the administration in the break-in, using "hush money" as the method to keep those convicted from talking. It was this hush money which later Dean claimed was one of the reasons that he began to talk to the special prosecutor's office as a witness against Nixon and his closest advisers.

On March 23, 1973, on the day the Watergate Seven were sentenced, District of Columbia federal judge John Sirica read a letter from one of them, James McCord, indicating that their trial had been fixed through pressures to plead guilty and that the burglary had been approved by the highest Nixon advisers.

Behind the roofline of the Howard Johnson's restaurant, the windows of the Democratic National Headquarters can be seen at the Watergate hotel. The break-in of these offices, orchestrated by high officials in President Nixon's reelection campaign committee, marked the beginning of Nixon's decline and a new era of public skepticism surrounding the highest office in the nation. (Copyright Washington Post. Reprinted by permission of the D.C. Public Library)

By April 15, 1973, Dean was also talking to federal prosecutors. On April 30, Haldeman, Assistant to the President for Domestic Affairs John Ehrlichman, and recently appointed Attorney General Richard Kleindienst tendered their resignations in the face of widening controversy and the growing evidence of their own complicity in at least the cover-up if not the actual planning of the burglary itself. Dean was fired by the president that same day. By May, Dean was openly providing the Sirica grand jury with documentation, and by June he was testifying to the Senate against the president, charging him with participating in the cover-up.

In July, 1973, the Watergate affair entered a new phase when the existence of the presidential tapes was revealed to the Senate committee during the testimony of White House staffer Alexander Butterfield. Special Prosecutor Archibald Cox and Judge Sirica opened a drive to subpoena the tapes as evidence. Nixon appealed Sirica's ruling, only to lose again at the Court of Appeals in October, 1973. Throughout this period, Nixon consistently claimed his innocence while refusing to release the tapes for what he claimed were both national security and executive privilege reasons. Suspicion was fanned by the infamous Saturday Night Massacre of October 20, 1973, when Cox and his task force were fired by the president with no warning, accompanied by the resignations of Attorney General Elliot L. Richardson (who had succeeded Kleindienst) and Deputy Attorney General William Ruckelshaus. In the flurry of activity that followed, the Nixon Administration came under immense pressure to turn over the tapes. On October 23, 1973, Nixon promised to give the tapes to Sirica's court.

The new special prosecutor, Leon Jaworski, and the House Judiciary Committee both pursued the tapes and evidence, receiving most of the transcripts by April, 1974. When the President refused to release the sensitive tape of June 23, 1972, a tape which would have Nixon's participation when previously he had claimed no direct involvement, Jaworski took the matter to the Supreme Court, which ruled that Nixon must turn over all tapes to Jaworski. By late July, 1974, the House had voted three separate articles of impeachment against Nixon. On August 5, 1974, the White House released the transcripts of the key June 23, 1974, conversation. Many of Nixon's friends heard this tape, including Senator Goldwater. His response after hearing these tapes was that Nixon's enemies did indeed have a "smoking gun" which pointed to his direct involvement in the scandal and that Nixon should resign to preserve the integrity of the office of the President.

Nixon had lied to the public, to his supporters, and to his own family for more than a year. Many of his supporters at last deserted him in anger or disappointment. His authority was gone. As Nixon prepared to leave the White House, he repeatedly said that while he was not a "quitter," he had been convinced that it was in the best interests of the nation that he resign and that all he wanted was what was best for the nation. On August 9, 1974, Richard Nixon became the first president of the United States to resign from office.

—*Edward A. Zivich, updated by Paul Barton-Kriese*

ADDITIONAL READING:

Colodny, Len. *Silent Coup: The Removal of a President.* New York: St. Martin's Press, 1991. Colodny portrays Nixon as a president betrayed and misinformed by his senior staff but who did the right thing in assuming the blame for Watergate and hence was forced from office.

Emery, Fred. *Watergate: The Corruption of American Politics and the Fall of Richard Nixon.* New York: Times Books, 1994. Emery makes the case that Nixon was not unaware, at least at the fringe of the Watergate affair, that some actions were being taken on his behalf that were not as aboveboard as they should have been.

Friedman, Leon, and William Levantrasser, eds. *Watergate and Afterward: The Legacy of Richard M. Nixon.* Westport, Conn.: Greenwood Press, 1992. The conclusions of a symposium held on what to make of Watergate. This collection explores all facets of the era and its main figures.

Liddy, G. Gordon. *Will: The Autobiography of G. Gordon Liddy.* New York: St. Martin's Press, 1995. Watergate as told by one of the Watergate Seven and one of its flashiest and most controversial figures. Liddy's account covers the break-in, the trials, and beyond.

McQuaid, Kim. *The Anxious Years: America in the Vietnam-Watergate Era.* New York: Basic Books, 1989. A good overview of the times in which the Watergate events took place: at the end of the "communist scare" years and the years of uncertainty over U.S. world power because of the nation's problems in Vietnam.

Nixon, Richard. *Selections.* New York: Harper & Row, 1988. Watergate in the words of the president whose administration was finally ended by the revelations of the crimes of the affair.

SEE ALSO: 1964, Vietnam War; 1967, Long, Hot Summer; 1968, Chicago Riots; 1968, Nixon Is Elected President; 1970, United States Invades Cambodia; 1973, U.S. Troops Leave Vietnam; 1974, Nixon Resigns.

1972 ■ TRAIL OF BROKEN TREATIES: *militant American Indians take over the Bureau of Indian Affairs to protest U.S. government treaty policies*

DATE: October 6-November 8, 1972

LOCALE: From Seattle to San Francisco to Los Angeles to Oklahoma City to Washington, D.C.

CATEGORIES: Native American history; Wars, uprisings, and civil unrest

KEY FIGURES:

Hank Adams, Assiniboine-Sioux negotiator

Dennis Banks (born 1935?), Ojibwa cofounder of the American Indian Movement (AIM)

Louis Bruce (1906-1989), Sioux-Mohawk and Bureau of Indian Affairs (BIA) commissioner

Carter Camp, Ponca negotiator and Oklahoma AIM leader

Frank C. Carlucci (born 1930), director of the Office of Management and Budget

Leonard Garment, special assistant to the president and White House minority affairs adviser

Harrison Loesch (born 1916), interior secretary, Bureau of Land Management

Russell Means (born 1939), Lakota cofounder of AIM

Rogers Morton (born 1914), U.S. secretary of the interior

Bradley Patterson, assistant to the minority affairs adviser

Leonard Peltier (born 1944), Ojibwa-Sioux security director

John Pratt, U.S. district court judge

Ralph Ware, Kiowa negotiator for the Indians

SUMMARY OF EVENT. Against the backdrop of political activism in 1969, the rise of Red Power began with the occupation of Alcatraz Island, which became a symbol of American Indian unity. New tribal alliances were formed around a common purpose: to bring attention to continuing failures in the bureaucratic administration of American Indian affairs. During the summer gathering at Rosebud Sioux Reservation, residents and members of the American Indian Movement (AIM) began plans for a caravan to Washington, D.C., just prior to election day.

Eight American Indian organizations planned the event, and four national groups endorsed its concept. The new alliance, including tribes from Canada and Latin America, was known as the Trail of Broken Treaties and Pan American Native Quest for Justice. Planning for the possibility of 150,000 participants, cochairs Reuben Snake, a Winnebago, and Robert Burnette, a Lakota, organized eleven committees, including media, medical, congressional contact, emergency legal needs, and participant accreditation.

The spiritual foundation of the caravan was declared in a public statement inviting "all Indians, spiritual leaders of the Western Hemisphere, and Indian interest groups to participate," but excluding all persons who would "cause civil disorder, block traffic, burn flags, destroy property, or shout obscenities in the street. . . . Each trail would be led by spiritual leaders who carried the Sacred Peace Pipe and Drum . . . and every pipe smoked was to remind America of the manner in which the treaties were signed." Burnette emphasized the serious purpose of the caravan: "We should be on our finest behavior . . . ban all alcohol and drugs, with expulsions guaranteed to violators. The Caravan must be our finest hour."

Departing for Washington, D.C., on October 6, caravans passed through historic sites, stopping to offer prayer. Requests had been made for a police escort into Washington, adequate housing, permission to conduct honoring ceremonies at Arlington, and presentation of the Twenty Points. The Twenty Points to be presented formally to the administration covered treaty reform, Bureau of Indian Affairs (BIA) reform, new land policies, improved cultural and economic conditions, and criminal jurisdiction over non-Indians on reservations.

Even as the caravan traveled, obstructions were being planned in Washington, D.C. In a memorandum to BIA commissioner Louis Bruce, dated October 11, Harrison Loesch of the Bureau of Land Management (BLM) stated, "This is to give you very specific instructions that the Bureau is not to provide any assistance or funding, either directly or indirectly" to the AIM demonstration in early November.

The caravan of the first five hundred participants arrived in Washington, D.C., at 4 A.M. on November 2. Denied the official recognition of a police escort, they proceeded through downtown blowing horns and stopping traffic. At 6 A.M., they paused in front of the White House to drum and sing a victory song, after which their police escort arrived. The early caravanners faced more barriers when the Army denied permission for Arlington ceremonies, and housing arrangements revealed a building full of rats. They headed for their only home—the BIA—where they were permitted to await accommodations.

With no solution by afternoon, confusion and hostility escalated. When the shifts changed at 4 P.M., the new guards were unaware of the agreement, and in trying to clear the area, began to remove the American Indians forcibly, attacking several with clubs. The misunderstanding escalated into panic as the injured Indians alerted others of impending attacks. Riot police surrounded the building, while Indians inside barricaded doorways with desks and chairs. They broke off table legs for clubs and stacked typewriters upstairs to drop out the windows on intruders. The Twenty Points and the significant spiritual purpose of the caravans were disregarded in the conflict over housing and food.

The likelihood of gaining public support for their cause was hindered by media attention to the unplanned takeover. Still, the presentation of the Twenty Points was attempted. Appeals for help were telegraphed to the United Nations and the Vatican, as negotiations with government officials were delayed or postponed daily. During the six-day occupation, BIA offices were ransacked, American Indian artifacts taken, files seized, and much damage done to the building.

AIM leaders claimed that federal agents had infiltrated the occupation and had done much of the damage. Some American Indians who had occupied the building and went on official tours of the site weeks later asserted that there was extensive damage in rooms where they were certain there had been no damage before. Slogans, names, and addresses covered walls where there had been no marks at the time of their departure.

American Indians received unexpected support from several people. Presidential candidate Dr. Benjamin Spock and African American activist Stokely Carmichael appeared at the scene. Representative Shirley Chisholm telegraphed support, and Judge John Pratt delayed holding a show-cause hearing demanded by the federal government to determine if American Indians were in contempt of his order to leave the building. LaDonna Harris, a Comanche and wife of Oklahoma senator Fred Harris, and Louis Bruce stayed the first night in the BIA; as a result of his support for the cause, Bruce was suspended from his post as BIA commissioner.

The protest ended on November 8. After several attempts at getting a response from White House officials and a series of court actions, demonstrators agreed to leave the BIA building. On behalf of the White House, Leonard Garment, White House minority affairs adviser, Frank Carlucci, director of the Office of Management and Budget, and Bradley Patterson, Garment's assistant, signed documents granting immunity for protestors, funding their transportation home, and committing to respond to the Twenty Points within sixty days.

The number of participants was estimated to have been five thousand. Although Secretary of the Interior Rogers Morton asserted that they were mostly urban activists, more than 80 percent of those who had made the journey were traditional reservation Indians. Among the elders were Frank Fools Crow and Charlie Red Cloud, both chiefs at Pine Ridge, and Tuscarora medicine man Mad Bear Anderson, also a leader at the Alcatraz occupation. Early estimates of damage ranged from half a million dollars to more than two million dollars; however, the final estimate was set at a quarter million dollars, because most artifacts and documents were returned.

The crisis had ended, but nothing had been resolved. Public reaction showed that much of the previous support for the American Indians' cause had been lost. Before winter had passed, echoes of the same demands were heard amid the gunfire during the occupation of Wounded Knee.

Six years later, in July, 1978, several hundred American Indians marched again into Washington, D.C., at the end of the Longest Walk from San Francisco. The event was intended to reveal continuing problems faced by American Indians and expose the backlash movement against treaty rights. Unlike earlier conflicts, it was a peaceful event. Red Power had come full circle—from lively Alcatraz days, through times of violent confrontation, to the spiritual unity celebrated at the end of the Longest Walk. —*Gale M. Thompson*

ADDITIONAL READING:

DeLoria, Vine, Jr. *Behind the Trail of Broken Treaties: An Indian Declaration of Independence.* 2d ed. Norman: University of Oklahoma, 1987. Lawyer-theologian DeLoria discusses the doctrine of discovery, treaty-making, civil rights, American Indian activism, sovereignty, and the Trail and Wounded Knee occupations.

Harvey, Karen D., and Lisa D. Harjo. *Indian Country: A History of Native People in America.* Discusses ten culture areas, historical perspectives, contemporary issues, and ceremonies. Presents timelines (50,000 B.C. to twentieth century), summaries, lesson plans, and resources. Appendices and index.

Trail of Broken Treaties: BIA, I'm Not Your Indian Anymore. Rooseveltown, N.Y.: Akwesasne Notes, 1973. Contains articles published during and after the Trail events; text of the Twenty Points; the White House response; replies suggested by Trail leadership; and an update on the BIA one year later.

Waldman, Carl. *Atlas of the North American Indian.* New York: Facts on File, 1985. Comprehensive coverage of history and culture, land cessions, wars, and contemporary issues. Maps, illustrations, and appendices.

SEE ALSO: 1924, Indian Citizenship Act; 1934, Indian Reorganization Act; 1953, Termination Resolution; 1969, Alca-traz Occupation; 1971, Alaska Native Claims Settlement Act; 1973, Wounded Knee Occupation; 1978, American Indian Religious Freedom Act; 1988, Indian Gaming Regulatory Act.

1973 ■ ROE V. WADE: *the U.S. Supreme Court rules that state laws prohibiting abortion are unconstitutional*

DATE: January 22, 1973
LOCALE: Washington, D.C.
CATEGORIES: Civil rights; Court cases; Women's issues
KEY FIGURES:

Harry Andrew Blackmun (born 1908), associate justice of the United States and author of the majority opinion

Warren Earl Burger (1907-1995), chief justice of the United States and author of a concurring opinion

William Orville Douglas (1898-1980) and

Potter Stewart (1915-1985), associate justices of the United States and authors of concurring opinions

Norma McCorvey, referred to as *Jane Roe* (born 1947), plaintiff in the district court case and the appellant in the Supreme Court case

William Hubbs Rehnquist (born 1924) and

Byron Raymond White (born 1917), associate justices of the United States and authors of dissenting opinions

Henry Wade (born 1911), district attorney in the Texas district where McCorvey filed suit and a defendant in the case

SUMMARY OF EVENT. By the early 1970's, abortion laws in the United States had become an issue of public controversy. Among the factors promoting this interest were concern for overpopulation, the vigorous women's rights movement, the overwhelming approval of physicians for liberalized abortion policies, and awareness that approximately one million illegal abortions occurred in the United States each year. Although by 1973, many states had revised and liberalized their abortion laws, arguments over these reforms were heated and bitter. On one side were those who argued that women should have unrestricted control over their bodies, and that this autonomy should include the freedom to terminate pregnancy medically. On the other side were those who maintained abortion was contrary to certain moral values and religious principles. The issue finally reached the United States Supreme Court in the case of *Roe v. Wade*, and was decided in January, 1973.

Norma McCorvey (Jane Roe) was an unmarried, impoverished pregnant woman who wanted to terminate her pregnancy by abortion in Texas, a state that prohibited abortion as a serious crime, except in cases where medical advice held that the life of the mother was otherwise endangered. The Texas statute was typical of state laws at the time. Roe first brought suit in the United States District Court for the Northern District of Texas, naming a district attorney, Henry Wade, as defendant. She received a judgment essentially in her favor when the Texas abortion statute was found unconstitutional.

Both parties then appealed the decision to the higher federal courts; ultimately, the case was argued before the Supreme Court. Roe's attorneys were seeking an order from the Supreme Court assuring that abortion laws could not be enforced in the future. By the time the case reached the higher courts, Roe was no longer pregnant. Her attorneys had anticipated this development and cast the issue as a class action on behalf of all women with unwanted pregnancies.

By a decision of seven to two, the Supreme Court affirmed the decision of the United States District Court and struck down the Texas law. The majority opinion was written by Justice Harry Blackmun. Concurring opinions were written by Chief Justice Warren Burger and by Justices William O. Douglas and Potter Stewart. The majority made the following significant points in its decision. Although there was no direct mention of abortion in the United States Constitution, the Court subjected the Texas statute to two tests. The first asked whether a fundamental right was violated. Blackmun's opinion identified this as the right to privacy, which was encompassed in the personal liberty protected by the due process clause of the Fourteenth Amendment. In support of this position, the Court cited several earlier decisions that maintained that an individual's right to decide matters pertaining to one's personal privacy usually was superior to the state's interest in restricting that right. Earlier decisions, for example, had held that the states were prohibited from passing laws restricting a person's right to marry whomever he or she chose, regardless of race, to educate his or her children in private schools, or to have access to and use contraceptives. The court had carved out a zone of privacy that included matters relating to marriage, procreation, and child rearing. Blackmun also pointed out that legislation criminalizing abortion dated only from the late nineteenth century. Thus, such laws were a relatively recent phenomenon in the United States. Such history put the *Roe* decision into the mainstream of traditional common law, allowing abortion during the early stages of pregnancy.

Having determined that the Constitution afforded women the right to determine whether to continue or terminate a pregnancy, the Court then dealt with the question of whether a state could overrule the constitutional right of the individual by demonstrating a compelling reason or reasons that it should pass laws regulating abortions.

In the one critical area, the Court ruled in favor of women's right to choose. The state of Texas had argued that it had a compelling reason to regulate abortion to protect the life of the fetus. The Court held, however, that "the unborn are not included within the definition of 'person' as used in the Fourteenth Amendment." Historically, the Court stated, the United States had never treated the rights of persons after birth the same as those of the unborn. The Constitution, for example, only regards "persons born or naturalized" as citizens. There is no provision for an income tax deduction for the unborn. Property rights usually begin at birth, and the unborn have no right of inheritance. Thus, a fetus, by law, was not a person, and the state had no compelling reason to pass laws to protect it.

The court also rejected the argument that the state had a compelling reason to prohibit abortions to protect the health of the mother. Blackmun's opinion cited statistics that legal, medical abortions early in pregnancy posed less of a threat to a woman's health than did normal childbirth.

The Court went further than establishing the constitutionality of abortion and laid down guidelines regarding the performing of abortions. In issuing these principles, the Court felt that it was dealing with a matter affecting the life and health of the pregnant woman and the potential for life of the unborn. The Court also sought to provide guidelines for state legislators in the drafting of abortion statutes in order to help stem the tide of future abortion cases in the federal courts.

The majority opinion stated that a woman did not have an absolute right to an abortion. The state had a legitimate interest in protecting a woman's health and potential human life and in maintaining proper standards. Before the end of the first trimester of pregnancy, the state could do nothing to prevent an abortion that had been decided upon by a woman in consultation with a physician licensed by the state. "From and after the end of the first trimester, and until the point in time when the fetus becomes viable," that is, able to live independently of the mother, the state could regulate the abortion procedure only to preserve and protect the life of the mother. After the fetus became viable, however, the state could prohibit abortions altogether, except in cases where the life or health of the mother was endangered.

Minority opinions written by Justices Byron White and William Rehnquist presented the anti-abortion position. White asserted that the Court's decision had sustained the position that the convenience of the prospective mother was superior to "the life or potential life that she carries. The Court," he continued, without constitutional sanction, "simply fashions and announces a new constitutional right for pregnant mothers" and in doing so, "invests that right with sufficient substance to override most existing state abortion statutes." White concluded by holding that the Court had interfered incorrectly with the legislative processes of the states. Abortion, he stated, was an issue that "should be left with the people and to the political processes the people have devised to govern their affairs."

Rehnquist held that there was no historical foundation for the Court's position that the right to abortion was to be found in the Fourteenth Amendment. History, he argued, established the fact that a majority of states had had abortion laws for at least a century, and that the legislators who had passed these laws represented the sentiments of the citizenry. There was, then, no historical support for Roe's argument of the universal acceptability of a woman's "right" to an abortion.

The Court left many issues relating to abortion undecided, because they had not been contested in this case. A victory, however, had been won by those who favored women's freedom of choice with regard to the continuation or termination of a pregnancy. Abortion on demand, which had been advocated by the more extreme advocates of the pro-abortion, pro-choice movement, had been prohibited. This part of the ruling gave hope to the anti-abortion, right-to-life group, which began a campaign to secure a constitutional amendment prohibiting abortion.

—*J. Stewart Alverson, updated by Mary Welek Atwell*

ADDITIONAL READING:

Garrow, David J. *Liberty and Sexuality: The Right to Privacy and the Making of Roe v. Wade*. New York: Macmillan, 1994. An exhaustive study of the people and legal issues involved in a series of court decisions related to privacy, that culminated in *Roe v. Wade*.

Goldstein, Leslie Friedman. *Contemporary Cases in Women's Rights*. Madison: University of Wisconsin Press, 1994. Contains a long section on court cases dealing with reproductive rights, in particular a meticulous discussion of the precedents and results of *Roe v. Wade*.

Mohr, James C. *Abortion in America: The Origins and Evolution of National Policy*. New York: Oxford, 1978. The most comprehensive history of the political and social forces that contributed to the development of anti-abortion legislation in the United States in the late nineteenth century.

Schneider, Carl E., and Maris A. Vinovskis, eds. *The Law and Politics of Abortion*. Lexington, Mass.: Heath, 1980. Legal scholars address, often critically, the principles underlying *Roe v. Wade*, as well as its political aftermath.

Siegel, Reva B. "Abortion as a Sex Equality Right: Its Basis in Feminist Theory." In *Mothers in Law*, edited by Martha Albertson Fineman and Isabel Karpin. New York: Columbia University Press, 1995. Argues for treating abortion rights as issues of sex equality rather than as part of the right to privacy.

Solinger, Rickie. *Wake Up Little Susie: Single Pregnancy and Race Before Roe v. Wade*. New York: Routledge, 1992. Discusses the political meaning of policies toward unwed motherhood prior to *Roe v. Wade*.

Tribe, Laurence H. *Abortion: The Clash of Opposites*. New York: W. W. Norton, 1990. A noted constitutional scholar examines abortion from philosophical, scientific, political, and legal perspectives.

SEE ALSO: 1868, Fourteenth Amendment; 1960, FDA Approves the Birth Control Pill; 1965, *Griswold v. Connecticut*; 1966, National Organization for Women Is Founded; 1978, Pregnancy Discrimination Act.

1973 ■ WOUNDED KNEE OCCUPATION:

Native Americans highlight their grievances against the U.S. government by staging an armed occupation at an old battle site

DATE: February 27-May 8, 1973

LOCALE: Pine Ridge Reservation, South Dakota

CATEGORIES: Native American history; Wars, uprisings, and civil unrest

KEY FIGURES:

Dennis Banks (born 1935?), co-founder of AIM

Lou Bean, sister of Buddy Lamont

Gladys Bissonnette, tribal elder

Grace Spotted Eagle Black Elk (1919-1987), tribal elder and wife of Wallace Black Elk

Wallace Black Elk (born 1921), Oglala medicine man

Frank Clearwater (died 1973), Indian casualty of the confrontation

Leonard Crow Dog (born 1942), Oglala medicine man on the Rosebud Reservation

Frank Fools Crow (born 1890), Teton Sioux ceremonial chief

Buddy Lamont (died 1973), Pine Ridge resident who died in the confrontation

Russell Means (born 1939), co-founder of AIM

Ellen Moves Camp, tribal elder

Richard Wilson, chairman of the BIA tribal council

SUMMARY OF EVENT. Internal strife on the Oglala reservation had reached the explosive stage by February, 1973, when the village of Wounded Knee, site of the last massacre of the Indian Wars in 1890, became the focal point for another confrontation between American Indians and U.S. military forces.

Tribal unemployment was at 54 percent, not counting those tribe members who lived in cities. Many of those with jobs worked for the government. One-third of the people were on welfare or similar pensions. Median income was around eight hundred dollars per year. Children were malnourished. Poverty, alcoholism, and suicide were widespread, and the average life span for Oglalas was forty-six years of age.

In February, 1972, an elderly American Indian had died after a public beating by two white men, who were charged with only second-degree manslaughter and released without paying bail. The American Indian Movement (AIM) was called in to support the family, and a full investigation showed evidence of misdealing in this and other incidents. As AIM's popularity increased nationally, the positions of Sioux tribal chairman Richard Wilson and other government-employed American Indians were being threatened.

The trouble at Wounded Knee began with the controversy over chairman Wilson, who had a heavy drinking habit, had been identified as a bootlegger, and nearly had been indicted on charges of misuse of federal funds. After his extravagantly funded campaign, Wilson awarded positions to more than nine hundred supporters, including his wife and sons, and had given a twenty-five thousand dollar job to his brother. He claimed that nothing was said in tribal law about nepotism.

Wilson used federal highway funds to arm his private police force. Known as the "goon squad" because of their brutality, they called themselves Guardians of the Oglala Nation (GOON) and suppressed with beatings or threats anyone who challenged Wilson. The Bureau of Indian Affairs (BIA), the Federal Bureau of Investigation (FBI), and the Justice Department gave full support to Wilson when he offered his goon squad's services to attack members of AIM.

Several elder Oglala women had spoken out about Wilson's incompetence. "[He] hasn't got the backbone to stand up and protect his Indians," declared Gladys Bissonnette. Grace Black

Elk said, "He hates AIM people because they are doing what he should have been doing." Ellen Moves Camp wondered, "Why is it that the government is backing him up so much?"

Wilson had fired the tribal vice president for supporting AIM and had banned AIM leader Russell Means from the reservation, threatening to "personally cut his braids off." Returning to his Pine Ridge home, Means was immediately arrested by BIA tribal police. Dennis Banks, with Means during the BIA takeover in Washington, D.C., was taken into custody upon his arrival. Both were released pending later trials. Citing suspicion of corruption, tribal members and AIM leaders began impeachment proceedings against Wilson, who illegally terminated the action. Attempts to speak out against this were quelled by further intimidation and violence.

In January, 1973, a young American Indian was stabbed to death by a white man. A riot ensued while AIM leaders were meeting with officials in the courthouse at Calico. In late February, traditional people marched on the Pine Ridge BIA building to protest Wilson's actions and the illegal presence of U.S. marshals on their reservation.

AIM again was summoned by spokesman Chief Fools Crow, and more than six hundred people were at the meeting led by Means and Banks. Lakota mothers pleaded for protection for the children, by asking that the fighting spirit return. One by one, the chiefs stood up. The Lakota would gather at the most symbolic spot on the reservation, Wounded Knee, for what was expected to be a two- or three-day stand. A public statement, signed by eight Oglala chiefs and medicine men, demanded treaty hearings and investigation of the BIA.

The next day, approximately two hundred Oglalas armed with hunting rifles were stationed at Wounded Knee. They were surrounded by the FBI, state police, and U.S. marshals armed with high-powered weapons and riding in armored personnel carriers. They were surrounded by BIA tribal police, while planes and helicopters circled the area. The media soon arrived.

Many separate factions were involved at Wounded Knee II: Wilson, his corrupt government, his GOON, and some older leaders in the tribal council who did not condone Wilson's methods, but were concerned about the possibility of losing federal support; the FBI, the BIA, U.S. marshals, and other government forces—all of whom were waging a war against AIM, the young militants, and the traditional elders who were trying to preserve the old ways.

On the third day, Fools Crow had just begun talks with traditionalists, AIM people, and federal authorities, when shots were exchanged. With military planes flying overhead, there was much confusion and many people were injured.

In the days and weeks that followed, much occurred at Wounded Knee: People hiked in at night to bring supplies and support; two U.S. senators visited; Wilson threatened to attack with nine hundred men; the Independent Oglala Nation (ION) was created; citizenships were granted; government agents were caught inside the compound; negotiations continued; a blizzard inundated the area; firefights continued; food and fuel ran out; airlifts arrived; medicine men Black Elk and Crow

Dog led a Ghost Dance and pipe ceremonies; a wedding was performed by Black Elk; an Iroquois Six Nation delegation arrived; a child was born; the trading post burned; a U.S. marshal was disabled; and two American Indian men died.

In spite of ongoing firefights, the leaders had helped to maintain the spiritual bonds of community. Wallace Black Elk or Leonard Crow Dog held prayer ceremonies with the sacred pipe before every meeting. Although Fools Crow went into Wounded Knee thirteen times, he remained neutral and continued to pray for peace throughout the long siege. He guided negotiations and carried in the peace document that finally ended the standoff.

More than two hundred Lakotas had begun the occupation and others had joined. Nearly four hundred American Indians were arrested as a result. According to Peter Matthiessen, author of *In the Spirit of Crazy Horse*, the U.S. Army was involved directly in behind-the-scenes operations as "military intelligence, and perhaps weapons and equipment, were provided to civilian authorities, with unofficial approval reportedly coming all the way from the White House." He also cited reports that the FBI requested two thousand soldiers to seize control of the reservation so arrests could be made, but the request was refused. The eight volunteers who had airlifted food and medical supplies were later charged with conspiracy and interfering with the official duties of federal troops.

Means and Banks were arrested later, but charges were dismissed because of evidence of perjury by government witnesses. In April, 1975, *The New York Times* reported that violence resulting from Wounded Knee II had continued. According to an FBI report, six people had been killed and sixty-seven assaulted on the Pine Ridge Reservation since January 1.

The fighting spirit of the Lakota had returned. As Black Elk declared, "Now, this is a turning point. The hoop, the sacred hoop, was broken here at Wounded Knee, and it will come back again."

—*Gale M. Thompson*

ADDITIONAL READING:

Harvey, Karen D., and Lisa D. Harjo, eds. *Indian Country: A History of Native People in America*. Golden, Colo.: North American Press, 1994. Discusses ten culture areas, historical perspectives, contemporary issues, major ceremonies; includes time lines (50,000 B.C. to twentieth century), summaries, and lesson plans. Appendices include "Threats to Religious Freedom," "Fort Laramie Treaty of 1868," and "Indian Activist Organizations and Events." Index. Written and illustrated by several American Indians.

Magill, Frank N., ed. *Ready Reference: American Indians*. Pasadena, Calif.: Salem Press, 1995. Survey of prehistory to late twentieth century. Discusses archaeology, architecture, arts, culture, history, language, religion, ten culture areas, well-known persons, events, acts, and treaties. Tables, maps, illustrations, photographs, listing of organizations.

Matthiessen, Peter. *In the Spirit of Crazy Horse*. 2d ed. New York: Viking Press, 1991. Covers Lakota struggles with the United States, including Little Big Horn, Wounded Knee I and

II, and the 1975 Pine Lodge shootout that resulted in Leonard Peltier's imprisonment. Personal accounts, trial records, chapter notes, index.

Voices from Wounded Knee, 1973: In the Words of the Participants. Rooseveltown, N.Y.: Akwesasne Notes, 1974. Includes daily events during occupation; logs kept by U.S. marshals; quotations, interviews, diaries, and taped radio conversations from a ten-day battle; negotiations; treaty meetings at Kyle; maps and photographs.

Waldman, Carl. *Atlas of the North American Indian.* New York: Facts on File, 1985. Comprehensive coverage of history and culture; land cessions and wars; and contemporary issues. Maps and illustrations; historical chronology; locations of tribes and reservations; place names; museums and archaeological sites in the United States and Canada.

Zimmerman, Bill. *Airlift to Wounded Knee.* Chicago: Swallow Press, 1976. Chronicle of eight airlift participants who delivered food and medical supplies during the occupation and were subsequently indicted for conspiracy and interfering with official duties of federal troops. Photos, notes, comments by author's attorney.

SEE ALSO: 1890, Battle of Wounded Knee; 1953, Termination Resolution; 1968, Indian Civil Rights Act; 1971, Alaska Native Claims Settlement Act; 1978, American Indian Religious Freedom Act; 1988, Indian Gaming Regulatory Act.

1973 ■ U.S. TROOPS LEAVE VIETNAM:
Americans withdraw from Vietnam in the first defeat of the United States in a foreign war

DATE: March, 1973
LOCALE: South Vietnam and Paris
CATEGORIES: Diplomacy and international relations; Wars, uprisings, and civil unrest
KEY FIGURES:

Henry Alfred Kissinger (born 1923), special assistant for national security affairs to President Nixon and chief negotiator of secret talks for the United States

Richard Milhous Nixon (1913-1994), thirty-seventh president of the United States, 1969-1974

Nguyen Van Thieu (born 1923), president of South Vietnam

Le Duc Tho (1911-1990), North Vietnamese revolutionary and chief negotiator of secret talks for North Vietnam

SUMMARY OF EVENT. In the United States' past, only the Civil War has aroused so many conflicting emotions among citizens, officials, and soldiers as did the Vietnam War. Debate in the United States began in the early 1960's over what means should be used to protect the Republic of South Vietnam. Division spread with time to questions of ends: What sort of peace was being sought in Asia? Were the Viet Cong really worse than the South Vietnamese government? Could the United States achieve an honorable withdrawal? The war posed such

dilemmas that the government was soon caught up in a charade of truth, obscuring issues and purposes even further.

From the time Richard M. Nixon became president in 1969, he was chiefly dependent upon the negotiating table for bringing the peace he had promised. His bargaining position was weak. With half a million U.S. troops in South Vietnam, the Viet Cong and North Vietnamese forces could not win a direct offensive, but their guerrilla techniques ensured that they could not lose, either. The war was essentially a waiting game, and the stakes were so much higher for the communists that they could afford to wait longer. Nor did the communists need a negotiated peace as much as Nixon did. The massive opposition at home to continued war required Nixon to deescalate, but strong popular support of U.S. intervention made total withdrawal an equally unacceptable policy.

Nevertheless, communist initiatives brought the first real breakthroughs in discussions over peace. From May, 1968, formal negotiations had been carried on in Paris, but these talks produced little more than rhetoric and repeatedly broke down in frustration. In June, 1971, Hanoi backed away from two earlier demands and agreed to discuss an in-place ceasefire and the conduct of internationally supervised elections without prior abolition of the Saigon government. Shortly afterward, the Viet Cong (South Vietnamese communists) made similar concessions, showing a conciliatory attitude towards the West. With these concessions, a second round of negotiations began, held between Le Duc Tho, a prominent North Vietnamese official, and Henry Kissinger, Nixon's national security adviser.

Although a subordinate of Nixon, Kissinger viewed his role in a different light. For Kissinger, the peace settlement would have to reflect the actual power situation, in which the North remained strong, the United States was to leave, and the government of the South lacked popular support and would probably collapse; domestic political considerations did not matter to him. Nixon, on the other hand, wanted to end the war without alienating his domestic political support and by reassuring allies that the United States would come to their aid if needed in the future.

The United States made several minor concessions in the ensuing discussions, but little real progress was made. President Nixon was feeling the pressure of an election year, and U.S. troop levels in Vietnam dropped rapidly, weakening his leverage at the talks. Although U.S. forces numbered ninety-five thousand, only six thousand were combat-ready. Despite the historic détentes Nixon achieved with China and the Soviet Union during 1972, neither of these two allies of North Vietnam pressured Hanoi to accept a compromise with the United States. Instead, the North launched a major offensive in the spring, overrunning Quang Tri province. In May, 1972, Nixon retaliated by ordering the bombing of North Vietnam to be stepped up, and the ports of the country mined and blockaded (bringing economic crisis to the communists); but at the same time, Kissinger offered major modifications of the United States bargaining position. For the first time, the United States was willing to permit North Vietnamese troops to remain in South

Vietnam after a cease-fire, and to modify the Saigon government before elections. Intensive talks between Kissinger and Le Duc Tho resumed, with special incentives for both sides. The Nixon Administration had to prove that its gamble in escalating the war was effective, and the North Vietnamese, watching the increasing likelihood of Nixon's reelection, wanted to reach an agreement before a safer Nixon became tougher.

In early October, Kissinger and Le Duc Tho agreed to a peace settlement along the lines of a proposal made by Hanoi in 1969, except that the confident North would allow the precarious government in the South to remain in place. The first step in the settlement was a cease-fire that would go into effect on October 24, 1972. When the text was revealed to Nixon, who was confident of reelection, the president insisted that South Vietnamese President Nguyen Van Thieu must also support the peace. Kissinger went to Saigon, but was unable to apply pressure on Thieu, who was intransigent. The North expressed its anger by releasing the text of the draft agreement and the history of the hitherto secret negotiations. Kissinger then flew back to Washington, D.C. Hoping to apply pressure on Saigon, he informed the U.S. press upon his arrival that "Peace is at hand," although not "in hand," but the South soon announced sixty-nine objections to the proposed text of the peace agreement.

In early November, Nixon won reelection in a landslide. In Paris, the North, believing that it had been duped by Kissinger, refused to make any concessions to the South. The talks became bitter and broke down in mid-December. When the talks collapsed, Nixon tried one more bold stroke and ordered the Christmas bombing of North Vietnam. Dozens of B-52 bombers were set upon the largest cities of the country, widely destroying industry. The communist antiaircraft defense was so vigorous, and U.S. anger at the attack so powerful, as to make the success of the bombing questionable. It was stopped in less than two weeks, and war-weary negotiators returned to Paris.

On January 31, 1973, peace accords were signed by North Vietnam, the Viet Cong, the United States, and a reluctant South Vietnam. The provisions of the treaty were substantially the same as those of the October agreement. By March 27, the United States was to withdraw its troops from Vietnam; exchanges of prisoners would go on during those two months. All Vietnamese forces would remain in place, and a cease-fire would be supervised by an International Commission of Control and Supervision, comprising representatives from Canada, Hungary, Indonesia, and Poland. All parties concurred on Vietnam's sovereignty and right of self-determination, and a council was established with responsibility for developing and executing plans for an open election. In 1973, Kissinger and Le Duc Tho were awarded the Nobel Peace Prize.

There is room for doubt concerning how seriously the treaty was taken by any of the concerned nations. Cease-fire lines never were clearly established, many of the provisions were vague and invited violation, and both sides broke the treaty almost as soon as it was signed. Kissinger's creative ambiguity in the wording of the peace treaty meant that all sides could interpret the text the way they wished, without being aware of alternative interpretations by others. The United States quickly withdrew, regained its captured prisoners, and could claim "peace with honor." Both President Thieu of South Vietnam and the scattered communist forces seemed to believe that their best prospects lay in renewed fighting. Congress had no intention of providing humanitarian aid to the North, as provided in the treaty, and Hanoi ignored the pledge to stop sending supplies to the Viet Cong. After U.S. troops withdrew on March 29, 1973, the United States sent the South some $2.6 billion in aid, resumed reconnaissance flights over Vietnam, and continued to bomb Cambodia. Upon learning that Kissinger had given secret assurances to Thieu to reenter the war if the South faltered, Congress required all military operations in and over Indochina to cease by August 15, 1973.

By the end of 1973, open war had returned to the nation. U.S. aid continued to flow to South Vietnam, and Thieu controlled a well-trained army of one million men. However, the Viet Cong and North Vietnamese seemed to have gained some critical psychological edge on their enemy, and their successes were self-reinforcing. During 1974, with Nixon distracted by investigations of his effort to cover up the burglary of Democratic Party headquarters at the Watergate apartments, Congress reduced military aid to the South to $907 million and then to $700 million in 1975. Accordingly, the communist positions were generally strengthened, and at the outset of 1975 they launched a last major offensive. After a major direct victory at Hue, communist forces drove rapidly over South Vietnam, pursuing an utterly demoralized army. By the end of April, Saigon was captured; the last U.S. advisers abandoned the country; and the Vietnam era of U.S. history was truly at an end.

—Richard H. Sander, updated by Michael Haas

ADDITIONAL READING:

Brown, Weldon A. *The Last Chopper: The Denouement of the American Role in Vietnam, 1963-1975*. Port Washington, N.Y.: Kennikat Press, 1976. A conventional U.S. explanation of motives and actions governing U.S. involvement.

Burchett, Wilfred. *Grasshoppers and Elephants: Why Vietnam Fell*. New York: Urizen Books, 1977. North Vietnam's view of the war, as interpreted by an Australian journalist.

Isaacs, Arnold R. *Without Honor: Defeat in Vietnam and Cambodia*. Baltimore, Md.: The Johns Hopkins University Press, 1983. A detailed account and analysis of peace negotiations and the departure of U.S. troops from Vietnam up to April 29, 1975.

Isaacson, Walter. *Kissinger: A Biography*. New York: Simon & Schuster, 1992. Chapters 9 through 21 provide a careful, balanced analysis of peace negotiations.

Kissinger, Henry A. *White House Years*. Boston: Little, Brown, 1979. Several chapters analyze the negotiations and explain Kissinger's motives.

SEE ALSO: 1964, Vietnam War; 1964, Berkeley Free Speech Movement; 1964, Johnson Is Elected President; 1967, Long, Hot Summer; 1968, Nixon Is Elected President; 1970, United States Invades Cambodia; 1995, United States Recognizes Vietnam.

1973 ■ DÉTENTE WITH THE SOVIET UNION: an important transitional stage in U.S.-Soviet relations marks the beginning of the end of the Cold War

DATE: May 26, 1973-December 26, 1991
LOCALE: United States and Soviet Union
CATEGORY: Diplomacy and international relations
KEY FIGURES:

Leonid Ilich Brezhnev (1906-1982), first secretary of the Communist Party of the Soviet Union, 1964-1982

George Herbert Walker Bush (born 1924), forty-first president of the United States, 1989-1993

James Earl "Jimmy" Carter, Jr. (born 1924), thirty-ninth president of the United States, 1977-1981

Anatoly Federovich Dobrynin (born 1919), Soviet ambassador to the United Nations

Mikhail Sergeyevich Gorbachev (born 1931), general secretary of the Communist Party, 1985-1991, and president of the Soviet Union, 1988-1991

Andrei A. Gromyko (1909-1989), Soviet foreign minister, 1946-1985

Henry Alfred Kissinger (born 1923), special assistant for national security affairs, 1969-1973, and U.S. secretary of state, 1973-1977

Mao Zedong (1893-1976), chairman of the Chinese Communist Party, 1949-1976

Richard Milhous Nixon (1913-1994), thirty-seventh president of the United States, 1969-1974

Ronald Wilson Reagan (born 1911), fortieth president of the United States, 1981-1989

Eduard A. Shevardnadze (born 1928), Soviet foreign minister, 1985-1990

SUMMARY OF EVENT. When détente (literally, "relaxation") became the prevailing framework of Soviet-United States relations in the early 1970's, neither its meaning nor its implications were clear. On the surface, its most important result was a series of nuclear arms agreements—with corollaries in trade, education, space research, and more—between the United States and the Soviet Union, beginning with the first Strategic Arms Limitation Talks (SALT I) Treaty signed by President Richard M. Nixon and Soviet leader Leonid I. Brezhnev in Moscow in May, 1972. At a deeper level, it reflected a new and more pragmatic turn in the long history of the Cold War; among European and Middle Eastern peoples, détente aggravated fears that the two superpowers would freeze their strategic options, thus precluding genuinely credible deterrence to protect them. By its very nature, détente, as manifested in SALT I, was encouraging to some and troublesome to others. Two other SALT treaties followed, culminating in the SALT III pact. SALT III was signed by President Jimmy Carter and Brezhnev in 1979 but never ratified by the U.S. Senate because of Soviet suppression of Jews and dissidents.

From the beginning, the SALT treaties, and even the notion of détente between the vastly different nuclear age superpowers, appeared contradictory and one-sided to those who considered it another ruse by the communists to lull the United States into dangerous passivity. Others, notably Senator Henry "Scoop" Jackson and exiled Soviet dissident writer Aleksandr Solzhenitsyn, believed that détente lowered the Soviet Union's risks of conflict while allowing it to continue building up its military and suppressing all political and ideological opposition at home. That the Soviet Union signed the 1975 Helsinki Accords, thus ostensibly endorsing the section called "Basket III" that theoretically guaranteed basic human and civil rights in the contracting countries, did not convince those who did not trust Soviet sincerity.

In the longer historical perspective, détente was a significant chapter in the history of global politics. Fundamental changes have marked the world of diplomacy in the twentieth century, including a steady and dramatic reduction in the number of true world powers. In 1900, the power bases in world politics were multipolar: Germany, Austria-Hungary, czarist Russia, Great Britain, France, and the United States all were engaged in empire-building. Similarly, between the two world wars, Nazi Germany, Japan, Great Britain, and the temporarily isolated United States occupied prominent positions as world powers. World War II, however, narrowed the field effectively to two major world powers—the United States and the Soviet Union—thus marking the advent of a bipolar world after 1945.

Bipolarism dominated the diplomacy of the Cold War years following World War II. Although the Soviet Union under Joseph Stalin's regime had been allied with the United States and Great Britain during the war, it was clear to most contemporaries of the war years that the alliance was one of convenience. At war's end, the world split into two basic camps, one allied with the Soviet Union, one with the United States. Tension increased markedly as the Communist Bloc was expanded by force in Eastern Europe and China. By the 1950's, the Cold War had erupted into a real conflict in Korea (1950-1953) and in the military alliances of Western nations in the North Atlantic Treaty Organization (NATO) and Eastern nations in the Warsaw Pact. Both sides ultimately were backed by the awesome power of nuclear weapons.

The Cold War, with its periodic military outbursts (the Bay of Pigs, Laos, Vietnam), had been characterized by military expenditures on both sides of the conflict throughout the 1950's and 1960's. This arms race had been the most massive in all of human history. The Soviet Union had given top social and economic priorities to military spending during these decades, at the obvious expense of civilian, consumer-oriented production. At the same time, the United States had given top priority to its defense expenditures, at the expense of its own social needs. This had led since the late 1960's to attempts by both Soviet and U.S. leaders to effect a rapprochement, or détente. The primary aim of this policy was to reduce the arms race and military tension in the world between the United States and the Soviet Union. In general, mistrust prevailed and worked against thorough cooperation. As long as the Soviet Union was ruled by an oppressive communist political structure, the United States and other supporters of détente had serious reservations, as did the Soviet leadership. Any concessions by one side or the other were viewed from the framework of national rather than mutual interest. Therein lay the greatest weakness of détente.

The first active application of the détente policy originated during the presidency of Richard M. Nixon. Although Nixon clearly initiated the policy, detailed negotiations were the work of Henry A. Kissinger, the key diplomatic figure of the Nixon presidency. Kissinger came to the administration from an academic background. A German-Jewish refugee from Nazi Germany, Kissinger had fully assimilated himself through the United States Army and as a student and faculty member at Harvard, where he gradually developed into an activist scholar who sought to influence foreign policy with his theory. He came to the public limelight through his friendship with Nelson Rockefeller. Based on his loyalty to Richard Nixon, once he entered Nixon's administration, Kissinger came to dominate the foreign policy of the Nixon years, both as national security adviser and as secretary of state.

Nixon and Kissinger both had excellent credentials for redirecting United States policy toward the Soviet Union. Both were conservatives and arch-foes of communism. If a liberal Democratic administration had proposed détente in earlier decades, it likely would have faced a massive Cold War onslaught in public opinion. Liberals, in effect, could not push for Soviet-U.S. agreements without suffering politically. A conservative such as Nixon, on the other hand, could strike up negotiations with the Russians without fanning domestic fears that he was "soft on communism."

The key concept launched by Kissinger and carried through in the presidency of Jimmy Carter was the insistence of the United States on linkage in any agreements with the Soviet Union. "Linkage" meant that any trade agreement, exchange program, credit—in effect, any concession—must be accompanied by (linked to) changes in Soviet policy. During the Kissinger years, the United States insisted on the elimination of ideology from Soviet foreign policy decisions. In negotiating the first Strategic Arms Limitation Treaties (SALTs I and II), the United States used its improved relations with Chairman Mao Zedong's China as leverage with Brezhnev's negotiators. In addition, the United States obtained Soviet aid in ending the Vietnam War through negotiations by tying the negotiations to SALT's prospects.

After SALT I, the United States linked ties with the Soviets to human rights for people in the Soviet sphere, but this effort bore little fruit until the rise of Mikhail Gorbachev as Soviet leader in 1985. Official commitment to détente waned after Nixon was forced to resign in 1974 in the wake of the Watergate scandal. His successor, Gerald Ford, visited the Soviet Union and continued the SALT negotiating process, but with less success than Nixon and Kissinger had had. President Carter's policy of upholding and reaffirming human rights had

few tangible results in the short run, which contributed to the Senate's refusal to ratify SALT II. The Soviet Union further eroded détente by deploying large numbers of its new, mobile SS-20 missiles targeted on all major European cities. That, more than the Soviet invasion of Afghanistan in December, 1979, disillusioned Carter and prompted him to cancel U.S. participation in the Olympics in Moscow in 1980.

Linkage, the cornerstone of détente, seemed to have reached its limits. The Soviet Union would not eliminate ideological considerations in either its domestic or foreign policies until the advent of Gorbachev as Soviet leader in March, 1985, and even then, only on a limited basis. Despite the 1975 Helsinki Accords, Soviet suppression of dissidents continued almost unabated until Gorbachev's *perestroika* (restructuring) opened the door to *glasnost* (publicity or openness), which invited public discussion and criticism of government policies. Under Gorbachev, détente took new turns, notably a more intense U.S. and Soviet interest in arms reduction. President Ronald Reagan, an old-style Cold Warrior, moved from his first term's blistering rhetoric, such as calling the Soviet Union an "evil empire," to a more accommodating position. This was reinforced by his projected Strategic Defense Initiative (SDI, popularly known as "Star Wars"), which aimed to protect the world from nuclear weapons through an elaborate system of space and land-based lasers that would provide a shield against incoming missiles.

Reagan proposed START (the Strategic Arms Reduction Talks) to replace the faltering SALT agreements, but a series of Reagan-Gorbachev summits in the middle 1980's foundered on Soviet fears that SDI would neutralize their nuclear deterrence and violate earlier SALT agreements. Nevertheless, the détente process continued as Gorbachev and his popular foreign minister, Eduard Shevardnadze, pursued arms reductions, and the Reagan and subsequent Bush Administrations remained open to credible, adequately guaranteed and equitable reductions. The most important tangible products were the INF (Intermediate Nuclear Force) Treaty of late 1987, which eliminated an entire class of nuclear weapons; the START Treaty of July, 1991; and the START II Treaty (January, 1993), negotiated by Bush and implemented early in the administration of President Bill Clinton. The Soviet Union was officially dissolved on December 26, 1991, with its East European Warsaw Pact allies already in disarray as communist regimes crumbled in that region. Détente outlived the Soviet Union, and the vision of a world safe from nuclear war again gained ground.

More than a declining Soviet system and U.S. vigilance, however, contributed to this radically new and unexpected twist of history. In retrospect, it is clearly important that Gorbachev and Shevardnadze made substantive changes of a scope that few would have believed possible in the early days of détente. The role that détente played in the overall process is not easy to estimate. What is clearer is that the long détente process contributed to new thinking about world peace and the national interests of the Soviet Union, the United States, and their allies. If the future of arms control has been uncertain in the post-Soviet period, there is little doubt that it will remain a pivotal concern of most nations, because of the continuing existence of thousands of nuclear weapons and the possibility that they might fall into the hands of states less restrained by Cold War considerations than the United States and the Soviet Union were for decades.

—*Edward A. Zivich, updated by Thomas R. Peake*

ADDITIONAL READING:

Gorbachev, Mikhail. *Perestroika: New Thinking for Our Country and the World.* Updated ed. New York: Perennial Library, 1988. A personal account of the origins and meaning of *perestroika* by its principal proponent. Contains sections on world peace and Soviet-U.S. relations, in which Gorbachev supports cooperation and arms reduction.

Kissinger, Henry A. *American Foreign Policy.* New York: W. W. Norton, 1969. Kissinger's views of U.S. foreign policy and the global balance of power, reflecting his historical, issue-specific approach to diplomacy.

_____. *Diplomacy.* New York: Simon & Schuster, 1994. A comprehensive analysis of diplomacy in early modern and recent periods. Extensive material on the period of détente and support for the approach, despite detractors' arguments.

Landau, David. *Kissinger: The Uses of Power.* Boston: Houghton Mifflin, 1972. A sympathetic biography by a colleague and friend. Presents Kissinger as one of the most creative modern diplomatic theorists, with both academic and experiential credentials.

Nixon, Richard M. *RN: The Memoirs of Richard Nixon.* New York: Grosset & Dunlap, 1978. A comprehensive personal account of Nixon's life and public career, in which the strongest elements are his foreign policy and détente. Shows his belief in a practical approach to peace, marked by mutual pragmatic agreements to avoid a nuclear war.

Ulam, Adam B. "Forty Years of Troubled Coexistence." *Foreign Affairs* 64, no. 1 (Fall, 1985): 12-32. A masterful overview of détente, with a scholarly analysis of SALT I and its aftermath. Argues that détente was essentially pragmatic; rejects the notion that détente was simply a Soviet ruse.

SEE ALSO: 1963, Nuclear Test Ban Treaty; 1979, United States and China Establish Full Diplomatic Relations; 1979, SALT II Is Signed; 1987, INF Treaty Is Signed; 1993, START II Is Signed.

1973 ■ ARAB OIL EMBARGO AND ENERGY CRISIS: *oil politics and a resulting oil embargo produce economic stagnation, inflation, and the need to develop alternative energy sources*

DATE: October 17, 1973-March 18, 1974
LOCALE: United States
CATEGORIES: Diplomacy and international relations; Economics; Transportation

KEY FIGURES:
James Earl "Jimmy" Carter (born 1924), thirty-ninth president of the United States, 1977-1981
James Rodney Schlesinger (born 1929), special assistant for energy matters to President Carter and first secretary of the Department of Energy, 1977-1979

SUMMARY OF EVENT. The consumption of oil by the Western world rose rapidly after World War II, as though there were no end to the supply. In 1973, the United States' policy of backing Israel against its oil-rich neighbors in the Middle East exacted a heavy penalty. On October 17, 1973, the Organization of Arab Petroleum Exporting Countries (OAPEC) began cutting the flow of oil to the United States by 5 percent every month; at the same time, OAPEC invoked an embargo on oil to the United States and other Israel-supporting countries. Overnight, the age of cheap and abundant oil ended, and an "energy crisis" began. The embargo was felt especially at the gas pump: Long lines of automobiles at service stations sparked tempers, and a business recession deepened. As the price of gasoline rose and shortages increased, consumers across the nation waited for hours in lines at the pumps, held hostage to the need for gasoline, the primary fuel for transportation. Other fuels, such as propane, kerosene, jet fuel, diesel oil, and home heating oil, were in increasingly short supply as well, and rationing nearly went into effect. Government measures that were instituted included year-round daylight savings time and passage of a federal highway speed limit of 55 miles per hour to conserve gasoline. Personal habits changed as individuals limited car travel, turned off lights and heat, and became interested in "economy" cars—high mileage-per-gallon vehicles whose subsequent growth in popularity changed consumers' postwar gas-guzzling tastes. The embargo was not lifted until March 18, 1974, at a meeting of the Organization of Oil Exporting Countries (OPEC) in Vienna, whose members included the OAPEC nations. OPEC, however, had flexed its muscles, and in January of 1974 had tripled the price of oil, increased royalties and taxes, changed its ways of computing these charges, and shocked oil-importing nations by announcing that henceforth it would control its production to maintain new, higher, price levels.

It has been argued that retaliation against U.S. support for Israel during the Yom Kippur War of 1967 was merely the catalyst that brought about the Arab oil embargo and that OPEC was merely at the mercy of worldwide political and economic forces that had existed for some time. The public's perception appeared different, however: Toward the end of the Arab oil embargo, *Business Week* published the results of an opinion poll showing that slightly more than a third of those sampled held the federal government most responsible for the energy shortage, while nearly one-third blamed the oil companies. Moreover, according to two somewhat contrasting arguments, gasoline lines could have been avoided. One, put forth by analyst Christopher Rand, focused on the fact that during the embargo, the nation's refineries were running at 10 percent below their normal-capacity rate of 93 percent and, more important, at 5 percent below the rate at which the domestic and imported raw feedstock for gasoline was accumulating. If the refineries had been operating up to a level that used the daily surplus without eating into existing inventories of crude oil and natural liquid gas (that is, at 88 percent of capacity, with about 53 percent of the yield as gasoline), there would have been "no cause for cutbacks, gasless weekends, damped thermostats, talk of rationing, or zany price hikes." In Rand's opinion, the lines were the result of deception by the U.S. oil industry.

Another analyst, Richard Mancke, agreed that the long lines at the gas stations were not necessary, but he placed the blame on the public sector instead of the private. Using the American Petroleum Institute's weekly reports on stocks of crude oil and refined products as reported in the *Oil and Gas Journal*, Mancke showed that at the beginning of the embargo period, petroleum stocks were 3 percent below what they had been a year earlier, and at its end, stocks were nearly 7 percent above the earlier figure. In other words, although 130 million fewer barrels of oil were imported than would have been the case had the embargo not occurred—assuming the continuation of pre-embargo levels—there was still an inventory of eight million barrels more than at the same time a year earlier. According to this argument, the "surplus" was the result of policies framed not by the oil industry but by the Federal Energy Office (FEO). The FEO sought and acquired an increased inventory. This surplus, Mancke argued, could and should have been used to eliminate the gasoline shortages. Rand identified the same surplus as not having been processed by the nation's refineries. Thus it appears that the oil industry was simply following the government's lead.

Gasoline shortages had occurred in the spring and summer before the embargo; moreover, domestic oil production was reduced by 3.4 percent between the second half of 1973 and the first half of 1974. Also, according to industry figures, oil imports for October-December, 1973, were 32 percent higher than for the same period of 1972. What is probably most relevant to any attempt to refute Mancke's casting of the FEO as the villain is Rand's contention that, because federal energy agencies employed many oil company executives, the oil industry exerted decisive influence over government energy policy. In any case, the fact of having to wait in line does not explain why the wait occurred, and the failure to avoid a shortage does not prove it was unavoidable.

On April 18, 1977, two days before presenting his energy proposals to a joint session of Congress, President Jimmy Carter addressed the American people in what one aide described as a "sky is falling" speech. Recognizing that the energy crisis was and would continue to be a problem, President Carter declared "war" on it and warned that delay in dealing with the situation would result in constant fear of embargoes and could endanger the United States' freedom as a sovereign nation and threaten its free institutions.

The public remained unmoved and unconvinced. Gallup polls taken a few weeks before and after the president's energy message showed only a marginal increase in the percentage of those who believed that the energy situation was very serious. Even this slight increase vanished as public opinion quickly returned to the roughly 40 percent level that had existed prior to the energy speech, and that still existed one year later. In July, 1977, October, 1977, and January, 1978, a *New York Times*-CBS News poll asked a scientifically selected sample of the public: "Do you think the shortage is real or are we just being told there are shortages so oil and gas companies can charge higher prices?" In each case, the public was sharply polarized. For every four out of ten respondents who accepted shortages as a fact, five did not. Furthermore, polarization of the public on energy issues was nothing new.

In April, 1977, just prior to Carter's energy speech to Congress, the CIA released an analysis predicting oil shortages by 1985; a few days after the speech, the United Nations released a report predicting enough oil and gas for at least another century. A Mobil Oil Company advertisement in a January, 1977, issue of the *Wall Street Journal* reaffirmed its numerous previous warnings about the worsening gas shortage; an August, 1977, editorial in the same newspaper cited government studies to support the claim that there were a thousand years of natural gas left in the United States alone. James R. Schlesinger, special assistant for energy matters to President Carter and first secretary of the Department of Energy from 1977 to 1979, gave an explanation for these contradictions. Since the mid-1960's, the major oil companies in the United States had been declaring that the world's oil was running out. In the mid-1970's, when the U.S. government agreed that this was the case, the oil companies requested higher prices and profits for their oil. The government responded that increased prices and profits were not necessary for existing oil fields, but only for newly developed ones. Recognizing that the federal government would not give them immediate rewards for their oil, some oil companies decided that there was really no oil emergency after all.

As of 1993, the United States relied on fossil fuels for almost 90 percent of its energy: about 45 percent from oil and 20 to 25 percent each from natural gas and coal. Whether it is a result of actual depletion of accessible resources, economic strategy, or political ploy, most petroleum industry experts agree that the world's oil and gas are being used up far faster than significant new supplies can be produced, and that known supplies of oil and gas have been seriously depleted in the United States. Despite a quadrupling in oil prices between 1970 and 1980 (after adjustment for inflation), a rise in petroleum prices in mid-1996, and exploration of more areas, the United States' proven reserves have continued to decline. Thus, higher prices have not automatically led to proportionate, or even appreciable, increases in fuel supplies. Furthermore, many major oil companies are branching out into other energy sources, which indicates their expectation of an essential shift away from petroleum to other energy alternatives in the future.

—*E. Gene DeFelice, updated by Alvin K. Benson*

ADDITIONAL READING:

Bailey, Thomas A., and David M. Kennedy. "The Stalemated Seventies." In *The American Pageant*. 8th ed. Lexington, Mass.: D. C. Heath, 1987. Reviews the events leading up to the Arab embargo, the resulting energy crisis, and the economic woes produced by the crisis.

Guertin, Donald L., W. Kenneth Davis, and John E. Gray, eds. *U.S. Energy Imperatives for the 1990's: Leadership, Efficiency, Environmental Responsibility, and Sustained Economic Growth*. Lanham, Md: University Press of America, 1992. Discusses energy-related economic and environmental issues, energy efficiency, and the need for the United States to be a leader in solving the energy crisis.

Hall, Charles A. S., Cutler J. Cleveland, and Robert Kaufmann. *Energy and Resource Quality: The Ecology of the Economic Process*. New York: John Wiley & Sons, 1986. Clear discussion of fossil fuel resource scarcity and the impact that the energy crisis has had and will have.

Mancke, Richard. *Squeaking By*. New York: Columbia University Press, 1976. Short update of the author's *Failure of U.S. Energy Policy*, in which he examines U.S. energy policies since the Arab oil embargo and defends the oil industry against charges of seeking excessive profits and market power.

Miller, E. Willard, and Ruby M. Miller. *Energy and American Society*. Santa Barbara, Calif.: ABC-CLIO, 1993. Examines the role of energy in modern U.S. society, including the evolution of energy discovery and demand in the United States, the effects of the Arab embargo, the energy crisis, and the evolution of energy laws and regulations. Tabular and statistical data.

Montgomery, Carla W. "Energy Resources—Fossil Fuels and Alternative Sources." In *Environmental Geology*. 3d ed. Dubuque, Iowa: Wm. C. Brown, 1992. Explores the energy crisis and renewable energy sources that might replace conventional sources in the future.

Rand, Christopher T. *Making Democracy Safe for Oil*. Boston: Little, Brown, 1975. Sparkling if partly polemical account of oil industry interactions with government, including one chapter devoted to the embargo.

Ruedisili, Lon C., and Morris W. Firebaugh, eds. "Background and Limitations," "Fossil-Fuel Energy Sources," and "Alternative Energy Sources." In *Perspectives on Energy*. 3d ed. New York: Oxford University Press, 1982. Describes the energy crisis and energy alternatives with the greatest capacity for sizable energy production. Includes some history, basic technical aspects, and economic, environmental, and political concerns in dealing with the energy crisis.

Yergin, Daniel. *The Prize: The Epic Quest for Oil, Money, and Power*. New York: Simon & Schuster, 1991. A broad-ranging history of oil and its impact on world events and politics.

SEE ALSO: 1974, Construction of the Alaska Pipeline; 1991, Persian Gulf War.

1974 ■ LAU V. NICHOLS: *the U.S. Supreme Court decides that school districts must provide bilingual education to limited-English-speaking students*

DATE: January 21, 1974
LOCALE: Washington, D.C.
CATEGORIES: Asian American history; Court cases; Education; Latino American history
KEY FIGURES:
William Orville Douglas (1898-1980), Supreme Court justice
Kinney Kinmon Lau (born 1964), San Francisco public school student
Alan Hammond Nichols (born 1930), president of the San Francisco Board of Education

SUMMARY OF EVENT. In 1954, the Supreme Court ruled in *Brown v. Board of Education of Topeka, Kansas* that the Fourteenth Amendment to the U.S. Constitution forbade school systems from segregating students into separate schools for only whites or African Americans. The decision effectively overturned a previous Court ruling, in *Plessy v. Ferguson* (1896), that such facilities could be "separate but equal." Instead of desegregating, however, Southern school systems engaged in massive resistance to the Court's order during the next decade. Congress then passed the Civil Rights Act of 1964, which prohibits many types of discrimination. Title VI of the law bans discrimination by recipients of federal financial assistance, including school systems.

In 1965, Congress adopted the Immigration and Nationality Act, under which larger numbers of Asian immigrants arrived in the United States than ever before, and their non-English-speaking children enrolled in public schools. In the San Francisco Unified School District, students were required to attend school until sixteen years of age, but in 1967, 2,856 students could not adequately comprehend instruction in English. Although 433 students were given supplemental courses in English on a full-time basis and 633 on a part-time basis, the remaining 1,790 students received no additional language instruction. Nevertheless, the state of California required all students to graduate with proficiency in English and permitted school districts to provide bilingual education, if needed. Except for the 433 students in the full-time bilingual education program, Chinese-speaking students were integrated in the same classrooms with English-speaking students but lacked sufficient language ability to derive benefit from the instruction. Of the 1,066 students taking bilingual courses, only 260 had bilingual teachers.

Some parents of the Chinese-speaking children, concerned that their children would drop out of school and experience pressure to join criminal youth gangs, launched protests. Various organizations formed in the Chinese American community, which in turn made studies, issued proposals, circulated leaflets, and tried to negotiate with the San Francisco Board of Education. When the board refused to respond adequately, a suit was filed in federal district court in San Francisco on March 25, 1970. The plaintiffs were Kinney Kinmon Lau and eleven other non-English-speaking students, mostly U.S. citizens born of Chinese parents. The defendants were Alan H. Nichols, president of the San Francisco Board of Education, the rest of the Board of Education, and the San Francisco Board of Supervisors.

On May 25, 1970, the Office for Civil Rights (OCR) of the U.S. Department of Health, Education, and Welfare issued the following regulation pursuant to its responsibility to monitor Title VI compliance: "Where inability to speak and understand the English language excludes national-origin minority group children from effective participation in the educational program offered by a school district, the district must take affirmative steps to rectify the language deficiency in order to open its instructional program to these students." OCR had sided with the Chinese-speaking students.

One day later, the court ruled that the school system was violating neither Title VI nor the Fourteenth Amendment; instead, the plaintiffs were characterized as asking for "special rights above those granted other children." Lawyers representing the Chinese Americans then appealed, this time supported by a friend-of-the-court brief filed by the U.S. Department of Justice. On January 8, 1973, the Court of Appeals also ruled adversely, stating that there was no duty "to rectify appellants' special deficiencies, as long as they provided these students with access to the same educational system made available to all other students." The appeals court claimed that the children's problems were "not the result of law enacted by the state . . . but the result of deficiency created by themselves in failing to learn the English language."

On June 12, 1973, the Supreme Court agreed to hear the case. Oral argument was heard on December 10, 1973. On January 21, 1974, the Supreme Court unanimously overturned the lower courts. Justice William O. Douglas delivered the majority opinion, which included the memorable statement that "There is no equality of treatment merely by providing students with the same facilities, textbooks, teachers, and curriculum; for students who do not understand English are effectively foreclosed from any meaningful education." The Court returned the case to the district court so that the school system could design a plan of language-needs assessments and programs for addressing those needs. In a concurring opinion, Chief Justice Warren E. Burger and Justice Harry A. Blackmun observed that the number of underserved non-English-speaking, particularly Chinese-speaking, students was substantial in this case, but they would not order bilingual education for "just a single child who speaks only German or Polish or Spanish or any language other than English."

The Supreme Court's decision in Lau ultimately resulted in changes to enable Chinese-speaking students to obtain equal educational opportunity San Francisco's public schools, although it was more than a year before such changes began to be implemented. The greatest impact has been among Spanish-speaking students, members of the largest language-minority group in the United States.

Subsequently, Congress passed the Equal Educational Opportunities Act in 1974, a provision of which superseded Lau by requiring "appropriate action to overcome language barriers that impede equal participation," which a federal district court later applied to the need for new methods to deal with speakers of "Black English" in Martin Luther King, Jr., Elementary School Children v. Michigan Board of Education (1979). Also in 1974, the Bilingual Education Act of 1968 was amended to provide more federal funds for second-language instruction so that school districts could be brought into compliance with Lau. Bilingualism was further recognized when Congress passed the Voting Rights Act of 1975, which established guidelines for providing ballots in the languages of certain minority groups.

In 1975, OCR established informal guidelines for four bilingual programs that would enable school districts to come into compliance with the Supreme Court ruling. The main requirement was first to test students to determine language proficiency. Students with no English proficiency at all were to be exposed to bilingual/bicultural programs or transitional bilingual education programs; secondary schools also had the option of providing "English as a second language" or "high intensive language training" programs. If a student had some familiarity with English, these four programs would be required only if testing revealed that the student had low achievement test scores.

Because the OCR guidelines were not published in the Federal Register for public comment and later modification, they were challenged on September 29, 1978, in the federal district court of Alaska (Northwest Arctic School District v. Califano). The case was settled by a consent decree in 1980, when the federal agency agreed to publish a "Notice of Proposed Rulemaking"; however, soon after Ronald Reagan took office as president, that notice was withdrawn. By 1985, a manual to identify types of language discrimination was compiled to supersede the 1975 guidelines, but it also was not published in the Federal Register for public comment. Meanwhile, methods for educating limited-English-speaking students evolved beyond the OCR's original conceptions, and further litigation followed. In 1981, a U.S. circuit court ruled in Castañeda v. Pickard that bilingual educational programs are lawful when they satisfy three tests: (1) the program is recognized by professionals as sound in educational theory; (2) the program is designed to implement that theory; and (3) the program actually results in overcoming language barriers.

During the presidency of Ronald Reagan, civil rights monitoring focused more on "reverse discrimination" than on violations of equal educational opportunities. Congressional hearings were held to goad OCR into action. Although in 1991

OCR's top priority was equal educational opportunities for national-origin minority and Native American students with limited-English proficiency (LEP) or non-English proficiency (NEP), results were difficult to discern, and a movement to make English the official language of the United States (the "English-only" movement) threatened to overturn *Lau* and related legislation. —*Michael Haas*

ADDITIONAL READING:

Biegel, Stuart. "The Parameters of the Bilingual Education Debate in California Twenty Years After *Lau v. Nichols.*" *Chicano-Latino Law Review* 14 (Winter, 1994): 48-60. The status of *Lau* in light of the 1990's English-only movement.

Bull, Barry L., Royal T. Fruehling, and Virgie Chatterg y. *The Ethics of Multicultural and Bilingual Education.* New York: Columbia University Teachers College Press, 1992. Contrasts how liberal, democratic, and communitarian approaches to education relate to bilingual and multicultural education.

Fineberg, Elliot M., et al. "The Problems of Segregation and Inequality of Educational Opportunity." In *One Nation Indivisible: The Civil Rights Challenge for the 1990's,* edited by Reginald C. Govan and William L. Taylor. Washington, D.C.: Citizens' Commission on Civil Rights, 1989. Reviews underenforcement of laws dealing with language-minority students during the Reagan years.

Moran, Rachel F. "Of Democracy, Devaluation, and Bilingual Education." *Creighton Law Review* 26 (February, 1993): 255-319. Contrasts special-interest bargaining and bureaucratic rule-making methods for dealing with needs for bilingual education.

Newman, Terri Lunn. "Proposal: Bilingual Education Guidelines for the Courts and the Schools." *Emory Law Journal* 33 (Spring, 1984): 577-629. Legal requirements of *Lau* presented as guidelines for school systems in establishing bilingual programs.

Orlando, Carlos J., and Virginia P. Collier. *Bilingual and ESL Classrooms: Teaching in Multicultural Contexts.* New York: McGraw-Hill, 1985. Discusses the need for bilingual education, alternative approaches available, and resources required.

United States Commission on Civil Rights. *A Better Chance to Learn: Bilingual-Bicultural Education.* Washington, D.C.: Author, 1975. Assesses the national impact of *Lau*; contains the text of the Supreme Court decision and related documents.

Wang, L. Ling-chi. "*Lau v. Nichols*: History of Struggle for Equal and Quality Education." In *Asian-Americans: Social and Psychological Perspectives,* edited by Russell Endo, Stanley Sue, and Nathaniel N. Wagner. Palo Alto, Calif.: Science & Behavior Books, 1980. Describes how the *Lau* case was pursued, especially the resistance to implementation.

SEE ALSO: 1954, *Brown v. Board of Education*; 1964, Civil Rights Act of 1964; 1965, Immigration and Nationality Act; 1968, Bilingual Education Act.

1974 ▪ CONSTRUCTION OF THE ALASKA PIPELINE: *a major engineering feat allows exploitation of a vast energy resource yet stirs controversy among competing economic and environmental interests*

DATE: January 23, 1974-June 20, 1977
LOCALE: Alaska
CATEGORIES: Economics; Science and technology
KEY FIGURES:
R. G. Dulaney, chairman of the Trans-Alaska Pipeline System
Charlie Edwardsen, executive director of the Arctic Slope Native Association
William Allen Egan (1914-1984), governor of Alaska
Walter J. Hickel (born 1919), U.S. secretary of the interior, 1969-1970
Thomas E. Kelly (born 1931), natural resources commissioner of Alaska

SUMMARY OF EVENT. In July, 1957, oil was discovered on the Kenai Peninsula of Alaska by the Richfield Company. The news initiated a rush on leases for land in the area in a fashion to which the Alaskan frontier is accustomed. Eleven years later, Thomas E. Kelly, Natural Resources Commissioner of Alaska, reclassified more than two million acres of North Slope land for competitive oil and gas leasing, whereupon the newly formed Atlantic-Richfield Company confirmed its findings of significant oil deposits on the North Slope. Even the most conservative estimates indicated that the oil in the North Slope was a major deposit, amounting to at least 9.6 billion barrels. Speculators poured into the state; approximately fourteen hundred corporations registered in Alaska to engage in the rush. Alaska experienced a boom not unlike the late 1800's gold rush, with all the accompanying excitement. This discovery was the advent of what was to be a significant landmark in the battle between environmental protection of natural resources and private interests.

A joint venture of Atlantic-Richfield, British Petroleum, and Humble Oil, simply called the Trans-Alaska Pipeline System (TAPS), applied for permission in 1969 to build a hot oil pipeline across the state from the North Slope to the port at Valdez. The proposal was met by organized opposition from conservationists posing questions that were not only environmental but also technical and economic. On the basis of a cursory investigation, TAPS opted for a conventional pipeline over a seemingly efficient route, discarding proposed alternatives, such as connecting with existing Canadian pipelines.

R. G. Dulaney, the Chairman of the Trans-Alaska Pipeline System, impatiently pushed for the approval and immediate completion of the pipeline over the route to the port at Valdez. Investigations and surveys were approved and under way when orders for the special forty-eight-inch pipe were placed with three Japanese companies. Meanwhile, the United States Department of the Interior set up a task force to oversee North

Slope oil development; this task force was modified by President Richard Nixon to include conservation and other interests. All this took place before an application was filed for permission to build a pipeline.

Meanwhile, apparent alliances were being formed for an anticipated confrontation. One issue, the technical feasibility of a buried pipeline over the proposed route, raised several problems which the task force was unable to solve satisfactorily: the impact of an underground pipeline on the permafrost; the incidence of earthquakes in this seismologically active area; the pollution which would result both from handling the oil and from increasing human activity in a wilderness region; and native land claims.

The ensuing political confrontations at both state and national levels developed into a classic confrontation of conflicting interests. Alaska was concerned for its future; and the lure of industrial prosperity was tempered by the problems industry would bring to the environment. At the national level, Congress adopted the National Environmental Policy Act in 1969, which was to be the major tool of conservationists in influencing public policy. The law required that information be made public on adverse environmental effects, and alternatives considered, for any federally supported project.

In the late summer of 1969, the Twentieth Science Conference met in Fairbanks to discuss the future of Alaska. From that conference, it was apparent that the final solution to the question of an Alaskan pipeline was not imminent. Dissident elements were organized and were not to be regarded as powerless. The political battles that were to follow focused on the two fundamental issues of environment and native land claims. Walter J. Hickel, secretary of the interior and former governor of Alaska, was thrust into a central role in these two conflicts.

On December 18, 1971, President Nixon signed into law the Alaska Native Claims Settlement Act. The bill provided Alaskan natives with full title to their land and first option on forty-four million acres of disputed territory. The act also required the oil companies to deposit $1 billion into the Alaskan state treasure so that all Alaskans would be able to benefit from the oil profits. William Egan, the governor of Alaska, who favored construction of the pipeline, was instrumental in the passage of this legislation. Charlie Edwardsen, principal spokesman of the Arctic Slope Native Association, was very critical of the act because it allowed the native Eskimos only surface rights to their oil-rich lands.

The focus then shifted to technical and environmental issues regarding the pipeline. The challenges, delays, and legal battles continued. Finally, on November 16, 1973, nearly five years after the initial TAPS proposal, President Nixon signed the Trans-Alaska Pipeline Authorization Act, and on January 23, 1974, the Department of the Interior issued the long-awaited construction permit. The pipeline was built by Alyeska Pipeline Service, a consortium of several large oil companies, including Atlantic-Richfield and British Petroleum.

Many problems remained. The tiny town of Valdez, swelled by the influx of pipeline workers and others rushing to a promising job market, simply had no facilities to deal with the large number of people. The struggle for land continued. The Alaskan natives sought to exercise options on the North Slope, while conservationists sought to enlarge the federal domain with parks, refuges, and national forests.

Three large mountain ranges had to be crossed as well as many rivers, including the Yukon. In many areas, because the land was frozen all year round, pipe could not be buried. If it were, the oil would melt the permafrost and destabilize the pipe. Other problems had to be considered also. Alaska is known for its beautiful tundra landscapes and many species of animals whose migration paths, grazing areas, or calving grounds might be threatened by the pipeline itself or by leakage from it. Also, Alaska is know to be seismologically active. Environmentalists and native peoples, as well as the regulations of the federal Environmental Protection Agency, placed many restrictions on the right of way and on the building of the pipeline. When the ground was disturbed, it was required that it be put back in its original condition. The ground had to be reseeded, and construction sites had to be cleaned. Construction crews were not to interfere with fish or their spawning beds. Aboveground pipe had to be elevated at least ten feet whenever migratory trails crossed the pipeline. Animals were not to be fed so that they would not become dependent on human presence. Builders were not permitted to fell trees near streams, and foresters ensured that no more trees were cut than necessary. The pipeline could not come nearer than one half mile to any city, wildlife refuge, or historic landmark. Archaeologists explored the area before the construction and found traces of Indian hunting camps. Most agree that the restrictions were beneficial, although some of them were attempts to stop the construction altogether.

Five thousand natives found jobs on the pipeline, and one thousand dollars per week was common pay. In all, Alyeska hired twenty-two thousand workers, who worked ten to twelve hours per day, seven days a week. These workers required large quantities of food, clothing, and shelter, all of which were supplied by Alyeska. The supplies, had to be flown into the area because Alaska grows very little of its own food. Where possible, the pipe was buried, but in permafrost areas it had to be thickly insulated. Where ground was warmer than the air, special heat pipes were installed underground to convey the heat to the outside air. In streambeds the pipe was either encased in about nine inches of concrete or was held down by concrete saddles weighing eighteen thousand pounds each. In other areas, where it was better to string the pipe above ground, care had to be taken that the warm oil would not melt the ground under it. Sometimes suspension bridges were built over the streams. A 2,300-foot bridge was built across the Yukon for both the pipeline and traffic. Occasionally, fleets of helicopters were used to carry personnel and to lower sections of pipe into places where no other transport was able to go.

On June 20, 1977, after several false starts, repairs, and accidents, oil began to flow into the pumping stations in Valdez. The first barrels of oil took about a month to travel the 800 miles, but soon 800,000 barrels a day and eventually 1,200,000 barrels a day would arrive in Valdez at a speed of four miles per hour and in about seven or eight days. Tankers at Valdez continually transported the oil to the lower forty-eight states and, beginning in November of 1995, to foreign countries directly, especially Japan. The amazing feat of engineering that helped solve the "energy crisis" of the mid-1970's, however, continued to be vexed by environmental problems. In 1990, for example, Joe Tracanna, an electrical inspector, noticed brown goo oozing from the thick electrical cables; in 1993, the Bureau of Land Management conducted an audit and found 4,300 electrical code violations and numerous other safety and operations errors. When the *Exxon Valdez* spilled eleven million gallons of oil into Prince William Sound in March of 1989, Alyeska was criticized for its response to the spill. Such incidents continued to provoke debate between environmental and economic interests.

—Jonathan M. Furdek, updated by Winifred O. Whelan

ADDITIONAL READING:

Allen, Lawrence. *The Trans-Alaska Pipeline South to Valdez.* Seattle, Wash.: Scribe Publishing Company, 1976. A detailed description of the plans and problems of constructing the pipeline.

Berry, Mary Clay. *The Alaska Pipeline: The Politics of Oil and Native Land Claims.* Bloomington: Indiana University Press, 1975. In a detailed account of events, the author provides an insight into the activities and happenings, the political pressures and issues, and the eventual compromise and outcome of an episode in American history that asserted public interests for environment and dramatically changed the direction of development of Alaska.

Bowermaster, David. "A Long, Blotted Record: New Criticism of the Trans Alaska Pipeline and the Firm That Runs It." *U.S. News & World Report* 115 (October 25, 1993): 38-39. Describes the "weeping wires" and other problems, such as the failure to properly install fittings designed to keep static electricity away from the pipeline.

Coates, Peter A. *The Trans-Alaska Pipeline Controversy: Technology, Conservation, and the Frontier.* Bethlehem, Pa.: Lehigh University Press, 1991. Describes the evolution of conservationist concern over Alaska since American acquisition in 1867.

Coombs, Charles. *Pipeline Across Alaska.* New York: William Morrow, 1978. This book discusses the history, construction, and economic and environmental impact of the eight hundred mile pipeline.

Mead, Robert Douglas. *Journeys Down the Line: Building the Alaska Pipeline.* Garden City, N.J.: Doubleday, 1978. A narrative of the discovery of Alaska oil, the building and history of the pipeline, and the controversies surrounding it.

Roscow, James P. *800 Miles to Valdez: The Building of the Alaska Pipeline.* Englewood Cliffs, N.J.: Prentice-Hall, 1977.

A detailed account of the events leading to the completion of the pipeline.

Skorupa, Joe. "Driving the Alaska Pipeline Road." *Popular Mechanics* 172 (October, 1995): 74-78. A description of scenery and mechanical difficulties experienced during a drive north from Fairbanks along the road that follows the pipeline.

SEE ALSO: 1971, Alaska Native Claims Settlement Act; 1973, Arab Oil Embargo and Energy Crisis.

1974 ∎ NIXON RESIGNS: *in the aftermath of the Watergate affair and the ensuing constitutional crisis, Nixon's resignation reaffirms the principle that no one, including the president, is above the law*

DATE: August 9, 1974
LOCALE: Washington, D.C.
CATEGORY: Government and politics
KEY FIGURES:

Archibald Cox (born 1912), Watergate special prosecutor
Samuel J. Ervin, Jr. (1896-1985), chair of the Senate select committee investigating Watergate
Gerald Rudolph Ford, Jr. (born 1913), fortieth vice president of the United States, 1973-1974, and thirty-eighth president of the United States, 1974-1977
Alexander M. Haig, Jr. (born 1924), White House chief of staff for Nixon
Leon Jaworski (1905-1982), Watergate special prosecutor
Richard Milhous Nixon (1913-1994), thirty-seventh president of the United States, 1969-1974
Peter W. Rodino, Jr. (born 1909), chairman of the House judiciary committee that approved impeachment
John J. Sirica (1904-1992), United States federal district Judge for the District of Columbia

SUMMARY OF EVENT. On August 9, 1974, Richard M. Nixon became the first president of the United States to resign that office, subsequently retiring to his estate in California. Nixon's resignation and the collapse of his administration were an outgrowth of the Watergate affair, which occupied increasing amounts of his time between June, 1972, and his forced resignation in August, 1974.

The Watergate scandal grew out of the arrest of five men who on June 17, 1972, broke into the national headquarters of the Democratic Party, which was then located in Washington's Watergate Hotel. Although three of the criminals, E. Howard Hunt, Jr., James W. McCord, Jr., and G. Gordon Liddy, worked for the Committee to Reelect the President (CRP, popularly known as CREEP), there was then no proof connecting their criminal activity with influential people at the Nixon White House. Starting in early 1973, others were implicated in the burglary because of the insistence of United States District Judge John J. Sirica, and the chain of conspirators eventually reached into the White House and the Justice Department, entangling the president himself. Some months later it was revealed that on June 23, 1972, Nixon had ordered the Central Intelligence Agency (CIA) to interfere with the investigation of this crime by the Federal Bureau of Investigation (FBI). The proof of Nixon's criminal obstruction of justice brought about the president's resignation.

The burglary was first investigated by the Senate Select Committee on Presidential Campaign Activities, chaired by Senator Sam J. Ervin, Jr., of North Carolina, while crusading *Washington Post* reporters Bob Woodward and Carl Bernstein persisted in their attempts to get to the bottom of the situation. The president's personal lawyer, John W. Dean III, in sworn testimony before the Ervin Committee, stated that the President and his advisers had tried to cover up for the burglars. This testimony launched a slow but steady momentum in the press, Congress, the courts, and the Justice Department to get to the bottom of the affair. Eventually, Dean's testimony was substantiated by the presidential audiotapes, whose existence was revealed to the public on July 16, 1973, when a White House aide named Alexander Butterfield told the Ervin Committee that all conversations in the Oval Office had been secretly recorded and that these tapes had been kept by order of President Nixon.

The President acccepted the resignations of his principal aides H. R. Haldeman and John D. Ehrlichman in April of 1973, following the early portions of Dean's damaging testimony. Dean himself was dismissed. Attorney General Richard G. Kleindienst and L. Patrick Gray III, acting director of the FBI, also resigned shortly thereafter. The new attorney general, Elliot L. Richardson, appointed a special Watergate prosecutor, Harvard University law professor Archibald Cox, with full authority to pursue the case wherever it might lead. Professor Cox fought a battle in the courts to force the president to surrender his taped conversations as material evidence. In a blatant effort to put an end to the investigation of his own involvement in the Watergate affair, President Nixon ordered Cox not to subpoena tapes or documents from the White House. When Cox refused to comply with this request, he was abruptly fired on October 20, 1973, in what has been called the Saturday Night Massacre. His firing was followed by the resignations of Attorney General Richardson and his deputy, William D. Ruckelshaus, both of whom refused to carry out the president's order to fire Cox. These events caused a public uproar and reaction against the president, and the House Judiciary Committee on February 6, 1974, began formal impeachment proceedings against him. Public pressure forced the president to relent, and his new attorney general, William B. Saxbe, appointed a new Watergate prosecutor, Leon Jaworski, who continued the battle to acquire the tapes.

The struggle on the part of the House Judiciary Committee under its chairman, Peter W. Rodino, Jr., from New Jersey, to enforce its subpoena that President Nixon turn over relevant tapes for the impeachment proceedings, and Jaworski to gain access to the entirety of the President's taped conversations, took many turns during the spring and summer of 1974 but

ended with an eight-to-nothing decision by the Supreme Court on July 24 that the president must surrender completely all the relevant and subpoenaed evidence in his possession. The high court's unanimous decision marked a total defeat for Nixon and his special counsel, James D. St. Clair from Boston, one of the best trial lawyers in the country. Meanwhile, the House Judiciary Committee, looking toward impeachment, had begun nationally televised hearings. Between July 27 and 30, 1974, the committee approved three articles of impeachment, charging Nixon with obstruction of justice, abuse of presidential powers, and impeding the impeachment process by defying committee subpoenas for evidence.

Even after the three articles of impeachment had been approved by the House Judiciary Committee, President Nixon still thought that enough Republican senators would support him during the impeachment trial to prevent his removal from office, but he was deceiving himself. At the insistence of James St. Clair, the president on August 5 released three taped conversations covered by the Supreme Court decision, which clearly indicated that he had tried to obstruct justice and cover up for the Watergate conspirators. The president's position was

Upon the resignation of President Nixon in disgrace on August 9, 1974, Gerald R. Ford became thirty-eighth president of the United States. One month later, Ford pardoned Nixon before the former president could be prosecuted on Watergate charges. (Library of Congress)

destroyed in both houses of Congress, and even prominent conservative Republicans and longtime Nixon supporters, such as Senator Barry Goldwater from Arizona, Senator Hugh Scott from Pennsylvania, and Congressman John Rhodes from Arizona, privately urged the president to face reality and resign. White House Chief of Staff Alexander M. Haig, Jr., devoted his energies and position to convincing the president that resignation was now the only way out. Nixon wavered for days, but on August 8, 1974, he went on nationwide television to announce that he would resign as president the following day, saying that his political base in Congress had eroded to the point that there was no longer any point in continuing to struggle.

Nixon's successor, Gerald R. Ford, on September 8, 1974, granted his predecessor a full and complete pardon for all federal crimes he might have committed as president. Nixon then issued a formal statement accepting the pardon and expressed regret only that he had not been more forthright and decisive in dealing with the Watergate scandal. He never admitted his personal guilt to the American public. A considerable public outcry arose, the feeling being that, as in the case of the earlier resignation of Vice President Spiro Agnew on October 10, 1973, justice had not been served because neither Agnew nor Nixon ever had to answer to juries for their crimes.

—*Jack L. Calbert, updated by Edmund J. Campion*

ADDITIONAL READING:

Ervin, Sam J., Jr. *The Whole Truth: The Watergate Conspiracy.* New York: Random House, 1980. A thoughtful analysis by Senator Ervin of the ethical and political implications of the Watergate scandal. Examines the seriousness of the constitutional crisis caused by Nixon's obstruction of justice.

Friedman, Leon, and William F. Levantrosser, eds. *Watergate and Afterward.* Westport, Conn.: Greenwood Press, 1992. Examines various legal and political dimensions of the dismissal of Archibald Cox, the July, 1974, Supreme Court ruling against Nixon, and the impeachment hearings in the House Judiciary Committee.

White, Theodore H. *Breach of Faith: The Fall of Richard Nixon.* New York: Atheneum Press, 1975. Describes Nixon's unsuccessful efforts at damage control during the unfolding of the Watergate scandal. A well-documented history of this constitutional crisis.

Wicker, Tom. *One of Us: Richard Nixon and the American Dream.* New York: Random House, 1991. Contains a thoughtful analysis of the possible reasons for Nixon's belief that he could violate the Constitution with impunity.

Woodward, Bob, and Carl Bernstein. *The Final Days.* New York: Simon & Schuster, 1976. Written by two *Washington Post* reporters who became famous for investigating the Watergate scandal, this volume describes events from the Saturday Night Massacre to Nixon's resignation.

SEE ALSO: 1964, Vietnam War; 1967, Long, Hot Summer; 1968, Chicago Riots; 1968, Nixon Is Elected President; 1970, United States Invades Cambodia; 1972, Watergate Affair; 1973, U.S. Troops Leave Vietnam.

1975 ■ EQUAL CREDIT OPPORTUNITY ACT:
financial institutions are required to make credit available without discrimination on the basis of sex or marital status

DATE: October 28, 1975
LOCALE: Washington, D.C.
CATEGORIES: Civil rights; Laws and acts; Women's issues
KEY FIGURES:
Bella Savitzky Abzug (born 1920), Democratic congresswoman from New York
Joseph Robinette Biden, Jr. (born 1942), Democratic senator from Delaware
William Emerson Brock (born 1930), Republican congressman from Tennessee, 1963-1970, and senator, 1971-1977
Gerald Rudolph Ford, Jr. (born 1913), thirty-eighth president of the United States, 1974-1977
William Proxmire (born 1915), Democratic senator from Wisconsin
Leonor Kretzer Sullivan (1904-1988), Democratic congresswoman from Missouri

SUMMARY OF EVENT. In 1968, Congress passed the Consumer Credit Protection Act. One provision of the law created the National Commission on Consumer Finance. In 1972, as a member of the commission, Congresswoman Leonor K. Sullivan persuaded the commission to investigate discrimination against women in the consumer credit industry. During commission hearings on the subject, testimony was presented about instances in which married women were denied credit cards and charge accounts except in their husbands' names, and about the fact that widows and divorced and separated women often were denied any sort of credit. Widows often continued to use their dead husband's name in order to continue to have credit, as if a live widow had less credit than a dead spouse. As a result, many women could buy neither cars nor houses on credit, even if they had been the bill payers in their families before the departure of their husbands.

The commission's report galvanized Congresswoman Bella S. Abzug to introduce a series of bills in 1972 to make credit discrimination illegal. Hearings were held in 1973, when a related bill, sponsored by Senator William E. Brock, passed the Senate, but more hearings in 1974 did not bear fruit in the House of Representatives. The issue was overshadowed by rampant inflation and developments in electronic bank transfers, which required a congressional reexamination of regulations in the banking and finance industry.

Congress was then working on the Depository Institutions Amendments of 1974, the most important provision of which was to raise the amount of federally guaranteed bank deposits from twenty thousand dollars to forty thousand dollars. On May 14, 1974, Brock and several cosponsors (Wallace F. Bennett, Edward W. Brooke, Alan Cranston, Robert W. Packwood,

William Proxmire, and John G. Tower) attached to the larger bill a provision known as Title V, which amended the Consumer Credit Protection Act by adding a new section, known as the Equal Credit Opportunity Act. When the larger bill was adopted overwhelmingly, the Equal Credit Opportunity Act of 1974 passed as well, going into effect on October 28, 1975.

The law prohibited any creditor from discriminating against any applicant on the basis of sex or marital status with respect to any aspect of a credit transaction. Although the Federal Reserve Board was empowered to issue implementing regulations, administrative enforcement by way of complaint investigation was assigned to many agencies. For national banks, enforcement is by the Comptroller of the Currency. The Federal Reserve Board handles all of its member banks, other than national banks. The Federal Deposit Insurance Corporation enforces the law for all banks that it ensures, other than members of the Federal Reserve System. The Federal Home Loan Bank Board, acting directly or through the Federal Savings and Loan Insurance Corporation, has jurisdiction over financial institutions subject to provisions of the Home Owners' Loan Act, the National Housing Act, and the Federal Home Loan Bank. The administrator of the National Credit Union enforces the law for any federal credit union. The Interstate Commerce Commission regulates any common carrier under its jurisdiction. The Civil Aeronautics Board monitors any air carrier subject to the Federal Aviation Act of 1958. The secretary of agriculture handles complaints regarding activities subject to the Packers and Stockyards Act of 1921. The Farm Credit Administration plays a similar role for any federal land bank, federal land bank association, federal intermediate credit bank, and production credit association. The Securities and Exchange Commission has jurisdiction over brokers and dealers. The Small Business Administration looks after small business investment companies. For all other matters, the Federal Trade Commission has responsibility under the law. In all cases, agencies can respond to complaints by initiating investigations; alternatively, they can monitor statistical patterns of reported loans for evidence that certain groups are disproportionately denied credit. If discrimination is documented, the agency can refer a case to the Department of Justice for legal action against the offending financial institution.

The bill put a cap on the amount to be obtained by victims of discrimination. Individuals could sue only up to $10,000, and class complaints were limited to $100,000 or 1 percent of net worth for willful violations. According to Sullivan, this provision made the law less effective, even diluting the force of the Truth in Lending Act by reducing the penalty for infractions.

Passage of the Equal Credit Opportunity Act was an easy victory: There were no public hearings and no opposition in Congress. After the law was signed by President Gerald R. Ford, Jr., on October 28, 1975, Sullivan urged Congress to amend the bill to remove the monetary caps and to broaden coverage so that credit discrimination based on race, color, religion, national origin, and age also would be illegal. She

soon introduced an expanded bill. Senators Joseph R. Biden, Jr., and William Proxmire assumed leadership on the bill in the Senate, modifying its text somewhat. On March 23, 1976, the Equal Credit Opportunity Act Amendments of 1976 passed, expanding coverage as Sullivan had asked, with a new cap of $500,000 for class-action suits; the statute of limitations for infractions was extended from one to two years.

The purpose of the law, as amended, is to require financial institutions to determine creditworthiness on the basis of finances, rather than on such nonfinancial grounds as age, sex, marital status, race, color, religion, or national origin. The law also protects recipients of public assistance funds from credit discrimination. The law immediately enabled millions of women to obtain credit cards, charge accounts, car loans, and home loans from financial institutions. However, the law had no effect on policies of insurance companies, and serious systemic credit discrimination has continued, especially based on race.

—*Michael Haas*

ADDITIONAL READING:

Burns, James A., Jr. "An Empirical Analysis of the Equal Credit Opportunity Act." *University of Michigan Journal of Law Reform* 13 (Fall, 1979): 102-142. According to a nationwide poll, those who suffer most from credit discrimination are younger persons, minorities, and women, in that order, although minorities complain the least.

Cronin, Lisa. "Equal Credit Opportunity Act: Some Good News, Some Not So Good." *Ms.* 5 (March, 1977): 95-97. Explains the politics of adopting the law and summarizes the coverage of the law.

Matheson, John H. "The Equal Credit Opportunity Act: A Functional Failure." *Harvard Journal of Legislation* 21 (Summer, 1984): 371-403. Posits that the law has failed to rectify much of the problem because the burden of proof is too heavy on the plaintiff, and there is administrative underenforcement.

Rogers, Laura L., and John L. Culhane, Jr. "Developments Under the Equal Credit Opportunity Act and Regulation B." *The Business Lawyer* 43 (August, 1988): 1571-1583. Discusses the regulation of the Federal Reserve Bank governing equal credit, as revised in 1985, and subsequent litigation.

Schafer, Robert T., and Helen F. Ladd. *Discrimination in Mortgage Lending.* Cambridge: MIT Press, 1981. Using data from California and New York, the authors show little gender discrimination, substantial age discrimination, and widespread discrimination based on ethnicity and race.

Smith, Dolores S. "Revision of the Board's Equal Credit Regulation: An Overview." *Federal Reserve Bulletin* 71 (December, 1985): 913-923. Explains the Federal Reserve Bank's implementing regulation for the law.

Taibi, Anthony D. "Banking, Finance, and Community Empowerment: Structural Economic Theory, Procedural Civil Rights, and Substantive Racial Justice." *Harvard Law Review* 107 (May, 1994): 1463-1545. Argues that the law failed to open credit for minorities because the banking industry continues to operate on the basis of neoclassical economics and seeks profits, not social equity.

SEE ALSO: 1963, Equal Pay Act; 1972, Equal Employment Opportunity Act.

1976 ▪ GREGG V. GEORGIA: *after declaring execution unconstitutional in 1972, the U.S. Supreme Court reinstates the death penalty contingent on protection against its arbitrary and capricious imposition*

DATE: July 2, 1976
LOCALE: Washington, D.C.
CATEGORIES: Civil rights; Court cases
KEY FIGURES:

William H. Furman, petitioner in *Furman v. Georgia*, 1972
Lucious Jackson, Jr., petitioner in *Jackson v. Georgia*, 1972
Elmer Branch, petitioner in *Branch v. Texas*, 1972
William Joseph Brennan, Jr. (born 1906) and
William Orville Douglas (1898-1980), associate justices of the United States and authors of the concurring majority opinion in the three 1972 cases
Troy Leon Gregg, petitioner in *Gregg v. Georgia*, 1976
Thurgood Marshall (1908-1993),
Potter Stewart (1915-1985), and
Byron R. White (born 1917), associate justices of the United States who joined in the majority opinion in the 1972 cases
Lewis F. Powell (born 1907) and
John P. Stevens (born 1920), associate justices of the United States and coannouncers, with Stewart, of the decision in the 1976 case

SUMMARY OF EVENT. The death penalty is a method of punishment that historically has been applied globally for both serious and relatively minor crimes against state, person, and property. During the medieval and early modern periods of European history, the death sentence was used as punishment for many crimes and usually was administered in public, often accompanied by torture of the most painful and gruesome kind. The greatest abuse of the use of the death penalty was probably reached in eighteenth century England when it was decreed, although not regularly applied, for several hundred offenses, most representing crimes against property.

The increased use of the death penalty and the resulting public desensitization, accompanied by the humanitarian movement in the West known as the Age of Enlightenment, led to a growing reaction to its use, especially among the intellectuals of the age. The most famous early attack on the death penalty came from an Italian, Cesare Beccaria, whose *Essay on Crimes and Punishments* (1764) led to a rapidly growing demand for reform. The results were quick to come. During the French Revolution, for example, the guillotine was used as a more humane instrument of execution than the less swift and sure ax or sword. By the 1830's, the number of cases in England for which the death penalty could be imposed had been reduced from the hundreds of a few decades earlier to

fifteen. The same trends followed in the United States, although the death penalty had never been imposed widely there.

By the middle of the twentieth century, the use of the death penalty had declined even further throughout most of the world, especially in Europe and the Americas. However, a large majority of the states in the United States still legislated its potential use in court sentences, although it seldom was actually imposed. A continuous attack on the imposition of the death penalty in criminal cases accompanied this decline in capital punishment. The opponents of the death penalty were never a majority, however, and all their arguments were countered by its proponents.

Generally, arguments for and against capital punishment can be divided into two basic categories—one based on religious belief and emotions, and the other founded on utilitarian or practical arguments. Supporters have argued, for example, that it is ordained by God as a means by which humans act as God's agents in ridding the world of the grossly undesirable, whereas opponents have held that justice belongs to God alone and cannot be delegated to people. In the category of practicality, supporters have held that capital punishment is a deterrent, protecting the community, prison staffs, and fellow prisoners from dangerous criminals. They also argue that those prisoners who receive the penalty of life imprisonment instead of death are an economic liability to the state. Opponents have countered these arguments by asserting that there is no proof that the threat of death deters criminals from committing capital offenses; that rehabilitation in prison rather than punishment could mitigate the problem of the dangerous criminal to society, prison staff, and prisoners; and that in well-run prisons, prisoners can be economic assets instead of liabilities. Most important, they have argued that judicial error can and has led to the execution of innocent persons, and that the imposition of the death penalty often has been socially and racially arbitrary and discriminatory. It was essentially on these arguments that the United States Supreme Court made its decisions on the death penalty in 1972 and 1976.

In 1972, two petitioners from Georgia, William H. Furman and Lucious Jackson, Jr., and a petitioner from Texas, Elmer Branch, brought suit in federal court against their respective states. Furman and Jackson had been convicted by juries in Georgia state courts of murder and rape, respectively, and had been sentenced to death by juries that had discretion over whether to impose the death penalty. Their sentences had been upheld by the Georgia Supreme Court. Branch had been sentenced to death for rape in Texas by a jury with the same discretionary power, and his sentence had been upheld by the Texas Court of Criminal Appeals. The United States Supreme Court, in a five-to-four decision, reversed the judgment of the state courts and remanded the cases for further proceedings. The cases were consolidated for argument and decision.

Furman, the plaintiff in the most renowned case, was an African American man who had attempted to enter a private home at night. He had shot and killed the homeowner through a closed door. Furman was twenty-six years of age and had a sixth-grade education. Prior to trial, Furman was committed to the Georgia Central State Hospital for a psychiatric examination on his plea of insanity. The hospital superintendent reported a diagnosis of mental deficiency with psychotic episodes. Although not psychotic at the time, Furman was not capable of cooperating with defense counsel, and they believed he needed further treatment. The superintendent later amended the report, saying Furman knew right from wrong and could cooperate with counsel.

Justices William O. Douglas, William Brennan, Potter Stewart, Byron White, and Thurgood Marshall composed the majority. They held that the death penalty, as it had been applied in these three cases, violated the Eighth and Fourteenth Amendments' prohibition of cruel and unusual punishment because, under the laws of Georgia and Texas, juries had an untrammeled discretion to impose or withhold the death penalty. In his opinion, Douglas held that the death penalty was cruel and unusual because, since it was imposed at the discretion of the jury, it had been applied selectively in a discriminatory fashion to members of a minority. Brennan, probably in an attempt to counter strict constructionists of the Constitution, held that the Eighth Amendment's prohibition of cruel and unusual punishment should not be considered as limited to torture or to punishments considered cruel and unusual at the time the Eighth Amendment was ratified. The prohibition should include all punishments that did not comport with the concept of human dignity held by society as a whole. Since society, according to Brennan, did not regard so severe a punishment as acceptable, its imposition represented a violation of the Eighth Amendment. It was now up to Georgia, Texas, and states with similar death penalty laws either to abolish capital punishment or to draft new laws that could be in agreement with the Court's decision in these three cases.

After the Supreme Court decision in *Furman v. Georgia*, thirty-five states and the federal government revised their capital punishment statutes to eliminate the equal protection problems. The revised statutes fell into two categories: those that made the death penalty mandatory for certain crimes and those that allowed the judge or jury to decide, under legislative guidelines, whether to impose the death penalty. Georgia, for example, amended its laws regarding imposition of the death penalty and attempted to make them fair, nondiscriminatory, and nonarbitrary. Under the new law, guilt or innocence was to be determined either by a jury, or by a trial judge in a case where there was no jury. In a jury trial, the judge was required to instruct the jury on lesser included offenses supported by the evidence.

After either a verdict, a finding, or a plea of guilty, a presentence hearing was to be conducted, at which the jury or judge would hear arguments and additional evidence in order to determine the punishment. At least one of two aggravating circumstances specified in the laws had to be found to exist beyond a reasonable doubt and had to be stated in writing before a jury or judge could impose the death penalty. The

death sentence then was appealed automatically to the Supreme Court of Georgia, which would determine if the sentence had been imposed under the influence of passion, prejudice, or any other arbitrary factor; whether the evidence supported the finding of a legally aggravating circumstance; and whether the sentence was excessive or disproportionate to the penalty imposed in similar cases. If the Georgia Supreme Court affirmed the death sentence, its decision was required to include reference to similar cases that the court had considered.

A case to test these revised Georgia statutes, *Troy Leon Gregg v. State of Georgia* (1976), was argued before the United States Supreme Court in March, 1976, and decided on July 2, 1976. Gregg and a companion were picked up by two motorists while hitchhiking in Florida. The bodies of the two motorists later were found beside a road near Atlanta, Georgia. When arrested the next day, a .25-caliber pistol was found in Gregg's possession and subsequently identified as the murder weapon. Gregg confessed, but claimed self-defense. Gregg had been convicted by a jury in a Georgia state court of two counts of armed robbery and two counts of murder. Throughout the trial and in the appeals process, the new Georgia statutes had been followed. The Georgia Supreme Court affirmed the conviction and the imposition of the death sentence for murder, although it vacated the sentence for the two counts of armed robbery.

The United States Supreme Court affirmed the decision of the Georgia Supreme Court. In a decision announced by Justices Stewart, Lewis Powell, and John P. Stevens, seven of the nine justices held that in this case, the imposition of the death penalty did not violate the prohibition of the infliction of cruel and unusual punishment under the Eighth and Fourteenth Amendments. The right of states to impose and implement the death penalty had been affirmed, so long as a state's statutes were fair, nondiscriminatory, and nonarbitrary. Although the restrictions had been lifted, society has continued to approach the death penalty with resistance, hesitation, and confusion.

—J. Stewart Alverson, updated by Janice G. Rienerth

ADDITIONAL READING:

Isenberg, Irwin, ed. *The Death Penalty*. New York: H. W. Wilson, 1977. A compilation of writings on the constitutional, legal, ethical, and philosophical aspects of capital punishment, taken from a wide variety of sources, mainly periodicals.

Jenkins, Nicholas. "Dirty Needle." *The New Yorker*, December 19, 1994, 5-6. Arguing against capital punishment, the article looks at different methods used to execute and the implications these methods have for society.

Johnson, Robert. *Condemned to Die: Life Under Sentence of Death*. Prospect Heights, Ill.: Waveland Press, 1989. An easily readable text with implications for current criminological thought. It deals with the warehousing of condemned prisoners.

Keplan, David. "Anger and Ambivalence." *Newsweek*, August 7, 1995, 24-28. Examines the contradiction between the growing popularity of capital punishment and the number of inmates who actually are put to death.

Nygaard, Richard. "Vengeance Is Mine, Says the Lord." *America* 8 (October, 1994): 6-8. Argues that revenge is the only reason for which a society uses the death penalty.

Reitan, Eric. "Why the Deterrence Argument for Capital Punishment Fails." *Criminal Justice Ethics* 12 (1993): 26-33. Examines the faults of the deterrence argument for capital punishment.

SEE ALSO: 1963, *Gideon v. Wainwright*.

1976 ■ CARTER IS ELECTED PRESIDENT:
weakening of party lines in the post-Vietnam, post-Watergate era results in a mixed mandate from a divided electorate

DATE: November 2, 1976
LOCALE: United States
CATEGORY: Government and politics
KEY FIGURES:

James Earl "Jimmy" Carter (born 1924), former governor of Georgia and Democratic presidential nominee

Robert Joseph "Bob" Dole (born 1923), Republican vice presidential nominee

Gerald Rudolph Ford (born 1913), thirty-eighth president of the United States, 1974-1977, and Republican presidential nominee

Eugene Joseph McCarthy (born 1916), independent third-party candidate

Walter Frederick Mondale (born 1928), Democratic vice presidential nominee

Ronald Wilson Reagan (born 1911), former governor of California

SUMMARY OF EVENT. Jimmy Carter took the presidency from Gerald Ford by a popular vote margin of only 2 percent—the same figure that one year earlier had represented the minuscule proportion of Democrats who preferred the former Georgia governor as their party's presidential nominee. It was the first time that an incumbent president had been defeated in forty-four years. Carter had come a long way, indeed, but just barely. Not only did Carter receive a bare majority of the popular vote and carry a minority of the states, but he also had a margin of only fifty-six electoral votes. It was the narrowest victory since Woodrow Wilson defeated Charles Evans Hughes by twenty-three electoral votes in 1916.

The very geography of the electoral vote seemed to reflect this narrow victory by presenting a symmetrical picture of a nation split roughly down the middle, with a solid South opposing a granite West. Yet the closeness of the national vote was really a closeness found mostly within, rather than between, the states. Relatively slight shifts of the popular vote in a few states easily could have altered the election results substantially. Independent candidate Eugene McCarthy's vote in Iowa, Maine, Oklahoma, and Oregon was greater than

Ford's plurality over Carter. It is likely that most supporters of McCarthy, a maverick liberal best known for his earlier anti-Vietnam War stand, would have gone to Carter. Polls consistently have shown the great majority of McCarthy's support had come from Democrats, so the Georgian very likely would have carried at least Oregon and Maine if McCarthy had not run there, and possibly Iowa and Oklahoma also.

The fifty-one electoral votes of Texas and Ohio might have been denied the Carter-Mondale ticket if Ford's running mate had been Ronald Reagan instead of Robert Dole. There is little doubt that as the Republican vice presidential candidate, Dole was more of a liability than an asset to Ford's campaign. A poll taken in late October found, for example, that while half the voters would choose Walter Mondale over Dole for vice president, only a third would choose Dole. Dole's hard-driving partisanship tended to subvert the image of presidential assuredness Ford was trying to project. Most injurious was a statement from Dole that seemed to attack the two world wars, Korea, and Vietnam as "Democratic wars." Mondale, on the other hand, added stability and the sense of being a known, Washington-tested element to Carter's essentially moral rather than political appeal. About two weeks before the Republican convention, Ford's campaign strategists gave him a 120-page memorandum that implicitly rejected Dole for the number two spot, because of his televised personal attack on Carter as being "Southern-fried McGovern." Yet Dole was picked and Reagan was not.

According to some accounts of the pursuit of the presidency, Reagan was not asked to join the ticket because his campaign manager in effect told Ford's chief of staff that the Californian would meet with the president only if it were assured that he not be asked. Others, however, assert that Reagan said he would have run with Ford had he been asked. According to this account, after losing the nomination, one of Reagan's supporters informed several of Ford's top staff that Reagan was available as a running mate, and so he half expected to be offered the vice presidency when he met with Ford. Still, Reagan's campaign manager maintained that, before the nomination, he explained to Ford's staff that the vice presidency should not be offered to Reagan, who did not want to embarrass the president by an outright refusal. There also is Reagan's handwritten note to his own California delegation: "There is no circumstance whatsoever under which I would accept the nomination for Vice-President. That is absolutely final." Because, Reagan says, the Ford people on the convention floor were promising the uncommitted delegates that Reagan would be on the ticket if Ford won, the Californians had to be assured it was not true. Nevertheless, Reagan later said that even though he did not want the job, if Ford had twisted his arm by claiming an obligation to party and country, "It would have been an impossibility to say no." In any event, if Reagan had run on the ticket, and Texas and Ohio had gone Republican, and no state for Ford defected, the only difference in the final outcome would have been an even closer race—with Carter winning by a hairline electoral vote margin of five.

Jimmy Carter, thirty-ninth president of the United States, out-bid incumbent Gerald Ford by only 2 percent of the popular vote during an election marked by a confused and disillusioned electorate. In the post-Watergate era, voters preferred the soft-spoken and morally upright Southern Democrat, who seemed to promise a return to the progressive policies of the Johnson era. (Library of Congress)

It is doubtful, though, that Ohio would have switched. As Gerald Pomper points out, the Democratic victory there "could be properly attributed to the union campaign." Nationwide, Carter held a nearly 25 percent lead over his opponent among voters from union households. This union support (which McGovern had lacked in 1972) reflected the fact that trivial matters—such as the campaign's semantic slips involving "ethnic purity"—had little lasting impact. Rather, for the first time in a generation, the electorate was sharply divided along partisan lines that ran parallel to the New Deal alignment. Four of every five Democrats voted for Carter, and almost nine of every ten Republicans for Ford. Since there were about twice as many Democrats as Republicans among the roughly two-thirds of the electorate identifying with a party, the reappearance of loyal party voting was critical to Carter's close victory.

After Richard Nixon resigned in disgrace from the presidency in 1974, and the Democrats swept the 1974 congressional election, it seemed likely that the next president would

be a Democrat. That an unknown Southern ex-governor would come out of the pack and surpass many other prominent Democrats to gain his party's nomination was a tremendous surprise, but Carter's forthrightness and apparent independence from entrenched interests made the Democrats' chances even stronger. Carter's unquestioned personal integrity and his enthusiasm as a campaigner quickly endeared him to the U.S. people. Ford, however, campaigned with surprising strength, although he had been bruised by his internecine party struggle with Reagan and was not particularly helped by having Dole as his running mate.

Ford managed to emerge from the tarnished aura given his party by Nixon and the associated Watergate incumbency, so often underrated in U.S. politics. The fact that Ford had been the president for more than two years and had presided over the nation's affairs with mild competence enabled him to capitalize on the inexperience of his opponent. Earlier in the campaign, Carter had gained popularity by the fact that he seemed to be a humble, honest peanut farmer from Plains, Georgia. By late October, Ford had managed to turn his equation around so that he seemed the veteran leader in contrast to Carter's inexperience and naïveté.

Carter's victory was attributable to several factors. The fact that he was potentially the first son of the Deep South to be elected president since Reconstruction caused a groundswell of support for him in Southern states that otherwise were growing more conservative and would, in fifteen years' time, be solidly Republican. Similarly, Carter's profession of born-again Christianity gave him popularity among evangelical and fundamentalist Christians that otherwise would have gone into his opponent's column. Several major ethnic groups—Jews, Latinos, African Americans—voted overwhelmingly for Carter, renewing traditional Democratic loyalties. Carter gained the crucial support of so-called ethnic Catholics in swing states such as Ohio and Pennsylvania. These voters, who had become Nixon Democrats in the wake of the excesses of the 1960's counterculture, were now ready to return to the Democratic fold.

Carter's election, however, was not a full renewal of the New Deal Democratic coalition. The voters were willing to prefer him in 1976, but that did not guarantee continuing enthusiasm either for Carter personally or for his party. What the 1976 election signified more than anything else was that traditional party loyalties were beginning to weaken on both sides. It was a mixed verdict that gave a mixed assessment of where the United States was going in the post-Watergate, post-Vietnam era. The fact that Carter, rather than a more traditional Democrat, had won in what seemed an obviously Democratic election year meant that the sway of party affiliation was weakening, to be replaced by an emphasis on ideology and on the candidate's image in the media.

—*E. Gene DeFelice, updated by Nicholas Birns*

ADDITIONAL READING:

Macdougall, Malcolm. *We Almost Made It.* New York: Crown, 1977. A perspective from inside the Ford campaign.

Reeves, Richard. *Convention*. New York: Harcourt Brace, 1977. A portrait of the Democratic Party that nominated Carter in 1976.

Schram, Martin. *Running for President: The Carter Campaign*. New York: Stein & Day, 1977. A journalistic history of the campaign.

Witcover, Jules. *Marathon: The Pursuit of the Presidency, 1972-1976*. New York: Viking, 1978. The best and most authoritative history of the 1976 campaign to date. An indispensable resource.

Wooten, James. *Dasher: The Roots and Rising of Jimmy Carter*. New York: Summit, 1978. The best post-campaign biography of Carter to date.

SEE ALSO: 1968, Nixon Is Elected President; 1974, Nixon Resigns; 1980, Reagan Is Elected President.

1977 ■ CANADA'S HUMAN RIGHTS ACT:
prohibition of discrimination based on race, national or ethnic origin, color, religion, age, sex, marital status, or conviction for an offense for which a pardon has been granted

DATE: August 10, 1977
LOCALE: Canada
CATEGORIES: Canadian history; Civil rights; Laws and acts
KEY FIGURES:
Stanley Ronald Basford (born 1932), Canadian minister of justice
Monique Begin (born 1936), minister of national revenue
Jules Léger (1913-1980), governor general of Canada
Aideen Nicholson (born 1927), member of the House of Commons
Pierre Elliott Trudeau (born 1919), prime minister of Canada
SUMMARY OF EVENT. Bill C-25, the Canadian Human Rights Act—first read in the House of Commons November 29, 1976, and first read in the Senate June 6, 1977—received the Royal Assent July 14, 1977, and was proclaimed to be in force August 10, 1977. The act was revised and expanded in 1985 to provide for those with physical disabilities and to clarify issues involving sexual harassment, the elderly, and women on maternity leave.

The Canadian Human Rights Act extends the laws that proscribe discrimination and that protect the privacy of individuals. The law is premised on the notion that every person should have an opportunity equal to that of other persons to make for himself or herself the life that he or she is able and wishes to have, consistent with his or her duties and obligations as a member of society, without being hindered in or prevented from doing so by discriminatory practices based on race, national or ethnic origin, color, religion, age, sex, marital status, or conviction for an offense for which a pardon has

been granted. The privacy of individuals, and their right of access to records containing personal information concerning them for any purpose, including the purpose of ensuring accuracy and completeness, should be protected to the greatest extent consistent with the public interest.

Part 1 of the Canadian Human Rights Act defines discrimination as the denial of goods, services, facilities, or accommodations customarily available to the general public. In employment, it is discriminatory to refuse to employ, to refuse to continue to employ, or to differentiate adversely in the course of employment. Part 1, Section 11, requires that equal wages be paid to men and women for equal work value, based on skill, effort, and responsibility.

Part 2 of the act created the Canadian Human Rights Commission to administer the Canadian Human Rights Act and to ensure that the principles of equal opportunity and nondiscrimination are followed within the areas of federal jurisdiction. This commission is composed of two full-time and six part-time commissioners. The commission is authorized to investigate complaints of discrimination in employment and in the provision of services, and complaints alleging inequities in pay between men and women based on equal work. The commission monitors annual reports filed by federally regulated employers under the Employment Equity Act, and programs, policies, and legislation affecting women, aboriginal peoples, visible minorities, and persons with disabilities, to ensure that their human rights are protected. It also develops and conducts information programs to promote public understanding of the Canadian Human Rights Act and the commission's activities.

Part 3 of the Canadian Human Rights Act explains the procedures to be used when a complaint is filed with the Canadian Human Rights Commission. Upon receipt of a complaint, the commission first determines whether or not its agency is the correct one to handle the complaint. The complaint is either accepted for investigation by the commission or sent to another federal agency for appropriate action. If the commission accepts the complaint for investigation, every effort is made to reach an early settlement between the two parties. If the complaint cannot be settled, the commission prepares an investigative report requesting the appointment of a conciliator to arbitrate the dispute.

If conciliation cannot be reached, the case is returned to the commission for a decision either to dismiss the case or to refer it to a human rights tribunal. A tribunal hearing results in a written decision, binding on all parties. Tribunal decisions may be appealed to a review tribunal or to the federal courts. In some discrimination cases, Canada's Supreme Court makes the final decision. Remedies for complainants include reinstatement and/or compensation for lost wages, letters of apology, or the issuance of antiharassment policy by an employer. The Canadian Human Rights Act provides for fines of up to fifty thousand dollars for threatening, intimidating, or discriminating against an individual who has filed a complaint, or for hampering the investigation process.

The act authorized the Canadian Human Rights Commission to create an administrative structure to administer the Human Rights Act. By 1994, the Canadian Human Rights Commission had delegated to the Office of the Secretary General of the Human Rights Commission the authority to oversee staff at headquarters and regional offices that investigate discrimination complaints throughout the country, except those dealing with employment and pay equity.

The Secretary General's office provides support to the Canadian Human Rights Commission and its seven specialized branch agencies: the Legal Services Branch, which represents the commission before tribunals, review tribunals, and the courts; the Anti-Discrimination Programs Branch, which handles all complaints filed with the commission, except employment and pay equity complaints; the Employment and Pay Equity Branch, which advises the Human Rights Commission on employment and pay equity matters, offers educational programs to employers and community groups, and investigates and conciliates equal pay complaints; the Policy and Planning Branch, which monitors and researches domestic and international human rights issues of interest to the commission; the Communications Branch, which explains the role and activities of the commission, discourages discriminatory practices, and fosters public understanding of the Act; the Corporate Services Branch, which provides headquarters and regional operations with support services; and the Personnel Services Branch, which provides headquarters and regional operations with support services in pay, benefits, staffing, resource planning, and health and safety.

Between 1985 and 1994, the Canadian Human Rights Commission received 464,535 inquiries. Actual complaints filed between 1991 and 1994 totaled 4,852, including all referrals to alternate redress. For the years 1991 to 1994, based on the number of discrimination complaints filed, the types of complaints were ranked in the following order: disability, sex, national or ethnic origin, race or color, family or marital status, age, religion, and discrimination after being pardoned. In the same years, the ranking order of methods of disposition of complaints was dismissal, settlement approved by all parties and the commission, sent to conciliation, no further proceedings, and early resolution.

The 1995 Canadian Human Rights Commission's annual report recommended the following changes: the adoption of amendments to the Canadian Human Rights Act to prohibit discrimination based on sexual orientation, to protect the human rights of Canada's aboriginal population, and to allow anyone present in Canada, not just those lawfully present, the right to file a discrimination complaint; that the commission report directly to Parliament instead of the Department of Justice and the Treasury Board; establishment of a permanent appeals tribunal to replace the existing system of ad hoc tribunals and review tribunals; that a mandatory retirement age be considered a discriminatory action; and that employers under federal jurisdiction be required to take the initiative in eliminating sex-based inequities from their compensation systems. These recommendations would enable the Canadian Human

Rights Act to provide the same protection against discrimination currently institutionalized in the Canadian Charter of Rights and Freedoms, international practice, and provincial legislation. —*William A. Paquette*

ADDITIONAL READING:
Acts of the Parliament of Canada. Vol. 2, pp. 887-930. Ottawa: Queen's Printer, 1976-1977. Contains the original Canadian Human Rights Act of 1977.

Canada Statute Citator. Aurora, Ont.: Canada Law Book, 1995. Provides monthly updates, revisions, and information of importance on Canadian laws.

Canadian Human Rights Commission. *Annual Report, 1994*. Ottawa: Minister of Supply and Service Canada, 1995. Provides a detailed self-examination of Canada's record on human rights.

Commerce Clearing House Canadian Limited. *Ottawa Letter*. Ottawa: Author, 1976-1977. Weekly reports chronicling the legislative progress of Bill C-25 (the Canadian Human Rights Act) in Canada's parliament.

House of Commons Debates, Official Report. Vol. 3. Ottawa: Queen's Printer, 1976-1977. Record of the Canadian parliamentary debates on Bill C-25, the Canadian Human Rights Act.

Revised Statutes of Canada, 1985. Vol. 5. Ottawa: Queen's Printer, 1985. Includes the complete and revised Canadian Human Rights Act.

SEE ALSO: 1968, Trudeau Era in Canada; 1969, Canada's Official Languages Act; 1978, Canada's Immigration Act of 1976; 1982, Canada's Constitution Act.

1977 ■ SPACEFLIGHTS OF VOYAGERS 1 AND 2: *interplanetary probes, equipped with instruments to gather scientific data and return visual images, make a "Grand Tour" of Jupiter, Saturn, Uranus, Neptune, and their moons*

DATE: August 20, 1977-September, 1989
LOCALE: Interplanetary space
CATEGORY: Science and technology
KEY FIGURES:
John R. Casani (born 1932), Voyager project manager
Bruce Murray (born 1931), director, Jet Propulsion Laboratory
Carl Sagan (born 1934), chair, Voyager Record Committee
Bradford A. Smith (born 1931), Voyager Imaging Team leader
Edward C. Stone (born 1936), Voyager project scientist
SUMMARY OF EVENT. In the late 1970's, the four large planets, Jupiter, Saturn, Uranus, and Neptune, were aligned so that a spacecraft could be sent to Jupiter, have its path bent by Jupiter's gravity, and then be sent to Saturn, Uranus, and, finally, Neptune. Such a fortuitous planetary alignment would

not occur again until 2159. Voyager 1 and Voyager 2, each carrying eleven scientific instruments and weighing 1,819 pounds, were sent on this "Grand Tour" of the outer planets. The Voyager project team at the Jet Propulsion Laboratory in Pasadena, California, designed them to be essentially identical, providing redundancy in case one spacecraft failed. Voyager 2 was launched from Cape Canaveral, Florida, by a Titan II-Centaur rocket on August 20, 1977, followed by Voyager 1 on September 5, 1977.

Voyager 1 made its closest approach to Jupiter, coming within 173,000 miles, on March 5, 1979. Cameras on Voyager 1 took more than eighteen thousand photographs of Jupiter and its moons, and other scientific instruments gathered data at an enormous rate. As Voyager 1 approached, the clouds in Jupiter's atmosphere were observed in more detail than ever before. A series of light- and dark-colored bands of clouds were seen, with swirling whirlpools within the clouds. A correlation was observed between the color of the bands and the direction of motion of the atmospheric wind. A ring system, similar to Saturn's rings but much less intense and invisible from the Earth, was photographed.

Each of Jupiter's large moons was different in surface features and texture from the next. An umbrella-shaped feature on the edge of Io, one of Jupiter's moons, was determined to be an erupting volcano, the first active volcano ever seen on any object other than Earth. The surface of Callisto, another moon, was pockmarked with impact craters, indicating that this surface had been preserved longer than any other Jovian satellite. The moon Europa, on the other hand, had an icy surface showing many cracks but little evidence of cratering.

Voyager 2, which approached Jupiter on July 6, 1979, confirmed and extended the results of Voyager 1. Voyager 2 was directed to make more detailed observations of Io, and at least six active volcanoes were observed. The spacecrafts' trajectories through the Jovian system were designed so that the force of Jupiter's gravity would change their paths and send them on to Saturn.

Voyager 1 came within seventy-seven thousand miles of Saturn on November 12, 1980. The atmosphere of Saturn was different from that of Jupiter, with no correlation between the wind direction and the color of the bands ringing the planet. High-resolution images of the ring system showed several hundred distinct rings, which, in photographs taken from Earth, all blur together into a few major rings. Clumps of material were seen in some rings; one ring, called the F-ring, appeared to be braided, as if strands of the ring had been twisted together.

Saturn's largest moon, Titan, was an important target for Voyager 1, because its atmosphere is similar in chemistry to the atmosphere of early Earth. Scientists had previously demonstrated that passage of an electric current, simulating a lightning discharge, through such an atmosphere produces organic chemicals that are the precursors to life. Instruments on board Voyager 1 identified several organic molecules, including methane and hydrogen cyanide, and a haze layer, attributed to microscopic particles of organic material, in Titan's atmosphere.

In order to pass close to Titan, Voyager 1 had to be put on a path that would eject it from the solar system, thus ending its planetary tour. The success of Voyager 1 enabled scientists to target Voyager 2 on a trajectory through Saturn's system that provided poor viewing of Titan but used Saturn's gravity to send the spacecraft to Uranus.

Voyager 2 reached Saturn on August 25-26, 1981, but developed a serious problem with its scan platform, which aims the cameras and other instruments at their targets, about halfway through the encounter. Planned high-resolution images of Enceladus, one of Saturn's moons, were missed when the camera aimed into space rather than at the moon. A planned six-picture mosaic of the moon Tethys captured only a small segment of the moon in one corner of a single picture.

National Aeronautics and Space Administration (NASA) engineers had several years to solve the problem with the scan platform as Voyager 2 headed to Uranus. Since the Voyagers had been designed only to operate at Jupiter, they faced other problems as well. The intensity of sunlight decreases with increasing distance from the sun, and very long exposures are needed to obtain photographs. Because the spacecraft would be moving at a high speed, engineers developed a procedure to rotate the camera in the opposite direction to minimize blurring.

Voyager 2 passed within sixty-seven thousand miles of Uranus on January 24, 1986, missing its aim point by only ten miles. Although clouds on Jupiter and Saturn were visible from Earth, no features on Uranus could be seen from Earth. Because the spin axis of Uranus points almost in the plane of its orbit, rather than perpendicular to the orbital plane as for the other eight planets, Uranus provided a test of whether planetary rotation or differences in solar heating dominate atmospheric motion. Voyager 2 observed cloud banding on Uranus, indicating a predominantly east-west wind circulation, similar to those of other planets that have atmospheres. This indicates that the direction of planetary rotation is the dominant effect in organizing weather circulation on the planets.

In 1977, scientists observing Uranus from NASA's Kuiper Airborne Observatory had produced evidence of nine rings around Uranus. Voyager 2 confirmed this and found myriad additional rings.

Voyager 2 reached Neptune on August 25, 1989, twelve years after leaving Earth. Photographs from Voyager 2 demonstrated that Neptune differs dramatically from the other three giant planets. Neptune appears deep blue in color, like the Earth, and most of the atmosphere is clear and transparent. Neptune has an atmospheric feature, called the Dark Spot, similar to the Red Spot in Jupiter's atmosphere. Gravitational interaction with Neptune sent Voyager 2 on a path out of the solar system.

The Voyagers had been preceded by the smaller Pioneer 10 and Pioneer 11 spacecraft, which reached Jupiter in December, 1973, and December, 1974, respectively. The first non-natural objects to leave the solar system, each Pioneer spacecraft carried a six-by-nine-inch gold-anodized aluminum plaque, with the images of a human male and female, as well as a pictorial representation of this solar system and its location relative to reference stars. These were intended as greetings and communication for any interplanetary beings who might discover the Pioneer spacecraft.

In December, 1976, John Casani, Voyager project manager, asked Carl Sagan to organize an effort to place similar messages on the Voyager spacecraft. Sagan intended to expand the Pioneer plaque to include more pictures, but Frank Drake, a radio astronomer at Cornell University, suggested that a record could store much more information in the same space. Each Voyager spacecraft carried a gold-coated phonograph record, instructions, and the cartridge and stylus needed to play the record.

The Voyager records included messages of greeting from U.S. president Jimmy Carter, U.N. secretary general Kurt Waldheim, and members of the United Nations Outer Space Committee, along with musical selections representing many of the Earth's cultures. The Voyager records will be pitted by impacts of micrometeorites during their travels through space, but scientists estimate most of the record's surface will survive for about a billion years, preserving examples of twentieth century humankind's words, music, and science essentially forever. The likelihood that the Voyager records will actually be recovered by an extraterrestrial civilization is low. Bernard Oliver, then vice president for research and development at Hewlett-Packard Corporation, emphasized that "its real function . . . is to appeal to the human spirit, and to make contact with extraterrestrial intelligence a welcome expectation of mankind."

—*George J. Flynn*

ADDITIONAL READING:

Burgess, Eric. *Far Encounter: The Neptune System.* New York: Columbia University Press, 1991. A well-illustrated, 192-page account of the scientific results obtained by Voyager at Neptune, the funding battle, and the technological struggle to overcome spacecraft system failures.

Cooper, Henry S. F., Jr. *Imaging Saturn: The Voyager Flights to Saturn.* New York: Holt, Rinehart and Winston, 1983. A well-illustrated account of the Voyager 1 and 2 encounters with Saturn, including the reactions of scientists as their theories were tested by Voyager observations.

Hunt, Garry, and Patrick Moore. *Atlas of Uranus.* New York: Cambridge University Press, 1989. Well-illustrated, ninety-six-page account of humankind's knowledge about Uranus and the measurements made by Voyager 2.

Poynter, Margaret, and Arthur L. Lane. *Voyager: The Story of a Space Mission.* New York: Atheneum, 1981. A behind-the-scenes account of the planning and design of the Voyagers and their encounters with Jupiter.

Sagan, Carl, et al. *Murmurs of Earth: The Voyager Interstellar Record.* New York: Ballantine, 1978. A firsthand account of the project to attach a record to the Voyager spacecraft, including texts of the messages it carries.

SEE ALSO: 1961, First American in Space; 1969, Apollo 11 Lands on the Moon; 1986, *Challenger* Accident; 1993, Astronauts Repair the Hubble Space Telescope.

1978 ■ PREGNANCY DISCRIMINATION ACT: *Congress passes a measure that defines sex discrimination to include discrimination on the basis of pregnancy*

DATE: 1978
LOCALE: Washington, D.C.
CATEGORIES: Civil rights; Laws and acts; Women's issues
SUMMARY OF EVENT. Congress passed the Civil Rights Act of 1964 to address discrimination on the basis of race. Those who opposed the bill proposed an amendment on the floor of the House of Representatives to also prohibit sex discrimination, thereby hoping to defeat it. The prohibition against sex discrimination thus lacked the firm foundation provided by the normal legislative process, which includes testimony during hearings and a committee report clearly spelling out the intentions of Congress. The courts then were faced with the problem of defining what constituted sex discrimination.

In 1974, the Supreme Court decided a case on whether a state disability plan that covered all disabilities except pregnancy and childbirth violated the U.S. Constitution's Fourteenth Amendment guarantee of equal protection of the laws. In *Geduldig v. Aiello*, the Supreme Court held that the state's policy was constitutionally permissible, because it did not employ a sex-based classification. Rather than treating men and women differently, the Court held, the state merely distinguished between pregnant and non-pregnant persons.

The Supreme Court was not legally required to make the same ruling on a statutory as opposed to a constitutional case, yet it did. In *General Electric Company v. Gilbert* (1976), the Court held that an employer's policy covering single-sex ailments and elective surgery, but excluding from coverage medical expenses arising from pregnancy and childbirth, did not violate Title VII's prohibition against discrimination on the basis of sex.

The courts developed two categories of sex discrimination. The first, disparate treatment, occurred when one's sex (overtly or covertly) was the basis of differential treatment—such as a state law that women could not work in bars. The second, disparate impact, occurred when a neutral requirement or condition, such as a height requirement, resulted in fewer women than men being able to comply. How courts categorized the cases determined how easy it was for an employer to justify its policy. To justify disparate treatment, an employer would have to show that sex was a bona fide occupational qualification for a job—for example, for a sperm donor or wet nurse. To justify disparate impact, on the other hand, an employer would merely have to show that such a restriction was necessary to the safe and effective operation of the business (and was not a pretext for sex discrimination). Because the Supreme Court had decided that pregnancy discrimination was not sex discrimination, it treated pregnancy discrimination as a case of disparate impact. In its 1977 ruling in *Nashville Gas*

Co. v. Satty, the Supreme Court upheld a requirement that pregnant employees take a leave of absence without pay, but found unlawful a company's practice of also stripping pregnant women of their accumulated seniority. The Court distinguished benefits to pregnant workers from burdens placed on them, but still treated pregnancy discrimination as a case of disparate impact.

The body that Title VII created to enforce discrimination law, the Equal Employment Opportunity Commission (EEOC) had offered interpretive guidelines in 1972, saying that discrimination because of pregnancy violated Title VII. Earlier, however, the EEOC's general counsel had said that because only women became pregnant, employers could exclude childbirth costs from insurance coverage. Five circuit courts had upheld the guidelines, maintaining that pregnancy discrimination was prohibited sex discrimination. In *Gilbert* and *Satty*, the Supreme Court rejected the EEOC's guidelines and overturned the lower courts.

Shortly after *Gilbert*, forty-three representatives from unions, civil rights groups, and feminist organizations formed the Campaign to End Discrimination Against Pregnant Workers. Congress responded swiftly. In 1978, it passed the Pregnancy Discrimination Act (PDA), which explicitly prohibited discrimination because of pregnancy. Title VII was amended to say:

> The terms "because of sex" or "on the basis of sex" include, but are not limited to, because of or on the basis of pregnancy, childbirth, or related medical conditions; and women affected by pregnancy, childbirth, or related medical conditions shall be treated the same for all employment-related purposes, including receipt of benefits under fringe benefit programs, as other persons not so affected but similar in their ability or inability to work, and nothing in section 703(h) of this title shall be interpreted to permit otherwise.

The effect of the PDA was apparent in the Supreme Court's decision in *Newport Shipping and Dry Dock Company v. EEOC* (1983). The Court held that companies could no longer offer reimbursement for the childbirth costs of female employees without also paying for the childbirth costs of the spouses of male employees. The Court declared that Congress had overruled the Court's decision in *Gilbert* by passing the PDA. Discrimination because of pregnancy now constituted disparate treatment (not disparate impact), justified only by the narrow defense of bona fide occupational qualification.

Supporters of the PDA thought that the amendment called for only equal treatment. Employers would be required to treat pregnant workers no worse and no better than other similarly incapacitated workers. If a company fired men who were temporarily disabled because of illness, it could also fire pregnant women. These feminists feared that if states or employers provided benefits to pregnant women only, rather than sickness benefits to all workers, companies would be less likely to hire women. Furthermore, treating women as special and deserving of protection in this case, they argued, would stigmatize them and justify less favorable treatment in other domains, as the history of protective legislation demonstrated. Other feminists argued that pregnancy was not an illness, and that pregnant workers deserved accommodation even if companies did not provide protection for sick workers. The debate became known as the special-versus-equal-treatment debate, and feminists lined up on both sides.

The issue came to a head in a challenge against a California law guaranteeing a limited right to reinstatement for women who were returning to work after giving birth. Lillian Garland had challenged the failure of California Federal Savings and Loan (Cal Fed) to reinstate her after childbirth. Cal Fed then challenged the California law as inconsistent with the Pregnancy Discrimination Act, because it offered a protection for pregnant women that was not available to other workers. Writing for a majority of the Supreme Court in 1987, Justice Thurgood Marshall held that the Pregnancy Discrimination Act "constructed a floor beneath which pregnancy benefits may not drop—not a ceiling above which they may not rise." The Court upheld the California law.

In 1991, the Supreme Court once again interpreted the Pregnancy Discrimination Act. In *United Autoworkers v. Johnson Controls*, however, the Court was asked whether an employer could ban women from jobs not because they were pregnant, but because they might become pregnant. Writing for a unanimous Court, Justice Harry Blackmun argued that the three circuit courts that analyzed exclusionary or "fetal protection policies" as neutral policies, allowing the employer to justify them under the business necessity defense, had mistakenly applied the law. Justice Antonin Scalia, in a concurring opinion, argued that Title VII prohibits employers from excluding nonsterilized women from hazardous work, not because men face reproductive hazards from lead, too, but because the Pregnancy Discrimination Act states unambiguously that employers may not exclude women from jobs because of their capacity to become pregnant. In *UAW v. Johnson Controls*, the Supreme Court held unequivocally that whether women can compare themselves to men or not, the law forbids employers from punishing women because they have the capacity to bear children.
　　　　　　　　　　　　　　　　　　　　—*Sally J. Kenney*

ADDITIONAL READING:

Eisenstein, Zillah. *The Female Body and the Law*. Berkeley: University of California Press, 1988. An exploration of the questions pregnancy discrimination raises for feminist theory.

Furnish, Hannah Arterian. "Prenatal Exposure to Fetally Toxic Work Environments: The Dilemma of the 1978 Amendments to Title VII of the Civil Rights Act of 1964." *Iowa Law Review* 66 (1980): 63-129. A legislative history of the PDA.

Kenney, Sally J. *For Whose Protection? Reproductive Hazards and Exclusionary Politics in the United States and Britain*. Ann Arbor: University of Michigan Press, 1992. Explores the history of pregnancy discrimination and cases of excluding fertile women from work.

Littleton, Christine A. "Reconstructing Sexual Equality." *California Law Review* 75 (1987): 1279-1337. Overview of cases and issues within the feminist community.

Vogel, Lise. *Mothers on the Job: Maternity Policy in the U.S. Workplace.* New Brunswick, N.J.: Rutgers University Press, 1993. Examines public policy debates over equality and difference.

Williams, Wendy. "Equality's Riddle: Pregnancy and the Equal Treatment/Special Treatment Debate." *New York University Review of Law and Social Change* 13 (1984-1985): 325-380. An article written by the most eloquent proponent of the equal treatment approach.

SEE ALSO: 1960, FDA Approves the Birth Control Pill; 1963, Equal Pay Act; 1965, Expansion of Affirmative Action; 1966, National Organization for Women Is Founded; 1970's, Rise of Women's Role in the Military; 1972, Equal Employment Opportunity Act; 1973, *Roe v. Wade*; 1975, Equal Credit Opportunity Act; 1988, Family Support Act; 1993, Family and Medical Leave Act.

1978 ■ PANAMA CANAL TREATIES: *after seventy-five years of domination in Panama, the United States relinquishes control of the canal*

DATE: March 16-April 18, 1978
LOCALE: Panama and Washington, D.C.
CATEGORIES: Diplomacy and international relations; Latino American history; Transportation; Treaties and agreements
KEY FIGURES:

Howard Henry Baker (born 1925), minority leader of the U.S. Senate

Robert Carlyle Byrd (born 1917), majority leader of the U.S. Senate

James Earl "Jimmy" Carter (born 1924), president of the United States, 1977-1981

Gerald Rudolph Ford (born 1913), president of the United States, 1974-1977

Henry Alfred Kissinger (born 1923), secretary of state, Nixon Administration

Juan Antonio Tack (born 1934), foreign minister of Panama

Omar Torrijos Herrera (1929-1981), chief of state of Panama and commander of its national guard

Cyrus Roberts Vance (born 1917), secretary of state, Carter Administration

SUMMARY OF EVENT. The Senate's ratification of the Treaty Concerning the Permanent Neutrality and Operation of the Panama Canal and the Panama Canal Treaty in the spring of 1978 was the culmination of a long and often dramatic effort to achieve mutually satisfactory new agreements between the United States and the Republic of Panama. Opponents fought the treaties with conviction and determination, leaving the outcome in doubt until the day of the vote. The Panama Canal had became a major political issue, and the debate was charged with emotion and intensity.

The history of the canal is colorful and long, dating back to the year 1513, when Vasco Núñez de Balboa first sighted the Pacific Ocean. The discovery that the territory called Darien was a relatively narrow land bridge between two great oceans prompted the Spanish emperor, Charles V, to order a survey for a possible canal across the isthmus. Periodically, the concept was revived, but not until the nineteenth century were efforts made to build a canal. Even an efficient overland crossing was not possible until 1855, when a U.S. company finished the Panama Railroad. In 1880, a French company under the direction of Ferdinand de Lesseps, the celebrated builder of the Suez Canal, decided to build the Panama Canal. However, the enterprise proved to be enormously more difficult than had been anticipated. Malaria, yellow fever, and financial ruin brought the French effort to a humiliating end.

U.S. interest in the gigantic project grew after the Spanish-American War of 1898, and specific plans were developed. Before buying out the French company's rights and resuming construction, the United States intended to ensure its complete control over the future canal. At the time, the Panamanian territory was a part of the Republic of Colombia, which was unwilling to make the kind of concessions sought by the United States. Thus, the United States saw its interests well served by assisting a Panamanian nationalist faction in forming the independent Republic of Panama in 1903. Two weeks after the independence proclamation, a treaty was signed between the new republic and the United States, granting the latter the use, occupation, and control of a ten-mile-wide strip of land across the isthmus in perpetuity. In return, Panama received ten million dollars and subsequent annual rent payments.

The building of the Panama Canal through the center of the Canal Zone required ten years, at a cost of more than $310 million and approximately four thousand lives, many of which were lost to sickness. It was formally opened to traffic on August 15, 1914. The construction of the canal was, and remains, one of the world's greatest engineering marvels. Through a series of locks, ships are raised or lowered for crossing from one ocean to the other. The canal has been immensely important for maritime transport and enormously beneficial to the Panamanian economy. Thousands of Panamanians have been employed in either the operation of or support services for the canal, or work for those living in the Canal Zone. The Republic of Panama, especially the cities of Cólon and Panama City, also has benefited from the presence of thousands of U.S. civilian and military personnel living in the Canal Zone. Cólon and Panama City are important centers of international banking and commerce.

The fact that Panama did not control its major resource became a fundamental issue in the country. A growing nationalistic sentiment generated vehement resentment of the "neo-colonial enclave." A bloody confrontation in January, 1964—precipitated by an attempt of Panamanian students to hoist their national flag in the Canal Zone and resulting in two dozen deaths and hundreds of injuries—convinced U.S. governmental leaders of the need to enter into negotiations with Panama for a new treaty. In 1967, after three years of deliberations, three treaties were drafted. They dealt with jurisdiction over the canal, defense and status of the military forces, and the possibility of a new sea-level canal. These tentative agreements subsequently were repudiated by Panama. The negotiations resumed in June, 1971, but remained intractable. Meanwhile, Panama succeeded in drawing worldwide attention to, and critical scrutiny of, the canal controversy. In March, 1973, the United Nations Security Council held a special meeting in Panama. A resolution calling for a just and equitable solution to the dispute and effective sovereignty for Panama over all its territory was introduced. The United States defeated the motion through the exercise of its veto power. Nevertheless, these actions gave Panama an important propaganda victory.

On February 7, 1974, Secretary of State Henry Kissinger and Foreign Minister Juan Antonio Tack of Panama met in Panama City and signed a joint statement of principle to serve as a framework for a new round of negotiations. The mutual goal was to arrive at a new treaty satisfying the basic concerns of both nations. This effort reached a successful conclusion on September 7, 1977, when the new Panama Canal Treaty and the Treaty Concerning the Permanent Neutrality and Operation of the Panama Canal were signed in Washington.

One treaty governs the operations and defense of the Panama Canal through December 31, 1999; the other guarantees the permanent neutrality of the canal. The treaties provide for the orderly and complete transfer of jurisdiction over the canal and the Canal Zone from the United States to Panama by the year 2000. A major point in the treaties is the removal of U.S. military forces, leaving Panamanian military forces as the sole guardians of the canal. A new United States government agency, the Panama Canal Commission, was to operate the canal for the rest of the century. Its board of directors would comprise five U.S. directors and four Panamanians. The plans called for a U.S. Director to be the administrator until 1990 and a Panamanian the deputy; thereafter, the roles would be reversed.

The new treaties encountered formidable opposition from conservative and rightist elements and required an intense public relations campaign, as well as vigorous lobbying, to ensure ratification by the United States Senate. President Jimmy Carter, Secretary of State Cyrus Vance, and other leading administration officials made every effort to persuade the country that the treaties were in the national interest. The agreements were presented as constituting a better defense against possible sabotage and terrorist attacks, because they gave the Panamanian people a greater stake in keeping the canal open. Moreover, the treaties were designed to promote a constructive, positive relationship between the United States and the other nations of the Western Hemisphere; a failure to ratify them could be expected to lead to an increasingly hostile, anti-American atmosphere. President Carter talked of "fairness, not force" in U.S. dealings with other nations, positing such a policy not as a mere moral imperative but as an element of pragmatic foreign policy.

The Senate ratified the Neutrality Treaty on March 16, 1978, by a vote of sixty-eight to thirty-two. Two "reservations"—instead of amendments, which might have required a repetition of the ratification process in Panama—were added. The first reservation was introduced by Senator Dennis De-Concini of Arizona, providing for U.S. armed intervention in Panama in the event the Panama Canal was closed. The second was introduced by Senator Sam Nunn of Georgia, allowing the United States and Panama to agree on stationing U.S. troops in Panama after 1999. Panamanian spokesmen indicated acceptance of these changes, but there was growing opposition in Panama to the Senate's efforts to alter the negotiated terms. The Panama Canal Treaty was ratified on April 18, 1978, also by a vote of sixty-eight to thirty-two. The added reservations included another by De Concini, allowing for U.S. troops to reopen the canal if operations were disrupted. Relieved that the long and intense process had finally come to an end, President Carter and Panamanian leader Omar Torrijos Herrera hailed the ratifications and predicted a new and amicable relationship between their countries. Both sides agreed to work toward making a smooth transition during the next two decades, allowing for Panama to work its way into running the canal and taking over the Canal Zone and the military installations.

The predictions of Carter and Torrijos were not realized, as the political stability of Panama deteriorated with each passing year. Political corruption and the growing influence of criminals resulted in widespread poverty and high crime rates. By 1989, the situation had become so severe that it was believed that U.S. civilian and military personnel were endangered. In December, President George Bush launched Operation Just Cause, sending U.S. military forces to arrest Panamanian dictator Manuel Antonio Noriega, whose administration was involved in drug dealing, money laundering, and murder. By 1995, only five years before the final transfer of the canal, little progress had been made by Panama. The United States had a timetable to turn over property so that by noon, December 31, 1999, it would all be under Panamanian control. There was hope of turning military bases into colleges, industrial parks, or tourist meccas. One of the first items turned over was the Panama Railroad, which had been in operation since 1855. By 1995, however, the railroad no longer operated. Depots were boarded up, engines sat rusting on the tracks, and the jungle had overtaken much of the track in the interior. Former railroad employees were without jobs, adding to unemployment rolls and street crime. One military installation had also been turned back to Panama, but squatters occupied it.

With the deadline for transfer of the Panama Canal at hand, calls for renegotiating the treaties were being heard in the United States and Panama. Many feared Panama was not yet able to operate, control, and guard the canal, and that the removal of U.S. military forces would further destabilize the government. Still, the United States seemed determined to press on with fulfilling its obligations under the Carter-Torrijos agreements of 1978.

—Manfred Grote, updated by Kay Hively

ADDITIONAL READING:

Buckley, Kevin. *Panama: The Whole Story*. New York: Simon & Schuster, 1991. Buckley, a seasoned reporter, tells the story of Operation Just Cause.

Crane, Philip M. *Surrender in Panama: The Case Against the Treaty*. New York: Dale Books, 1978. Examines the Panama Canal treaties as seen by those who opposed them.

Koster, R. M., and Guillermo Sanchez Borbon. *In the Time of the Tyrants: Panama, 1968-1990*. New York: Putnam, 1990. A look at internal politics in Panama and U.S.-Panama relations.

LeFeber, Walter. *The Panama Canal*. New York: Oxford University Press, 1978. Gives a brief history of the canal and closely examines the 1978 treaties.

McCullough, David. *The Path Between the Seas*. New York: Simon & Schuster, 1977. One of the finest, most readable books on the Panama Canal.

SEE ALSO: 1889, First Pan-American Congress; 1903, Acquisition of the Panama Canal Zone; 1933, Good Neighbor Policy.

1978 ■ CANADA'S IMMIGRATION ACT OF 1976: *for the first time in Canadian history, legislation delineates national responsibility for immigration*

DATE: April 10, 1978
LOCALE: Ottawa
CATEGORIES: Canadian history; Immigration; Laws and acts
KEY FIGURE:
Robert Andras (born 1909), chief architect of the act
SUMMARY OF EVENT. The Immigration Act of 1976 is a landmark in Canadian immigration policy and history. It delineated national responsibility for immigration for the first time in Canada's history, and it pledged government commitment to family reunification and to Canada's international obligations to ease the plight of refugees, the displaced, and the persecuted. It also reflected Canada's changing economic circumstances, ethnic composition, humanitarian considerations, and place in the international community.

Canada had traditionally restricted immigration to northern and western Europeans. After World War II, Canada's economy boomed and the business lobby was exerting pressure to open immigration channels. Starting in the 1950's, Canada needed immigrants in order to have sufficient people to maintain her economy. On the other hand, there was a desire to maintain the predominance of northern and western Europeans in the population.

The Immigration Act of 1952 had contributed to European domination in the Canadian population by giving the minister of immigration and immigration officials wide discretionary powers to open and close off immigration to any group. However, in the 1950's, many Third World countries gained independence, and Canada had to consider their growing importance as trading partners and their influence in the United Nations. Thus, Canada started by assigning small quotas to Asian Commonwealth partners. When the expected inflow from northern and western Europe did not materialize, Canada set up offices in Italy, which started the large Italian influx that climbed into the hundreds of thousands. By the mid-1960's, Italians were the dominant laborers in Canada's construction industry.

The need for laborers and the refugee issue challenged Canadian immigration policy. The change started in 1956, when Hungarian refugees, following the communist takeover in Hungary, poured into Australia. By sending teams to refugee settlements and setting aside established procedures, Canada successfully resettled thirty-seven thousand Hungarians in Canada. In the early 1960's, the Canadian market for laborers began to shrink, and active immigration work fell by 50 percent. De facto segregation existed during this period: Immigration offices were established in Europe and North America, but only two in Asia.

In the 1960's, illegal entrants became a problem. The numerous illegals caused the creation of a government commission to review all aspects of immigration. The White Paper on Immigration released in 1966 called for a complete and final overhaul of Canadian immigration policy. This policy should be free of discrimination based on race or ethnicity. The white paper also advocated the right of Canadian citizens to sponsor immediate relatives, if their educational and occupational standards met those of regular immigrants.

When the report came up for discussion in parliamentary committee, ethnic communities exhibited surprising strength. By 1970, they represented one-third of Canada's population and had become a "third force" in Canadian politics. They were confident, had economic affluence, and demanded a new deal for themselves, which included a society that demanded less conformity to the Anglo culture and a more pluralistic focus. One response to these demands, in the later 1960's, was the development and implementation of an equitable immigration system based on domestic economic requirements and on prospects for short-term and long-term integration. From 1967 to the mid-1970's, the key immigration issues for Canada were refugees (Czechoslovakian, Ugandan, Asian, and Chilean) and illegal immigration.

In 1972, Robert Andras, who was to be the chief architect of the Immigration Act of 1976, became minister of manpower and immigration. Andras not only revitalized his department but also energetically worked for immigration reform. In September, 1973, he initiated a major review of immigration and population policies, which resulted in the publication of a green paper on the subject. Because there was a lack of scholars and scholarship on the subject, the document was a disappointing, overcautious, and inadequate. Consequently, a Special Joint Committee of the Senate and House of Commons was appointed in March of 1975. The committee held fifty public hearings, heard four hundred witnesses, and received fourteen hundred briefs. The report it presented to Parliament in November, 1975, was warmly received, and sixty of its sixty-five recommendations were accepted. Its principal recommendation was that Canada continue to be a country of immigration, for demographic, economic, family, and humanitarian reasons. The report argued that a new immigration act should contain a clear and formal statement of principal objectives concerning admission, nondiscrimination, sponsorship of relatives, refugees, and classes of persons prohibited. Operational details should be specified in the regulations.

The report communicated that immigration should be a central variable in Canada's population policy to forestall the decline of Canada's population, especially of Francophones. In relation to population policy, immigration should be linked to population growth and economic conditions. However, the policy and target figures should be determined and presented for parliamentary scrutiny after consulting with the provinces. Other recommendations were that the point system be retained but modified to encourage settlement in underdeveloped areas, and that more staff be hired and better enforcement procedures be instituted.

These recommendations were incorporated into the immigration bill, which had its first reading on November 22, 1976 (hence that year has become linked with the name of the act), received royal assent on August 5, 1977, and became law on April 10, 1978. The act contained constructive provisions and was politically sensitive and forward-looking. It made a positive contribution to the Canadian public image in the area of immigration management. Its most significant provisions were included in a clear statement of the basic principles of Canadian immigration policy, as recommended by the Special Joint Committee—the first time that had been attempted in Canadian immigration law.

The act created a new system of planning and managing Canadian immigration. It sought to involve the provinces in immigration planning and decision making, as well as to open process to parliamentary and public discussion. The act established three classes of immigrants: family, refugee, and others selected on the basis of the point system. Ministerial discretion was reduced in areas of exclusion, control, and enforcement. Other provisions dealt with refugees, revising the point system and ensuring that actual immigrant landings were consistent with announced immigration levels.

The Immigration Act of 1976 was praised as a responsible and forward-looking piece of legislation. In some respects, the act has proved worthy of that praise. In 1979, Canada's commitment to easing the distress of refugees, displaced persons, and the persecuted was seriously challenged by the "boat people" of Southeast Asia. There was a great outpouring of public concern for the situation. The government dispatched immigration officials to the refugee camps and, by the end of 1980, admitted more than sixty thousand ethnic Vietnamese, Cambodians, Laotians, and Chinese from Southeast Asia—the highest per capita "boat people" resettlement program of any nation. One group that has become highly visible has been

entrepreneurs, who, with an investment of $250,000, can immigrate to Canada. Hong Kong Chinese have been particularly noticeable in this category.

All has not gone as expected, however. Sympathy for those entering Canada and then claiming refugee status has waned, because undocumented immigration continues to be a major problem. The law has resulted in a mounting backlog of more than twenty thousand refugee status-determining cases. The provinces, except for Quebec and Ontario, did not cooperate in setting up population guidelines. The potentially valuable Demographic Policy Steering Group and Demographic Policy Secretariat disappeared, and federal government efforts to develop a population policy were initially stalled. There has been a long-term trend of fertility falling in the industrialized world, especially in Canada, and rising in the nonindustrialized countries. Thus, by the mid-1980's, Canada had to develop a population policy for falling birth rates and emigration to the United States; she had to use immigration as a vital part of her population policy. Because western and northern European countries were no longer significant sources of immigration, Canada has turned to Asia a means of maintaining a sufficient population level. The Immigration Act of 1976 has nevertheless provided the framework for Canada to adapt to changing circumstances and exhibit humanitarian behavior by providing refuge to the dispossessed in the world. —*Arthur W. Helweg*

ADDITIONAL READING:

Hawkins, Freda. *Canada and Immigration: Public Policy and Public Concern.* 2d ed. Kingston, Ont.: McGill-Queen's University Press, 1988. The most complete account to date of Canadian immigration policy.

Palmer, Howard, ed. *Immigration and the Rise of Multiculturalism.* Vancouver, B.C.: Copp Clark, 1975. Analyzes the relationship of immigrant communities and the development of multiculturalism in Canada.

Trouper, Harold. "Immigration and Multiculturalism." In *Canada,* edited by Mel Watkins. New York: Facts On File, 1993. Bibliography and index.

Whitaker, Reginald. *Double Standard: The Secret History of Canadian Immigration.* Toronto: Lester & Orpen Dennys, 1987. Good discussion of the unequal application of immigration policies to different ethnic groups.

1978 ■ REGENTS OF THE UNIVERSITY OF CALIFORNIA V. BAKKE: *the U.S. Supreme Court defines racial quotas in preferential admissions programs to be unconstitutional yet also declares that an applicant's race can be a consideration*

DATE: June 28, 1978
LOCALE: Washington, D.C.
CATEGORIES: Civil rights; Court cases; Education

KEY FIGURES:

Allan Paul Bakke (born 1940), the respondent

William J. Brennan, Jr. (born 1906), Supreme Court justice, author of an opinion supported by three other justices

Warren Burger (1907-1995), chief justice of the United States

Reynold Colvin, attorney who the presented oral argument for the respondent

Archibald Cox (born 1912), Harvard law professor who presented the oral argument for the plaintiff

Lewis F. Powell (born 1907), Supreme Court justice and author of a separate and decisive opinion

John Paul Stevens (born 1920), Supreme Court justice and author of an opinion supported by three other justices

SUMMARY OF EVENT. The case of *Regents of the University of California v. Bakke*, better known as the *Bakke* case, led to a significant U.S. Supreme Court civil rights decision. It was the first case concerning the constitutionality of preferential college admissions programs to be heard by the Supreme Court. Although the decision of the Court settled some questions concerning the legality of race-conscious admissions processes, the lack of a majority opinion in the case left other questions unresolved.

At the time of this decision, the defendant in the case, a white man by the name of Allan Paul Bakke, was thirty-eight years of age. In 1973, he had been an applicant for a space in the fall entering class at the University of California at Davis' Medical School (UCDMS); he also applied later that year for a space in the 1974 entering class. While one hundred spaces were available for the entering class, sixteen of these spaces had been set aside each year since 1971 for a special admissions program intended to benefit disadvantaged applicants who had identified themselves on their applications as belonging to one of several minority groups. Despite the fact that Bakke's grade point average as well as his scores on the Medical College Admission Test were far above those of the applicants accepted under the special admissions program for 1973 and 1974, he was not admitted to UCDMS. Charging that he had been the victim of racial discrimination that constituted "reverse discrimination," he sued UCDMS on the grounds that, were it not for the racial quotas involved with the special admission program, his application would have been accepted.

In 1975, the Superior Court of California ruled against Bakke, stating that he did not prove that the program's existence was the cause of his rejection from the medical school. The court did, however, rule that the special admissions program was unconstitutional. On appeal, the California Supreme Court went further, declaring in its 1976 ruling that UCDMS must use an entirely race-blind admissions process to achieve the goal of greater minority student representation. The court also agreed with Bakke that he had been the victim of reverse discrimination and ordered that he be admitted to UCDMS. The University of California then appealed to the U.S. Supreme Court to rule on the constitutionality of its preferential admissions program. In February, 1977, the Court agreed to hear the *Bakke* case.

The *Bakke* case attracted much national attention, because in it, two interests vital to many people in the United States met head-on: the interest in correcting past injustices resulting from discrimination and moving the process of integration forward thorough affirmative action, and the interest in ensuring equal opportunity for all citizens. Many medical schools historically had discriminated against minority applicants; although UCDMS, founded in 1968, had not, the ratio of minority physicians to the substantial minority population in California still was far lower than that of white physicians to California's white population. During oral argument, Archibald Cox (famous for his role as a special prosecutor during the Watergate scandal) stressed UCDMS's responsibilities as a public educational institution to raise the number of minority physicians working within California. He argued that this goal could not be achieved unless the preferential admissions program remained in effect. Reynold Colvin, a San Francisco attorney who had never before argued a case in front of the Supreme Court, downplayed the constitutional issues to emphasize the facts associated with Bakke's rejection, particularly the fact that he was excluded from competing for sixteen open spaces in the class on the basis of his race alone.

The 4-1-4 judgment of the Supreme Court on June 28, 1978, revealed its members to be deeply divided over the issues raised by *Bakke*. Justice John Paul Stevens, in an opinion joined by Justices Warren Burger, William Rehnquist, and Potter Stewart, upheld the ruling at the state level, declaring that Bakke's civil rights had been violated and that the preferential admissions program was illegal. To support this opinion, Stevens pointed to the guarantee under Title VI of the 1964 Civil Rights Act that no one could be excluded on the basis of race from a program receiving federal funding. This opinion was opposed by four other justices (William Brennan, Harry Blackmun, Thurgood Marshall, and Byron White) who saw the admissions program as violating neither Title VI nor the equal protection clause of the Fourteenth Amendment. In Brennan's opinion, the admissions program was justified because its goal of correcting an imbalance in the number of minority physicians was a worthwhile one for a public medical school to have, and letting racial preferences play a role in the admissions process was a direct and necessary way of bringing that goal about.

Justice Lewis Powell agreed with neither side. In a separate opinion, he maintained UCDMS's admissions program reflected the use of racial quotas and so violated Title VI and the equal protection clause. He was unpersuaded by the reasoning that preferential admissions were necessary either to right the wrongs caused by past discrimination or for the purposes of producing more minority physicians to serve minority populations. Turning to the First Amendment, however, Powell found a justification for giving weight to an applicant's race in admissions decisions. Using preferential admissions as a means to achieve the goal of creating a student body with increased racial diversity and thus an educational climate marked by a greater diversity of ideas and opinions was, Powell claimed, constitutional. The government had a valid interest in creating this climate, he argued, in order to better shape the education of future leaders.

Justice Powell's vote was crucial. In the absence of a majority opinion among the Supreme Court justices concerning *Bakke*, it created a majority of votes that brought about a decision in the case. Part of that decision was to admit Bakke to UCDMS and to strike down the special admissions program at the medical school, because it involved racial quotas. Equally important was the second part of the decision: a declaration that race could be considered in admissions in order to further the state's interests in creating educational diversity. The decision disappointed those supporters of affirmative action who believed reverse discrimination was necessary to correct the injustices of the past and pleased others who saw the Court as giving university administrators a wide leeway in developing future policies of affirmative action. The majority vote in the decision was established by the slimmest of margins, the justices who agreed on the legality of race-conscious admissions did not agree for the same reasons, and not all of the justices based their opinions on constitutional considerations. For these reasons, the *Bakke* decision, despite its undeniable significance, did not set a clear direction for the nation in the matter of affirmative action.   *—Diane P. Michelfelder*

ADDITIONAL READING:

Dworkin, Ronald. "What Did *Bakke* Really Decide?" In *A Matter of Principle*. Cambridge, Mass.: Harvard University Press, 1985. A brief, clearly argued defense of the claim that the *Bakke* decision did not settle as many issues about the legitimacy of affirmative action as anticipated.

McCormack, Wayne. *The Bakke Decision: Implications for Higher Education Admissions*. Washington, D.C.: American Council on Education and the Association of American Law Schools, 1978. Contains a thoughtful discussion of the case's implications for educational institutions.

Sindler, Allan P. *Bakke, Defunis, and Minority Admissions: The Quest for Equal Opportunity*. New York: Longman, 1978. A comprehensive account of the *Bakke* case from start to finish, including a balanced analysis of the social and legal issues associated with it along the way. Index.

Tribe, Laurence. "Dismantling the House that Racism Built: Assessing Affirmative Action." In *Constitutional Choices*. Cambridge, Mass.: Harvard University Press, 1985. A Harvard law professor provides a short, clear analysis of the significance of the *Bakke* decision in the light of other decisions by the Supreme Court.

Wilkinson, J. Harvie, III. *From "Brown" to "Bakke": The Supreme Court and School Integration: 1954-1978*. New York: Oxford University Press, 1979. A lively description and analysis of the *Bakke* case from within the larger context of the U.S. Civil Rights movement and the history of desegregation. Index.

SEE ALSO: 1954, *Brown v. Board of Education*; 1957, Little Rock School Desegregation Crisis; 1962, Meredith Registers at "Ole Miss"; 1965, Expansion of Affirmative Action.

1978 ■ TOXIC WASTE AT LOVE CANAL:
a community suffering from chemically induced illness discovers that it is built on a hazardous waste site

DATE: August 7, 1978
LOCALE: Niagara Falls, New York
CATEGORIES: Environment; Health and medicine; Science and technology
KEY FIGURES:
Hugh Leo Carey (born 1919), governor of New York
Lois Gibbs (born 1951), leader of the Love Canal activist movement
William C. Hennessy (born 1926), commissioner of the New York State Department of Transportation and chairman of the Love Canal Task Force
Robert P. Whalen (born 1925), New York State commissioner of health, who declared the town a medical emergency site

SUMMARY OF EVENT. The inherent conflict between a benign environment fit for human habitation and the disposal of the toxic waste effluents of a technological society is a rapidly spreading problem. The pervasive environmental threat of chemical contamination results from the insidious penetration of toxic materials leeched from dump sites into groundwater or into the atmosphere.

During the first half of the twentieth century, laws regulating the disposal of toxic wastes were virtually nonexistent in North America. Industrial plants found that the easiest and least expensive means of disposing of the growing mounds of chemical waste products was to dump them directly into the atmosphere or the waterways. If this were not feasible, an only slightly more benign alternative was to dispose of them in landfills, following the maxim "out of sight, out of mind." Because no attempt was made to contain the chemical wastes in the landfill, it was only a matter of time until the toxins leaked into the environment. In the United States, when toxic waste landfills were filled, they were often capped off with soil and used for other purposes, such as housing developments.

Thousands of toxic dump sites have been festering sores for towns throughout North America, and debates continue over who should shoulder the cost of cleaning them up or relocating the residents who live in proximity to them. When a toxic waste site is discovered near a residential community, the health risks are assessed. If the risks are moderate, people who cannot afford to sell their house at a loss may decide to accept the increased risk and remain. If the toxic contamination is severe enough, however, residents may be forced to relocate, causing entire communities to become ghost towns.

Love Canal, at Niagara Falls, New York, was just such a community. An uncompleted abandoned canal (three thousand feet long by one hundred feet wide) that had been planned as a link between the upper and lower Niagara River in 1890 by

William T. Love (from whom the canal derives its name) began to be used as a landfill and municipal dump in the 1920's. In 1945, the site was put to a more ominous use, as a legal chemical waste dump site by the Hooker Chemicals and Plastics Corporation of Niagara Falls. By 1953, when the site was filled, more than twenty-one thousand tons of at least eighty different types of toxic waste had been buried in the abandoned canal bed. In addition to processed sludges and fly ash, some of the toxic chemicals disposed of included highly carcinogenic PCBs (polychlorinated biphenyls) and dioxin, one of the most deadly synthetic chemicals known. After the site was closed, it was sealed with a clay cap (the accepted procedure at that time), covered with top soil, and donated, along with the neighboring property, to the growing city of Niagara Falls. The land was zoned for development as a residential area, homes were constructed adjacent to the landfill, and in 1954, the Board of Education built an elementary school directly above the chemical dump site.

By 1972, all homes abutting the landfill were completed and occupied. By the mid-1970's, however, the buried chemicals occasionally would surface, causing strange odors in the air and water and peculiar substances in the soil, or appearing as a corrosive liquid sludge that sporadically seeped into basements. During these years, a rash of neighborhood sicknesses was reported, but a connection was not made between the buried toxic wastes and the high incidence of health problems. Then Lois Gibbs, an unassuming housewife with two young children, took up the battle. Although Gibbs and her family occupied her middle-class dream house, she was goaded into action after her son developed epilepsy, blood disease, asthma, and pneumonia in rapid succession. Each of these can be symptomatic of toxic poisoning, but the local politicians did not believe there was any connection. Gibbs was seen by the authorities as a hysterical malcontent. Nevertheless, the incidence of serious diseases continued to mount, affecting Gibbs's daughter too. Residents organized, demanding a full-scale investigation. After holes filled with a foul-smelling liquid began to appear in lawns, and soil subsidence resulted in the surfacing of barrels of toxic waste, an extensive investigation was undertaken by the New York State Health Department.

The results exonerated Gibbs. Highly toxic chemicals from the canal indeed had leaked into the soil and contaminated the groundwater of most of the neighboring homes. Laboratory analyses confirmed the presence of more than two hundred distinct organic chemical compounds. Although not all compounds were equally toxic, the complex mixture of chemical compounds escaping from the canal raised the specter of unpredictable synergistic effects.

Because of the high levels of contaminants in the water, soil, and air, residents who lived in proximity to the canal were experiencing a high incidence of chromosomal damage, most clearly manifested as miscarriages and birth defects. In addition, the long-term exposure to toxic chemicals caused increases in the rate of occurrence of cancer, nerve damage, and other severe disorders. In 1978, after studying the problem and

obtaining conclusive data, the Department of Health ordered the evacuation of pregnant women and young children from 239 homes; on August 7, the site was declared a disaster area. Eventually, all but eighty-six of the nine hundred families living in Love Canal were evacuated. As a result of the unrelenting pressure put upon government bureaucrats by Gibbs and her NIMBY ("Not In My Back Yard") activist movement, the federal government eventually agreed to purchase the abandoned homes of evacuated citizens at a cost of twenty million dollars. Another two hundred million dollars was appropriated to detoxify the region. A study by the U.S. Environmental Protection Agency (EPA) in 1980 revealed that among the last eighteen pregnancies for area residents, there were only two normal births, but four miscarriages, three stillbirths, and nine children born with congenital defects.

Although Love Canal was termed the worst environmental disaster involving chemical wastes in U.S. history, it proved to be just the first of thousands of similar cases of contamination by legally and illegally dumped wastes across North America. Realizing that the burden of cleaning up these sites would have to be shared by government and industry, the U.S. Congress enacted the Superfund program in 1980. A "superfund" of $1.6 billion was created in order to detoxify an estimated twenty-two thousand abandoned hazardous waste sites. Some of this money was used to relocate 1,390 families in forty-two communities. The federal government increasingly has opted to relocate people rather than detoxify areas when this option is feasible. Relocation protects residents more quickly and is considerably less expensive.

The saga of Love Canal not only was the first highly publicized toxic waste disposal situation in North American history but also was probably the most expensive and certainly the most unusual case to date. Few hazardous chemical waste dump sites are entombed directly under a residential community. Both the citizens of Love Canal and government officials were drawn into this environmental disaster with no previous experience to refer to and no particular expertise, but the knowledge gained was invaluable not only for other specific sites but also as an impetus for the legislation that created the Superfund, and as a means of helping to ensure that more toxic time bombs were not created in the future. Nevertheless, in succeeding years budgetary constraints limited measures to reduce at the source the huge volumes of toxic waste materials being generated by industrial operations. —*George R. Plitnik*

ADDITIONAL READING:

Brown, Michael. *Laying Waste: The Poisoning of America by Toxic Chemicals*. New York: Pantheon Books, 1979. Written by a reporter living in the Niagara Falls area during the event. Emotional but essential.

_____. "Love Canal Revisited." *The Amicus Journal* 10, no. 3 (Summer, 1988). A look at the Love Canal crisis a decade after its apex.

Epstein, Samuel S., Lester O. Brown, and Carl Pope. *Hazardous Waste in America*. San Francisco: Sierra Club Books, 1982. An overview of the history, politics, and economics of hazardous waste in the United States. Index and useful appendices.

Gibbs, Lois. *Love Canal: My Story*. New York: Grove Press, 1982. Gibbs's own perspective on the Love Canal incidents.

Kronewetter, Michael. *Managing Toxic Wastes*. Englewood Cliffs, N.J.: Messner, 1989. A concise, well-organized discussion of toxic-waste problems and issues. Photographs, index, bibliography.

Levine, Adeline Gordon. *Love Canal: Science, Politics, and People*. Lexington, Mass.: Lexington Books, 1982. One of the better books on Love Canal available. Excellent references.

New York State Department of Health. *Love Canal: Public Health Time Bomb*. Albany, N.Y.: Author, September, 1978. Presents the causes and devastating effects of this tragedy in terms of human health, suffering, and environmental damage.

_____. *Love Canal: A Special Report to the Governor and Legislature*. Albany, N.Y.: Author, April, 1981. Presents the history and demographics of the Love Canal disaster, and the results of the toxicological investigations and epidemiological studies.

Shaw, L. Gardner, and L. W. Milbrath. *Citizen Participation in Government Decision Making: The Toxic Waste Threat at Love Canal, Niagara Falls, New York*. Albany, N.Y.: Nelson A. Rockefeller Institute of Government, State University of New York, no. 8, Spring, 1983. An EPA-sponsored study detailing the role of citizen participation at toxic waste sites.

SEE ALSO: 1979, Three Mile Island Accident; 1981, Ozone Hole Is Discovered; 1989, *Exxon Valdez* Oil Spill.

1978 ■ AMERICAN INDIAN RELIGIOUS FREEDOM ACT: *the U.S. Congress recognizes its obligation "to protect and preserve for American Indians their inherent right of freedom to believe, express, and exercise traditional religions"*

DATE: August 11, 1978
LOCALE: Washington, D.C.
CATEGORIES: Civil rights; Laws and acts; Native American history; Religion
KEY FIGURES:
John Collier (1884-1968), commissioner of Indian affairs who issued a 1934 policy statement affirming American Indian religious freedom
Scott Leavitt (1879-1966), Montana congressman who sponsored a 1926 bill to extend federal law over American Indians
Richard Milhous Nixon (1913-1994), president of the United States, 1969-1974, who made a statement in support of American Indian religious freedom
SUMMARY OF EVENT. Throughout most of U.S. history, the federal government has discouraged and abridged the free exercise of traditional American Indian religions. The federal gov-

ernment provided direct and indirect support to a variety of Christian denominations who sought to Christianize and "civilize" American Indians. In 1883, bowing to pressure from Christian churches, the federal government forbade "the savage and barbarous practices that are calculated to continue [American Indians] in savagery, no matter what exterior influences are brought to bear on them." The Sun Dance, rites of purification, other religious ceremonies, and the practices of medicine men were forbidden. Violators could be prosecuted and receive ten days in jail if they continued their "heathenish practices." Such a law restricting freedom of religion was possible because tribes were regarded as distinct political units separate and apart from the United States, and so were not covered by the protections of the Constitution or the Bill of Rights.

In the 1920's, there was a crusade for reform in federal American Indian policy, and there were outspoken concerns for the support of freedom of religion for American Indian peoples. In 1933, John Collier was appointed Commissioner of Indian Affairs under Franklin Roosevelt. On January 31, 1934, he circulated a pamphlet entitled *Indian Religious Freedom and Indian Culture* among employees of the Indian Service. This pamphlet, which stressed that "the fullest constitutional liberty, in all matters affecting religion, conscience, and culture" should be extended to all American Indians, established policies for Indian Service employees to follow. Collier directed unequivocally, "No interference with Indian religious life or ceremonial expression will hereafter be tolerated. The cultural liberty of Indians in all respects is to be considered equal to that of any non-Indian group." Two weeks later, Collier issued a second order, which dealt with religious services at government-operated schools. It had been common practice to require students in government schools to attend church services. This new policy statement, "Regulations for Religious Worship and Instruction," prohibited compulsory attendance at services, although it did allow religious denominations to use school facilities for services. Religious instruction was permitted one hour per week in the day schools; however, parents had to give written permission for their children to attend. This policy was especially controversial, because these regulations extended to representatives of native religions as well as to Christian missionaries.

These policy statements were not well received by missionaries who had been active on various reservations, and many regarded Collier's move to protect American Indian religious freedoms as a direct attack on the churches and Christianity. Collier was accused of being an atheist and of being antireligious. Criticism of Collier was especially strong among Protestant missionary societies and included attacks from Christian Indians who decried this return to the old ways as subverting American Indian progress. Nevertheless, Collier insisted that American Indians be granted complete constitutional liberty in all matters affecting religion, conscience, and culture, and he asserted that religious liberty extended to all people, not just Christians.

Most tribal governments endorsed Collier's policy of religious freedom, and, on many reservations, there was a revival of the older spiritual traditions. However, federal and state laws have not endorsed or permitted freedom of religion for American Indians consistently. Certain state and federal laws and policies prevented the free exercise of religion for many American Indian people. A large area of concern was that many areas that were considered to be sacred lands by the tribes had passed from Indian control to state or federal jurisdiction. Access to such sacred sites often was limited or not permitted. The use of peyote in Native American Church ceremonies was a contentious issue, because peyote is a restricted substance because it has hallucinogenic properties. The use of eagle feathers in a variety of rituals was another source of friction with federal officials, because eagles were protected under endangered species laws. There also have been occasions of interference in religious ceremonies by government agents and curious onlookers. American Indian people had little recourse to remedy these situations, and tribal governments had no powers of prosecution or enforcement.

As a result of continuing problems with the free exercise of traditional American Indian religions, Congress passed a broad policy statement, Senate Joint Resolution 102, commonly known as the American Indian Religious Freedom Act (AIRFA), on August 11, 1978. After noting the U.S. right to freedom of religion and the inconsistent extension of that right to American Indian people, Congress acknowledged its obligation to "protect and preserve for American Indians their inherent right of freedom to believe, express, and exercise the traditional religions of the American Indian, Eskimo, Aleut, and Native Hawaiian, including but not limited to access to sites, use and possession of sacred objects, and the freedom to worship through ceremonial and traditional rites." AIRFA also required all federal agencies to examine their regulations and practices for any inherent conflict with the practice of American Indian religions. These agencies were required to report back to Congress and recommend areas in which changes in policies and procedures were needed to ensure that American Indian religious freedoms were protected.

The American Indian Religious Freedom Act is a key element in self-determination and cultural freedom in the United States. However, even with passage of this act, Native Americans have continued to experience problems in access to sacred sites and the use of peyote. The right of Native Americans to use peyote is an unsettled issue in both federal and state courts. Although peyote is subject to control under the Federal Comprehensive Drug Abuse Prevention and Control Act, a number of states exempt its use in Native American Church ceremonies. Some courts uphold the right of Native Americans who are church members to possess and use peyote; other courts do not. Likewise, American Indians are not guaranteed access to sacred sites that are located outside the bounds of Indian lands, even when these lands are under federal control.

The United States Supreme Court has ruled that AIRFA is a policy statement only, and it does now allow American Indians to sue when federal agencies disregard native religious prac-

tices or when agencies pursue plans that will have an adverse impact on Native American religion or beliefs. In 1988, in *Lyng v. Northwest Indian Cemeteries Association*, the United States was granted the right to build a logging road through federal lands that were central to the traditional religions of the Yurok, Karuk, and Talowac tribes. In 1990, the United States Supreme Court ruled, in *Department of Human Resources of Oregon v. Smith*, that the state of Oregon could prohibit a member of the Native American Church from using peyote, because that state regarded peyote as an illegal substance. These Supreme Court decisions make clear that if federal or state agencies fail to comply with the policies established in AIRFA, American Indian people have no legal recourse to sue or claim adverse impact on their religion. The extension of full religious freedom to Native American people is an evolving concept in U.S. jurisprudence, and the American Indian Religious Freedom Act constitutes an important philosophical foundation toward ensuring the free exercise of religion and access to sacred areas.
—*Carole A. Barrett*

ADDITIONAL READING:

Deloria, Vine, Jr., ed. *American Indian Policy in the Twentieth Century*. Norman: University of Oklahoma Press, 1985. These essays interpret American Indian policy through important legal decisions. One essay explores AIRFA and its ineffectiveness in protecting access to sacred sites.

Deloria, Vine, Jr., and Clifford Lytle. *The Nations Within: The Past and Future of American Indian Sovereignty*. New York: Pantheon Books, 1984. A thorough examination of the Collier years and their impact on later American Indian poetry.

Echo-Hawk, Walter E. "Loopholes in Religious Liberty. The Need for a Federal Law to Protect Freedom of Worship for Native American People." *NARF Legal Review* 14 (Summer, 1991): 7-14. An important analysis of what AIRFA should provide in the way of legal protection of religious freedoms for American Indian peoples.

Josephy, Alvin M. *Now That the Buffalo's Gone: A Study of Today's American Indians*. Norman: University of Oklahoma Press, 1984. Contains a chapter on American Indian efforts to retain their spirituality and provides American Indian perspective on this issue.

SEE ALSO: 1968, Indian Civil Rights Act; 1969, Alcatraz Occupation; 1972, Trail of Broken Treaties; 1973, Wounded Knee Occupation; 1988, Indian Gaming Regulatory Act.

1979 ■ UNITED STATES AND CHINA ESTABLISH FULL DIPLOMATIC RELATIONS: *relations with China gains greater leverage for the United States in negotiations with the Soviet Union*

DATE: January 1, 1979
LOCALE: Washington, D.C., and Beijing, China
CATEGORY: Diplomacy and international relations

KEY FIGURES:

Zbigniew Brzezinski (born 1928), U.S. national security adviser

James Earl "Jimmy" Carter, Jr. (born 1924), thirty-ninth president of the United States, 1977-1981

Deng Xiaoping (born 1904), Chinese vice premier and vice chairman of the Chinese Communist Party

Richard Milhous Nixon (1913-1994), thirty-seventh president of the United States, 1969-1974

SUMMARY OF EVENT. In 1949, guerrilla leader Mao Zedong completed his long struggle to overthrow the nationalist government of China. Mao consolidated his victory by establishing a communist government on the Chinese mainland. The nationalists, led by Chiang Kai-shek, fled to the island of Taiwan, where they established a rival Chinese government. Both Chiang and Mao claimed to represent all of China. The United States officially recognized Chiang's government in Taipei as the sole legitimate Chinese government.

As the Cold War intensified in subsequent years, the United States sought to isolate and weaken the communist Chinese government, just as Washington had sought to contain the power and influence of the Soviet Union. By the end of the 1950's, however, the nominal ideological affinity between the world's two largest communist countries, the People's Republic of China (PRC) and the Soviet Union, was unable to prevent a widening rift in their bilateral relations. In the 1960's, the growing Sino-Soviet split led policymakers in Washington, D.C., to consider improving relations with the PRC as a way of isolating the Soviet Union, which was seen as the larger threat to U.S. security. By 1971, the Foreign Relations Committee of the U.S. Senate held hearings on the possible establishment of official ties with the PRC, and on admitting it to the United Nations as the proper representative of China. The United Nations recognized the PRC that year, coincident with Taiwan's expulsion from that seat.

A major breakthrough in U.S.-PRC relations came with President Richard Nixon's state visit to Beijing in 1972. As a champion of the realist school of foreign policy, Nixon believed that the PRC's ideological rhetoric and its disagreeable domestic behavior (including human rights abuses and intolerance of dissent) mattered less to U.S. interests than the PRC's foreign policy. By establishing contact with the PRC, Nixon sought to give the communist government a stake in friendly relations with the United States. Nixon's official visit opened the door to increased U.S.-PRC trade and a variety of military and security agreements. Nevertheless, the Nixon Administration stopped short of granting the PRC full diplomatic recognition.

Ironically, it was President Jimmy Carter, noted for his self-professed commitment to human rights and morality in international affairs, who officially recognized the PRC. The political environment in which Carter found himself was fundamentally altered from the time of Nixon's visit to Beijing. Nixon had resigned the presidency in 1974 in disgrace as a result of the Watergate scandal. Mao had died in 1976. The leadership in the PRC came to be dominated by Deng Xiao-

ping, who promoted modernization, economic reform, and improved ties with the West. Although the PRC under Deng still was seen as a communist state guilty of continuing human rights abuses, it was considered to be an improvement over the Mao era. In addition, the PRC's improving economy presented enticing trade and business opportunities to the United States. U.S.-PRC relations were continually improving.

Washington made overtures to Beijing on the subject of establishing full diplomatic relations. Although formal recognition was attractive to the PRC, the communist leadership steadfastly demanded of the United States three conditions: the termination of official relations with Taiwan, the removal of U.S. troops from Taiwan, and the abrogation of the U.S.-Taiwan mutual defense treaty. These conditions would be difficult for the pro-Taiwanese and anticommunist groups who forcefully, and often successfully, lobbied Congress.

Nevertheless, the Carter Administration was motivated to reach an agreement with Beijing. As a result of a number of factors, including renewed Soviet military involvement in Africa and stalled arms control talks, U.S.-Soviet relations were worsening. Playing the "China card" therefore became increasingly attractive to the Carter Administration. Behind-the-scenes negotiations continually sought a compromise on the various issues. National Security Adviser Zbigniew Brzezinski held numerous and regular discussions with PRC officials in Washington, D.C.

By the end of 1978, a breakthrough had occurred. On December 15, the White House announced that full diplomatic relations with China would be established on the first of the new year. It formally acknowledged "the Chinese position that there is but one China and Taiwan is part of China." It also recognized the People's Republic of China as "the sole legal Government of China." As a small concession to Taiwan, the United States proclaimed that "the people of the United States will maintain cultural, commercial, and other unofficial relations with the people of Taiwan." All this largely had been kept secret, and even much of the Congress had been kept in the dark.

Shortly thereafter, Deng Xiaoping was officially received in Washington, D.C. In their joint statements, the leaders of the United States and the PRC emphasized a shared anti-Soviet perspective. Despite scattered protests, most notably from Taiwan, the establishment of official ties between the United States and the PRC was widely applauded by governments around the world as a move that squared diplomacy with reality.

Within the United States itself, however, the Carter Administration came under heavy criticism for "selling out" Taiwan. Making good on his promises to Beijing, Carter sought to replace the U.S.-Taiwan mutual defense treaty with a Taiwan Enabling Act, which did not guarantee Taiwan's security and which would replace the U.S. embassy in Taipei with an American Institute in Taiwan to represent U.S. interests. Senator Barry Goldwater challenged the president's right to terminate the mutual defense treaty without Senate approval. Although Goldwater failed in that effort, the final bill passed by the U.S.

Congress in the spring of 1979, the Taiwan Relations Act, provided several concessions to Taiwan. It expressed an intent to ensure that Taiwan receive enough defensive arms to protect itself and guaranteed that the lack of formal diplomatic relations would not disqualify Taiwan from various aid programs.

The establishment of relations between Washington and Beijing consolidated the tripolar diplomacy that had been begun under Nixon. U.S.-PRC relations remained largely cooperative, although by no means was the PRC pulled into the United States' political orbit. In fact, when the Soviet Union and most other communist countries implemented radical reforms in the late 1980's and renounced communism altogether a short time later, China remained a committed communist state. Aside from a few anomalies like Cuba and Vietnam, in the mid-1990's the PRC was the only globally significant communist state in existence.

Despite continued human rights abuses, including the mass murder of student demonstrators at Tiananmen Square in 1989, U.S.-PRC relations have remained relatively steady, with Washington regularly granting Beijing "most favored nation" trade status. —*Steve D. Boilard*

ADDITIONAL READING:

Daley, John Charles, moderator. *The Future of Chinese-American Relations*. AEI Forum 29. Washington, D.C.: American Enterprise Institute for Public Policy Research, 1979. Brief booklet presenting comments from Senators Barry Goldwater, Alan Cranston, and Bob Dole, and Representative Jonathan Bingham, on the then-developing normalization of relations with China. The forum took place about eight months before the establishment of full diplomatic relations.

Garrett, Banning N., and Bonnie S. Glaser. "From Nixon to Reagan: China's Changing Role in American Strategy." In *Eagle Resurgent? The Reagan Era in American Foreign Policy*, edited by Kenneth A. Oye, Robert J. Lieber, and Donald Rothchild. Boston: Little, Brown, 1987. The first half of this article discusses the U.S. rapprochement with the PRC, including the establishing of official ties. A scholarly article with extensive footnotes.

Garson, Robert. *The United States and China Since 1949: A Troubled Affair*. London: Pinter, 1994. Chapter 6 examines the normalization of relations between the United States and China between 1972 and 1979. Notes and bibliography.

Gregor, A. James. *The China Connection: U.S. Policy and the People's Republic of China*. Stanford, Calif.: Hoover Institution Press, 1986. A history of U.S. involvement with China, focusing on the establishment of the PRC, China's foreign policy, and rapprochement with the United States. Presents a skeptical view of China's predictability and the coincidence of interests between the United States and China.

Harding, Harry. *A Fragile Relationship: The United States and China Since 1972*. Washington, D.C.: Brookings Institution, 1992. Chapter 3 focuses on the normalization of relations between the United States and China. A smooth, historical narrative; appendices and notes.

Starr, John Bryan, ed. *The Future of U.S.-China Relations*.

New York: New York University Press, 1981. Written shortly after the establishment of full diplomatic relations, these essays present a variety of perspectives on normalization. More analytical than historical.

SEE ALSO: 1950, Korean War; 1955, Formosa Resolution; 1972, Rapprochement with China; 1973, Détente with the Soviet Union.

1979 ■ THREE MILE ISLAND ACCIDENT: *an accident at a nuclear power plant spurs growing concerns over the potential hazards of nuclear power*

DATE: March 28, 1979
LOCALE: Three Mile Island, Pennsylvania
CATEGORY: Environment
KEY FIGURES:
James Earl "Jimmy" Carter, Jr. (born 1924), thirty-ninth president of the United States, 1977-1981
Joe Deal, chief of environmental protection and public safety, Department of Energy
Harold Denton, director of reactor regulations, Nuclear Regulatory Commission

SUMMARY OF EVENT. At 4:00 A.M. on the morning of March 28, 1979, operations began to unravel at the Metropolitan Edison Company's nuclear power plant located on Three Mile Island in the Susquehanna River, just south of the Pennsylvania capital of Harrisburg. A pump malfunctioned in the water-cooled nuclear reactor facility, and the operators on duty, misled by a faulty instrument, turned off the emergency cooling system. Without adequate coolant, the reactor overheated quickly to the danger level, igniting fears of a catastrophic core meltdown.

At the time of the accident, Three Mile Island was already a troubled plant in a troubled power industry. Shortly after World War II, a three-pronged structure had emerged to spearhead the development of a nuclear power industry in the United States. The first element was the Atomic Energy Commission (AEC), created by the Atomic Energy Act of 1946 and charged with the incompatible tasks of both promoting and regulating the peaceful use of nuclear power. Its congressional overseer was also its ally, the Joint Committee on Atomic Energy (JCAE), staffed throughout most of its existence (1946-1977) with proponents of nuclear energy. The third part of this subgovernment was the private utility companies, subsidized and sheltered by the AEC when adopting the nuclear option for electrifying the postwar United States.

With the increase in environmental awareness in the United States during the late 1960's, the nuclear power plants being built throughout the country belatedly came under close scrutiny, because of the environmental risks posed by nuclear power. Several states eventually adopted more rigorous standards for the licensing and construction of nuclear power plants than existing federal AEC standards required. Nevertheless, the big blows to nuclear power in the United States prior to the Three Mile Island incident were struck not by the environmentalists but by the energy crises of 1973 and 1979.

On the one hand, these crises boosted the case for an enlarged nuclear power industry worldwide. Greater reliance on nuclear energy could be an important step toward reducing dependency on unreliable supplies of foreign oil. On the other hand, the inflationary pressures unleashed by these crises made the price of constructing nuclear power plants much greater. When combined with the expense of overcoming the growing number of restrictions being placed on the nuclear industry in the United States, the inflationary factor stripped away the economic advantage that nuclear power had previously enjoyed over coal-produced electricity.

When the energy crises politicized the issue of energy, it became too important a subject for Congress to leave nuclear power in the hands of the existing, small, subgovernmental system. In the public debate over energy options that followed the first energy crisis, the AEC was attacked repeatedly for monopolizing information about nuclear power. In the Energy Reorganization Act of 1974, the AEC was split along functional lines, its regulatory responsibilities given to a newly created Nuclear Regulatory Commission (NRC) and its industry-promotion and subsidy roles delegated to the Energy Research and Development Authority (ERDA, later absorbed into the Department of Energy). Three years later, Congress disbanded the JCAE. As a result of these actions, funds earmarked for nuclear energy decreased abruptly, from 68 percent of the ERDA's 1977 budget to 55 percent in 1979.

On the regulatory front, however, environmentalists criticized the NRC for being not much more aggressive than the AEC had been in holding nuclear power plants to strict public safety regulations. Their arguments found support in the preaccident history of Three Mile Island. As the postaccident analysis of NRC files revealed, Three Mile Island had remained a troubled installation even after the NRC's 1975 decision to exempt it from the stiffer safety regulations that the NRC had adopted, on the grounds that the plant was already under construction when those rules were promulgated. Between then and December 30, 1978, when the plant was hurried on line, apparently so that Metropolitan Edison could claim a tax depreciation allowance for it on its 1978 tax return, Three Mile Island was the site of several safety violations and mechanical failures. Furthermore, according to postaccident investigators, its operators had never been trained to cope with the mechanical failure that they faced on March 28, 1979.

The accident that resulted at that time became an instant watershed in the history of nuclear power in the United States. The danger of a core meltdown or major release of radioactive vapor was sufficiently high to warrant the evacuation of large numbers of the resident population near the plant's site. The Office of the Governor of Pennsylvania actively monitored events until the danger advisory was lifted on April 9. Harold Denton, NRC director of reactor regulations, was dispatched

to Three Mile Island to take personal charge of the NRC's on-site crisis management operation. Even President Jimmy Carter, once trained as a nuclear engineer, journeyed to the plant at the end of the danger period to demonstrate that matters were under control and that the plant no longer posed any threat to public safety. Interwoven among these men was a maze of national, state, and local officials, and an army of media personnel who made Three Mile Island the most covered nuclear accident in the country's history.

The publicity was not entirely negative. After the initial mechanical breakdown was catapulted into a crisis by human error, management personnel responded well to the crisis and no serious environmental or human harm occurred. Three Mile Island thus remained a warning of the dangers of nuclear power, not an example of the horrors and costs of a core meltdown, as would occur seven years later at Chernobyl in the Soviet Union. Perhaps for this reason, a plurality of the general public continued to favor nuclear energy as an energy option in public opinion polls throughout 1979 and 1980.

On the other hand, the numbers taking a not-in-my-backyard (NIMBY) approach to the issue rose substantially, active support for nuclear power dropped nearly ten points between 1978 and 1979, and the number of people who were opposed to nuclear power rather than unsure about it substantially increased following the Three Mile Island accident. This overall hardening in the opposition to nuclear energy after the Three Mile Island accident, combined with the disincentives already working against the construction of new nuclear power plants and the short-term certainty of more and stricter regulation of nuclear power plants, paralyzed the industry in the United States. Even the pro-nuclear-power position of President Ronald Reagan's administration could not dissuade most electrical companies across the country from following the lead of the Public Service Company of Oklahoma after the Three Mile Island accident and aborting further commitment to even those nuclear power stations already under construction.   —Joseph R. Rudolph, Jr.

ADDITIONAL READING:

Cantelon, Philip L., and Robert C. Williams. *Crisis Contained: The Department of Energy at Three Mile Island*. Carbondale: Southern Illinois University Press, 1982. A balanced account of the events, which concludes that the Department of Energy generally managed the crisis effectively.

Davis, David Howard. *Energy Politics*. 4th ed. New York: St. Martin's Press, 1993. Characterizes the Three Mile Island crisis as less a cause than a climax of the nuclear debate in the United States.

Ford, Daniel. *Three Mile Island: Thirty Minutes to Meltdown*. New York: Viking Press, 1982. Divides blame for the accident between builders more concerned with costs than safety and federal guidelines that were too easily circumvented.

Goldsteen, Raymond, and John K. Schorr. *Demanding Democracy After Three Mile Island*. Gainesville: University of Florida Press, 1991. Views the Three Mile Island affair as the product of citizens allowing themselves to become politically disempowered.

Houts, Peter S., et al. *The Three Mile Island Crisis: Psychological, Social, and Economic Impacts on the Surrounding Population.* University Park: Pennsylvania State University Press, 1988. Focusing on the strains of citizens living with an energy system that they have reason to believe endangers them.

Martin, Daniel. *Three Mile Island: Prologue or Epilogue?* Cambridge, Mass.: Ballinger, 1980. An excellent account of both the accident and the human and organizational errors in the operation of nuclear power plants in the United States that led to it.

Nuclear Regulatory Commission. *The Status of Recommendations of the President's Commission on the Accident at Three Mile Island: A Ten-Year Review.* Washington, D.C.: Executive Director for Operations, U.S. National Research Council, 1989. The official response to the accident.

Office of Policy and Planning. *The Socio-Economic Impacts of the Three Mile Island Accident: Final Report.* Harrisburg, Pa.: Governor's Office of Policy and Planning, 1980. An official analysis of the impact of the accident.

Starr, Philip, and William Pearman. *Three Mile Island Sourcebook: Annotations of a Disaster.* New York: Garland, 1983. A useful chronology of the controversy surrounding Three Mile Island from 1966 to 1981, based largely on articles in the local press near the plant site.

SEE ALSO: 1978, Toxic Waste at Love Canal; 1981, Ozone Hole Is Discovered; 1989, *Exxon Valdez* Oil Spill.

1979 ■ CLARK ELECTED CANADA'S PRIME MINISTER: *Canada's Conservative Party makes a temporary dent in Liberal Party control*

DATE: May 23, 1979
LOCALE: Canada
CATEGORIES: Canadian history; Government and politics
KEY FIGURES:
John Edward Broadbent (born 1936), New Democratic Party leader
Charles Joseph "Joe" Clark (born 1939), leader of the Progressive Conservative Party
John Crosbie (born 1931), shadow finance minister for the Progressive Conservatives
Flora MacDonald (born 1926), shadow foreign minister for the Progressive Conservatives
Pierre Elliott Trudeau (born 1919), incumbent Canadian prime minister and Liberal Party leader
SUMMARY OF EVENT. In 1979, Pierre Elliott Trudeau had been prime minister of Canada for eleven consecutive years. During those years, he had achieved much in terms of social and economic programs. He had become prominent in international circles because he was, at that time, the best-known Canadian prime minister ever in foreign eyes. His popularity at home was beginning to flag, however. In 1976, Trudeau had

received a huge boost in the polls when the sovereignist Parti Québécois had come to power in Trudeau's native province of Quebec. The English Canadian population, especially, hoped that Trudeau, a French Canadian himself, could convince his fellow Quebecers that it was in their best interest to stay within Canada, and that his own status as prime minister was evidence of the lengths to which French Canadians could rise in a united Canada. Several years had passed since the Parti Québécois had come to power, and there was no immediate sign that Quebec planned to seriously investigate sovereignty. In the meantime, Canada's economy, along with that of the entire Western world, was sluggish, victim to "stagflation," in which high inflation and growing unemployment coexisted.

Trudeau's Liberal Party faced an invigorated opposition in the Progressive Conservatives. The Tories' previous leader, Robert Stanfield, was affable and well respected but it was thought that Stanfield was perhaps a bit too content to be the number two man, to be Leader of the Opposition rather than prime minister. His replacement was the young Charles Joseph Clark, known universally as Joe, a vigorous, hard-hitting politician who did not shrink from taking on Trudeau personally during question time in Parliament. Clark was less than forty years of age when he led the party into the election—unusually young for a politician in the Western world. To many, Clark's youth was just what the Tories needed.

Trudeau, somewhat in the manner of John F. Kennedy in the United States, was unusually charming, charismatic, and debonair for a Canadian politician, and had tended to make his Tory opponents look old-fashioned and dowdy by comparison. Although Clark looked a bit stiff and unimaginative when compared with Trudeau, he gave the impression of being sharper and more defined. He gave the Progressive Conservatives a good position in the personality battle for the first time since Trudeau's ascendancy. Although a fiscal conservative, Clark was socially liberal on some issues, which made him more attractive to an undecided voter than his predecessors had been, putting the word "progressive" back into the name Progressive Conservative. Clark's wife, Maureen McTeer, had kept her maiden name and was a professional woman of repute. Clark's shadow cabinet (a list of people who would be ministers if he won the election and was asked to form a government) included Flora MacDonald, the shadow foreign minister, who was one of the most prominent women in Canadian politics. Clark hoped to attract more of the women's vote than the Progressive Conservatives had in the past.

Trudeau suffered from the family problems he had experienced in the late 1970's. His young, attractive wife, Margaret, had grown tired of the political lifestyle, and the couple had separated. Margaret Trudeau was a fixture in Canadian and international gossip columns, and was reputed to be romantically involved with other men. Although this did not cause a major diminution in Trudeau's levels of popular support, it certainly did not enhance his image. Trudeau also fell behind on the issues. This was particularly true in the case of economic issues, where Clark's more free-market policies, ably promoted by John Crosbie of Newfoundland, his shadow finance minister, seemed to many likely to revitalize the Canadian economy. Aware of his problems when it came to economic issues, Trudeau conjured up the idea of an "Economic Olympics" (an image fashioned to appeal to the Canadian public, because the 1976 Summer Olympic Games had been held in Montreal) where the economic performance of Canada was compared to that of other industrial nations. Many people, however, believed Trudeau was merely manipulating statistics and was not taking into account the economic malaise felt by Canadian people in general.

Foreign policy, seldom an issue in Canadian elections, was also terrain on which Clark seemed to have the advantage. Trudeau had stood for a lessening in Cold War tensions with the Soviet Union, to the point where some considered him a neutralist. Clark, on the other hand, saw a pattern of increasing Soviet aggression around the world. This made him popular among certain constituencies, particularly Ukrainian-Canadians in the Prairie Provinces.

Trudeau stressed a less immediate, more abstract issue: the need for constitutional reform in Canada. Although independent in fact for decades, Canada's constitution still was subject to amendment by the British Parliament. Trudeau wanted to change this and to develop a constitution that would ensure French Canadians equal rights within Canada, thus solving the country's linguistic problem as well. Most voters agreed with Trudeau's ideals, but they were more inclined to vote on the basis of the bread-and-butter issues stressed by Clark.

Canada's third party, the Social Democrats, aspired to play an enlarged role in the campaign. Despite the best efforts of their dedicated leader, John Edward Broadbent, the electorate's attention remained on the two major parties. Although Clark seemed better positioned on the issues, many observers thought that Trudeau could still ride the advantages of incumbency to victory. On May 23, 1979, they were proven wrong, as the Progressive Conservatives took the most seats in the House of Commons, and Clark became prime minister. The Progressive Conservatives were particularly helped by Clark's popularity in the western provinces, which were alienated from Trudeau and his perceived preoccupation with a Quebec-Ontario axis.

Clark's victory was by no means a total one. For one thing, he did not receive a majority of seats in the House of Commons, because the rest of the chamber was divided between several different parties, and therefore could not rally to oppose the Progressive Conservatives as a bloc. Being a minority government meant that Clark's government could fall by losing a vote of confidence in which all the other parties opposed him, as happened seven months later.

That Clark and the Progressive Conservatives gained only a minority in the 1979 elections can be attributed to regional divisions. Overall, the Progressive Conservatives won 136 seats, the Liberals 114, the New Democrats 26, and minor parties 7. The strength of the Tories was concentrated in Ontario and the West. In Ontario, the Progressive Conservatives won 57 seats, compared to 32 for the Liberals and 6 for the New Democrats. In the West, the Progressive Conservative success was even more sweeping, with 57 seats compared to 3 for the Liberals (traditionally weak in the West) and 17 for the New Democrats. It was these provinces that were the most responsive to Clark's free-market message. In the Atlantic Provinces, the Progressive Conservatives won 18 out of a possible 30 seats. In Quebec, they failed miserably, garnering only two seats. The Westerner, Clark, had no appeal for Quebecers when running against the native, bilingual Trudeau; it would take a Quebec native to win the province for the Tories, as Brian Mulroney did in 1984.

For all the success of his campaign against Trudeau, Clark entered office with only a partial mandate. It soon turned out that the Canadian populace was more excited by the rhetoric of privatization and free-market economics than the actuality, which led to Clark's government being short-lived and to Trudeau's return to office.
—*Nicholas Birns*

ADDITIONAL READING:

Fotheringham, Allen. *Look Ma—No Hands: An Affectionate Look at Our Wonderful Tories*. Toronto, Ont.: Key Porter Books, 1983. An entertaining and irreverent look at the party Clark led to power in 1979.

Kelly, Fraser. *The Canadian Voter's Guide: Election '79*. Toronto, Ont.: McClelland and Stewart, 1979. A convenient summary of the primary issues at stake in the 1979 parliamentary campaign.

Nolan, Michael. *Joe Clark, The Emerging Leader*. Toronto, Ont.: Fitzhenry and Whiteside, 1978. A campaign biography of Clark.

Penniman, Howard, ed. *Canada at the Polls, 1979 and 1980: A Study of the General Elections*. Washington, D.C.: American Enterprise Institute, 1981. A collection of academic analyses of the campaign.

Troyer, Warner. *Two Hundred Days: Joe Clark in Power: The Anatomy of the Rise and Fall of the Twenty-first Government*. Toronto, Ont.: Personal Library, 1980. Examines the policies of the government elected in 1979.

Trudeau, Pierre Elliott. *Memoirs*. Toronto, Ont.: McClelland & Stewart, 1993. The Liberal leader's perspective on the campaign. Gives a surprisingly high estimate of Clark.

SEE ALSO: 1968, Trudeau Era in Canada.

1979 ■ SALT II Is Signed: *a significant step in a long process toward arms reductions commits the United States and the Soviet Union to limitations in strategic weapons but fails to see ratification*

DATE: June 18, 1979
LOCALE: Vienna, Austria
CATEGORIES: Diplomacy and international relations;
 Treaties and agreements

KEY FIGURES:

Leonid Ilich Brezhnev (1906-1982), general secretary of the
   Communist Party of the Soviet Union
James Earl "Jimmy" Carter, Jr. (born 1924), thirty-ninth
   president of the United States, 1977-1981

SUMMARY OF EVENT. The SALT II treaty signed by Jimmy
Carter and Leonid Brezhnev in Vienna on June 18, 1979,
committed the United States and the Soviet Union to the first
significant reduction in nuclear weapons since the beginning
of the nuclear arms race after World War II. The Strategic
Arms Limitations Talks (SALT) process started November 17,
1969, with negotiations between the United States and the Soviet Union and produced the first SALT agreement (SALT I),
signed in Moscow on May 26, 1972. SALT I comprised two
separate agreements: an antiballistic missile treaty, prohibiting
both countries from building a nationwide defense against
ballistic missiles; and an interim agreement establishing a
five-year moratorium on the construction of strategic ballistic
missile launchers. SALT I was intended to be the first of
several arms control agreements to end the arms race in strategic weapons.

Following ratification of the SALT I agreements by the
United States in the summer of 1972, negotiations for SALT II
began in November. Almost immediately, the two sides found
themselves stalemated on a number of difficult issues. Each
party wanted to legalize a strategic force structure that maxi-
mized its advantages against the other. Thus, a principal objective of the United States was to eliminate the Soviet numerical
superiority by equalizing the number of launchers each side
could possess. At the time of the moratorium, the Soviet Union
possessed 1,618 intercontinental ballistic missiles (ICBMs)
compared to 1,054 in the United States, and 740 submarine-
launched ballistic missiles (SLBMs) compared to the United
States' 656. This U.S. deficit was compensated for by the fact
that the United States had the ability to deploy more than one
warhead in a single missile. Technically, that capacity is referred to as a multiple independently targeted reentry vehicle
(MIRV). Thus, at the time of SALT I, the United States could
hit more targets with nuclear weapons than could the Soviet
Union. However, it was only a matter of time before the Soviet
Union would acquire MIRV ability for its missiles; then its
total destructive capacity would exceed that of the United
States.

The Soviets wanted to include in the total calculations
weapons systems that were deployed in the European theater,
which had not been included in the SALT I accord. These were
known as forward-based systems (FBS) and consisted of tactical aircraft based in Europe or on aircraft carriers in waters
around Europe. Because the United States considered FBS
forces to be dedicated to the defense of Europe, it had refused
to count them as strategic weapons.

The United States wanted to limit indirectly the anticipated
Soviet deployment of MIRV'd missiles by mandating deep
reductions in the total weight (called throwweight) of Soviet
missiles. Soviet missiles were larger than U.S. missiles and

had greater throwweight. Other difficult issues were what to
do about cruise missiles (air-breathing guided missiles developed first by the United States); whether to require the Soviets
to include their Backfire bomber in the totals permitted to
them; and what kinds of modernization of weapons to permit.

Compounding the difficulty of the military-technical issues
was a deteriorating political climate. In 1973, war in the Middle East had exacerbated tensions in U.S.-Soviet relations. In
1974, the Watergate trauma had eroded the political authority
of the Nixon Administration, undercutting both public and
congressional support for the SALT process. The mood of
détente produced by SALT I had deteriorated during the mid-
1970's. A renewed effort to negotiate was undertaken by the
Ford Administration, which came into office in 1974. In December, Gerald Ford and Leonid Brezhnev met in the Soviet
city of Vladivostok to sign an interim agreement. The Vladivostok agreement simply set a number of goals for a future
SALT treaty: a maximum of 2,400 strategic nuclear vehicles
for each side, with a subceiling of 1,320 that could be MIRV'd.

The SALT II negotiations were completed during the administration of Jimmy Carter, but only after a series of tense
and acrimonious exchanges between the two sides. After a
comprehensive review of the negotiations, President Carter's
advisers came up with a comprehensive proposal to reduce
strategic nuclear launchers well below the figures agreed to at
Vladivostok. Presented to the Soviets in March, 1977, the new
plan was harshly rejected by the Soviet leaders, who charged
the United States with repudiating previously agreed-upon
positions. That setback proved to be only temporary, however.
In October, 1977, when the five-year period of the SALT I
moratorium expired, both countries agreed to abide by its
terms, although not formally bound to do so. By May, 1979,
the text of the SALT II treaty was completed, and Carter and
Brezhnev journeyed to Vienna to sign the treaty in an elaborate
ceremony.

The SALT II treaty was a lengthy and complex agreement,
comprising four parts. The treaty itself contained numerical
ceilings and subceilings on launchers and was to remain in
force until 1985. SALT II set a limit of 2,400 for strategic
launchers (ICBMs, SLBMs, and strategic bombers), to decline
to 2,250 by 1981. This provision would have required the
Soviet Union to dismantle 250 launchers but would not have
affected the United States' arsenal, which was then under the
ceiling. A subceiling of 1,320 was established for MIRV'd
systems; within that limit, a further subceiling of 1,200 applied
to all ballistic missiles and a further subceiling of 820 was set
for all ICBMs. Other provisions in the treaty placed qualitative
restraints on the development of new weapons and prohibited
mobile launchers for heavy missiles. To meet U.S. demands,
limits were set for the number of warheads that could be
placed in MIRV'd missiles; to satisfy the Soviets, limits were
placed on the number of cruise missiles that could be deployed
on an airplane. A protocol to the treaty provided for limitations
that would apply for only two years. In a separate document,
Leonid Brezhnev promised to build no more than thirty Back-

fire bombers per year. The final part of the treaty specified principles for future SALT negotiations.

For all the effort that went into the negotiations, SALT II was never ratified. The single most important factor in derailing SALT II was the Soviet invasion of Afghanistan in December, 1979. In response to the invasion, President Carter withdrew the treaty from Senate consideration. Even before the Afghan crisis, opposition to the treaty had been building in the U.S. Congress and in the public at large. Support for arms control during the mid- to latter 1970's declined as a result of the collapse of détente in Soviet-United States relations. A major factor in the collapse was the spurt of Soviet activism in the Third World, particularly in Africa. Between 1975 and 1978, the Soviet Union and Cuba became active participants in the civil and regional wars in Angola and the Horn of Africa. Their involvement contributed to the strengthening of Marxist, anti-Western regimes in Angola and Ethiopia, which led to an intensification of anti-Soviet sentiment in the United States. In the face of that sentiment, the prospects for arms control declined.

There was still widespread agreement in Washington and Moscow that the substance of SALT II served the security interests of both countries well. As a result, both governments agreed that they would continue to observe its provisions, if the other side continued to do so. This observance continued even under the administration of Ronald Reagan, who, in his presidential campaign, called SALT II fatally flawed. The failure of SALT II's ratification was only a temporary setback in the long effort to reduce the nuclear arsenals of the two superpowers. U.S.-Soviet relations changed dramatically during the 1980's, following the accession to power of Mikhail Gorbachev in Moscow. In the 1980's and 1990's, treaties such as the INF (intermediate nuclear force) and START I and START II (strategic arms reduction talks) agreements brought about nuclear arms reduction unimaginable during the 1970's.

—*Joseph L. Nogee*

ADDITIONAL READING:

Blacker, Coit D. "The Soviets and Arms Control: The SALT II Negotiations, November 1972-March 1976." In *The Other Side of the Table: The Soviet Approach to Arms Control*, edited by Michael Mandelbaum. New York: Council on Foreign Relations Press, 1990. Provides detailed description of Soviet objectives in SALT II.

Blacker, Coit D., and Gloria Duffy, eds. *International Arms Control, Issues and Agreements*. 2d ed. Stanford, Calif.: Stanford University Press, 1984. Detailed analysis of SALT II agreement and the agreements that preceded and followed it.

Bundy, McGeorge. *Danger and Survival: Choices About the Bomb in the First Fifty Years*. New York: Random House, 1988. A comprehensive and authoritative history of nuclear issues by an important policymaker.

Flanagan, Stephen J. "SALT II." In *Superpower Arms Control: Setting the Record Straight*, edited by Albert Carnesale and Richard N. Haass. Cambridge, Mass.: Ballinger, 1987. Focuses on the political context of U.S.-Soviet relations.

Talbott, Strobe. *Endgame: The Inside Story of SALT II*. New York: Harper & Row, 1979. A journalistic but reliable study of the domestic politics of SALT II.

U.S. Arms Control and Disarmament Agency. *Arms Control and Disarmament Agreements: Texts and Histories of Negotiations*. Washington, D.C.: Author, 1982. Contains official texts of SALT and all prior arms control agreements.

SEE ALSO: 1973, Détente with the Soviet Union; 1985, U.S.-Soviet Summit; 1987, INF Treaty Is Signed; 1993, START II Is Signed.

1980 ■ ABSCAM AFFAIR: *the conviction of seven members of Congress on bribery-related charges spurs public cynicism toward elected officials*

DATE: February, 1980-March 11, 1982
LOCALE: Washington, D.C.
CATEGORY: Government and politics
KEY FIGURES:

John W. Jenrette, Jr. (born 1936), Democratic congressman from South Carolina

Richard Kelly (born 1924), Republican congressman from Florida

Raymond F. Lederer (born 1938), Democratic congressman from Pennsylvania

John M. Murphy (born 1926), Democratic congressman from New York

John P. Murtha (born 1932), Democratic congressman from Pennsylvania

Michael J. "Ozzie" Myers (born 1943), Democratic congressman from Pennsylvania

Larry Pressler (born 1942), Democratic senator from South Dakota

Frank Thompson, Jr. (born 1918), Democratic congressman from New Jersey

Harrison A. "Pete" Williams (born 1919), Democratic senator from New Jersey

SUMMARY OF EVENT. In February, 1980, the U.S. public was shocked to learn that the Federal Bureau of Investigation (FBI) had conducted a probe that allegedly had uncovered serious violations of the law by at least seven members of Congress and other politicians. During the probe, undercover agents had posed as Arab men operating a business called Abdul Enterprises. These agents met with members of Congress and local officials, offering them cash or other bribes in exchange for political favors. As hidden video cameras were filming the transactions, several congressmen cheerfully accepted bribes, while promising to help Abdul Enterprises and to introduce legislation to help one of the corporate officers achieve permanent residency in the United States.

The first Abscam trial took place before a jury in Brooklyn, New York, in August of 1980. The defendants included Representative Michael "Ozzie" Myers of Pennsylvania, a mayor, a city council member, and an attorney. Congressman Myers admitted to taking the cash gift but said the payment did not constitute bribery, because he never intended to make good his promise to help the supposed Arab business executives. The jury, however, was impressed by video footage showing Myers accepting fifty thousand dollars in cash, then coming back later and asking for more. After ten hours of deliberation, the jury returned a guilty verdict. The House of Representatives moved quickly to expel Myers. By a vote of 376-30, Myers became the first member of Congress to be expelled since 1861, and the only one to be expelled for a cause other than treason.

Subsequent trials added to the public's growing revulsion toward dishonesty in government. At the trial of Congressman John W. Jenrette, Jr., a videotape showed Jenrette discussing a bribe, then joking that he had larceny in his blood. His defense attorneys stressed that Jenrette had drinking problems. Jenrette was convicted, but he insisted on continuing his bid for reelection. His South Carolina constituents repudiated him at the polls, and Jenrette resigned before his term's end to prevent formal expulsion by the House of Representatives.

Public cynicism reached a new height with the trial of Congressman Richard Kelly of Florida. Kelly admitted to receiving twenty-five thousand dollars from undercover agents, but he claimed that he had done so to enable him to conduct his own investigation. When incredulous reporters asked why he had never reported the incidents to law enforcement officers, Kelly replied that he had not wanted to blow his cover. Images of Kelly gleefully stuffing currency into his pockets stayed in the jury's minds, however, and Kelly was convicted. Kelly's reelection bid was halted by his defeat in the Republican primary before his conviction.

Three other members of the House of Representatives also were convicted in Abscam cases: Raymond F. Lederer and Frank Thompson, Jr., of New Jersey, and John M. Murphy of New York. Thompson and Murphy went down to defeat at the polls as their cases were moving to trial. Lederer was reelected, but he resigned to prevent his expulsion.

The case of the only U.S. senator caught up in the Abscam scandal moved forward slowly. Senator Harrison A. "Pete" Williams, unlike the members of the House of Representatives, was fortunate in that he was not up for reelection in 1980. Williams' case was more complex than that of the other defendants, because he did not receive cash in exchange for his promises to help a supposed sheik to secure permanent residency status. Instead, Williams received what were purported to be shares of stock, as well as a favorable business loan from the corporation represented by the stock shares. Williams defended himself by saying that he had believed the shares of stock to be worthless, while he believed the loan was a legitimate loan and not a bribe. The senator was convicted, however; after a number of delays, he resigned on March 11, 1982, hours before the Senate was expected to expel him. If he had been expelled, Williams would have been the first senator ousted since the Civil War.

There were few bright spots in the Abscam story. One member of the House, John P. Murtha of Pennsylvania, did meet with the FBI undercover agents and did discuss bribes and favors, but he stopped short of accepting a bribe. The only hero in the story appeared to be Senator Larry Pressler of South Dakota. Pressler was captured on videotape telling the agents posing as Arab business executives that the steps they were suggesting were wrong and illegal. Pressler finally left the meeting in disgust. Yet the fact remained that seven members of Congress had been convicted, fined, and sent to jail. All were either defeated by their constituents, resigned under pressure, or (in the case of Myers) expelled.

The six House members and one senator who were convicted had few supporters. Yet the FBI also came under criticism, and few embraced this sting operation unreservedly. Many feared that in the Abscam probe the FBI had initiated crimes, rather than working to prevent crime. Did Abscam fall under the legal term "entrapment"? Criminal defendants may win acquittal if they can prove that they had no previous disposition to violate the law, but had been pressured into such violations by the urging of law officers. Various appeals courts ruled repeatedly that Abscam did not constitute entrapment. Other critics feared that this kind of case could be used to punish members of one particular political party or faction. At least one Abscam defendant claimed his prosecution was motivated by the desire of officials in President Jimmy Carter's administration to punish him for supporting Edward Kennedy's bid for the 1980 Democratic presidential nomination. Arab Americans complained that Abscam was founded on U.S. stereotypes about Arab culture, and made those stereotypes worse.

Images of members of Congress stuffing their pockets with cash, joking all the while, soured citizens' image of the federal government at a time when it was still tarnished from the Watergate scandal and the resignation of President Richard Nixon only six years earlier. The public's perception of Congress was darkened even further by a number of unrelated charges, indictments, and convictions at the same time the Abscam cases were moving forward. The charges against various members of the House of Representatives included financial irregularities, accepting illegal gifts, pocketing parts of employees' salaries, buying votes, drug possession, and various sex-related crimes. Coupled with scandals within the Reagan Administration shortly after Abscam, the net effect of Abscam and the other congressional scandals was to lower public's esteem of their elected officials. —*Stephen Cresswell*

ADDITIONAL READING:

Berman, Jerry J. *The Lessons of Abscam*. Washington, D.C.: American Civil Liberties Union, 1982. Takes a critical look at Abscam and the potential use of Abscam-like tactics to suppress civil liberties.

Caplan, Gerald M., ed. *Abscam Ethics: Moral Issues and Deception in Law Enforcement*. Cambridge, Mass.: Ballinger, 1983. The authors of seven essays use Abscam as the starting point for their analyses of the ethical issues of entrapment, enticement, and deception by law officers.

Congressional Quarterly Almanac. Washington, D.C.: Congressional Quarterly, 1980-1983. This annual reference book is the best source of detailed information about the Abscam cases.

Greene, Robert W. *The Sting Man: Inside Abscam.* New York: Dutton, 1981. A first-person account by a key participant in the Abscam cases.

Shaheen, Jack G. *Abscam: Arabiaphobia in America.* Washington, D.C.: American-Arab Anti-Discrimination Committee, 1980. Scores the Justice Department for using U.S. stereotypes of Arab culture as a tool in the Abscam cases.

U.S. Senate. 97th Congress. 2d session. *Final Report of the Select Committee to Study Law Enforcement Undercover Activities of Components of the Department of Justice to the U.S. Senate.* Senate Report 97-682. Washington, D.C.: Government Printing Office, 1981. A basic compendium of primary sources. Contains analysis of ethical issues raised by the Abscam prosecutions.

SEE ALSO: 1972, Watergate Affair; 1986, Iran-Contra Scandal.

1980 ■ MARIEL BOAT LIFT: *a massive influx of Cuban refugees provokes an agonizing reappraisal of U.S. refugee policy*

DATE: April 1-September, 1980
LOCALE: Cuba, Florida, and waters between
CATEGORIES: Diplomacy and international relations; Immigration; Latino American history
KEY FIGURES:
James Earl "Jimmy" Carter (born 1924), thirty-ninth president of the United States, 1977-1981
Fidel Castro (born 1926 or 1927), revolutionary leader and dictator of Cuba
Robert "Bob" Graham (born 1936), governor of Florida
Wayne S. Smith, head of the U.S. Interests Section in Havana
Peter Tarnoff, U.S. Department of State negotiator
SUMMARY OF EVENT. After Fidel Castro became dictator of Cuba in January, 1959, relations between the United States and Cuba steadily deteriorated, as Castro turned his country into a communist state allied with the Soviet Union, the United States' rival in the Cold War (1947-1991). Diplomatic relations with Cuba were broken, and an economic embargo was imposed upon the country.

The communization of Cuba alienated Cubans as well. From 1959 to 1962 (when Castro halted all further airplane flights from the island), about two hundred thousand Cubans fled their homeland, most of them settling in Miami, Florida. In late 1965, special freedom flights of refugees were organized with the cooperation of the Castro government; although registration for these flights was closed off in 1966, the flights themselves continued until 1973. The early refugees were

disproportionately from Cuba's professional and white-collar classes; with extensive financial assistance from the U.S. government, and their own hard work, they achieved a remarkable level of prosperity in the United States in a short time.

Hopes for rapprochement with Castro rose in 1977, when Jimmy Carter became president of the United States. A United States Interests section of the Swiss Embassy was established in Havana, under a State Department official, Wayne Smith, to handle relations between Cuba and the United States. When Castro persisted in his military intervention in Angola, however, plans for lifting the U.S. embargo were shelved indefinitely. In October, 1979, relations with Castro deteriorated when Washington, D.C., welcomed the hijacker of a Cuban boat as a freedom fighter.

Between January and March, 1979, Castro, to polish his image abroad and to gain badly needed foreign currency, allowed more than 115,000 Cuban Americans to visit their relatives in Cuba. The apparent prosperity of the Cuban Americans caused discontent among Cubans on the island because of the austerity and lack of consumer choices in the island's socialist economy.

On April 1, 1980, six Cubans commandeered a city bus and drove it through the gate of the Peruvian Embassy, demanding asylum; in the ensuing melee, one Cuban guard was killed. Castro responded by removing the police guards from the embassy. By April 9, 1980, about ten thousand more Cubans had crowded into the embassy, demanding the right of political asylum. On April 16, with Castro's permission, airplane flights began to take asylum-seekers to Costa Rica; on April 18, however, Castro, embarrassed by the blow to his image abroad, suddenly canceled these flights. On April 20, he opened the port of Mariel to all those who wished to leave the island and to anyone who wished to ferry discontented Cubans to Florida.

Persons sympathetic to the plight of the would-be emigrants chartered boats to sail to Mariel, pick up those who wanted to leave, and bring them to Key West, Florida. Once in Mariel, the boats' skippers were forced to accept everyone whom Cuban authorities wanted to be rid of, including criminals, the mentally ill, and homosexuals. Because some of the boats were not seaworthy, a tragic accident was always a possibility; and the U.S. Coast Guard sometimes had to rescue refugees from boats in danger of sinking.

President Carter, distracted by the Iranian hostage crisis and the worsening of relations with the Soviet Union after the latter's occupation of Afghanistan, vacillated in regard to the boat lift. In a speech given on May 5, Carter urged the people of the United States to welcome the refugees with open arms. On May 14, however, he threatened criminal penalties for those who used boats to pick up Cubans, and ordered the Coast Guard to stop the boat lift by arresting and fining the skippers and seizing the boats. Without cooperation from Castro, this order was largely ineffective. It was not until September 25, after hard bargaining between Castro and State Department negotiators Wayne Smith and Peter Tarnoff, that Castro ended the boat lift; several hundred would-be refugees who had missed the boat lift were allowed to take air flights out of Cuba in November.

Between April and September, 1980, south Florida bore the brunt of the tidal wave of refugees, which is estimated to have reached as high as 125,000. In the Miami area, social services, health services, schools, and law enforcement authorities found their resources strained to the breaking point by the sudden influx. Housing was suddenly in short supply; quite a few Mariel refugees in Florida had to sleep in the Orange Bowl, underneath a highway overpass, or in tent cities. On May 6, Carter, in response to pleas from Florida governor Bob Graham, declared Florida a disaster area, and authorized ten million dollars in relief for that state to help defray the cost of the refugee influx; U.S. Marines were sent to Florida to help process the refugees.

In June, 1980, President Carter ordered all those refugees who had not found relatives or others willing to sponsor them placed in detention camps in Wisconsin, Pennsylvania, and Arkansas. In Pennsylvania and Arkansas, the refugees, bored and fearful about their future, rioted. By October, the majority of the Marielitos had been released into various communities, and the detention camps were closed.

News of the riots fueled a growing backlash in U.S. public opinion against the Mariel refugees. The much-publicized presence of criminals among the refugees also helped generate a feeling of revulsion against the entire group: Marielitos were blamed for the upsurge in violent crime in Miami in 1981. In 1980, a year of economic downturn, many people in the United States feared that more Cuban refugees would mean higher unemployment.

Once released from custody, Marielitos faced a difficult adjustment. Unlike earlier Cuban refugees, the Marielitos did not arrive in the midst of general prosperity; they came when the twin plagues of inflation and recession were besetting a U.S. economy still struggling to absorb refugees from Vietnam, Laos, and Cambodia. Hence, Marielitos did not receive as much financial assistance from the federal government as earlier Cuban refugees. In addition, more of the Marielitos were poorly educated people from blue-collar backgrounds; more of them were single men without family ties; and a larger percentage of them were black or mulatto. Marielitos of all colors faced prejudice and discrimination, not merely from Euro-Americans but also from longer-settled Cuban Americans, who saw the Marielitos as insufficiently hard-working and feared that popular U.S. resentment of the Marielitos might rub off on them as well. In 1983, Marielitos in Miami had an unemployment rate of 27 percent; although the rate had been cut to 13 percent by 1986, they still lagged behind longer-settled Cuban Americans in employment and income.

Marielitos who ran afoul of the law quickly discovered that, however minor their offenses, they had fewer rights than native-born U.S. criminals. Marielitos who had criminal records in Cuba or who committed crimes in the United States faced incarceration for an indefinite term in federal prisons. In 1985,

President Ronald Reagan secured a promise from Castro to take back Marielito criminals; only a few hundred had been deported when Castro, enraged by U.S. sponsorship of Radio Marti—an anti-Castro radio broadcast—canceled the agreement. In November, 1987, a new agreement provided for the deportation to Cuba of Marielito criminals in return for the acceptance by the United States of Cuban political prisoners; upon hearing of the agreement, Marielitos held in federal prisons in Oakdale, Louisiana, and Atlanta, Georgia, rioted, taking hostages. The riots ended only when the Reagan Administration promised that no prisoner would be sent back to Cuba without individual consideration on his or her case, and that some of those whose offenses were relatively minor would be released into the community. In 1995, however, eighteen hundred Marielitos were still incarcerated in federal prisons.

When the Mariel boat lift began, Islamic militants in Iran had already publicly humiliated the United States government by seizing and holding captive U.S. diplomatic personnel. The seemingly uncontrollable Cuban refugee influx came to be seen as a symbol, not of the bankruptcy of Communism, but of Carter's alleged ineptitude in conducting U.S. foreign policy. U.S. voters' anger over the refugee influx, together with widespread frustration over economic recession and the Iranian hostage crisis, helped doom Carter's bid for reelection in November, 1980.

The Mariel boat lift of 1980 revived xenophobia among people in the United States. Until 1980, much of the U.S. public had seen Cuban refugees as courageous freedom fighters, comparable to Czechs or Hungarians fleeing Soviet tanks rather than to Puerto Ricans or Mexicans fleeing poverty; the presence of criminals and misfits among the Marielitos shattered the benign Cuban stereotype. After 1980, sentiment would build steadily for reducing the number of immigrants and refugees admitted into the United States. The ultimate consequence of the Mariel boat lift of 1980 was President Bill Clinton's decision in August, 1994, when faced with a new exodus from Cuba, to eliminate the privileged status of Cuban asylum-seekers.

—*Paul D. Mageli*

ADDITIONAL READING:

Hamm, Mark S. *The Abandoned Ones: The Imprisonment and Uprising of the Mariel Boat People*. Boston, Mass.: Northeastern University Press, 1995. The best study to date of the Marielito prison riots of 1987; also contains much information on the 1980 boat lift itself. Argues that federal policy denied the prisoners basic human rights. Chronology; endnotes; bibliography; index.

Larzelere, Alex. *Castro's Ploy, America's Dilemma: The 1980 Cuban Boat Lift*. Washington, D.C.: National Defense University Press, 1988. A detailed study on the boat lift, especially valuable for its look at the decision-making process within the Carter Administration. Relies heavily on interviews conducted in 1986 with Carter-era officials. Chronology; maps; figures; photographs; endnotes; index.

Loescher, Gil, and John A. Scanlan. *Calculated Kindness:*

Refugees and America's Half-Open Door, 1945-Present. New York: Free Press, 1986. Chapter nine examines the effect of the Mariel boat lift on the shaping of U.S. refugee policy in general. Criticizes Carter's response to the boat lift as indecisive. Endnotes; bibliography; index.

Pedraza-Bailey, Silvia. *Political and Economic Migrants in America: Cubans and Mexicans.* Austin: University of Texas Press, 1985. Chapter two compares the demographic portrait of the Marielitos with that of earlier Cuban refugees. Explains why the proportion of Afro-Cubans among the Marielitos was greater than in previous refugee flows. Endnotes; bibliography; index.

Portes, Alejandro, and Alex Stepick. *City on the Edge: The Transformation of Miami.* Berkeley: University of California Press, 1993. Chapter two shows that Miami's English-speaking whites and better-established Cuban Americans were both guilty of prejudice and discrimination against Marielitos. One of the few deep studies of the Marielitos' adjustment problems; regional focus, however, limits the book's usefulness for those interested in the Marielito experience throughout the United States. Map; tables; bibliography; index.

Smith, Wayne S. *The Closest of Enemies: A Personal and Diplomatic History of the Castro Years.* New York: W. W. Norton, 1987. Chapter eight provides a first-hand account of the intergovernmental talks that ended the boat lift. One must be skeptical, however, of the author's tendency to blame U.S. policy failures on his superiors' refusal to follow his advice. Photographs; endnotes; index.

SEE ALSO: 1980, Miami Riots.

1980 ■ MIAMI RIOTS: *simmering racial and ethnic hostility explodes under pressures from new immigration*

DATE: May 17-19, 1980
LOCALE: Miami, Florida
CATEGORIES: African American history; Immigration; Latino American history; Wars, uprisings, and civil unrest
KEY FIGURES:
Maurice Ferre (born 1935), mayor of Miami
Robert "Bob" Graham (born 1936), governor of Florida
Arthur McDuffie (1947?-1979), insurance salesman and victim of police brutality
Janet Reno (born 1938), state attorney for Dade County
SUMMARY OF EVENT. The Miami riots of 1980 constituted the most murderous urban disorder in the United States since the 1960's. The random killing of whites, not merely the looting of stores, was the goal of the rioters. Yet if the excesses of the rioters were terrible, the provocation that moved them to these acts was also severe. The roots of the violence lay deep in the past.

African Americans had lived in Miami, Florida, since the founding of the city in 1896. As in other Southern states,

blacks were subjected to legalized segregation and discrimination for many years. In the 1950's and 1960's, because of their relative lack of political power, Miami's African Americans were unable to prevent a superhighway from being built through the hitherto thriving black neighborhood of Overtown, displacing many of the inhabitants into a newer ghetto, Liberty City. In 1980, Miami's African American middle class was small compared with that of other metropolitan areas; unemployment among African Americans in Liberty City was 40 percent, and unemployment among the youth of that ghetto was even higher, despite the fact that Dade County (in which Miami was located) was more prosperous than the nation as a whole. Destitute single-parent African American families were common.

In another Southern city, Atlanta, Georgia, African Americans gradually had gained greater political power: An African American mayor had been elected in 1973 and blacks had gained greater access to employment opportunities in local government. However, in Dade County in 1980, African Americans comprised only about 16 percent of the registered voters. African Americans were stymied in attempts to achieve political power on the local level by the fragmentation of the main black neighborhood, Liberty City, between two governments: that of the city of Miami, and that of Dade County, which had jurisdiction over that part of Liberty City outside the Miami city limits. The legislative bodies of both the city of Miami and of Dade County were elected on an at-large basis, further retarding the growth of African American political power. In February, 1980, the relative political powerlessness of African Americans was emphasized when one of the few black officials at the county level, school superintendent Johnny Jones, was convicted of stealing public funds in a trial many African Americans believed to be unfair.

From 1959 on, south Florida had experienced an influx of Cuban refugees; African Americans in Miami came to see these refugees as yet another obstacle to their progress. Before 1980, most Cuban refugees were of white (Spanish) origin; many were from the upper economic and educational strata of the island. The refugees presented African Americans with unwelcome competition for jobs and housing; the refugees' entrepreneurial success soon far outpaced the accomplishments of African American business operators. African Americans resented what they saw as the generous financial benefits bestowed by the federal government on the refugees, as compared with the meager assistance offered to poor United States-born blacks. By the late 1970's, Cubans were vying with African Americans in both the political and economic spheres. Although the frustration of having to compete with foreigners probably helped fuel the fury of the rioters in 1980, the immediate causes of the disturbance were an especially outrageous instance of police brutality and the failure of the judicial system to punish the perpetrators.

In all metropolitan communities, police have the right to use force as a last resort to compel citizens to obey lawful orders. In many urban areas of the United States in the second half of the twentieth century, however, racial differences between the police and the citizens had led to bitter disputes over police exercise of the use of force. Miami, Florida, where police brutality against African Americans had a long history, was one such city.

That part of Liberty City within the Miami city limits was patrolled by the Miami Police Department (MPD); that outside of Miami's boundaries, by the Public Safety Department (PSD) of Dade County. On December 17, 1979, Arthur McDuffie, a thirty-three-year-old African American insurance agent with no criminal record, was riding along the highway on his motorcycle when several officers of the PSD ordered him to stop. When he refused to do so, he was pursued; when captured, he was beaten severely with nightsticks and heavy flashlights. McDuffie died a few days later from the injuries he had sustained at the hands of the police. This was the last of several incidents of alleged police brutality in Dade County in 1979: These included the shooting death of a teenager in Hialeah; the alleged sexual abuse of a prepubescent African American girl by a white police officer; and the severe beating administered by police to a black schoolteacher, after the police had raided his house in search of illicit drugs.

The state attorney for Dade County, Janet Reno, prepared a case against four Dade County police officers who had beaten McDuffie. When the case was brought to trial, on March 31, 1980, it was in the town of Tampa, on the state's gulf coast; it was believed that the officers could not get a fair trial in Miami. Because of peremptory challenges by the defense attorney, the jury before which the case was tried was all white. The jury's decision, handed down on the hot, dry afternoon of Saturday, May 17, 1980, shocked Miami's African American community: The police officers were acquitted of all charges.

In the early evening hours of May 17, the anger of the black Miamians boiled over into violence, rocks began to fly, and mobs began to attack individuals. Later that evening, after a mob attempt to set fire to the Metro Justice Building was barely repulsed, the governor of Florida, Bob Graham, ordered the National Guard sent to Miami; it did not arrive in full force, however, until Tuesday. It was not until May 23 that the situation was returned to normal. As a result of the riots, eighteen people died; hundreds were injured: there was eighty million dollars' worth of property damage; and eleven hundred people were arrested. Many Miami businesses were burned: African American, Cuban, and native-born white business owners all suffered.

Major arteries of traffic, used by motorists of all races and ethnic backgrounds, ran through Liberty City, In the evening hours of May 17, several white motorists, presumably unaware of the verdict, drove through that neighborhood, where they encountered maddened crowds, composed mostly of young people, bent on revenge. About 250 whites were injured that night in attacks by rioters; seven whites died as a result of the injuries sustained. Of those who died, one middle-aged woman perished from severe burns when her car was set afire; a young sales clerk, a teen-ager, and a sixty-three-year-old

Cuban refugee butcher died as the result of severe beatings. The reign of terror that night was mitigated only by the willingness of some courageous African Americans to rescue persons threatened by the mobs. The deliberate attacks on whites distinguished the Miami riot from the urban riots of the late 1960's, in which most deaths had occurred by accident.

In the days following that bloody Saturday, blacks were riot victims as well. Some of those killed were rioters; others were law-abiding individuals mistaken for rioters by the police; still others appear to have been random shooting victims of unknown white assailants. Most Miami-area African Americans were neither rioters, nor heroes, nor victims; they simply waited for the disturbances to end.

The McDuffie riot seemed, for a while, to threaten Reno's career. A Dade County Citizens' Committee, appointed by Governor Graham on May 23, 1980, to investigate the causes of the riots, issued a report in October, 1980, that criticized Reno's handling of the prosecution of the police officers from March through May of 1980, as well as her treatment of other racially sensitive police brutality cases that arose in 1979. At the time of the May, 1980, verdict, and for some time thereafter, many Miami-area African Americans accused Reno, probably unfairly, of being a racist. She eventually succeeded both in mending her political fences with the African American community and in being reelected as state attorney for Dade County; in February, 1993, she was appointed attorney general of the United States.

In the decade after the riot, the PSD tried to develop ways to train its officers to use violence less often. Both the Miami and Dade County police departments also made efforts to hire more African Americans. During the 1980's, local businessmen worked to help Miami's African American entrepreneurs. As of 1995, however, the latter were still not as prosperous, on the average, as Miami's Cuban entrepreneurs, and the poverty rate of African Americans in Miami remained high. In the 1980's, African Americans gained slightly greater influence in the area's politics: For example, an African American was named chief of police of the city of Miami. In 1985, Puerto Rican-born Maurice Ferre, who had been mayor of Miami since 1973, was replaced by Cuban-born Xavier Suarez. As of 1996, however, no African American had been elected mayor of Miami.

For the United States, the Miami Riot of 1980 ended twelve years of freedom from major urban riots; it was not, however, accompanied by rioting in any other U.S. city. Riots broke out again in Miami's African American ghetto in December, 1982; in January, 1989 (when a Hispanic police officer, William Lozano, shot an African American motorcyclist to death); and in July, 1995. The later riots, however, were not as costly in lives or property as the 1980 outburst; and in May, 1993, Lozano's acquittal by a jury in Orlando was not followed by violence.

The Miami Riot of 1980 was an alarm bell, warning the United States of the sharp tensions between the races that still persisted a decade and a half after the legislative victories of the Civil Rights movement, and of the combustible possibilities that existed wherever blacks, native-born whites, and Hispanic immigrants lived side by side. The triggering of the Miami riot by an unpopular jury verdict rather than by immediate actions by the police foreshadowed the trajectory of the disastrous riot of April 29-May 1, 1992, in Los Angeles, California. —*Paul D. Mageli*

ADDITIONAL READING:

Anderson, Paul. *Janet Reno: Doing the Right Thing*. New York: John Wiley and Sons, 1994. Although this biography is otherwise nearly hagiographic in tone, the author does criticize Reno's strategy for prosecuting the police officers in 1980. Offers insights into the character and personality of a key player in the 1980 events. Photographs; index.

Mohl, Raymond A. "On the Edge: Blacks and Hispanics in Metropolitan Miami Since 1959." *Florida Historical Quarterly* 69, no. 1 (July, 1990): 37-56. Traces the riots of 1980, 1982, and 1989 back to African American anger at Cuban success. Comparing African Americans in Miami with those elsewhere in the Civil Rights-era South, concludes that African Americans' complaints of being unfairly displaced by Cubans were justified. Based on newspapers and secondary sources. Footnotes.

Porter, Bruce, and Marvin Dunn. *The Miami Riot of 1980: Crossing the Bounds*. Lexington, Mass.: D. C. Heath, 1984. The only detailed book-length account of the 1980 riot to date. Glosses over neither the brutality of white police officers nor the cruelty of black rioters. Based on extensive interviews. Photographs; map; figures; tables; chapter notes; index.

Portes, Alejandro, and Alex Stepick. *City on the Edge: The Transformation of Miami*. Berkeley: University of California Press, 1993. Two sociologists see the May, 1980, riot as part of a long process by which Miami-area blacks came to see Cuban refugees, as well as native-born whites, as their oppressors. Analyzes statistical data and argues that the economic displacement of African Americans by pre-1980 Cuban refugees was not as great as blacks believed. Based on interviews, newspapers, and census data. Tables; figures; photographs; endnotes; index.

Skolnick, Jerome H., and James J. Fyfe. *Above the Law: Police and the Excessive Use of Force*. New York: Free Press, 1993. Compares the McDuffie incident with cases of police brutality in other U.S. cities and provides a good account of efforts within the Dade County police department, after 1980, to control the use of force by police. Endnotes; index.

Stack, John F., Jr., and Christopher Warren. "The Reform Tradition and Ethnic Politics: Metropolitan Miami Confronts the 1990's." In *Miami Now! Immigration, Ethnicity, and Social Change*, edited by Guillermo J. Grenier and Alex Stepick III. Gainesville: University Press of Florida, 1992. Asserts that the riots of 1980, 1982, and 1989 were predictable reactions to Miami blacks' relative political powerlessness, which the authors trace to a system of local government designed by white reformers for reasons unrelated to race. Figures; endnotes; bibliography; index.

SEE ALSO: 1943, Urban Race Riots; 1965, Watts Riot; 1968, Chicago Riots; 1980, Mariel Boat Lift; 1992, Los Angeles Riots.

1980 ■ REAGAN IS ELECTED PRESIDENT: *the birth of a reassessment of the government's role and the ascendancy of conservative forces in the Republican Party and the nation as a whole*

DATE: November 4, 1980
LOCALE: United States
CATEGORY: Government and politics
KEY FIGURES:
John Bayard Anderson (born 1922), Independent Party candidate
George Herbert Walker Bush (born 1924), Republican candidate and vice president
James Earl "Jimmy" Carter, Jr. (born 1924), thirty-ninth president of the United States, 1977-1981
Ronald Wilson Reagan (born 1911), fortieth president of the United States, 1981-1989

SUMMARY OF EVENT. The election of former California governor Ronald Reagan to the presidency was a major event in U.S. political history. It offered the first compelling evidence that the U.S. electorate was in the process of a realignment of the national majority assembled by Franklin Delano Roosevelt in 1932. Realignments in U.S. politics often are generational and reflect the emergence of new voters, new coalitions and voting patterns, and new issues that point to a changing political consensus over public policy. These long-standing trends crystallized in the 1980 election, in which a narrowly elected incumbent president was challenged for renomination, and there was deep unrest among the electorate.

In order to understand Reagan's election in 1980, one should note that there was great dissatisfaction with his predecessor's presidency. Jimmy Carter's Democratic administration was marred by weak appraisals of his performance in public opinion polls: Only 21 percent of the population gave him favorable ratings in July, 1980. This reaction to his administration reflected a record of high inflation, high unemployment rates, and economic challenges from foreign business. Carter also was confronted by an energy crisis, challenges from the Organization of Petroleum Exporting Countries (OPEC) in the Middle East, the fall of Shah of Iran Mohammad Reza Pahlavi, the subsequent taking of U.S. hostages, and the Soviet Union's invasion of Afghanistan. These events combined to create a sense of frustration and even humiliation among voters, resulting in challenges to Carter's renomination from California governor Jerry Brown and Massachusetts senator Edward Kennedy.

Given the vulnerability of President Carter, a large number of Republicans sought the nomination in 1980. Competing against Reagan were Representatives John Anderson and Philip Crane; Senators Howard Baker and Robert Dole; John Connelly, a former governor of Texas and a former Democrat; and former ambassador George Bush. After the Iowa caucuses and the New Hampshire primary, all but Bush and Anderson withdrew. Neither was able to sustain his drive, because of party infighting among moderates and the solidarity of the party's conservatives. Anderson, however, had attracted a large following among younger voters, independents, moderate Republicans, and even Democrats. He became an Independent candidate, running on the platform of "national unity." With Democrat Patrick Lucey as his running mate, Anderson appeared on the ballot in all fifty states. The popularity of his third party indexed the dissatisfaction of voters and threatened the possibility of a president who did not have a majority of the popular vote.

By May of 1980, however, Reagan had sewn up the Republican nomination and was nominated almost unanimously at the Republican convention. He selected George Bush as his running mate. The campaign was bitter, with extreme rhetoric on all sides. There were sharp differences between the two major candidates on abortion, the ratification of the Equal Rights Amendment for women, welfare, education, taxes, economic policy, and foreign affairs. Nevertheless, the election became a referendum on the Carter years. Ronald Reagan was one of the most ideological candidates in history but succeeded in identifying himself with the fundamental U.S. values of individualism and self-reliance and a strong sense of optimism about the future. In his final television speech before the election, Reagan promised a "new era of reform" and an "era of national renewal."

Reagan won in forty-four states, with 489 electoral votes to Carter's 49—the third largest electoral college victory in modern times. Reagan received 43,901,812 votes, for 50.7 percent of the total for all three major candidates. President Carter received 35,483,820 votes (40.6 percent). Anderson received no electoral votes and 6.6 percent of the popular vote. Although Reagan enjoyed an overwhelming victory in the electoral college, he had won only a bare majority in terms of the popular vote. The voter turnout was 52.6 percent of the voting-age population, the lowest since 1948. The Republicans also won control of the Senate for the first time since 1952, gaining twelve seats, and gained seats in the House of Representatives. Reagan's election was both a repudiation of the Carter Administration and a vote for a more conservative philosophy.

Demographic analysis of the presidential vote, based on election-day exit polls, shows that the African American vote was 11 percent for Reagan, 85 percent for Carter, and 3 percent for Anderson. Reagan received 55 percent of the white vote, with 36 percent going to Carter and 7 percent to Anderson. Of those identifying themselves as Hispanic, 56 percent voted for Carter, 35 percent for Reagan, and 8 percent for Anderson. Men gave 55 percent of their vote to Reagan, 36 percent to Carter, and 7 percent to Anderson; women voted 47 percent for Reagan, 45 percent for Carter, and 7 percent for Anderson.

Fortieth president of the United States Ronald Reagan, a former actor who proved to have a superior rapport with the media and the American people, returned Republican conservative idealism to the presidency, promising to cut big government and government spending. While successful in passing sweeping tax and budget reforms, including cuts in social programs, Reagan adhered to Cold War foreign policies that resulted in increased defense spending and a soaring federal budget deficit. (Library of Congress)

Ronald Reagan's election marked a significant change in U.S. public philosophy. The essence of this shift can be seen in a phrase from his inaugural address: "In the present crisis, government is not the solution to our problems; government is the problem. It is my intention to curb the size and influence of the federal establishment. . . ." Reagan was reelected in 1984 in a landslide victory over President Carter's vice president, Walter Mondale.

The eight years of the Reagan presidency were marked by several major events, achievements, and difficulties. In foreign affairs, Reagan's major goal was to challenge and engage the Soviet Union. The Reagan Doctrine attempted to do this by actively aiding anticommunist forces around the world and containing Soviet influence. These goals led to the support of rebels fighting in Afghanistan and to involvement in Latin America against Marxist insurgents. The support of anti-Sandinista forces (Contras) in Nicaragua and of any government with an anti-government stance proved a source of major controversy. During Reagan's administration the United States maintained an increased military presence in the Middle East and a willingness to use force to protect U.S. interests in that region. This policy led to confrontations with Syria and Libya, deployment of Marines in Lebanon, and clashes with Iran.

A consequence of the Reagan Doctrine was support for covert actions and the diversion of funds from arms sales to the Contras, which led to the Iran-Contra scandal, involving several highly placed government officials. Other major foreign policy events included the signing of the Intermediate Nuclear Forces Treaty, a important step toward reducing the number of nuclear weapons, and summit meetings with Soviet Union president Mikhail Gorbachev in Reykjavik, Iceland, and in Washington, D.C. These policies led to a large increase in defense spending and to programs such as the Strategic Defense Initiative (SDI, popularly known as "Star Wars"), aimed at defending against possible missile attacks.

Perhaps the most significant aspect of Reagan's domestic policy was his achievement of major tax cuts and other tax reforms, which he hoped would lead to less government spending. Reagan attempted an ambitious conservative agenda to refocus spending and policy priorities. He proposed cuts in discretionary spending in the general areas of education, welfare, and related programs. Nevertheless, government spending, the size of government, and the federal budget deficit all greatly increased during Reagan's presidency, in part because of increased defense spending, the expansion of Medicare, and the political difficulties of achieving cuts in popular programs for the poor, the elderly, and other constituency groups. Therefore, although Reagan achieved some success in slowing the rate of increase of spending, the cuts he implemented were offset by increases in other programs. Together with massive tax cuts, these factors contributed to an unprecedented increase in the federal deficit. In short, President Reagan was less than successful in his domestic agenda. He did change the nature of public policy debate but did not successfully legislate his conservative agenda. This may have been in part because of his style of disengagement from administrative detail, as well as political opposition.

President Reagan left office with nearly 68 percent of the population approving his performance. He survived an assassination attempt, policy failures, and political scandals. He remained popular because of his personality, his skillful use of the media, and his fundamental optimism. Perhaps most significant, he succeeded in his main goal, the redefinition of the role of government for the first time since the New Deal.

—Melvin Kulbicki

ADDITIONAL READING:

Barrett, Laurence I. *Gambling with History*. Garden City, N.Y.: Doubleday, 1983. A balanced account the 1980 election and Reagan's first two years in office, with emphasis on his personal convictions and ideology.

Berman, Larry, ed. *Looking Back on the Reagan Presidency*. Baltimore: The Johns Hopkins University Press, 1990. A collection of perspectives on Reagan's domestic and foreign policy failures and achievements.

Jones, Charles O., ed. *The Reagan Legacy: Promise and Performance*. Chatham, N.J.: Chatham House, 1988. Essays assessing the political and institutional strengths and weaknesses of Reagan's presidency.

Mayer, Jane, and Doyle McManus. *Landslide: The Unmaking of the President, 1984-1988*. Boston: Houghton Mifflin, 1988. An authoritative account of Reagan's reelection and the political difficulties in his second term.

Pomper, Gerald M., ed. *The Election of 1980: Reports and Interpretations*. Chatham, N.J.: Chatham House, 1981. Essays on the political context of the 1980 election. Excellent accounts of the difficulties affecting both political parties.

Sandoz, Ellis, and Cecil V. Crabb, eds. *A Tide of Discontent: The 1980 Elections and Their Meaning*. Washington, D.C.: Congressional Quarterly Press, 1981. Discusses the significance of Reagan's first presidential election, emphasizing analysis of the electorate's voting behavior.

SEE ALSO: 1973, Arab Oil Embargo and Energy Crisis; 1976, Carter Is Elected President; 1981, Reagan's Budget and Tax Reform; 1985, U.S.-Soviet Summit; 1986, Iran-Contra Scandal; 1987, INF Treaty Is Signed; 1988, Bush Is Elected President.

1981 ■ IBM MARKETS THE PERSONAL COMPUTER: *mass marketing of portable personal computers marks the beginning of a revolution in business practices and communications*

DATE: April, 1981

LOCALE: Boca Raton, Florida

CATEGORIES: Business and labor; Communications; Cultural and intellectual history; Science and technology

KEY FIGURES:

Frank Taylor Cary (born 1920), chairman of IBM's management committee

Phillip Donald Estridge (1935-1985), head of the IBM Entry Systems Division, charged with developing and marketing the personal computer

William H. "Bill" Gates (born 1955), head of Microsoft, a major developer of software

Timothy Paterson, head of Seattle Computer Products, author of the Q-DOS operating system

Marcian "Ted" Hoff (born 1937), inventor of the 4004 microprocessor chip

William Lowe, leading advocate and planner of the early IBM personal computer program

William B. Shockley (born 1910), developer of the theory of the junction transistor, which led to the field effect transistor

Ed Roberts, small businessman who developed the Altair 8800

Stephen Wozniak (born 1951), Hewlett-Packard engineer who developed the Apple computer

SUMMARY OF EVENT. Although the historical roots of computers lay in ancient calculating devices of Babylonia and centuries of gradual enlargement of information storage and processing, the personal computer (PC) is a distinctly modern development. Its immediate ancestors were the World War II-era computers developed out of military necessity, notably the huge British Colossus, an electronic computer that enabled a secret decoding system known as Ultra to decode German military plans.

Meanwhile, U.S. inventors at the Massachusetts Institute of Technology (MIT), the Stanford Research Institute, the Xerox Palo Alto Research Center, and the University of Pennsylvania, among others, reached new plateaus of computer technology. In 1946, an important breakthrough came with the ENIAC (Electronic Numerical Integrator and Calculator) at the University of Pennsylvania. It is considered the world's first general-purpose electronic computer, because the Colossus had a single military cryptographic purpose.

Military computers, like their postwar successors, were large, extremely expensive, and impractical for personal and routine business use. Widely marketable personal computers, or PCs, had to await the development of the transistor (1947-1948), which provided the miniature switches essential to computer, radio, television, and other electronic circuitry; and microprocessor silicon chips with the ability to use at least 32,000 (32K) bytes of memory operating in miniaturized circuits. The transistor emanated from the work of three U.S. physicists—Walter H. Brattain, John Bardeen, and William B. Shockley—at Bell Laboratories in New Jersey in 1947 and 1948. The trio shared the 1956 Nobel Prize for their work. Called the point-contact transistor, the first transistor proved to be seminal. The next year, Shockley developed the theory of the junction transistor, and by 1952 he had published the theory that made possible the field effect transistor, which is basic to miniaturized computer circuits.

Intel's 8080 microprocessor (1974), developed as an improved version of its 1972 8008 invented by Marcian (Ted) Hoff, could address 64K bytes of memory. It triggered a growing number of steadily improving Intel microprocessors and spurred other companies to develop their own.

An important catalyst in the early history of personal computers was a January, 1975, cover story in the hobbyist journal *Popular Electronics* that featured Ed Roberts and his new Altair 8800 computer kit. It had been built in a small storefront operation in Albuquerque, New Mexico by Micro Instrumentation Telemetry Systems (MITS), and it had been named, at the suggestion of Roberts' teenage daughter, for a fictitious planet on the popular television series *Star Trek*. The Altair 8800 sold for less than four hundred dollars in kit form without operational attachments, and it soon attracted phenomenal interest in developing a small, versatile computer for businesses and personal use. Roberts produced a simple computer that was hardly more than a box with a microprocessor, lights and toggle switches on the front, and a scant 256 bytes of memory. Among the many units that soon appeared, with accessories to make them practically functional, was the IMSAI, thirteen thousand of which were sold by 1978 to small businesses and hobbyists, making it the leader in world production.

By 1977, the Tandy Corporation (Radio Shack), Commodore, and the new Apple company, developed by Hewlett-Packard engineer Stephen Wozniak, had outdistanced the earlier personal computers with attractive, fully functional PCs. The Commodore PET, Tandy's TRS-80, and the Apple II had keyboards, extensive addressable memory, and software that enabled a wide range of functions. Apple II beat Commodore and Radio Shack to market and became the first major electronics company to produce a personal computer. Its computers were complete with keyboards and cassette storage devices.

IBM's production of personal computers began with internal divisions over its feasibility. Apple's stunning success bothered management committee chairman Frank Cary, because IBM had been the industry leader in the large mainframe computers used by the military and big corporations. After turning to Bill Lowe and other supporters, Cary and IBM finally made the commitment and, significantly, decided to focus on the end product rather than internal development of the operational software or hardware components; those would be assembled from various producers.

Thus, IBM's meteoric rise in the personal computer industry was based on earlier innovations by hobbyists, new and rapidly growing companies like Apple, and its own long history in computer technology. Large IBM computers already were pacesetting market items, backed by the strong guarantees of Big Blue, as IBM was known. By 1975, IBM had developed its Systems Network Architecture (SNA). SNA software ran in the host mainframe 370 system, closely linked with its 3705 communications controller, but it proved inadequate for the burgeoning microcomputer market, as numerous and better networking options followed quickly in the wake of the PC revolution.

IBM entered the small personal computer market in 1981 with its popular IBM PC and soon took a commanding lead in the industry. IBM's policy of buying components from other companies (as far away as Taiwan) and its securing of software arrangements with Bill Gates—one of the founders and the head of Microsoft—and Tim Paterson of Seattle Computer Products, who developed the disk operating system (DOS), gave the corporation distinct advantages, although it also meant that IBM missed some lucrative opportunities. Another important advantage was the widespread production of IBM-compatible computers and software. Under Phillip (Don) Estridge, IBM's Entry System Division, based in Boca Raton, Florida, directed the rapidly expanding PC production and marketing. As early as 1983, the IBM PC had become the industry standard, with more than one million computers in place.

If not the first, IBM's PC was the most influential in the market. The dramatic increase in computer use by businesses, governments, schools, colleges, and private individuals was spurred to a great degree by the availability of IBM-compatible units. In 1982, the IBM PC-XT—with its "hard" disk drive, resident in the computer, and memory expanded from the original PC's 64K to 256K—marked a significant upgrade. Only two years later, the PC-AT expanded memory to 512K, and in 1987, the PS/2 reached 1-2 megabytes (one megabyte equals 1,000 kilobytes). IBM did not take full control of the industry, as other companies—notably Apple—expanded their operations. IBM's market share peaked at about 24 percent, but its influence as the standard and major producer made it singularly influential. Serious problems plagued IBM in the late 1980's, as much of the small computer market passed it by, leading to restructuring under Chairman John F. Akers that did not solve many of the giant corporation's problems.

The personal computer was a revolution within a revolution that gave personal computers a central role in virtually every aspect of life in the industrialized countries, and IBM played a pivotal role in that transformation with both its mainframes and its personal computer line. PCs many times faster and smaller than the large mainframes were in one hundred million homes and businesses by the early 1990's, with promise that the number would increase. Prodigy, CompuServe, America Online, the World Wide Web, and other network interface systems drew hundreds of thousands of new customers into the "cyber world." People met friends, even marriage partners, through computer networks on the Internet. Small businesses and libraries increased their contacts geometrically, with access to a virtually endless array of resources. Scholars, poets, mothers, and scout leaders were among the millions who used computers to work, play, and study. Propelled by both technology and commercial interests, the personal computer became a global phenomenon, with long-range social, economic, intellectual, and even spiritual significance.

The impact of the personal computer eludes confident analysis. From business and medical records to home finances, from helping children with their school assignments to enabling people to meet dating partners, the PC has revolutionized contemporary life. Many people with communication handicaps are enabled by their personal computers to write via electronic mail (e-mail) and chat with others with increased confidence through computer networks. Others are developing their artistic skills, and millions more are finding entertainment, inspiration, and guidance.

The widespread use of personal computers is not an unqualified blessing. Computer networks can be, and are, abused both for criminal and morally questionable purposes such as pornography and extortion. The growth of the Internet has raised the perceived need for regulation, and thus another area of government responsibility and expense. Some critics worry that the use of PCs will lead to an erosion of privacy. Despite these dangers, however, the personal computer is here to stay. With it, unimaginable possibilities lie ahead for private individuals, schools and colleges, and small and large businesses to tap into the burgeoning information revolution that marks the dawning of the twenty-first century.   —*P. Ann Peake*

ADDITIONAL READING:

Bitter, Gary. *Computers in Today's World.* New York: John Wiley & Sons, 1984. Readable textbook on computer use

traces computer history through four basic stages, culminating in the age of personal computers.

Carroll, Paul. *Big Blues: The Unmaking of IBM.* New York: Crown, 1993. A lively history of IBM's personal computer industry from 1980 to 1993, and the economic and structural woes of IBM in the 1980's and early 1990's.

DeLamarter, Richard Thomas. *Big Blue: IBM's Use and Abuse of Power.* New York: Dodd, Mead, 1986. This hard-hitting analysis of IBM and its problems includes much valuable material on the background of T. J. Watson, the founder and chief executive of IBM for forty years, as well as the development of PC technology and markets. Argues that the computer industry needs more intense competition.

Forester, Tom. *High-Tech Society: The Story of the Information Technology Revolution.* Cambridge, Mass.: MIT Press, 1988. A popular overview; readable, comprehensive, and balanced in its approach.

Langlois, Richard N. "External Economies and Economic Progress: The Case of the Microcomputer Industry." *Business History Review* 66 (Spring, 1992): 1-50. Thoroughly chronicles the microcomputer industry, with focus on the broader economic factors affecting the computer industry. Includes valuable information on the evolution of personal computers.

Large, Peter. *The Micro Revolution Revisited.* Allanheld, N.J.: Rowman, 1984. With a rather unusual focus on the computer's effect on society and individual life, explains the basic technology of computers and points out dangers to computer users, such as threats to privacy and high-tech crime in the age of computer networks.

SEE ALSO: 1947, Invention of the Transistor; 1990's, Rise of the Internet.

1981 ■ FIRST AIDS CASES ARE REPORTED:
the escalating epidemic of a life-threatening virus changes the way people view sexual behavior, privacy issues, and public policy

DATE: June 5, 1981
LOCALE: North America
CATEGORY: Health and medicine
KEY FIGURES:

Anthony Stephen Fauci (born 1940), research scientist and administrator at the National Institute for Allergy and Infectious Diseases

Robert Charles Gallo (born 1937), research scientist and administrator at the National Cancer Institute in Tumor Cell Biology

Luc Montagnier (born 1932), French research scientist and professor at the Pasteur Institute

SUMMARY OF EVENT. On June 5, 1981, a brief note in the *Morbidity and Mortality Weekly Report* (*MMWR*) described five cases of pneumonia caused by *Pneumocystis carinii* in five homosexual men at three different hospitals in Los Angeles. The *MMWR* has been a vital week-to-week monitor of the nation's health and an active instrument for detecting new and unusual threats to public health—the first reports of Legionnaires' disease, Lyme disease, and other diseases were relayed there. If a new disease appeared in one location last week, news of it is disseminated this week, and next week, physicians elsewhere who have been alerted update the Centers for Disease Control (CDC) on the extent of its spread. *Pneumocystis* pneumonia (PCP) was rare and almost never found, except in patients with compromised immune systems. Such clusters of serious illness might be due to random chance, but could also be the vanguard of a new epidemic.

Suspicions increased in the next weeks, as ten additional cases, again among male homosexual patients, were confirmed by biopsy. Another uncommon disease, a cancer called Kaposi's sarcoma (KS), had been diagnosed in twenty-six homosexual men, two cases overlapping with the *Pneumocystis carinii* pneumonia cases. This was published in the July 4, 1981, *MMWR*, although it was "not clear if or how the clustering of KS, pneumocystis, and other serious diseases in homosexual men is related." By August 28, the *MMWR* scaled up concerns by reporting data on 108 persons with either or both diseases, noting that the data indicated "a common underlying factor" and announcing that state and local health departments were conducting active surveillance for additional cases, and a national case-control study was being implemented.

The CDC established a task force on Kaposi's sarcoma and opportunistic infections (KSOI), which reported the epidemiological aspects of the outbreak in the *New England Journal of Medicine* in 1982. The May, 1982, *MMWR* reported abnormal T-lymphocyte helper-to-suppressor ratios among a small sample of male homosexuals, indicating that something was causing a persistent problem with their immune systems. Since an immunodeficiency disease can result in varied problems, the *MMWR* ran brief case descriptions of diffuse, undifferentiated non-Hodgkins lymphoma found among homosexual males on June 4, 1982. The rapidly increasing numbers of KS, PCP, and related opportunistic infections were reported in the June 11 and 18 issues. Every week saw dramatic increases in the number of cases reported, as well as extensions to Haitians and persons with hemophilia.

On September 3, 1982, the *MMWR* declared that this group of clinical entities, previously called KSOI, would be called "acquired immune deficiency syndrome" (AIDS). By now, it was firmly suspected that the agent was blood-borne, and in the November *MMWR*, the CDC issued precautions and procedures for clinical and laboratory staff. In December, 1982, blood transfusion was appearing as a risk factor among the approximately 5 percent of AIDS cases occurring to those not in a known risk group. December *MMWR*s also reported infant cases. By January, 1983, cases of previously healthy women who had developed AIDS had accumulated; some were intravenous drug users—an emerging high-risk group—

but some were not, suggesting that AIDS could be transferred heterosexually. By June, 1983, 1,641 cases of AIDS had been reported to the CDC, only 109 of which were in women.

Luc Montagnier and other researchers at the Pasteur Institute in France had now isolated a virus from the lymph nodes of a male homosexual, which they called lymphadenopathy virus (LAV). In the United States, Robert Gallo was leading a research team that had investigated earlier human retroviruses, a type of virus that invaded cells and read the viral genetic code "backward" into the coding of the host cell. In mid-1983, Gallo and fellow researchers reported the isolation of a third human T-cell leukemia virus (HTLV) in AIDS cases, and by early 1984, Gallo's team concluded that HTLV-III was the sole primary cause of AIDS.

A prototype blood test for antibodies to the virus was available from Gallo's laboratory in early 1984 and was approved by the Food and Drug Administration (FDA) and put into effect one year later. The Pasteur Institute filed a patent for a test for AIDS shortly before the U.S. researchers filed a patent on a test for checking blood supplies for AIDS.

With names such as AIDS-related virus (ARV) also in print and joining HTLV-III and LAV, the scientific community moved to avoid further confusion by renaming the new agent "human immunodeficiency virus" (HIV). A second HIV, with a different genetic sequence, designated HIV-2, was soon discovered from West Africa, with its first U.S. case reported in 1987.

On August 1, 1985, the CDC refined the case definition of AIDS to exclude other known causes of cellular immunodeficiency. In 1987, because the $CD4^+$ lymphocyte was now understood to be the primary target of HIV infection, the CDC expanded the case definition of AIDS to include all HIV-infected persons with fewer than two hundred $CD4^+$ lymphocytes per cubic millimeter of blood. It further refined the definition in 1992, when effective management of *Pneumocystis carinii* pneumonia and antiviral therapies had become effective in slowing the onset of symptoms that previously had been relied on for case definition.

Not all researchers accepted the conclusion that HIV caused AIDS. Most vocal was Peter Duesberg, who noted that research did not show HIV present in all infected persons, and some HIV-infected persons remained free of AIDS symptoms. Duesberg pointed to extensive drug use and to the immunosuppressant effects of heroin, cocaine, and other drugs commonly used by at-risk populations. Other researchers questioned the "HIV-only" position and pointed to the possibility of co-factors acting together with HIV to produce a failure in the immune system, and pointed to other infectious agents.

The definition of the disease that came to be known as AIDS was critical in securing early data that characterized the disease, and further discoveries modified this definition, affecting the medical care, insurance status, and public perception of the disease. The disease had ramifications that went beyond health and public policy issues, however: The sociological impact was enormous. Whereas a generation earlier the "sexual revolution" of the 1960's—in part engendered by medical technology in the birth control pill—had opened the way for sexual relations with multiple partners and socially accepted sex outside marriage, the advent of AIDS caused a new generation to reevaluate such behavior and to call for "safe sex": monogamous relationships combined with use of condoms. Questions of moral responsibility now more than ever arose in the context of sexual relations, raising questions about the culpability of individuals who knowlingly spread the AIDS virus and about issues or privacy versus the "need to know." While some used the disease to castigate lifestyles and behaviors they found morally taboo, the fact remained that the AIDS virus was not a disease confined to homosexuals and drug addicts but rather a disease tied to unsafe behaviors, and one that was spreading throughout the general population.

—*John Richard Schrock*

ADDITIONAL READING:

Bart, Sandra. *An Annotated Bibliography of Scientific Articles on AIDS for Policymakers.* Washington, D.C.: Government Printing Office, 1987. Abbreviated and accurate summary of research on AIDS, written for the layperson.

Centers for Disease Control. *Reports on AIDS: Published in the Morbidity and Mortality Weekly Report, June 1981 Through May 1986.* Atlanta, Ga.: Department of Health and Human Services, Public Health Service, Centers for Disease Control, 1986. Presents, in chronological order, the reports that drew medical scientists' attention to the newly emerging viral disease and coordinated clinical reporting across the United States.

Gallo, Robert C. *Virus Hunting: AIDS, Cancer, and the Human Retrovirus—A Story of Scientific Discovery.* New York: Basic Books, 1991. A readable narrative by the principal U.S. researcher, who gives his perspective on the unfolding of the AIDS virus story.

Gallo, Robert C., and Luc Montagnier. "AIDS in 1988." *Scientific American* 259, no. 4 (October, 1988): 41-48. The codiscoverers of the AIDS virus recount their discovery and provide excellent illustrations of HIV. This whole issue of *Scientific American* is devoted to AIDS articles of interest.

Root-Bernstein, Robert S. *Rethinking AIDS: The Tragic Cost of Premature Consensus.* New York: Free Press, 1993. Provides a representative minority viewpoint on alternative hypotheses for explaining AIDS.

Shannon, Gary W., Gerald F. Pyle, and Rashid L. Bashur. *The Geography of AIDS: Origins and Course of an Epidemic.* New York: Guilford Press, 1991. A brief summary of the AIDS virus discovery is followed by more extensive analysis of the expansion of the epidemic.

U.S. National Commission on AIDS. *AIDS: An Expanding Tragedy.* Washington, D.C.: Author, 1993. Analyzes the state of the HIV epidemic and future trends; discusses prospects for prevention, therapy, and cure; gives specific interim reports and recommendations based on science.

SEE ALSO: 1952, Development of a Polio Vaccine; 1960, FDA Approves the Birth Control Pill.

1981 ■ REAGAN'S BUDGET AND TAX REFORM: *the Economic Recovery Act and the Omnibus Budget Reconciliation Act reduce personal income taxes and cut federal spending on social programs*

DATE: August 13, 1981
LOCALE: Washington, D.C.
CATEGORY: Economics
KEY FIGURES:
James Earl "Jimmy" Carter, Jr. (born 1924), thirty-ninth president of the United States, 1977-1981
Ronald Wilson Reagan (born 1911), fortieth president of the United States, 1981-1989
David Stockman (born 1946), director of the Office of Management and Budget

SUMMARY OF EVENT. During the 1980 election campaign, Republican candidate Ronald Reagan taunted President Jimmy Carter by asking voters: "Are you better off than you were four years ago?" Carter had struggled with declining productivity rates, double-digit inflation, 20 percent interest rates, nearly eight million people unemployed, and a 5 percent drop in real hourly wages over the previous five years.

Reagan defeated Carter in November, 1980, largely by promising new solutions to economic problems. He championed free-market, supply-side economic theory rather than the use of governmental power to fine-tune the economy. Government regulations weighed down the natural tendency of a capitalist economy to grow, Reagan asserted: Government was the problem, not the solution. Reagan's economic policies over the next several years would come to be known as Reaganomics.

When Reagan took office in January, 1981, he subordinated all issues to economic recovery. David Stockman, director of the Office of Management and Budget, became the lead figure in formulating Reagan's program. Stockman, bright and hard-working, used his knowledge of budgetary details to dominate economic policy making in 1981.

While Reagan left the details to his economic experts, he established the basic elements of the programs: a massive tax cut, a huge increase in military spending, reduced nondefense spending, and a balanced budget by 1984. He believed that lower taxes would lead to economic growth and that that growth, along with cuts in nondefense programs, would allow a balanced budget. However, when Reagan succumbed to political pressure and ruled that there would be no cuts in social security or other major entitlement programs, Stockman's reductions could only come from a small part of the budget. Stockman's final figures projected a balanced budget in 1984 only by using overly optimistic forecasts of revenue gains and economic growth.

On February 18, 1981, Reagan presented his program to a joint session of Congress. He proposed a four-part program:

cutting government spending, reducing taxes, eliminating unnecessary and unproductive economic regulations, and encouraging a consistent anti-inflationary monetary policy. Reagan labeled government as the main source of the nation's
economic problems and promised that his program would
return government to its proper province, while restoring to
the people the right to decide how to dispose of their earnings.
He predicted that his recovery plan would create thirteen million new jobs and control inflation, while achieving a balanced
budget by 1984. He asked Congress to cut $41.4 billion from
eighty-three programs, without cutting social security, Medicare, or veterans' pensions. He increased defense spending,
the president said, because even in its straitened economic
condition, the United States had to respond to the Soviet
military buildup. Reagan proposed 10 percent reductions in
individual income taxes in each of the next three years and an
increase in tax depreciation allowances for business.

After Reagan made his initial proposals, the hard political
work began. Many Washington insiders did not take the former movie star seriously, but Reagan quickly gave the old
guard a lesson in politics. Voters responded to his televised
appeals by flooding Congress with telegrams supporting the
president's program. Reagan used both charm and intimidation in dealing with individual members of Congress. During
his first few months in office, despite being seriously wounded
in an assassination attempt, Reagan met ninety-six times with
senators and representatives and spent hours with them on the
telephone. He engaged in artful deal-making, pledging not to
close a military base in one key representative's district, pleas-
ing another by retaining price supports for peanut farmers, and
promising those from the "oil patch" (Texas, Oklahoma, and
Louisiana) that he would oppose a windfall profits tax on the
petroleum industry. After Reagan promised protection for the
sugar industry, one important Louisiana Democrat admitted
that while he could not be bought, he could be rented. The first
step toward a Reagan victory came when Congress decided to
use the relatively new budget reconciliation process, by which
appropriations were packaged into one omnibus bill rather
than voted on as separate items.

The Democratic-dominated House Budget Committee had
formulated its own budget, which made less than half the
spending cuts that the president wanted. Reagan's work paid
off on May 7, when sixty-three Democrats revolted against
party leaders and joined the Republicans to support the administration bill. On July 31, Congress agreed to the most
widespread package of budget cuts in its history.

The final bill cut nearly $35.2 billion from a spending
level of $740 billion projected by the Congressional Budget
Office for fiscal year 1982, and it trimmed $130.6 billion
of expected outlays for fiscal years 1981-1984. The bill tight-
ened eligibility for food stamps and public assistance, cut
funds for subsidized housing programs, reduced school lunch
subsidies, instituted a "needs test" for student loans, limited
pay raises for federal employees, and made hundreds of other
changes.

The battle over Reagan's tax legislation was even more
hard-fought than that over the budget bill. Reagan said government was a kind of organism with an insatiable appetite for
money and a tendency to grow forever, unless he could starve
it by reducing its food—tax revenue. In his February 18 message, Reagan asked for a 10 percent reduction in individual
income taxes on July 1, 1981, followed by two additional 10
percent cuts in 1982 and 1983. He also called for more liberal
depreciation allowances for business.

Two days before the vote, the outcome was still considered
too close to call, but Reagan's skillful deal-making again
brought him crucial Democratic support. Congress gave him
most of what he wanted. The final bill reduced all individual
income tax rates by 5 percent on October 1, 1981, 10 percent
on July 1, 1982, and an additional 10 percent on July 1, 1983.
The bill liberalized depreciation allowances for business; reduced the top rate on investment income from 70 percent to 50
percent; and indexed individual tax brackets to inflation, preventing inflation from pushing people into higher brackets. On
August 13, 1981, Reagan signed the Economic Recovery Act
of 1981 and the Omnibus Budget Reconciliation Act of 1981.
He told reporters that over the next three years, the budget bill
represented $130 billion in savings and the tax bill $750 billion in tax cuts.

Reagan's economic program had mixed results. In late
1981, the economy entered a severe recession, with the unemployment rate peaking at 10.3 percent in early 1983. The
recession was followed by the longest period of sustained
economic growth in U.S. history, but half the millions of new
jobs created paid less than poverty-level wages. Reagan's most
important economic success came through working with the
Federal Reserve Board to bring inflation under control. His
greatest failure was the exploding national debt. Although he
had projected a balanced budget by 1984, deficits rose to
record heights. From George Washington through Jimmy Carter's administration, the United States had accumulated $1.1
trillion in national debt; under Reagan the United States added
$1.8 trillion to its debt. Reagan's legacy placed several con-
straints on his successors, which resulted in the need to allo-
cate more than 10 percent of the nation's yearly budgets required to pay the interest on the debt, rather than being
available to be reinvested in the country's social and economic
infrastructure.

—*William E. Pemberton*

ADDITIONAL READING:

Boskin, Michael J. *Reagan and the Economy: The Successes, Failures, and Unfinished Agenda*. San Francisco: Institute for Contemporary Studies Press, 1987. An overview of
Reaganomics and an evaluation of supply-side theory, which
asserts that Reagan supporters and opponents overstated the
revolutionary effects of the president's policies.

Campagna, Anthony S. *The Economy in the Reagan Years:
The Economic Consequences of the Reagan Administrations*.
Westport, Conn.: Greenwood Press, 1994. Finds the Reagan
economic program to be contradictory in its provisions and
fraudulent in its promises. Argues that its legacy of massive

budget deficits trapped the nation and prevented Reagan's successors from dealing with fundamental economic problems.

Friedman, Benjamin M. *Day of Reckoning: The Consequences of American Economic Policy Under Reagan and After*. New York: Random House, 1988. Argues that Reaganomics undermined the moral foundations of the nation, as the older generation refused to tax itself and instead borrowed from generations to come, leaving them a blighted future.

Stockman, David A. *The Triumph of Politics: How the Reagan Revolution Failed*. New York: Harper & Row, 1986. This brutally honest account by one of the chief architects of Reaganomics is the starting place to study Reagan's economic program.

Wilber, Charles K., and Kenneth P. Jameson. *Beyond Reaganomics: A Further Inquiry into the Poverty of Economics*. Notre Dame, Ind.: University of Notre Dame Press, 1990. Places Reaganomics in the context of contrasting Keynesian and conservative views of the economic world.

SEE ALSO: 1980, Reagan Is Elected President.

1981 ■ OZONE HOLE IS DISCOVERED: *the British Antarctic Survey's discovery of a hole in Earth's protective ozone layer raises environmental concerns in North America and around the globe*

DATE: October, 1981
LOCALE: Halley Bay, Antarctica
CATEGORIES: Environment; Science and technology
KEY FIGURES:
Joseph C. Farman, head of the Geophysical Unit of the British Antarctic Survey
James E. Lovelock (born 1919), inventor who demonstrated the global atmospheric distribution of chlorofluorocarbons
Frank Sherwood Rowland (born 1927), discoverer of the catalytic pathway for ozone depletion by chlorine from chlorofluorocarbons
Susan Solomon (born 1956), leader of the National Ozone Expedition at Antarctica's McMurdo Station
SUMMARY OF EVENT. The sun's energy is derived from a nuclear fusion process fueled by hydrogen. The electromagnetic radiation from this process constantly bathes Earth, affecting major physical, chemical, and biological processes. Although many of the sun's rays have wavelengths and frequencies (in the visible light range) that are essential to living organisms, there is a wide range of radiation—for example, X-rays and ultraviolet rays—that is detrimental. Earth's atmosphere prevents the incidence of most detrimental radiation on the terrestrial and aquatic surface, thereby shielding living organisms from the potential effects of ionizing radiation. Therefore, it is of extreme importance to understand and monitor the properties of the atmosphere that serve the life-saving function of selective radiation shield.

Several distinct layers of gas mixtures are found at different altitudes of the atmosphere. All living organisms thrive in the bottom layer, which consists of nitrogen (75 percent by volume), oxygen (23 percent), argon (1.3 percent), carbon dioxide (0.04 percent), and varying concentrations of water vapor. The presence of oxygen in Earth's atmosphere is largely a result of photosynthesis by terrestrial plants and oceanic phytoplankton. Sometime in Earth's history, diatomic oxygen accumulated to the extent that it was slowly converted (with the assistance of incident ultraviolet light and a catalytic molecule) to triatomic oxygen, also known as ozone. Because ultraviolet light is required in both the production and destruction of ozone, a steady-state concentration of ozone exists at approximately fifteen to thirty kilometers above Earth's surface in the stratosphere. Because ozone is capable of absorbing and emitting electromagnetic radiation from the sun, its occurrence in the stratosphere affects living organisms in two important ways: The ozone layer causes a temperature inversion that impacts weather and climate, and it prevents harmful ultraviolet radiation from reaching Earth's surface.

Although ozone was named in 1840 by the Swiss chemist Christian Schönbein, its presence and function in the stratosphere were not recognized until 1879, when Marie-Alfred Cornu in Paris theorized that the cutoff of natural ultraviolet radiation is caused by gases in the upper atmosphere. The presence of ozone in the upper atmosphere was confirmed in 1913 by physicist Charles Fabry at Marseilles. The invention of a prism spectrophotometer for taking precise measurements of stratospheric ozone by Gordon Dobson in 1926 led to illuminating studies by an English geophysicist, Sydney Chapman, who in 1931 devised a set of equations to describe ozone dynamics and function in the stratosphere. Soon after the confirmation of the significance of the ozone layer, the American public became aware of the danger to humanity if the ozone layer could not be sustained, as noted by Charles Abbot of the Smithsonian Institution, writing in the October 10, 1933, issue of *The New York Times*.

The first modern concern about the effects of human activities on the integrity of the ozone layer occurred as a result of the attempt to introduce supersonic air transportation by European and American aeronautical engineers in the 1960's. Design constraints for such supersonic airplanes demand a flight altitude of about forty-five kilometers and speeds of more than six thousand kilometers per hour. In addition to widespread public concern regarding unpleasant sonic booms associated with such speeds, speculations within the scientific community about the impact of supersonic flights on global climate was growing. James McDonald, an atmospheric physicist acting for the National Academy of Science, conducted experiments that indicated that the water vapor and other trace gases (such as nitrogen oxides) produced by supersonic airplanes could have a significant impact on ozone concentrations in the stratosphere. Halstead Harrison of the Boeing Science Research Laboratories in Seattle estimated in 1970 that a 3.8

percent depletion of global ozone concentrations could result from about nine hundred supersonic flights. By March, 1971, James McDonald and Harold Johnston of the University of California, Berkeley, presented larger persuasive estimates of global ozone loss as a result of supersonic flights; perhaps more important, they linked such ozone losses to potential increases in cases of skin cancer within the population. Consequently, despite concerns for loss of jobs and national technological competitive edge, the U.S. House of Representatives voted on March 17, 1971, to discontinue funding for supersonic transportation.

Almost immediately after the diffusion of concerns over the environmental impacts of supersonic flights, the problem of ozone depletion by other trace compounds introduced into the atmosphere by domestic and industrial activities was raised by scientists at a January, 1972, workshop of the Atomic Energy Commission in Fort Lauderdale, Florida. At the conference, Lester Machta of the National Oceanic and Atmospheric Administration discussed the previous work of James Lovelock, the inventor of the electron-capture detector for gas chromatographic measurements of atmospheric chemicals, who had determined the presence of chlorofluorocarbon-11 (CFC-11) at concentrations ranging from forty parts per trillion in the Southern Hemisphere to seventy parts per trillion in the Northern Hemisphere. The hemispheric difference in CFC-11 concentration is explained by the manufacture and use of the compound as a refrigerator coolant and as a propellant in aerosol sprays, activities linked to industrialized countries of the Northern Hemisphere. Present at the 1972 workshop was F. Sherwood Rowland of the University of California, Irvine, who later showed in laboratory experiments with Mario Molina that the stratosphere could act as a "sink" for CFCs, in which they supply chlorine atoms that catalyze the destruction of ozone.

The 1974 publication of the Rowland-Molina theory of CFC-mediated depletion of stratospheric ozone met with opposition in the industrial sector, which depends on the manufacture and marketing of chlorofluorocarbon compounds that had otherwise proven safe since their invention by Thomas Midgley, Jr., in the late 1930's. Global appreciation of the significance of CFCs' role in ozone depletion was not immediately apparent, because routine measurements of ozone in the stratosphere had been conducted since the mid-1950's, and the data did not show any ozone depletion as of 1974, when the theory was published. In 1978, the National Aeronautics and Space Administration (NASA) developed Nimbus 7, a satellite that orbited Earth with a type of ozone-monitoring equipment called the total ozone mapping spectrometer (TOMS). Although the satellite detected low ozone concentrations, the computerized equipment was designed to regard such extraordinarily low measurements as erroneous. It was Joseph Farman, leader of the Geophysical Unit of the British Antarctic Survey, which had been monitoring the concentration of ozone of the Antarctic stratosphere since the 1950's, who first recorded significant seasonal reduction of ozone concentrations

over Halley Bay during the Antarctican spring of 1981. Farman's data, eventually published on May 16, 1985, linked the seasonal depletion of the ozone layer to chemical pollutants. His results were confirmed by NASA scientists after retrospective evaluation of Nimbus 7 TOMS measurements.

The publication of Farman's work prompted intense activity by NASA scientists to develop sensitive models of ozone-related atmospheric chemistry, an effort led by Michael Prather of NASA's Goddard Institute for Space Studies. By August 21, 1986, the first National Ozone Expedition (NOZE), led by Susan Solomon of the National Oceanic and Atmospheric Administration, arrived at the U.S. research base McMurdo Station to investigate thoroughly the problem of ozone concentrations over the Antarctic. NOZE confirmed that there was severe depletion of ozone at altitudes between twelve and twenty kilometers in the Antarctic stratosphere. The NOZE report, made public on October 20, 1986, also intimated the involvement of chemical pollutants in the creation of the ozone hole.

A major consequence of the scientific discovery of the ozone hole in Antarctica was the international agreement to freeze production of CFCs at 1986 levels, beginning in 1989. The freeze was to be followed by a 20 percent reduction in 1994, and another 30 percent reduction by 1999. The Montreal Protocol on Substances That Deplete the Ozone Layer, as the agreement is officially known, was adopted by representatives of twenty-four countries on September 16, 1987.

—*O. A. Ogunseitan*

ADDITIONAL READING:

Cagin, Seth, and Philip Dray. *Between Earth and Sky*. New York: Pantheon Books, 1993. Provides detailed information on the history of issues leading to the discovery of the ozone hole and the chemistry of CFCs.

Lovelock, James E. *Gaia: A New Look at Life on Earth*. Rev. ed. Oxford, England: Oxford University Press, 1995. Summarizes the author's seminal findings regarding global distribution of CFCs.

Roan, Sharon. *Ozone Crisis*. New York: John Wiley, 1989. Documents the struggle between academic scientists and industrialists over the control of CFC production.

U.S. Congress. Senate. Committee on Environment and Public Works. Subcommittee on Environmental Protection. *Stratospheric Ozone Depletion and Chlorofluorocarbons*. Washington, D.C.: Government Printing Office, 1987. Transcript of joint hearings before subcommittees on Environmental Protection and Environment and Public Works.

U.S. Environmental Protection Agency. *CFCs and Stratospheric Ozone*. Cincinnati, Ohio: EPA Center for Environmental Research Information, December, 1987. Government version of findings and recommendations regarding stratospheric ozone depletion.

SEE ALSO: 1908, White House Conservation Conference; 1916, National Park Service Is Created; 1974, Construction of the Alaska Pipeline; 1978, Toxic Waste at Love Canal; 1979, Three Mile Island Accident; 1989, *Exxon Valdez* Oil Spill.

1982 ■ CANADA'S CONSTITUTION ACT:

Canada assumes control over its own constitution, ushering in an era of intense debate over the division of powers between the federal and provincial governments and a confrontation between advocates of Quebec's sovereignty and Canadian nationalists

DATE: April 17, 1982

LOCALE: Ottawa, Ontario, Canada

CATEGORIES: Canadian history; Laws and acts

KEY FIGURES:

René Lévesque (1922-1987), premier of the province of Quebec, 1976-1985, and leader of the Parti Québécois

Brian Mulroney (born 1939), prime minister of Canada, 1984-1993

Jacques Parizeau (born 1930), premier of the province of Quebec, 1994-1995

Pierre Elliott Trudeau (born 1919), prime minister of Canada, 1968-1979 and 1980-1984

SUMMARY OF EVENT. In 1841, English-speaking Upper Canada and French-speaking Lower Canada were joined in a political union, but by the 1860's, these two culturally distinct groups encountered difficulties in cooperation. A new constitution, the British North America Act of 1867, brought together French-speaking Quebec and English-speaking Ontario, along with the previously self-governing British colonies of Nova Scotia, New Brunswick, and Prince Edward Island, into a confederation called Canada. This confederation established a decentralized political system, with much of the power retained by the individual provinces.

Following World War II, Canada emerged on the world scene as a significant international power, but its constitution, the basic set of laws by which it was governed, was still in the hands of Great Britain. The patriation of the constitution—that is, Canada's assuming full control over its content and amendment—became a national issue.

Quebec's Liberal premier, Jean Lesage, proposed discussions on patriation and an amending formula at a federal-provincial conference held in Ottawa in July, 1960. Lesage spoke of the need for a special status for Quebec, an arrangement by which the Quebec government would negotiate directly with the federal government for exemption from certain national policies. In addition, Lesage described Quebec as a distinct society within Canada, asking: "What objection would there be if Canada were to adopt a constitutional regime which would take into account the existence of two 'nations' or 'societies' within one Canada?" The issues of special status for Quebec and its recognition as a distinct society became the objectives of future Quebec governments, as debate over patriation of the constitution continued for two decades.

In the November 15, 1976, provincial election, the Parti Québécois, which called for a referendum on separation from Canada, was elected to govern Quebec. Parti Québécois leader René Lévesque called for a provincial referendum on sovereignty-association, under which, within its boundaries, Quebec would have exclusive power to make laws, administer taxes, and establish diplomatic relations, but would maintain an economic association with Canada and continue to use the Canadian currency.

Protection of the French language and culture became an important issue in Quebec. On August 26, 1977, the Quebec National Assembly passed Bill 101, which severely restricted the use of languages other than French in Quebec. On December 13, 1979, the Supreme Court of Canada unanimously struck down those provisions of Bill 101 that restricted the use of English in the National Assembly and the courts of Quebec. Quebec voters rejected the sovereignty-association proposal by a margin of 60 to 40 percent, in a provincial referendum held on May 20, 1980.

With the national election of the Liberal Party in February, 1980, the Liberal prime minister, Pierre Elliott Trudeau, made constitutional reform and patriation major objectives of the new government. Trudeau promised during the campaign that "we will immediately take action to renew the Constitution and we will not stop until we have done that." Trudeau's proposal included new economic powers for the federal government and a broad charter of rights for all Canadians. A four-day meeting of the premiers of the provinces, beginning September 8, 1980, failed to reach agreement on the content of a new constitution.

Prime Minister Trudeau, in a nationally televised address to the Canadian people on October 2, 1980, announced his decision to proceed unilaterally, asking the Canadian Parliament to petition the British Parliament on the patriation issue. Revisions to the constitution were to be decided after patriation. By October 14, Lévesque and several other premiers had announced their opposition to unilateral action by the federal government on patriation, and court challenges to this federal action were begun in Manitoba, Quebec, and Newfoundland.

Lévesque and the Parti Québécois opposed four major aspects of the federal government's plan to patriate and reform the constitution. First, they wanted clear agreement on both the division of powers between the federal government and the provinces, and the charter of rights, before patriation. Second, they wanted Quebec to have broad veto power over future changes to the constitution. Third, they insisted on inclusion of an opting-out provision, allowing individual provinces to elect not to participate in certain federally mandated programs. Fourth, they opposed a national charter of rights that might restrict the powers of the provinces. The Supreme Courts of Manitoba and Quebec supported the federal government's legal right to proceed unilaterally, but Newfoundland's Supreme Court condemned the federal procedure. On September 28, 1981, the Supreme Court of Canada ruled that unilateral federal action was legal, but that such action violated the standard procedure for constitutional change.

Prime Minister Trudeau called another conference with the premiers at which, on November 5, 1981, they reached agreement on a package including patriation, a modified amending formula, and a weakened Charter of Rights and Freedoms. Quebec and Ontario would no longer have a veto over future constitutional change. The amendment formula required approval by both houses of the federal Parliament, plus approval by the legislatures of at least two-thirds of the provinces having at least half of the total population of all the provinces. The new Charter of Rights and Freedoms would include a provision allowing individual provinces to opt out of fundamental freedoms, legal rights, and equality rights mandated under the federal charter. Lévesque asserted Quebec's right to veto the new agreement, but the Supreme Court of Canada ruled that Quebec had no such right of veto.

In March, 1982, the British Parliament, by the Canada Act of 1982, renounced any future legislative role in amending the Canadian Constitution after April 17, 1982. On that day, Queen Elizabeth II came to Canada to proclaim Canada's new Constitution on Parliament Hill in Ottawa. Lévesque charged that his fellow premiers had abandoned Quebec in a time of crisis, and he indicated Quebec did not agree to the new Constitution.

In April, 1987, the premiers met with Prime Minister Brian Mulroney at Meech Lake, in Ontario, where they drafted an agreement that would have permitted special status for Quebec and acknowledged Quebec as a distinct society within Canada. The Meech Lake Accord also allowed provinces to opt out of certain federal shared-cost programs and gave the provinces increased control over immigration. Some Canadians opposed Quebec's becoming "more equal" than the other provinces, having powers not granted to the other provinces. The Meech Lake Accord required unanimous approval of the ten provincial governments. The National Assembly of Quebec accepted the Meech Lake Accord on June 23, 1987, but its adoption was blocked by the opposition of the legislatures in Manitoba and New Brunswick. Canada's failure to come to terms with Quebec resulted in increased tension between the federal and Quebec provincial governments.

A second attempt to meet Quebec's demands was drafted by the premiers in Charlottetown, Prince Edward Island, in 1992. The Charlottetown Accord recognized Quebec as a distinct society with a unique civil law system; provided for an elected Senate, a demand of the western provinces; and permitted individual provinces to negotiate directly with the federal government for increased control over immigration and regional development. The Charlottetown Accord was rejected in a national referendum on October 26, 1992. The leader of the Parti Québécois, Jacques Parizeau, responded the next day, saying, "It is clear that between Quebec and Canada there is not only a lasting misunderstanding, but a solution is hopeless."

The Parti Québécois was returned to power in the Quebec provincial elections on September 12, 1994, and the new pre-

mier, Jacques Parizeau, called for a second vote on separation from Canada. The sovereignist forces were defeated by a narrow margin of about 1 percent of the ballots cast in the fall, 1995, Quebec referendum, but Parizeau promised that the fight for separation was not over.   —*George J. Flynn*

ADDITIONAL READING:

Banting, Keith, and Richard Simeon. *And No One Cheered: Federalism, Democracy, and the Constitution Act.* Toronto: Methuen, 1983. Seventeen essays by Canadian scholars on the struggle over constitutional reform and what patriation of the constitution is likely to mean for Canada's future.

Gangon, Alain-G. *Quebec: Beyond the Quiet Revolution.* Scarborough, Ont.: Nelson Canada, 1989. Includes an in-depth account of the Quebec perspective on the debate over the Canadian Constitution.

Green, Ian. *The Charter of Rights.* Toronto: James Lorimer, 1989. A comprehensive discussion of the Charter of Rights and Freedoms, with chapters focusing on legal rights, equality, and language rights.

McWhinney, Edward. *Canada and the Constitution 1979-1982.* Toronto: University of Toronto Press, 1982. An in-depth account of the meetings, court rulings, and deals that shaped the 1982 Constitution. Written by a professor of law.

Sheppard, Robert, and Michael Valpy. *The National Deal.* Toronto: Fleet Books, 1982. A comprehensive history of the constitutional debate in Canada.

SEE ALSO: 1867, British North America Act; 1875, Supreme Court of Canada Is Established; 1931, Statute of Westminster; 1940, Ogdensburg Agreement; 1947, Canada's Citizenship Act; 1960, Quebec Sovereignist Movement; 1968, Trudeau Era in Canada; 1969, Canada's Official Languages Act; 1970, October Crisis; 1990, Meech Lake Accord Dies; 1992, Defeat of the Charlottetown Accord.

1982 ■ PLYLER V. DOE: *the U.S. Supreme Court extends the equal protection clause of the Fourteenth Amendment to guarantee the right of noncitizens to public social services*

DATE: June 15, 1982

LOCALE: Washington, D.C.

CATEGORIES: Civil rights; Court cases; Education; Health and medicine; Immigration

KEY FIGURES:

William Joseph Brennan, Jr. (1906-1995), associate justice who delivered the *Plyler* decision

Warren Earl Burger (1907-1995), dissenting chief justice in *Plyler*

Roger Brooke Taney (1777-1864), chief justice who rendered the *Dred Scott* decision

SUMMARY OF EVENT. In May, 1975, the Texas legislature enacted a law that denied financial support for the public education of the children of undocumented aliens. The state's local school districts, accordingly, were allowed to exclude such children from public school enrollment. The children of noncitizen aliens who henceforth paid for their public school education still were permitted to enroll. Despite the statute, Texas public school districts continued enrolling the children of undocumented aliens until 1977-1978, when, amid a continuing economic recession and accompanying budget tightening, the law was enforced. An initial challenge to the 1975 law arose in the Tyler Independent School District in Smith County, located in northeastern Texas, but similar challenges in other school districts soon produced a class-action suit.

The problem that had inspired the state law was the massive influx—principally of Mexicans but also of persons from other Central American countries—into Texas, as well as into New Mexico, Arizona, and California. Some of these people entered the United States for seasonal agricultural jobs, while others, undocumented, remained. Most were poor and seeking economic opportunities unavailable to them in Mexico and Central America. Figures released by the U.S. Immigration and Naturalization Service estimated that when the *Plyler* case arose, between two and three million undocumented aliens resided in Texas and other southwestern portions of the United States. Texas claimed that 5 percent of its population, three-quarters of a million people, were undocumented aliens, roughly twenty thousand of whose children were enrolled in Texas public schools. With recession adversely affecting employment, many of the state's taxpayers asked why they should bear the financial burdens of educating illegal aliens, as well as providing them with other benefits, such as food stamps and welfare payments.

The U.S. Supreme Court's 5-4 decision on *Plyler v. Doe* was delivered by Associate Justice William Joseph Brennan, Jr., a justice whom many observers considered a liberal but whose overall record was moderate. The *Plyler* majority ruling upheld a previous decision by the U.S. Fifth Circuit Court that had ruled for the defendants. Chief Justice Warren Burger vigorously dissented from the majority opinion, along with justices Byron White, William Rehnquist, and Sandra Day O'Connor.

On behalf of the Court's majority, Brennan declared that the 1975 Texas statute rationally served no substantial state interest and violated the equal protection clause of the Fourteenth Amendment. Ratified along with the Thirteenth and Fifteen Amendments during the post-Civil War Reconstruction Era, the Fourteenth Amendment guaranteed "that no State shall . . . deny to any person within its jurisdiction the equal protection of the laws." Although the overriding concern of Reconstruction politicians, judges, and states ratifying the Fourteenth Amendment was to afford protection to newly emancipated African Americans, the equal protection clause increasingly had been interpreted to mean what it stated: guaranteeing equal protection of the laws to any person—precisely the line of reasoning taken by Brennan. Brennan and the Court majority likewise disagreed with the Texas argument that undocumented aliens did not fall "within its jurisdiction," thus

excluding them and their children from Fourteenth Amendment guarantees. Such an exclusion, Brennan declared, condemned innocents to a lifetime of hardship and the stigma of illiteracy.

The *Plyler* decision was novel in two important respects. It was the first decision to extend Fourteenth Amendment guarantees to each person, irrespective of that person's citizenship or immigration status. Second, the Court majority introduced a new criterion for determining the applicability of Fourteenth Amendment protections: the doctrine of heightened or intermediate scrutiny. The Court avoided applying its previous standard of strict scrutiny. It recognized that education was not a fundamental right and that undocumented aliens were not, as it had previously phrased it, a "suspect class," in the sense that they, like African Americans, historically had been victims of racial discrimination. Heightened scrutiny was warranted, Brennan and the majority agreed, because of education's special importance to other social benefits and because children of undocumented aliens were not responsible for their status.

Chief Justice Burger and the three other dissenting, generally conservative, justices, who were staunch advocates of judicial restraint, strongly criticized Brennan and the majority for what the dissenters considered to be arguing political opinions instead of adhering to sound jurisprudence. The dissenters seriously questioned heightened scrutiny as a viable judicial standard and found that the Texas statute substantially furthered the state's legitimate interests.

The *Plyler* decision represented a significant departure from the decision rendered by Chief Justice Roger B. Taney in *Dred Scott v. Sandford* (1857), a decision that the Fourteenth Amendment was designed in part to nullify by political means. *Plyler*'s heightened standard of scrutiny, however, continued through the mid-1990's to be controversial and confusing, both within the Supreme Court and among legal observers. The issue arising when the equal protection clause was applied to cases not involving racial discrimination had been raised in *Buck v. Bell* (1927), when Justice Oliver Wendell Holmes denounced such decision making as "the usual last resort of constitutional arguments."

In *Plyler*, Brennan and the majority saw no chance to apply the Court's already accepted classification of strict scrutiny to equal protection cases, because *Plyler*'s defendants, the undocumented aliens, were not victims of institutionalized racial discrimination or of reverse discrimination. They were illegals as a consequence of their own conscious actions. Nevertheless, as legal scholars observed, in order to prevent hardship and stigmas from afflicting schoolchildren, who were not responsible for their parents' actions, the *Plyler* majority introduced an intermediate level of classification with their standard of heightened scrutiny. Such a standard raised questions about whether undocumented aliens and their families enjoyed rights to other government benefits, such as welfare assistance, medical care, and food stamps.

The difficulties confronted by Texas, by other Southwestern states, and by illegal aliens and their children were alleviated

somewhat by a broad federal amnesty program launched in 1992.
—*Clifton K. Yearley*

ADDITIONAL READING:

Aleinikoff, Thomas A., and David A. Martin. *Immigration: Process and Policy*. 2d ed. Saint Paul, Minn.: West, 1991. A careful review of modern U.S. immigration policies. Discusses the problems posed by illegal, undocumented aliens and the difficulties faced by government policymakers in coping with illegals.

Blasi, Vincent, ed. *The Burger Court*. New Haven, Conn.: Yale University Press, 1983. An authoritative yet readable analysis of the Chief Justiceship of Warren Burger, which did little to modify civil rights decisions of his predecessors. Also clarifies Brennan's attitudes and decisions.

Curtis, Michael Kent. *No State Shall Abridge*. Durham, N.C.: Duke University Press, 1986. A clear, scholarly exposition of the role played by the Fourteenth Amendment and the Bill of Rights in modern U.S. jurisprudence, including civil and criminal rights, racial and reverse discriminations, and interpretations of due process.

Hull, Elizabeth. *Without Justice for All*. Westport, Conn.: Greenwood Press, 1985. A precise study bearing on the problems raised in *Plyler*, the historical plight of resident and illegal aliens and their families, and the varying status of their constitutional rights.

Mirande, Alfredo. *Gringo Justice*. Notre Dame, Ind.: University of Notre Dame Press, 1990. A spirited, dismaying critique of U.S. judicial and political treatment of Hispanic immigrants by both the states and the federal government. Provides excellent context for understanding important aspects of the *Plyler* case.

Nelson, William. *The Fourteenth Amendment*. Cambridge, Mass.: Harvard University Press, 1988. An authoritative analysis of the evolution of the Fourteenth Amendment from a set of political principles to a vital part of twentieth century judicial decisionmaking. Good analyses of the Supreme Court's standards of scrutiny, including the intermediate or "heightened" scrutiny applied in *Plyler*.

SEE ALSO: 1868, Fourteenth Amendment; 1964, Civil Rights Act of 1964; 1968, Bilingual Education Act; 1974, *Lau v. Nichols*.

1982 ■ DEFEAT OF THE EQUAL RIGHTS AMENDMENT: *although the amendment fails to achieve ratification, it prompts the passage of other legislation designed to curtail discrimination against women and minorities*

DATE: July 7, 1982
LOCALE: Washington, D.C.
CATEGORIES: Laws and acts; Women's issues

KEY FIGURES:

Bella Savitzky Abzug (born 1920), congresswoman and vocal supporter of the ERA

Samuel J. Ervin, Jr. (1896-1985), senator and opponent of the ERA

Jerry L. Falwell (born 1933), leader of the Moral Majority and opponent of the ERA

Jesse Helms (born 1921), senator and opponent of the ERA

Alice Paul (1885-1977), social reformer and author of the ERA

Phillis Stewart Schlafly (born 1924), author and right-wing activist who founded Stop-ERA

Gloria Steinem (born 1935), prominent feminist, author, and promoter of the ERA

SUMMARY OF EVENT. On March 22, 1972, Senator Sam Ervin, a leading ERA opponent, acknowledged his "overwhelming defeat." Raising his fists, he intoned, "Father, forgive them, they know not what they do." Minutes later, the Senate passed the Equal Rights Amendment (ERA) by 84 to 8. The House of Representatives had already passed it by 354 to 23.

The ERA had been pending in Congress since 1923, when Alice Paul, founder of the National Woman's Party, introduced the first version to Congress. The modern ERA campaign began in 1967, when a stubborn Alice Paul, then eighty-two years of age, persuaded the National Organization for Women (NOW) to endorse the amendment. The amendment's language had remained the same since its last modification in 1943:

> Equality of rights under the law shall not be denied or abridged by the United States or by any State on account of sex.

In 1970, the amendment passed the House but not the Senate. A substitute was introduced in an attempt to save it; neither the original nor the substitute generated sufficient support. The debate continued more intensely in 1971, and media attention made the whole nation aware of it.

Gloria Steinem, Bella S. Abzug, Shirley Chisholm, and Betty Friedan advocated that the guiding principle for women was to build a nationwide, nonpartisan coalition of female voters. Thus, the Women's Political Caucus met for the first time, on July 10, 1971, in Washington, D.C. The leaders pointed out that 53 percent of the voting population were women, but women held only 1.6 percent of top government jobs. The caucus hoped to get more women elected and appointed to public offices. Its most immediate goal, however, was to gain passage of a proposed ERA.

The pro-ERA campaign was fierce and widespread. The House began debate on October 11, 1971. Unlike the long, fruitless debate of the previous year, the 1971 debate was efficient, passionate, and decisive. The House passed the ERA proposal that summer. On the Senate side, it seemed that the amendment might stumble on its own uncompromising language. Nevertheless, final senate approval came in the 84-8 vote on March 22, 1972. A seven-year deadline was set for ratification by two-thirds (thirty-eight) of the states. By the end of

1972, twenty-two states had passed the amendment. Women's groups were hopeful it would be ratified by mid-1973.

Congressional passage of the ERA in 1972 was a great accomplishment for women in the face of apathy, ridicule, and organized opposition. In a real sense, however, the amendment was a weak symbolic gesture. It was used by many politicians as a "throwaway vote" to appease female constituents. Most votes were not indicative of conviction on the issue.

Many related pieces of essential legislation affecting women were diluted or defeated by narrow margins, with most opposition coming from Republicans. A crucial child-care bill, for example, was approved by Congress but vetoed by President Nixon. The House, which had approved the ERA overwhelmingly, voted against prohibiting discrimination in undergraduate admissions to colleges and universities, against the Equal Pay Act, against increasing the enforcement powers of the Equal Employment Opportunity Commission, and against support for day care. The House also voted against a minimum wage for some 1.5 million domestics, 98 percent of whom were women and 80 percent of whom had annual incomes of less than two thousand dollars.

At the same time, women gained many victories in other ERA-related issues. Executive positions and other well-paying jobs were opening to women as never before. There was a general optimism that, even if the ratification drive failed, women were winning the fight. A flood of profeminist congressional, state, and local legislation was introduced, and often passed, ahead of ERA ratification. The hope for ERA ratification, however, dwindled in the November, 1972, election: Only seven months after passage of the ERA, fourteen women were elected to the House (an increase of only two over 1971) and the Senate lost both its women senators.

As early as 1974, there were strong indications that ratification would be more difficult than anticipated. On February 7, Ohio lawmakers approved the amendment, bringing the number of ratifying states to thirty-three, with five more to go. There was no further progress.

ERA opponents, meanwhile, had methodically eroded legislators' confidence in the amendment. They magnified potential adverse effects of the ERA, claiming that a thousand laws designed to protect women could be invalidated. They argued that the ERA would subject women to military draft and eliminate alimony, child support, and the customary granting of child custody to women in divorces.

At this time, "men's lib" became a national phenomenon. Women's campaigns for full equality prompted American men to reassess their own situations. Liberation was becoming a double-edged sword. Men launched counterattacks, moving into fields once reserved for women, including jobs as telephone operators, nurses, and flight attendants.

Opposition to the ERA was not limited to men. Many women on the political right were against the ERA, believing that the women's movement devalued the career of homemaking. A leading ERA critic was Phillis Schlafly, an author and mother of six. She described feminists as antichildren, anti-

men, and antifamily. She wrote that modern technology had helped make a noble, satisfying, and creative profession out of being a housewife and mother. Schlafly's followers and other opposition groups prevented the ERA from being ratified by more states and helped persuade five of the states that had ratified the amendment to rescind.

More feminine opposition came from African American women, such as Ida Lewis and poet Nikki Giovanni, who both believed that most black women did not respond to the white-dominated movement because of its alleged insensitivity to African American problems. They charged that sexism was less important than racism, and that the same white women who were fighting for women's rights came out to shout, spit, and throw rocks at black children who were bused into white schools.

As the 1979 cutoff date approached, the ERA was still three states short of ratification. Intense lobbying by women's groups persuaded Congress to extend the deadline to June 30, 1982. By March of 1979, opponents had succeeded in getting Tennessee, Kentucky, Idaho, Nebraska, and South Dakota to rescind their ratifications. In December, 1981, in a long-awaited decision, U.S. District Court Judge Marion J. Callister ruled that states could legally rescind passage of a constitutional amendment and that Congress had violated the Constitution by granting the extension.

Pro-ERA forces clearly share blame for the amendment's defeat. Feminists relied too heavily on impassioned rhetoric, displaying little of the political savvy needed to wage a state-by-state ratification drive. In contrast, the opposition—including the Eagle Forum, fundamentalist Christian churches, the Moral Majority, the John Birch Society, the Church of Jesus Christ of Latter-day Saints (Mormons), and the American Farm Bureau—were well financed and effectively organized.

On July 7, 1982, ten years after the ERA was passed by Congress, it died, three states short of the thirty-eight needed for ratification. Celebrations were held throughout the United States by opposition groups. "Special service" awards were given to outstanding ERA opponents, including Moral Majority leader Jerry Falwell, Undersecretary of State James Buckley, and Senator Jesse Helms. ERA supporters believed they had the majority on their side. Women constituted more than half the U.S. population, and in 1972 polls had shown that the amendment was favored by more than two-thirds of U.S. citizens.

One week after the demise of the ERA, a new effort began when 157 representatives and 46 senators reintroduced the amendment. Women's groups heaped invective on President Ronald Reagan, who, unlike his six predecessors, opposed the amendment. They promised to redouble efforts and vowed to become a "third force" in the U.S. political scene.

—Chogollah Maroufi

ADDITIONAL READING:

Faludi, Susan. *Backlash: The Undeclared War Against American Women.* New York: Crown, 1991. An impassioned and articulate account of the complex backlash against women's rights that took place during the Reagan-Bush era.

Feinberg, Renee, ed. *The ERA: An Annotated Bibliography of the Issues, 1976-1985.* Westport, Conn.: Greenwood Press, 1986. Describes and evaluates books and articles on the many political and social issues involved in the ERA controversy.

Mansbridge, Jane J. *Why We Lost the ERA.* Chicago: University of Chicago Press, 1986. Argues that the lost cause had many beneficial effects, including consciousness raising, the formation of women's activist organizations, and influencing other legislation affecting women's lives.

Mathews, Donald G., and Jane Sherron De Hart. *Sex, Gender, and the Politics of ERA: A State and the Nation.* New York: Oxford University Press, 1990. Focuses on the complexities of the fight for ratification of the ERA in North Carolina, one of three critical states hotly contested by both sides in the struggle.

Steiner, Gilbert Y. *Constitutional Inequality: The Political Fortunes of the ERA.* Washington, D.C.: Brookings Institution, 1985. A well-researched and cogently written account of the ERA from a constitutional perspective.

SEE ALSO: 1920, U.S. Women Gain the Vote; 1923, Proposal of the Equal Rights Amendment; 1965, Expansion of Affirmative Action; 1966, National Organization for Women Is Founded; 1972, Trail of Broken Treaties; 1978, Pregnancy Discrimination Act.

1983 ■ UNITED STATES INVADES GRENADA: *a late Cold War confrontation on a Western Hemisphere island nation, aimed at communist containment*

DATE: October 25-November 2, 1983
LOCALE: Republic of Grenada
CATEGORIES: Diplomacy and international relations; Latino American history; Wars, uprisings, and civil unrest
KEY FIGURES:
Maurice Bishop, founder of the Grenadian New Jewel Movement
Eugenia Charles (born 1919), prime minister of Dominica and chair of the Organization of Eastern Caribbean States
Bernard Coard, leader of the radical coup against Bishop
Ronald Reagan (born 1911), fortieth president of the United States, 1981-1989
Margaret Thatcher (born 1925), prime minister of Great Britain

SUMMARY OF EVENT. Relations between Grenada, an independent republic within the British Commonwealth of Nations, and the United States began to deteriorate in the late 1970's with the creation of a Grenadian Marxist government, the New Jewel Movement (NJM), led by moderate socialist Maurice Bishop. Beginning in 1979, Bishop established cordial relations with the Soviet Union and Cuba, including an exchange of diplomatic recognition and the beginnings of extensive Cuban-Soviet military and financial aid to Grenada.

As a result, the United States government initiated a boycott of the Bishop government, refused to accept the credentials of the Grenadian ambassador in Washington, D.C., and withdrew the United States ambassador to Grenada. The United States also attempted to block loans to Grenada from Western Europe, the World Bank, and the Caribbean Development Bank. Grenada was excluded from U.S. regional assistance programs available to other Caribbean and Latin American states. Soviet and Cuban assistance for Central American rebellions hostile to the United States strengthened the United States' resolve to prevent further possible Soviet threats to U.S. interests in Latin America and the Caribbean.

The immediate cause of heightened U.S.-Grenadian tensions, however, was the construction of an international airport at Point Salines, southwest of St. George's, Grenada's capital. According to U.S. intelligence sources, the airport was being built with assistance from Cuba, as well as several European nations. Cuban engineers were alleged to be in the process of lengthening and strengthening the airport runways for the possible use of Cuban and Soviet military aircraft. The alleged military application of the new Grenadian airport was used from 1981 to 1983 by President Ronald Reagan, a longtime critic of Soviet influence and a staunch supporter of Cold War diplomacy, to focus attention on the alleged Soviet and Cuban direction of Bishop's NJM. The Reagan Administration claimed that the Soviet Union had established a missile base in Grenada's central mountains, and that sophisticated Soviet monitoring equipment might be installed in Grenada to track U.S. submarine movements in the Caribbean.

The Reagan Administration's decision to use military force was reinforced by an October, 1983, coup against Bishop, sparked by Bernard Coard, the leader of an extremist revolutionary faction within the New Jewel Movement and an ardent admirer of Cuban communism. Coard also was accused of being responsible for Bishop's murder during the fighting between NJM factions and Grenadian government forces. Coard's extremist revolutionary regime immediately requested increased Cuban and Soviet military assistance and ordered the creation of a people's militia, the jailing of political opponents, and an end to Bishop's pledge of free elections by the beginning of 1984. Following several weeks of ineffective diplomatic negotiations between the Reagan Administration and the Coard regime, on October 25, 1983, U.S. Marines and U.S. Army Rangers, plus a small military police force from six Caribbean nations, invaded Grenada. The U.S. military force included nineteen hundred Marines, the helicopter carrier *Saipan*, a sixteen-ship battle group led by the aircraft carrier *Independence*, and the amphibious assault ship *Guam*.

President Reagan's official announcement of the invasion included a statement that the United States was responding to an October 23 request from the Organization of Eastern Caribbean States (OECS) to help restore law and order in Grenada and guarantee political freedom and free elections for the Grenadian population. Reagan also maintained that information from the OECS and reports that U.S. citizens, many of them medical students enrolled at the Medical University of St. George's, were trying to escape the island and could be held hostage by the Coard regime or Cuban military advisers had persuaded him that the United States had no choice but to act decisively. Reagan's assertions were seconded by Prime Minister Eugenia Charles of Dominica, chairwoman of the OECS. Charles asserted that the Coard-led coup against Bishop was inspired and directed by Cuban advisers who feared that free elections in Grenada would result in a repudiation of revolutionary Marxism and the end of Cuban influence on the island.

Armed resistance to the U.S.-led invasion was stronger than anticipated. U.S. military intelligence concluded that between six hundred and eleven hundred Cuban construction workers, military advisers, and militia were in Grenada. U.S. Marines reported that the airport, government buildings, and other strategic areas were heavily defended. By October 26, however, most opposition had been subdued and, once the major U.S. military objectives were attained, three hundred members of a joint eastern Caribbean police force landed on the island to begin security operations. By October 29, all Cuban personnel on the island had been captured, and Coard and other members of his regime had been arrested. Under OECS auspices, a new interim government was announced under British Commonwealth jurisdiction. Sir Paul Scoon, Commonwealth governor general, on November 1 announced plans for elections and revealed his intention to bring to trial those responsible for the murder of Maurice Bishop. Scoon also delivered diplomatic messages to the Soviet Union and Cuba that Grenada was cutting all ties with the two nations, and that approximately 650 captured Cubans would be repatriated.

By early November, the U.S. Department of State had revealed the contents of thousands of secret documents discovered by U.S. and Caribbean security forces. The documents included three Soviet supply agreements with the Bishop regime. U.S. officials also cited evidence that the Soviet Union had agreed to provide military training for the Grenadian militia. Other documents indicated that Cuba had long-range plans to take over the island and initiate a terrorist training camp to be used to foment revolutionary movements in the Caribbean and Central America. The Central Intelligence Agency released captured Cuban communications indicating that Cuba had planned to send 341 additional officers and 4,000 reservists to Grenada by the end of 1983. Reagan Administration officials also cited documentary evidence to show that Cuba and the Coard regime planned to hold U.S. citizens hostage in the event of hostile U.S. actions.

International reaction to the U.S. invasion was almost universally negative. British prime minister Margaret Thatcher expressed considerable doubt regarding the invasion and advised Reagan to reconsider using military action as a substitute for economic sanctions against the Coard regime. Thatcher also announced publicly that the Grenada situation should be considered a British Commonwealth affair and therefore outside the interests of the United States. By November 1, how-

ever, the Thatcher government announced limited support for Reagan's decision to invade, based on the prime minister's understanding that the United States was entitled to act at the request of the OECS. The French government, on October 25, declared the U.S. invasion a violation of international law. The Canadian government also announced its regret for the invasion in light of the lack of substantial evidence to show that U.S. citizens in Grenada were in danger. The governments of the Soviet Union and Cuba, and the Sandinista regime in Nicaragua issued pro forma condemnations of U.S. actions, which asserted that the Reagan Administration was interested solely in subordinating Grenada to U.S. neocolonialist rule. On October 28, the United Nations Security Council approved, by a vote of eleven to one, with three abstentions, a resolution condemning the armed intervention in Grenada. The United States vetoed the resolution.

In the United States, political opinions regarding the invasion split along party lines. Democratic congressmen and senators generally condemned the invasion as unprovoked, hasty, an overreaction, and tantamount to an act of war. Other Democratic Party leaders in Washington ridiculed Reagan as having a "cowboy mentality" and criticized the president for relying too heavily on the military solution to diplomatic problems. Republican political leaders, however, praised Reagan's "decisive actions." Most proinvasion sentiment centered on arguments for enforcement of the Monroe Doctrine, the thwarting of Soviet-inspired terrorism, and the necessity for backing the president and the U.S. Armed Forces during a time of crisis. U.S. public opinion generally favored President Reagan's decision to invade Grenada and eliminate Soviet and Cuban influence.

—*William G. Ratliff*

ADDITIONAL READING:

Gilmore, William C. *The Grenada Intervention: Analysis and Documentation.* New York: Facts on File, 1984. Examines the legal arguments for the U.S. invasion of Grenada.

Lewis, Gordon K. *Grenada: The Jewel Despoiled.* Baltimore: The Johns Hopkins University Press, 1987. A sober assessment of the background of the U.S. invasion of Grenada, which focuses on Grenadian political developments.

O'Shaughnessy, Hugh. *Grenada: An Eyewitness Account of the U.S. Invasion and the Caribbean History That Provoked It.* New York: Dodd, Mead, 1985. A journalist's account of the political maneuvering in Grenada that brought the New Jewel Movement to power and subsequent Grenadian political radicalization.

Payne, Anthony, et al. *Grenada: Revolution and Invasion.* New York: St. Martin's Press, 1984. A scholarly investigation of the Grenada crisis, which is highly critical of the Reagan Administration's motives and pretexts for the invasion.

Payne, Anthony. *The International Crisis in the Caribbean.* Baltimore: The Johns Hopkins University Press, 1984. An effort to place the U.S. intervention into Grenada in the context of overall Caribbean political and economic development.

SEE ALSO: 1823, Monroe Doctrine; 1980, Reagan Is Elected President.

1983 ■ JACKSON BECOMES FIRST MAJOR AFRICAN AMERICAN CANDIDATE FOR PRESIDENT: *more than one hundred years after the Civil War, an African American becomes a serious contender for the presidency*

DATE: November 3, 1983

LOCALE: Washington, D.C.

CATEGORIES: African American history; Government and politics

KEY FIGURES:

Geraldine Anne Ferraro (born 1935), Democratic representative and 1984 vice presidential nominee

Gary Warren Hart (born 1936), Colorado senator who sought the Democratic presidential nomination

Jesse Louis Jackson (born 1941), veteran civil rights activist who sought the Democratic presidential nomination

Walter Frederick Mondale (born 1928), 1984 Democratic presidential nominee

Ronald Wilson Reagan (born 1911), fortieth president of the United States, 1981-1989

SUMMARY OF EVENT. In a memorable speech of November 3, 1983, the Reverend Jesse Jackson became the first major African American candidate for the presidency of the United States. Using the rhythms and tones of the Southern Baptist preacher that he was, Jackson lashed out at the administration of President Ronald Reagan, charging that it was anti-black, anti-Hispanic, pro-rich, and pro-military. He also attacked his own party, accusing the Democrats of having been too weak in opposing the many threats posed by the Reagan presidency. The new candidate urged formation of a "rainbow coalition," in which Americans of all races and ethnic groups would come together to oppose policies that hurt the poor and middle classes.

Jackson entered the race under a number of handicaps. Many people saw him as "a black candidate," but far less than half the electorate was African American. Many African American leaders were already backing other Democratic hopefuls, and they made no move to switch to Jackson. While Jackson was a respected minister, community activist, and former associate of Martin Luther King, Jr., he had never held political office and could offer only modest evidence of expertise in foreign policy. The two strongest Democratic contenders, former vice president Walter Mondale and U.S. Senator Gary Hart, both had abundant experience as elected officials.

On the other hand, Jackson could boast of a remarkably successful life of devoted public service and prolific achievements in civil rights. While a student at North Carolina Agricultural and Technical State College, Jackson was simultaneously student body president, an honors student, and quarterback of the football team. After graduation, he was on the staff of North Carolina's governor, Terry Stanford, and he attended Chicago Theological Seminary. While working for the Chicago office of Operation Breadbasket, he led protests that forced Chicago stores to hire more African Americans and to stock more goods made by black-owned firms. Soon Jackson was national director of Operation Breadbasket. Jackson was with King the night of the latter's assassination, and he soon went to work as a top executive for King's Southern Christian Leadership Conference. At the time he announced his candidacy for the presidency, Jackson was heading Operation PUSH (People United to Save Humanity), a group designed primarily to help minority-group children excel in school.

Only seven weeks into the campaign, Jackson seized an opportunity to prove his abilities in the foreign policy arena. Syria was holding prisoner a downed U.S. pilot named Robert O. Goodman, Jr. Jackson charged that the Reagan Administration was doing little to secure the pilot's release, and stories in the press seemed to support Jackson's charges. Jackson sent a message concerning the pilot to Syrian president Hafez al-Assad, and in response, Assad invited Jackson to come to Syria. Jackson did so and won the release of the pilot. While President Reagan and a number of other politicians initially criticized Jackson for interfering with U.S. foreign policy, all praised Jackson after his success.

The first African American to make a serious bid for the presidency of the United States, Jesse Jackson was not elected but broke ground for future candidates. (Library of Congress)

Back on the campaign trail, Jackson was hampered by an inexperienced and disorganized staff and by a scarcity of funds for running television spots. With only a modest advertising budget, Jackson had to rely on reporters for his public exposure. Soon his photograph was on the covers of dozens of magazines, and his voice was heard in scores of radio and television interviews. Jackson benefited from his speaking skills, which seemed to captivate audiences more than did the efforts of his main rivals, Mondale and Hart.

In the first two contests for the Democratic nomination (those in Iowa and New Hampshire), Jackson was hurt by the lack of large minority populations in those states. In the Iowa caucuses, Jackson finished seventh, with less than 2 percent of the vote; in the New Hampshire primary, he placed fourth, with 6 percent of the total vote. Jackson's first major test came with the Super Tuesday contests in a number of states, held on March 13, 1984. On that day, Jackson won 21 percent of Georgia's vote and 20 percent in Alabama. A number of Democratic hopefuls dropped out of the presidential race, leaving only Mondale, Hart, and Jackson.

As the primary season wore on, Jackson continued to show some real strength. In the important New York primary, Jackson won more than one-quarter of the vote. He placed first in the District of Columbia primary, taking 67 percent of the vote. While this District of Columbia win was expected, given the black majority in the nation's capital, Jackson surprised most observers with his strong victory in Louisiana, where he captured 43 percent of the total vote. In Mississippi, Jackson finished ahead of Hart; in South Carolina, Jackson did better than either of his two rivals. Even in the industrial state of Illinois, Jackson won a respectable 21 percent.

Jackson's biggest stumble came over allegations that he was bigoted. An African American journalist reported that he had overheard Jackson referring to Jews as "Hymies" and to New York City as "Hymietown." Jackson at first ducked reporters' questions about the comments, but later admitted having used the terms. He did say that the remarks were simply slang, and that he used the terms with no animosity. Jackson's reputation as a coalition-builder was also hurt by his friendship with Louis Farrakhan, an African American leader of the Nation of Islam. Farrakhan seemed to make threats against the life of the reporter who broke the "Hymietown" story, and he later referred to Judaism as a "gutter religion." Jackson eventually distanced himself completely from Farrakhan's words, but many liberal Democrats grew lukewarm toward the Jackson candidacy.

Going into the Democratic National Convention in San Francisco, it was clear that Mondale had enough delegates to secure his nomination. Still, Jackson remained a significant force: Many party leaders feared that Jackson would remain aloof from the Democratic campaign. Others feared that he might consider running as an independent. Jackson was able to play on these fears to get the Democratic convention to declare its support for affirmative action and to appoint a committee to consider the changes Jackson sought in delegate selection procedures. When the roll was called, Mondale had the support of 2,191 delegates, Hart 1,200, and Jackson 465. While Jackson fell well short of a victory, he had broken the color barrier by becoming the nation's first major presidential hopeful who was African American. Jackson won more than three times as many delegates as had an earlier African American candidate, Representative Shirley Chisholm, who had run in 1972.

The 1984 Democratic convention also broke a gender barrier, as it tapped the first woman to appear on a major party ticket. Geraldine Ferraro was the convention's choice for vice president. Jackson campaigned on behalf of the Mondale-Ferraro ticket, but the Democrats went down to defeat in 1984. Still, the Jackson candidacy had offered an unusually strong voice on behalf of the poor and minority groups. Such voices have appeared only infrequently on the presidential campaign trail.

—Stephen Cresswell

ADDITIONAL READING:

Barker, Lucius J. *Our Time Has Come: A Delegate's Diary of Jesse Jackson's 1984 Presidential Campaign*. Urbana: University of Illinois Press, 1988. Particularly strong first-person account of the Jackson campaign and the 1984 Democratic National Convention.

Barker, Lucius J., and Ronald W. Walters, eds. *Jesse Jackson's 1984 Presidential Campaign: Challenge and Change in American Politics*. Urbana: University of Illinois Press, 1989. Presents the Jackson campaign's history from a variety of perspectives.

Jackson, Jesse. *A Time to Speak: The Autobiography of the Reverend Jesse Jackson*. New York: Simon & Schuster, 1988. A good starting point for any study of Jackson's 1984 presidential bid.

Kimball, Penn. *Keep Hope Alive: Super Tuesday and Jesse Jackson's 1988 Campaign for the Presidency*. Washington, D.C.: Joint Center for Political and Economic Studies, 1989. Covers the background and key events of Jackson's 1988 presidential bid.

Reed, Adolph L. *The Jesse Jackson Phenomenon: The Crisis of Purpose in Afro-American Politics*. New Haven, Conn.: Yale University Press, 1986. Reed puts the 1984 Jackson campaign in the larger context of African American political history.

SEE ALSO: 1980, Reagan Is Elected President; 1988, Bush Is Elected President.

1984 ■ MULRONEY ERA IN CANADA:
a Progressive Conservative leader assumes the office of prime minister, ending three decades of Liberal Party control of Canada's government

DATE: September 4, 1984-February 24, 1993
LOCALE: Canada
CATEGORIES: Canadian history; Government and politics

KEY FIGURES:

John Edward Broadbent (born 1936), leader of the New
Democratic Party

Charles Joseph Clark (born 1939), leader of the Progressive
Conservative Party until 1983; prime minister, 1979-1980

Brian Mulroney (born 1939), prime minister, 1984-1993

Pierre Elliott Trudeau (born 1919), Liberal Party leader;
prime minister, 1968-1979 and 1980-1984

John Turner (born 1929), Liberal Party leader who served as
prime minister from June-September, 1984

SUMMARY OF EVENT. The landslide election victory of the
Progressive Conservative Party (PCP) on September 4, 1984,
ended decades of political dominance by Canada's Liberal
Party. The election victory of PCP leader Brian Mulroney
astounded political forecasters. The final count gave the Progressive Conservatives 211 of 282 seats in Canada's House of
Commons. Stunned Liberals had elected only forty members
to Commons, and John Edward Broadbent's New Democratic
Party won only thirty seats. The PCP won almost 50 percent of
the national vote, compared to the Liberals' 28 percent and the
New Democratic Party's 19 percent. Mulroney had spent
much of the 1984 campaign talking about the need for better
relations with the United States and stronger Canadian support
for western alliance policies. His conservative victory may be
seen as a continuation of Western governments abandoning
liberal/socialist governments for conservative ones, after the
election of Margaret Thatcher in the United Kingdom (1978)
and Ronald Reagan in the United States (1980).

Mulroney was sworn in as Canada's eighteenth prime minister on September 14, 1984. This represented a dramatic rise in
politics for a man little known in Canadian circles until 1983.
Mulroney's election campaign stressed his humble beginnings
in Baie Comeau, Quebec, where he was born March 20, 1939,
to Irish parents. The Mulroneys were a devout Catholic family,
who had emigrated from Ireland during the potato famine in
the 1840's. Mulroney's father worked in the Baie Comeau's
pulp mill and worked at night as an electrician. Prime Minister
Mulroney's parents scraped together enough money for him to
attend a boarding school, believing that education was their
son's only way out of a tough blue-collar existence.

English was spoken at home by the Mulroneys, but Brian
learned the French spoken by Baie Comeau's Quebecer majority. His bilingual ability served him well at St. Francis Xavier
Universities, where he earned a bachelor of arts degree in
political science, and later at Dalhousie and Laval Universities,
at which he studied law. Brian Mulroney was the first anglophone student at Laval to take all of his courses in French.

Mulroney's politics increasingly shifted to the Progressive
Conservative Party in college, because he found the Liberal
Party closed to a son of the working classes. Throughout his
academic career and later while practicing law, Mulroney
made extensive contacts within the Progressive Conservative
Party. It was as a labor lawyer that Mulroney earned his
reputation as a skillful negotiator and conciliator. He received
a 1974 appointment to the three-member Cliche Commission,
which was authorized to investigate the destruction caused by
workers at a hydroelectric dam on James Bay. The commission
issued a lengthy report recommending major changes in labor
relations and union practices in Quebec.

Mulroney's work on the Cliche Commission gained him
national prominence and led his colleagues to urge him to run
for the leadership of the PCP in 1976. The attempt failed, and
Mulroney accepted the position of executive vice president,
and later president, of the Iron Ore Company of Canada, which
he temporarily turned from an unprofitable company into a
money-making operation. In 1983, economic reversals forced
Iron Ore of Canada to scale back its mining operations. Resul-
tant layoffs led to worker protests, but Mulroney won the
workers' favor by giving them generous compensation pack-
ages. Mulroney's actions gained the national press's attention.

In January, 1983, PCP leader Joe Clark announced his intention to step down as chairman of the party and allow a party
convention to select his replacement. Clark, the former prime
minister, was taking a gamble, hoping to gain a renewed
pledge of party support against the Liberal Party, whose popularity was plummeting in the national polls. However, Clark's
resignation gave Mulroney the opportunity to resign his corporate presidency and announce his candidacy for party leader,
without antagonizing the PCP leadership.

The Progressive Conservative Party's June, 1983, convention offered conservatives a choice between former leader and
prime minister Clark, newcomer Mulroney, and John Crosbie.
There were no backroom deals or power plays, but frequent
refusals to alter allegiances. On the third ballot, Crosbie was
eliminated because of his third-place finish and because he
could not speak French. The PCP wanted to appeal to Quebecers. On the fourth and final ballot, Mulroney won 1,584
votes to Joe Clark's 1,325 votes. Mulroney's election was
attributed to his youth and vigor, his skillful organizational
talents, his bilingualism, and the desire of the party to seek a
winner and a future.

In a Nova Scotia by-election held on August 29, 1983, Mulroney won his first seat in Parliament, with 18,882 votes to the
Liberal Party's 7,828 votes. Mulroney's win signaled rising
disenchantment with both the Liberal Party and Prime Minister
Pierre Trudeau. In 1984, Mulroney united the PCP's ideological
wings and established an election platform advocating support
of the North Atlantic Treaty Organization alliance and a close
relationship with the United States. Mulroney publicly lauded
Ronald Reagan's invasion of Grenada; was willing to let the
United States test its cruise missiles in Canada; and advocated
a balanced budget, spending cuts, and business incentives,
while continuing government support for medicare, social programs, and publicly owned enterprises. On July 1, Trudeau
resigned and was replaced by an unelected prime minister,
John Turner. Trudeau hoped that his belated resignation would
reinvigorate the Liberal Party under a new leader.

In the resulting Turner-Mulroney campaign, Mulroney
stressed that he was an agent of change, while the Liberals
represented the past without any new ideas. Mulroney played

the "Baie Comeau card," presenting himself as a man of the people against Toronto and the establishment. Mulroney capitalized on Turner's campaign mistakes of acknowledging billions of dollars in government waste and the appointment of wealthy Canadians to patronage positions in return for political contributions.

In a series of televised debates, Prime Minister Turner appeared ill at ease, rigid, and badly dressed. A well-dressed and poised Mulroney focused on the Quebecers, by speaking in the French Quebec idiom and acknowledging Quebec's nationalistic concerns. At the end of the three debates, Turner had lost his advantages of prime ministerial posturing and the perception that he was more competent than Mulroney to lead Canada. Throughout the campaign, the tarnished legacy of Trudeau continued to haunt Liberal Party fortunes. When Turner hired the legendary Keith Davey after the debates to reinvent his campaign, Canadians became convinced that the Liberal Party had returned to old-style politics and manipulation.

Throughout the election, Mulroney consistently displayed his ability to synthesize issues, understand personalities, and resolve disputes. Mulroney set the campaign agenda and appealed for support from Canada's minorities and the Quebecers. His organizational skills, charisma, and his U.S.-style election campaigning gave the Progressive Conservative Party its first significant victory since the 1950's. Mulroney's stunning 1984 election upset was repeated in 1988.

The Mulroney years (1984-1993) in Canada were an era of social revolution and near economic collapse. For many Canadians, the federal authority no longer offered peace, order, and good government, but instead aroused increasing hostility and controversy. As prime minister, Mulroney quickly established a strong rapport with U.S. presidents Reagan and George Bush. Mulroney signed the Free Trade Agreement (FTA) with the United States and later the North American Free Trade Agreement (NAFTA), which included Mexico. Canadian budgets were slashed; national industries were closed, downsized, or privatized. Oil prices were decontrolled, tougher regulations for financial institutions were imposed, and foreign investment was encouraged with the creation of the Foreign Investment Review. Mulroney developed better relations with the United States, boycotted South Africa until apartheid fell, and gave Canada a more international role in world affairs.

Mulroney's accomplishments were overshadowed after the 1988 election by the imposition of a Goods and Services Tax, which Canadians soon despised; the failure of the 1987 Meech Lake and the 1992 Charlottetown Accords, which attempted to create a new status for Quebec; and the provincial rejection of further constitutional reforms. Increasing questions about Mulroney's expensive habits and finances, charges of Progressive Conservative corruption, and provincial demands for more autonomy led to Mulroney's resignation on February 24, 1993. The position of party leader for the Progressive Conservative Party and the office of prime minister went to Canada's first woman prime minister, Kim Campbell, on June 13; Campbell went down to an election defeat on October 25 to the Liberal Party, under Jean Chrétien. The Progressive Conservative Party lost 152 of its 154 parliamentary seats. In spite of the recent allegations against Mulroney, he had drawn Canada irrevocably into a closer relationship with both the United States and Mexico, made Canada an international player in foreign policy, and made a serious effort to resolve the issue of Quebec's continued association within Canada.

—*William A. Paquette*

ADDITIONAL READING:

Cameron, Stevie. *On the Take: Crime, Corruption, and Greed in the Mulroney Years*. Toronto: MacFarlane Walter and Ross, 1994. Chronicles a multitude of corruption charges leveled against Mulroney after his departure from office.

Hoy, Claire. *Friends in High Places: Politics and Patronage in the Mulroney Government*. Toronto: Key Porter Books, 1987. A no-holds-barred account of Mulroney's government, which catalogs a long list of government scandals.

MacDonald, L. Ian. *Mulroney: The Making of the Prime Minister*. Toronto: McClelland and Stewart, 1984. A detailed account of the years 1983 and 1984, when Mulroney gained the leadership of the Progressive Conservative Party and won election to the prime ministership.

Murphy, Rae, Robert Chodos, and Nick Auf der Maur. *Brian Mulroney, the Boy from Baie-Comeau*. Toronto: James Lorimer, 1984. A well-written account of Mulroney's life before becoming prime minister.

Sawatsky, John. *Mulroney: The Politics of Ambition*. Toronto: MacFarlane Walter and Ross, 1991. This political biography contains 660 interviews conducted by a seasoned Canadian investigative reporter, Richard Guyn, to determine the accuracy of corruption charges against Mulroney's administration.

SEE ALSO: 1968, Trudeau Era in Canada; 1987, Canada's Pay Equity Act; 1990, Meech Lake Accord Dies; 1990, Bloc Québécois Forms; 1992, Defeat of the Charlottetown Accord; 1993, Campbell Becomes Canada's First Woman Prime Minister.

1985 ■ U.S.-SOVIET SUMMIT: *the first summit meeting in six years between the leaders of the United States and the Soviet Union prompts a series of summits that will end in arms reductions*

DATE: November 19-21, 1985
LOCALE: Geneva, Switzerland
CATEGORY: Diplomacy and international relations
KEY FIGURES:
Mikhail Gorbachev (born 1931), leader of the Soviet Union
Richard Norman Perle (born 1941), assistant secretary of state
Ronald Wilson Reagan (born 1911), fortieth president of the United States, 1981-1989
Eduard Shevardnadze (born 1928), Soviet foreign minister
George Shultz (born 1920), U.S. secretary of state

SUMMARY OF EVENT. U.S.-Soviet relations were deteriorating in the early 1980's, with President Ronald Reagan overseeing a buildup of the U.S. military and a series of aging Soviet leaders overseeing an expansionist foreign policy. U.S. and Soviet troops, advisers, and weapons faced each other in such places as Angola, Afghanistan, and Nicaragua. Negotiations to limit the two countries' nuclear weapons—a mainstay of U.S.-Soviet diplomacy since the late 1960's—had been broken off in 1983.

Mikhail Gorbachev's ascension to the post of general secretary of the Communist Party in March, 1985, spawned some hopes in the West that the hard-line Soviet stance might be open to revision. Gorbachev began ambitious domestic reform programs in the Soviet Union and stated his intention to establish a rapprochement with the West. Arms control negotiations, called the Nuclear and Space Talks, were resumed in Geneva. As a sign of a new dialogue between the two countries, Gorbachev and Reagan agreed to meet face to face in the Swiss capital in the fall of 1985. It would be the first meeting between a U.S. president and his Soviet counterpart since the 1970's.

The Geneva summit began on November 19, 1985. The subject of arms control was the most closely watched aspect of the discussions between the two leaders. In particular, the two sides sought to limit, and possibly reduce, the number of intermediate-range nuclear forces (INFs) based in Europe. Prior to the summit, the Soviet Union had staked out a position that these weapons should be reduced by 50 percent on each side. That position had three conditions, however. First, only nuclear weapons deployed in Europe would be counted; weapons based on U.S. and Soviet soil would be exempt. U.S. negotiators had routinely opposed such provisions, arguing that INFs in the Soviet Union could reach Western Europe, but such weapons based in the United States could not reach Eastern Europe. Second, the Soviets demanded that French and British nuclear forces be reduced by the same proportion, arguing that those forces were essentially under U.S. control through NATO. The United States rejected that logic. Third, the Soviet negotiating position required that the United States terminate its program to research and develop a nuclear defense system. This so-called Strategic Defense Initiative (SDI), popularly known at the time as "Star Wars," had been proposed by Reagan in 1983 and had been opposed continuously by the Soviet Union ever since. The Reagan Administration stood by its decision to research and develop a strategic nuclear defense, although it remained vague on the question of deployment.

Such was the diplomatic history leading up to the Geneva summit. The talks began with the formal meeting of the two heads of state before cameras on the morning of November 19. Breaking with traditional practice for superpower summits, Reagan and Gorbachev quickly left to meet privately, without advisers or negotiators, for an hour. At other points during the two-day summit, these private meetings were repeated, for a total of six hours of face-to-face discussions between Reagan and Gorbachev with no one but translators present. The summit also was unique for the news blackout that kept the talks shrouded in secrecy until a joint statement was issued on November 21.

A number of agreements were signed at the Geneva summit, covering such areas as environmental protection, and educational, cultural, and scientific exchanges. Of particular interest were the agreements concerning security and nuclear weapons. In their joint statement, the two leaders pronounced their belief that "a nuclear war cannot be won and must never be fought," reaffirmed their commitment to the nuclear nonproliferation treaty and to the principle of a 50 percent reduction in nuclear arms, and promised to seek an interim agreement reducing INF. The two leaders also stated their intention to meet twice more over the next two years. Observers made references to the "Spirit of Geneva"—an optimistic (and short-lived) sense of cooperation that had come out of the Geneva summit meeting in July, 1955, between President Dwight Eisenhower and Soviet leader Nikita Khrushchev.

Despite the air of civility and the photos of the two leaders speaking amicably by a fire, the 1985 summit produced little of immediate substance. No formal agreement on arms control had been achieved, and virtually no progress was made on the major issues that had divided the two sides prior to the summit. Reagan remained committed to the Strategic Defense Initiative, and Gorbachev continued to stress that no arms control treaty could be signed until Reagan relented on SDI. Those who had expected the meeting of the new, vigorous Soviet leader and the second-term president to bring an immediate breakthrough in the superpowers' nuclear impasse were disappointed. At the same time, those who had feared that one or the other leader would "give away the store"—a fear that would be especially pronounced after the Reykjavik summit the following year—were relieved.

The Geneva summit thus ended on a note of guarded hope. After a decade of increasingly strained relations between Moscow and Washington, the highest officials of the two countries were again speaking to each other face to face. They had found some common ground on the principle of nuclear arms reductions and other subjects. They saw the necessity of communication and cooperation. Gorbachev had established his credentials as a world leader important enough to secure a private audience with the president of the United States. Reagan maintained his strong commitment to SDI but also was depicted as someone willing to talk and negotiate with the Soviet leadership. It later would become clear that the Geneva summit marked the beginning of a new, and, it turned out, final, era in superpower relations.

In the months following the Geneva summit, arms control talks continued in Geneva, and the vague commitment to a 50 percent arms reduction in Europe began to take form. True to their stated intentions, Gorbachev and Reagan met several more times in subsequent years, each time reaffirming their shared desire to normalize relations and secure peace in Europe. By the end of 1987, a treaty to eliminate all U.S.

and Soviet intermediate-range nuclear missiles in Europe—including those based in the Soviet Union west of the Ural mountains, and excluding those owned by France and Britain—had been signed. Reagan's commitment to SDI remained intact. Clearly, the Soviet Union's resolve had eroded since the time of the Geneva summit.   —*Steve D. Boilard*

ADDITIONAL READING:

Arms Control Association. *Arms Control and National Security: An Introduction.* Washington, D.C.: Author, 1989. A basic explanation of arms control negotiations and treaties. Chapter 10 examines nuclear forces in Europe, including the 1987 INF Treaty.

Dallin, Alexander, and Gail W. Lapidus. "Reagan and the Russians: American Policy Toward the Soviet Union." In *Eagle Resurgent? The Reagan Era in American Foreign Policy*, edited by Kenneth A. Oye, Robert J. Lieber, and Donald Rothchild. Boston: Little, Brown, 1987. Covers Reagan's Soviet policy since 1981, with several pages devoted to events leading up to the Geneva summit and to the summit itself. A scholarly, analytical article; extensive footnotes.

"The Flickering Glow from the Fireside Summit." *The Economist* 297, no. 7421 (November 23, 1985): 31-32. A brief analysis of the 1985 Geneva summit, including a comparison with the 1955 Geneva summit.

Mandelbaum, Michael, and Strobe Talbott. *Reagan and Gorbachev.* New York: Vintage Books, 1987. Examines the issue of how the separate agendas of Reagan and Gorbachev, as well as their attempts to find a common ground, influenced the future of Soviet-U.S. relations in the mid-1980's. Especially thorough treatment of SDI.

Rueckert, George L. *Global Double Zero: The INF Treaty from Its Origins to Implementation.* Westport, Conn.: Greenwood Press, 1993. Good background on the INF negotiations, of which the Geneva summit was a significant watershed. Explains the context of arms control and diplomacy in the 1970's and 1980's.

"World Press Report: Beyond Geneva." *World Press Review* 33, no. 1 (January, 1986): 39-44. A compilation of articles concerning the Geneva summit, culled from newspapers in Great Britain, Germany, Brazil, Israel, Japan, and France.

SEE ALSO: 1973, Détente with the Soviet Union; 1979, SALT II Is Signed; 1987, INF Treaty Is Signed; 1993, START II Is Signed.

1986 ■ CHALLENGER ACCIDENT: *after nearly twenty-five years of safe spaceflight, a stunned nation witnesses the explosion of the space shuttle and the deaths of its crew*

DATE: January 28, 1986
LOCALE: Off Cape Canaveral, Florida
CATEGORY: Science and technology

KEY FIGURES:
Gregory Jarvis (1944-1986), payload specialist
Christa McAuliffe (1948-1986), mission participant and the first private citizen to go into space
Ronald E. McNair (1950-1986), African American mission specialist
Ellison Onizuka (1946-1986), Japanese American mission specialist
Judith Resnick (1949-1986), mission specialist
Francis R. "Dick" Scobee (1939-1986), shuttle commander
Michael Smith (1945-1986), pilot

SUMMARY OF EVENT. On the morning of January 28, 1986, an explosion pierced the unusually crisp winter air above Cape Canaveral and disrupted the United States' most promising technological enterprise. The destruction of the space shuttle *Challenger* and the loss of its seven crew members were swift and catastrophic. Subsequent investigation concluded that U.S. efforts to sustain an ambitious space program needed to be seriously evaluated.

Challenger had been expected to study Halley's Comet and launch a sophisticated TDRS communications relay satellite. This twenty-fifth shuttle mission was the first scheduled in an ambitious year, when planned missions included a satellite that would study Jupiter, the launch of the Hubble Space Telescope, at least four missions sponsored by the Pentagon, and countless commercial payloads. The reputations of the shuttle and of the National Aeronautics and Space Administration (NASA) were on the line.

In the days prior to the launch, the mission seemed plagued by bad weather. After several delays caused by doubtful forecasts, the crew entered the shuttle on January 27, only to leave again because a handle on the crew entry/exit hatch jammed and replacing it took so long that the launch was scrubbed for a third time. The morning of January 28 did not seem much more promising. With early morning temperatures hovering near the freezing mark, engineers expressed concern. No shuttle had ever been launched with temperatures only a few degrees above freezing, but after consultations with senior advisers, shuttle mission director Jesse Moore gave the green light. At 11:38 A.M. on a clear, cold Florida day, Cape Canaveral reverberated to the familiar roar of main engine ignition, followed by clouds of smoke and flame from the solid-rocket boosters. In a matter of seconds, *Challenger* cleared the tower and began the roll that would carry the craft to the east across the ocean. Spectators watched while a calm voice from the public address system narrated the launch.

Unknown to anyone in the cabin or on the ground, there was already a jet of flame hungrily licking around the giant orange fuel tank from the right-hand booster rocket. "*Challenger*, go with throttle up," reported mission control. "Roger, go with throttle up," came the reply from Commander Dick Scobee. These were the last words received from the seven astronauts. Seconds later, the shuttle suddenly disappeared amid a cataclysmic explosion that ripped the fuel tank from nose to tail. The delta-winged craft that had been perched on the side of this tank was torn free by the blast and disintegrated in midair. Scobee had time to open his radio channel but was cut off before he could speak. Pilot Michael Smith, suddenly aware that something was terribly wrong, exclaimed, "Uh oh." Some of the crew activated emergency oxygen supplies but with no effect. Although the crew's cabin seemed to have remained largely intact, the aerodynamic pressure exerted on the passengers killed any who survived the explosion. The remnants of the craft plummeted nine miles into the ocean.

Relatives, friends, and pupils in the viewing area could only watch spellbound as the hideous white cloud and its two horns grew in the otherwise cloudless sky. Adding to the tension, the calm voice of the public address announcer continued reading off the altitude and velocity. Then the worst fears of everyone were confirmed. "Flight controllers here looking very carefully at the situation," continued the still-calm voice on the PA, "obviously a major malfunction. We have no downlink. We have a report from the flight dynamics officer that the vehicle has exploded." It was the worst accident in nearly twenty-five years of manned spaceflight, and the first time U.S. astronauts had been lost during a mission. A shock wave spread throughout the nation. A presidential commission was set up to investigate the accident. Chaired by former Secretary of State William Rogers, it included such dignitaries as Nobel Prizewinner Richard Feynman; former astronaut Neil Armstrong; the first U.S. woman in space, Sally Ride; and former test pilot General Chuck Yeager. The *Challenger* accident brought most of the space program to a temporary halt.

In the weeks of confusion following the accident, NASA administrators struggled to comprehend the disaster. The immediate explanation seemed quite simple and direct. A solid-rocket booster was thought to have burned a break through the adjacent wall of the external tank, thereby releasing the tank's load of hydrogen on a leaking joint in one of the two solid-rocket boosters that propelled the shuttle into space.

To the public, it appeared that this accident was a painful but inevitable consequence of a complex technology. Sooner or later, accidents were bound to happen because of unanticipated technical problems and errors in judgment by managers and operators in the system. However, the investigation report of the Rogers Commission concluded that *Challenger*'s solid-rocket booster problem originated with the faulty design of its joint and was exacerbated as both NASA and contractor management first failed to recognize the problem, then failed to fix the problem, and finally treated the problem as an acceptable flight risk. In 1979, contractor Morton Thiokol had reported problems in the design of the O-ring used to seal joints in the solid-rocket booster. While engineers at Morton Thiokol concluded that the flaws posed no significant problem, engineers at NASA expressed real concern. Real attention to the problem, however, did not arise until 1985, when joint failure was noticed on two returning shuttle flights. Still, the failure of the O-rings was not attributed to temperature extremes. Neither Morton Thiokol nor NASA responded adequately to internal warnings about the faulty seal design, nor did either make a timely attempt to develop and test a new seal after the initial design was shown to be deficient. Instead, Morton Thiokol and NASA management accepted O-ring failure as unavoidable and an acceptable flight risk.

The commission's conclusions that administrators at NASA were informed of the problematic joint early enough for its agencies to have responded appropriately suggested that this accident was neither unanticipated nor inevitable. The commission called for a more active role for astronauts and engineers in assessing and approving launches. Other recommendations included a complete redesign of the solid-rocket booster joints; the study of astronaut escape systems and greater safety margins for shuttle landings; and a realistic flight schedule that was more consistent with available resources, placed safety as its top priority, and reduced the risks to astronauts' lives as much as possible.

Perhaps NASA officials miscalculated the risks by underestimating the dangers associated with the flawed seal joint. Still, the *Challenger* accident not only revealed organizational problems within NASA but also became a vivid witness to the consequences of savage budget reductions. The space shuttle program had ended a six-year U.S. drought in space and was to be a stepping-stone to spectacular scientific progress and profitable new manufacturing facilities in space. Yet, from its inception, the United States' space shuttle program had endured budget reductions at the expense of production standards. Meanwhile, under the impetus of the presidential directive, the U.S. space agency was pressing ahead as quickly as possible to meet the demands for the Strategic Defense Initiative and an operational space station by the early 1990's, as well as the demands of its civilian and scientific customers.

After two years of investigations and an agonizing reorganization, NASA resumed the shuttle program. However, after the *Challenger* accident, NASA did not regain completely its status as the standard bearer of U.S. excellence. The space program remained active but did not recapture the imagination of the U.S. public as its creators had once hoped. —*Kathleen Carroll*

ADDITIONAL READING:

Cassamayou, Maureen Hogan. *Bureaucracy in Crisis: Three Mile Island, the Shuttle Challenger, and Risk Assessment*. San Francisco, Calif.: Westview Press, 1993. Although this work is a critique of the politics of governmental agencies, the assessment of the *Challenger* incident is helpful for understanding the collapse of communication between NASA's engineers and Morton Thiokol.

Lindee, Susan, and Dorothy Nelkin. "*Challenger*: The High Cost of Hype." *Bulletin of the Atomic Scientists* (November, 1986): 16-18. Examines the *Challenger* accident from the perspective of media pressure. Suggests that NASA's reputation with the public might have compelled officials to rush to a decision to launch.

Logsdon, John M. "The Decision to Develop the Space Shuttle." *Space Policy* 2, no. 2 (1986): 103-112. Scholarly, authoritative insight into the development of the space shuttle program.

Miller, Christine M. "Framing Arguments in a Technical Controversy: Assumptions About Science and Technology in the Decision to Launch the Space Shuttle *Challenger*." *Journal of Technical Writing and Communication* 23, no. 2 (Spring, 1993): 99-115. Scrutinizes the structure of NASA's decision-making process.

Report of the Presidential Commission of the Space Shuttle "Challenger" Accident. Springfield, Va.: National Aeronautics and Space Administration, June, 1986. Provides the most complete view of what caused the accident and what happened as a result of this tragedy.

Schwartz, Howard S. *Narcissistic Process and Corporate Decay: The Theory of the Organizational Ideal*. New York: New York University Press, 1990. Uses several case studies, including NASA, to assess the corporate structure.

SEE ALSO: 1961, First American in Space; 1969, Apollo 11 Lands on the Moon; 1993, Astronauts Repair the Hubble Space Telescope.

1986 ■ IMMIGRATION REFORM AND CONTROL ACT: *a new immigration law provides for the legalization of illegal aliens and establishes sanctions against employers who hire undocumented workers*

DATE: November 6, 1986
LOCALE: Washington, D.C.
CATEGORIES: Business and labor; Immigration; Laws and acts
KEY FIGURES:

Theodore M. Hesburgh (born 1917), chairman of the Select Committee on Immigration and Refugee Policy

Edward M. Kennedy (born 1932), Democratic senator from Massachusetts

Romano L. Mazzoli (born 1932), Democratic congressman from Kentucky

Leon E. Panetta (born 1938), Democratic congressman from California

Ronald Wilson Reagan (born 1911), fortieth president of the United States, 1981-1989

Peter W. Rodino (born 1909), Democratic congressman from New Jersey

Charles E. Schumer (born 1933), Democratic congressman from New York

Alan K. Simpson (born 1931), Republican senator from Wyoming

SUMMARY OF EVENT. The 1986 Immigration Reform and Control Act (IRCA) was signed into law by President Ronald Reagan on November 6, 1986. The act (Public Law 99-603) amended the Immigration and Nationality Act and was based in part on the findings and recommendations of the Select Commission on Immigration and Refugee Policy (1978-1981). In its 1981 report to Congress, this commission had proposed that the United States continue to accept large numbers of immigrants and enact a program of amnesty for undocumented aliens already in the United States. To deter migration of undocumented aliens to the United States, the commission also proposed to make the employment of illegal aliens a punishable offense.

These proposals were incorporated into the Simpson-Mazzoli bill, a first version of which was enacted by the Senate in 1982. In the five years between its introduction and its enactment, the bill ran into opposition from a variety of quarters. Agricultural interests, especially growers of perishable commodities, were concerned that the proposed employer sanctions would jeopardize their labor supply. Mexican American advocacy groups also opposed employer sanctions, while organized labor and restrictionists who were concerned about the massive influx of foreign workers favored employer sanctions. Many liberals and humanitarians supported the notion of legalizing the status of undocumented aliens and expressed concerns over potential discrimination against them.

In the 1980's, the bill repeatedly was pronounced dead only to be revived again as various lawmakers, notably Representatives Leon Panetta, Charles Schumer, and Peter Rodino, introduced compromises and amendments to respond to their constituencies or to overcome opposition by congressional factions. Differences also developed between the House Democratic leadership and the Republican White House over funding the legalization program. On October 15, 1986, the House at last approved the bill, by a vote of 238 to 173; the Senate approved the bill on October 17, by a vote of 63 to 24.

The major components of the Immigration Control and Reform Act provided for the control of illegal immigration (Title I), the legalization of undocumented aliens (Title II), and the reform of legal immigration (Title III). Other sections of the act provided for reports to Congress (Title IV), state assistance for the incarceration costs of illegal aliens and certain Cuban nationals (Title V), the creation of a commission for the study of international migration and cooperative economic development (Title VI), and federal responsibility for deportable and excludable aliens convicted of crimes (Title VII).

A major objective of the IRCA, the control of illegal immigration, was to be achieved by imposing sanctions on employers. IRCA made it unlawful for any person knowingly to hire, recruit, or refer for a fee any alien not authorized to work in the United States. Before hiring new employees, employers would be required to examine certain specified documents to verify a job applicant's identity and authority to work.

The act established civil and criminal penalties, and employers could be fined up to two thousand dollars per unauthorized alien, even for a first offense. Employers who demonstrated a pattern of knowingly hiring undocumented aliens could face felony penalties of up to six months' imprisonment and/or a three-thousand-dollar fine per violation. Employers also were required to keep appropriate records. Failure to do so could result in a civil fine of up to one thousand dollars. In order to allow time for a public education campaign to become effective, penalties against employers for hiring undocumented aliens were not phased in until June, 1987.

The second major objective of the IRCA, the legalization of undocumented aliens, was to be realized by granting temporary residence status to aliens who had entered the United States illegally prior to January 1, 1982, and who had resided in the United States continuously since then. They could be granted permanent residence status after eighteen months if they could demonstrate a minimal understanding of English and some knowledge of the history and government of the United States. After a five-year period of permanent residence, they would become eligible for citizenship.

The act also permitted the attorney general to grant legal status to aliens who could show that they had entered the United States prior to January, 1972, and lived in the country since then. Newly legalized aliens were barred from most forms of public assistance for five years, although exceptions could be made for emergency medical care, aid to the blind or disabled, or other assistance deemed to be in the interest of public health.

To assure passage of the bill, support of the growers in the West and Southwest was essential. After protracted negotiations, the growers succeeded in getting the kind of legislation that assured them of a continued supply of temporary agricultural workers. The new program differed from earlier bracero programs by providing for the legalization of special agricultural workers who could work anywhere and who could become eligible for permanent resident status or for citizenship. The IRCA granted temporary residence status to aliens who had performed field labor in perishable agricultural commodities in the United States for at least ninety days during the twelve-month period ending May 1, 1986, as well as to persons who could demonstrate to the Immigration and Naturalization Service that they had performed appropriate agricultural field labor for ninety days in three successive previous years while residing in the United States for six months in each year.

The act also revised and expanded an existing temporary foreign worker program known as H-2. In case of a shortage of seasonal farmworkers, employers could apply to the secretary of labor no more than sixty days in advance of needing workers. The employer also was required to try to recruit domestic workers for the jobs. H-2 also provided that during fiscal years 1990-1993, additional special agricultural workers could be admitted to temporary residence status as "replenishment workers." Their admission was contingent upon certification of the need for such workers by the secretaries of labor and of agriculture. Replenishment workers who performed ninety days of field work in perishable agricultural commodities in each of the first three years would be eligible for permanent resident status. They were, however, disqualified from public assistance. In order to become eligible for citizenship, they would have to perform seasonal agricultural services for ninety days during five separate years.

The IRCA also provided permanent resident status for a hundred thousand specified Cubans and Haitians who entered the United States prior to January 1, 1982. The law increased quotas from former colonies and dependencies from five hundred to six thousand and provided for the admission of five thousand immigrants annually for two years, to be chosen from nationals of thirty-six countries with low rates of immigration. Altogether, the Immigration Reform and Control Act led to the legalization of some three million aliens; however, IRCA was not as successful in curbing illegal immigration as had been anticipated.

Mindful of the potential for discrimination, Congress established an Office of Special Counsel in the Department of Justice to investigate and prosecute charges of discrimination connected with unlawful immigration practices. The act also required states to verify the status of noncitizens applying for public aid and provided that states be reimbursed for the implementation costs of this provision. To reimburse states for the public assistance, health, and education costs resulting from legalizing aliens, the act provided for the appropriation of one billion dollars in each of the four fiscal years following its enactment.   —Helmut J. Schmeller

ADDITIONAL READING:

Bean, Frank D., Georges Vernez, and Charles B. Keely. *Opening and Closing the Doors: Evaluating Immigration Reform and Control*. Washington, D.C.: Rand Corporation and the Urban Institute, 1989. Scholarly study of the IRCA of 1986, its implementation, and its impact on illegal immigration.

Daniels, Roger. "The 1980s and Beyond." In *Coming to America: A History of Immigration and Ethnicity in American Life*. New York: HarperCollins, 1990. Brief, critical discussion of the IRCA, with special emphasis on the act's amnesty provision.

Fuchs, Lawrence H. *The American Kaleidoscope: Race, Ethnicity, and the Civic Culture*. Hannover, N.H.: University Press of New England, 1990. Concise, well-documented discussion of the act by the executive director of the staff of the Select Commission on Immigration and Refugee Policy.

Ueda, Reed. *Postwar Immigrant America: A Social History*. Boston: St. Martin's Press, 1994. Discusses the IRCA and related immigration legislation in the broader context of worldwide immigration. Useful charts and maps.

Zolberg, Aristide R. "Reforming the Back Door: The Immigration Reform and Control Act of 1986 in Historical Perspective." In *Immigration Reconsidered: History, Sociology, and Politics*, edited by Virginia Yans-McLaughlin. New York: Oxford University Press, 1990. Comprehensive, well-documented account of the genesis of the IRCA, with particular emphasis on the legislative history.

SEE ALSO: 1943, Magnuson Act; 1952, McCarran-Walter Act; 1965, Immigration and Nationality Act.

1986 ■ IRAN-CONTRA SCANDAL: *U.S. government officials violate national policy by conducting the secret sale of arms to Iran and diverting the profits to Contra guerrillas attempting to overthrow the Nicaraguan government*

DATE: November 13, 1986-May 4, 1988
LOCALE: Washington, D.C.
CATEGORIES: Diplomacy and international relations; Government and politics
KEY FIGURES:
Robert Carl "Bud" McFarlane (born 1937), national security adviser
Oliver L. North (born 1943), National Security Counsel staff member
John M. Poindexter (born 1936), McFarlane's successor as national security adviser
Ronald Wilson Reagan (born 1911), fortieth president of the United States, 1981-1989
Richard V. Secord (born 1932), Air Force general

SUMMARY OF EVENT. In November, 1986, secret operations conducted in Iran and Nicaragua by the staff of the National Security Counsel (NSC) became public, and the ensuing Iran-Contra scandal endangered the presidency of Ronald Reagan. Reagan was the key figure in the Iran-Contra affair. He set policy for his administration, but left the daily operations of government to his subordinates. In 1985, Donald T. Regan became chief of staff, and Robert C. McFarlane was national security adviser, succeeded in December, 1985, by John M. Poindexter. These hardworking but politically insensitive men carried out Reagan's policy without questioning its wisdom or legality.

Reagan inherited two problems that, together, led to Iran-Contra. On January 16, 1979, followers of the Muslim leader in Iran, the Ayatollah Ruhollah Khomeini, overthrew the shah of Iran, Mohammad Reza Pahlavi, a longtime U.S. ally. The Reagan Administration believed that the new government of Iran supported international terrorist organizations, including groups that had kidnapped several U.S. citizens who were being held in Lebanon. Through Operation Staunch, Washington pressured its allies not to sell arms to Iran. On June 30, 1985, Reagan proclaimed that the United States would not bargain with kidnappers: "The United States gives terrorists no rewards. We make no concessions. We make no deals."

The second problem began on July 17, 1979, when the Nicaraguan dictator, Anastasio Somoza, was overthrown by the Sandinista forces, led by Daniel Ortega. The Reagan Administration believed that the Sandinistas were communists, and on November 17, 1981, Reagan approved covert support for the anti-Sandinista guerrilla groups that came to be known as the Contras, whom Reagan regarded as heroic freedom fighters. Many members of Congress believed that U.S. in-

volvement in a Nicaraguan civil war could lead to a quagmire similar to the Vietnam War. Beginning in late 1982, Congress passed legislation, called the Boland Amendments, that prohibited the Department of Defense and the Central Intelligence Agency from conducting military operations in Nicaragua. Reagan then instructed National Security Adviser McFarlane to keep the Contras together, "body and soul."

The Iran and Contra covert operations became joined because they were both conducted by the staff of the National Security Council (NSC). Those who were involved in Iran-Contra had varied motives. McFarlane was concerned that the United States had no policy in place to try to influence events when the aged Khomeini died. Others, especially President Reagan, became obsessed with the plight of the U.S. hostages held in Lebanon. Israel also influenced events. In July, 1985, the Israeli government informed McFarlane that it had established contact with moderate elements in Tehran who wanted to improve relations with the United States. To demonstrate the seriousness of both parties, the Iranian moderates would persuade the Lebanese to release the U.S. hostages, and the United States would sell arms to Iran, then engaged in a long and bloody war with Iraq. If Washington approved, Israel would act as intermediary, selling Iran the arms and replenishing its stock by purchases from the United States.

Secretary of State George Shultz and Secretary of Defense Caspar Weinberger opposed the transfer, which they recognized as an arms-for-hostage trade that violated United States policy. Reagan, however, approved the sale. In August and September, 1985, Israel transferred 504 TOW missiles to Iran. Only one kidnap victim was freed, rather than all seven as the U.S. had expected.

In November, 1985, the United States began to handle the arms shipments directly, rather than using Israel as an intermediary. McFarlane asked NSC staff member Lieutenant Colonel Oliver L. North to manage the operation, and North turned for assistance to retired Air Force general Richard Secord.

In December, 1985, McFarlane resigned as national security adviser and was replaced by John Poindexter, who left North in charge of the operation. Despite repeated disappointments in getting hostages released, the NSC staff, with Reagan's support, continued shipping weapons. In May, 1986, Reagan asked McFarlane to conduct a special mission that secretly took him to Tehran. After fruitless negotiations with various shadowy figures, McFarlane broke off talks and came home. Two hostages were freed in July and one in October, but two additional U.S. citizens were kidnapped in September, 1986.

While the Iranian initiative unfolded, Poindexter struggled to carry out President Reagan's directive to hold the Contras together. North, who handled operational details, brought Secord in to help in the Contra operation. The two men set up an organization they called the Enterprise to help carry out their activities. As Congress cut off funds for Contra military operations, North headed a campaign to raise money from private donors, and he secretly funneled millions of dollars from

Saudi Arabia to the Contras through a network of nonprofit organizations and Swiss bank accounts. North and Secord's Enterprise owned aircraft, warehouses, arms and other supplies, ships, and boats, and even had a hidden runway located in Costa Rica. North, with McFarlane's and Poindexter's knowledge, had created a secret government organization operating outside the authority of Congress.

In his search for funds, North intermingled the Iran and Contra operations. He diverted profits from Iranian arms sales to the Contras. This diversion of funds became the focal point of the investigations that began when news of the operations surfaced.

On October 6, 1986, the Sandinistas shot down an Enterprise airplane and captured a U.S. crew member. Four weeks later, on November 3, 1986, a Lebanese newspaper published an account of the secret McFarlane mission to Tehran. Investigative reporters scrambled for information on both stories. Because North had intermingled the secret operations, uncovering one endangered the other.

On November 13, Reagan spoke to the nation in a televised speech, followed a few days later by a press conference. The media scoffed at his claim that the Iranian operation was not an arms-for-hostages deal, and his press conference was riddled with misstatements of facts. Many Reagan advisers, who had watched Richard Nixon's presidency destroyed during the Watergate scandal, pressed the president to get the full, accurate story before the public as quickly as possible. On November 21, 1986, Reagan asked Attorney General Edwin Meese to investigate the matter. As Meese started his probe, North began to destroy potentially incriminating documents. On November 22, however, Meese's aides uncovered a memo that disclosed North's diversion of funds from the Iranian arms sales to the Contras. After Meese informed Reagan of the diversion, Poindexter resigned and North was fired from the NSC staff.

Several investigations got under way, but Reagan's quick action helped minimize the damage to his presidency. The diversion of Iranian funds to the Contras became the focal point of the investigation, and the media and Congress searched for evidence that Reagan had known of North's activity. This search diverted attention from the broader problems raised by White House bargaining with a terrorist nation and conducting operations hidden from Congress. The highly publicized congressional investigation floundered when John Poindexter testified that Reagan did not know of the diversion. Poindexter said that he had not told Reagan of the diversion because he wanted to protect the president in case the operation were ever disclosed.

Reagan's presidency was damaged, but his popularity began to recover as he and Soviet premier Mikhail Gorbachev held a series of summit meetings that resulted in agreements to control nuclear arms. As the Cold War tensions eased, Iran-Contra became less worrisome to the public, and Reagan left office as one of the most popular presidents in history.

—*William E. Pemberton*

Lieutenant Colonel Oliver North testifies before Congress that he and President Reagan "did not discuss" the illegal Iran-Contra operation: The Cold War foreign policies of the Reagan Administration encouraged aid to anticommunist forces around the world. These goals led the U.S. to support the Nicaraguan Contras, a guerrilla group whom Reagan regarded as freedom fighters against the Marxist Sandinista government. At the same time, the Reagan Administration covertly engaged in the sale of arms to Iran as a bargaining tool to negotiate the release of hostages in Lebanon. A member of the National Security Council, North was assigned to manage the Iranian arms sales and diverted profits to aid the Nicaraguan Contras in the face of funding cuts by Congress. Questions regarding the president's knowledge of this illegal operation were put down by later testimony of National Security Adviser John Poindexter—diverting attention from an even thornier issue: the United States' willingness to negotiate with terrorists. (AP/Wide World Photos)

ADDITIONAL READING:

Cohen, William S., and George J. Mitchell. *Men of Zeal: A Candid Inside Story of the Iran-Contra Hearings.* New York: Viking Press, 1988. A forthright account of the Iran-Contra hearings by two senators, a Republican and a Democrat, who served on the investigating committee.

Draper, Theodore. *A Very Thin Line: The Iran-Contra Affairs.* New York: Hill & Wang, 1991. The starting place for a study of Iran-Contra, by a journalist who has mastered the available documentary evidence.

Ledeen, Michael A. *Perilous Statecraft: An Insider's Account of the Iran-Contra Affair.* New York: Charles Scribner's Sons, 1988. An account of the Iranian operation from a person who worked closely with the Israelis during the early part of the affair.

North, Oliver L. *Under Fire: An American Story.* New York: HarperCollins, 1992. A controversial book, as many of its key claims have been disputed by others.

Wroe, Ann. *Lives, Lies, and the Iran-Contra Affair.* London: I. B. Tauris, 1991. An even-handed account of Iran-Contra by a British journalist.

SEE ALSO: 1972, Watergate Affair; 1980, Abscam Affair; 1991, Persian Gulf War.

1987 ■ CANADA'S PAY EQUITY ACT:
employers in the public and private sectors are required to provide equal pay for jobs requiring comparable skill, effort, and responsibility

DATE: June, 1987
LOCALE: Ontario, Canada
CATEGORIES: Business and labor; Canadian history; Laws and acts; Women's issues
KEY FIGURES:
David Peterson (born 1943), Liberal premier of Ontario when the Pay Equity Act was passed
Ian B. Scott (born 1930), justice minister who introduced the Pay Equity Act in the Ontario legislature in 1986
William Wrye (born 1944), labor minister who introduced the Public Service Pay Equity bill in the Ontario legislature in 1986

SUMMARY OF EVENT. By the 1960's, there was clear economic evidence of differential pay for male-dominated and female-dominated jobs in Canada. In 1979, the average earned income of Canadian women who worked for the full year was 63 percent of the full-year earnings of men. There were widely divergent views on the reasons for these pay differences. At one extreme, the wage gap was regarded as resulting from years of wage discrimination against women in the workplace. At the other extreme, the wage difference was explained as a natural outcome of market supply and demand, with women choosing careers requiring lower levels of skill or education and thus earning lower pay.

In 1980, more than one-third of the female workers in Canada were employed in traditionally low-paying clerical occupations, compared to 6 percent of the male workers, suggesting that at least part of the pay differential resulted from different types of occupations. However, a study published by the Ontario Ministry of Labour in 1982 concluded that when the salaries of men and women employed in the same occupation for the same firm were compared, the women still earned almost 10 percent less than the men. This study confirmed that part, but not all, of the pay difference was due to wage discrimination.

In the 1970's and 1980's, growing activism by the women's movement focused attention on the differential pay issue. Disagreements about the cause of the pay differential were resolved by focusing on comparable worth or pay equity, the demand for equal pay for equal work. The goal of instituting pay equity is to end wage discrimination by requiring a comparison of the wages of women and men who hold jobs requiring similar skills and education and who have the same length of experience in those jobs.

In Canada, the New Democratic Party championed the cause of workers' rights and supported legislation on pay equity. A long period of Conservative Party rule in the province of Ontario came to an end in 1985, with the formation of a minority Liberal government. To obtain a working majority and maintain power, the Liberals needed the support of either the Conservative Party or the New Democratic Party. In May, 1985, the New Democratic Party agreed to support the Liberals in return for a promise that the Liberal leadership would introduce several pieces of legislation, including a bill on pay equity for both the public and the private sectors.

In the fall of 1985, the Liberal government consulted with organizations representing women, labor, and business in order to work out the details of the proposed legislation. The Public Service Pay Equity bill, Bill 105, was introduced in the Ontario legislature by Labor Minister William Wrye on February 11, 1986. As written, the bill would have covered only twenty-nine thousand women in public service jobs, but the New Democratic Party and the Conservatives offered a series of amendments expanding the scope of the coverage to 340,000 women in public sector jobs. Widespread criticism of Bill 105 by women's and labor groups prompted the Liberal government to introduce the Pay Equity Act, covering both public and private sector jobs. This bill was introduced by Ian Scott, the attorney general and the minister responsible for the status of women, on November 24, 1986.

Debate focused on the scope of the legislation, with three sectors considered: the narrow public sector (only civil service employees), the broader public sector (including education, health, and municipal workers), or the entire public and private sector. Many businesses opposed legislation affecting the private sector, because it would mandate an increase in wages for some workers in the private sector. The Ontario Chamber of Commerce estimated that implementation of the proposal could cost as much as five billion dollars within the province.

Despite these objections, Conservative Party attempts to limit the scope of the bill failed, and the Pay Equity Act received final approval in June, 1987, taking effect in Ontario on January 1, 1988.

The law required that employers having more than ten workers assess all jobs in which more than 60 percent of the employees are women. About 1.7 million women in Ontario were covered by the act. The wages paid for these jobs had to be compared to the wages paid for male-dominated jobs found to be similar based on four criteria: skill, effort, responsibility, and working conditions. Using the four criteria, the York Board of Education, for example, determined that secretaries in media resources, earning $9.26 per hour, were in an equivalent job to caretakers, earning $10.64 per hour.

Women working in the public sector were affected almost immediately, with the first salary adjustments to be made by January 1, 1990, and complete pay equity to be achieved by January 1, 1995. For workers in the private sector, the time for implementing the pay adjustments depended on the size of the business. Companies having 500 employees or more had to make their first pay adjustments by January 1, 1991, while companies with 100 to 499 employees had until January 1, 1992, companies with 50 to 99 employees had until January 1, 1993, and companies with 10 to 49 employees had until January 1, 1994. Private companies with fewer than ten employees were exempt from compliance. In the private sector, no company was required to pay out more than 1 percent of its previous year's payroll as equity adjustments, with additional adjustments of 1 percent of total payroll each year until equity is achieved. There was no deadline for private firms to reach pay equity, so long as they made adjustments of at least 1 percent of payroll each year.

More than eight hundred Ontario companies had five hundred or more employees, and were required to begin implementation by the first deadline. The law produced substantial raises for women, particularly those in secretarial and clerical jobs. After evaluating the skill, effort, responsibility, and working conditions of a receptionist earning $6.81 per hour and a warehouseman earning $9.38 per hour, an automobile company in Toronto found these to be comparable positions. They were required to make a series of adjustments in the salaries of their receptionists to bring the two jobs' salaries into balance. The Bruce Telephone Company adjusted the wages of its female service representatives by about $2.50 per hour, to match that earned by male telephone installers. Werner-Lambert Canada, a pharmaceutical company, indicated it would make minor upward adjustments in the salaries of about a dozen female employees.

The province of Manitoba had passed a pay equity act in 1985, but its coverage was restricted to a narrow part of the public sector, excluding school boards, nursing homes, and many other public institutions. Following passage of the Ontario Pay Equity Act, the governments of Nova Scotia, Prince Edward Island, and New Brunswick passed their own pay equity acts in 1988 and 1989; however, these acts also were restricted to covering certain groups of public employees. The executive director of the National Committee on Pay Equity, Claudia Wayne, based in Washington, D.C., said "Ontario has gone the furthest in the world" in mandating pay equity for employees within the province. —*George J. Flynn*

ADDITIONAL READING:

Curtis, James, Edward Grabb, and Neil Guppy, eds. *Social Inequality in Canada: Patterns, Problems, Policies.* Scarborough, Ont.: Prentice-Hall Canada, 1988. A collection of essays, including one titled "Employment Opportunities for Women" that addresses salary differential and its causes.

Freudenheim, Milt. "A New Ontario Law Matches Women's Wages with Men's." *The New York Times*, July 27, 1989, A1, A18. An in-depth description of how the Pay Equity Act is being implemented in Ontario. Discusses the criteria for assessing comparable jobs and indicates the pay increases expected for women under the law.

Fudge, Judy, and Patricia McDermott, eds. *Just Wages: A Feminist Assessment of Pay Equity.* Toronto: University of Toronto Press, 1991. A collection of papers presented at the 1990 Pay Equity conference at York University, focusing on the results of the 1987 Ontario Pay Equity Act.

Gunderson, Morley. "Male and Female Wage Differentials and Policy Responses." *Journal of Economic Literature* 27 (March, 1989): 46-72. An in-depth description of the wage differentials between men and women, with comparisons showing how equivalent work is established.

Gunderson, Morley, and W. Craig Riddell. *Labour Market Economics: Theory, Evidence, and Policy in Canada.* Toronto: McGraw-Hill Ryerson, 1988. Includes a ten-page discussion of the Ontario Pay Equity Act and its effects.

SEE ALSO: 1963, Equal Pay Act.

1987 ■ INF Treaty Is Signed: *a nuclear arms control agreement eliminates an entire class of American and Soviet missiles in the European theater*

DATE: December 8, 1987
LOCALE: Washington, D.C.
CATEGORY: Diplomacy and international relations
KEY FIGURES:
Leonid Brezhnev (1906-1982), general secretary of the Communist Party, 1964-1982, and president of the Soviet Union, 1977-1982
Frank C. Carlucci (born 1930), U.S. secretary of defense
James Earl "Jimmy" Carter (born 1924), thirty-ninth president of the United States, 1977-1981
Mikhail Gorbachev (born 1931), general secretary of the Communist Party, 1985-1991, and president of the Soviet Union, 1988-1991
Yuli Aleksandrovich Kvitsinskiy (born 1936), head of the Soviet delegation to the Intermediate Nuclear Force talks

in Geneva, 1981-1983, and chief of the Soviet Space
Arms Group, Geneva, 1985-1986

Roland Lajoie (born 1936), major general in the U.S. Army
and first director of the U.S. On-Site Inspection Agency

Paul Nitze (born 1907), head of the U.S. negotiating team at
the Arms Control Talks in Geneva, 1981-1984, and
special adviser to the president and the secretary of state,
1984-1989

Ronald Reagan (born 1911), fortieth president of the United
States, 1981-1989

Helmut Schmidt (born 1918), chancellor of the Federal
Republic of Germany, 1974-1982

SUMMARY OF EVENT. In the late 1950's and early 1960's, the
Union of Soviet Socialist Republics deployed nuclear missiles—SS-4's and SS-5's—capable of reaching Western European countries. U.S. nuclear missiles capable of reaching Soviet targets were deployed in small numbers in the United
Kingdom, Italy, and Turkey in the early 1960's. These missiles
were removed after Soviet missiles in Cuba were withdrawn in
the wake of the 1962 Cuban Missile Crisis. Thereafter, there
were no land-based intermediate-range missiles in Europe until 1983.

Beginning in the late 1970's and early 1980's, the Soviet
Union began to deploy new and modernized intermediate-
range missiles, the SS-20's. Coupled with the simultaneous
deployment of the new Backfire bomber, these nuclear forces
roused concerns in Western Europe about security and the
credibility of the North Atlantic Treaty Organization
(NATO)'s nuclear deterrent. Led by West German chancellor
Helmut Schmidt, NATO leaders concluded that the increased
threat posed to Europe by the mobile and highly accurate
SS-20 missiles, each capable of carrying three independently
targetable nuclear warheads, needed a strong NATO response.
In December, 1979, NATO foreign and defense ministries
adopted a dual-track strategy of deploying U.S. intermediate-
range ballistic and cruise missiles with a total of 572 nuclear
warheads, while negotiating with the Soviets on arms control
treaties to reduce the overall nuclear threat as well as the
SS-20 threat. Pershing II and ground-launched cruise missiles (GLCM) were to be deployed in Belgium, the Netherlands, the Federal Republic of Germany, the United Kingdom, and Italy. The first deployment of these missiles began
in late 1983.

The negotiations on an intermediate-range nuclear forces
(INF) treaty began in November, 1980, at the end of Jimmy
Carter's presidency. With the election of Ronald Reagan as
U.S. president, these talks proceeded fitfully. In November,
1981, Reagan presented his new zero-option proposal in the
INF talks, offering to cancel planned deployment of the
Pershing II and GLCMs if the Soviets would dismantle their
SS-20, SS-4, and SS-5 missiles. In response, Soviet president
Leonid Brezhnev sought a moratorium on the deployment of
new intermediate-range launchers in Europe.

Faced with U.S. and Soviet negotiating positions unacceptable to both sides, chief U.S. and Soviet negotiators in Ge-

neva—Paul Nitze and Yuli Kvitsinskiy—after many private
talks culminating with an informal walk in the woods, devised
a compromise formula. It called for a two-thirds reduction in
the SS-20's directed at Western Europe in exchange for the
elimination of Pershing II deployments, but not the GLCMs.
The compromise formula was rejected by both Moscow and
Washington, D.C. When, in November, 1983, the German
Bundestag voted in favor of the deployments of the Pershing II
and cruise missiles, the Soviet Union walked out of the INF
talks, thus ending the first phase of these negotiations.

The INF talks did not resume until March, 1985, by which
time two significant developments had occurred. Mikhail Gorbachev had assumed leadership of the Soviet Union and, over
the period of the next several years, made a series of concessions that eliminated the major differences in positions in the
INF talks between the United States and the Soviet Union. On
the U.S. side, there was mounting popular pressure to pursue
serious arms control negotiations with the Soviet Union, and
Reagan, during his second term in office, gave this issue
priority. The INF negotiations were complex and featured
prominently in the Reagan-Gorbachev summits in Geneva in
November, 1985, and Reykjavik in October, 1986. In April,
1987, Gorbachev proposed an INF treaty that would eliminate
both long-range and shorter-range intermediate missiles in
Europe, a proposal expanded later to include such missiles
globally—in effect, a global zero-option. With U.S. and German acceptance of the global zero option and Soviet acquiescence to on-site verification, the last stumbling blocks to the
treaty were removed.

This second phase ended with the signing by President
Reagan and General Secretary Gorbachev of the INF Treaty
on December 8, 1987, at a summit meeting in Washington,
D.C. The treaty consisted of seventeen articles, supplemented
by two protocols and a memorandum of understanding
(MOU). The first protocol defined the elimination procedures.
The second protocol spelled out the purpose, rules, and procedures for conducting on-site inspections regarding treaty compliance. The MOU provided for an accounting by each party of
the number and location of missiles and other systems and
facilities covered in the treaty.

The treaty called for elimination of all ground-launched
missiles, of which there were approximately twenty-seven
hundred with ranges between five hundred and five thousand
kilometers (approximately three hundred to thirty-three hundred miles). On the U.S. side, the intermediate long-range
missiles slated for elimination were the Pershing II and the
BGM-109 GLCM; the intermediate shorter-range missiles included the Pershing IA. On the Soviet side, the intermediate
long-range missiles were the SS-20, SS-4, SS-5, and SSC-X-
4; the intermediate shorter-range missiles were the SS-23 and
SS-12. All U.S. and Soviet INF missile systems had to be
eliminated by the third treaty year.

The INF Treaty was ratified by the U.S. Senate on May 27,
1988, and was ratified by the Presidium of the Supreme Soviet
of the U.S.S.R. the following day. At the Moscow summit on

June 1, 1988, Reagan and Gorbachev exchanged the instruments of ratification, and the INF Treaty entered into force.

In order to assist the mission of on-site inspections and escort responsibilities under the provisions of the INF Treaty, on January 18, 1988, Reagan instructed Secretary of Defense Frank Carlucci to establish the On-Site Inspection Agency. Its first director, Major General Roland Lajoie of the U.S. Army, was appointed on February 1, 1988. Together with their counterparts from the Soviet Union, Lajoie's staff adhered to the meticulous timetable for elimination of the affected intermediate-range missiles. All such missiles were eliminated by the target year of 1991.

The INF Treaty represented a significant milestone in the history of U.S.-Soviet arms control talks. It eliminated, for the first time, an entire class of missiles; more important, it set a precedent for intensive on-site inspections to monitor treaty compliance. The treaty required or permitted the United States and the Soviet Union to conduct several hundred such inspections at operational missile sites, repair facilities, storage depots, training sites, and former missile production or assembly facilities. Soviet INF sites in the Soviet Union, Czechoslovakia, and East Germany, and United States INF sites in West Germany, Belgium, the Netherlands, Italy, Great Britain, and the United States were targeted for inspections.

The INF Treaty set in motion the U.S.-Soviet arms control agenda for the future and was an important precursor to the Strategic Arms Reduction Treaty I (START I), which was signed in 1991; the Conventional Forces in Europe (CFE) Treaty of 1992; and START II in 1993. Together, these treaties laid the groundwork for significant reductions in Soviet and U.S. nuclear arsenals.   —*Vidya Nadkarni*

ADDITIONAL READING:

Brady, Linda P. *The Politics of Negotiation: America's Dealing with Allies, Adversaries, and Friends.* Chapel Hill: University of North Carolina Press, 1991. Covers negotiations on the INF Treaty in detail in chapter 6.

Bunn, George. *Arms Control by Committee: Managing Negotiations with the Russians.* Stanford, Calif.: Stanford University Press, 1992. Investigates case histories of U.S.-Soviet arms control negotiations, including the INF talks, from a U.S. perspective.

Dewitt, David, and Hans Rattinger, eds. *East-West Arms Control: Challenges for the Western Alliance.* London: Routledge, 1992. Examines NATO strategy and alliance politics, and the role of public opinion and domestic policies on arms control.

Mayers, Teena Karsa. *Understanding Weapons and Arms Control: A Guide to the Issues.* Rev. 6th ed. McLean, Va.: Brassey's, 1991. A succinct account of postwar U.S. nuclear strategy. Contains a detailed glossary of arms control terms.

Rueckert, George L. *Global Double Zero: The INF Treaty from Its Origins to Implementation.* Contributions in Military Studies 135. Westport, Conn.: Greenwood Press, 1993. Discusses the negotiations and implementation procedures of the INF Treaty. Charts, maps, and tables.

SEE ALSO: 1973, Détente with the Soviet Union; 1979, SALT II Is Signed; 1985, U.S.-Soviet Summit; 1991, Bush Announces Nuclear Arms Reductions; 1993, START II Is Signed.

1988 ■ CIVIL RIGHTS RESTORATION ACT:
recipients of federal financial assistance are obligated by nondiscriminatory requirements in all respects, not merely in activity aided by federal funds

DATE: March 22, 1988
LOCALE: Washington, D.C.
CATEGORIES: Civil rights; Laws and acts
KEY FIGURES:
Terrel Howard Bell (born 1921), secretary of education, 1981-1985
William Joseph Brennan, Jr. (born 1906),
Thurgood Marshall (1908-1993), and
Byron Raymond White (born 1917), Supreme Court justices
Patricia Roberts Harris (1924-1985), secretary of health, education, and welfare, 1979
Augustus Freeman Hawkins (born 1907), Democratic representative
Edward Moore Kennedy (born 1932), Democratic senator from Massachusetts
Ronald Wilson Reagan (born 1911), fortieth president of the United States, 1981-1989

SUMMARY OF EVENT. Title VI of the Civil Rights Act of 1964 mandated that federal funds could not be used to support segregation or discrimination based on race, color, or national origin. The law did not affect a number of other civil rights problems, however. At Cornell University's School of Agriculture, for example, women could not gain admission unless their entrance exam scores were 30 to 40 percent higher than those of male applicants. Epileptics were often barred from employment, and persons in wheelchairs had difficulty gaining access to libraries and schools. Persons in their fifties were often told that they were qualified for a job but too old. To rectify these problems, Congress extended the scope of unlawful discrimination in federally assisted schools in Title IX of the Education Amendments Act of 1972 to cover gender; the Rehabilitation Act of 1973 expanded the same coverage to the disabled; and the Age Discrimination Act of 1975 added age as a protected class.

Enforcement of the statute regarding education was initially assigned to the Office for Civil Rights (OCR) of the U.S. Department of Health, Education, and Welfare, which later became the U.S. Department of Education. OCR ruled that the statute outlawed not only discrimination in the particular program supported by federal funds but also discrimination in programs supported by nonfederal funds. All recipients of federal financial assistance were asked to sign an agreement with OCR, known as the "Assurance of Compliance with Title IX of the Education Amendments of 1972 and the Regulation Issued by the Department of Health, Education and Welfare in Implementation Thereof," as a condition of receiving a federal grant.

From 1974 to 1984, Grove City College, located in western Pennsylvania, received $1.8 million in tuition grants and guaranteed student loans but was the only such recipient to refuse to sign an assurance of compliance. The college argued that the funds were for students, not the college, but OCR insisted that the financial aid was administered as a part of the college's financial aid program, so the college must pledge as a whole not to discriminate on the basis of race, color, national origin, or gender. OCR instituted enforcement proceedings against Grove City College, and an administrative law judge ruled in 1978 that the college could no longer receive federal student loan moneys.

Grove City College and four students desiring financial aid (Marianne Sickafuse, Kenneth J. Hockenberry, Jennifer S. Smith, and Victor E. Vouga) then sued. The original defendant was Patricia Roberts Harris, secretary of health, education, and welfare. In 1980, when the case was first tried, the federal district court ruled in favor of Grove City College on the grounds that no sex discrimination had actually occurred. On appeal, the court of appeals reversed the lower court's decision, and the matter was taken up by the Supreme Court of the United States, this time with Terrel H. Bell, head of the newly created federal Department of Education, as the defendant.

In *Grove City College v. Bell* (1984), Justice Byron R. White delivered the majority opinion of the court, which held that OCR did not have sufficient congressional authority to withhold funds from Grove City College for failure to sign the assurance of compliance. Moreover, according to the court, violations of Title VI could occur only in the specific program or activity supported directly with federal funds, a judgment that went beyond the question raised by the case. Justices William J. Brennan, Jr., and Thurgood Marshall dissented, arguing that the Court's ruling gutted Title VI.

Shortly after the Supreme Court ruling, OCR dropped some seven hundred pending enforcement actions, resulting in an outcry from civil rights groups over the decision. Representative Augustus F. Hawkins then authored the Civil Rights Restoration Act in the House, and Senator Edward M. Kennedy sponsored the bill in the Senate. Their aim was to amend all the affected statutes—Title VI of the Civil Rights Act of 1964, Title IX of the Education Amendments of 1972 Act, the Rehabilitation Act of 1973, and the Age Discrimination Act of 1975. According to the bill, any agency or private firm that wanted to receive federal financial assistance would have to comply with the nondiscrimination requirement as a whole, even if the aid went to only one subunit of that agency or firm.

The road toward passage of the proposed statute was full of potholes, however. Although Hawkins' version quickly passed in the House of Representatives, the measure was caught up in the politics of abortion, and the bill died in the Senate. Opponents advanced more than one thousand amendments over a period of four years, and representatives of the administration of President Ronald Reagan testified against passage of the law. A group known as the Moral Majority broadcast the fear that the bill would protect alcoholics, drug addicts, and homosexuals from discrimination, although there were no such provisions in the proposal.

More crucially, the Catholic Conference of Bishops, which was traditionally aligned with the Civil Rights movement, wanted two amendments to the bill. One proposed amendment, which was unsuccessful, would have exempted institutions affiliated with religious institutions from complying with the law if religious views would be compromised thereby. The other proposed amendment, which was opposed by the National Organization for Women, was an assurance that no federal funds would be spent on abortion. With two parts of the Civil Rights movement at loggerheads, Congress delayed finding a compromise.

In 1987, leaving out references to abortion, Congress finally adopted the Civil Rights Restoration Act, which then went to President Ronald Reagan for his signature to become law. Reagan, however, became the first president to veto a civil rights bill since Andrew Johnson. Instead, he sent a substitute bill to Congress, which would have exempted farmers, grocery stores, ranchers, and religious institutions.

Supporters of the act next sought to gain sufficient votes to override the presidential veto, and the act had sufficient support. With the gallery filled with persons in wheelchairs, opponents in the Senate tried to destroy the bill by various amendments in debate on the floor of the Senate on January 28, 1988. An amendment by Senator Orrin G. Hatch, for example, would have legislatively exempted organizations closely identified with the tenets of a religious organization, although the bill enabled such groups to obtain exemptions from OCR. He also sought to restrict coverage to the specific affected statutes. Both efforts were defeated. Senators Thomas R. Harkin and Gordon J. Humphrey gained support for an amendment that permitted employers to discriminate against persons with an infection or contagious disease whose presence on the job might threaten the health or safety of others or could not otherwise perform the duties of the job. This reflected the hysteria then common about acquired immunodeficiency syndrome (AIDS).

Senator John C. Danforth proposed an amendment that would disallow federal payments for abortion. This amendment passed, providing that neither Title VI nor Title IX was intended to require an abortion or payment for an abortion. With the passage of the act by the Senate on March 22, 1988, Congress overrode Reagan's veto, and the law went into effect immediately. The law restored civil rights enforcement to where it was before the *Grove* case.   —*Michael Haas*

ADDITIONAL READING:

Blow, Richard. "Don't Look NOW." *New Republic* 198 (April 11, 1988): 11-12. Explains why the National Organization for Women opposed the law.

Gillespie, Veronica M., and Gregory L. McClinton. "The Civil Rights Restoration Act of 1987: A Defeat for Judicial Conservatism." *National Black Law Journal* 12 (Spring, 1990): 61-72. Explains the politics and facets of the law.

Robinson, Robert K., Billie Morgan Allen, and Geralyn McClure Franklin. "The Civil Rights Restoration Act of 1987: Broadening the Scope of Civil Rights Legislation." *Labor Law Journal* 40 (January, 1989): 45-49. Discusses coverage of the law.

Watson, Robert. "Effects of the Civil Rights Restoration Act of 1987 upon Private Organizations and Religious Institutions." *Capital University Law Review* 18 (Spring, 1989): 93-118. Discusses conservative objections to the law.

Willen, Mark. "Congress Overrides Reagan's Grove City Veto." *Congressional Quarterly Weekly Review* 46 (March 26, 1988): 774-776. Explains the parliamentary maneuvers required to get the law passed.

SEE ALSO: 1964, Civil Rights Act of 1964; 1965, Expansion of Affirmative Action; 1991, Civil Rights Act of 1991.

1988 ■ FAMILY SUPPORT ACT: *the first overhaul of the welfare system in more than half a century, the act cements a link between welfare and work*

DATE: October 13, 1988
LOCALE: Washington, D.C.
CATEGORIES: Laws and acts; Social reform
KEY FIGURES:

William L. Armstrong (born 1937), Republican senator from Colorado

Hank Brown (born 1940), Republican representative from Colorado

Michael Newbold Castle (born 1939), Republican governor of Delaware

William Jefferson "Bill" Clinton (born 1946), Democratic governor of Arkansas

Thomas J. Downey (born 1949), Democratic representative from New York

Daniel Patrick Moynihan (born 1927), Democratic senator from New York

SUMMARY OF EVENT. After years of debate, Congress cleared welfare reform legislation on September 30, 1988, and on October 13, President Ronald Reagan signed Public Law 100-485, known as the Family Support Act of 1988 (FSA). The new law affirmed an evolving vision of the responsibilities of parents and government for the well-being of poor adults and their dependent children.

FSA left intact the basic entitlement nature of the federal-state Aid to Families with Dependent Children (AFDC) program and even expanded it by requiring states to extend coverage to certain two-parent families. The anchoring principle of FSA was that parents should be the primary supports of their

children and that, for many people, public assistance should be coupled with encouragement, support, and requirements to aid them in moving from welfare to self-support. FSA placed a responsibility both on welfare recipients to take jobs and participate in employment services, and on government to provide the incentives and services to help welfare recipients find employment. For noncustodial parents, usually absent fathers, this was reflected in greater enforcement of child support collections. For custodial parents, usually mothers, this meant new obligations to cooperate in child collection efforts, as well as new opportunities for publicly supported child care, education, training, and employment services, coupled with obligations to take a job or cooperate with the program.

FSA was Congress' third attempt in twenty years to overhaul the welfare system. Two previous efforts, in 1969 and 1977, foundered over many of the same philosophical differences and technical issues about how best to reduce welfare dependency that threatened to defeat the new law. Most elusive was how to maintain an economic safety net for government-assisted poor parents and their children, while discouraging nonsubsidized working-poor parents from becoming welfare-dependent and preventing the underwriting of low-wage labor. President Reagan's vow in his 1986 state of the union message to make welfare reform a priority buoyed advocates of the law. A commitment by the nation's governors to overhaul welfare also encouraged reformers.

A consensus emerged around the idea that work was better than welfare, but it proved fragile in 1987 when the White House proposed that states should experiment with existing programs without benefit of new federal funds, while House Democrats pushed through a bill that expanded benefits and cost more than $7 billion. Senators Daniel P. Moynihan (Democrat, New York) and Lloyd Bentson (Democrat, Texas), chairman of the Senate Finance Committee, steered a more modest $2.8 billion plan through the Senate on June 16, 1988. To gain White House and Republican support, Moynihan and Bentson accepted work and participation requirements added by Senate Minority Leader Robert Dole (Republican, Kansas) and Senator William L. Armstrong (Republican, Colorado). Liberal Democrats recoiled at the thought of work requirements, and many governors worried about increased costs associated with meeting job training and other requirements.

FSA established the Job Opportunities and Basic Skills (JOBS) training program to assure that needy families with children would obtain the education, training, and employment necessary to help them avoid long-term welfare dependency. The JOBS program replaced several other work-incentive programs, such as the Work Incentive (WIN) and WIN DEMO projects of the 1980's. Child care and supportive services were provided to enable individuals to accept employment or receive training.

State JOBS programs were required to include appropriate educational activities, such as high school or equivalent education, combined with training as needed; basic and remedial education to achieve functional literacy, and education for individuals with limited English proficiency; job skills training; job readiness activities; and job development and placement. State programs also included, but were not limited to, two of the four following services: group and individual job search; on-the-job training, during which the recipient would be placed in a paid job for which the employer provided training and wages and, in return, would be paid a supplement for the employee's wages by the state Social Security Act Title IV-A (AFDC) agency; work supplementation, in which the employed recipient's AFDC grant could be diverted to an employer to cover part of the cost of the wages paid to the recipient; and community work experience programs or other Department of Health and Human Services-approved work programs, which generally provided short-term work experience in public projects.

The JOBS program also amended the unemployed-parent component of AFDC to provide that at least one parent in a family must participate for a minimum of sixteen hours a week in a work program specified by the state. If a parent was less than twenty-five years of age and had not completed high school, the state could require the parent to participate in educational activities directed at attaining a high school diploma or in another basic education program. The second parent could be required to participate at state option, unless he or she met another exemption criteria. At the outset, many AFDC parents were excluded from participation in JOBS, and the legislation called for gradually increasing the participation rates throughout the 1990's from 5 to 20 percent.

Early critics of FSA's design and implementation noted that many JOBS requirements did not apply to AFDC recipients in two-parent families. Where they did, fathers were placed mainly in on-the-job training or "workplace" programs and provided with far fewer services than were available to mothers. A possible reason for this differential treatment is that work training and placement experiments with men receiving AFDC have resulted, at best, in only marginal, if at all measurable, gains when experimental groups are compared with controls. Another criticism has been that funding for JOBS is a "capped" entitlement: The federal government matches expenditures by each state up to a fixed amount. Congressional appropriations for this part of FSA cannot legally exceed the cap, regardless of state need or demand.

The other major provision of FSA concerned child-support enforcement. FSA required automatic withholding of child support from an absent parent's paycheck for all new and modified support orders, commencing two years after enactment, regardless of whether the payments were in arrears, as had been specified in 1984 legislation. Initially this provision applied only to all cases being enforced by the state child-support agency, but after January 1, 1994, it covered all orders, regardless of whether a parent had sought assistance from the state child-support agency. FSA also required states, beginning in fiscal 1992, to meet federal standards in establishing paternity for children born out of wedlock. States must either establish paternity for half of all children born out of wedlock who were receiving state child-support services (with some exceptions for good cause); equal or exceed the average paternity-establishment percentage for all states; or have increased their paternity-establishment percentage by three percentage points or more from fiscal 1988-1991 or in any year thereafter.

Groups representing divorced fathers complained that automatic wage withholding could lead to their losing jobs, and that actually handing over the monthly support check was the only leverage they had to ensure that mothers obeyed visitation orders. Congress overruled such objections in the light of evidence showing that 52 percent of all women with children less than twenty-one years of age did not receive part or all of the child support legally due to them, and that nearly 40 percent of households with children in need of support did not have court orders or legal support agreements.

—*Richard K. Caputo*

ADDITIONAL READING:

Berry, Mary Frances. *The Politics of Parenthood: Child Care, Women's Rights, and the Myth of the Good Mother*. New York: Viking Press, 1993. This history of parenthood in the twentieth century shows how increased labor force participation among women undermined any incentive to support poor, unemployed mothers on public assistance. Notes, bibliography, and index.

Caputo, Richard K. "Limits of Welfare Reform." *Social Casework* 70, no. 2 (February, 1989): 85-95. Discusses the 1988 welfare reform and job training efforts in light of the impact that structural shifts in the economy and society had on employment and quality of life for the working poor and hard-to-employ.

Chilman, Catherine S. "Welfare Reform or Revision? The Family Support Act of 1988." *Social Service Review* 66, no. 3 (September, 1992): 349-377. Outlines the chief provisions of FSA and discusses its background, implementation—especially its Job Opportunities and Basic Skill (JOBS) training program and child-care components—and plans for evaluation. Notes.

Congressional Quarterly Almanac 1988. Vol. 44, pp. 349-364. Washington, D.C.: Congressional Quarterly Inc., 1988. Describes background, provisions, Senate committee action, Senate floor action, and final conference actions on FSA legislation.

Gueron, Judith M., and Edward Pauly. *From Welfare to Work*. New York: Russell Sage Foundation, 1991. Reviews the welfare demonstration projects whose results informed the debates leading to passage of FSA. Appendices; references; author and subject indexes.

Handler, Joel, and Yeheskel Hasenfeld. *The Moral Construction of Poverty: Welfare Reform in America*. Newbury Park, Calif.: Sage Publications, 1991. Highlights the symbolic significance of distinguishing between worthy and nonworthy recipients of public assistance, culminating with the FSA. References and index.

SEE ALSO: 1935, Social Security Act; 1993, Family and Medical Leave Act.

1988 ■ Indian Gaming Regulatory Act:

Congress regulates gaming on Indian lands by dividing it into three classes and authorizing compacts between tribes and states

Date: October 17, 1988

Locale: Washington, D.C.

Categories: Economics; Laws and acts; Native American history

Key figures:

Dennis DeConcini (born 1937), Democrat from Arizona who introduced the Indian Gaming Control Act in the United States Senate

Daniel Inouye (born 1924), Democrat from Hawaii who chaired the Senate Select Committee on Indian Affairs

Ross Swimmer (born 1943), assistant secretary for Indian Affairs

Morris Udall (born 1922), Democratic congressman from Arizona who introduced the first of a series of proposed Indian gaming bills in 1983

Summary of event. The Indian Gaming Regulatory Act (IGRA), Public Law 100-497, signed into law on October 17, 1988, by President George Bush, represents an amalgamation of ideas presented in various bills introduced in Congress from 1983 through 1987 and provides a system to permit and regulate gaming on American Indian lands.

The IGRA divides gaming into three classes. Class I gaming includes social games of minimal value, as well as traditional games played as a part of tribal ceremonies or celebrations. Class I gaming is exclusively regulated by the tribes. Class II gaming includes bingo, and if played within the same location, pull tabs, lotto, tip jars, instant bingo, games similar to bingo, and certain card games. A tribe may engage in Class II games if the state in which the tribe is located permits such gaming for any purpose by any person, organization, or entity. Class III gaming includes all forms of gaming other than Class I or II, for example, banking card games like blackjack, baccarat and chemin de fer, slot machines, craps, parimutuel horse racing, and dog racing. Class III gaming is prohibited unless authorized by a tribal-state compact.

In addition to classifying games, the IGRA established a three-member National Indian Gaming Commission within the Department of the Interior. The commission chairman is appointed by the president of the United States with Senate approval; the other two members are appointed by the secretary of the interior. At least two members must be enrolled members of an American Indian tribe. The commission has the power to approve all tribal gaming ordinances and resolutions, shut down gaming activities, levy and collect fines, and approve gaming management contracts for Class II and III gaming. The commission has broad power to monitor Class II gaming by inspecting gaming permits, conducting background investigations of personnel, and inspecting and auditing books and records. Regulation and jurisdiction of Class III gaming is more complicated. Class III gaming is lawful when it is authorized by a tribal ordinance, approved by the chairman of the commission, located in a state that permits such gaming (whether for charitable, commercial, or government purposes), and conducted in compliance with a tribal-state compact that is approved by the secretary of the interior.

A tribe seeking to conduct Class III gaming must request that the state in which its lands are located negotiate a tribal-state compact governing the conduct of gaming activities. The compact may include provisions concerning the application of tribal or state criminal and civil laws directly related to gaming, the allocation of jurisdiction between the state and tribe, state assessments to defray the costs of regulation, standards for operation and maintenance of the gaming facility, and other subjects related to the gaming activity. The state is not authorized to impose a tax or assessment upon a tribe unless the tribe agrees. The state cannot refuse to negotiate a compact based on its inability to impose a tax, fee, or other assessment.

The question of gaming on American Indian reservations is one that involves both sovereignty and economic issues for tribes and states alike. The IGRA grants United States district courts jurisdiction over actions by tribes. Reasons for such action include failure of a state to negotiate with a tribe seeking to enter a compact; failure of the state to negotiate in good faith; or any violation of the tribal-state compact. The IGRA provides that a federal district court may order a tribe and state to reach a compact if the state fails to meet its burden of proving that it negotiated in good faith. If no compact is forthcoming, a court may appoint a mediator to recommend a compact. In March, 1996, the United States Supreme Court ruled in *Seminole Tribe of Indians v. Florida* that Congress cannot force states into federal court to settle disputes over gambling on reservations. Federal law, through the IGRA, still permits tribes to seek help from the secretary of the interior when state officials balk at tribal plans for gaming operations.

The IGRA requires that all gaming facilities be tribally owned and that revenue from gaming operations be directed for specific tribal programs, such as education, elderly programs, or housing. Restriction of gaming to tribal governments ensures that American Indian gaming remains a government function rather than a personal endeavor.

The most controversial aspect of the IGRA involves the tribal-state compacting required for Class III gaming. Tribal sovereignty is diminished by the IGRA, because it forces states and tribes into an agreement. Most laws recognize that tribes have a government-to-government relationship with the federal government and are not under state jurisdiction unless there is prior agreement (as in Public Law 280 states). The IGRA specifically requires negotiations between tribes and states, a relationship they do not normally have.

States objected to the tribal-state compacting on the grounds that it violated their sovereignty under the Eleventh Amendment of the Constitution, which protects states from

Bay Mills Gambling Casino, Michigan, run by the Ojibway tribe under the regulations of the Indian Gaming Regulatory Act of 1988. (Raymond P. Malace)

being sued in federal court against their will. In a 1996 Supreme Court decision, it was ruled that Congress cannot attempt to resolve stalled negotiations between states and tribes over on-reservation gambling by making states and their officials targets of federal lawsuits. The Eleventh Amendment rights of states were upheld.

The IGRA has been embraced by many tribes in the United States as a way to bolster reservation economies. Some of the most poverty-stricken areas in the United States are American Indian reservations, and gaming revenues give tribes income to reinvest in other business ventures. However, the compacting process can result in conflict of interest for some states that rely heavily on gaming revenues. In addition, the issue of untaxed revenues resulting from American Indian gaming operations is a factor in establishing compacts, and states in need of such revenue cannot act dispassionately with tribes when they negotiate those compacts. Gaming on American Indian reservations is fraught with issues of competing interests for both tribes and states. —*Carole A. Barrett*

ADDITIONAL READING:

Canby, William C. *American Indian Law in a Nutshell.* Minneapolis: West, 1981. Provides simple explanations of complex legal issues that inhere in dealings between the federal government, states, and tribal nations.

MacFarlan, Allan A. *Book of American Indian Games.* New York: Associated Press, 1958. Discusses and describes various games, including gambling games, played by a variety of North American tribes.

Pommersheim, Frank. "Economic Development in Indian Country: What Are the Questions?" *American Indian Law Review* 12 (1987): 195-217. Explains the need for revenue in American Indian country and the possibilities gaming provides tribes.

Santoni, Roland J. "The Indian Gaming Regulatory Act: How Did We Get Here? Where Are We Going?" *Creighton Law Review* 26 (1993): 387-447. Provides a comprehensive chronology of the legislation, pertinent legal cases, suggested amendments, and a table of tribal-state compacts.

Turner, Allen C. "Evolution, Assimilation, and State Control of Gambling in Indian Country: Is *Cabazon v. California* an Assimilationist Wolf in Preemptive Clothing?" *Idaho Law Review* 24, no. 2 (1987-1988): 317-338. Explores the seminal case that influenced involvement of states in the compacting process.

Wilkinson, Charles F. *American Indians, Time, and the Law: Native Societies in a Modern Constitutional Democracy.* New Haven, Conn.: Yale University Press, 1987. Discusses tribal sovereignty as a preconstitutional right and how this inherent right can be diminished.

Wunder, John R. *"Retained by the People": A History of American Indians and the Bill of Rights.* New York: Oxford University Press, 1994. A chronicle and comprehensive history of the relationship between American Indians and the federal government. Gives detailed analysis of the tribal-federal relationship.

SEE ALSO: 1953, Termination Resolution; 1968, Indian Civil Rights Act; 1969, Alcatraz Occupation; 1971, Alaska Native Claims Settlement Act; 1972, Trail of Broken Treaties; 1973, Wounded Knee Occupation; 1978, American Indian Religious Freedom Act.

1988 ■ BUSH IS ELECTED PRESIDENT: *the conservative agenda inaugurated by Ronald Reagan's presidency is continued by George Bush*

DATE: November 8, 1988
LOCALE: United States
CATEGORY: Government and politics
KEY FIGURES:

Lloyd Millard Bentson, Jr. (born 1921), Democratic vice presidential nominee

George Herbert Walker Bush (born 1924), incumbent vice president and Republican presidential nominee

Michael Stanley Dukakis (born 1933), Massachusetts governor and Democratic presidential nominee

Jesse Louis Jackson (born 1941), African American candidate for the Democratic presidential nomination

James Danforth Quayle (born 1947), Republican senator and vice presidential nominee

SUMMARY OF EVENT. George Bush was the first sitting vice president of the United States to win the presidency since Martin Van Buren in 1836. His election to the presidency marked the first time that the same party had won three consecutive elections since Franklin Delano Roosevelt. The election of 1988 was also unique for the large number of candidates contesting for each party's nomination. Republicans running included Bush, Senate Minority Leader Robert Dole, Representative Jack Kemp, Delaware governor Pierre (Pete) DuPont, former secretary of state Alexander Haig, and religious broadcaster Marion (Pat) Robertson. Democratic hopefuls running included senators Joseph Biden, Albert Gore, Gary Hart, and Paul Simon, Representative Richard Gephardt, governors Bruce Babbitt and Michael Dukakis, and African American minister and civil rights activist Jesse Jackson. This large number of candidates was a result of changes in the rules of both parties for delegate selection, the rise in primaries, the

availability of public campaign money, and the arrival of new campaign, media, and fund-raising technologies. In addition, it was thought that the political definition and future of both parties was at stake.

The Republican Party was divided over what President Ronald Reagan's legacy should be and who should carry the legacy forward. Vice President Bush was the front-runner, but he was seen as a vacillating moderate by the conservative core of the party. DuPont and Kemp claimed that they would be able to institute the limited national government, tax reduction, and market-oriented economic and regulatory policies of the Reagan agenda. Dole also emphasized these traits and had the second highest ratings in the polls in 1987, after Bush. Haig was the weakest candidate, because he had no electoral base or constituency. The Reverend Pat Robertson represented a new force in electoral politics. As a television preacher with a large audience, he had a potentially large political base, because of his visibility and his stance on moral issues.

Bush stressed the need for loyalty to him as Reagan's vice president. After some early campaign setbacks, Bush won a clear victory in the New Hampshire primary and then won decisively on Super Tuesday, a day on which sixteen primaries were scheduled. He selected a little-known, second-term senator from Indiana, J. Danforth Quayle, as his running mate. His campaign theme became "a kinder, gentler America."

The race for the Democratic nomination was more complicated. The party was deeply split between those who wanted to continue the activist government social and economic programs of the Great Society of President Lyndon Johnson and those who espoused a stance that was more moderate or less liberal, yet preserved the party's traditional ideals. Gary Hart was the initial front-runner, but personal scandal involving a liaison with an aspiring model scuttled his campaign. Biden withdrew because of accusations that he had made a plagiarized speech. The remaining candidates suffered from lack of name recognition, fund-raising difficulties, and an inability to differentiate themselves from one another and to reconcile the liberal and moderate forces within the party. Jackson was very visible and had a solid constituency among African Americans, but he was too closely linked to the policies of the liberal wing of the party for most voters.

The Democratic primaries were chaotic. Michael Dukakis prevailed because of superior organization, ample campaign funds, and an ability to bring together a national coalition of Democratic groups and voters. The nomination evolved into a three-way contest among him, Gore, and Jackson, who attracted significant white support to his campaign. Dukakis continued to expand his base, and his momentum eventually gave him the nomination. Dukakis selected Senator Lloyd Bentson of Texas as his running mate.

Since the advent of television, electoral politics had been sensitive to the needs and demands of the mass media. The election of 1988 continued and expanded on this trend. Both sides focused on negative advertising and mudslinging, as each attempted to define the other with negative connotations

George Herbert Walker Bush, forty-first president of the United States. Among the achievements of the Bush Administration are passage of the Americans with Disabilities Act (1990), antidrug legislation, and nuclear arms reductions. Bush also presided over the brief Persian Gulf War against Iraq in defense of U.S. ally Kuwait. (Library of Congress)

and associations. While there were televised national debates among the candidates, most observers would not characterize the campaign as driven by substantive debate on either side.

Bush won in 40 states with 426 electoral votes, to Dukakis' 111 electoral votes (one elector cast his vote for Lloyd Bentson). Bush received 47,946,422 votes, for 53.89 percent of the total; Dukakis received 41,016,429 votes, or 46.11 percent. Voter turnout was 50.2 percent of the eligible voting-age population, the lowest since 1948.

Demographic analysis of the presidential vote, based on election-day exit polls, shows that the African American vote was distributed 12 percent for Bush and 86 percent for Dukakis, with 2 percent going to other candidates. Those who identified themselves as Hispanic voted 30 percent for Bush and 69 percent for Dukakis. White voters gave 59 percent of their vote to Bush and 40 percent to Dukakis. Women gave 50 percent of their vote to Bush and 49 percent to Dukakis. Overall, Bush did almost as well in areas of the country and among groups in which President Reagan had done well in his two elections, and did not do well where Reagan had not.

As the forty-first president, George Bush had policy and political failures and successes. Foreign affairs is his strongest legacy. His crowning achievement in this area was the orchestration in 1990 of the world response to the invasion of Kuwait by Saddam Hussein of Iraq, which threatened the stability of the Middle East as well as the supply of oil. Through intense personal diplomacy, Bush convinced a reluctant Congress and hesitant allies to mount what became a military victory, known as Operation Desert Storm, or the Persian Gulf War, over Iraq.

The second major event during Bush's administration was the assault on Panama to depose Manuel Noriega. While this was a popular decision, the long-term impact it would have on Panama's domestic political and economic problems was unclear. Nevertheless, these policies signaled an end to the Vietnam syndrome—the reluctance to use U.S. military force.

Bush was heavily engaged in the management of the new international order brought on by the collapse of the Soviet Union and the ending of the Cold War. This marked the shift from nuclear deterrence and containment of communism to problems of drug trafficking, the environment, Third World development, and the increasing interdependence of nations.

In domestic affairs, Bush's presidency was an attempt to consolidate the Reagan program. His efforts in this area were limited by the demands of foreign affairs; the controversy over his selection of Clarence Thomas for the Supreme Court, along with the controversial testimony by Anita Hill; and the collapse of the savings and loan industry, which necessitated a massive government bailout. Perhaps most important, the large deficit of the Reagan years led Bush to break his pledge not to raise taxes, but to allow a large tax increase.

These factors, coupled with a perceived lack of domestic vision and political and management disarray in the White House, led to Bush's defeat by Arkansas governor Bill Clinton in 1992. Ultimately, George Bush lacked the ideological conviction and comforting rhetoric of President Reagan. At the same time, his election confirmed the existence of a strong conservative movement in U.S. politics.   —*Melvin Kulbicki*

ADDITIONAL READING:

Abramson, Paul R., John H. Alrich, and David W. Rohde, eds. *Change and Continuity in the 1988 Election.* Washington, D.C.: Congressional Quarterly Press, 1990. Essays with a strong focus on voter behavior historically, as well as in 1988.

Campbell, Colin, and Bert A. Rockman, eds. *The Bush Presidency: First Appraisals.* Chatham, N.J.: Chatham House, 1991. Focuses on President Bush's leadership style in the context of divided government.

Drew, Elizabeth. *Election Journal: Political Events of 1987-1988.* New York: William Morrow, 1989. A chronicle of the major events and personages in this election year, along with a solid account of the role of the media in politics.

Germond, Jack, and Jules Witcover. "Betraying the Revolution." In *Mad as Hell: Revolt at the Ballot Box, 1992.* New York: Warner Books, 1993. An analysis of the root causes of Bush's fall from great popularity in fewer than two years.

Pomper, Gerald M., ed. *The Election of 1988: Reports and Interpretations.* Chatham, N.J.: Chatham House, 1989. Essays on the electoral and political context of the Bush election.

Simon, Roger. *Road Show*. New York: Farrar, Straus & Giroux, 1991. A lively account of the candidates and their managers in a campaign environment dominated by the mass media.

Will, George. *The New Season: A Spectator's Guide to the 1988 Election*. New York: Simon & Schuster, 1989. An often witty analysis of the ideology and political forces at work in this election, from a conservative's point of view.

See also: 1980, Reagan Is Elected President; 1983, Jackson Becomes First Major African American Candidate for President; 1990, Americans with Disabilities Act; 1991, Persian Gulf War; 1991, Bush Announces Nuclear Arms Reductions; 1991, Civil Rights Act of 1991; 1992, Clinton Is Elected President.

1989 ■ Exxon Valdez Oil Spill: *the largest oil spill in U.S. waters focuses attention on the environmental, economic, and political consequences of tanker ship operations*

Date: March 24, 1989
Locale: Prince William Sound, Alaska
Categories: Business and labor; Environment
Key figures:

Gregory T. Cousins (born 1951), third mate of the *Exxon Valdez*

Joseph J. Hazelwood (born 1947), captain of the *Exxon Valdez*

Frank Iarossi, president of Exxon Shipping

Robert Kagan, helmsman on the *Exxon Valdez*

Dennis Kelso, Alaska's environmental conservation commissioner

Steve McCall, commandant, U.S. Coast Guard, Valdez

Summary of event. At 12:27 A.M., March 24, 1989, Captain Joseph J. Hazelwood reported the *Exxon Valdez* aground on Bligh Reef, twenty-eight miles from Valdez, Alaska, in Prince William Sound. Eight of eleven cargo tanks and three of five ballast tanks were punctured, spilling about 258,000 of the 1,480,000 barrels of oil aboard the tanker.

At one time, stringent restrictions had been placed on tanker operation in Prince William Sound. These included an emergency clean-up crew permanently on duty at Valdez, Coast Guard monitoring of traffic through Prince William Sound, pilotage from Valdez to the open sea, restricted inbound and outbound traffic lanes, and State Department of Conservation oversight of all operations. However, the requirement of double-bottomed tankers was not initiated, and traffic monitoring was limited to the northern end of the sound. As 8,549 tanker transits were completed without serious mishap, restrictions progressively eased. Piloting was reduced to the Valdez Narrows, the clean-up crew was scaled

back and staffed on a contingency basis by Alyeska (the consortium of oil companies responsible for such cleanup), Coast Guard supervision was diminished, and tankers were routinely allowed to cross into the inbound lane when avoiding ice.

The *Exxon Valdez* arrived after dark at Valdez on March 22. While the ship was loading, Captain Hazelwood and part of the crew went ashore, returning around 8:30 P.M., March 23. The ship sailed at approximately 9:30 P.M. The pilot left the ship at the entrance to Valdez Narrows. At 11:30, Captain Hazelwood radioed the Coast Guard, obtaining clearance to enter the inbound lane to avoid floating ice. Shortly thereafter, he changed course another 20 degrees, going outside the established lanes. These were routine maneuvers for avoiding ice. At 11:50, the bridge watch changed and helmsman Robert Kagan came on duty. The third mate, Gregory Cousins, remained on watch because his assigned successor was exhausted after supervising loading. At 11:53, Captain Hazelwood gave Cousins control of the ship and left the bridge for a few minutes. Cousins was licensed only for open-sea operation, but short-term use of unlicensed officers was routine and tolerated.

Hazelwood gave Cousins detailed orders to turn to the right, thus avoiding Bligh Shoal, when he came abeam of the Busby Island light. This point was reached two or three minutes after the captain left. After about another minute, the lookout reported that the Bligh Island light, which should have been to port, was to starboard. The tanker hit the reef at 12:04 A.M. According to an automatic recording device, Hazelwood's order was executed five minutes too late. It is unclear whether Cousins or Kagan caused the delay. Following the captain's instructions would have prevented grounding.

Both the pilot and the Coast Guard investigating officer who boarded the tanker at 3:00 A.M. thought they smelled alcohol on the captain's breath. A state law enforcement officer administered blood alcohol tests to Hazelwood, Cousins, and Kagan about ten hours after the grounding. Hazelwood's blood alcohol level tested at 0.061, below the 0.1 level commonly applied in drunk-driving tests, but above 0.04 Coast Guard limits. On March 28, *The New York Times* and the *Anchorage Daily News* reported that Hazelwood had had three license suspensions for drunken driving, and that his license was suspended at the time of the grounding. On March 26, 1990, in Superior Court in Anchorage, Hazelwood was acquitted of operating a ship under the influence of alcohol and two other charges, but was convicted of negligently discharging oil. He was fined fifty thousand dollars and sentenced to one thousand hours of beach-cleaning. Later, the Coast Guard suspended his and Kagan's licenses for six months. Sixteen months later, the official accident report of the National Traffic Safety Board ruled that Hazelwood was "impaired" when the ship ran aground. They also cited crew fatigue, the third mate's failure to make the turn on time, improper crew oversight by Exxon, and inadequate equipment, staffing, and management by the Valdez Coast Guard office as factors causing the accident.

On March 26, spilled oil covered an elliptical area across the middle of Prince William Sound southwest of the *Exxon*

Valdez. By mid-day, March 30, floating oil had moved into the islands in the western sound. Observations and modeling indicated that, after two weeks, about 30 percent of the oil had evaporated; 40 percent was on beaches or in the intertidal zone, mostly on islands in western Prince William Sound; and about 25 percent had entered the Gulf of Alaska between Prince William Sound and about half-way to Cook Inlet. Only 5 percent remained afloat in Prince William Sound. Oil in decreasing amounts ultimately reached Chignik on the Aleutian Peninsula. About 10 percent of the oil entering the Gulf of Alaska floated beyond Cook Inlet. Only 2 percent reached the Shelikoff Strait between Kodiak and the mainland, and six tar balls were found at Chignik. Beach oiling beyond Cook Inlet was sporadic and light to negligible.

Alyeska was immediately notified and had a helicopter in the air at 1:30 A.M. At the same time, Frank Iarossi, president of Exxon Shipping, began mobilizing men and equipment to be sent to Alaska. Alyeska's equipment barge took fourteen hours, instead of the promised five, to reach the scene. Alyeska's equipment and personnel were designed and governmentally approved for spills of about two thousand barrels—grossly inadequate for the *Exxon Valdez* spill. Local fishermen placed booms that kept oil away from four fish hatchery sites.

On March 25, Exxon accepted financial responsibility for the spill and took control of the cleanup. Exxon began removing oil from the *Exxon Valdez* on March 25, completing the job and towing the ship away on April 4. Attempts at containing and skimming the oil were ineffective, because of inadequate equipment. Only three thousand barrels of oil were removed. Exxon's use of dispersants and burning, delayed for two days by Coast Guard commander Steve McCall and Alaska Department of Environmental Control director Dennis Kelso, contributed little before these efforts were terminated as a result of severe weather on March 26.

Exxon began shoreline cleanup on April 2, continuing until winter, and resumed in spring, 1990. For the most part, oil was washed from the beaches with cold to hot water and thereafter skimmed or sucked from the sea. Fertilizers were spread to stimulate natural organisms feeding on oil. In some cases, chemical dispersant was applied, but was discontinued as ineffective and counterproductive. Oil-soaked debris, mousse (water in oil emulsions), and tar balls were manually removed. From 1989 through 1992, local communities undertook cleansing or containment efforts. After 1992, recovery was generally left to natural processes. By 1994, the beaches appeared clean.

An estimated 269,000 to 580,000 sea birds were killed; 3,600 dead birds were collected. Bird rescuers captured many birds and undertook to clean and return them to the wild, but with little success. About three thousand sea otters probably died. Sixteen hundred dead otters were counted in the summer of 1989; 348 were rescued and treated, but only 226 survived, at an estimated cost of eighty thousand dollars each. About 50 electronically tagged animals died shortly after release. Seal and whale mortality estimates are less reliable, but it appears that these animals largely escaped. It was feared that damage

to fish and fisheries would be extensive, and salmon and herring fisheries were closed in 1989. Tests, however, indicated little damage to fish, and subsequent salmon and herring runs were normal. Shellfish, however, did accumulate hydrocarbons. By 1994, Exxon had spent more than $3.5 billion in damages, fines, cleanup expenses, research, and investigation.

—Ralph L. Langenheim, Jr.

ADDITIONAL READING:

Davidson, Art. *In the Wake of the Exxon Valdez*. San Francisco: Sierra Club Books, 1990. Describes the grounding, responses to it, and its environmental effects. Contains many small factual errors and is biased against industry and government.

Hodgson, Bryan. "Alaska's Big Spill: Can the Wilderness Heal?" *National Geographic* 177, no. 1 (January, 1990): 5-43. Straightforward account of environmental damage and remediation.

"Industry's Oil Spill Response Capability Crucial Test in '90's." *The International Petroleum Encyclopedia: 1994* 27 (1994): 205-211. Update on environmental recovery and regulatory action to prevent spills at Valdez.

Keeble, John. *Out of the Channel: The Exxon Valdez Oil Spill in Prince William Sound*. New York: HarperCollins, 1991. Describes the accident and pertinent events before and after. Biased against industry and government.

Loughlin, Thomas R., ed. *Marine Mammals and the Exxon Valdez*. San Diego, Calif.: Academic Press, 1994. A factual account of spill effects on marine mammals and of responses to the accident.

Piper, Ernest. *The Exxon Valdez Oil Spill*. Anchorage: Alaska Department of Environmental Conservation, 1993. Final report on the spill and the response to it.

Smith, Conrad. *Media and Apocalypse: News Coverage of the Yellowstone Forest Fires, Exxon Valdez Oil Spill, and Loma Prieta Earthquake*. Westport, Conn.: Greenwood Press, 1992. Describes the *Exxon Valdez* grounding and analyzes news coverage.

"The Valdez Spill." *The International Petroleum Encyclopedia: 1990* 23 (1990): 32-40. Factual account of the spill, its control and remediation, and political effects.

SEE ALSO: 1971, Alaska Native Claims Settlement Act; 1973, Arab Oil Embargo and Energy Crisis; 1974, Construction of the Alaska Pipeline; 1978, Toxic Waste at Love Canal; 1979, Three Mile Island Accident.

1989 ■ LINCOLN SAVINGS AND LOAN DECLARES BANKRUPTCY: *criminal activities in the manipulation of the Lincoln concern are symptomatic of deeper problems in the thrift industry*

DATE: April 13, 1989
LOCALE: Phoenix, Arizona, and Washington, D.C.
CATEGORIES: Business and labor; Economics

KEY FIGURES:

Charles H. Keating, Jr. (born 1923), principal owner of Lincoln Savings and Loan

Carl Henry Lindner, Jr. (born 1919), Keating's client and associate in American Financial Corporation

SUMMARY OF EVENT. Charles H. Keating, Jr., a champion swimmer, antipornography crusader, and attorney who built a financial empire through takeovers and stock sales, acquired control of a Southern California savings and loan (S&L), Lincoln Savings and Loan, in 1983. In April, 1989, the holding company for that S&L, American Continental Corporation, declared bankruptcy, causing the S&L to collapse. The Lincoln S&L episode convinced many people that the S&L industry's problems were caused by criminal behavior on the part of owners and managers.

Keating had worked as an attorney in Cincinnati, building relationships with important clients, such as Carl Lindner, Jr., who acquired and sold other companies as a feared "takeover" artist. Through Lindner, Keating acquired part ownership in American Financial Corporation, which had a network of businesses. One of the businesses that attracted Keating was a Phoenix, Arizona, homebuilder, Continental Homes. Keating acquired Continental Homes directly from Lindner in 1976, after a federal suit against their companies resulted in a consent decree.

At first, Keating had planned to liquidate Continental Homes, but upon closer inspection, he decided to continue it as a viable operation. In fact, the business boomed, moving from deep in the red into the black. Keating moved to Arizona in 1978 to manage Continental Homes more closely. As a result of the Securities and Exchange Commission suit that had resulted in the consent decree against American Financial Corporation, Keating assumed many of that defunct company's debts. Lindner remained in charge of the company, and gradually appeared to rescue it. American Financial Corporation was touted as the fastest-growing public company in the United States, but federal regulators remained skeptical. At the very time that national news magazines hailed American Financial Corporation as a rising giant, federal auditors concluded that Lindner-owned businesses lost almost ten million dollars a month.

Keating, physically and managerially removed from American Financial Corporation, concentrated on Continental Homes. He concluded that while home construction provided good returns, financing of home construction could be even more lucrative. Keating found the perfect vehicle for such financial operations in a Lindner-owned, California-based S&L, Lincoln Savings and Loan. He purchased the S&L in 1983, at a time when Continental Homes built three thousand to five thousand homes a year, and assumed possession of Lincoln S&L in 1984. Lincoln S&L had assets of $1.2 billion, and after a year under Keating's management, it boasted assets of $2.5 billion. It failed, however, along with its holding company, in 1989, and Keating was investigated under a full range of charges.

Like other S&Ls—often referred to as thrift associations or simply thrifts—Lincoln suffered from long-term problems that had started to beset the industry in the 1970's. Most of those problems had originated in the New Deal regulations that established or governed the thrift industry. In the Great Depression, Congress attempted to support the nation's sagging thrift associations by allowing them special advantages over commercial banks, the most important of which was the authority to pay higher interest rates on deposits than banks could offer. In return, S&Ls were prohibited from consumer lending (such as making auto loans) and from offering checking accounts (called demand deposits). S&Ls concentrated almost exclusively on long-term mortgage loans, often up to thirty years in length. As long as inflation remained low, or at least steady in its increase, the S&Ls could adapt their long-term rates. Beginning in the late 1960's, when inflation suddenly surged, the S&Ls found that they had to pay 3 to 5 percent more on deposits than they earned on mortgage loans. Had the phenomenon been short-lived, the S&Ls could have handled it, but when inflation rates continued to rise, the S&Ls were pushed to the brink. They could not refinance their mortgage loans at higher interest rates.

By the late 1970's, the thrift industry faced deep losses, and it lobbied Congress for relief from the restrictions on lending. Congress enacted several laws, such as the Garn-St. Germain Act, that permitted S&Ls to engage in consumer and commercial lending and to offer demand deposits. The several revisions of banking laws taken together were referred to as deregulation, but little mention was made of the fact that regulation itself had caused the turmoil.

Suddenly freed to lend on consumer items, commercial properties, and even low-grade bonds (usually referred to as junk bonds), the S&Ls had to make up substantial losses in a short time or collapse. S&L owners and managers, therefore, sought the riskiest investments, but such investments often have the potential for the highest return. In the early 1980's, those investments included junk bonds and, more frequently, speculations in land. Prior to the New Deal, owners and managers had been restrained by the fact that they knew their depositors' funds were at risk in such speculative ventures; if the S&L failed, the depositors lost their money. During the New Deal, however, the federal government created deposit insurance for banks through the Federal Deposit Insurance Corporation (FDIC) and for S&Ls and thrift associations through the Federal Savings and Loan Insurance Corporation (FSLIC). Those government entities insured deposits, ultimately to amounts of $100,000 per individual account. Deposit insurance, therefore, separated the S&L owners and managers from the potential plight of the depositors if there were trouble.

Owners correctly deduced that if they continued on their present course, their institutions would go out of business, but if they guessed wrong on their investments, their institutions would go out of business. In either case, the depositors would get their money. Only if the owners invested in high-risk ventures that succeeded could the S&Ls and the depositors all win. Deposit insurance therefore had the effect of motivating the owners to seek the riskiest investments.

With the majority of deposits insured, S&L owners and managers, facing certain collapse without a dramatic turn-around, invested in the riskiest land speculations and, to a much lesser degree, in junk bonds. Areas with the potential for rapid growth offered the most tempting targets for S&L funds, such as land for development in Arizona, Texas, California, Florida, and Colorado. Texas, Colorado, and California all suffered as a result of the fall in oil prices in the early 1980's, while cities in Arizona, California, and Colorado found they had overbuilt office space. The subsequent collapse of land prices destroyed the asset value of the largest investments for most of the thrifts. Land values in Phoenix, Houston, Denver, and Los Angeles fell significantly, and with each new drop in land values came new S&L bankruptcies.

In 1979, there were 5,147 S&Ls or thrift associations in business. By 1989, the number had fallen to 3,347 institutions covered by FSLIC (or its successor fund, SAIF) or the Bank Insurance Fund (BIF). No direct evidence exists on the eighteen hundred thrifts that failed were due to criminal activity by operators such as Keating, but an assessment of significant investments in junk bonds—usually blamed as the primary culprit for S&L problems—has revealed that investments in junk bonds and commercial holdings grew at a slower rate than either land loans or consumer loans by S&Ls. Nontraditional holdings as a percentage of total S&L assets rose by 10 percent from 1982 to 1985 alone. Consumer loans doubled and land loans tripled, suggesting that land and consumer loans were most responsible for the falling asset value of the S&Ls.

Criminal activity, however, was present in numerous S&L cases, particularly in Texas, where Democratic Speaker of the House of Representatives Jim Wright used his influence to deflect regulators from S&Ls run by his associates. Wright was forced to resign.

Charles Keating was indicted on racketeering charges, tried, and convicted. In April, 1992, he was sentenced to ten years in prison, having to serve five years before he was eligible for parole. Only those who had invested directly in American Continental Corporation or Lincoln lost significant amounts of money in the long run: Deposit insurance protected most of the average depositors.

The Keating affair broadened amid revelations that in 1984, Keating had met with five U.S. senators—Democrats John Glenn of Ohio, Alan Cranston of California, Don Riegle of Michigan, Dennis DeConcini of Arizona, and Republican John McCain of Arizona. Those senators told investigators that no promises were involved and that Keating provided only information. None of the five suffered much political damage, but others, such as Wright, were tarred by their connection to S&Ls.

In broader terms, the S&L crisis had not produced the dreadful results many had predicted for the economic system. As land values returned, the government was able to sell many

of the S&Ls it held in receivership for more than analysts originally had expected. S&Ls that had not failed gradually returned to health in the deregulated atmosphere. Keating continued to maintain that he had not committed any crimes, but served his prison sentence. —*Larry Schweikart*

ADDITIONAL READING:

Adams, James Ring. *The Big Fix*. New York: John Wiley, 1990. Emphasizes internal corruption, political ties, and fraud as the causes for S&L difficulties. Relates Texas scandals and apparent violations of the regulatory/examination process. Fails to appreciate the effect of deposit insurance, the original interest rate mismatch, and simple fluctuations in land prices.

Binstein, Michael, and Charles Bowden. *Trust Me*. New York: Random House, 1993. Rambling and disjointed, but contains numerous quotations from Keating and has as much biographical information as exists in a single source. Posits that deregulation and criminal elements caused the industry's woes.

Brumbaugh, R. Dan, Jr. *Thrifts Under Siege*. Cambridge, Mass.: Ballinger, 1988. Comprehensive study of the problems of thrifts and the role of deposit insurance and regulation, published before the restoration of land values undercut some of the effect of calls for immediate action to forestall further disaster.

Pilzer, Paul Zane, and Robert Deitz. *Other People's Money*. New York: Simon & Schuster, 1989. Blames poor judgment by S&L managers and bad luck, in addition to corruption, for industry troubles. Written by Texas authors close to the real estate business, who attempt to analyze the effects of regulation.

White, Lawrence J. *The S&L Debacle*. New York: Oxford University Press, 1991. An excellent scholarly study of S&L problems. Analyzes the portfolio changes in the industry, showing that commercial, consumer, and land loans, not junk bonds, caused the asset value to fall, while regulatory problems allowed the S&Ls to weaken.

1989 ■ HUMAN GENOME PROJECT BEGINS:
an ambitious project to map and sequence the entire human genome promises medical advances but raises social and ethical concerns

DATE: October 1, 1989
LOCALE: Bethesda, Maryland
CATEGORIES: Health and medicine; Science and technology
KEY FIGURES:
Charles DeLisi (born 1941), associate director of the Office of Health and Environment Research at the U.S. Department of Energy
Bernadine Healy (born 1944), director of the National Institutes of Health, 1991-1993
Robert L. Sinsheimer (born 1920), molecular biologist and former chancellor, University of California, Santa Cruz
Louis Sullivan (born 1933), secretary of Health and Human Services, 1989-1993

James D. Watson (born 1928), first director of the National Center for Human Genome Research

James B. Wyngaarden (born 1924), director of the National Institutes of Health, 1982-1989

SUMMARY OF EVENT. The ability of a living organism to reproduce anatomically, physiologically, and behaviorally consistent offsprings is encoded in the genetic material collectively referred to as the organism's genome. The human genome is organized as twenty-three pairs of chromosomes. Each chromosome is made up of tightly packaged strands of the molecule called deoxyribonucleic acid (DNA). There are two complimentary strands in human DNA, with each strand essentially made up of a sequence of four nucleotides, guanine (G), adenine (A), thymine (T), and cytosine (C). A sequence of nucleotides that specifically encode for the production of a discrete characteristic of the organism is known as the "gene" for that characteristic or trait. Hence, in metaphorical terms, there are genes for eye color, skin color, ability to digest certain food items, resistance or susceptibility to hereditary diseases, and a host of other traits. The Human Genome Project seeks to determine the relative position of each of the estimated fifty to one hundred thousand human genes and to determine the sequence of the approximately three billion nucleotides constituting the entire human genetic material.

The simultaneous occurrence of related events at different locations makes it difficult to pinpoint a beginning date for the human genome research. However, as early as September, 1987, the U.S. secretary of energy, prompted by Charles De-Lisi, instructed three national laboratories (Lawrence Berkeley and Lawrence Livermore in California, and Los Alamos in New Mexico) to establish human genome research centers dedicated to chromosome mapping and the development of automated techniques for sequencing large segments of DNA. In December, 1987, the United States Congress, acting on a bill introduced by Senator Pete Domenici of New Mexico, awarded almost thirty million dollars to the National Institutes of Health (NIH) and the Department of Energy (DOE) to organize the federal human genome program in 1988. By October, 1988, NIH director James Wyngaarden announced the creation of an NIH Office for Human Genome Research, to be headed by James D. Watson, Nobel laureate and head of the Cold Spring Harbor Laboratory in New York. On October 1, 1989, Secretary of Health and Human Services Louis Sullivan elevated Watson's office to the National Center for Human Genome Research, and by 1991 the federal human genome program was formally established with an annual budget of approximately $135 million. The entire project was expected to cost three billion dollars over fifteen years.

Watson served as the first director of the Human Genome Project during his temporary tenure at the National Institutes of Health. He successfully dealt with one of the early concerns of molecular biology researchers, the fear that the scale of the Human Genome Project would threaten funds for smaller studies that constituted the major part of NIH support for basic science. Watson resigned on April 10, 1992, in the wake of controversy over conflict-of-interest regulations. Francis Collins, one of the key researchers who located the gene for cystic fibrosis, was appointed the second director of the Center for Human Genome Research, on April 7, 1993.

Most of the early discussion and organizational activities concerning the Human Genome Project took place in the United States, but soon after the recognition that only international collaboration could attain the outlined goals, several European countries, especially France, Germany, England, Italy, the Netherlands, and Denmark, launched contemporaneous Human Genome Projects. A flurry of activities in support of the Human Genome Project also took place in Japan and the former Soviet Union.

The conceptualization of goals for the Human Genome Project evolved through scientific discussions initiated in the mid-1980's by Robert Sinsheimer, distinguished molecular biologist and chancellor of the Santa Cruz campus of the University of California, and Charles DeLisi, director of the Office of Health and Environment at the Department of Energy. The specific formulation of goals for the Human Genome Project was precipitated by several decades of scientific curiosity concerning the nature of heredity, as initially illuminated by Gregor Mendel's laws of inheritance, and the molecular identity of the genetic material, as elucidated by the work of James Watson and Francis Crick, winners of the 1962 Nobel Prize in Physiology or Medicine.

Several technical and conceptual advances in molecular biology during the 1960's and early 1970's led directly to the feasibility of the Human Genome Project. Probably the most consequential event was the invention of DNA sequencing techniques by Walter Gilbert and Allan Maxam at Harvard University in Cambridge, Massachusetts, and Fred Sanger at Cambridge University in England. In the early days of DNA sequencing, the procedure was tedious and time-consuming, with considerable margins of error. By the end of the 1980's, automated DNA sequencing had become a reality largely as a result of the work of Leroy Hood, a molecular biologist then at the California Institute of Technology. Another major development that led to the feasibility of mapping and sequencing the entire human genome was the development of recombinant DNA techniques that made it possible to introduce (by cloning) large pieces of human DNA into bacteria that can subsequently produce large quantities of the cloned DNA for sequencing. The construction of biologically functional hybrid (chimeric) DNA molecules in 1973 by Stanley Cohen and Herbert Boyer led to the invention of DNA cloning and genetic engineering. This invention and subsequent technical improvements persuaded many leading molecular biologists not only that large genomes can be sequenced in small parts, but also of the possibility of gene therapy, which is the replacement of erroneous DNA segments in individuals suffering from hereditary diseases. It is arguable that the promise of gene therapy persuaded key members of Congress to earmark fiscal resources for the Human Genome Project.

During the 1980's, proponents of the Human Genome Project predicted beneficial repercussions from improved prenatal or postnatal diagnosis and possible treatment for several hereditary diseases, such as cystic fibrosis, Huntington's disease, familial hypercholesterolemia, and hereditary cancers. However, several prominent scientists concerned about the social implications of genetic knowledge have continued to call for caution and, in some cases, for prohibition of the Human Genome Project. The major concerns stem from prior social experimentation with eugenics, the pseudoscientific effort to control human reproduction on the basis of preferential genetic matching, and the potential pressure for sterilization of individuals carrying undesirable hereditary traits. Opponents of the Human Genome Project (for example, Ruth Hubbard and Richard Lewontin at Harvard University, and Troy Duster at the University of California, Berkeley) argued that the risks of social discrimination based on genetic sequence identity outweigh any potential medical benefits associated with sequencing the human genome. These skeptics seriously doubted the general preparedness of U.S. society to sustain confidentiality of genetic sequence information, in particular because health insurance agencies and labor employers had expressed interest in obtaining information about genetic traits that announce predisposition to certain disease conditions. Even staunch proponents of the Human Genome Project agreed that laws must be drafted to prevent genetic discrimination and to ensure public education regarding genetic testing and therapy.

—O. A. Ogunseitan

ADDITIONAL READING:

Duster, Troy. *Backdoor to Eugenics.* New York: Routledge, 1990. Highlights ethical dilemmas and potential societal pitfalls inherent in applying molecular genetic technologies to medical issues and population screening programs.

Frankel, Mark S., and Albert H. Teich, eds. *The Genetic Frontier: Ethics, Law and Policy.* Washington, D.C.: American Association for the Advancement of Science, 1994. Eighteen authors tackle issues of family relationships, privacy and confidentiality, behavioral genetics, and property rights as they are affected by the Human Genome Project.

Hubbard, Ruth, and Elijah Wald. *Exploding the Gene Myth.* Boston: Beacon Press, 1993. Vibrant discussion and ultimate rejection of the geneticization of human social and health problems. Skeptical about the expensive big-science approach to the Human Genome Project.

Kevles, Daniel J., and Leroy Hood, eds. *The Code of Codes: Scientific and Social Issues in the Human Genome Project.* Cambridge, Mass.: Harvard University Press, 1992. Balanced discussion by eleven authors on the technical and social challenges faced in the early stages of the Human Genome Project.

Lee, Thomas F. *Gene Future: The Promise and Perils of the New Biology.* New York: Plenum Press, 1993. Places the Human Genome Project within a larger scientific revolution concerning increasingly efficient manipulation and commercialization of living organisms.

Lewontin, Richard, Leon Kamin, and Steven Rose. *Not in Our Genes: Biology, Ideology, and Human Nature.* New York:

Pantheon, 1984. Authored by proponents of a dialectical philosophy of biologists that rejects genetic determinism and favors an inseparable interaction between genetics and environment.

U.S. National Research Council Committee on Mapping and Sequencing the Human Genome. *Mapping and Sequencing the Human Genome.* Washington, D.C.: National Academy Press, 1988. The authoritative source on early concepts of mainstream scientists commissioned by the National Academy of Sciences to outline goals for the Human Genome Project.

SEE ALSO: 1952, Development of a Polio Vaccine; 1960, FDA Approves the Birth Control Pill; 1981, First AIDS Cases Are Reported.

1990 ■ MEECH LAKE ACCORD DIES:
Canadian leaders fail in an attempt to reform the Constitution of 1982 by incorporating Quebec

DATE: June 22, 1990
LOCALE: Canada
CATEGORY: Canadian history
KEY FIGURES:

Robert Bourassa (born 1933), premier of Quebec

Elijah Harper (born 1949), only Native Canadian member of Manitoba's legislature

Brian Mulroney (born 1939), prime minister of Canada, 1984-1993

Jacques Parizeau (born 1930), leader of the sovereignist Parti Québécois

Pierre Elliott Trudeau (born 1919), prime minister of Canada 1968-1979 and 1980-1984

Clyde K. Wells (born 1937), premier of Newfoundland

SUMMARY OF EVENT. Constitutionally, much unfinished business faced Canada in the 1980's. The nature of the country's Senate had not been agreed upon. Fueled by sovereignist impulses, Quebec remained outside the 1982 constitution and demanded that specific conditions be met before it would approve the document. Canadian prime minister Brian Mulroney of the Progressive Conservative Party sought to break the long deadlock on these matters.

On April 30, 1987, following ten hours of intense negotiations at Meech Lake, a resort in Quebec, Mulroney and the ten provincial premiers reached a unanimous agreement designed to bring Quebec into the constitution. Acting in the role of mediator, Mulroney was able to engineer a compromise enhancing the power of all provinces. The belief that Quebec should be no more than equal to the other provinces was advanced by the leaders of Nova Scotia, Alberta, Manitoba, and Saskatchewan. Quebec's premier, Robert Bourassa, a Harvard-trained economist and advocate of federalism, eased tensions by indicating a willingness to be flexible. Agreement was made possible when Alberta's premier, Donald Getty, who wanted a powerful, elected Senate representing all the provinces equally, softened his demand that Senate reform be resolved before the Quebec question.

The key provision of the Meech Lake Accord was the recognition of Quebec as a distinct society within Canada. This was an important concession that would afford certain protections for Quebec's Francophone culture. The agreement also included other important provisions. Constitutional changes in federal institutions and provincial boundaries would require the unanimous consent of Ottawa and the provinces. The federal government committed itself to addressing the Senate reform issue in the near future. The prime minister and provincial premiers would be required to meet at least twice annually, with one conference devoted to constitutional matters and the other to economic issues. Quebec was guaranteed three judges on the nine-member Canadian Supreme Court. This had been customary but now would be constitutionally entrenched. In most instances, the Parliament in Ottawa would be obligated to choose justices from among candidates proposed by provinces. Within quite broad limitations, any province would be allowed to opt out of federally funded programs under provincial jurisdiction. Quebec would not have to accept immigrants out of proportion to its percentage of the national population.

The Meech Lake Accord was to be final when ratified by Parliament, all ten provincial legislatures, and the premiers at a follow-up conference. A three-year deadline, expiring June 23, 1990, was set for the process.

The pact, characterized as a milestone in federal-provincial relations, was a triumph for Mulroney. Quebec's premier described the pact as "a historic breakthrough for Quebec as a Canadian partner." William Vander Zalm, premier of British Columbia and a leading spokesman for Western Canada, stated that the accord "changes the nature of the relationships and responsibilities of our national and provincial governments in a manner that bodes well for our collective future."

Opposition surfaced in various quarters. The leaders of sovereignist Parti Québécois accused Bourassa of selling out Quebec. Bourassa's Liberal Party had ousted the Parti Québécois from power in 1985. However, the Quebec public did not appear to share the Parti Québécois' outrage. René Lévesque-sovereignist, former Quebec premier, and former leader of the Parti Québécois—and former Canadian prime minister Pierre Trudeau, who opposed Quebec's demands, both declined to comment on the accord. Liberal Party leader John Turner commented, "I have the feeling that Mr. Mulroney gave away too much to achieve that deal." He criticized the idea of provinces choosing senators and Supreme Court justices, and worried about the ability of the federal government to initiate national programs if the provinces were able to opt out.

Having not been invited to participate in the conference, Anthony Penikett, leader of the Yukon territorial government, expressed opposition to the agreement because each province would have veto power over the Yukon's aspirations of becoming a full province. Numerous conferences were convened

and studies initiated to iron out difficulties. Eight provinces endorsed the accord. However, in 1989, Newfoundland elected a new premier, Liberal Clyde K. Wells, who had campaigned against the agreement. Under Wells, the Newfoundland House of Assembly voted to rescind its earlier approval of Meech Lake.

Newfoundland, Manitoba, and New Brunswick argued that the clause declaring Quebec to be a distinct society would give Quebec too much power and enable it to pass laws conflicting with the nation's 1982 Charter of Rights and Freedoms. Those fears were strengthened in 1988, when Quebec overruled a Canadian Supreme Court decision striking down a law restricting the use of any language other than French on public signs. The holdout provinces also objected to what they saw as a failure to address the issues of Senate reform and minority rights. Following the adoption of a compromise designed to answer some of those concerns, New Brunswick's legislature voted unanimously to approve the accord. However, opposition remained strong in Manitoba and Newfoundland.

Manitoba, with its large population of native peoples, had sought the inclusion of a "Canada clause" that would have emphasized the entire nation's multicultural characteristics. The Manitoba legislature's sole native member, Elijah Harper, sought to block passage of the accord, arguing it had ignored native concerns. On June 22, Harper refused to give his consent to an extension of the legislature's Meech Lake debate. Since the extension would have required unanimous approval, Harper's move effectively killed the accord. Harper's action was hailed by other native Canadian leaders.

In Newfoundland, Wells canceled a scheduled vote on the accord, criticizing what he called the pressure tactics of Mulroney. Wells had been outraged to learn that Mulroney's government had offered a plan to extend the approval deadline in Manitoba but not in Newfoundland. He argued that Mulroney was attempting to make his province a scapegoat for the accord's failure.

The Meech Lake Accord died on June 22, 1990, when Newfoundland and Manitoba failed to ratify the agreement. The defeat of the accord was viewed as a major blow to Mulroney, who had twice been elected on promises to unite the country. Mulroney's popularity plummeted. In a rare televised address, Mulroney acknowledged his disappointment but reaffirmed "a truly united tolerant Canada endures and will eventually prevail." The Liberal Party accused Mulroney of deliberately fostering a crisis atmosphere in the last days of the debate by delaying talks on a possible compromise in order to create last-minute pressures on the holdout provinces.

The failure of Meech Lake generated speculation about Quebec's future and prompted a cautious response from Robert Bourassa, who repeatedly stressed that his government would take no action jeopardizing Quebec's economy. Jacques Parizeau, leader of Parti Québécois, jubilantly described the crisis as "the moment of truth." The Parti Québécois had been campaigning to hold a provincial referendum on "sovereignty association" for Quebec, which was generally understood to mean that Quebec would retain economic ties with Canada while gaining political independence. A similar referendum had failed in 1980, but more recent polls had found nearly 60 percent of Quebecers favored political sovereignty.

Instead of regretting the accord's failure, many Quebecers were elated by the outcome. The failure of Meech Lake had fallen just one day before St. Jean-Baptiste Day, Quebec's national holiday. Expressing their support for an independent Quebec, nationalists celebrated. Nearly two hundred thousand people turned out for a parade in Montreal, many of them waving Quebec's fleur-de-lis flag and chanting, "Vive le Quebec libre" (Long live free Quebec). This was the first such parade held in twenty years, following the event's discontinuation after violent demonstrations in 1968 and 1969. Many in Anglophone Canada also celebrated. In a rare venture into Canadian politics, Queen Elizabeth II pleaded for unity, but Canada was to plunge headlong into a political crisis. —*Randall Fegley*

ADDITIONAL READING:

Cohen, Andrew. *A Deal Undone*. Vancouver, B.C.: Douglas and McIntyre, 1990. An in-depth look at the negotiations and politics surrounding the making and breaking of the Meech Lake Accord.

Coyne, Deborah. *Roll of the Dice*. Toronto: Lorimer, 1992. An examination of the Meech Lake Accord that concentrates on Clyde Wells and the politics of Newfoundland.

Mathews, Georges. *Quiet Resolution: Quebec's Challenge to Canada*. Toronto: Summerhill, 1990. Presents Robert Bourassa's comments on Quebec, Canadian politics, and Meech Lake.

Milne, David. *The Canadian Constitution*. Toronto: Lorimer, 1990. A review of Canadian constitutional history through the 1980's.

Monahan, Patrick. *Meech Lake: The Inside Story*. Toronto: University of Toronto Press, 1991. A thorough overview of the accord and the politics that surrounded it.

Trudeau, Pierre Elliott. *Pierre Trudeau Speaks Out on Meech Lake*. Toronto: General Paperbacks, 1990. The critical views of the former prime minister.

Vipond, Robert. *Liberty and Community*. Albany: State University of New York Press, 1991. Examines the inability of Canadians to agree on constitutional reforms.

SEE ALSO: 1960, Quebec Sovereignist Movement; 1970, October Crisis; 1984, Mulroney Era in Canada; 1990, Bloc Québécois Forms; 1992, Defeat of the Charlottetown Accord.

1990 ■ BLOC QUÉBÉCOIS FORMS: *a new political party is created to contest Canadian general elections on the exclusive issue of sovereignty for Quebec*

DATE: July 25, 1990
LOCALE: Montreal
CATEGORIES: Canadian history; Government and politics
KEY FIGURES:
Lucien Bouchard (born 1938), leader of the Bloc Québécois

Robert Bourassa (born 1933), premier of Quebec, 1970-1976 and 1985-1994
Gilles Duceppe (born 1947), first Bloc Québécois candidate elected to Parliament
Mario Dumont (born 1970), leader of the Action Démocratique Party
Jacques Parizeau (born 1930), premier of Quebec in 1994

SUMMARY OF EVENT. The creation of the Bloc Québécois was a direct result of the constitutional turmoil that gripped Canada in the 1980's. Canada had adopted a new constitution in 1982, but the French-speaking province of Quebec refused to accept its legitimacy. Quebec's refusal was mainly on the grounds that the Constitution failed to give Quebec adequate powers to protect its French language and unique Québécois culture. In order to secure Quebec's assent, Brian Mulroney, the Canadian prime minister, and all ten provincial leaders met at Meech Lake, Quebec, in 1987, and crafted a series of amendments favorable to Quebec. However, it became increasingly apparent that not all the provincial legislatures would ratify the Meech Lake Accord by the deadline date of June 23, 1990, no doubt accurately reflecting English-speaking Canada's belief that the accord granted too many concessions to Quebec.

Faced with impending defeat, a number of Members of Parliament (MPs) from Quebec, regardless of party affiliation, began to lose hope that the federal government would grant their province enough concessions to justify their remaining within the Canadian federation. If federalism would not work, then full political sovereignty for Quebec was the only plausible alternative. Lucien Bouchard, minister of environment in the Conservative government of Mulroney, resigned on May 21, 1990, citing a loss of faith in the way the government had handled the crisis. Other defections, from both the Liberal Party and the Conservative Party, followed. Soon there was talk of forming a bloc of Quebec MPs whose principal task would be to fight for Quebec's sovereignty. Lucien Bouchard later claimed that Robert Bourassa, the Liberal premier of Quebec's provincial government, encouraged him to embark upon such a project.

On July 25, 1990, the newly formed Bloc Québécois (BQ) announced its manifesto. It stated that the BQ's primary allegiance was to the nation of Quebec and recognized the province's legislature, the National Assembly, as the supreme democratic institution of the Québécois people. Its mission was to defend Quebec's interests in the federal parliament and to promote sovereignty within Quebec. All BQ members would be given a free vote in the Canadian House of Commons; there would be no party discipline, save on the exclusive issue of sovereignty for Quebec. In June, 1991, the BQ transformed itself into a political party at a conference held in Sorel-Tracy. Now sovereignists could be consistent in their voting patterns. On the provincial level, they could vote for the Parti Québécois, a nationalist party established in 1968, and for the Bloc Québécois in federal elections.

Lucien Bouchard was personally responsible for much of BQ's success. Born in the ultranationalist region of Lac St.

Jean in northern Quebec, he was trained as a lawyer and practiced law in Chicoutimi. He voted in favor of the 1980 provincial referendum on the issue of sovereignty, although it was defeated by a decisive margin. After serving on numerous high-profile commissions related to labor relations, he was appointed as Canada's ambassador to France, in which capacity he served from 1985 to 1988. In 1988, he was elected to Parliament as a Conservative, and the following year he was appointed minister of environment. Handsome, charismatic, and a fine speaker, Bouchard tended to be more intellectual than emotional, although he knew how to tap the impatience and frustrations of the Québécois people. Serving him well was an extraordinary ability to stay in tune with public opinion. Since the foundation of the BQ, opinion polls consistently showed him to be by far the most popular politician in Quebec.

The Bloc Québécois experienced a good deal of electoral success in its early years. Shortly after it announced its new manifesto, a federal by-election was held in east Montreal on August 13, 1990. The BQ put up an attractive candidate in Gilles Duceppe, a former labor activist. He captured 66 percent of the vote to become the first sovereignist candidate elected to the Canadian Parliament. In 1992, there was another attempt to appease Quebec on the constitutional issue. The Canadian prime minister and the provincial premiers hammered out a series of concessions to Quebec at Charlottetown, Prince Edward Island. Similar in scope to the Meech Lake Accord, these proposals had to be endorsed in referenda held in every province. The Bloc Québécois took the position that the Charlottetown Accord did not go far enough in meeting Quebec's minimum demands and campaigned against it. The accord was voted down in six out of the ten provinces, and the vote in Quebec was 57 percent against.

When a general election was called for October, 1993, the BQ fielded candidates in all of Quebec's seventy-five constituencies. This was a daunting task, given the fact that the BQ was still a small group, consisting of only eight MPs. In some cases, the BQ encouraged legislative staff from the Parti Québécois to run for office. While the Liberals and Conservatives in Quebec campaigned on the issues of jobs and employment, the BQ was the only party to speak consistently on the sovereignty issue. The BQ won a stunning victory, capturing 49 percent of the vote in Quebec and winning fifty-four seats. The BQ did very well among former Conservatives, took 60 percent of the French-speaking vote, and had strong appeal among trade unionists and the educated urban elites. Nationwide, the Liberal Party under the leadership of Jean Chrétien won easily, gaining 177 seats, but because of the complete collapse of the Conservative Party vote, the Bloc Québécois emerged as the second largest party in Parliament and therefore earned the formal status of Official Opposition.

Canadians understandably found it disconcerting that the Official Opposition was a party dedicated to the breaking up of Canada. Compounding the problem was that many MPs of the Bloc Québécois were new to Parliament and had little interest in pan-Canadian or foreign affairs. Nevertheless,

Bouchard had stated he would responsibly fulfill his role as the government's chief critic and act on behalf of all Canadians. So successful was Bouchard that he elicited respect in formerly hostile quarters, and some political analysts suggested that the BQ was more protective of mainstream Canadian values than some of the more established federal parties. Although BQ never developed a detailed party program, it emerged as a party that tended to be fiscally conservative and left-of-center on social welfare issues. It gained popularity by opposing the cuts in popular benefit programs proposed by some economy-minded MPs. Ironically, the electoral success of the BQ and the respect it generated within the House of Commons increased Quebecers' interest in federal affairs.

In 1994, sovereignists in Quebec scored another victory when the Parti Québécois was elected to power in provincial elections. The victory was undoubtedly more a result of the unpopularity of the outgoing Liberal Party than any dramatic upsurge in sovereignist sentiment. Nevertheless, the new Parti Québécois premier, Jacques Parizeau, promised to hold a referendum on sovereignty during his term of office. In preparation for the forthcoming referendum, a new sovereignist alliance was forged that included the Parti Québécois, the Bloc Québécois, and the Action Démocratique Party, a small splinter party led by Mario Dumont. On June 12, 1995, they agreed that if the sovereignists won the referendum, there would be a year's time in which to negotiate a new political and economic arrangement with the rest of Canada. Should those talks fail, then Quebec would issue a unilateral declaration of independence.

The promised referendum was held on October 30, 1995. Prior to the voting, opinion polls showed the sovereignists trailing, but when Bouchard was in effect put in charge of the campaign instead of the heavy-handed Parizeau, there was an upsurge in support. More than 92 percent of Quebec's electorate voted, with those opposed to sovereignty winning by a narrow margin of 50.6 percent to 49.4 percent. Fewer than 54,000 votes out of a total of 4,700,000, separated the two sides. On the day after the election, a disappointed Parizeau announced his intention to resign as Quebec's premier, and on January 29, 1996, he was succeeded by Lucien Bouchard. Because Bouchard had to resign his seat in the House of Commons, Michel Gauthier was chosen leader of the Bloc Québécois. Although the sovereignists were defeated, their response was one of total defiance, confidently believing that the next referendum would finally yield the desired result. Thus, the referendum of 1995 essentially settled nothing, and both Quebec and Canada faced an uncertain future.

—*David C. Lukowitz*

ADDITIONAL READING:

Bouchard, Lucien. *On the Record.* Translated by Dominique Clift. Toronto: Stoddart, 1994. In this interim memoir, the leader of the Bloc Québécois discusses his career, the founding of the new party, and the aspirations of the Québécois people.

Johnson, William. *A Canadian Myth: Québec, Between*

Canada and the Illusion of Utopia. Montreal: Robert Davies, 1994. A readable, informative account of Quebec politics in the early 1990's. Marked by a strong anti-Québécois bias.

Noël, Alain. "Distinct in the House of Commons: The Bloc Québécois As Official Opposition." In *Canada: The State of the Federation*, edited by Douglas M. Brown and Janet Hiebert. Kingston, Ont.: Institute of Intergovernmental Relations, 1994. Argues that the Bloc Québécois behaved responsibly during its first year in Parliament and was frequently more in tune with mainstream Canadian values than the more established parties.

Valaskakis, Kimon, and Angéline Fournier. *The Delusion of Sovereignty.* Translated by George Tombs. Montreal: Robert Davies, 1995. Authors attempt to expose what they believe are the myths and fallacies held by sovereignists, arguing that sovereignty would be detrimental to Quebec's economy and culture.

Young, Robert. *The Secession of Quebec and the Future of Canada.* Montreal: McGill-Queen's University Press, 1995. A thoughtful and scholarly analysis on the impact that Quebec's secession would have, concluding that it would not be catastrophic for either Canada or Quebec.

SEE ALSO: 1960, Quebec Sovereignist Movement; 1968, Trudeau Era in Canada; 1969, Canada's Official Languages Act; 1970, October Crisis; 1982, Canada's Constitution Act; 1990, Meech Lake Accord Dies; 1992, Defeat of the Charlottetown Accord.

1990 ■ AMERICANS WITH DISABILITIES ACT: *landmark legislation provides comprehensive civil rights protections for persons with disabilities*

DATE: July 26, 1990
LOCALE: Washington, D.C.
CATEGORIES: Civil rights; Disability rights; Laws and acts
KEY FIGURES:
George Herbert Walker Bush (born 1924), forty-first president of the United States, 1989-1993
Anthony "Tony" Coelho (born 1942), representative from California
Thomas "Tom" Harkin (born 1939), senator from Iowa
Steny Hoyer (born 1939), representative from Maryland
SUMMARY OF EVENT. The Americans with Disabilities Act (ADA) of 1990 provides civil rights protections that prohibit discrimination against people with disabilities in employment, public services, public accommodations, transportation, and telecommunications. Prior to passage of the ADA, discrimination against people with disabilities was prohibited only in federally funded programs by authority of the Rehabilitation Act of 1973 and the Fair Housing Act Amendments of 1988. The ADA was far more expansive in scope. Passage of the ADA gave people with disabilities similar protections to those

that are provided to persons on the basis of race, sex, national origin, and religion by the 1964 Civil Rights Act. The passage of the ADA marked a shift in the making of civil rights policy from the judicial branch to the legislative branch of government. It has been considered the most significant piece of civil rights legislation since the passage of the Civil Rights Act of 1964. The stated purpose of the ADA is "to provide a clear and comprehensive national mandate for the elimination of discrimination against individuals with disabilities."

It is estimated that forty-three million people in the United States have physical and/or mental disabilities. The social and economic conditions of people with disabilities indicate significant disadvantage. For example, in the late 1980's, 25 percent of U.S. households earned less than fifteen thousand dollars per year, but the household incomes for 50 percent of persons with disabilities were less than fifteen thousand dollars per year. In other words, people with disabilities were twice as likely to live on very low incomes. The ADA grew from the realization that people with disabilities faced significant barriers that inhibited the opportunity to be fully employed, the choice to live independently, and the ability to access public services and public spaces. Equal access, treatment, and opportunities had not been provided to people with disabilities. Growing public sentiment that the rights of people with disabilities were not being protected was illuminated in a 1989 Gallup News poll. The poll found that 81 percent of the U.S. public believed that insufficient attention had been given to the civil rights of people with disabilities. The ADA documents in its findings on the conditions of people with disabilities that "historically society has tended to isolate and segregate individuals with disabilities, and, despite some improvements, such forms of discrimination against individuals with disabilities continue to be a serious and pervasive social problem." In order to address this social injustice, Congress passed the Americans with Disabilities Act and President George Bush signed it into law.

Years of discussions and attempts at enacting various components of the ADA had occurred before its passage. The National Council on Disability, a federal agency that provides recommendations to the legislature regarding the needs of people with disabilities, first proposed the need for antidiscrimination legislation in 1986. The council provided draft legislation to the Congress in 1988, and a joint House and Senate committee hearing was held. In May of 1989, the bill was introduced in both the House and Senate. The Senate passed the measure on September 7, 1989. Considerable time and energy was needed to pass the House version of the ADA, but the bill passed the House on May 22, 1990. One advantage that helped in the passage of the ADA was that it had strong support from both political parties. Thus passage of the ADA in both the House (403-20) and the Senate (76-8) was overwhelming. The bill then went to a conference committee, where the final differences between the House and Senate versions were worked out and a compromise was reached. On July 12 and 13, the House and Senate voted to pass the final version of the ADA, which was sent to President Bush and signed into law on July 26, 1990.

The major components of the ADA include the definition of disability and the requirements for compliance in the employment, public accommodations, transportation, state and local government operations, and telecommunications provisions. The ADA defines a person as having a disability according to the following criteria: "A) a physical or mental impairment that substantially limits one or more of the major life activities of such individual; B) a record of such an impairment; or C) being regarded as having such an impairment." The major employment provisions of the ADA prohibit employers with fifteen or more employees from discriminating against people with disabilities. Reasonable accommodations must be made in the workplace for qualified applicants with disabilities. Reasonable accommodation includes modifying workstations and equipment, unless this would result in undue hardship.

The public accommodation provisions state that people with disabilities cannot be discriminated against in public accommodations, which include restaurants, hotels, theaters, doctors' offices, retail stores, museums, libraries, parks, private schools, day care centers, pharmacies, and other similar places of public accommodation. Physical barriers in facilities must be removed if possible, and if not, alternatives for service delivery must be developed. All new buildings that provide public services and all new commercial facilities must be accessible. Individuals with vision or hearing impairments must be provided with auxiliary aids in order that they may have equal opportunities to participate in or benefit from services. The transportation provisions require new buses and bus stations and new rail vehicles and rail stations to be accessible. Existing rail services must have at least one accessible car per train. Paratransit transportation services must be available for people with disabilities who cannot use fixed-route services, unless this would result in undue hardship. State and local governments may not discriminate against people with disabilities, and all facilities, services, and communications must be accessible.

Telecommunication relay services for people with hearing and/or speech impairments must be provided twenty-four hours a day by all companies offering telephone services to the general public. Provisions of the ADA were phased in over several years, beginning with the public services components, which became effective January 26, 1992, and the employment provisions, which became effective on July 26, 1992. By July of 1995, the majority of provisions were in effect.

The overall response to the ADA has been positive. The spirit of the law, to end discrimination and provide equal opportunities for people with disabilities, has been embraced by the general public. A 1995 Louis Harris poll assessing the corporate response to the ADA found that 78 percent of businesses thought that the ADA should remain in place or be strengthened. The ADA has resulted in many more people being able to maintain their jobs after acquiring a disability. It is estimated that prior to the passage of the ADA, more than 50 percent of people who acquired disabilities lost their jobs as a result of the disability. With the ADA in place, more than 75 percent of such persons are staying on the job. In addition, the ADA has made higher education a possibility for people with disabilities who previously were unable to succeed because of social and physical barriers. The ADA has brought a great deal of visibility and understanding to the needs of people with disabilities. There are still improvements to be made, however. For example, employment opportunities for people with disabilities are still limited. While more work needs to be done to ensure equal opportunities for people with disabilities, the ADA has provided significant progress toward that goal.

—*Stephanie Brzuzy*

ADDITIONAL READING:

Perritt, Henry H. *Americans with Disabilities Act Handbook.* New York: John Wiley & Sons, 1990. Analyzes the ADA from a legal perspective, including the obligations of employers and procedural issues.

"Sweeping Law for Rights of Disabled: Private Discrimination Barred; Access Mandated." *Congressional Quarterly Almanac* 46 (1990): 447-461. Includes the legislative history and provisions of the ADA.

West, Jane, ed. *The Americans with Disabilities Act: From Policy to Practice.* New York: Mill Bank Memorial Fund, 1991. Provides comprehensive coverage of all aspects of the ADA, from policy and practice implications to implementation issues.

SEE ALSO: 1964, Civil Rights Act of 1964.

1991 ■ PERSIAN GULF WAR: *under U.S. leadership, the international community upholds international law by reversing Iraq's invasion of Kuwait, but questions concerning the U.S. role in world affairs remain*

DATE: January 17-February 28, 1991
LOCALE: Kuwait, Iraq, and Saudi Arabia
CATEGORY: Wars, uprisings, and civil unrest
KEY FIGURES:
Tariq Aziz (born 1936), minister of foreign affairs and deputy prime minister of Iraq
James A. Baker (born 1930), U.S. secretary of state
George Herbert Walker Bush (born 1924), forty-first president of the United States, 1989-1993
April Glaspie (born 1942), U.S. ambassador to Iraq
Saddam Hussein (born 1937), president of Iraq and head of the ruling Baath Party
Javier Pérez de Cuéllar (born 1920), secretary-general of the United Nations
Jabir al-Ahmad al-Jabir al-Sabah (born 1926), emir of Kuwait

PERSIAN GULF WAR, 1991

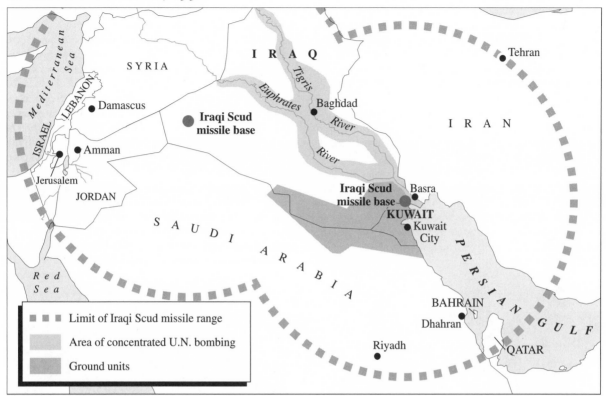

Legend:
- ▪ ▪ ▪ Limit of Iraqi Scud missile range
- Area of concentrated U.N. bombing
- Ground units

SUMMARY OF EVENT. In August, 1990, a number of factors contributed to Iraqi president Saddam Hussein's decision to invade and annex neighboring Kuwait. Since Kuwait's independence, in June, 1961, Iraqi leaders had questioned the legitimacy of Kuwait's sovereignty and the border demarcating the two countries. An important oil field straddled the ill-defined frontier, and Kuwait had been tapping it. Iraq also charged Kuwait with exceeding its oil quota set by the Organization of Petroleum Exporting Countries (OPEC), thereby increasing supplies and depressing prices. Iraq had pressed Kuwait unsuccessfully for the latter to make available to Baghdad two islands, Warba and Babiyan, strategically located across from Umm Qasr, Iraq's only outlet on the Persian Gulf proper.

Most important, 1990 was a time of acute financial hardship for Iraq because of the great indebtedness it had incurred following its murderous eight-year war with Iran, which had concluded in 1988. Iraq had to rebuild its devastated economy, especially its crucial oil industry.

Several factors led Saddam Hussein to decide that this was a good time to force Iraq's creditors, especially Kuwait, to relinquish their claims on their wartime "loans": Iranian-Iraqi relations were improving; Iraqi economic problems were becoming more pressing; he had misread the degree of U.S.-Soviet cooperation possible in the post-Cold War era; and he apparently misinterpreted U.S. ambassador April Glaspie's statement to him on July 25, 1990, that the Bush Administra-

tion was neutral in matters of inter-Arab disputes "like your border disagreement with Kuwait." Hussein also hoped to punish those who had brought down the price of oil by overproduction or committed other "offenses."

Various meetings of leaders and conferences involving Iraq, Kuwait, and others were fruitless, partly because Kuwait refused to give ground on substantive issues and partly because Saddam Hussein seemed to be determined to invade Kuwait. The invasion occurred at 2:00 A.M. on August 2, 1990. Token resistance by the tiny Kuwaiti army and the escape of most members of the extended al-Sabah ruling family to Saudi Arabia followed within hours. Kuwait was occupied by Iraq and soon declared to be its nineteenth province.

Saddam Hussein proved to be wrong in his estimate of the response of the international community, which insisted that his invasion of the neighboring country be rolled back. The United States, the Soviet Union, and United Nations Security Council Resolution 660 called for Iraq's immediate withdrawal from Kuwait. Four days later, on August 6, the Security Council imposed mandatory trade sanctions by members of the international organization, including a ban on Iraqi and Kuwaiti oil (Resolution 661).

Despite Saddam Hussein's reassurances to Joseph Wilson, the U.S. chargé d'affaires in Baghdad, President George Bush ordered the Eighty-second Airborne Division to protect neighboring Saudi Arabia in case Iraq was contemplating monopolizing the bulk of Middle Eastern oil production. Spearheading the emerging international response, Operation Desert Shield became the largest deployment of U.S. troops overseas since the Vietnam War. Iraq's formal annexation of Kuwait brought several Arab and other Muslim countries to side with the U.N.-sponsored, U.S.-led coalition. Westerners in Iraq and Kuwait were moved as human shields to sites that could become potential coalition targets in Iraq.

On November 29, the U.N. Security Council, acknowledging that its Resolution 660 of August 2 ordering Iraq to evacuate Kuwait had not been followed, mandated that all necessary means be used to expel Iraq after January 15, 1991 (Resolution 678). One last meeting between U.S. secretary of state James Baker and Iraqi foreign minister Tariq Aziz in Geneva on January 9, 1991, proved unsuccessful, as Aziz refused to accept Baker's renewed call for Iraq's unconditional withdrawal from Kuwait. The same was true of U.N. Secretary-General Javier Pérez de Cuéllar's visit to Saddam Hussein on January 13.

The Persian Gulf War is usually broken down into four stages. Operation Desert Shield covered the period from the invasion of Kuwait on August 2, 1990, to the unleashing of the U.S.-led U.N. coalition's air war on January 17, 1991. The next phase, Operation Desert Storm, had two components: the air war through February 23 and the ground war from February 24 through February 28. The aftermath following the cease-fire saw the withdrawal of Iraqi forces from Kuwait; the redrawing of the Iraqi-Kuwaiti border by a U.N. commission; the creation of U.N.-sponsored safe zones and no-fly zones in Iraq to protect Kurds and other minorities; U.N. inspection of Iraqi facilities to monitor and force the destruction of any nuclear, biological, or chemical weapons; and the continued imposition of U.N. trade sanctions on Iraq.

The military operations involved more than three-quarters of a million troops on the coalition side (some 541,000 from the United States and about 254,000 from a number of the twenty-nine other countries participating in Desert Storm at its peak) facing some one million Iraqis. The Iraqi numerical advantage was not translated into battlefield successes; the technological edge of the coalition greatly offset other factors.

General Norman Schwarzkopf stands among soldiers of the First Infantry Division during a visit to troops in Saudi Arabia on the eve of the Persian Gulf War of 1991. Controversy continues to surround the question of whether the war, a ground and air conflict with Iraq, was an advisable strategy and met its goals, although its brevity and relatively low number of casualties did assuage fears of another prolonged involvement such as that in Vietnam a generation earlier. (Library of Congress)

As news reporters from CNN broadcast the events of the airwar live, a world audience watched and wondered whether the high-tech advantage of the coalition forces had spawned a new type of "bloodless" war. Such expectations proved illusory: The disproportionate Iraqi casualties not only testified to this fact but also raised the question of a just war among some observers. On March 3, senior military representatives from both sides met to finalize the cease-fire, whose terms the Iraqis accepted unconditionally.

In the aftermath, a protracted controversy continued over the Bush Administration's decision to halt the ground war after a hundred hours, allowing Saddam Hussein and his Baathist regime to remain in power and the Iraqi army to suppress the Kurdish and Shiite uprisings soon after the cease-fire. President George Bush was aware that any longer-term entanglement might antagonize his constituency back home, as presidential elections were already on the horizon. He was unable to capitalize on his spectacular victory and soaring postwar popularity in the polls, however, because by November, 1992, economic problems had become the electorate's primary concern.

Questions also were raised as to whether enough time had been given for the economic embargo to take effect before Operation Desert Storm was initiated. A debate regarding the high cost in Iraqi civilian suffering and lives that the U.N. embargo was exacting also continued. Despite the suspected contraband with its next-door neighbors Jordan and Iran, Iraq, deprived of its major export and foreign currency earner, oil, was becoming impoverished and unable to provide for the needs of the masses. Controversy also continued regarding the degree of encouragement that the earlier tilt toward Iraq of the Reagan and Bush administrations and the ambivalent words of Ambassador April Glaspie had given to Saddam Hussein. United Nations agencies were saddled with additional responsibilities and outlays in their several missions, especially the caring for many internal and external refugees.

As for the overall significance of the Persian Gulf War, there was no consensus either on whether it was the defining moment of President Bush's "New World Order" to uphold international law or the event simply reflected oil politics as usual, packaged to appear as a stand for what was right with a few Arab members in the coalition providing an appropriate cover.

—Peter B. Heller

ADDITIONAL READING:

Clark, Ramsey. *The Fire This Time: U.S. War Crimes in the Gulf.* New York: Thunder's Mouth Press, 1992. A spirited indictment by the former U.S. attorney general and peace activist of the U.S. role in military operations and its "corrupting" of the United Nations to maintain the trade embargo.

Heikal, Mohammed Hassanein. *Illusions of Triumph: An Arab View of the Gulf War.* New York: HarperCollins, 1992. Interesting account by Egypt's top political observer, arguing that Iraq is only a small part of much deeper Arab problems, many of them of Western origin.

Hilsman, Roger. *George Bush vs. Saddam Hussein: Military Success! Political Failure?* Novato, Calif.: Lyford Books,

1992. A Columbia University foreign policy expert critiques what he considers to be the U.S. president's predilection to resort too readily to military force.

Hiro, Dilip. *Desert Shield to Desert Storm: The Second Gulf War.* New York: Routledge, 1992. Well researched. Includes informative maps and appendices of all kinds.

Moore, Molly. *A Woman at War: Storming Kuwait with the U.S. Marines.* New York: Charles Scribner's Sons, 1993. The senior military corespondent of the *Washington Post* describes the war and what it meant for a woman to cover it in a conservative Muslim environment.

U.S. News & World Report. *Triumph Without Victory: The Unreported History of the Persian Gulf War.* New York: Times Books, 1992. Includes the texts of all U.N. resolutions from August 2, 1990, through August 15, 1991, as well as the Joint Congressional Resolution of January 12, 1992, authorizing the U.S. president to help implement them.

SEE ALSO: 1988, Bush Is Elected President.

1991 ■ BUSH ANNOUNCES NUCLEAR ARMS REDUCTIONS: *evidencing improved relations with the Soviet Union, the United States unilaterally announces reductions of its nuclear armaments and level of military readiness*

DATE: September 27, 1991
LOCALE: Washington, D.C.
CATEGORY: Diplomacy and international relations
KEY FIGURES:
George Herbert Walker Bush (born 1924), forty-first president of the United States, 1989-1993
Mikhail Gorbachev (born 1931), president of the Soviet Union and general secretary of the Communist Party
Ronald Wilson Reagan (born 1911), fortieth president of the United States, 1981-1989

SUMMARY OF EVENT. After four decades of Cold War suspicion and periodic confrontations between the United States and the Soviet Union, an era of significantly improved relations between the two nuclear superpowers developed after 1985. A major foreign and military policy speech by President George Bush on September 27, 1991, marked the efforts of both nations to reduce their nuclear armaments and lessen the dangers of nuclear confrontation and possible war. What was especially striking about the president's policy statement was that the reductions he announced were not the result of specific negotiations with the Soviet government, but were taken unilaterally by the United States.

Since atomic weapons first appeared in 1945, nuclear weapons' designs, destructive power, and possible uses had expanded greatly. By the 1970's, both superpowers possessed large numbers of these destructive devices. Initial negotiations to limit the rate of growth of certain types of nuclear weapons earlier had resulted in two groundbreaking agreements, the Strategic Arms Limitation Treaties of 1972 (SALT I) and 1979 (SALT II), and U.S.-Russian negotiations sporadically continued during the 1980's, culminating in a 1987 treaty to eliminate intermediate range nuclear missile systems located in Europe.

The greatest danger to both nations, in size and destructive power, involved the powerful intercontinental ballistic missiles (ICBMs), which possessed the necessary range to reach each other's territory. Negotiations to limit this class of strategic weapons continued between the U.S. and Soviet governments for several years, leading to an agreement in July, 1991. Mikhail Gorbachev and George Bush signed the Strategic Arms Reduction Treaty (START) in Moscow as the first step to beginning the numerical reduction of these powerful strategic missiles. (The treaty would be ratified in early 1992.) This atmosphere for greater cooperation, building on prior arms control efforts, provided the background for the president's dramatic announcement in September.

Other favorable conditions in 1990 and 1991 also signaled an improved relationship between the two Cold War rivals. Soviet military intervention in neighboring Afghanistan had ended in 1989; communist governments in Central and Eastern Europe had fallen from power in 1989 with minimal violence; the nations of East and West Germany had united in 1990; and growing economic ties between the Soviet Union and the West promised more cooperation. A significant agreement to limit military forces and non-nuclear weapons in Europe was adopted in November, 1990, by the Warsaw Pact (the Soviet Union and its European communist allies) and the North Atlantic Treaty Organization (NATO), of which the United States was a member. The following year, the Warsaw Pact itself ended.

The Soviet Union's cooperation with the United Nations and the West during the Persian Gulf War against Iraq in early 1991 also showed a willingness to work together in common purpose. An annual meeting of the leading economic nations, known as the Group of Seven (G7), invited Gorbachev to attend as an eighth participant in London in July, 1991. A few days later, Bush flew to Moscow to sign the START treaty. Thus the conditions were favorable for additional proposals from each side to continue the trend to reduce the threshold of nuclear danger.

President Bush's September, 1991, televised speech discussed a broad range of nuclear weapons systems and outlined the changes in military policies he unilaterally adopted. Bush first described changes in the Cold War environment and the growing cooperation between the superpowers. He argued that the possibility of a Soviet attack on Western Europe was no longer likely. Essentially Bush declared the Cold War was over and said that the two nations could work together in the future. This opportunity to improve the relationship now required both sides to undertake additional positive steps toward increased cooperation and peace. Building on previous arms control agreements, the president specified steps he intended

to adopt for the U.S. military. Some decisions were immediate and unilateral, falling under Bush's authority as U.S. commander in chief. For example, approximately twenty-one hundred U.S. nuclear artillery shells and short-range nuclear missiles located in Europe, originally designed for tactical battlefield use in case of war with the Soviet Union and its Warsaw Pact allies, were ordered withdrawn and destroyed. More than eight hundred nuclear weapons were removed from U.S. surface warships and naval aircraft. Bush also gave orders for the U.S. long-range bomber force to end its twenty-four-hour alert status. This policy, in place since the 1950's, had required war planes with nuclear weapons to be continually ready in case of crisis and possible nuclear war. A category of ICBMs scheduled to be eliminated under the START treaty, 450 Minuteman IIs, would be dismantled immediately rather than during the longer period specified in START. Further development and deployment of several new types of nuclear missiles, including the controversial MX missile with ten nuclear warheads, was canceled.

Bush's speech also identified several long-term objectives requiring future negotiations with the Soviet government. He proposed joint talks to seek the eventual elimination of all land-based multiwarhead nuclear missiles, as well as to improve procedures for the future supervision and dismantling of nuclear weapons of both nations. He recommended consideration of joint efforts to develop antiballistic missile defense systems for each nation.

The dramatic announcement of September 27 caught the world by surprise, because of its sweeping provisions and important implications for the future. Western military analysts interpreted the president's overture as having several purposes. In addition to the arms cuts and other steps, the United States hoped to support Gorbachev, who faced the imminent collapse of the Soviet Union. If that occurred, Soviet nuclear armaments would be even more difficult to negotiate, control, and eliminate. The president, prior to making his public speech, had privately communicated its contents to major world leaders, including Gorbachev. The Soviet response was considered to be the most significant. On September 28, Gorbachev gave cautious support to the U.S. proposals and reiterated Soviet interests in reducing nuclear weapons. He regretted that the U.S. president had not gone further, however, such as suspending U.S. underground nuclear testing. The Soviet leader promised careful consideration of the U.S. declaration, and the Moscow government indicated it would present its own proposals.

On October 5, the Gorbachev government announced a comparable set of reciprocal policies and unilateral cuts in Soviet military forces. Several steps paralleled Bush's orders, including removal of the Soviet strategic bomber force from ready-alert status, removal and destruction of tactical battlefield nuclear armaments, and a promise to dismantle more than five hundred ICBMs. Several missile projects also were canceled. Additional Soviet proposals even went beyond Bush's September announcement, including adoption of a one-year moratorium on Soviet nuclear weapons testing.

The two governments, within a two-week period, had announced substantial reductions in nuclear weapons systems and the general level of military preparedness. The extent of the decisions and the rapidity of their implementation signified continued cooperation between the two superpowers. The decisions announced by both leaders in their September 27 and October 5 statements provided the basis for further advances in shrinking the arms race and resolving the potential dangers of nuclear conflict.   *—Taylor Stults*

ADDITIONAL READING:

"Arms Control: U.S. and Soviet Announcements and Proposals of Major Reductions on Nuclear Weapons." *Foreign Policy Bulletin* 2, no. 2 (September/October, 1991): 47-51. Complete texts of three documents: Bush's September 27 speech, a September 27 "White House Summary of U.S. Initiatives on Nuclear Arms," and Gorbachev's October 5 response.

Beschloss, Michael R., and Strobe Talbott. *At the Highest Levels: The Inside Story of the End of the Cold War*. Boston: Little, Brown, 1993. Assesses the major leaders and events between 1989 and 1991.

Bush, George. "New Initiatives to Reduce U.S. Nuclear Forces." *U.S. Department of State Dispatch* 2, no. 39 (September 30, 1991): 715-718. Complete text of the president's September 27, 1991, speech.

Crockatt, Richard. *The Fifty Years War: The United States and the Soviet Union in World Politics, 1941-1991*. New York: Routledge, 1995. Shows the shift from confrontation to cooperation in nuclear weapons agreements and on other issues.

Gaddis, John L. *The United States and the End of the Cold War: Implications, Reconsiderations, Provocations*. New York: Oxford University Press, 1992. Broad interpretation of the changing Cold War relationships by the 1990's.

Oberdorfer, Don. *The Turn: From the Cold War to a New Era: The United States and the Soviet Union, 1983-1990*. New York: Poseidon Press, 1991. Covers the period of improved U.S.-Soviet Union relations under Reagan and Gorbachev.

SEE ALSO: 1973, Détente with the Soviet Union; 1979, SALT II Is Signed; 1985, U.S.-Soviet Summit; 1987, INF Treaty Is Signed; 1993, START II Is Signed.

1991 ■ CIVIL RIGHTS ACT OF 1991: *the act restores equal-opportunity law to its status before 1989, the year in which several Supreme Court decisions weakened two decades of legal precedents*

DATE: November 7, 1991
LOCALE: Washington, D.C.
CATEGORIES: Civil rights; Laws and acts
KEY FIGURES:
George Herbert Walker Bush (born 1924), forty-first president of the United States, 1989-1993

John Claggett Danforth (born 1936), Republican senator from Missouri
Edward Moore "Ted" Kennedy (born 1932), Democratic senator from Massachusetts

SUMMARY OF EVENT. The Civil Rights Act of 1991 has been described as among the most sweeping civil rights laws to be passed by Congress. In response to several adverse decisions by the Supreme Court, Senators Edward M. Kennedy and John C. Danforth jointly sponsored the Civil Rights Act of 1991, which was drafted with the objective of overturning these decisions. President George Bush, who had vetoed a similar bill in 1990, signed the bill into law in 1991.

Through congressional hearings, Congress concluded that additional remedies under federal law were needed to deter unlawful harassment and intentional discrimination in the workplace; decisions of the Supreme Court had weakened the effectiveness of federal civil rights protection; and legislation was necessary to provide additional protection against unlawful discrimination in employment. The expressed purpose of the Civil Rights Act of 1991 was to restore the state of discrimination law to what it had been before 1989, the year in which a conservative Supreme Court issued several decisions that seriously threatened the enforceability of equal opportunity laws. The act further expanded the scope of coverage of relevant civil rights statutes to include individuals or plaintiffs who sued under the Age Discrimination Act (ADA) or the Rehabilitation Act, and granted coverage to federal employees of Congress and employees of U.S. companies located in foreign countries.

Title VII of the Civil Rights Act of 1964 had made it unlawful to discriminate in employment because of race, ethnicity, color, sex, or religion. The primary issue facing judicial bodies empowered to adjudicate claims of discrimination was to define what employment practices violated Title VII and other antidiscrimination laws. Traditionally, employers screened potential employees by the use of general intelligence and aptitude tests, word-of-mouth recruiting, and other subjective criteria that disproportionately excluded or disparately impacted minorities from employment and promotion. In *Griggs v. Duke Power Company* (1971), which is considered the most important decision in the evolution of equal employment opportunity law, the Supreme Court had articulated the major principle that invalidated general intelligence tests and other criteria that had the effect of excluding minorities, regardless of the intent of the employer. The Court stated that if any criteria had a disparate impact upon the protected group, the criteria were unlawful and could be sustained only if they were related to the job and necessary for business. The burden of proof to rebut the claim shifted to the employer once the possibility of discrimination had been shown through statistical or other evidence.

In 1989, the Supreme Court issued several decisions that reversed the *Griggs* burden-of-proof standard and several other major legal principles governing unlawful discrimination. In *Ward Cove v. Atonio Company*, the Supreme Court changed the *Griggs* standard by holding that employees not only must show that they were disparately and discriminatorily impacted but also must prove that the employer could have employed alternate ways with less disparate impact. In *Price Waterhouse v. Hopkins*, the Court held that even after the employer has been found guilty of unlawful discrimination, it could still escape liability by showing that the employee would have been dismissed or treated differently for another nondiscriminatory reason. These changes made it significantly more difficult for plaintiffs to prevail in suits.

The Civil Rights Act of 1991 restored the *Griggs* principle. It also reversed the *Price Waterhouse* decision, stipulating that an unlawful practice is established when the complaining party demonstrates that race, color, religion, or national origin was a motivating factor for any employment practice, even though other factors also motivated the decision.

In *Paterson v. McLean Credit Union* (1989) the Supreme Court severely limited Section 1981 of the Civil Rights Act of 1866 when it held that the act covered only unlawful discrimination with regard to race and national origin at the time of hiring. Acts of discrimination that occurred after hiring were no longer illegal under the Civil Rights Act of 1866. The Civil Rights Act of 1991 reversed this decision by prohibiting pre- and post-employment discrimination.

In *Lorance v. AT&T Technologies* (1989) the Supreme Court upheld the dismissal of discrimination charges by female employees who charged that the implementation of a new seniority system discriminated against them. This decision established the principle that although women had been adversely affected by a new seniority policy, their complaint was barred because the statute of limitations had expired. The Supreme Court ruled that the timing began at the time of the policy change and not when the women became aware of the discriminatory effects of the policy. This reasoning was criticized on the grounds that an individual often may not know the discriminatory impact of the policy change until long after the statute of limitations for filing has passed. The Civil Rights Act of 1991 restored the legal principle that the statute of limitations began when the individual becomes aware of the discrimination.

Many municipalities have entered into consent decrees that grant relief to minority employees to avoid lengthy and costly litigations. Such consent decrees may adversely affect the interests of white male employees. However, all parties affected by the decree are notified and given an opportunity to intervene to protect the interests of their members. Once the consent decree has been approved by the court, it cannot be challenged in the future. In *Martin v. Wilks* (1989) the Supreme Court established a new principle. It allowed new white firefighters who were not a party to the original consent decree and judgment to reopen the decision. Had this new principle been allowed to stand, it would have threatened the validity of hundreds of consent decrees in the United States. The Civil Rights Act of 1991 reversed this decision. The act precluded any later challenge by a present employee, former employee, or applicant to a consent decree granting affirmative rights to minority employees.

Several major differences existed between Section 1981 of the Civil Rights Act of 1866 and other equal opportunity laws with respect to remedies available to plaintiffs. Whereas a plaintiff had a right to a jury trial and compensatory and punitive damages under Section 1981 of the 1866 act, plaintiffs who sued under Title VII, the ADA, and the Rehabilitation Act had no right to a jury trial and could only seek compensatory damages. The Civil Rights Acts of 1991 expanded these rights accorded to plaintiffs under Section 1981 to plaintiffs who were subjected to intentional discrimination under Title VII, the Americans with Disabilities Act of 1990, and the Rehabilitation Act of 1973.

Another notable limitation in the equal opportunity law was the absence of protection from discrimination for federal employees and U.S. citizens working in U.S. firms overseas. The Civil Rights Act of 1991 extended the right to sue to federal employees in the legislative and executive branches under Title VII, ADA, and the Rehabilitation Act. One exception was made to the definition of unlawful practices: that party affiliation and political compatibility may not be attacked as unfair employment practices. Furthermore, the act extended coverage to U.S. employees employed in foreign lands by U.S. firms.

Civil service examinations are required for most jobs and promotions in the public sector. Applicants are supposed to be chosen based on competitive scores earned. It has been charged, however, that these tests are biased in favor of white men in particular and white applicants and employees in general. Generally, a higher proportion of whites will score more highly than members of minority groups, including white women. To ensure that a larger number of minorities will be hired and promoted, the scores are adjusted for minorities such that some minorities with lower scores occasionally may be selected over whites with higher scores. This adjustment of test scores, which is referred to as race norming, emerged as a contentious issue in the United States. The Civil Rights Act of 1991 expressly prohibits compensatory adjustments to test scores in employment based upon race or other protected characteristics. —*Richard Hudson*

ADDITIONAL READING:

Kmiec, D. W., et al. "The Civil Rights Act of 1991: Theory and Practice—A Symposium." *Notre Dame Law Review* 68 (1993): 911-1164. Six critical articles on different aspects of the act.

Practising Law Institute. *The Civil Rights Act of 1991: Its Impact on Employment Discrimination Litigation*. New York: Author, 1992. This manual, written for lawyers and legal professionals, offers an analysis of the Civil Rights Act of 1991.

Rutgers Law Review 45, no. 4 (Summer, 1993): 887-1087. Contains eight critical articles delivered at the symposium "The Civil Rights Act of 1991: Unraveling the Controversy," on different aspects of the act.

U.S. Commission on Civil Rights. *Affirmative Action in 1980's: Dismantling the Process of Discrimination: A Statement of the United States Commission on Civil Rights*. Washington, D.C.: Author, 1981. Offers an analysis of affirmative action policies, structural and organizational discrimination, and the various civil rights statutes passed to protect minorities from job discrimination.

U.S. Equal Employment Opportunity Commission. *EEOC Compliance Manual*. Chicago: Commerce Clearing House, 1995. Clear, comprehensive descriptions of unlawful practices, types of proofs and evidence that establish discrimination, and procedures to pursue claims of unlawful discrimination.

SEE ALSO: 1964, Civil Rights Act of 1964; 1965, Voting Rights Act; 1965, Expansion of Affirmative Action; 1967, Freedom of Information Act; 1968, Bilingual Education Act; 1968, Indian Civil Rights Act; 1972, Equal Employment Opportunity Act; 1975, Equal Credit Opportunity Act; 1978, Pregnancy Discrimination Act; 1978, *Regents of the University of California v. Bakke*; 1988, Civil Rights Restoration Act.

1992 ■ LOS ANGELES RIOTS: *a police brutality trial reveals the wide gap between African American and Euro-American views of the criminal justice system, sparking the worst violence in the city's history*

DATE: April 29-May 1, 1992
LOCALE: Los Angeles, California
CATEGORY: Wars, uprisings, and civil unrest
KEY FIGURES:
Reginald Denny, white truck driver severely beaten by African Americans
Daryl F. Gates (born 1926), chief of the Los Angeles Police Department
Rodney King (born 1966), African American subject of a videotaped beating by Los Angeles police
Stacey Koon (born 1950), sergeant-in-charge of the Los Angeles police involved in the beating of Rodney King
Damien Williams, African American charged with participating in the beating of Denny

SUMMARY OF EVENT. Before the Rodney King beating on March 3, 1991, many in the Los Angeles community believed that the Los Angeles Police Department (LAPD) had demonstrated a pattern of excessive force, particularly against minority groups. One significant example was Operation Hammer, begun in 1989, during which the LAPD allegedly rounded up African Americans and Hispanics without probable cause that they had had committed a crime, simply because of the way the suspects looked and because the police wanted to avert the threat of gang violence. As a result, the chief of the LAPD, Daryl Gates, was despised by many in the African American community. The videotape of Rodney King's beating by members of the LAPD, therefore, came as no surprise to the African American community of Los Angeles. It merely confirmed what they already thought: that police brutality and use of excessive force against minorities was a common practice.

The videotape, recorded by private citizen George Holliday in the morning hours of March 3, 1991, contained eighty-one seconds of footage. The footage that was seen throughout the United States was of King, a six-foot, three-inch African American weighing 225 pounds, prone on the ground, sustaining blows to his head, neck, kidney area, and legs from four policemen, who were kicking and smashing at him with their truncheons. Not in full view on the videotape were nineteen other police officers surrounding the four who were administering the beating. Also not in view were the onlookers who were pleading that the beating stop. The police paid no attention to them. As a result of the beating, King sustained eleven fractures to his skull, a crushed cheekbone, a broken ankle, internal injuries, a burn on his chest, and some brain damage.

Television viewers also did not see what preceded the beating. During the evening, King had consumed the equivalent of a case of beer. His blood alcohol level was twice the legal limit. He was on parole at the time and ran the risk of landing back in jail if he were caught speeding. Police, led by Stacey Koon, started chasing King as he sped through the streets of Los Angeles. The chase escalated to one hundred miles per hour at one point, before the police were able to stop King and force him out of his car. Nor did television viewers see King fighting with the police, even standing up after being stunned twice with a taser gun. People saw only the prone body of an African American man being assaulted repeatedly by white police officers.

Four of the officers, including Koon, were charged with the beating at the end of March, 1991, in Los Angeles. Their attorneys moved for a change of venue for the trial, which was granted. The trial was held in the spring of 1992 in Simi Valley, a suburban town an hour's drive north of Los Angeles. The town was the home for a large proportion of LAPD officers and retirees and was dominated by law-and-order conservatives. Six men and six women, none of whom was African American, made up the jury. According to those who were present, the prosecution presented a weak and diffuse case. The defense, however, was strong. It played the videotape in slow motion over and over until its effect became trivialized. The defense also emphasized how King presented a threat to the police. Koon testified about King's "hulk-like strength and how he groaned like a wounded animal," conjuring up for the jury the image of police representing the "thin blue line" that protects the forces of civilization from the savagery represented by King. To those who had likely settled in Simi Valley to get away from the alleged evils and crime of the inner city, the message resounded. After thirty-two hours of deliberation, on April 29, 1992, the jury acquitted the four officers. The verdict was announced on television at 2:50 P.M.

At 4:00 P.M., in the South Central Los Angeles district near Florence and Normandie Boulevards, five African American gang members went to get some malt liquor at the Payless Liquor Store. They started to take it without paying, when the owner's son tried to stop them. One of the gang members smashed the son on the head with a bottle and allegedly said,

"This is for Rodney King." Other gang members hurled the bottles they held through the store windows, while the owner pressed the alarm for the police. When two officers came, the suspects were not there.

At 5:30, at the corner of Florence and Normandie, eight black men wielding baseball bats started breaking the car windows of passing motorists. Eighteen police cars and thirty-five officers from the LAPD sped to the area. They arrested three suspects but left at 5:45. In the next hour, the crowd attacking cars grew to two hundred people. One of the victims was Reginald Denny, a white truck driver, who was pulled from his truck and beaten by African Americans, including Damien Williams, with a fire extinguisher. The police from the 77th district of the LAPD still stayed away. Chief Gates had left police headquarters at 6:30 to attend a fund-raising event in the affluent suburb of Brentwood.

By 7:30, the crowd at Florence and Normandie had started lighting fires. An hour later, the LAPD finally returned to the area and began to disperse the crowd. By that time, the fires, rioting, and looting had spread to other parts of the city. The riots continued for two more days, local news coverage flooding the airwaves with helicopter views of hundreds of fires throughout the city and normally law-abiding citizens looting goods from stores. On Friday, May 1, 1992, Rodney King appeared on television with the plea, "Can't we all get along?" When the riots ended that day in Los Angeles, fifty-eight people had died, more than twelve thousand people had been arrested, and the property damage was estimated to be $1 billion. Throughout the nation, uprisings had started in Atlanta, Las Vegas, Minneapolis, New York, Omaha, and Seattle.

The riots in Los Angeles following the Rodney King trial caused more damage and spread across a wider area than those of the 1960's. Gates subsequently was replaced by an African American chief of police, Koon and a fellow officer were convicted of violating King's civil rights in federal court, Williams was acquitted of most of the charges in the beating of Reginald Denny, and King won a civil suit against the city of Los Angeles. These actions reinforced the perception of many that the criminal justice system treats whites and African Americans differently, whereas others argued that the riots were less the result of racial tensions than of a widening gap between "haves" and "have-nots" in U.S. society.   —*Jennifer Eastman*

ADDITIONAL READING:

"Can't We All Get Along?" "The Fire This Time," and "Anatomy of an Acquittal." *Time* 139, May 11, 1992. Articles give good overview of the events on April 29, 1992, and following.

"Los Angeles, April 29, 1992, and Beyond: The Law, Issues, and Perspectives." *Southern California Law Review* 66, May, 1993. A panoply of views on the trial and the riots, from why the videotape did not guarantee a guilty verdict to the role the federal government should play in monitoring police brutality. The most comprehensive view of the issues involved.

"Symposium on Criminal Law, Criminal Justice, and Race."

Tulane Law Review 67, no. 6, June, 1993. Discusses the use of racist imagery in the acquittal of the police officers and the conclusion that there are two systems of justice in the United States, "one black, one white—separate and unequal."

"Symposium: The Urban Crisis: The Kerner Commission Report Revisited." *North Carolina Law Review* 71, no. 5 (June, 1993). Articles discuss how the riots of 1992 differed from those of the 1960's. Explains that there were different minority groups involved and areas affected.

"The Untold Story of the L. A. Riot." *U.S. News and World Report* 114 (May 31, 1993): 34-39. An objective account of the facts that led to the beginning of and the escalation of the riots at Florence and Normandie Boulevards.

SEE ALSO: 1943, Urban Race Riots; 1965, Watts Riot; 1967, Long, Hot Summer; 1980, Miami Riots.

1992 ■ ASIAN PACIFIC AMERICAN LABOR ALLIANCE: *a new labor-activist organization forms to address the needs of a growing Asian and Pacific Islander community in the United States*

DATE: May 1, 1992
LOCALE: United States
CATEGORIES: Asian American history; Business and labor
KEY FIGURES:
Ah Quan McElrath (born 1915), organizer of the Longshore Workers Union in Hawaii
Jay Mazur (born 1932), chair of APALA's American Labor Committee, 1991-1992
Art Takei (born 1922), founder and president of the Alliance of Asian Pacific Labor
Philip Vera Cruz (1905-1994), vice president of the United Farm Workers during the 1930's
Kent Wong (born 1956), national president of APALA

SUMMARY OF EVENT. On May 1, 1992, the Asian Pacific American Labor Alliance (APALA) held its founding convention in Washington, D.C. That gathering drew five hundred Asian, American, and Pacific Island unionists and laborers from around the United States, including garment factory workers from New York City, hotel and restaurant workers from Honolulu, longshore laborers from Seattle, nurses from San Francisco, and supermarket workers from Los Angeles. The establishment of the APALA was the culmination of several decades of Asian American unionization activity.

Since the mid-1970's, Asian American labor activists in California had worked to strengthen unionization attempts by holding organizational meetings in the larger Asian American communities within San Francisco and Los Angeles. Through the efforts of such neighborhood-based organizations as the Alliance of Asian Pacific Labor (AAPL), stronger ties between labor and the community were forged, and Asian union staff members were united more closely with rank-and-file labor leaders. Those too-localized efforts of the Alliance of Asian Pacific Labor, however, failed to organize significant numbers of Asian American workers. In order to begin unionizing on the national level, AAPL administrators, led by Art Takei, solicited organizational aid from the American Federation of Labor-Congress of Industrial Organizations (AFL-CIO), a key U.S. labor collective.

Upon the invitation of the AFL-CIO executive board, AAPL vice president Kent Wong attended the 1989 national AFL-CIO convention in Washington, D.C., to lobby for the establishment of a national labor organization for Americans of Asian and Pacific Island descent. In addressing Wong's request, AFL-CIO president Lane Kirkland acknowledged the local accomplishments of the AAPL in California and recognized the organizing potential of the growing Asian American workforce. In 1991, Kirkland appointed a national Asian Pacific American labor committee. This group of thirty-seven Asian and American labor activists met for more than a year to create the Asian Pacific American Labor Alliance. In planning for the 1992 convention, the Asian Pacific American labor committee released a nationwide invitation for Asian, American, and Pacific Island unionists, labor activists, and workers to gather in Washington, D.C., to take on the responsibility for bridging the gap between the national labor movement and the Asian Pacific American community.

The response to that invitation exceeded the committee's expectations. At the May 1, 1992, convention, more than five hundred delegates participated in adopting an Asian Pacific American Labor Alliance constitution and in setting up a governmental structure with a national headquarters in Washington, D.C., and local chapters throughout the United States. Organized in this manner, the APALA could receive recognition and control from a national administration guided by the AFL-CIO, while still using its powerful techniques of community organization at the local level.

During the convention, APALA organizers and delegates also recognized and honored Asian Pacific American labor pioneers whose achievements they believed had melded national and local unionization efforts successfully. Among them was Philip Vera Cruz, the eighty-seven-year-old former vice president of the United Farm Workers Union. Vera Cruz had worked since the 1930's to create local unions for farmworkers in the southwestern United States, and continuously lobbied for national support of farmworkers' unionization. Other honorees included those who were seen by APALA to have made significant contributions toward heightening the recognition of Asian American laborers, such as Ah Quan McElrath of the Hawaiian Longshore Workers Union. As a result of McElrath's efforts throughout the 1950's, sugar and pineapple plantation workers in Hawaii achieved greater workplace and community status.

In addition to recognizing the history of Asian American labor activism and honoring the achievements of Asian American and Pacific Islanders, APALA looked ahead toward its role in continuing such activism and achievement. To this extent,

APALA drafted a Commitment to Organizing, to Civil Rights, and to Economic Justice. This document called for empowerment of all Asian and Pacific American workers through unionization on a national level; it also called for the provision of national support for individual, local unionization efforts. The APALA also promoted the formation of AFL-CIO legislation that would create jobs, ensure national health insurance, reform labor law, and channel financial resources toward education and job training for Asian and Pacific Island immigrants. Toward that end, a revision of U.S. governmental policies toward immigration also was called for. APALA's commitment document supported immigration legislation that would promote family unification and provide improved immigrant access to health, education, and social services. Finally, the document promoted national government action to prevent workplace discrimination against immigrant laborers; vigorous prosecution for perpetrators of racially motivated crimes was strongly supported. To solidify their commitment, APALA delegates passed several resolutions, which they forwarded to the AFL-CIO leadership. These documents decried the exploitative employment practices and civil rights violations alleged against several United States companies.

Convention delegates also participated in workshops that focused on individual roles in facilitating multicultural harmony and solidarity, enhancing Asian American participation in unions, and advancing a national agenda to support more broadly based civil rights legislation and improved immigration policies and procedures. From these APALA convention workshops, two national campaigns were launched. The first involved working with the AFL-CIO Organizing Institute to recruit a new generation of Asian Pacific American organizers, both at the national and local levels. The second campaign involved building a civil and immigration rights agenda for Asian Pacific American workers, based upon APALA's commitment document and its convention resolutions.

Through the legislative statement of its goals and in lobbying for their substantive societal implementation, the Asian Pacific American Labor Alliance was the first Asian American labor organization to achieve both national and local success. Although by the time of the 1992 APALA convention Asian Americans had been engaged in various forms of unionization activity for more than 150 years, establishment of APALA within the ranks of the AFL-CIO provided it with more powerful organizational techniques. The Asian Pacific American Labor Alliance was able to solidly unite Asian Pacific workers, simultaneously integrating them into the larger U.S. labor movement.

—*Thomas J. Edward Walker and Cynthia Gwynne Yaudes*

ADDITIONAL READING:

Aguilar-San Juan, Karin, ed. *The State of Asian America: Activism and Resistance in the 1990s.* Boston, Mass.: South End Press, 1994. Explores the connection between race, identity, and empowerment within the workplace and the community. Covers Euro-American, African American, and Asian American cultures. Bibliographical references; index.

Chang, Edward, and Eui-Young Yu, eds. *Multiethnic Coalition Building in Los Angeles.* Los Angeles: California State University Press, 1995. Suggests ways to build multicultural harmony within the community and the workplace. Discusses labor union organization among African Americans, Chicanos, and Asian Americans in California. Bibliographical references.

Friday, Chris. *Organizing Asian American Labor.* Philadelphia: Temple University Press, 1994. Analyzes the positive impact of Asian Pacific immigration upon the formation of industries on the West Coast and in the Pacific Northwest between 1870 and 1942. Bibliographical references; index.

Omatsu, Glenn, and Edna Bonacich. "Asian Pacific American Workers: Contemporary Issues in the Labor Movement." *Amerasia Journal* 8, no. 1 (1992). Discusses the advance in status that Asian American workers have achieved in recent decades; summarizes the political, economic, and social issues that still impede their progress.

Rosier, Sharolyn. "Solidarity Starts Cycle for APALA." *AFL-CIO News* 37, no. 10 (May 11, 1992): 11. Summarizes the AFL-CIO conference report on the establishment of the Asian Pacific American Labor Alliance.

Wong, Kent. "Building Unions in Asian Pacific Communities," *Amerasia Journal* 18, no. 3 (1992): 149-154. Assesses the difficulties of Asian American unionization and gives suggestions for overcoming those problems.

SEE ALSO: 1886, American Federation of Labor Is Founded; 1899, Hay's "Open Door Notes"; 1935, Congress of Industrial Organizations Is Founded.

1992 ■ TAILHOOK SCANDAL: *inappropriate behavior during the convention reveals the hostile environment for women in the military and results in the resignation of the secretary of the Navy*

DATE: June 24, 1992
LOCALE: Washington, D.C., and Las Vegas, Nevada
CATEGORY: Women's issues
KEY FIGURES:
Paula Coughlin (born 1962?), aide to Rear Admiral John W. Snyder, and Tailhook whistleblower
H. Lawrence Garrett (born 1939), secretary of the U.S. Navy
Frank B. Kelso II (born 1933), chief naval officer and acting secretary of the Navy
John W. Snyder, Jr., commanding officer at the Naval Air Test Center, Patuxent River
SUMMARY OF EVENT. Tailhook, the September meeting of the Tailhook Association, a naval aviators' organization, was a well-known bacchanal. At the yearly meetings of the Navy's elite "top guns," drunkenness, pranks, and lewd behavior were de rigueur. Named for the arresting device that helps stop a Navy jet landing on an aircraft carrier at sea, Tailhook celebrated aviator "machismo" and skill. Aviators expected the

1991 convention at the Las Vegas Hilton to be the bawdiest yet—a reward for their heroism in the Gulf War.

In September, 1991, two incidents occurred at Tailhook, both reflecting women's status in the military. At the panel that provided a forum for aviators to question admirals, a female aviator asked when women would be allowed to fly tactical or combat operations. The mostly male audience of aviators laughed and heckled Lieutenant Monica Rivadeneira, and the panel of admirals responded minimally without admonishing the audience. Women in the military and those who have studied women's integration maintain that only when women are permitted to serve in combat will their male peers treat them with due respect. One indication of the disrespect accorded to women in the military during the 1990's has been the sexual harassment that many have endured. Sexual harassment of women in the armed forces has a long history, and Tailhook was only one in a series of events that drew nationwide attention to the issue in the early 1990's.

On the evening of September 7, 1991, Lieutenant Paula Coughlin, an aide to Rear Admiral John W. Snyder, went to the third floor of the Las Vegas Hilton. What Coughlin saw and experienced there became the first part of the Tailhook scandal. Immediately after she exited the elevator, fellow officers lining either side of the thirty-foot-long hotel corridor surrounded her. Naval aviators assumed the Tailhook formation, the gauntlet. Aviators closed in on her, preventing her escape. Coughlin was shoved down the hall, fondled by her assaulters as she passed them. Calls of "admiral's aide" preceded her, demonstrating that her assailants knew her identity and her rank. The aviators ignored her pleas for help, her angry shouts, and her attempts to fight back. Covered with beer, clothes disheveled and torn, and bruised, Coughlin emerged from the gauntlet and fled. The next day she reported her experience to her commanding officer, noting that she had feared gang rape. Her complaint was dismissed with an offhand comment that one had to expect such things at Tailhook. After repeated attempts to get action from Snyder, Coughlin decided to go over his head.

Upon learning of the assaults, Secretary of the Navy H. Lawrence Garrett denounced the convention, ordered a Naval investigation, and seeming to pursue the Navy's policy of "zero tolerance" for sexual harassment. In June of 1992, when Garrett responded to the Naval Investigative Service (NIS) report with a call for complete accountability of squadron commanders at the Tailhook convention, NIS released a supplemental report that was Garrett's undoing: It placed Garrett at Tailhook and said he had turned a blind eye to the sexual antics and violations of junior officers. After the Navy's internal investigation failed to uncover any culprits and called into question the ability of the Navy to police itself, Garrett called on the Office of the Inspector General of the Department of Defense (DOD) to do its own probe of Tailhook.

On June 24, 1992, Paula Coughlin went public, taking her story to the national media. Frustrated by the Navy's failure to punish the perpetrators nine months after the event, Coughlin hoped to spur on the investigation by coming forward. Two days later, Garrett resigned, taking full responsibility for the Tailhook scandal. This was the Navy's first real step toward accountability for Tailhook.

The DOD report of April, 1993, detailed the second scandalous revelation of Tailhook, the cover-up. The findings showed that eighty-three women (revised up from the original NIS figure of twenty-six) had been involved and that excesses at Tailhook 1991 extended beyond the gauntlet. The hospitality suites on the third floor of the hotel had been the sites of further exploits, including phallic drink spigots dispensing white russians, indecent exposure, and pornographic movies. The DOD report also disclosed that the sexual misconduct occurred with the knowledge of Navy higher-ups. The cover-up—aimed at damage control and closing ranks to protect those at all levels within the Navy and the Navy itself—made a mockery of zero tolerance, demonstrating the pervasiveness of the attitudes behind the Tailhook abuse.

Although Tailhook was the result of a masculine military culture that viewed sexual exploits as the reward for the risks Navy fliers took on a daily basis, it was more than that. The U.S. military in the early 1990's was at a crossroads, and the Tailhook episode was an example of deep resistance to changes in the gender composition of the armed forces. By 1991, many well-trained female pilots had hit the "glass ceiling" in the military, a glass ceiling upheld by the Combat Exclusion Act of 1948. Military women exerted steady pressure through various channels to overturn the law that banned women from combat and, by extension, from promotion and equal treatment.

In 1991, in the Persian Gulf War, women in the military again had served bravely and with valor, but in greater numbers and in great danger. As a result, gender and military service was on the nation's mind. Finally, the Department of Defense was reducing the size of the armed forces, shaping a national defense in line with the post-Cold War world. Men and women in all branches of the service wondered where they would fit in the new downsized Navy. With fewer positions available at all levels, military men eyed women as competitors.

Tailhook therefore called attention to the plight of women in the military. The Navy severed its thirty-five-year-long support of the Tailhook Association. The congressional Armed Services Committee held a hearing on gender discrimination in the military in its wake. Garrett created the Standing Committee on Women in the Navy and Marine Corps in June, 1992. In January, 1993, the Navy revised its sexual harassment policy, defining it and making any violation of the code a punitive offense. It defined sexual harassment along the guidelines of civilian society, noting both the "sex for promotion" and "hostile environment" components. On April 28, 1993, the Navy opened competition for combat assignments, excluding ground fighting. Forty percent of the jobs were still closed to women, but flying combat and going to sea—the most important aspects of naval service—were finally open to women.

Only one aviator was formally censured for his behavior at Tailhook. Rear Admiral Snyder was removed from command in 1991 for not responding to Coughlin's complaint. Several of the most zealous participants at Tailhook benefited from the investigator general's frustration with aviator stonewalling. In return for immunity, they testified, but did not provide enough evidence against their peers to result in courts-martial. Admiral Frank Kelso, acting secretary of the Navy, retired early because of his presence at Tailhook, but kept his stars. Paula Coughlin resigned from the Navy, finding it impossible to do her job in a climate of hostility. She filed a civil suit against Hilton Hotels and won. —*Jessica Weiss*

ADDITIONAL READING:

Chema, J. Richard. "Arresting 'Tailhook': The Prosecution of Sexual Harassment in the Military." *Military Law Review* 140 (Spring, 1993): 1-64. Argues that existing naval codes, if enforced, cover sexual harassment, and that no new guidelines are required.

Ebbert, Jean, and Marie-Beth Hall. *Crossed Currents: Navy Women from World War I to Tailhook.* Washington, D.C.: Brassey's, 1993. Encompasses the first women clerks during World War I, the WAVES of World War II, and the women of the 1990's who fought for the right to fly combat missions and serve at sea.

Holm, Jeanne. *Women in the Military: An Unfinished Revolution.* Rev. ed. Novato, Calif.: Presidio Press, 1993. A history by one of the highest-ranking women in the Navy.

United States Congress. House Committee on Armed Services. Military Personnel and Compensation Subcommittee. *Gender Discrimination in the Military: Hearings Before the Military Personnel and Compensation Subcommittee and the Defense Policy Panel of the Committee on Armed Services, House of Representatives, 102nd Congress, 2nd Session.* Washington, D.C.: Government Printing Office, 1992. Transcript provides background on women in the military as well as contemporary attitudes within and outside the military toward women's role in the national defense and toward the Tailhook scandal.

Zimmerman, Jean. *Tailspin: Women at War in the Wake of Tailhook.* New York: Doubleday, 1995. Places Tailhook in the context of the changes within the military in the 1980's and 1990's. Discusses the changing role of women in combat operations and post-Cold War downsizing.

SEE ALSO: 1982, Defeat of the Equal Rights Amendment.

1992 ■ DEFEAT OF THE CHARLOTTETOWN ACCORD: *Canada's constitutional crisis deepens with the electorate's rejection of an intensely negotiated package of reforms*

DATE: October 26, 1992
LOCALE: Canada
CATEGORY: Canadian history

KEY FIGURES:

Robert Bourassa (born 1933), premier of Quebec

Joe Clark (born 1939), constitutional affairs minister; prime minister of Canada, 1979-1980

Brian Mulroney (1939), prime minister of Canada, 1984-1993

Jacques Parizeau (born 1930), leader of the sovereignist Parti Québécois

Pierre Elliott Trudeau (born 1919), prime minister of Canada, 1968-1979 and 1980-1984

SUMMARY OF EVENT. The 1990 failure of the Meech Lake Accord plunged Canada into a serious constitutional crisis. Political parties saw much turmoil. A Quebec-based reform party, the Bloc Québécois, was formed by Progressive Conservative and Liberal defectors. The leaders of western Canada forged links to face off against both Quebec and the federal government in Ottawa.

On November 1, 1990, Prime Minister Brian Mulroney created a national commission to study the future of Canada. This move was criticized by native Canadians who were in the midst of a dispute with the government and by the Quebecers who had established their own panel to examine the future. The leaders of French-speaking Quebec remained cool to federal efforts to proceed on constitutional and trade issues. Quebec premier Robert Bourassa introduced a Liberal Party plan to radically decentralize the country. Meanwhile, Prime Minister Mulroney pleaded for unity. On September 24, 1991, Mulroney unveiled a series of constitutional reforms, entitled Shaping Canada's Future Together. These proposals came under immediate criticism, not only by the usual Quebecers and native critics but also by those from the Canadian West who felt the reforms weakened their provinces' economies.

Attitudes hardened throughout 1992, with Alberta premier Donald Getty opposing policies of bilingualism, while he and Newfoundland's Clyde Wells pressed for a strong Senate based on provincial equality. Five conferences on constitutional reform attempted to hammer out the differences between provinces. Numerous plans were debated in a nationwide discussion on Canada's future, with criticism arising throughout the country: Quebecers, native Canadians, residents of the western provinces, and feminists who feared an undermining of the Canadian Bill of Rights. Hopes rose and fell as detailed debates revolved around highly theoretical concepts, such as "asymmetrical federalism," senatorial equality, and the exact nature of Quebec's distinct society.

On August 27, 1992, Mulroney, the provincial premiers, territorial leaders, and representatives from four native associations unanimously agreed on a constitutional reform package, known as the Charlottetown Accord, named after the capital of Prince Edward Island, where it was signed.

The accord's provisions included the Canada Clause, a statement of principles on which the country was founded, which was to serve as a guide for the courts to interpret the constitution. It decreed that Quebec constituted "within Canada a distinct society," with a French-speaking majority, a unique culture, and a civil-law tradition (in contrast to the common-law tradition prevailing elsewhere in Canada). The federal and provincial governments would be committed to the development of minority-language communities. The nation would be committed to respecting individual and collective human rights and freedoms. In the words of the document, "Canadians confirm the principle of the equality of the provinces at the same time as recognizing their diverse characteristics."

An elected Senate with expanded powers was to be created to replace the appointed body that had been convened since 1982. Each province would be equally represented with six senators, and the territories would each have one senator. Additional seats were to be apportioned to native peoples. The House of Commons, Canada's lower house, would be expanded to reflect population distribution more closely. Ontario, Quebec, British Columbia, and Alberta would gain seats. In recognition of its distinctiveness, Quebec would be guaranteed at least 25 percent of the seats. The nine Supreme Court justices would be named by the federal government from lists submitted by the provinces, as opposed to the practice of being appointed at the sole discretion of the federal government. Three would always be from Quebec.

The accord provided constitutional recognition that the native peoples had "the inherent right of self-government within Canada." Although there was no agreement on what the concept meant, it did not include the notion of separate sovereignty for native peoples, who were to negotiate the details of the concept with federal and provincial governments. If the natives' rights had not been defined after five years, the courts could issue a final determination.

The federal government would retain control of national entities, such as the Canadian Broadcasting Corporation and unemployment insurance. Provincial governments would have exclusive jurisdiction over culture and job retraining programs. The federal government would withdraw completely, whenever provincial authorities requested, from forestry, mining, tourism, recreation, housing, and municipal and urban affairs. Provinces could negotiate administrative agreements with the federal government for increased control over immigration and regional development.

The accord's opponents were numerous. Former prime minister Pierre Trudeau denounced what he saw as Quebec's unduly large role. Even more scathing in their criticisms, Western Canadians tended to oppose the accord because they did not favor concessions to Quebec, whereas Quebecers voted no because they thought the accord did not deliver them enough concessions. Native Canadians, women's groups, and others also had their doubts.

On October 26, 1992, Canadian voters overwhelmingly defeated the accord. Ending an often divisive national campaign, a majority of voters in the provinces of Quebec, Nova Scotia, Alberta, British Columbia, Saskatchewan, Manitoba, and the Yukon Territory voted no to the question, "Do you agree that the Constitution of Canada should be renewed on the basis of the agreement reached on August 28, 1992?" The yes side won in Ontario, New Brunswick, Newfoundland, Prince Edward

In the wake of the 1992 defeat of the Charlottetown Accord, voters gather in October, 1995, at Hull, Quebec, across the Ottawa River from Parliament Hill, after voting in a referendum on splitting Quebec from Canada. Although supporters of national unity prevailed, the sovereignist movement remained strong and the bloodless but bitter struggle for secession continued. (AP/Wide World Photos)

Island, and the Northwest Territories. Nationwide, the no side out-polled the yes side 54.4 percent to 44.6 percent, with a 74.9 percent turnout of eligible voters. The referendum was technically a nonbinding guide for the ten provincial assemblies, each of whose approval was needed for formal ratification of the accord. A no vote in any one province had been widely viewed as all that would be necessary to kill the accord.

Constitutional Affairs Minister Joe Clark offered a bleak assessment of what the no vote meant: "We thought after two decades of failure, the failure of six rounds of constitutional discussions, we had found in the Charlottetown Accord a way to resolve these deep and dividing problems in Canada, or begin their resolution. . . . It's clear tonight that that solution has not been accepted. What's not clear tonight is what solution might be available to us." A few hours after the no had become evident, Prime Minister Mulroney declared, "The Charlottetown agreement is history." Canadians and their governments should now set aside the constitutional issue, he said, and concentrate on fostering "strong and durable economic renewal."

On October 26, Jacques Parizeau, leader of the sovereignist Parti Québécois, told supporters in Montreal that Quebec's rejection of the accord "said what we didn't want—the next time we will say what we want. Québécois are a people, they are a nation, and very soon they will be a country." Parizeau had made clear during the referendum campaign that if the Parti Québécois won the next provincial election in Quebec, he would call for a referendum on independence. He argued that the nationwide no vote had effectively been a plea to abandon efforts to revise the constitution. He insisted that the only options remaining for Quebec were sovereignty or a vastly revised federal arrangement. The leader of the Bloc Québécois, Lucien Bouchard, offered a different appraisal of the options facing Quebec. Bouchard reasoned, "There were two roads for Québécois before the referendum—profoundly renewed federalism and sovereignty. These two options must now find a convergence." Robert Bourassa, Quebec's Liberal premier who had led the yes campaign in that province, pointed to the results of two polls indicating most Quebecers preferred to remain part of the Canadian confederation, and reiterated his party's goal to "Build Quebec within Canada," saying that federalism would "advance the cause of Quebec."

Many Canadians voted no to Charlottetown to vent their anger against the political and business establishment in general and the Progressive Conservative Party and Mulroney in particular. The most significant victim of the accord's failure was Brian Mulroney. Facing growing pressure to step down, given the implicit "no-confidence" nature of the referendum, he resigned as the leader of the Progressive Conservative Party and as prime minister on February 24, 1993, after a frustrating decade-long campaign for Canadian unity, during which the country's worst recession raged.   —*Randall Fegley*

ADDITIONAL READING:

Hurley, James Ross. *The Canadian Constitutional Debate.* Ottawa: Privy Council Office, 1994. A good look at Canadian constitutional history from 1987 to 1992.

McRoberts, Kenneth, and Patrick Monahan. *The Charlottetown Accord: The Referendum and the Future of Canada.* Toronto: University of Toronto Press, 1993. An excellent examination of the negotiations and politics surrounding the Charlottetown Accord and its subsequent failure to be approved by the Canadian electorate.

Smith, David, et al. *After Meech Lake.* Saskatoon, Sask.: Fifth House, 1991. A look at the possibilities facing Canada following the 1990 failure of the Meech Lake Accord.

Sutherland, Kate. *Referendum Round-Table.* Edmonton, Alberta: Centre for Constitutional Studies, 1992. A good monograph analyzing the Charlottetown Accord.

Vipond, Robert. *Liberty and Community.* Albany: State University of New York Press, 1991. Examines the inability of Canadians to agree on constitutional reforms.

SEE ALSO: 1960, Quebec Sovereignist Movement; 1970, October Crisis; 1984, Mulroney Era in Canada; 1990, Meech Lake Accord Dies.

1992 ■ CLINTON IS ELECTED PRESIDENT: *a Democrat captures the White House for the first time in a decade, promising change and meeting with intense congressional resistance*

DATE: November 3, 1992
LOCALE: Washington, D.C.
CATEGORY: Government and politics
KEY FIGURES:
George Herbert Walker Bush (born 1924), forty-first president of the United States, 1989-1993
William Jefferson "Bill" Clinton (born 1946), forty-second president of the United States
Newton Leroy "Newt" Gingrich (born 1943), Republican leader in the House of Representatives
H. Ross Perot (born 1930), independent candidate for president

SUMMARY OF EVENT. On January 20, 1993, Bill Clinton was sworn in as the forty-second president of the United States. In a three-cornered race, he had won a substantial electoral victory over the incumbent Republican president, George Bush, and independent candidate H. Ross Perot, a Texas billionaire. Clinton's victory can be traced back to events in the late 1960's that reshaped both major U.S. political parties. Since the Great Depression, the Democratic Party had been the country's dominant political force. A coalition of Southern white politicians and Northern urban and labor leaders had been formed. The Democrats could rely on votes from large cities, minorities, unionized workers, Southerners, Catholics, and Jews. The Republicans were led by Northeastern and Midwestern Protestants. They could usually count on support from the business community and middle- and upper-class suburban voters.

Two powerful political struggles of the 1960's brought

about a reconstruction of both national party coalitions. Opposition to the war in Vietnam induced many liberal Democrats to attack and ultimately weaken or destroy the big-city Democratic machines and labor leaders. Liberal activists for a variety of other causes began to support special-interest groups rather than the party itself. The Civil Rights movement weakened Democratic strength in the South. Although liberals controlled many congressional districts, the party's strength in presidential campaigns was diminished. For thirty years, the pattern of Republican presidents and Democratic Congresses was established; before Clinton, only Jimmy Carter had been able to overcome the trend.

During the first days of his administration, Clinton seemed to be well positioned to produce new programs and initiatives. Not only had the election ended twelve years of Republican control of the executive branch, but the Democrats also were in control of both houses of Congress. Many observers believed that the coalition assembled by President Ronald Reagan—right-wing Republicans together with Republican and Democratic centrists—finally had come unraveled as a result of the weakened U.S. economy. Clinton's campaign promises had included restoration of economic health, deficit reduction, health care reform, campaign spending reform, and support for the North American Free Trade Agreement (NAFTA). Taken as a whole, the elements of Clinton's program seemed to be well calculated to expand or restore the power of the Democratic Party in national politics.

However, the president found within a few months that there were severe limits on what he could accomplish. Solid Republican opposition to his proposals, coupled with the defection of many Democrats whose interests were adversely impacted by Clinton's program, prevented him from achieving much in the early days of his administration. His efforts to find compromises acceptable to Congress often made him appear to vacillate, further weakening his political influence. Moreover, he had invested a great deal of political capital to persuade the armed forces to accept the presence of homosexuals in the military. Clinton found the going tough on this issue and was forced to accept a compromise that satisfied neither side in the dispute.

By the end of the first two years of Clinton's term, he had achieved only two major legislative victories: passage of his budget and approval of NAFTA. The president's budget was a success, resulting in a real reduction in the projected budget deficit and a real reduction in the number of federal employees. The unemployment rate dropped substantially, as many new jobs were created. In the case of NAFTA, Clinton found it necessary to appeal to Republicans for additional legislative support. Although the treaty passed, its results were unclear and controversy continued over its impact on U.S. workers. The president failed to persuade Congress to pass an elaborate health care reform plan, which had been his highest most publicly visible priority. So many interests had been consulted in the formation of the plan and so many compromises made that the proposal lost clarity and focus; public support waned,

and the president and Mrs. Clinton, who had assumed a large role in orchestrating the plan, had to accept defeat.

Both before and after the election, the president's greatest political challenge had come from opponents who made a variety of charges: the president and the First Lady, Hillary Rodham Clinton, were charged with conflicts of interest and financial improprieties in connection with the Whitewater real estate development in Arkansas years before Clinton's presidency. After the senior staff of the White House Travel Office was dismissed and replaced with people known to the Clintons, Mrs. Clinton was charged with cronyism in what became known as the "Travelgate" matter. In 1993, President Clinton was charged with propositioning and sexually harassing a former Arkansas state employee, Paula Jones. Jones, with the financial support of conservative groups opposed to the president, filed a suit against him, in spite of his denials. In the meantime, Mrs. Clinton—having been attacked for her ground-

Bill Clinton, forty-second president of the United States, campaigned on a platform of "change" after twelve years of Republican policies. Although he struggled with the appearance of inconsistent political ideals, delays in cabinet appointments, inexperienced staff, and debacles such as Travelgate and the Whitewater affair, he made progress in lowering a mushrooming federal budget deficit, in bringing health care reform to the Congress as a serious issue, and in working with a midterm Republican Congress toward welfare and other social reforms. (Library of Congress)

breaking role in health care reform and for impropriety in the Travelgate and Whitewater matters—was forced to redefine her role as First Lady in a more traditional way, and her participation in the affairs of government became less visible.

President Clinton also faced strong factional opposition among Democrats. He had campaigned for office as a centrist New Democrat, but in order to prevail with Congress and the bureaucracy, he found it necessary to adopt a much more liberal stance as president than he had presented as a candidate. His new positions on rights for homosexuals, abortion, and minority representation were not generally popular with the public. They also made the president appear to be waffling on a variety of campaign promises. The administration's abandonment of a promised middle-class tax cut and welfare reform were particularly damaging.

President Clinton's apparent inability to prevail in the legislative process or to become popular enough to silence the critics of his personal behavior made him appear weak and vacillating. In the midterm elections of 1994, the Democrats suffered a stunning reversal, losing control of both houses of Congress for the first time in more than forty years. After that election, President Clinton moved back toward the political center. This second major turnabout did little at first to reestablish his reputation for principled and steadfast political leadership. By late 1995 and early 1996, however, the president had rebounded. Republican measures, part of the 1995-1996 budget bill, which would have shifted the administration of the welfare and Medicare programs from the national to the state governments, were vetoed. There were not enough Republican votes in Congress to override the president's veto. The president's success in the public relations battle that followed did much to restore his political standing.

Although the crucial decisions of the second half of Clinton's 1992 term were legislative rather than administrative, the president also had some very visible foreign policy and administrative successes. Clinton successfully withdrew the troops sent to Somalia by President Bush in 1992. U.S. military intervention in Haiti proved successful, bringing about peaceful elections and a peaceful presidential transition for the first time in that country's history. Clinton's administration also established a coalition to intervene militarily to end the savage war between Bosnia and Serbia in the former Yugoslavia. On the administrative side, the Federal Emergency Management Agency (FEMA), which had not acquitted itself well after hurricanes during the Bush Administration, was reorganized in the first years of Clinton's administration. When severe flooding struck the Pacific Northwest in 1996, FEMA did an excellent job of rushing federal aid to flood victims.

The political situation after 1994—a Democratic President and a Republican Congress—had been practically unknown in the United States since before the Great Depression of 1929. There were unusually sharp administrative and policy differences between the Clinton Administration and the Republican majorities in Congress. The new group of Republicans in the House of Representatives, under the leadership of House Speaker Newt Gingrich of Georgia, were both highly ideological and highly disciplined. The fierce struggle between President Clinton and the Republicans established the critical and defining nature of the 1996 election to the future of U.S. politics. Had either party captured both elected branches of government, the direction of U.S. public policy would have been determined for years to come. However, the parties split control of the government. With Congress and the White House each controlled by a different party, analysts expected the continuation of centrist or compromise government.

—Robert Jacobs

ADDITIONAL READING:

Campbell, Colin, and Bert A. Rockman, eds. *The Clinton Presidency: First Appraisals*. Chatham, N.J.: Chatham House, 1995. Excellent essays on the Clinton presidency by political scientists. Harold Stanley's "The Parties, the President, and the 1994 Midterm Elections" is particularly insightful.

Cohen, Richard E. *Changing Course in Washington: Clinton and the New Congress*. New York: Macmillan, 1994. Documents Clinton's shift toward the conservative side of the Democratic Party.

Denton, Robert E., Jr., and Rachel L. Holloway, eds. *The Clinton Presidency: Images, Issues, and Communications Strategies*. Westport, Conn.: Praeger, 1996. Expert analysis of Clinton's images, issues, and rhetoric during and after the 1992 presidential campaign.

Drew, Elizabeth. *On the Edge: The Clinton Presidency*. New York: Simon & Schuster, 1994. Recounts the internal policy struggles of the Clinton Administration during its first two years.

Greenberg, Stanley B. *Middle Class Dreams: The Politics and Power of the New American Majority*. New York: Times Books, 1995. Thoughtful analysis of the central trends in U.S. public opinion. Suggests that the electorate is becoming more conservative.

Hohenberg, John. *The Bill Clinton Story: Winning the Presidency*. Syracuse, N.Y.: Syracuse University Press, 1994. Scholarly analysis of Clinton's 1992 campaign strategy.

SEE ALSO: 1988, Bush Is Elected President; 1993, North American Free Trade Agreement; 1994, Brady Handgun Violence Protection Act; 1994, U.S.-North Korea Pact; 1994, Republicans Return to Congress; 1994, General Agreement on Tariffs and Trade; 1995, United States Recognizes Vietnam.

1992 ■ U.S. MARINES IN SOMALIA: *under the auspices of the United Nations, U.S. forces enter a nation in anarchy to secure humanitarian operations*

DATE: December 9, 1992-March 31, 1994
LOCALE: Somalia
CATEGORY: Diplomacy and international relations
KEY FIGURES:
Mahammad Farah Aideed, prominent Somali military leader

Boutros Boutros-Ghali (born 1922), secretary general of the United Nations

George Herbert Walker Bush (born 1924), forty-first president of the United States, 1989-1993

William Jefferson "Bill" Clinton (born 1946), forty-second president of the United States

Ali Mahdi Mahammad (born 1939), prominent leader in the Hawiye clan

Robert B. Oakley (born 1931), U.S. special envoy to Somalia

Mahammad Siad Barré (born 1921), former president of Somalia

SUMMARY OF EVENT. President George Bush announced on December 4, 1992, that U.S. forces would be sent to Somalia in order to provide security for the provision of emergency humanitarian assistance. This announcement followed months of civil war and famine in Somalia and many months of international debate about how best to deal with that country's deteriorating situation. On December 3, 1992, the U.N. Security Council authorized a member state to intervene in Somalia, where anarchy reigned. The intervening power was authorized to use all necessary means to provide security for humanitarian relief. The Bush Administration, which had been preparing for this eventuality, took formal steps to mount a peacekeeping operation, called Operation Restore Hope, under U.S. command. The first troops landed in Mogadishu, Somalia's capital and largest city, in the early morning hours of December 9. U.S. forces remained in Somalia until March 31, 1994, when President Bill Clinton formally called for the withdrawal of all but a handful of U.S. troops, in the face of ongoing civil strife and discord. Although the operation failed to produce a political resolution to the Somali civil war, it did restore considerable order to the Somali countryside and ended the famine.

Although Somalia is a largely homogeneous country in terms of ethnicity, religion, and language, its people are divided into six major clans and numerous subclans. The majority of Somalis are fiercely independent nomads, with strong loyalty to the family and clan. Traditionally, clans and subclans have engaged in disputes over pasture and water resources, but significant interclan marriage has muted such conflict, as has the mediating authority of clan elders. This traditional capacity for conflict resolution was weakened during the 1980's, as President Mahammad Siad Barré, who had seized power in a coup in 1969, nine years after Somalia's independence, sought to manipulate the clan system to maintain his increasingly unpopular regime. Siad Barré's policies of reform in his early years were welcomed by most Somalis. After the failure of his attempt to capture the predominantly Somali-inhabited Ogaden region in Ethiopia, his regime gradually became more authoritarian and increasingly brutal. As opposition to Siad Barré grew, he responded by rewarding fellow Marehan clan members with positions of power. Other clans responded with determined resistance. The northwestern part of Somalia fell into open rebellion in May, 1988. Siad Barré responded ruthlessly with aerial bombings of Hargeisa,

the regional capital, and hundreds of thousands of Isaq Somali took refuge in nearby Ethiopia. The civil war in the north continued for three years, culminating in a declaration of independence on May 17, 1991, and the formation of Somaliland Republic. During the latter months of 1990, civil war had spread throughout southern Somalia. Awash in arms from years of military assistance during the Cold War, opposition groups flourished. Mahammad Farah Aideed's well-armed Somali National Army (SNA) gradually gained the upper hand against Siad Barré's forces, which had been reduced by defections to Marehan clan units. Aideed's forces captured Mogadishu in late January, 1991, as Siad Barré fled from the capital city after plundering it and retreated into the southern countryside, where pitched battles were fought with Aideed's forces in fertile agricultural areas, interrupting local farming and precipitating the famine.

If Siad Barré's opposition had been united, Somalia might not have devolved into anarchy. However, disputes over who should govern the country developed immediately after Siad Barré's flight, the principal contest being between Aideed and Ali Mahdi Mahammad, a Mogadishu businessman. Both men were members of the Hawiye clan of the United Somali Congress (USC), but they hailed from different subclans. Ali Mahdi Mahammad had considerable political support, especially among his Agbal subclan, but Aideed had a more effective fighting force. In late 1991, the two sides clashed for several months in the streets of Mogadishu. International relief organizations of the United Nations withdrew from the country because of the complete lack of security, leaving only the International Committee of the Red Cross and some private agencies to cope with the growing famine. Regional diplomatic efforts failed. By February, 1992, a cease-fire was agreed upon and a special coordinator was appointed to reinitiate a U.N. presence. These efforts failed, and U.N. Secretary General Boutros Boutros-Ghali called for a more concerted international effort.

The U.N. Security Council responded by creating the United Nations Operation in Somalia (UNOSOM I), under the direction of Mohamed Sahnoun. This ill-fated effort was underfunded and met with strong Somali resistance. The famine deepened during 1992, and relief supplies could not be delivered, owing to the ongoing civil war. Boutros-Ghali and Sahnoun clashed over how the United Nations should respond, and the latter resigned in September, just before a planned national reconciliation conference.

Matters deteriorated further as death rates from starvation and disease skyrocketed. Facing this grim humanitarian situation, the Bush Administration, in its waning months in office, offered to deploy U.S. troops to provide security for relief supplies. Special envoy Robert Oakley was dispatched by Bush to negotiate a smooth entry for U.S. forces with Somali factional leaders, and U.S. forces, designated the Unified Task Force (UNITAF), were on the ground by December 9, 1992, with assistance from military units of Canada, France, Italy, Belgium, and Morocco. The troops initially received a hero's

Between December, 1992, and the spring of 1994, U.S. forces participated in Operation Restore Hope, an intervention in Somalia, an east African nation ravaged by famine and the anarchy of civil war. (AP/Wide World Photos)

welcome from the Somali people and cautious acquiescence from the Somali factions. Within a month, Mogadishu and key regional cities had been secured, relief supplies were reaching famine-stricken areas, and the emergency situation had been greatly stabilized—but the political situation remained tenuous. Diplomatic efforts to restore the local elders' influence, to establish an interim police force, and quietly to impound the large caches of weapons were initiated.

Initially, public support in the United States for the Operation Restore Hope was strong. Most U.S. citizens perceived the operation as being consistent with U.S. humanitarian policies, even though the United States paid for three quarters of the UNITAF expenses. The problems came after the United States handed over authority to a reconstituted UNOSOM II. President Clinton, a newcomer to foreign policy, was eager to reduce the U.S. presence in the region and for the U.N. to take

overall operational control. Robert Oakley finished his assignment in March, 1993. Later in the same month, UNITAF functions were transferred formally to UNOSOM II, and the U.S. marines began to withdraw from Somalia, leaving a much smaller U.S. contingent of four thousand to join UNOSOM II.

With the United Nations taking a more direct role, Aideed's forces became bolder in resistance to UNOSOM II. Aideed greatly resented U.N. Secretary General Boutros-Ghali and took an early opportunity to challenge him. SNA forces attacked a Pakistani patrol in early June, 1993, killing many. Boutros-Ghali called the action a war crime and Aideed a criminal. U.N. forces began a cat-and-mouse effort to capture Aideed, and UNOSOM II became increasingly unpopular among Somalis.

In early October, 1993, U.S. units of UNOSOM II engaged in a running gun battle with Aideed forces, suffering more than ninety casualties, including eighteen dead. This event stirred outrage in the United States and sparked calls for complete U.S. withdrawal. Bowing to the political pressures, the Clinton Administration agreed to withdraw all U.S. forces by March 31, 1994. The vast majority of U.S. forces were withdrawn from Somalia by the summer of 1994, although several thousand U.S. troops were deployed in 1995 to provide security for the complete withdrawal of U.N. forces, leaving Somalis to work out a political solution for themselves.

—Robert F. Gorman

ADDITIONAL READING:

Ghalib, Jama Mohammed. *The Cost of Dictatorship: The Somali Experience.* New York: Lilian Barber, 1995. A fascinating autobiographical account of life under the Siad Barré regime.

Hirsch, John L., and Robert B. Oakley. *Somalia and Operation Restore Hope.* Washington, D.C.: U.S. Institute for Peace, 1995. An informative account of Operation Restore Hope by two men with practical experience.

Makinda, Samuel M. *Seeking Peace from Chaos: Humanitarian Intervention in Somalia.* An Occasional Paper of the International Peace Academy. Boulder, Colo.: Lynne Rienner, 1993. A brief analysis of the Somalia civil war and the early phases of Operation Restore Hope.

Sahnoun, Mohamed. *Somalia: The Missed Opportunities.* Washington, D.C.: U.S. Institute for Peace, 1994. A somewhat biased critique of the U.N. handling of the Somali humanitarian crisis, written by the U.N. diplomat responsible for implementation of UNOSOM I.

Samatar, Ahmed I., ed. *The Somali Challenge: From Catastrophe to Renewal?* Boulder, Colo.: Lynne Rienner, 1994. A collection of perceptive essays that assess why Somalia collapsed and how it might restore itself.

1993 ■ START II Is SIGNED: *the United States and the Soviet Union commit to deep reductions in their nuclear arsenals and inaugurate a post-Cold War environment of reduced superpower threats*

DATE: January 3, 1993
LOCALE: Moscow, Russia
CATEGORY: Diplomacy and international relations
KEY FIGURES:
James Baker (born 1930), previous U.S. secretary of state
George Herbert Walker Bush (born 1924), forty-first president of the United States, 1989-1993
Lawrence Eagleburger (born 1930), U.S. secretary of state
Andrei Kozyrev (born 1941), foreign minister of the Russian Federation
Boris Yeltsin (born 1931), president of the Russian Federation
SUMMARY OF EVENT. For four decades after the end of World War II, the United States and the Soviet Union amassed ever-increasing numbers of weapons. For most of that time, arms control agreements were elusive. The continuous improvement in East-West relations in the late 1980's paved the way for unprecedented agreements to reverse the arms race in Europe, including the treaty to eliminate intermediate-range nuclear forces (INF) in 1987 and to significantly cut conventional forces in Europe (CFE) in 1990. A year later, culminating almost a decade of arms control talks initiated by U.S. President Ronald Reagan, the United States and the Soviet Union signed an agreement to reduce strategic nuclear weapons, which by definition threaten the territory of the superpowers themselves. Only months after START (the Strategic Arms Reductions Treaty) was signed, however, the Soviet Union disintegrated into fifteen sovereign countries.

The United States and the former Soviet republics—particularly Russia—set about to restructure their relationships in the post-Soviet, post-Cold War world. In terms of nuclear arms, two issues were paramount. First, how could START be implemented when one of its signatories no longer existed? It was agreed at a meeting in Lisbon, Portugal, on May 23, 1992, that all the former Soviet republics would be bound by the treaty, that Russia would possess the remaining, permitted nuclear weapons, and that the other former Soviet republics would commit to forgo the acquisition of any nuclear arms. The second issue was how the nuclear reductions called for in START could be extended, acknowledging that the Cold War's nuclear legacy posed an unacceptable threat that must be reduced even more severely. Accordingly, the United States and Russia began work on a START II treaty.

The president of the Russian Federation, Boris Yeltsin, was absorbed by numerous issues during his country's first year as a sovereign state. Russia was threatened by ethnic and national tensions, economic collapse, burgeoning crime, societal instability, tense relations with its newly independent neighbors, and a variety of other problems. Yeltsin, like Soviet President Mikhail Gorbachev before him, sought above all else to stabilize relations with the West, particularly the United States. Western cooperation, technical assistance, and financial aid would be critical to Yeltsin's efforts to address his country's problems. The United States, as the world's sole superpower, clearly approached the START II talks from a position of strength.

In a Washington, D.C., summit on June 17, 1992, scarcely six months after the collapse of the Soviet Union, the United States and Russia signed a joint understanding to reduce their strategic nuclear arsenals by two-thirds. In Moscow, six months later, on January 3, 1993, Yeltsin and U.S. president George Bush signed the Treaty Between the United States of America and the Russian Federation on Further Reduction and Limitation of Strategic Offensive Arms (START II).

One of the key features of START II was that it called for the complete elimination of heavy intercontinental ballistic missiles (ICBMs) and all ICBMs with multiple warheads. These land-based ICBMs are considered particularly threatening to international stability because they are effective offensive weapons and are relatively vulnerable to destruction by a preemptive strike. As a result, logic compels leaders in charge of these weapons to favor using them in a time of heightened international tensions. Therefore, eliminating these weapons can be expected to enhance stability in crisis situations. Because the Soviet Union, and thus Russia, traditionally had placed a large proportion of their nuclear warheads on heavy ICBMs, this provision of START II was seen to be of greater benefit to the United States.

Although START II was to eliminate the most destabilizing ICBMs, single-warhead ICBMs were still permitted. So were nuclear weapons deployed on aircraft and on submarines. The Central Limits provision of START II placed ceilings on the total number of strategic nuclear weapons, irrespective of deployment. The first phase of this provision, to be completed seven years after implementation of the first START treaty (now known as START I), required that Russia and the United States reduce their number of deployed strategic warheads to 3,800 and 4,250, respectively. (START I had set a limit of 6,000 for each country.) The second phase of START II, which was to be concluded by January 1, 2003, requires a further reduction to 3,000 for Russia and 3,500 for the United States. By this date, all heavy and multiwarhead ICBMs must be eliminated. Unlike its predecessor, START II required that certain classes of decommissioned missiles be destroyed. In general, START I allowed undeployed, decommissioned missiles to be stored or converted.

START II could not be implemented until START I was ratified by the respective legislatures and entered into force. In many ways, START II built upon and complemented START I. Specific sublimits placed on submarine- and plane-deployed warheads by START I remain in effect under START II. START I's ceiling of sixteen hundred total strategic nuclear delivery vehicles (such as missiles and bombers, as opposed to the warheads deployed on them) also remains in effect. START II did, however, change the way that bombers are counted. Under START I, each bomber would count toward the country's nuclear ceilings as one warhead, regardless of how many warheads were actually on board. START II counts the actual number of warheads on board.

Compliance with the provisions of START II was to be ensured by a series of highly intrusive verification measures. U.S. and Russian representatives would be permitted to observe the removal, conversion, and destruction of missiles. Heavy bombers could be inspected to confirm weapon loads. Various other remaining weapons systems must be exhibited to confirm their compliance with the treaty's provisions. The verification regime of START II built substantially upon that of START I.

Although START II was signed by the Russian and U.S. presidents, ratification of the treaty was not assured. Several factors interacted to complicate the situation. The first START treaty, a precondition for START II, had not gone into force at the time START II was signed. In addition, the Republican Bush Administration was replaced by Democrat Bill Clinton's

only weeks after the Moscow summit. Although Yeltsin remained president of Russia, his policies and international agreements, including START II, were seen as too hasty and pro-Western by the new, independent Russian Parliament—a far cry from the compliant Soviet-era legislature. Finally, the legal questions arising from the disintegration of the Soviet Union complicated the question of precisely who was bound by START. For these reasons, the Clinton Administration withdrew the treaty from Senate consideration until a more opportune political environment could be achieved.

START I finally went into force on December 5, 1994. Controlled by the new Republican majority, Senate hearings on START II resumed in early 1995. The Russian Parliament also was considering the treaty, but had not ratified it as of the summer of 1995.   —*Steve D. Boilard*

ADDITIONAL READING:

Arbotov, Alexei. "START II, Red Ink, and Boris Yeltsin." *Bulletin of the Atomic Scientists* 49, no. 3 (April, 1993): 16-21. Suggests that the treaty is biased in favor of the United States; therefore, ratification by the Russian Parliament should not be expected.

Mendelsohn, Jack. "Next Steps in Nuclear Arms Control." *Issues in Science and Technology* 9, no. 3 (Spring, 1993): 28-34. Places START II in the broader context of world politics and nuclear stability. Argues that the United States should push for ratification of START I and II, as well as other nuclear arms control treaties.

Quester, George H., and Victor A. Utgoff. "Toward an International Nuclear Security Policy." *Washington Quarterly* 17, no. 4 (Autumn, 1994): 5-19. One of the first comprehensive articles on the United States' role in stopping nuclear arms proliferation after the signing of START II. Posits that the disintegration of the Soviet Union probably will not create new nuclear states, but identifies new and continuing nuclear threats.

"START II Treaty Approval Urged." *U.S. Department of State Dispatch* 4, no. 20 (May 17, 1993): 345-347. A transcript of Secretary of State Warren Christopher's speech calling on the U.S. Senate to ratify the treaty.

"START II: Treaty Between the United States of America and the Russian Federation on the Further Reduction and Limitation of Strategic Offense Arms." *Arms Control Today* 23, no. 1 (January-February, 1990): S5-S8. A supplemental section presenting the treaty language. The issue also includes a variety of articles concerning the treaty.

Winkler, Allan M. "Keep Pressing for Arms Control." *The Chronicle of Higher Education* 39, no. 37 (May 19, 1993): B1-B4. Assesses arms control efforts in the post-Cold War era. Suggests that START II provides significant progress toward an arms control regime, but that it does not address several important nuclear threats.

SEE ALSO: 1973, Détente with the Soviet Union; 1979, SALT II Is Signed; 1985, U.S.-Soviet Summit; 1987, INF Treaty Is Signed; 1991, Bush Announces Nuclear Arms Reductions.

1993 ■ FAMILY AND MEDICAL LEAVE ACT:

Congress passes a measure to guarantee job security and adequate leave for workers in times of family and medical emergency

DATE: February 5, 1993
LOCALE: Washington, D.C.
CATEGORIES: Civil rights; Health and medicine; Laws and acts; Social reform
KEY FIGURES:
George Herbert Walker Bush (born 1924), forty-first president of the United States, 1989-1993
William Jefferson "Bill" Clinton (born 1946), forty-second president of the United States
Christopher John Dodd (born 1944), Democratic senator from Connecticut and cosponsor of the act
Patricia Scott "Pat" Schroeder (born 1940), Democratic representative from Colorado, a major proponent of the act

SUMMARY OF EVENT. On February 3, 1993, the Congress of the United States passed the Family and Medical Leave Act of 1993, a comprehensive plan to ensure job security and leave opportunities for U.S. employees in times of family and medical need or crisis. President Bill Clinton signed the act into law on February 5, and it took full effect on August 6, 1993.

Through much of the twentieth century, the paradigm for families in North America was clearly defined: Husbands worked in the marketplace and provided financial support, and wives stayed home managing domestic life and child care. Women looked after children or ailing family members. Husbands tended to be "company men," so employers were not likely to accommodate family crises. Extended families were concentrated; there was often a grandparent, cousin, or other relative nearby who could help with family caretaking.

Shifts in lifestyles and work patterns had rendered this paradigm virtually meaningless by the 1980's. The number of women in the workforce increased dramatically during the wartime 1940's, declined temporarily after the war's end, but then grew again. Economic realities engendered double-income families, and the women's movement encouraged women to establish their own careers. Only 19 percent of women in the United States worked outside the home in 1900, but by the early 1990's, that figure was as high as 74 percent. With increased rates of divorce and unmarried parenthood, single-parent families became common, especially in inner-city, impoverished, and minority communities. In 1988, 27 percent of families had a single parent, twice the percentage of 1970.

Another change was the increase in life expectancies as a result of advances in medical technology, both in general and in the treatment of serious illnesses. People lived longer, and the U.S. population as a whole had aged dramatically. In 1993, the thirty-two million citizens over the age of sixty-five constituted 12 percent of the populace and was its fastest-growing segment. Home care of the elderly often was viewed as prefer-

able to institutionalization, and many serious illnesses could be treated without hospitalization. According to the National Council on Aging, at least 20 percent of the workforce had some caregiving responsibilities.

As a result of these factors, a vast majority of U.S. workers potentially faced difficult choices between work and family. A 1990 study by the Southport Institute for Policy Analysis estimated that 11 percent of caregivers were forced to quit their jobs to care for relatives. The U.S. Small Business Administration estimated that 150,000 workers were losing their jobs annually because they could not take medical leave. Others found their jobs less than secure upon returning from leave. In the absence of a national policy, even sympathetic employers could change policy without notice. The employee had little true protection.

The Civil Rights Act of 1964 and the Pregnancy Discrimination Act of 1978 provided certain guarantees, but comprehensive federal legislation was needed. Prior to the Family and Medical Leave Act of 1993, the United States was the only industrialized nation in the world without such a law; Japan provided twelve weeks of pregnancy leave with partial pay, and Canadian women were given forty-one weeks. Sweden offered eighteen months of family leave for use at the time of birth and when a child entered school. Norway, Austria, France, England, and Luxembourg had laws that provided leave for the care of an elderly parent.

Family and medical leave legislation was proposed several times during the 1980's, only to meet congressional gridlock and presidential vetoes. Earlier versions of the act were very strong, offering up to twenty-six weeks of leave. Conservatives of both parties feared that such legislation would weigh heavily on businesses and strongly opposed any federally mandated employee policies. Although President George Bush claimed to carry the mantle for traditional family values, he vetoed the watered-down 1992 bill, offering instead his own plan based on refundable tax credits for employers. Even the 1993 measure was almost blocked by Senate Republicans with an extraneous amendment reaffirming the ban on homosexuals in the military. However, in the opening weeks of the Clinton Administration, the 1993 act was passed by healthy bipartisan margins in both houses.

The Family and Medical Leave Act required U.S. employers to offer limited unpaid leave in four circumstances: upon the birth of an employee's child; upon the arrival of an adopted child; in cases where the employee is needed to provide care for a spouse, child, or parent with a serious health condition; or in cases where the employee is afflicted with a debilitating health condition. The act also provided definitions and restrictions to balance employers' and employees' interests. It ensured that employees returning from leave be given the same or a comparable position and salary with full benefits reinstated. The act exempted businesses with fewer than fifty employees, which could be seriously impaired by the loss of essential employees, and established employee eligibility according to length of employment. It also dealt with issues such as the substitution of available paid leave, advance notification of leave-taking, and formal certification of debilitating health conditions. The act established a bipartisan, sixteen-member Commission on Leave and gave the secretary of labor investigative authority for enforcement. It also opened the door for employees to initiate civil actions to remedy alleged violations.

The act was viewed by many as a halfway measure that achieved more by its mere existence than by its specific guarantees. The national policy stopped short of numerous state laws and countless corporate policies already in effect. Conversely, an estimated 50 percent of U.S. workers did not work enough hours or for large enough companies to be covered. The cost to the employee of unpaid time off remained too high for many workers to afford to leave to take care of family problems.

In 1992, the Family and Work Institute released a three-year study of a thousand companies in Rhode Island, Oregon, Minnesota, and Wisconsin regarding compliance with state leave laws. Ninety-one percent reported no trouble adapting to state rules; 94 percent of leave-takers had returned to their positions; and 75 percent of supervisors reported a positive effect on company business. It was estimated to be two to five times as expensive to replace an employee permanently as to grant temporary leave. A large number of companies with established leave policies, including such giants as DuPont, AT&T, and Aetna, reported limited problems and favorable results—including cost-effectiveness—from their family leave programs.

The Family and Medical Leave Act of 1993 established important guarantees without a major overall effect on either the nation's economic health or its business practices. It helped to standardize those practices and relieve family leave policy making of the pressures of business competitiveness. Since the act has taken effect, hundreds of lawsuits and complaints have been brought to the courts and the Department of Labor. In 1995, new rules were issued to clarify the situations covered by the act and the procedures required of both employees and employers in requesting and granting leave.   —*Barry Mann*

ADDITIONAL READING:

Bauer, Gary L. "Leaving Families Out." *National Review* 45, no. 6 (March 29, 1993): 58-60. Argues that the Family and Medical Leave Act is a betrayal of conservative approaches to strengthening the family.

"Family and Medical Leave Legislation." *Congressional Digest* 72, no. 1 (January, 1993): 2-32. An overview of family and medical leave legislative history and prospects as of the start of the 103rd Congress. Presents arguments for and against the policy by thirteen lawmakers, including President George Bush and senators Bob Dole and Edward Kennedy.

Maynard, Roberta. "Meet the New Law on Family Leave." *Nation's Business* 81, no. 4 (April, 1993): 26. Explains the act in lay terms and explores its potential problems.

Murray, Marjorie. "Family Leave: Read This Before You Take (or Give) It." *Working Woman* 20, no. 5 (May, 1995): 15. An update on the law and the clarifying rules issued two years after its passage. Emphasizes the limits of the act and the confusion it has engendered in a variety of situations.

Saltzman, Amy. "Time Off Without Pain." *U.S. News & World Report* 115, no. 5 (August 2, 1993): 52-55. A practical discussion on the new law, including anecdotes about several workers who experienced the types of difficulties that the law was passed to address.

SEE ALSO: 1964, Civil Rights Act of 1964; 1978, Pregnancy Discrimination Act; 1988, Family Support Act; 1990, Americans with Disabilities Act.

1993 ■ WORLD TRADE CENTER BOMBING: *the bombing proves that the United States is not immune to international terrorism*

DATE: February 26, 1993
LOCALE: Downtown Manhattan Island, New York City
CATEGORY: Diplomacy and international relations
KEY FIGURES:
Mahmoud Abouhalima (born 1960),
Ahmad M. Ajaj (born 1967),
Nidal A. Ayyad (born 1968),
Mohammed A. Salameh (born 1968), West Bank Palestinians and co-conspirators
Kevin Thomas Duffy (born 1933), a U.S. federal district court judge who tried the first four defendants
Eyad Ismail, (Iyad Mahmoud Ismail Nijm, born 1971), a West Bank Palestinian and the driver of the van that carried the explosives
Omar Abdel Rahman (born 1938), an Egyptian Muslim fundamentalist cleric and spiritual leader
Abdul Rahman Yasin (born 1961), a suspect who remained at large
Ramzi Ahmad Yousef (born 1968), thought to be the mastermind behind the plot

SUMMARY OF EVENT. At 12:17 P.M. on February 26, 1993, a yellow rental van loaded with some twelve hundred pounds of nitrate explosives blew up in the garage of the World Trade Center's North Building, in lower Manhattan Island, New York City. The van, driven by Eyad Ismail, had a twelve-minute fuse located between the front seats. Once it was lit, Eyad Ismail and Ramzi Ahmad Yousef, a friend with whom he had grown up in Kuwait, jumped into another car driven by a third companion.

The 110-story tower, like its twin, was part of a seven-structure complex where some fifty thousand people were employed and which also saw some eighty thousand visitors per day. The blast created a huge crater and tore through four levels of the multilayered basement. The maelstrom of smoke, darkness, and chaos left six individuals dead and more than a thousand injured—mostly from smoke inhalation, debris, and psychological trauma. The explosion, felt several miles away, knocked out the twin towers' generators, ripped doors off elevators, silenced radio and television stations, and nearly damaged the wall that holds back the waters of New York Harbor.

It took some of the occupants of the higher floors as long as five hours to climb down the quarter mile of stairways, much of it in pitch darkness. Windows were smashed to provide relief from the smoke, which had risen through elevator and ventilation shafts. Emergency crews responded quickly in helping the occupants out of the building, plucking some from the roof by helicopter.

Four days after the bombing, *The New York Times* received a letter from a group calling itself the Liberation Army Fifth Battalion. Although the group was unknown to law enforcement agencies, the letter was authenticated by the Federal Bureau of Investigation (FBI) as originating with one of the suspects, Nidal A. Ayyad. The message stated that the attack was "in response to the American political, economical, and military support to Israel, the state of terrorism, and to the rest of the dictator countries in the region." The letter continued: "The American people are responsible for the actions of their government and they must question all of the crimes that their government is committing against other people. Or they— Americans—will be the targets of our operations that could diminish them."

Four Arab Muslim militants were eventually arrested. All had been influenced by blind Egyptian cleric Sheikh Omar Abdel Rahman, who earlier had been charged in his native country with involvement in the assassination of former president Anwar al-Sadat but later was released. The first arrest, of Mohammed A. Salameh, was made by tracing the person who had rented the van and then asked for his $400 deposit back because the vehicle allegedly had been stolen. Arrests of three other conspirators—Nidal A. Ayyad, Mahmoud Abouhalima, and Ahmad M. Ajaj—followed. Abdul Rahman Yasin, also named in the case, remained a fugitive.

Their five-month trial began in October, 1993. On March 4, 1994, the four were found guilty on all thirty-eight counts of conspiracy to blow up the building, explosive destruction of property, and interstate transport of explosives. Some ten thousand pages of testimony from 207 witnesses were collected. Each of the men was sentenced to 240 years in prison without parole by Judge Kevin Thomas Duffy of U.S. federal district court in Manhattan. Because there were no eyewitnesses, the convictions hinged mostly on forensic evidence extricated from the rubble, such as shards of the van, along with telephone and bank records and other documentary evidence. Most of the conspirators had connections with El Sayyid A. Nosair, an Egyptian convicted of assault and weapons charges for a shooting at the time of the assassination of militant Rabbi Meir Kahane in 1990.

Long after the bombing, fugitives and additional suspects were apprehended, extradited, and eventually tried. Ramzi Ahmad Yousef, who was believed to be the mastermind of the bombing, was located in Pakistan and returned to New York in February, 1995. He was considered to be a trained professional terrorist, unlike those he recruited, entering countries under different aliases, with false papers, cash, and connections. Eyad Ismail was traced to Jordan and returned to New York in July, 1995.

After the blast, the tower and other areas in the complex were closed for varying lengths of time as the federal government made low-interest loans available to many small businesses to offset their forgone earnings. The hundreds of millions of dollars' worth of structural damage to property was covered, in part, by insurance carriers and federal assistance. The extensive damage provided reconstruction and renovation work for local contractors. The psychological trauma—both to many individuals at the blast site and, more generally, to the collective American psyche—was much longer-lasting. The attack on a symbol of American commerce evidenced the fact that the earlier American sense of immunity from foreign terrorism on home territory had largely disappeared.

There continued to be a lurking suspicion that some fundamental questions had not been fully answered. Who was behind the conspiracy? Who had transferred $8,500 from Europe to some of the defendants? Why was the bombing carried out? Were the eleven persons accused in 1995 of plotting to bomb the United Nations headquarters, the FBI office in Washington, two Hudson River tunnels, and a bridge across the river part of this larger montage?

As the authorities pondered these fundamental questions, the more practical and immediate concerns of securing possible future targets from terrorists also were addressed. What had been being done—checking identities and parcels, restricting the use of space, exchanging information with other law enforcement agencies, and so forth—could be intensified, and possibly done better, but there was no fail-safe system against terrorism, any more than against other forms of crime. For one thing, the terrorists were using advanced technology in their operations. For another, a number were sufficiently motivated to undertake attacks no matter how risky to their own lives.

Because terrorism is often the result of deeply nursed grievances whose solution lies in difficult political remedies, angry and determined individuals and groups were likely to continue to exist. Furthermore, in an open society such as that of the United States, eager media looking for the newsworthy often have been too willing to publicize such groups' causes and air their grudges. Most citizens resigned themselves to living with the hope that they would not meet the fate of Steven Knapp, William Macko, Robert Kirkpatrick, Monica Smith, John DiGiovanni, and Wilfredo Mercado, the six who died in the basement of the World Trade Center on that fateful winter day.

—Peter B. Heller

ADDITIONAL READING:

Behar, Richard. "The Secret Life of Mahmud the Red." *Time* 142, no. 14 (October 4, 1993): 54-61. Describes the role of defendant Mahmud Abouhalima in the World Trade Center bombing.

Dwyer, Jim, et al. *Two Seconds Under the World: Terror Comes to America—The Conspiracy Behind the World Trade Center Bombing.* New York: Crown, 1994. A spotty account by several reporters from *New York Newsday*. Has fairly good photographs.

Gauch, Sarah. "Terror on the Nile." *Africa Report* 38, no. 3 (May, 1993): 32-35. Connects the World Trade Center bombing in New York and terrorist attacks in Cairo, Egypt, focusing attention on the rise of Islamic radicalism.

MacDonald, Eileen. *Shoot the Women First*. New York: Random House, 1991. Provides insight into the role of women in terrorist groups around the world, including Palestinian groups.

Nacos, Brigitte L. *Terrorism and the Media: From the Hostage Crisis to the World Trade Center Bombing*. New York: Columbia University Press, 1994. Argues that even if terrorism relies on media coverage as the most effective ammunition, government censorship is the least desirable option.

Simon, Jeffrey D. *The Terrorist Trap: America's Experience with Terrorism*. Bloomington: Indiana University Press, 1994. Chapter 1 treats the World Trade Center bombing under the title of "Welcome to Reality," which epitomizes the book's content.

Weaver, Mary Anne. "The Trail of the Sheikh." *New Yorker* 69, no. 8 (April 12, 1993): 71-89. Discusses the shadowy, blind Muslim cleric who has been mentioned in various terrorist plots, and his Egyptian connections.

See also: 1995, Oklahoma City Federal Building Is Bombed.

1993 ■ Branch Davidians' Compound Burns: *an FBI raid on a religious cult results in the deaths of more than eighty persons, leads to an investigation of the government agencies involved, and becomes a rallying point for antigovernment sentiment*

Date: April 19, 1993
Locale: Waco, Texas
Categories: Civil rights; Religion; Wars, uprisings, and civil unrest
Key figures:
David Koresh (born Vernon Wayne Howell, 1959-1993), leader of the Branch Davidian cult
Janet Reno (born 1938), attorney general of the United States
William Sessions (born 1930), director of the Federal Bureau of Investigation

Summary of event. On April 19, 1993, more than eighty members of the Branch Davidians, a religious sect, died during a government raid on their compound in Waco, Texas. The fiery battle was exactly what cult leader David Koresh had predicted; the loss of life fulfilled Attorney General Janet Reno's greatest fear.

The tragedy occurred at Mt. Carmel, called Ranch Apoca-

lypse, in the wake of a decision by the Federal Bureau of Investigation (FBI) to end a fifty-one-day standoff with force. The decision had been a difficult one, and the results convinced Attorney General Janet Reno that it had been the wrong one. The Mt. Carmel residents were members of the Branch Davidian cult, an offshoot of the Seventh-day Adventist church. The group had lived peacefully in Waco since 1935, with only one flare-up of unrest—when Vernon Howell (later known as David Koresh) challenged George Rodon's leadership during the 1980's. When Rodon was institutionalized on murder charges, Howell took over the Davidians, and peace seemed to reign. Then reports of unusual events began to surface. Neighbors complained of hearing machine-gun fire. It was reported that children were being sexually abused. A delivery man informed authorities of grenade shipments. Finally, the Bureau of Alcohol, Tobacco, and Firearms (ATF) began to investigate.

The ATF leadership became alarmed when they substantiated reports that the cult had amassed nearly $200,000 worth of guns and other weapons. On February 28, 1993, the agency moved to take control of Mt. Carmel. Their attempt failed, and four agents and six Davidians died during a shootout. It was uncertain who had fired first, but the ATF received great criticism for its show of force. Because Koresh was often seen in the community, many people questioned why he had not been arrested in town. Some critics accused the ATF of tipping off the media in order to gain publicity and protect the agency from budget cuts. Other sources believed that ATF leaders knew they had lost the element of surprise, yet sent their agents into a seeming death trap. Whatever the truth behind the failed raid, the result was a nerve-wracking standoff.

In the weeks that followed, the FBI surrounded the compound and attempted to persuade the Davidians to surrender. First, the agency gave Koresh whatever he requested, including broadcast of a rambling, fifty-eight-minute speech. In exchange, Koresh allowed thirty-seven Branch Davidians, including twenty-one children, to leave the compound. When conciliation yielded no more results, the FBI began to flood the compound with annoying bright lights and loud sounds. The agents even attempted to smuggle listening devices into Mt. Carmel to gather intelligence that would enable agents to devise better strategies. Koresh and the remaining cult members held their ground.

A ninth-grade dropout and disappointed rock musician, Koresh had become convinced that he was God incarnate. He claimed that he was a sinful Jesus whom God had sent to earth to experience the vices of man—training that would prepare Koresh to stand in judgment for the sinners of the world on the final Judgment Day. True to his convictions, Koresh denied himself nothing. He enjoyed beer, fast cars, and promiscuous sex but denied them to his followers. He isolated the men and took every female he desired as a wife—even girls as young as eleven years of age—claiming he was the only one holy enough to sire children. His followers gave in to these demands, surrendered their possessions, and submitted themselves to hours of rambling sermons. Koresh maintained his control over the adults through the withholding of food. There was a spanking room to ensure the proper behavior of children.

During the siege, the FBI consulted psychological experts who became increasingly alarmed at Koresh's behavior. They told the agency that Koresh saw himself as invincible. They predicted that he would never free the remaining hostages. The FBI searched for a plan to bring the standoff to a conclusion. It was rumored that the entire compound was booby-trapped and thus that any attack had to proceed cautiously. The ATF had proof that the Davidians possessed powerful weapons and night-vision scopes. Sentries appeared to guard the windows at all times and would hold children up to the windows whenever agents approached. Strategists considered attacking with a water cannon, but the force of the blow could have caused the building to collapse on the children. FBI director William Sessions and his top deputies put together a plan based on the use of gas to cause confusion, then approached Attorney General Reno.

Reno questioned the FBI about the danger of exposing people to gas. She was concerned that an anesthetic gas might be too strong for the children, causing their deaths. The FBI brought in an expert who persuaded Reno that tear gas would not be carcinogenic, cause birth defects, or otherwise inflict permanent harm. Reno also wanted to know how Koresh would react to this type of pressure. No one could say for sure if he would lead his followers to death. Negotiators had questioned Koresh about his plans for suicide more than once, and each time he denied such plans. On the other hand, a warning concerning Davidians in Australia had been received the year before, predicting they would never be taken alive. Reno weighed the evidence and demanded the FBI restate its justification. Finally, she contacted President Bill Clinton and made her recommendation to attack.

At 6:00 A.M., April 19, the barrage began. Two armored combat engineer vehicles (CEVs) began moving toward the compound. Loudspeaker announcements urged the cult members to surrender. Koresh ordered his followers to don their gas masks. Then the shooting began. The CEVs began breaking holes in the walls and pumped gas throughout the building. The women and children gathered in the center of the second floor, where there was no exit. Around noon, the announcements urging surrender were repeated. Gas was so thick, the agents urged the people to walk toward the sound of the loudspeaker. Then explosions shook the area: The ammunition stores had exploded.

Winds began gusting to thirty miles per hour. The buildings disappeared beneath a blaze of fire. Construction materials were flimsy and very flammable. Bales of hay that had been placed against windows for warmth fueled the fire. A propane tank that had been used to block the door also fed the flames. As the agents watched helplessly, several people suddenly remembered hearing about a school bus that had been buried on the grounds for use as a bunker. They investigated to see if the children had been hidden there, but it was empty. By the time the blaze was out, nothing was left but ashes and bodies.

Later that day, Reno stood before the media. She took full responsibility for the decision that had precipitated the Waco disaster. Many people thought she was committing political suicide, but Reno stood firm. She deeply regretted the loss of life, and she insisted that the decision had been hers alone. Some analysts held that Reno could not be completely to blame, speculating that Koresh had planned to set the fires from the very beginning. His few surviving disciples, however, denied any plans of mass suicide. One young man who had lived in the compound for a year insisted that the residents had intended to evacuate the compound—that many of them were near the front of the building when a tank caused it to collapse, starting a fire that filled the area with black smoke so no one could see; children and adults fled for the interior areas, but the fire spread too quickly and they were trapped. Another survivor told of trying to get to the children but finding the way blocked with debris caused by government vehicles.

FBI agents insisted that their tanks did not start the blaze. They contended that the fire began in several locations at the same moment and believed that Koresh deliberately murdered his followers to fulfill his prophecy. Some experts who have been trained to deal with terrorists, however, remained critical of the FBI's handling of the Branch Davidians, contending that the use of gas was a mistake and suggesting that the FBI never considered seriously the possibility of the cult members' willingness to die for Koresh. Some theologians, moreover, have argued that the cult's religious leanings were neglected and could have been used to approach a peaceful resolution. Regardless of who was at fault—or whether (as seems more likely) both Koresh and the FBI agents contributed to the events that resulted in the deaths—the Waco debacle soon assumed symbolic importance, appealing to antigovernment sentiments awakened by similar incidents at Ruby Ridge, Idaho, and, in the spring of 1996, near Jordan, Montana, in some U.S. citizens who believed that the federal government was taking too much control of their lives.

—*Suzanne Riffle Boyce*

ADDITIONAL READING:

Breault, Marc. *Inside the Cult: A Member's Exclusive Chilling Account of Madness and Depravity in David Koresh.* New York: Dutton, 1993. Written by a former recruiter for the Branch Davidians. Photographs.

Gibbs, Nancy, et al. "Oh My God, They're Killing Themselves!" *Time* 141, no. 18 (May 3, 1993): 26-42. A series of articles detailing the events at Waco.

Gotschal, Mary G. "A Marriage Made in Hell." *National Review* 46, no. 6 (April 4, 1994): 57-60. Discusses the legal background of the Branch Davidians' clash with government agencies.

Lindedecker, Clifford L. *Massacre at Waco: The Shocking Story of Cult Leader David Koresh and the Branch Davidians.* New York: St. Martin's Press, 1993. A paperback resource, with photographs.

Long, Robert E., ed. *Religious Cults in America*. New York: H. W. Wilson, 1994. A collection of reprinted articles on the Branch Davidians and American cults in general. Bibliography.

1993 ■ CAMPBELL BECOMES CANADA'S FIRST WOMAN PRIME MINISTER: *the decisive defeat of the Progressive Conservatives yields the first administration headed by a woman*

DATE: June 13, 1993
LOCALE: Ottawa, Ontario, Canada
CATEGORIES: Canadian history; Government and politics; Women's issues
KEY FIGURES:
Kim Campbell (born 1947), prime minister of Canada, June-November, 1993
Jean Chrétien (born 1934), elected prime minister of Canada in November, 1993
Brian Mulroney (born 1939), prime minister of Canada, 1984-1993

SUMMARY OF EVENT. Three individuals served as Canada's prime minister during 1993, including Kim Campbell, the first woman to hold this office. Born on March 10, 1947, in British Columbia, Campbell studied at the University of British Columbia and the London School of Economics. She earned a law degree in 1983. Between 1983 and 1988, Campbell participated in British Columbia's politics, and was elected to the provincial legislative assembly. Campbell was elected to Canada's House of Commons in 1988 to represent a Vancouver district. As a Progressive Conservative Party member, she supported the leadership and program of Prime Minister Brian Mulroney.

Her abilities and reputation eventually led to several cabinet appointments. After working in the Department of Indian and Northern Affairs, she was named Canada's minister of justice in 1990. In January, 1993, she became minister of national defence. After more than eight years in office, Mulroney, in February, 1993, announced his decision to resign as Canada's prime minister and as leader of the Progressive Conservative Party. His decision was for personal reasons, compounded by low public opinion polls indicating his continuing as prime minister would be a serious detriment to the party's chances in the 1993 parliamentary elections. Through the spring of 1993, the party considered several candidates as Mulroney's successor. Kim Campbell won the party's top post on June 13 and was sworn in as prime minister on June 25.

Upon assuming office, the new prime minister energetically began placing her mark on the nation. The new federal cabinet was reduced in size, and several government departments were abolished or consolidated for greater efficiency. She attended the G7 conference of major industrialized nations in July in Tokyo, earning praise for her skills. Trade relations with other nations, especially with the United States on the proposed North American Free Trade Agreement (NAFTA), continued in a positive and cooperative atmosphere. Domestically, the prime minister proposed programs to retrain workers who were losing jobs as a result of plant closings or reductions. She also promised to eliminate the government's deficit within five years, without increasing taxes. Most social programs would be continued, but with some consolidation or reduction. Campbell suggested constitutional reform, especially in the selection and authority of the Canadian Senate.

Public opinion polls in early July showed wide support (40 percent) for the new prime minister, even higher than public support for her party (33 percent). As Canada's national leader, she faced economic challenges. Sizable government deficits inherited from the prior administration had to be tackled, and Campbell was held partly responsible for those problems as a result of her association with the Mulroney Administration. Efforts to reduce or eliminate budget deficits required reductions in well-established and heavily funded programs, such as defense, transfer payments to provinces, pensions, and programs for the native peoples. Many groups and constituencies feared they would be affected adversely by such reductions. The Campbell Administration, during the summer of 1993, took an active role in foreign policy issues. Canada supported expansion of the permanent members of the United Nations Security Council and promised to continue its peacekeeping presence in the Bosnian civil war. On trade issues, negotiations resolved NAFTA "side deals" on labor and environmental questions, and obtained significant rulings affecting Canada-United States trade in softwood lumber, beer, and steel.

Within her own party, the prime minister made news headlines by the expulsion of three Progressive Conservative members from their party after they had been charged with corruption during her predecessor's tenure. This enhanced the party's image as a clean, reputable political organization, but critics questioned her decision because the individuals had not yet been found guilty of the allegations in court. In a major policy speech in August, she criticized the influence of lobbyists, promised to make political appointments based on merit, and indicated a possible change in the pension rules for Members of Parliament (MPs). She supported openness in providing full information before government decisions were made, hoping to convince Canadians that her administration was more democratic than its predecessors. Parliamentary committees also would have more authority in shaping proposed legislation. Considering the history of strong party discipline in Canadian politics, her support of permitting MPs to vote based on their own conscience rather than following the call of the party was an unusual departure from tradition. Her call for reforms in the educational sector also attracted public support.

By August, Campbell's reputation had grown significantly, raising hopes of a solid Progressive Conservative win in the fall parliamentary election. Polls showed Campbell, at 51 percent, had the highest approval as a prime minister in three decades. They also indicated Canadians favored her by a two-to-one margin over Jean Chrétien, the Liberal Party leader. A Gallup poll predicted a close race between the Progressive Conservatives and the Liberals, but this represented a substantial gain for the former party over its low standing in polls earlier in the year.

After the prime minister, in early September, announced the federal election date for October 25, campaigning began in earnest, with an estimated ten million dollars in the Progressive Conservatives' war chest. The five major parties agreed to several television debates in early October, to provide the electorate with a view of party agendas, issues, and leaders. The Progressive Conservatives, seeing Campbell as their most popular and effective advocate, scheduled her to appear throughout the nation in an extensive political campaign. By mid-September, polls showed the Progressive Conservatives taking a slight lead over the Liberals, 36 percent to 33 percent. Other parties lagged behind.

Campaign issues, in addition to the personalities of the party leaders, increasingly focused on economic issues: NAFTA, the deficit, and unemployment. On the campaign trail, the prime minister promised to eliminate the deficit in five years but not at the expense of social services. By late September, polls began to show erosion of Progressive Conservative strength. Canadians appeared more concerned about jobs than deficit reduction. The 1.6 million unemployed made job creation a strong campaign issue, and opposition parties hammered the point home to Canadians voters.

As the campaign intensified and the Progressive Conservative momentum began to weaken, Campbell moved away from providing specifics on many controversial issues and vaguely promised to present the government's policies following the election. Her opponents promptly accused the government of hiding possible deep cuts in social services that would adversely affect many Canadians. In addition, her sharp comments and abrasive manner (some accused her of arrogance) appear to have undercut voter support. Several television advertisements from her party struck viewers as particularly offensive.

Following the scheduled television debates in early October, in which Campbell aggressively took the offensive against her opponents, polls showed the Liberals moving ahead of the Progressive Conservatives by a margin of 37 percent to 22 percent. By the week before the election, polls revealed an even larger Liberal lead (44 percent), with the Reform Party (19 percent) in second place, and Progressive Conservatives in third place (16 percent). An estimated 18.5 million Canadians were eligible to vote in the October 25 general election, and 69 percent cast their ballots. For the first time, thanks to a revision of election laws, Canadians living outside the country on election day were able to submit absentee ballots.

The results were a Liberal landslide and a Progressive Conservative debacle. The Progressive Conservatives received only 16 percent of the popular vote, compared to 50 percent in the 1984 and 43 percent in the 1988 elections. The number of party seats in the new House of Commons actually determined the future of Canadian politics. Jean Chrétien's Liberals won 177 seats, followed by the Bloc Québécois (54), Reform Party (52), and New Democrats (9). Kim Campbell's Progressive Conservatives won only two seats: one in Quebec and one in New Brunswick. This number, compared to the 154 seats held before the election, shows the extent of the party's disaster. To add to the humiliation, the prime minister lost her own district seat in Vancouver.

No party in power in Canadian history had ever suffered such a crushing electoral defeat. Campbell's controversial leadership may partly explain the results, but public alienation from the Progressive Conservatives had deeper roots. The transfer of office occurred on November 4, 1993, when Jean Chrétien took the oath as Canada's twentieth prime minister. Nine years of Progressive Conservative Party rule, including Kim Campbell's 134 days in office as Canada's first woman prime minister, now had ended. On December 13, 1993, she resigned as head of the Progressive Conservative Party.

—Taylor Stults

ADDITIONAL READING:

Campbell, Kim. *Sayings of Chairman Kim*. Montreal: Davies, 1993. Compilation of Campbell's candid comments on many subjects.

Dobbin, Murray. *The Politics of Kim Campbell: From School Trustee to Prime Minister*. Toronto: Lorimer, 1993. A short biography.

Fife, Robert. *Kim Campbell: The Making of a Politician*. Toronto: HarperCollins, 1993. Another quick biography of Campbell.

Frizzel, Alan, et al. *The Canadian General Election of 1993*. Ottawa: Carleton University Press, 1994. An excellent analysis of the campaign.

Martin, Lawrence. *Chrétien*. 2 vols. Toronto: Lester, 1995. An extended biography of the Liberal Party leader, including a discussion of the 1993 campaign.

SEE ALSO: 1984, Mulroney Era in Canada; 1993, North American Free Trade Agreement.

1993 ■ NORTH AMERICAN FREE TRADE AGREEMENT: *reducing barriers to the flow of goods, services, and investment among Canada, Mexico, and the United States, the agreement and its effects are hotly debated*

DATE: November 20, 1993
LOCALE: Washington, D.C.
CATEGORIES: Business and labor; Diplomacy and international relations; Economics; Treaties and agreements

KEY FIGURES:

George Herbert Walker Bush (born 1924), forty-first
president of the United States, 1989-1993

William Jefferson "Bill" Clinton (born 1946), forty-second
president of the United States

H. Ross Perot (born 1930), businessman and candidate for
president in 1992

Carlos Salinas de Gortari (born 1948), president of Mexico,
1988-1994

SUMMARY OF EVENT. Approval of the North American Free
Trade Agreement (NAFTA) in 1993 was one in a long series of
policy actions reflecting a commitment by the United States
government to relatively unrestricted international trade and
finance. This commitment began in 1934, when, in the depths
of a deep depression, the United States adopted a policy of
reciprocal trade agreements. Agreements were negotiated by
which the United States reduced tariffs on the products of
other countries that agreed to the do the same for U.S. products. This helped trade to expand and gave each country an
opportunity both to sell more exports and to buy more imports.
At the end of World War II, this policy was extended by the
formation of the General Agreement on Tariffs and Trade
(GATT), which involved many countries negotiating at once.
GATT negotiations involved a series of "rounds," with the
Uruguay round ending in new agreements in 1994.

Policy toward international trade has always been controversial. Most economists argue that relatively free international
trade encourages each country to specialize in the products it
can produce most efficiently—that competition is intensified
and innovation encouraged, allowing consumers to benefit
from lower prices and higher productivity. Such benefits were
evident in products such as automobiles (after the 1950's) and
electronic products (after the 1970's). However, within each
country there are industries that believe they would not be able
to compete with imports. U.S. companies producing clothing
and shoes, for example, have complained that they are under-
sold by imports from low-wage countries such as China. One
reason that wages are low in China, however, is that labor
productivity is also low there.

As NAFTA was being developed, many firms and labor
unions opposed the liberalization of trade, arguing that competition from imports would reduce job opportunities. These
issues were strongly debated in the presidential election of
1992. President George Bush had initiated and encouraged the
formulation of NAFTA, and Democratic candidate Bill Clinton supported it, but independent H. Ross Perot strongly opposed NAFTA. He claimed there would be a "giant sucking
sound" as U.S. jobs were transferred to Mexico. Many environmentalists also opposed NAFTA, claiming that Mexican
products had another unfair advantage because requirements
for environmental protection were lax in Mexico. Some liber-
tarian groups opposed NAFTA on the basis that it did not
really provide free trade, because of the substantial bureaucratic involvement required to carry out its many complex
provisions.

Supporters of NAFTA argued that many U.S. business firms
would gain by improved access to Mexican markets. For example, privatization of the Mexican telephone system in 1991
created profit opportunities for U.S. firms who were among
the world leaders in this high-tech sector. U.S. firms producing
motion pictures, recorded music, television programs, and
computer software received much revenue from sales to other
countries and often were damaged by intellectual piracy.
NAFTA offered them the prospect of improved protection of
their intellectual property rights. Pro-NAFTA forces also argued that the treaty would increase the prosperity of the Mexican economy, increasing wage levels and decreasing the large
flow of Mexican immigrants across the southern border of the
United States. They also pointed out that the economies of
Canada and Mexico were far smaller than that of the United
States, and thus were unable to flood U.S. markets with goods.

The treaty was first approved in Canada, where it was
supported by the ruling Progressive Conservative Party, completing legislative approval June 23, 1993. In the U.S. Congress, there was considerable opposition, but strong lobbying
by President Clinton secured the treaty's approval on November 20, 1993. In Mexico, support by the dominant Institutional
Revolutionary Party of President Carlos Salinas de Gortari
assured relatively easy approval on November 22, 1993.

As finally approved, the agreement was a long and complex
document. It had four major types of provisions. First, NAFTA
reduced, and promised to eliminate, all tariffs (taxes on imports) and most nontariff barriers (such as quantitative quotas
on imports) among the three countries. These liberalizations
were to be spread over fifteen years, but two-thirds of Mexican
imports to the United States and half of U.S. exports to Mexico
were duty-free or became so immediately. Government contracts were to be open to competitive bidding by firms from all
three countries.

Second, NAFTA provided rules to protect investment and
intellectual property rights. NAFTA expanded Canadian and
U.S. companies' ability to set up or buy a business in Mexico
and made it easier for them sell out if they wanted to quit. U.S.
and Canadian banks were given greater freedom to invest in
Mexican banks. Restrictions on bringing profits back were
removed. Protection of intellectual property rights involved
patents, copyrights, trademarks, and computer software. U.S.
firms strongly desired protection against people copying
books, records, videotapes and audiotapes, and software without permission or payment of royalties. This had been more of
a problem in Mexico than in Canada.

Third, NAFTA reduced barriers to trade in services, such as
banking and finance, transportation, telecommunications, and
audiovisual activities. Mexico extended temporary work permits to service providers from Canada and the United States.

Last, NAFTA provided administrative procedures to settle
disputes over the way each country applied the rules. Special
commissions were created to exert influence over environmental policies and over labor-market conditions.

NAFTA did not have a large immediate impact on economic

relations between the United States and Canada, since their trade, services, investment, and intellectual property conditions were already on a relatively harmonious basis. For the first year after NAFTA's adoption, both the United States and Mexico appeared to benefit. U.S. export sales to Mexico and imports from Mexico increased substantially. Mexico benefited from substantial capital inflow, increasing production capacity, and improving technology. In December, 1994, however, Mexico was hit by a financial crisis that resulted in a devaluation of the Mexican peso by about one-half. The International Monetary Fund attributed the panic to a reaction by Mexican investors to a large government deficit and declining foreign reserves. Inflation in Mexico had been running at a rate of nearly 200 percent per year. Feeling the peso was overvalued, investors sold Mexican securities and used the proceeds to buy dollars and other foreign currency.

Previous NAFTA opponents pointed to the panic as justification for their views, although the panic could not be directly traced to NAFTA. The panic led to severe economic depression in Mexico. As Mexican prices and incomes fell, Mexicans reduced their purchases of imports and U.S. export sales to Mexico fell by 40 percent in the spring of 1995. NAFTA did help cushion the impact of the crisis on the Mexican economy. Export-oriented areas, such as the city of Juarez, found their sales to the United States greatly increased. In 1995, there was a large inflow of direct investment by U.S. firms eager to buy or build factories and take advantage of the momentarily inexpensive Mexican property, labor, and materials.

—*Paul B. Trescott*

ADDITIONAL READING:

Belous, Richard S., and Jonathan Lemco, eds. *NAFTA as a Model of Development.* Washington, D.C.: National Planning Association, 1993. Twenty-one conference papers presenting a good variety of viewpoints, including several from the perspective of Canada and Mexico.

Grayson, George W. *The North American Free Trade Agreement: Regional Community and the New World Order.* Lanham, Md.: University Press of America, 1995. This narrative history of debates and negotiations covers most of the issues but ends with the approval of the treaty.

Orme, William A., Jr. *Continental Shift: Free Trade and the New North America.* Washington, D.C.: Washington Post, 1993. Although written before NAFTA's final adoption, this "briefing book" gives a clear and unbiased view of the history of NAFTA, deflating exaggerated claims on both sides.

Weintraub, Sidney. *NAFTA: What Comes Next?* Westport, Conn.: Praeger, 1994. Examines broad issues of foreign investment, economic structure within the three countries, possible addition of members, and diplomacy.

Zangari, B. J., ed. *NAFTA: Issues, Industry Sector Profiles and Bibliography.* Commack, N.Y.: Nova Science, 1994. Devotes approximately one hundred pages to the details of the agreements and nearly two hundred pages to the probable impact on various U.S. industries.

SEE ALSO: 1994, General Agreement on Tariffs and Trade.

1993 ■ ASTRONAUTS REPAIR THE HUBBLE SPACE TELESCOPE: *images of unprecedented detail and clarity reveal secrets of the universe*

DATE: December 2-13, 1993
LOCALE: Earth orbit
CATEGORY: Science and technology
KEY FIGURES:
Thomas D. Akers (born 1951) and
Kathryn C. Thornton (born 1952), crew members who assisted in replacing solar panels
Kenneth D. Bowersox (born 1956), pilot of the space shuttle on its mission to repair the Hubble Space Telescope
Richard O. Covey (born 1946), commander of the space shuttle on the repair mission
Jeffrey A. Hoffman (born 1944), crew member who assisted in replacing optical instruments
F. Story Musgrave (born 1935), payload commander of the space shuttle during the repair
Claude Niccolier (born 1944), Swiss astronaut and operator of the space shuttle remote arm

SUMMARY OF EVENT. One of the earliest envisioned scientific applications of space exploration was placing a large telescope beyond the optical distortions imposed by earth's atmosphere. The Hubble Space Telescope (HST), the first realization of this dream, experienced many setbacks before finally becoming operational. The launch of the telescope was delayed by two years after the explosion of the space shuttle *Challenger* in 1986. When the telescope was launched in April, 1990, astronomers discovered to their horror that its optics contained a major defect.

Like most large astronomical telescopes, the HST uses a large concave mirror, the primary mirror, to focus incoming light to an image. The primary mirror of the HST is 2.4 meters in diameter. Secondary mirrors are used to reflect the image to its final viewing location. The secondary mirrors often are curved to assist in focusing the image. The primary and secondary mirrors must be fabricated to exactly the right shape and their curvatures precisely coordinated. The primary mirror in the HST was ground to the wrong shape, resulting in an optical defect called spherical aberration. Light reflected off different parts of the primary mirror focused in different locations, making it impossible to focus the telescope perfectly.

Ironically, it was the very magnitude of the error that prevented its detection. Telescope mirrors are given their basic shape by grinding, then polished to dimensions accurate to within a small fraction of a wavelength of light, or within the width of a few hundred atoms. The optical instrument used in testing the primary mirror during grinding had a lens about a millimeter out of position, causing the primary mirror to be slightly too flat. The later optical tests applied to the HST mirror were designed to monitor the perfection of the mirror surface; it never occurred to any of the builders of the telescope that a gross error in the basic shape of the mirror was possible. Severe as it was, the error in the HST's primary mirror was only 0.002 millimeter. Nevertheless, the error was 100,000 times as great as any surface irregularities in the mirror. At the level of accuracy routinely required in the design of astronomical telescopes, a flaw such as that in the Hubble Space Telescope might be likened to building a bridge across the wrong river. Scientist Robert Shannon called it "the single largest mistake that's ever been made in optics." A crude optical test of the telescope did reveal the problem, but the test results initially were thought to be a result of the relative crudeness of the test, not a flaw in the telescope.

Popular media accounts of the problem often created the impression that the telescope was useless. In reality, the effects of spherical aberration often could be largely removed by computer processing. For bright objects, such as planets in the solar system, the Hubble Space Telescope returned extremely detailed images, even with flawed optics. The problem was most acute for faint objects. Because spherical aberration spreads light out over a larger area than a perfect image, it took about five times longer to make observations on faint objects than would have been the case with the originally designed system. The original design of the HST called for 70 percent of the light from a star to be concentrated in the central core of the image; the flawed HST achieved only 15 percent. It was impossible to collect enough light to observe the faintest objects, such as galaxies at the edge of the observable universe. Observing such faint objects had been one of the principal reasons for launching the telescope.

Replacing the flawed primary mirror was out of the question, but many of the observing instruments aboard the HST were made to be easily replaced. Mirrors in replacement instruments could be shaped to compensate for the flaw in the primary mirror. However, tests showed that the replacement mirrors had to be aligned with great precision or other optical errors would be introduced, making the HST's images even worse. Two of the imaging cameras on the HST were redesigned to correct the HST's optical problems.

Flawed optics were not the only problem aboard the HST. Its large solar panels vibrated every time the satellite passed in or out of the earth's shadow, because of expansion and contraction of the panels. Ground controllers had developed ways of compensating for the vibration, but the compensations taxed the HST's on-board computer. Also, three of the HST's six gyroscopes had failed, leaving the telescope with the bare minimum needed for operation. If another failed, the telescope would be completely inoperable. Replacement of the gyroscopes was a higher priority than even repair of the optics.

On December 2, 1993, the space shuttle *Endeavor* lifted off on flight STS-61, one of the most complex space missions in history. The crew, six men and one woman, comprised six U.S. astronauts and a Swiss astronaut from the European Space Agency. Beginning on December 5, shuttle astronauts made six-hour spacewalks on five successive days. They replaced

two imaging cameras with corrected optics, replaced the solar cell panels, replaced the failed gyroscopes and their electronics, and added a processor to the HST's computer. *Endeavor* landed on December 13 after eleven days in orbit. The mission proceeded so flawlessly that author R. T. Fienberg, writing about the mission, referred readers to an article written before the mission and simply told readers to "change all the verbs to past tense."

Images returned by the refurbished HST showed that the telescope's problems were completely fixed and that image quality equaled or exceeded its original specifications. In the solar system, the HST succeeded in clearly revealing Pluto and its moon Charon and returning the most detailed images ever of the large asteroid Vesta. It also showed that the atmospheric storm patterns on Neptune had changed greatly in the few years since the Voyager encounter in 1989. One unsuccessful observation dramatically illustrated the quality of the telescope. Astronomers imaged a globular star cluster, hoping to find large numbers of extremely small faint stars. As seen from earth, globular star clusters are so tightly packed with stars that the images overlap, creating a solid mass of light. Although the HST did not find the hoped-for faint stars, its images were so sharp that they peered through the cluster to reveal faint galaxies far beyond.

Another widely published image showed a distant cluster of galaxies surrounded by thin, sharp arcs of light. These arcs are the distorted images of more remote galaxies, an example of gravitational lensing and dramatic support for Albert Einstein's general theory of relativity. In gravitational lensing, massive objects like clusters of galaxies bend light much like a crude lens, creating the distorted images that the HST showed with unprecedented clarity. In another confirmation of general relativity, observations with the HST in May, 1994, indicated the presence of a giant black hole at the center of the galaxy M87.

The repair of the Hubble Space Telescope ended one of the most trying periods for the United States space program, which had been plagued by a seemingly endless string of problems and mission failures since the loss of the space shuttle *Challenger* in 1986. The almost perfect execution of an extraordinarily complex space flight and the equally perfect performance of the repaired Hubble Space Telescope greatly aided in restoring public confidence in the space program.

—*Steven I. Dutch*

ADDITIONAL READING:

Fienberg, Richard Tresch. "Endeavour's Excellent Adventure." *Sky and Telescope* 87, no. 4 (April, 1994): 20-23. A photographic history of the repair of the Hubble telescope in space.

"Gravity's Lens at Work." *Sky and Telescope* 90, no. 1 (June, 1995): 11. Includes a spectacular image of gravitational lensing caused by distant galaxies.

Hoffman, Jeffrey A. "How We'll Fix the Hubble Space Telescope." *Sky and Telescope* 86, no. 5 (November, 1993): 23-29. A schedule of repairs to the Hubble Telescope, written by one of the participating astronauts. The mission proceeded almost exactly as projected in this article.

"Hubble's Image Restored." *Sky and Telescope* 87, no. 4 (April, 1994): 24-27. Mainly devoted to a gallery of images made with the repaired Hubble telescope.

"Hubble's Road to Recovery." *Sky and Telescope* 86, no. 5 (November, 1993): 16-22. A history of the problems with the Hubble telescope and the development of solutions. Assumes familiarity with telescopes and imaging terminology.

"Missing Mass Still Missing." *Sky and Telescope* 89, no. 2 (February, 1995): 11. Accompanied by an image that dramatically illustrates the resolving power of the HST as it looks through a dense star cluster to reveal faint galaxies beyond.

SEE ALSO: 1961, First American in Space; 1969, Apollo 11 Lands on the Moon; 1977, Spaceflights of Voyagers 1 and 2; 1986, *Challenger* Accident.

1994 ■ BRADY HANDGUN VIOLENCE PROTECTION ACT: *legislation establishes a mandatory five-day waiting period and background check before a handgun can be purchased in the United States*

DATE: March 1, 1994
LOCALE: Washington, D.C.
CATEGORY: Laws and acts
KEY FIGURES:

James Brady (born 1940), press secretary to President Ronald Reagan

Sarah Brady (born 1942), chairperson of Handgun Control, Inc.

William Jefferson "Bill" Clinton (born 1946), forty-second president of the United States

Robert J. Dole (born 1923), Senate minority leader

Edward Feighan (born 1947), Democrat from Ohio who introduced the bill in the House

Howard Metzenbaum (born 1917), Democrat from Ohio who introduced the bill in the Senate

George Mitchell (born 1923), Senate majority leader

Ronald Wilson Reagan (born 1911), fortieth president of the United States, 1981-1989

Charles Schumer (born 1950), Democrat from New York who reintroduced bill in the House in 1993

SUMMARY OF EVENT. On November 30, 1993, President Bill Clinton signed the Brady Handgun Violence Protection Act into law—the first significant federal gun control legislation passed since 1968. Its passage came after a six-year campaign by James and Sarah Brady and Handgun Control, Inc., which was fiercely opposed by the National Rifle Association.

James Brady had been active in Republican Party politics from the early 1960's. He had held posts in the administrations of presidents Richard Nixon and Gerald Ford. In 1980, he joined the presidential campaign of Ronald Reagan as director of public affairs. When Reagan became president in January, 1981, Brady was named White House press secretary. On March 30, 1981, a mentally disturbed young man shot at President Reagan and his entourage as they left a Washington, D.C., hotel at which the president had delivered a speech. Reagan was seriously wounded, as were a Washington police officer and a secret service agent. James Brady was the most seriously injured, with a gunshot wound to the head. For several days, Brady was near death. His recovery was long and painful. He was not allowed to go home for eight months and did not return to work for almost two years. Even then, he continued to suffer paralysis of the left side, problems with speech, and memory difficulties.

Sarah Kemp Brady was a Republican Party activist when she met James in 1970. They were married in 1973. At the time Brady was shot, they had a two-year-old son, Scott. Sarah helped her husband in his long recovery. In 1984, when Scott was five years of age, Sarah found him playing with a friend's loaded pistol. This event, along with her husband's experience, convinced her to become active in the gun control movement. She called Handgun Control, Inc., the most influential gun control advocacy group, and offered to help. From that point on, Sarah Brady became a tireless advocate for stricter gun control laws.

A proposed federal gun control law, called the Brady bill because of the activism of Jim and Sarah Brady, was first introduced in Congress by Democratic representative Ed Feighan of Ohio, on February 4, 1987. The main provision of the bill was a seven-day waiting period for the purchase of handguns. Polls at the time showed that the American public favored such a measure, but the bill was strongly opposed by the National Rifle Association (NRA). The position of the NRA was that any new gun control legislation violated the Second Amendment to the Constitution.

The Second Amendment is part of the Bill of Rights, which was ratified in 1791. It says simply, "A well regulated Militia, being necessary to the security of a free State, the right of the people to keep and bear Arms, shall not be infringed." Legal interpretations of the amendment have usually concluded that some restrictions on firearms are constitutional. During the 1930's, violence perpetuated by organized crime had led to the passage of the first federal gun control laws. These laws banned private ownership of submachine guns and banned the sale of firearms to known criminals. In 1939, in *Miller v. United States*, the Supreme Court found that these restrictions were constitutional, since such weapons had no relationship to the formation of a well-regulated militia. The next significant piece of federal gun control legislation was passed in 1968, in response to the assassinations of Martin Luther King, Jr., and Robert Kennedy. This law prohibited interstate sales of firearms and required gun dealers to keep records of sales.

The NRA worked throughout the 1970's and 1980's to repeal some provisions of the 1968 Gun Control Act. They had some success in 1986, when Congress voted to repeal the ban on interstate sales of rifles and shotguns. In 1987, the NRA mounted an intense lobbying campaign to defeat the Brady bill and spent approximately two million dollars in the effort. The

Brady bill was to be voted on in the House of Representatives in September of 1988. Handgun Control, Inc. and the Bradys lobbied hard for it, and on September 7, a group of 120 uniformed police officers marched on the Capitol in support of it. However, the bill was defeated by a vote of 228 to 182.

The Brady bill was reintroduced in Congress in 1990, but it was never brought to a vote because of opposition from powerful members of Congress, including House Speaker Tom Foley (Democrat, Washington). The bill was introduced again in 1991. On May 8, 1991, the House of Representatives passed a bill requiring a seven-day waiting period for gun purchases. The Senate version, passed on June 28, called for a five-day waiting period. The compromise bill, incorporating the Senate requirements, was passed by the House on November 27, but Republican senators launched a filibuster against it and it never came to a vote in the Senate. In 1992, supporters of the Brady bill once again tried to bring it up for a vote in the Senate, but were unable to get enough votes to end the filibuster.

By 1993, public support for gun control legislation had increased dramatically. A poll conducted in March of that year showed that 70 percent of all Americans and 57 percent of gun owners felt that there should be more restrictions on the sale of firearms. Passage of the Brady bill was favored by 88 percent of people in the United States. The bill was introduced in the House by Democrat Charles Schumer of New York on February 22, 1993, and in the Senate by Ohio Democrat Howard Metzenbaum on February 24. The NRA and Handgun Control, Inc. kept up their intensive lobbying efforts.

On November 10, 1993, the House passed the bill by a vote of 238 to 182. Ten days later, the Senate passed its bill by a vote of 63 to 36. There were significant differences in the bills passed by the two houses of Congress, and a conference committee negotiated for two days before presenting a conference report to both houses. On November 22, the House of Representatives passed the compromise bill by a vote of 238 to 187. In the Senate, minority leader Robert Dole (Republican, Kansas) threatened to block passage of the bill with a filibuster. Dole negotiated with Senate Majority Leader George Mitchell of Maine, and finally agreed not to block passage of the bill if the Senate would consider modifications to it early in the new year. The Senate passed the bill by voice vote on November 24. Jim Brady called it a "Thanksgiving present for the American people." The law went into effect on March 1, 1994.

Assessments of the effectiveness of the Brady bill after its first year of enforcement were mixed. The NRA and other antigun-control groups asserted that the law not only was a clear violation of the Second Amendment but also was ineffective, because it did not keep criminals from buying guns illegally. They pointed to the fact that the Department of Justice prosecuted only four cases under the Brady bill it its first year. They also pointed out several loopholes that have allowed limitations on law enforcement record-keeping and have exempted pawn shops from some of the rules. Several judges found some provisions of the law unconstitutional, although it has remained in effect pending appeal. The Bradys

and other supporters of the bill maintain that it was a success. They pointed to government figures showing that seventy thousand convicted felons were prevented from buying guns under the law in its first year. They admitted that the bill was weak, but asserted that it was an important first step in stopping handgun violence. Jim Brady called his namesake bill "the end of unchecked madness and the commencement of a heartfelt crusade for a safer and saner country."

—*Deborah D. Wallin*

ADDITIONAL READING:

Cozic, Charles P., ed. *Gun Control*. San Diego, Calif.: Greenhaven Press, 1992. Contains articles written by those on all sides of the issue, including Sarah Brady and the NRA.

Davidson, Osha Gray. *Under Fire: The NRA and the Battle for Gun Control*. New York: Henry Holt, 1993. An attempt to provide a balanced view of the history of the NRA and its recent confrontations with gun control advocates.

Dickenson, Mollie. *Thumbs Up: The Life and Courageous Comeback of White House Press Secretary Jim Brady*. New York: Wiliam Morrow, 1987. Includes photographs and a bibliography.

LaPierre, Wayne. *Guns, Crime and Freedom*. Washington, D.C.: Regnery, 1994. This book, written by a lobbyist for the NRA, presents the arguments against gun control. Extensive bibliography.

Siegel, Mark A., et al. *Gun Control: Restricting Rights or Protecting People?* Wylie, Tex.: Information Plus, 1995. A study guide with many tables and charts to help in interpreting the information.

1994 ■ U.S.-NORTH KOREA PACT: *the threat of North Korean nuclear arms prompts the United States to develop incentives for the complete dismantling of that nation's nuclear program*

DATE: October 21, 1994
LOCALE: Geneva, Switzerland
CATEGORY: Diplomacy and international relations
KEY FIGURES:
William Jefferson "Bill" Clinton (born 1946), forty-second president of the United States
Robert Joseph Dole (born 1923), Republican senator from Kansas
Kim Il Sung (1912-1994), former North Korean president
Kim Jong Il (born 1942?), Kim Il Sung's chosen successor
Kim Young Sam, president of South Korea
SUMMARY OF EVENT. The isolated communist dictatorship of North Korea signed a pact with the United States on October 21, 1994, outlining a timetable for steps by each side that would end in the complete dismantling of North Korea's nuclear program within ten years. In return, the United States promised to reduce trade barriers, supply North Korea with

oil to fill its energy needs, and assist in the replacement of North Korea's old graphite reactors with new, safer, light-water reactors.

Experts said the new reactors would be less well suited to producing weapons-grade plutonium, the raw material for making nuclear bombs. However, U.S. officials admitted that the agreement posed a risk that North Korea could discard the agreement during the ten-year period and obtain fuel to make nuclear weapons. Sources at the Central Intelligence Agency (CIA) asserted that there was a better than even chance that North Korea had already developed a nuclear weapon but believed that, without the pact, it would have developed many more bombs—as many as one hundred over the subsequent ten years.

Tension had grown between the United States and North Korea as a result of North Korea's repeated refusal to allow international inspection of its nuclear facilities, which some U.S. experts believed were being used to extract plutonium for nuclear bombs. This refusal was in violation of the Nuclear Non-Proliferation Treaty (signed in 1968, entered into force in 1970), an international agreement to prevent the spread of nuclear weapons that had been signed by many countries, including North Korea. Moreover, in defiance of International Atomic Energy Agency regulations, North Korea had removed eight thousand highly radioactive fuel rods from a major nuclear complex at Yongbyon. If the rods were reprocessed, which the North Koreans said was necessary for safety reasons, they would yield enough plutonium to make five nuclear bombs.

The United States responded to these violations by pushing for trade sanctions against North Korea, which in turn said it would interpret any U.S.-led embargo as an act of war. The standoff was eased by a peace mission in early summer, led by former U.S. president Jimmy Carter. The North Korean president, Kim Il Sung, agreed to open negotiations with U.S. government representatives. Kim also suggested a meeting with the South Korean president, Kim Young Sam, which would have been the first meeting between the two leaders since Korea was divided at the end of World War II. After a promising start, however, negotiations were halted by the sudden death in July of Kim Il Sung. They were resumed under the leadership of his chosen successor, his fifty-two-year-old son Kim Jong Il, and the agreement was signed.

The agreement would take about ten years to be fully implemented, allowing at least five years before international monitors would carry out inspections to determine how much weapons-grade plutonium had been extracted by the North Koreans. It was expected to be at least eight years before all of North Korea's eight thousand plutonium-laden fuel rods could be removed from the country. This delay in the pact was criticized by the United States' ally, South Korea, and by some U.S. Republicans, who feared that North Korea would take Western aid money and later renege on the pact. The North Koreans feared that the United States' commitment to aid would evaporate as soon as North Korea relinquished its nuclear potential. To alleviate fears on both sides, President Bill Clinton's ad-

ministration pointed to the pact's carefully synchronized steps. It also said that North Korea would not possess a functioning nuclear reactor until it fulfilled its side of the pact.

The pact was a three-phase plan. In the first phase, scheduled to begin at the time of signing the pact and expected to take five years to carry out, North Korea was to freeze its nuclear program while the United States and its allies undertook a massive aid effort to provide North Korea with new sources of energy. The North Koreans would not refuel their Yongbyon reactor and would stop building two larger reactors. The fuel rods already removed were to be properly stored and regularly inspected. In return for the North Korean freeze, the United States and its allies were to begin work on the first of two light-water reactors, at a cost of four billion dollars, most of which would be provided by South Korea and Japan. At this stage, no nuclear components of the reactor would be installed. Pending completion of the new reactors, the United States and its allies would provide up to half a million metric tons of free oil per year.

In the second phase, North Korea would allow monitors to inspect the two waste sites that were previously off limits, so that it could be determined how much weapons-grade plutonium had been removed. The North Koreans would also begin sending their rods to a third country. Removal of all the rods was expected to take up to eight years. In return, the United States was to complete work on the first light-water reactor, which would begin producing electricity.

In the third and final phase, the North Koreans were to dismantle the plants that were involved in its nuclear weapons program. In return, the United States and its allies would complete work on the second light-water reactor.

The progress of the pact after the signing was far from smooth. On December 17, 1994, a U.S. Army helicopter that had strayed five kilometers north of a demilitarized zone into North Korean air space was shot down by the North Koreans. One of the two pilots was killed; the second was held by the North Koreans before being released on December 30, after U.S. warnings that any further delay could jeopardize the pact. In early 1995, another problem was encountered. On March 8, North Korea threatened to jettison the agreement if the United States continued to insist that South Korea build the two new light-water reactors. Observers said that it would be humiliating for North Korea to obtain reactors from its long-term enemy, South Korea, because that would prove that South Korea was richer and more technologically advanced than North Korea. North Korea also feared that South Korea would somehow use the deal to gain control over North Korea. The Clinton Administration pointed out, however, that South Korea was the only country willing to take the lead in financing the light-water reactors.

Furthermore, the Clinton Administration protested the diversion of some of the fifty thousand tons of heavy fuel oil supplied by the United States to North Korea for heating and electricity. Intelligence reports suggested that the oil was diverted by officials unconnected with the pact. This type of oil cannot be used to power planes and tanks in North Korea's army, but it may have been used in industrial sites. According to U.S. officials, the diversion meant either that North Korea's leadership could not control the implementation of the accord or that it had chosen not to do so. In either case, the incident fueled the fears of some analysts that the leadership of North Korea was unstable or uncertain.

Fears escalated in early April, 1996, when for three consecutive days heavily armed North Korean troops entered the demilitarized zone between North and South Korea. The zone had been established in 1953 as part of the armistice agreement ending the Korean War. The incursions followed an announcement by the North Korean government that it no longer recognized the demilitarized zone. A few days later, on April 16, President Clinton and South Korean president Kim Young Sam proposed talks to bring about a permanent peace deal replacing the 1953 armistice. U.S. officials believed that North Korea's incursions into the buffer zone may have been intended to force such talks rather than as a serious threat of war against South Korea.

Nevertheless, the United States remained concerned about North Korea's military intentions. In late April, the United States began talks with North Korea on its missile program, prompted by reports that North Korea was developing long-range missiles and selling them to politically unstable countries such as Iran and Syria. In this atmosphere of mistrust and uncertainty, the United States hoped that the U.S.-North Korea nuclear pact would prove a factor in preventing, or lessening, the possibility of another Korean war.   —*Claire J. Robinson*

ADDITIONAL READING:

Albright, David. "How Much Plutonium Does North Korea Have?" *Bulletin of the Atomic Scientists* 50, no. 5 (September/October, 1994): 46-53. The president of the Institute for Science and International Security, Washington, D.C., analyzes where North Korea's nuclear program stands.

Bunge, Frederica M., ed. *North Korea: A Country Study.* Washington, D.C.: The American University, Foreign Area Studies, 1981. An analysis of North Korea's economic, national security, political, and social systems, and how they are shaped by cultural factors.

Powell, Bill, and Russell Watson. "Headless Beast: North Korea After Kim." *Newsweek* 124, no. 3 (July 18, 1994): 18-23. Summarizes Western fears of North Korea and its nuclear weapons program.

Tai Sung An. *North Korea: A Political Handbook.* Wilmington, Del.: Scholarly Resources, 1983. For the student requiring background to the pact, a useful overview of the nation's social, political, and economic history and foreign relations.

Watson, Russell. "Home for New Year's Eve." *Newsweek* 125, no. 2 (January 9, 1995): 49. Explores the ramifications of the 1994 incident in which a U.S. helicopter was shot down over North Korean soil.

SEE ALSO: 1973, Détente with the Soviet Union; 1979, SALT II Is Signed; 1985, U.S.-Soviet Summit; 1987, INF Treaty Is Signed; 1991, Bush Announces Nuclear Arms Reductions; 1993, START II Is Signed.

1994 ■ REPUBLICANS RETURN TO CONGRESS: *a growing conservative constituency elects a Republican majority to both houses of Congress for the first time in forty years*

DATE: November 8, 1994
LOCALE: United States
CATEGORY: Government and politics
KEY FIGURES:
William Jefferson "Bill" Clinton (born 1946), forty-second
    president of the United States
Newton Leroy "Newt" Gingrich (born 1943), Republican
    representative from Georgia

SUMMARY OF EVENT. In the fall of 1994, as the midterm congressional elections approached, the U.S. electorate was in volatile mood. People were disillusioned and skeptical about political institutions and political leaders. It seemed to many people that government was out of touch and no longer responsive to the needs of ordinary people. Voter anger against the federal establishment made 1994 a difficult year to be an incumbent.

Republicans were optimistic that they would benefit from voter dissatisfaction, pointing to the sharp drop in popularity of President Bill Clinton in public opinion polls. To win control of the House of Representatives, the Republicans needed to win forty new seats. To take the Senate, seven new seats were needed. As a divisive and bitter campaign drew to a close, the conventional wisdom was that the Republicans would make gains, but these probably would fall short of winning majorities in either house.

Few people expected the political earthquake that followed. Democrats tumbled to defeat all across the country, and the Republicans seized control of both the House of Representatives and the Senate for the first time since 1954. In the House, Republicans won 230 seats to the Democrats' 204. In the Senate, Republicans secured a 53 to 47 advantage, reversing a pre-election situation of 56 to 44 in favor of the Democrats. Some of the most powerful Democrats were defeated. These included Speaker of the House Thomas Foley and Representative Don Rostenkowski of Illinois, chairman of the Ways and Means Committee (whose reelection campaign was especially difficult, because he had been indicted for misappropriation of funds). Other, younger figures such as Representatives Jim Slattery of Kansas and Jim Cooper of Tennessee, both of whom had been considered future Democratic leaders, also were defeated.

This voting pattern was repeated at state level, where the Republicans gained twelve governorships, making a total of thirty, including seven of the eight largest states. The Republicans also made big gains in state legislatures across the country. It was the biggest GOP success since 1946, and it left the Democrats confused and leaderless.

As the Republicans rejoiced, some Democrats were quick to blame President Clinton for the debacle. They pointed out that he had failed to keep his promise of a middle-class tax cut, and that he had failed to make the fundamental changes in the way government works that he had promised in his 1992 campaign. Although he had claimed to be a centrist New Democrat, his policies closely resembled traditional liberalism—which the public had come to associate with high taxes and excessive government spending, the kind of "big government" that was now being identified as the problem rather than the solution to the nation's ills.

The architect of the Republican victory was Georgia representative Newt Gingrich, formerly the House minority whip and after the election, set to become the Speaker of the House. An aggressive, fiercely partisan figure, Gingrich was instrumental in drawing up the Republican platform, the main plank of which was the Contract with America. This was a ten-point plan that the Republicans promised to bring before Congress in their first hundred days if they were in charge of the new Congress.

The contract called for the enactment of a constitutional amendment that would mandate a balanced federal budget by 2002. The idea was to promote fiscal responsibility by reining in a Congress that was perceived as out of control on spending. The contract also promised a tougher anticrime bill than the one President Clinton had signed the previous September; sharp cuts in welfare programs, including the power to cut off benefits to unmarried mothers who were less than twenty-one years of age; term limits on members of Congress, which would replace career politicians with "citizen legislators"; legal reforms; a tax cut for the middle class and a 50 percent cut in the capital gains tax; an increase in defense spending; and a reorganization of the way the House does business, involving a cut in the number of congressional committees and a reduction of Congressional staff by one-third.

This agenda was so radical that after the Republican victory, commentators said the country was about to undergo the biggest reversal of direction in government policy since President Franklin Roosevelt's New Deal program, which had begun in 1933. Since the New Deal, there had been a consensus that central government should intervene to remedy the social and economic ills of the country. This had culminated in President Lyndon Johnson's Great Society social programs of the 1960's.

House minority whip Newt Gingrich of Georgia, addressing Republican congressional candidates approximately one month prior to the November, 1994, elections that swept in a new Republican Congress, announces a "Contract with America" to bring to a vote such issues as tax cuts, term limits, and a balanced budget amendment. (AP Photo/John Duricka)

The conservative Republicans who triumphed in 1994 believed this long period of liberal government activism had led to the social problems of the 1990's, such as welfare dependency and an erosion of moral values. They made no secret of their desire to dismantle the welfare state and return many of the accumulated powers of the federal government to the states.

The elections left President Clinton weakened and returned the nation to another period of divided government, in which the executive branch is controlled by a different party than the one that controls the legislature. Divided government had been the norm for more than twenty years until Clinton's election in 1992, which coincided with firm Democratic control of Congress. In the days after the election, Clinton struggled for a response to the debacle. At first, the White House claimed that voters were merely lashing out at incumbents in a display of antigovernment anger. However, it was clear that the statistics did not support such an interpretation, since primarily Democratic incumbents were voted out. A more considered response came in a postelection speech to the Democratic Leadership Council, in which Clinton defended his record. He pointed out he was the first president since Harry Truman to cut the federal budget deficit, which had quadrupled during the presidencies of Ronald Reagan and George Bush. Clinton also took credit for promoting free trade, which traditionally has been supported by Republicans, and for his anticrime bill, which provided funds for more than a hundred thousand more police officers. Clinton pointed out that he already had reduced the size of the federal government by more than a quarter of a million employees. In other speeches, the president said that although he was willing to cooperate with the Republican Congress, he would not compromise on matters of principle. One such matter was the ban on certain kinds of assault weapons, which was enacted as part of the anticrime bill, but which many Republicans wanted to repeal.

Anticipating many legislative battles ahead, analysts suggested that the nation might have to endure two years of gridlock. They pointed out that although the Republicans had majorities in both houses of Congress, they lacked the two-thirds majority needed to override a presidential veto. It also was expected that the Democrats would use many procedural maneuvers in Congress to block the Republicans, as the Republicans themselves had done when they were in the minority.

When the 104th Congress convened in January, 1995, the Republicans delivered on their promise of a dynamic hundred days. They succeeded in bringing all the major points in their Contract with America to a vote in the House of Representatives, and all but one measure passed there. Many Democrats voted with the Republicans. The one failure was the proposal for a constitutional amendment to mandate a federal balanced budget, which failed to secure the two-thirds majority required for a constitutional amendment. Although many of these proposals faced a much tougher fight in the Senate, it was clear that the Republicans had profoundly shifted the focus of political debate for a long time to come.

—*Bryan Aubrey*

ADDITIONAL READING:

Beschloss, Michael R. "What Took Them So Long?" *Newsweek* 124, no. 21 (November 21, 1994): 49. Analyzes the resurgence of conservatism in the United States since the 1970's and discusses why that has taken so long to produce Republican majorities in Congress.

Fineman, Howard. "The Warrior." *Newsweek* 125, no. 2 (January 9, 1995): 28-34. Discusses House Speaker Newt Gingrich's life and career. Points out the consistency of Gingrich's conservative message since he first ran for Congress in 1974, but also describes some of the contradictions in his personality and philosophy.

Galen, Michele. "How the Election Looks from the Corner Office." *Business Week*, no. 3400 (November 21, 1994): 36. Interviews with business leaders who welcome the GOP victory, although some express fears that the bitter election will lead to divisiveness and gridlock.

Kaus, Mickey. "They Blew It." *The New Republic* 211, no. 23 (December 5, 1994): 14-19. Argues that had President Clinton made welfare rather than health care reform his priority, the Democrats would not have suffered such a crushing defeat.

Kelly, Michael. "You Say You Want a Revolution." *The New Yorker* 70, no. 38 (November 21, 1994): 56-63. Detailed analysis of voting patterns, the response of the Clinton Administration, and the difficulty Clinton was expected to have in regaining the political initiative.

SEE ALSO: 1992, Clinton Is Elected President.

1994 ■ GENERAL AGREEMENT ON TARIFFS AND TRADE: *the most ambitious trade agreement to date is designed to facilitate free trade and increase exports worldwide*

DATE: December 1, 1994
LOCALE: Washington, D.C.
CATEGORIES: Business and labor; Diplomacy and international relations; Economics; Treaties and agreements
KEY FIGURES:
William Jefferson "Bill" Clinton (born 1946), forty-second president of the United States
Robert Joseph "Bob" Dole (born 1923), Republican senator from Kansas

SUMMARY OF EVENT. On December 1, 1994, the U.S. Senate joined the House of Representatives in voting overwhelmingly in favor of what was widely considered to be the most far-reaching trade agreement reached to date. The General Agreement on Tariffs and Trade (GATT) slashed tariffs (taxes on imports) by an average of 40 percent in the 124 participating countries. Cuts in tariffs were expected to bring a boom in U.S. exports, leading to more jobs. In addition, American consumers would have access to cheaper imported goods. GATT, which had taken eight years to negotiate, represented a huge leap toward free trade worldwide.

A version of GATT had governed most international trade since 1948, but negotiations to expand the agreement began only in 1986. The new GATT was governed by a new organization, the World Trade Organization, located in Geneva. This organization had more power over signatory nations than its predecessor, the GATT Secretariat, and had the authority to enforce agreements through the imposition of trade penalties.

The Senate's and House of Representatives' vote in favor of GATT sounded a rare note of unity between Democrats and Republicans. They were brought together by their confidence that the agreement would revitalize the economy. President Bill Clinton's administration estimated that the agreement would create half a million new jobs. The administration also predicted an annual increase of $150 billion in U.S. economic growth when the agreement was fully implemented, after ten years. Worldwide, the Organization for Economic Cooperation and Growth estimated that GATT's lower tariffs and higher import quotas (limits on amounts of goods permitted to be imported) would increase world income by $270 billion per year.

Tariffs have been used by almost all nations in the world to protect their own farmers and native industries against competition from cheaper foreign goods. Increasingly, however, many economists have come to oppose such self-protectionist measures. They believe that free trade, without the barriers of tariffs, is the key to worldwide economic growth. The principles of free trade that inspired GATT hold that a country that is good at producing a given product will profit from exporting it to countries that are less efficient at producing that product. In return, a country can use the wealth it gains from exports to buy goods and services that are produced more efficiently elsewhere. It is theorized that, when each country focuses on what it does best, market forces of supply and demand organize distribution for maximum economic growth and consumers benefit from lower prices. However, governments have interfered with these market forces by imposing tariffs and strict quotas limiting the amounts of a product that can be imported, giving the product a false scarcity value that pushes up its price.

Not all economists are convinced that promoting free trade through initiatives such as GATT is the answer to the world's economic problems. Some argue that free trade benefits developed nations more than developing nations, since the richer nations can import goods from countries where labor and materials are cheaper. Critics of this view cite the Asian nations as proof of the benefits of free trade for developing nations. During the early 1960's, these countries were in serious economic trouble. Those that favored free trade (Hong Kong, Taiwan, South Korea, and Singapore) experienced more growth than countries that did not (India, North Korea, and Vietnam). Manufacturing did tend to flow toward sources of cheap labor, but this tendency helped develop the local economy and raise the standard of living.

Concerns over the possible negative effects of GATT are not restricted to economics. Cultural conflicts have arisen from the agreement, such as a disagreement between the United States and Japan over rice. The Japanese have always banned the import of rice to protect their own rice crop, which occupies a central position in their culture and religion, but under GATT the Japanese agreed to allow the import of some rice. Although the conflict was resolved, the episode presented an important challenge to advocates of free trade: How far should a country's cultural traditions be compromised to facilitate world trade?

Resistance to GATT also came from within the United States. Critics expressed fears that the World Trade Organization could attack U.S. consumer protection laws (such as the labeling of food product ingredients), worker protection laws, and environmental regulations as trade barriers. Among those who raised questions about the power of the World Trade Organization were Republican Senator Bob Dole, consumer advocate Ralph Nader, and various environmental lobby groups. Critics have presented many scenarios to back up their arguments. For example, if the United States decided on ethical grounds to ban the import of South Asian rugs made using child labor, countries that suffered from the decision could take their case to a panel of three World Trade Organization judges. If the judges ruled against the United States, then Congress or the state whose regulation was under challenge would have to decide whether to change that regulation. If the lawmakers refused, trade sanctions could be imposed against U.S. exports. As another example, environmentalists have expressed concern that under GATT, the United States could not impose its own stringent environmental laws on other nations. In 1991, under existing GATT rules whose enforcement provisions were far weaker than those ratified in 1994, the United States lost a case brought against one of its federal laws banning the importation of tuna fish caught in nets that also trapped dolphins. A GATT panel ruled that the United States could not impose its environmental restrictions on the rest of the world. Otherwise, the panel said, the United States could use those restrictions to keep out foreign competitors. In an attempt to allay fears about the World Trade Organization and its possible threat to U.S. sovereignty, President Clinton reached an agreement with Senator Dole to create a commission in the United States to review judgments that the organization makes against the United States.

The main areas of trade affected by GATT and its stipulations are as follows. In agriculture, U.S. GATT negotiators were at odds for years with the European Community over agricultural issues. The Europeans wanted to maintain subsidies to their farmers, but the United States wanted subsidies eliminated because they gave an unfair advantage in the marketplace at high cost to taxpayers. GATT produced a compromise that stipulates that agricultural tariffs be reduced by 36 percent in industrial nations and 24 percent in developing nations. Regarding intellectual property, GATT required all member countries to respect patents, trademarks, and copyrights. This requirement was expected to eradicate the pirated computer programs, records, videocassettes, and prescription drugs rampant in developing nations. Regarding automobiles, restrictions on auto exports, such as those that the United

States imposed on Japan, were eliminated. The agreement also banned the widespread practice of requiring high local content in some products, such as cars, a practice that protects local jobs but discourages imports. The agreement also limited the ability of countries to favor domestically owned factories at the expense of foreign-owned ones. Finally, richer nations were required to phase out quotas on clothing imports over a ten-year period. Quotas were to be replaced by less restrictive tariffs. Some of the strongest opposition to GATT in the United States had come from textile states such as North Carolina and South Carolina, which feared that their industries would suffer as a result of cheap foreign imports.

It seemed inevitable that GATT would continue to provoke conflicts of nationalistic self-interest, but there is little doubt that its ratification marked the beginning of a new era of increased global cooperation and trust between its signatory nations.　　　　　　　　　　　　　　　*—Claire J. Robinson*

ADDITIONAL READING:

Boskin, Michael J. "Pass GATT Now." *Fortune* 130, no. 12 (December 12, 1994): 137-138. A Republican economist gives reasons why members of his party in Congress should put politics aside and approve what he considers to be a vital trade agreement.

Dentzer, Susan. "A New Tapestry of Protectionism." *U.S. News and World Report* 117, no. 22 (December 5, 1994): 83. Points out the protectionist potholes built into GATT by some of its signatory nations.

Harbrecht, Douglas. "GATT: Tales from the Dark Side." *Business Week*, no. 3404 (December 19, 1994): 52. Cautions that global trade promoted by GATT may cause protectionist backlash in some nations as a result of trade moving to pools of cheap labor elsewhere in the world.

Nader, Ralph. "Drop the GATT." *The Nation* 259, no. 11 (October 10, 1994): 368-369. Consumer advocate Nader warns against the power of the World Trade Organization, which he believes is undemocratic and a threat to U.S. sovereignty.

Thomas, Rich. "Tempest over Trade." *Newsweek* 124, no. 23 (December 5, 1994): 50. Answers objections to GATT, including the issue of U.S. sovereignty and the power of the World Trade Organization.

SEE ALSO: 1993, North American Free Trade Agreement.

1995 ■ OKLAHOMA CITY FEDERAL BUILDING BOMBED: *one of the worst terrorist attacks in U.S. history demonstrates Americans' vulnerability to attack by rogue ideologues*

DATE: April 19, 1995
LOCALE: Oklahoma City, Oklahoma
CATEGORY: Wars, uprisings, and civil unrest
KEY FIGURES:
Frank Keating (born 1944), governor of Oklahoma
Timothy James McVeigh, principal suspect in the bombing

Terry Lynn Nichols, indicted for allegedly assisting McVeigh in construction of the bomb

SUMMARY OF EVENT. On April 19, 1995, a truck bomb parked before the Alfred P. Murrah Federal Office Building in downtown Oklahoma City exploded, shattering the foundation and lower floors of the nine-story concrete edifice that housed fifteen federal agencies, more than five hundred employees, and a second-floor day-care center. Direct casualties included 168 dead as a result of the blast, and more than six hundred injured. These numbers made the bombing the worst incident of terrorism in U.S. history, but they do not fully recount the level of injury. The longer list was the one of indirect victims, stretching from the more than 250 children who lost a parent in the blast, to the tens of thousands in the Oklahoma City community who counted among their friends and loved ones those killed or wounded by the explosion, to the worried federal workers, and to citizens across the country trying to adjust to their vulnerability to terrorism, wherever they might work or live.

Rescue workers from states as far away as Virginia joined with those in Oklahoma City in seeking survivors amid the rubble. State, local, and federal law enforcement agencies joined in what was reportedly the largest criminal investigation in United States' history. Initial news stories suggested a Middle Eastern connection with the bombing, and Arab Americans received intense scrutiny in airports across the country. Lobbyist groups would later protest that these news releases stereotyped Middle Easterners as terrorists and exposed them to abuse by an outraged U.S. public; however, circumstantial evidence did point in that direction. The explosive, a mixture of fuel oil and an ammonium nitrate fertilizer, was the same compound that Arab terrorists had employed in the February 26, 1993, bombing of the World Trade Center in New York, which killed six and injured another thousand. So too did the mode of delivery: a parked rental van. Moreover, because of Oklahoma's links with the international oil community, people from the Middle East had long been familiar sights on its cities' streets. Even the initial leads developed in the same way as those leading to the apprehension of the Arabs involved in the World Trade Center bombing: identifying the vehicle containing the explosives and tracking it to the agency that rented it. The day following the blast, however, to the shock of much of the U.S. public, the Federal Bureau of Investigation (FBI) released composite sketches of the men renting the van—John Does 1 and 2—two white Americans.

Although violence is not unusual in the United States, political violence has been. Assassinations of political leaders have been relatively infrequent, and then invariably the work of alienated and often psychotic individuals. Similarly, while U.S. history is replete with the names of legendary villains, they have tended to be criminals such as bank robbers Jesse James and Bonnie and Clyde. Political criminals such as John Brown have been few, and even such violent political organizations as the Ku Klux Klan and the Minutemen, and more recent emotional groups such as the anti-abortionist advocates, overwhelmingly have had as their targets either individuals or corporate America, not the federal government. The 1970 bombing of the Army Math Research Center at the University of Wisconsin by antiwar protestors thus stood as the major postwar instance of political violence by United States citizens against an arm of the United States government prior to the Oklahoma City explosion, and statistics still indicate that of the more than three thousand bombs detonated in anger in the United States each year, virtually all are set off by persons because of personal grievances, with the overwhelming majority finding their targets at the municipal level. For most people in the United States, the idea that U.S. citizens could have conspired to have killed so many federal workers in Oklahoma City was nearly as hard to absorb as the bombing itself.

With sketches of the prime suspects in hand, investigators moved swiftly. John Doe 2 was eventually cleared of involvement in the terrorist attack; John Doe 1, identified as Timothy McVeigh, was quickly captured and charged with the bombing. As authorities reconstructed events, the planning of the attack had begun as early as the previous December, when McVeigh and an army buddy, Michael Fortier, allegedly cased the nine floors of the federal building. During the following weeks, Fortier allegedly assisted McVeigh in raising the money needed to buy the tons of fertilizer used in the blast by selling guns (possibly stolen) at a series of gun shows, while another army friend, Terry Nichols, allegedly assisted McVeigh in constructing the bomb. The momentarily popular theory that the blast was the work of the Michigan citizen militia, an ultra-right-wing anti-Washington group counting Nichols among its devoted members, remained unsubstantiated.

As the investigation proceeded from arrest to the indictment of McVeigh, Fortier, and Nichols, the national political process mobilized for action against domestic and foreign terrorist threats to the United States. The destruction in Oklahoma City testified grimly to the vulnerability of democratic societies to terrorism, given the freedom to travel and associate that they accord to those within their borders, the ease with which the ingredients for bombs such as that used in Oklahoma City can be obtained, and the modern revolutions in transportation and communications that enable transnational terrorists to operate ever more easily and even to network with one another. Within the same week as the bombing in Oklahoma City, a gas attack in a Tokyo subway attributed to a Japanese Buddhist cult hospitalized four hundred people; and in Canada, the bombing of the historic provincial legislative building in Charlottetown on Prince Edward Island killed one person in an incident feared to be a copycat act inspired by the Oklahoma City tragedy. Most ominously, by the end of April, a State Department report entitled "Patterns of Terrorism: 1994" noted the increasing tendency of international terrorists to develop ties with domestic groups, including the Mafia and drug gangs in the United States. The future, intelligence analysts concluded, is apt to be one of more, not less, terrorism, with the terrorists placing a greater emphasis on mass casualties than has been the case historically.

The Omnibus Counterterrorism Act of 1995, previously placed before Congress by the Clinton Administration as a response to the growing menace of international terrorism, initially benefited from the events in Oklahoma City. Congressional leaders vowed to join with the White House in a bipartisan effort to pass the measure, and provisions were added to give the bill a wider reach. Boasts were made that the enlarged, $1.5 billion bill would be enacted by the end of May. The wheels of the U.S. political system, however, like those of justice, grind very sluggishly. Slowed by opposition from domestic Muslim American and militia lobbyists, who attacked the bill as an unconstitutional restraint on individual freedoms, the bill came to a halt in May, 1995, when the Senate rejected the president's proposal to permit emergency roving wiretaps in cases involving terrorism or potential terrorism, and Republicans saddled the bill with the capital punishment debate by including in it exceedingly stringent curbs on appeals by death row inmates. As a consequence, nearly a year after the Oklahoma City bombing, none of the suspects had been placed on trial nor had the political process produced a single piece of counterterrorism legislation. —*Joseph R. Rudolph, Jr.*

ADDITIONAL READING:

Crenshaw, Martha, ed. *Terrorism in Context.* University Park: Pennsylvania State University Press, 1995. An outstanding collection of background papers on the topic.

Hansen, Jon. *Oklahoma Rescue.* New York: Ballantine, 1995. A human-interest account, written by one of Oklahoma's City's pivotal rescue workers.

Irving, Clive, ed. *In Their Name: Dedicated to the Brave and the Innocent, Oklahoma City, April, 1995.* New York: Random House, 1995. A good set of essays on the bombing and the victims of terrorism in Oklahoma City.

MacLean, Nancy. *Behind the Mask of Chivalry: The Making of the Second Ku Klux Klan.* New York: Oxford University Press, 1994. For background reading, an excellent study of the country's oldest right-wing terrorist organization.

Riley, Kevin Jack, and Bruce Hoffman. *Domestic Terrorism: A National Assessment of State and Local Preparedness.* Santa Monica, Calif.: Rand Corporation, 1995. Sixty-six pages of chilling reading prepared for the Department of Justice.

United States Customs Service. *The Oklahoma City Tragedy.* Washington, D.C.: Government Printing Office, 1995. A special issue of *Customs Today* (volume 30, number 2) dedicated to the victims of the Oklahoma City bombing.

SEE ALSO: 1993, World Trade Center Bombing.

1995 ■ UNITED STATES RECOGNIZES VIETNAM: *U.S. diplomatic recognition of Vietnam marks the end of the traumatic and divisive Vietnam War era*

DATE: July 11, 1995
LOCALE: Washington, D.C.
CATEGORY: Diplomacy and international relations

KEY FIGURES:

George Herbert Walker Bush (born 1924), forty-first
president of the United States, 1989-1993

James Earl "Jimmy" Carter (born 1924), thirty-ninth
president of the United States, 1977-1981

William Jefferson "Bill" Clinton (born 1946), forty-second
president of the United States

J. Robert "Bob" Kerrey (born 1943), Democratic senator
from Nebraska

Vo Van Kiet (born 1922), prime minister of Vietnam

John McCain (born 1936), Republican senator from Arizona

SUMMARY OF EVENT. President Bill Clinton, on July 11, 1995, announced the diplomatic recognition of the Socialist Republic of Vietnam by the United States. Recognition of Vietnam brought to a close a war that officially had ended more than twenty years before. In announcing his decision, Clinton said, "We can now move on to common ground. Whatever divided us before, let us consign to the past."

Concerning Vietnam, moving away from the past had proved a long and agonizing process for the United States. The Vietnam War took the lives of more than fifty-eight thousand U.S. personnel between 1961 and the fall of Saigon on April 30, 1975. The United States government had hoped that the peace agreement of January, 1973, which provided for a cease-fire, withdrawal of foreign troops, return of prisoners of war, and a peaceful reunification of Vietnam, might prevent a communist takeover of all of Vietnam.

North Vietnamese forces, however, remained in South Vietnam after the agreement and, after consolidating their areas of control, launched an offensive in March, 1975, that would lead, by the end of April, to complete victory and establishment of one Vietnam, with Hanoi as its capital. The final resolution of the war intensified United States resentment toward Vietnam and made reconciliation with the former enemy even more difficult. An embargo on trade with North Vietnam, imposed in 1964, was extended to all of Vietnam. Nevertheless, President Jimmy Carter, elected in 1976, took some first steps toward a rapprochement by lifting the prohibition on travel to Vietnam, beginning discussions with the Vietnamese government, and accepting Vietnam as a member of the United Nations.

These initial steps were halted by the Vietnamese demand in 1978 for reconstruction aid promised in the 1973 Peace Accords. Hostility between Vietnam and the United States was increased in the same year by a Vietnamese friendship treaty with the Soviet Union, recognition of China (Vietnam's historic enemy) by the United States, and Vietnam's invasion of Cambodia. From the United States' perspective, improved relations with Vietnam henceforth were dependent on that nation's withdrawal from Cambodia, its recognition of an independent Cambodian government, commitment to basic human rights for its own citizens, and, most important, a strict accounting of all U.S. servicemen missing in action or taken prisoner in Vietnam.

The Vietnamese agreement in 1989 to withdraw from Cambodia opened the way for a sequence of steps that ultimately would lead to normalization of relations. In 1991, President George Bush defined the incremental steps, known as the "Roadmap," that Vietnam would have to take before the United States would grant diplomatic recognition. One of these steps, a peace agreement between Vietnam and Cambodia, was completed in October, 1991.

The United States reciprocated in 1992 by permitting U.S. companies to open offices in Vietnam. With the trade embargo still in effect, however, there was little incentive for companies to do so. The next significant development was Clinton's decision in 1993 to end U.S. opposition to international institutions and other nations making money available to Vietnam. Soon afterward, U.S. businesses were declared free to bid on projects funded by international financial institutions, so that they would not be shut out of business opportunities partially financed by U.S. dollars.

Throughout the early 1990's, the Vietnamese had been increasingly helpful in locating the remains of missing U.S. servicemen. Teams from the United States were permitted to search the Vietnamese countryside; and war records, including the archives of the war museum in Hanoi, were turned over to the United States.

One major step short of diplomatic recognition remained: lifting the trade embargo. Debate centered on several issues, including the economic implications of maintaining the trade embargo. The U.S. business community recognized Vietnam's resources, including oil reserves estimated to be the fourth largest in the world and a labor force with one of the highest literacy rates in Southeast Asia. It also was obvious that other nations were gaining significant investment advantages in the country. Impediments to foreign investments also were recognized, among them inadequate distribution capabilities, state control of businesses, and both a market philosophy and legal system still in flux.

The continuing communist nature of the government and restrictions on individual rights raised concerns with many persons in the United States, but others noted that the United States had long done business with a variety of repressive regimes, including China. From a geopolitical perspective, it was argued that an economically strengthened Vietnam would be a counterbalance to Chinese domination in the region.

The most emotional issue surrounding the trade embargo and diplomatic recognition of Vietnam was continuing uncertainty over the fate of U.S. troops still listed as missing in action or known to have been taken prisoner. The trade embargo was viewed by many as a means to pressure the Vietnamese government into cooperating on the prisoner-of-war/missing-in-action (POW/MIA) issue. On the other hand, many argued that improving relations with Hanoi would both reward the country for past cooperation and encourage future efforts.

On February 3, 1994, President Clinton announced an end to the United States' trade embargo against Vietnam. This decision, Clinton stated, had been based on only one criterion: "gaining the fullest possible accounting for our prisoners of war and our missing in action." The president continued, "To-day I am lifting the trade embargo against Vietnam because I am absolutely convinced it offers the best way to resolve the fate of those who remain missing and about whom we are not sure." Lifting the embargo did not involve granting most fa-vored nation trade status to Vietnam, so tariffs on Vietnamese goods imported into the United States remained high. In addi-tion, U.S. businesses operating in Vietnam would not have the support afforded by a U.S. embassy.

Diplomatic recognition was the next logical step, but it also excited controversy. The arguments for and against lifting the trade embargo, especially regarding POW/MIA issues, were also applied to normalization of relations. President Clinton's announcement on July 11, 1995, was boycotted by the Ameri-can Legion and by several family groups, including the Na-tional League of Families of American Prisoners and Missing in Southeast Asia. Members of Congress were divided, argu-ing either that recognition acknowledged Vietnam's coopera-tion and would further the effort to reach as final an account-ing as possible, or that it would remove the final incentive for Vietnamese cooperation.

As Clinton spoke, he was accompanied by politicians from both parties, including Republican Senator John McCain, a former prisoner of war, and Democratic Senator Bob Kerrey, who had lost part of a leg in combat during his tour of duty. "Never before in the history of warfare has such an extensive effort been made to resolve the fate of soldiers who did not return," the president said. He promised that "normalization of our relations with Vietnam is not the end of [that] effort."

The U.S. business community generally welcomed the president's decision but called for additional steps, such as granting most favored nation status to reduce tariffs and mak-ing insurance available from the Overseas Private Investment Corporation in order to protect U.S. investments.

Prime Minister Vo Van Kiet of Vietnam greeted the resump-tion of diplomatic relations with an expression of gratitude to President Clinton and a promise that Vietnam would continue to help the United States resolve questions concerning the fate of the missing U.S. servicemen. —*Edward J. Rielly*

ADDITIONAL READING:

Castelli, Beth. "The Lifting of the Trade Embargo Between the United States and Vietnam: The Loss of a Potential Bar-gaining Tool or a Means of Fostering Cooperation?" *Dickin-son Journal of International Law* 13, no. 1 (Winter, 1995): 297-328. A reasoned discussion of background, considerations involved in lifting the trade embargo, and projections for the future.

Chang, Tim Tien-Chun. "Joint Ventures in Vietnam." *Com-mercial Law Bulletin* 9, no. 4 (July 1, 1994): 17-19. Offers a succinct, clear explanation of types of investments and of challenges facing foreign investors.

Howes, Craig. *Voices of the Vietnam POWs.* New York: Oxford University Press, 1993. Provides important context for understanding the continuing importance of the POW/MIA issue.

Moss, George Donelson. *Vietnam: An American Ordeal.* Englewood Cliffs, N.J.: Prentice-Hall, 1990. Although no sin-gle book can adequately cover the Vietnam War, this book is among the most thorough.

Sutter, Robert G. *Vietnam-U.S. Relations: The Debate over Normalization.* Washington, D.C.: Library of Congress, 1992. A detailed view of political debate regarding normalization of relations with Vietnam.

U.S. Congress. House. Committee on Foreign Affairs. Sub-committee on Asian and Pacific Affairs. *U.S. Economic Em-bargo on Vietnam.* Washington, D.C.: Government Printing Office, 1993. Congressional testimony addressing important issues associated with U.S.-Vietnam relations.

SEE ALSO: 1964, Vietnam War; 1964, Berkeley Free Speech Movement; 1964, Johnson Is Elected President; 1967, Long, Hot Summer; 1968, Tet Offensive; 1968, Nixon Is Elected President; 1970, United States Invades Cambodia; 1973, U.S. Troops Leave Vietnam.

1990's ■ RISE OF THE INTERNET: *a revolu-tionary communications network mush-rooms as low-cost personal computers, software, and network services flood the mass market*

DATE: Mid-1990's
LOCALE: Worldwide and "cyberspace"
CATEGORIES: Business and labor; Communications; Cultural and intellectual history; Science and technology
KEY FIGURES:
Tim Berners-Lee (born 1945), creator of the World Wide Web
Vannevar Bush (1890-1974), early computer pioneer
Vinton Cerf (born 1943), Stanford University researcher who developed the protocols used by computers on the Internet
James Clark, cofounder of Netscape
William H. "Bill" Gates (born 1955), founder of Microsoft, a key computer software provider
Al Gore (born 1948), U.S. vice president who encouraged investment in the critical infrastructure of the information superhighway

SUMMARY OF EVENT. The Internet is a loose collection of interconnecting commercial and noncommercial computer networks, including on-line information services, to which users can subscribe, that use standard protocols (or rules) to exchange information.

The Internet began as ARPAnet, an electronic messaging and research tool put together in the late 1960's by the United States' Defense Department's Advanced Research Projects Agency. ARPAnet linked together computers at universities doing military-funded research and other research facilities around the world. ARPAnet was designed to allow uninter-rupted data routing in the event of a nuclear war, bypassing failed connections. Although people at these institutions discovered the enormous utility of a network that linked them with their peers around the world, the network did not have a major effect outside this sphere because few businesses and individuals had computers. When the first commercial on-line service, CompuServe, started in 1969, there were few computers to participate.

The ARPAnet scheme depended on being able to send messages by any available path, so protocols had to be devised to control and monitor data delivery. Use of Transmission Control Protocol/Internet Protocol (TCP/IP), developed by Vinton Cerf at Stanford University, was important in creating compatibility among a variety of computer equipment. By the early 1980's, a number of networks had developed, with interconnections following. These interconnections led to the term "Internet." In 1986, the National Science Foundation created NSFNET to connect supercomputer sites around the United States. It also connected computers at schools and research sites. Soon NSFNET absorbed ARPAnet.

In 1991, Senator Al Gore promoted legislation that expanded NSFNET and renamed it NREN, the National Research and Education Network, which brought it into more schools and colleges. The legislation also allowed businesses to purchase part of the network for commercial uses. Mass commercialization followed. Gore proposed creating a National Information Infrastructure of a telecommunications network, "information appliances" connected to the network, and information stored in digital libraries and databases filled with text images and videos. He said that rapid advances in telecommunications and computer technology were causing the information and telecommunications industries to converge.

Rapid growth of the Internet required the bringing together of several elements: readily available terminal devices, networks to link them, user-friendly software, and substantial content. These elements came together in the 1990's. While such development could have happened with a telephone or cable television add-on, the key factor was the growth of personal computer (PC) ownership and the connection of these computers to on-line services. Many students were introduced to Internet service through their schools' computer network. As it became easier for nonexperts to navigate this information stream, more new users were attracted each year.

Microsoft's founder, Bill Gates, has said the Internet's popularity is the most important single development in the computing world since IBM introduced the PC in 1981. He asserts that the Internet will evolve into a more powerful information highway that will forever change the way people buy, work, learn, and communicate.

The Internet is not owned or funded by any one institution, organization, or government. Rather this "organized anarchy" is directed by the Internet Society, which works out such issues as standards, resources, and addresses. The computers, routers, and communication links are owned by many parties. By the mid-1990's, the Internet had evolved into a network composed of millions of host computers, all but a few of them privately maintained. Tens of millions of PC users would roam the "information highway" and tap into this vast amount of data, thanks to its ease of use.

The many alternative routing possibilities have made it almost impossible to block certain types of information selectively. At the same time, it has empowered many groups, because use of the Internet is possible at low cost. Messages can be sent via various communication services to other users on the Internet, if one knows their computer address. Users can access the Internet through various "dial-up" providers, through corporate or educational systems, and via on-line information providers such as CompuServe and America Online.

Four basic processes can be carried out on the Internet: communication (electronic mail or e-mail), document or file transfer, interactive browsing, and reading and posting to topic-specific bulletin boards. E-mail is the cornerstone of the Internet; it allows two people to send messages to each other in a near-real-time manner. The ability to communicate with someone in an unobtrusive but effective and comprehensive way has tremendous advantage for both senders and receivers; it is one of the most popular uses of the Internet. E-mail users can also route or forward information to others.

In addition to a huge base of mail users, the Internet provides access to large amounts of data on subjects ranging from the trivial to the most serious. The Internet can be used as a global bulletin board through thousands of topical newsgroups that electronically discuss various issues. A message posted to a newsgroup can be read, forwarded elsewhere, or responded to.

One 1995 survey found 9.5 million people in the United States used the Internet, including 1.1 million children less than eighteen years of age. Half had first gotten online that year. Other estimates indicated higher numbers and that about 20 to 30 million computers around the world are connected. Columbia Broadcasting System (CBS) radio began providing a regular feature called an "Internet Minute." The ease with which companies and individuals can place information on the Internet has changed the whole idea of what it means to publish. As Internet access became important to businesses, Internet addresses appeared on business cards, in catalogs, and in advertisements. Many state governments have placed documents online, and many candidates and elected officials used e-mail addresses for voter education and constituent communication.

The World Wide Web (WWW or Web) is a user-friendly "front end" to the information already on the Internet. Tim Berners-Lee, an expert in communications and text-handling programs, wrote the basic Web software while at the CERN physics laboratory in Geneva, Switzerland, in 1990, and placed it on the Internet the next year. He came up with the standards for addressing, linking language, and transferring multimedia documents on the Web. This software provides a protocol for requesting readable information (including text, graphics, figures, and databases) stored on remote computer systems, using networks.

The key to the Web's success is hypertext, which is information that can be stored and retrieved in a nonhierarchical structure. The concept of hypertext had been suggested by

Vannevar Bush in 1945. Every hypertext item has an address of its own, meaning one can move from one file to the next through a series of links created by someone. The next file accessed through "point-and-click" connections could be half-way around the world. All the technical aspects of moving from one computer to the other are transparent to the user, who can simply explore without interference by using appropriate "browsers," software that helps the user to find the topic of interest.

Many institutions and individuals now have established Web sites. In late 1995, for example, the Vatican opened up a Web site, with the ultimate intent to make papal messages and church documents available for downloading by scholars, clerics, and laity around the world. More than a million people logged on the Vatican's Web site during the first two weeks. An Orthodox Jewish group has provided a site that would provide Torah readings. The Internal Revenue Service opened up its Web site in early 1996. Some 220,000 computer users visited it during the first twenty-four hours, and more than a million in its first week—even before the debut was officially announced.

The protocols that control information transmission on the Internet and the Web have worked exceptionally well, despite rapid growth of usage. The Web has experienced tremendous growth and diversification, becoming a library, marketplace, stage, and funhouse. By 1995, it was the Internet's center of activity, as thousands of companies, organizations, and individuals set up sites. In two years, the Web grew from 100 to 100,000 sites. Tremendous energy and creativity was channeled into the Web, with sites even including video and audio programs. The Internet's vast and unexplored possibilities—social, economic, and scientific—promised to revolutionize human society during the twenty-first century.

—*Stephen B. Dobrow*

ADDITIONAL READING:

Cady, Glee Harrah, and Pat McGregor. *Mastering the Internet*. Alameda, Calif.: Sybex, 1995. One of many definitive guides to using the Internet.

Diamond, Edwin, et al. "The Ancient History of the Internet." *American Heritage* 46, no. 6 (October, 1995): 34-41. Discusses the background of the Internet.

Gates, Bill. *The Road Ahead*. New York: Viking, 1995. Discusses the changes that computer usage will bring to everyday life.

Godin, Seth, ed. *Information Please Business Almanac and Sourcebook*. Boston: Houghton Mifflin, 1995. A source of business references on the Internet.

Goodman, Danny. *Living at Light Speed*. New York: Random House, 1994. A survival guide to using Internet and other on-line resources.

Thomas, Brian. *The Internet for Scientists and Engineers: Online Tools and Resources*. New York: IEEE Press, 1995. Explains how to use the Internet and where to find scientific information.

SEE ALSO: 1947, Invention of the Transistor; 1981, IBM Markets the Personal Computer.

GREAT EVENTS FROM HISTORY
NORTH AMERICAN SERIES

KEY WORD INDEX

CATEGORY LIST

NOTE: The entries in this publication are listed below under all categories that apply. The chronological order under each category corresponds to the chronological order of the entries in these volumes.

AFRICAN AMERICAN HISTORY

1619, Africans Arrive in Virginia
1641, Massachusetts Recognizes Slavery
1661, Virginia Slave Codes
1712, New York City Slave Revolt
1739, Stono Rebellion
1773, African American Baptist Church Is Founded
1775, Pennsylvania Society for the Abolition of Slavery Is Founded
1777, Northeast States Abolish Slavery
1784, Hall's Masonic Lodge Is Chartered
1787, Free African Society Is Founded
1787, Northwest Ordinance
1791, Haitian Independence
1793, Whitney Invents the Cotton Gin
1793, First Fugitive Slave Law
1804, First Black Codes
1807, Congress Bans Importation of African Slaves
1816, AME Church Is Founded
1820's, Social Reform Movement
1820, Missouri Compromise
1830, Proslavery Argument
1830, Webster-Hayne Debate
1831, *The Liberator* Begins Publication
1831, Nat Turner's Insurrection
1833, American Anti-Slavery Society Is Founded
1839, Amistad Slave Revolt
1847, *The North Star* Begins Publication
1850, Underground Railroad
1850, Compromise of 1850
1850, Second Fugitive Slave Law
1853, National Council of Colored People Is Founded
1854, Kansas-Nebraska Act
1856, Bleeding Kansas
1857, First African American University
1857, *Dred Scott v. Sandford*
1858, Lincoln-Douglas Debates
1859, Last Slave Ship Docks at Mobile
1859, John Brown's Raid on Harpers Ferry
1863, Emancipation Proclamation
1863, Reconstruction
1865, Freedmen's Bureau Is Established

1865, New Black Codes
1865, Thirteenth Amendment
1866, Rise of the Ku Klux Klan
1866, Civil Rights Act of 1866
1866, Race Riots in the South
1868, Fourteenth Amendment
1890, Mississippi Disfranchisement Laws
1895, Booker T. Washington's Atlanta Exposition Address
1896, *Plessy v. Ferguson*
1909, National Association for the Advancement of Colored People Is Founded
1910, Great Northern Migration
1917, Universal Negro Improvement Association Is Established
1930, Nation of Islam Is Founded
1931, Scottsboro Trials
1941, Executive Order 8802
1942, Congress of Racial Equality Is Founded
1944, *Smith v. Allwright*
1954, *Brown v. Board of Education*
1955, Montgomery Bus Boycott
1957, Southern Christian Leadership Conference Is Founded
1957, Little Rock School Desegregation Crisis
1960, Civil Rights Act of 1960
1962, Meredith Registers at "Ole Miss"
1963, King Delivers His "I Have a Dream" Speech
1964, Civil Rights Act of 1964
1965, Assassination of Malcolm X
1965, Voting Rights Act
1965, Watts Riot
1965, Expansion of Affirmative Action
1967, Long, Hot Summer
1968, Assassinations of King and Kennedy
1968, Fair Housing Act
1971, *Swann v. Charlotte-Mecklenberg Board of Education*
1972, Equal Employment Opportunity Act
1980, Miami Riots
1983, Jackson Becomes First Major African American Candidate for President

ASIAN AMERICAN HISTORY

1849, Chinese Immigration
1854, Perry Opens Trade with Japan
1868, Burlingame Treaty
1875, Page Law
1882, Chinese Exclusion Act
1882, Rise of the Chinese Six Companies
1892, Yellow Peril Campaign
1895, Chinese American Citizens Alliance Is Founded
1898, *United States v. Wong Kim Ark*
1899, Philippine Insurrection
1899, Hay's "Open Door Notes"
1901, Insular Cases
1907, Gentlemen's Agreement
1913, Alien Land Laws
1917, Immigration Act of 1917
1922, *Ozawa v. United States*
1930, Japanese American Citizens League Is Founded
1934, Tydings-McDuffie Act
1942, Censorship and Japanese Internment
1943, Magnuson Act
1959, Alaska and Hawaii Gain Statehood
1968, Bilingual Education Act
1974, *Lau v. Nichols*
1992, Asian Pacific American Labor Alliance

BUSINESS AND LABOR

1790, Slater's Spinning Mill
1793, Whitney Invents the Cotton Gin
1808, American Fur Company Is Chartered
1810, *Fletcher v. Peck*
1825, Erie Canal Opens
1833, Rise of the Penny Press
1842, *Commonwealth v. Hunt*
1842, Dorr Rebellion
1846, Howe's Sewing Machine
1859, First Commercial Oil Well
1882, Standard Oil Trust Is Organized
1886, American Federation of Labor Is Founded
1887, Interstate Commerce Act
1890, Sherman Antitrust Act
1894, Pullman Strike

1918, Demobilization After World War I
1924, Dawes Plan
1929, Stock Market Crash
1929, Great Depression
1930's, Mass Deportations of Mexicans
1930, Baltimore and Ohio Railroad
Begins Operation
1931, Empire State Building Opens
1932, Reconstruction Finance
Corporation Is Created
1932, Ottawa Agreements
1932, Bonus March
1933, The Hundred Days
1933, Tennessee Valley Authority Is
Established
1933, National Industrial Recovery Act
1934, Tydings-McDuffie Act
1934, The Dust Bowl
1935, Works Progress Administration Is
Established
1935, Black Monday
1935, National Labor Relations Act
1935, Social Security Act
1936, Reciprocity Treaty
1939, Mobilization for World War II
1941, 6.6 Million Women Enter the
U.S. Labor Force
1942, Bracero Program
1943, Inflation and Labor Unrest
1943, Urban Race Riots
1946, Employment Act
1955, AFL and CIO Merge
1959, St. Lawrence Seaway Opens
1961, Peace Corps Is Established
1967, Long, Hot Summer
1971, Devaluation of the Dollar
1973, Arab Oil Embargo and Energy
Crisis
1974, Construction of the Alaska Pipeline
1981, Reagan's Budget and Tax Reform
1988, Indian Gaming Regulatory Act
1989, Lincoln Savings and Loan
Declares Bankruptcy
1993, North American Free Trade
Agreement
1994, General Agreement on Tariffs
and Trade

EDUCATION

1650, Harvard College Is Established
1785, Beginnings of State Universities
1802, U.S. Military Academy Is
Established
1820's, Free Public School Movement
1820's, Social Reform Movement

1823, Hartford Female Seminary Is
Founded
1833, Oberlin College Is Established
1837, Mt. Holyoke Seminary Is
Founded
1857, First African American University
1862, Morrill Land Grant Act
1865, Vassar College Is Founded
1867, Office of Education Is Created
1912, U.S. Public Health Service Is
Established
1925, Scopes Trial
1929, League of United Latin American
Citizens Is Founded
1944, G.I. Bill
1954, *Brown v. Board of Education*
1957, Little Rock School
Desegregation Crisis
1962, Meredith Registers at "Ole Miss"
1963, *Abington School District v.
Schempp*
1964, Berkeley Free Speech Movement
1965, Expansion of Affirmative Action
1968, Bilingual Education Act
1971, *Swann v. Charlotte-Mecklenberg
Board of Education*
1974, *Lau v. Nichols*
1978, *Regents of the University of
California v. Bakke*
1982, *Plyler v. Doe*

ENVIRONMENT

1872, Great American Bison Slaughter
1908, White House Conservation
Conference
1916, National Park Service Is Created
1924, Halibut Treaty
1934, The Dust Bowl
1978, Toxic Waste at Love Canal
1979, Three Mile Island Accident
1981, Ozone Hole Is Discovered
1989, *Exxon Valdez* Oil Spill

EXPANSION AND LAND
ACQUISITION

1626, Algonquians "Sell" Manhattan
Island
1670, Hudson's Bay Company Is
Chartered
1673, French Explore the Mississippi
Valley
1702, Queen Anne's War
1711, Tuscarora War
1728, Russian Voyages to Alaska
1737, Walking Purchase

1754, French and Indian War
1763, Proclamation of 1763
1763, Paxton Boys' Massacres
1769, Rise of the California Missions
1774, Lord Dunmore's War
1774, Quebec Act
1784, Fort Stanwix Treaty
1785, Ordinance of 1785
1787, Northwest Ordinance
1790, Nootka Sound Convention
1790, Little Turtle's War
1793, Mackenzie Reaches the Arctic
Ocean
1794, Battle of Fallen Timbers
1794, Jay's Treaty
1795, Pinckney's Treaty
1803, Louisiana Purchase
1804, Lewis and Clark Expedition
1806, Pike's Southwest Explorations
1808, American Fur Company Is
Chartered
1810, *Fletcher v. Peck*
1810, Astorian Expeditions
1811, Construction of the National Road
1813, Creek War
1815, Westward Migration
1819, Adams-Onís Treaty
1820, Land Act of 1820
1821, Santa Fe Trail Opens
1823, Jedediah Smith Explores the Far
West
1830, Webster-Hayne Debate
1830, Indian Removal Act
1830, Trail of Tears
1835, Texas Revolution
1840's, "Old" Immigration
1841, Preemption Act
1842, Frémont's Expeditions
1842, Webster-Ashburton Treaty
1846, Mormon Migration to Utah
1846, Mexican War
1846, Oregon Settlement
1846, Occupation of California and the
Southwest
1848, California Gold Rush
1850, Compromise of 1850
1853, Pacific Railroad Surveys
1853, Gadsden Purchase
1858, Fraser River Gold Rush
1862, Homestead Act
1864, Sand Creek Massacre
1866, Chisholm Trail Opens
1867, Purchase of Alaska
1872, Great American Bison Slaughter

1952, Eisenhower Is Elected President
1957, Diefenbaker Era in Canada
1960, Quebec Sovereignist Movement
1960, Kennedy Is Elected President
1961, Peace Corps Is Established
1962, Reapportionment Cases
1963, Pearson Becomes Canada's Prime Minister
1963, Assassination of President Kennedy
1964, Twenty-fourth Amendment
1964, Johnson Is Elected President
1968, Assassinations of King and Kennedy
1968, Trudeau Era in Canada
1968, Chicago Riots
1968, Nixon Is Elected President
1969, Alcatraz Occupation
1972, Rapprochement with China
1972, Watergate Affair
1974, Nixon Resigns
1976, Carter Is Elected President
1979, Clark Elected Canada's Prime Minister
1980, Abscam Affair
1980, Reagan Is Elected President
1982, Canada's Constitution Act
1983, Jackson Becomes First Major African American Candidate for President
1984, Mulroney Era in Canada
1986, Iran-Contra Scandal
1988, Bush Is Elected President
1990, Bloc Québécois Forms
1992, Clinton Is Elected President
1993, Campbell Becomes Canada's First Woman Prime Minister
1994, Republicans Return to Congress

HEALTH AND MEDICINE
1846, Surgical Anesthesia Is Safely Demonstrated
1857, New York Infirmary for Indigent Women and Children Opens
1900, Suppression of Yellow Fever
1912, U.S. Public Health Service Is Established
1921, Sheppard-Towner Act
1952, Development of a Polio Vaccine
1960, FDA Approves the Birth Control Pill
1978, Toxic Waste at Love Canal
1981, First AIDS Cases Are Reported
1982, *Plyler v. Doe*

1989, Human Genome Project
1993, Family and Medical Leave Act

IMMIGRATION
1798, Alien and Sedition Acts
1840's, "Old" Immigration
1844, Anti-Irish Riots
1848, California Gold Rush
1849, Chinese Immigration
1868, Burlingame Treaty
1882, Chinese Exclusion Act
1882, Rise of the Chinese Six Companies
1892, Yellow Peril Campaign
1892, "New" Immigration
1895, Chinese American Citizens Alliance Is Founded
1898, *United States v. Wong Kim Ark*
1907, Gentlemen's Agreement
1913, Anti-Defamation League Is Founded
1917, Immigration Act of 1917
1919, Red Scare
1922, Cable Act
1922, *Ozawa v. United States*
1924, Immigration Act of 1924
1927, Sacco and Vanzetti Are Executed
1930's, Mass Deportations of Mexicans
1942, Bracero Program
1943, Magnuson Act
1945, War Brides Act
1952, McCarran-Walter Act
1953, Refugee Relief Act
1954, Operation Wetback
1965, Immigration and Nationality Act
1978, Canada's Immigration Act of 1976
1980, Mariel Boat Lift
1980, Miami Riots
1982, *Plyler v. Doe*
1986, Immigration Reform and Control Act

JEWISH AMERICAN HISTORY
1654, First Jewish Settlers
1913, Anti-Defamation League Is Founded

LATINO AMERICAN HISTORY
A.D. 200, Mayan Civilization
A.D. 700, Zapotec Civilization
1428, Aztec Empire
1492, Columbus' Voyages
1519, Cortés Enters Tenochtitlán

1528, Narváez's and Cabeza de Vaca's Expeditions
1540, Coronado's Expedition
1542, Settlement of Alta California
1598, Oñate's New Mexico Expedition
1632, Zuñi Rebellion
1810, El Grito de Dolores
1819, Adams-Onís Treaty
1821, Mexican War of Independence
1823, Monroe Doctrine
1835, Texas Revolution
1839, Amistad Slave Revolt
1846, Mexican War
1846, Occupation of California and the Southwest
1848, Treaty of Guadalupe Hidalgo
1850, Bloody Island Massacre
1853, Gadsden Purchase
1857, Cart War
1877, Salt Wars
1889, First Pan-American Congress
1895, Hearst-Pulitzer Circulation War
1898, Spanish-American War
1903, Platt Amendment
1910, Mexican Revolution
1912, Intervention in Nicaragua
1916, Pershing Expedition
1917, Jones Act
1929, League of United Latin American Citizens Is Founded
1930's, Mass Deportations of Mexicans
1933, Good Neighbor Policy
1942, Bracero Program
1948, Organization of American States Is Founded
1952, Puerto Rico Becomes a Commonwealth
1954, Operation Wetback
1956, Cuban Revolution
1962, Cuban Missile Crisis
1965, Delano Grape Strike
1968, Bilingual Education Act
1972, United Farm Workers Joins with AFL-CIO
1974, *Lau v. Nichols*
1978, Panama Canal Treaties
1980, Mariel Boat Lift
1980, Miami Riots
1983, United States Invades Grenada

LAWS AND ACTS
1641, Massachusetts Recognizes Slavery
1649, Maryland Act of Toleration
1660, British Navigation Acts

NATIVE AMERICAN HISTORY

1790, Little Turtle's War
1793, Mackenzie Reaches the Arctic Ocean
1794, Battle of Fallen Timbers
1799, Code of Handsome Lake
1808, Prophetstown Is Founded
1810, *Fletcher v. Peck*
1812, War of 1812
1813, Creek War
1813, Battle of the Thames
1815, Westward Migration
1815, Treaty of Ghent
1815, Red River Raids
1817, Seminole Wars
1821, Santa Fe Trail Opens
1828, *Cherokee Phoenix* Begins Publication
1830, Indian Removal Act
1830, Trail of Tears
1831, Cherokee Cases
1837, Rebellions in Canada
1847, Taos Rebellion
1861, Stand Watie Fights for the South
1861, Apache Wars
1862, Great Sioux War
1863, Long Walk of the Navajos
1864, Sand Creek Massacre
1866, Bozeman Trail War
1867, Medicine Lodge Creek Treaty
1868, Washita River Massacre
1869, First Riel Rebellion
1871, Indian Appropriation Act
1872, Great American Bison Slaughter
1874, Red River War
1876, Canada's Indian Act
1876, Battle of the Little Bighorn
1877, Nez Perce Exile
1885, Second Riel Rebellion
1887, General Allotment Act
1890, Closing of the Frontier
1890, Battle of Wounded Knee
1903, *Lone Wolf v. Hitchcock*
1924, Indian Citizenship Act
1934, Indian Reorganization Act
1953, Termination Resolution
1959, Alaska and Hawaii Gain Statehood
1965, Voting Rights Act
1968, Indian Civil Rights Act
1969, Alcatraz Occupation
1971, Alaska Native Claims Settlement Act
1972, Trail of Broken Treaties
1973, Wounded Knee Occupation

1978, American Indian Religious Freedom Act
1988, Indian Gaming Regulatory Act

ORGANIZATIONS AND INSTITUTIONS

1627, Company of New France Is Chartered
1650, Harvard College Is Established
1670, Hudson's Bay Company Is Chartered
1768, Methodist Church Is Established
1775, Pennsylvania Society for the Abolition of Slavery Is Founded
1784, Hall's Masonic Lodge Is Chartered
1785, Beginnings of State Universities
1787, Free African Society Is Founded
1789, Episcopal Church Is Established
1790's, First U.S. Political Parties
1802, U.S. Military Academy Is Established
1816, Second Bank of the United States Is Chartered
1816, AME Church Is Founded
1819, Unitarian Church Is Founded
1823, Hartford Female Seminary Is Founded
1833, American Anti-Slavery Society Is Founded
1833, Oberlin College Is Established
1834, Birth of the Whig Party
1837, Mt. Holyoke Seminary Is Founded
1846, Independent Treasury Is Established
1846, Smithsonian Institution Is Founded
1853, National Council of Colored People Is Founded
1854, Birth of the Republican Party
1857, New York Infirmary for Indigent Women and Children Opens
1865, Freedmen's Bureau Is Established
1866, Rise of the Ku Klux Klan
1867, Office of Education Is Created
1867, National Grange of the Patrons of Husbandry Forms
1869, Rise of Woman Suffrage Associations
1871, Barnum's Circus Forms
1875, Supreme Court of Canada Is Established
1886, American Federation of Labor Is Founded

1889, Hull House Opens
1890, Women's Rights Associations Unite
1895, Chinese American Citizens Alliance Is Founded
1905, Industrial Workers of the World Is Founded
1905, Niagara Movement
1913, Anti-Defamation League Is Founded
1916, National Woman's Party Is Founded
1916, National Park Service Is Created
1917, Universal Negro Improvement Association Is Established
1918, Republican Resurgence
1919, Black Sox Scandal
1920, League of Women Voters Is Founded
1929, League of United Latin American Citizens Is Founded
1930, Nation of Islam Is Founded
1930, Japanese American Citizens League Is Founded
1935, Works Progress Administration Is Established
1935, Congress of Industrial Organizations Is Founded
1942, Congress of Racial Equality Is Founded
1955, AFL and CIO Merge
1957, Southern Christian Leadership Conference Is Founded
1960, Quebec Sovereignist Movement
1966, National Organization for Women Is Founded
1968, Chicago Riots

PREHISTORY AND ANCIENT CULTURES

15,000 B.C., Bering Strait Migrations
1500 B.C., Olmec Civilization
700 B.C., Ohio Mound Builders
300 B.C., Hohokam Culture
A.D. 200, Mayan Civilization
A.D. 200, Anasazi Civilization
A.D. 700, Zapotec Civilization
A.D. 750, Mogollon Culture
A.D. 750, Mississippian Culture
1428, Aztec Empire

RELIGION

1620, Pilgrims Land at Plymouth
1630, Great Puritan Migration
1632, Settlement of Connecticut

1636, Rhode Island Is Founded
1649, Maryland Act of Toleration
1654, First Jewish Settlers
1662, Half-Way Covenant
1681, Pennsylvania Is Founded
1692, Salem Witchcraft Trials
1730's, First Great Awakening
1768, Methodist Church Is Established
1769, Rise of the California Missions
1773, African American Baptist Church Is Founded
1774, Quebec Act
1786, Virginia Statute of Religious Liberty
1789, Episcopal Church Is Established
1790's, Second Great Awakening
1799, Code of Handsome Lake
1816, AME Church Is Founded
1819, Unitarian Church Is Founded
1820's, Social Reform Movement
1836, Rise of Transcendentalism
1844, Anti-Irish Riots
1846, Mormon Migration to Utah
1930, Nation of Islam Is Founded
1963, *Abington School District v. Schempp*
1978, American Indian Religious Freedom Act
1993, Branch Davidians' Compound Burns

SCIENCE AND TECHNOLOGY

1776, First Test of a Submarine in Warfare
1790, Slater's Spinning Mill
1793, Whitney Invents the Cotton Gin
1807, Voyage of the *Clermont*
1825, Erie Canal Opens
1831, McCormick Invents the Reaper
1836, Rise of Transcendentalism
1844, First Telegraph Message
1845, Era of the Clipper Ships
1846, Howe's Sewing Machine
1846, Smithsonian Institution Is Founded
1846, Surgical Anesthesia Is Safely Demonstrated
1858, First Transatlantic Cable
1859, First Commercial Oil Well
1861, Transcontinental Telegraph Is Completed
1862, *Monitor* vs. *Virginia*
1869, Transcontinental Railroad Is Completed
1876, Bell Demonstrates the Telephone

1879, Edison Demonstrates the Incandescent Lamp
1883, Brooklyn Bridge Opens
1893, World's Columbian Exposition
1900, Teletype Is Developed
1903, Acquisition of the Panama Canal Zone
1903, Wright Brothers' First Flight
1913, Ford Assembly Line Begins Operation
1920, Commercial Radio Broadcasting Begins
1926, Launching of the First Liquid-Fueled Rocket
1927, Lindbergh's Transatlantic Flight
1930, Baltimore and Ohio Railroad Begins Operation
1931, Empire State Building Opens
1934, Development of Radar
1938, First Xerographic Photocopy
1939, Debut of Commercial Television
1942, Manhattan Project
1945, Atomic Bombing of Japan
1947, Invention of the Transistor
1952, Development of a Polio Vaccine
1952, Hydrogen Bomb Is Detonated
1959, St. Lawrence Seaway Opens
1960, FDA Approves the Birth Control Pill
1961, First American in Space
1969, Apollo 11 Lands on the Moon
1974, Construction of the Alaska Pipeline
1977, Spaceflights of Voyagers 1 and 2
1978, Toxic Waste at Love Canal
1981, IBM Markets the Personal Computer
1981, Ozone Hole Is Discovered
1986, *Challenger* Accident
1989, Human Genome Project
1990's, Rise of the Internet
1993, Astronauts Repair the Hubble Space Telescope

SETTLEMENTS

1565, St. Augustine Is Founded
1584, Lost Colony of Roanoke
1603, Champlain's Voyages
1607, Jamestown Is Founded
1620, Pilgrims Land at Plymouth
1626, Algonquians "Sell" Manhattan Island
1630, Great Puritan Migration
1632, Settlement of Connecticut

1636, Rhode Island Is Founded
1663, Settlement of the Carolinas
1670, Charles Town Is Founded
1681, Pennsylvania Is Founded
1732, Settlement of Georgia
1808, Prophetstown Is Founded
1814, New Harmony and the Communitarian Movement
1846, Mormon Migration to Utah
1846, Oregon Settlement
1848, California Gold Rush
1858, Fraser River Gold Rush

SOCIAL REFORM

1730's, First Great Awakening
1775, Pennsylvania Society for the Abolition of Slavery Is Founded
1777, Northeast States Abolish Slavery
1787, Free African Society Is Founded
1790's, Second Great Awakening
1808, Prophetstown Is Founded
1814, New Harmony and the Communitarian Movement
1819, Unitarian Church Is Founded
1820's, Social Reform Movement
1828, *Cherokee Phoenix* Begins Publication
1831, *The Liberator* Begins Publication
1833, American Anti-Slavery Society Is Founded
1850, Underground Railroad
1851, Akron Woman's Rights Convention
1857, New York Infirmary for Indigent Women and Children Opens
1867, National Grange of the Patrons of Husbandry Forms
1889, Hull House Opens
1920, Prohibition
1921, Sheppard-Towner Act
1935, Social Security Act
1935, Congress of Industrial Organizations Is Founded
1938, Fair Labor Standards Act
1941, 6.6 Million Women Enter the U.S. Labor Force
1955, Montgomery Bus Boycott
1960, FDA Approves the Birth Control Pill
1963, King Delivers His "I Have a Dream" Speech
1965, Expansion of Affirmative Action
1988, Family Support Act
1993, Family and Medical Leave Act

TRANSPORTATION

1807, Voyage of the *Clermont*
1811, Construction of the National Road
1815, Westward Migration
1821, Santa Fe Trail Opens
1823, Jedediah Smith Explores the Far West
1825, Erie Canal Opens
1845, Era of the Clipper Ships
1853, Pacific Railroad Surveys
1860, Pony Express
1866, Chisholm Trail Opens
1869, Transcontinental Railroad Is Completed
1887, Interstate Commerce Act
1903, Acquisition of the Panama Canal Zone
1903, Wright Brothers' First Flight
1913, Ford Assembly Line Begins Operation
1927, Lindbergh's Transatlantic Flight
1930, Baltimore and Ohio Railroad Begins Operation
1959, St. Lawrence Seaway Opens
1973, Arab Oil Embargo and Energy Crisis
1978, Panama Canal Treaties

TREATIES AND AGREEMENTS

1778, Franco-American Treaties
1783, Treaty of Paris
1784, Fort Stanwix Treaty
1790, Nootka Sound Convention
1794, Jay's Treaty
1795, Pinckney's Treaty
1803, Louisiana Purchase
1815, Treaty of Ghent
1819, Adams-Onís Treaty
1842, Webster-Ashburton Treaty
1848, Treaty of Guadalupe Hidalgo
1853, Gadsden Purchase
1867, Purchase of Alaska
1867, Medicine Lodge Creek Treaty
1868, Burlingame Treaty
1871, Treaty of Washington
1907, Gentlemen's Agreement
1919, Treaty of Versailles
1921, Washington Disarmament Conference
1924, Halibut Treaty
1928, Kellogg-Briand Pact
1932, Ottawa Agreements
1936, Reciprocity Treaty
1940, Ogdensburg Agreement
1942, Bracero Program

1948, Organization of American States Is Founded
1949, North Atlantic Treaty
1978, Panama Canal Treaties
1979, SALT II Is Signed
1987, INF Treaty Is Signed
1993, START II Is Signed
1993, North American Free Trade Agreement
1994, U.S.-North Korea Pact
1994, General Agreement on Tariffs and Trade

WARS, UPRISINGS, AND CIVIL UNREST

1495, West Indian Uprisings
1598, Oñate's New Mexico Expedition
1622, Powhatan Wars
1632, Zuñi Rebellion
1636, Pequot War
1642, Beaver Wars
1664, British Conquest of New Netherland
1675, Metacom's War
1676, Bacon's Rebellion
1680, Pueblo Revolt
1702, Queen Anne's War
1711, Tuscarora War
1712, New York City Slave Revolt
1714, Fox Wars
1739, Stono Rebellion
1739, King George's War
1754, French and Indian War
1759, Cherokee War
1763, Pontiac's Resistance
1763, Paxton Boys' Massacres
1765, Stamp Act Crisis
1767, Townshend Crisis
1768, Carolina Regulator Movements
1770, Boston Massacre
1773, Boston Tea Party
1774, Lord Dunmore's War
1775, Battle of Lexington and Concord
1775, Second Continental Congress
1776, Indian Delegation Meets with Congress
1776, First Test of a Submarine in Warfare
1777, Battle of Oriskany Creek
1777, Battle of Saratoga
1781, Cornwallis Surrenders at Yorktown
1790, Little Turtle's War
1791, Haitian Independence
1793, Whiskey Rebellion

1794, Battle of Fallen Timbers
1797, XYZ Affair
1804, Burr's Conspiracy
1810, El Grito de Dolores
1811, Battle of Tippecanoe
1812, War of 1812
1813, Creek War
1813, Battle of the Thames
1815, Battle of New Orleans
1815, Red River Raids
1817, Seminole Wars
1821, Mexican War of Independence
1831, Nat Turner's Insurrection
1835, Texas Revolution
1837, Rebellions in Canada
1839, Amistad Slave Revolt
1842, Dorr Rebellion
1844, Anti-Irish Riots
1846, Mexican War
1846, Occupation of California and the Southwest
1847, Taos Rebellion
1850, Bloody Island Massacre
1857, Cart War
1859, John Brown's Raid on Harpers Ferry
1860, Confederate States Secede from the Union
1861, Stand Watie Fights for the South
1861, Apache Wars
1861, First Battle of Bull Run
1862, *Monitor* vs. *Virginia*
1862, Great Sioux War
1863, First National Draft Law
1863, Battles of Gettysburg, Vicksburg, and Chattanooga
1864, Sherman's March to the Sea
1864, Sand Creek Massacre
1865, Surrender at Appomattox and Assassination of Lincoln
1866, Race Riots in the South
1866, Bozeman Trail War
1868, Washita River Massacre
1869, First Riel Rebellion
1874, Red River War
1876, Battle of the Little Bighorn
1877, Nez Perce Exile
1877, Salt Wars
1885, Second Riel Rebellion
1890, Battle of Wounded Knee
1898, Spanish-American War
1899, Philippine Insurrection
1910, Mexican Revolution
1912, Intervention in Nicaragua
1916, Pershing Expedition

TIME LINE

Date	Event	Date	Event
15,000 B.C.	Bering Strait Migrations	Apr., 1670	Charles Town Is Founded
1500-300 B.C.	Olmec Civilization	May 2, 1670	Hudson's Bay Company Is Chartered
700 B.C.-A.D. 500	Ohio Mound Builders	1671-1730	Indian Slave Trade
300 B.C.-A.D. 1400	Hohokam Culture	1673-1740's	French Explore the Mississippi Valley
A.D. 200-900	Mayan Civilization	Jun. 20, 1675	Metacom's War
A.D. 200-1250	Anasazi Civilization	May 10, 1676-Oct. 18, 1676	Bacon's Rebellion
A.D. 700-900	Zapotec Civilization	Aug. 10, 1680	Pueblo Revolt
A.D. 750-1250	Mogollon Culture	Mar. 4, 1681	Pennsylvania Is Founded
A.D. 750-1500	Mississippian Culture	Jun., 1686-Apr., 1689	Dominion of New England Forms
A.D. 986-1008	Norse Expeditions	Jun. 2, 1692-May, 1693	Salem Witchcraft Trials
1428-1521	Aztec Empire	May 15, 1702-Apr. 11, 1713	Queen Anne's War
Oct. 12, 1492-1504	Columbus' Voyages	Sep. 22, 1711-Mar. 23, 1713	Tuscarora War
1495-c. 1510	West Indian Uprisings	Apr. 6, 1712	New York City Slave Revolt
Jun. 24, 1497-May, 1498	Cabot's Voyages	Summer, 1714-1741	Fox Wars
c. 1500-1777	Iroquois Confederacy	Jul., 1728-1769	Russian Voyages to Alaska
Mar. 3, 1513-Feb., 1521	Ponce de León's Voyages	1730's-1760	First Great Awakening
Nov. 8, 1519	Cortés Enters Tenochtitlán	Jun. 20, 1732	Settlement of Georgia
Apr. 12, 1528-Apr., 1536	Narváez's and Cabeza de Vaca's Expeditions	Aug. 4, 1734	Trial of John Peter Zenger
		Sep. 19, 1737	Walking Purchase
Apr. 20, 1534-Jul., 1543	Cartier and Roberval Search for a Northwest Passage	Sep. 9, 1739	Stono Rebellion
		Oct. 19, 1739-Oct. 18, 1748	King George's War
May 28, 1539-Sep. 10, 1543	De Soto's Expeditions	May 28, 1754-Feb. 10, 1763	French and Indian War
Feb. 23, 1540-c. Oct. 13, 1542	Coronado's Expedition	Jun. 19, 1754-Jul. 10, 1754	Albany Congress
Jun. 27, 1542-Apr. 21, 1782	Settlement of Alta California	Oct. 5, 1759-Nov. 19, 1761	Cherokee War
Sep. 8, 1565	St. Augustine Is Founded	May 8, 1763-Jul. 24, 1766	Pontiac's Resistance
1570's-1644	Powhatan Confederacy	Oct. 7, 1763	Proclamation of 1763
Jun. 7, 1576-Jul., 1578	Frobisher's Voyages	Dec. 14, 1763-Dec. 27, 1763	Paxton Boys' Massacres
Jun. 17, 1579	Drake Lands in Northern California	Mar. 22, 1765-1766	Stamp Act Crisis
Jul. 4, 1584-Aug. 17, 1590	Lost Colony of Roanoke	Jun. 29, 1767-Apr. 12, 1770	Townshend Crisis
Jan., 1598-Feb., 1599	Oñate's New Mexico Expedition	1768-May 16, 1771	Carolina Regulator Movements
Mar. 15, 1603-Dec. 25, 1635	Champlain's Voyages	Oct. 30, 1768	Methodist Church Is Established
May 14, 1607	Jamestown Is Founded	Jul. 17, 1769-1824	Rise of the California Missions
Jun., 1610	Hudson Explores Hudson Bay	Mar. 5, 1770	Boston Massacre
Jul. 30, 1619-Aug. 4, 1619	First General Assembly of Virginia	1773-1788	African American Baptist Church Is Founded
Aug. 20, 1619	Africans Arrive in Virginia		
Dec. 16, 1620	Pilgrims Land at Plymouth	Dec. 16, 1773	Boston Tea Party
Mar. 22, 1622-Oct., 1646	Powhatan Wars	Apr. 27, 1774-Oct. 10, 1774	Lord Dunmore's War
May 6, 1626	Algonquians "Sell" Manhattan Island	May 20, 1774	Quebec Act
Apr. 27, 1627	Company of New France Is Chartered	Sep. 5, 1774-Oct. 26, 1774	First Continental Congress
May, 1630-1643	Great Puritan Migration	Apr. 14, 1775	Pennsylvania Society for the Abolition of Slavery Is Founded
Feb. 22, 1632-Feb. 27, 1632	Zuñi Rebellion		
Fall, 1632-Jan. 5, 1665	Settlement of Connecticut	Apr. 19, 1775	Battle of Lexington and Concord
Jun., 1636	Rhode Island Is Founded	May 10, 1775-Aug. 2, 1775	Second Continental Congress
Jul. 20, 1636-Jul. 28, 1637	Pequot War	May 24 *and* Jun. 11, 1776	Indian Delegation Meets with Congress
Nov., 1641	Massachusetts Recognizes Slavery		
1642-1685	Beaver Wars	Jul. 2, 1776	New Jersey Women Gain the Vote
Sep. 8, 1643	Confederation of the United Colonies of New England	Jul. 4, 1776	Declaration of Independence
		Sep. 6, 1776-Sep. 7, 1776	First Test of a Submarine in Warfare
Apr. 21, 1649	Maryland Act of Toleration	Jul. 2, 1777-1804	Northeast States Abolish Slavery
May 30, 1650-May 31, 1650	Harvard College Is Established	Aug. 6, 1777	Battle of Oriskany Creek
Aug., 1654-Sep., 1654	First Jewish Settlers	Oct. 8, 1777-Oct. 17, 1777	Battle of Saratoga
Sep. 13, 1660-Jul. 27, 1663	British Navigation Acts	Feb. 6, 1778	Franco-American Treaties
Mar., 1661-1705	Virginia Slave Codes	Mar. 1, 1781	Articles of Confederation
1662	Half-Way Covenant	Oct. 19, 1781	Cornwallis Surrenders at Yorktown
Mar. 24, 1663-Jul. 25, 1729	Settlement of the Carolinas	Sep. 3, 1783	Treaty of Paris
Mar. 22, 1664-Jul. 21, 1667	British Conquest of New Netherland	Sep. 29, 1784	Hall's Masonic Lodge Is Chartered

Date	Event	Date	Event
Oct. 22, 1784	Fort Stanwix Treaty	Jun., 1815-Aug., 1817	Red River Raids
1785	Beginnings of State Universities	Apr., 1816	Second Bank of the United States Is Chartered
May 20, 1785	Ordinance of 1785		
Jan. 16, 1786	Virginia Statute of Religious Liberty	Apr. 9, 1816	AME Church Is Founded
Apr. 12, 1787	Free African Society Is Founded	Nov. 21, 1817-Mar. 27, 1858	Seminole Wars
Jul. 13, 1787	Northwest Ordinance	1819	Unitarian Church Is Founded
Sep. 17, 1787	U.S. Constitution Is Adopted	Feb. 22, 1819	Adams-Onís Treaty
Oct. 27, 1787-May, 1788	*Federalist* Papers Are Published	Mar. 6, 1819	*McCulloch v. Maryland*
Apr. 30, 1789	Washington's Inauguration	1820's-1830's	Free Public School Movement
Jul. 28, 1789-Oct. 16, 1789	Episcopal Church Is Established	1820's-1850's	Social Reform Movement
Sep. 24, 1789	Judiciary Act	Mar. 3, 1820	Missouri Compromise
1790's	First U.S. Political Parties	Apr. 24, 1820	Land Act of 1820
1790's-1830's	Second Great Awakening	Aug. 24, 1821-Sep. 28, 1821	Mexican War of Independence
Jan., 1790	Hamilton's *Report on Public Credit*	Sep., 1821	Santa Fe Trail Opens
Oct., 1790	Nootka Sound Convention	1823	Hartford Female Seminary Is Founded
Oct. 18, 1790-Jul., 1794	Little Turtle's War	Sep., 1823-1831	Jedediah Smith Explores the Far West
Dec. 20, 1790	Slater's Spinning Mill	Dec. 2, 1823	Monroe Doctrine
1791	Canada's Constitutional Act	Mar. 2, 1824	*Gibbons v. Ogden*
Aug. 22, 1791-Jan. 1, 1804	Haitian Independence	Dec. 1, 1824-Feb. 9, 1825	U.S. Election of 1824
Dec. 15, 1791	U.S. Bill of Rights Is Ratified	Oct. 26, 1825	Erie Canal Opens
1793	Whitney Invents the Cotton Gin	Feb. 21, 1828	*Cherokee Phoenix* Begins Publication
Feb. 12, 1793	First Fugitive Slave Law	Nov., 1828	Webster's *American Dictionary of the English Language*
Jul. 22, 1793	Mackenzie Reaches the Arctic Ocean		
Jul., 1794-Nov., 1794	Whiskey Rebellion	Dec. 3, 1828	Jackson Is Elected President
Aug. 20, 1794	Battle of Fallen Timbers	1830-1865	Proslavery Argument
Nov. 19, 1794	Jay's Treaty	Jan. 7, 1830	Baltimore and Ohio Railroad Begins Operation
Oct. 27, 1795	Pinckney's Treaty		
Sep. 19, 1796	Washington's Farewell Address	Jan. 19, 1830-Jan. 27, 1830	Webster-Hayne Debate
Oct. 4, 1797-Sep. 30, 1800	XYZ Affair	May 28, 1830	Indian Removal Act
Jun. 25, 1798-Jul. 14, 1798	Alien and Sedition Acts	May 28, 1830-1842	Trail of Tears
1799	Code of Handsome Lake	Jan. 1, 1831	*The Liberator* Begins Publication
Feb. 17, 1801	Jefferson Is Elected President	Mar. 18, 1831 *and* Mar. 3, 1832	Cherokee Cases
Mar. 16, 1802	U.S. Military Academy Is Established		
Feb. 24, 1803	*Marbury v. Madison*	May 11, 1831-Feb. 20, 1832	Tocqueville Visits America
May 9, 1803	Louisiana Purchase	Summer, 1831	McCormick Invents the Reaper
Jan., 1804-Jan., 1807	First Black Codes	Aug. 21, 1831	Nat Turner's Insurrection
May 14, 1804-Sep. 23, 1806	Lewis and Clark Expedition	Jul. 10, 1832	Jackson vs. the Bank of the United States
Jul. 11, 1804-Sep. 1, 1807	Burr's Conspiracy		
Sep. 25, 1804	Twelfth Amendment	Nov. 24, 1832-Jan. 21, 1833	Nullification Controversy
Jul. 15, 1806-Jul. 1, 1807	Pike's Southwest Explorations	Sep. 3, 1833	Rise of the Penny Press
Mar. 2, 1807	Congress Bans Importation of African Slaves	Dec., 1833	American Anti-Slavery Society Is Founded
		Dec. 3, 1833	Oberlin College Is Established
Aug. 17, 1807	Voyage of the *Clermont*	Apr. 14, 1834	Birth of the Whig Party
Apr., 1808	Prophetstown Is Founded	Jun. 30, 1835-Oct. 22, 1836	Texas Revolution
Apr. 6, 1808	American Fur Company Is Chartered	1836	Rise of Transcendentalism
Mar. 16, 1810	*Fletcher v. Peck*	Oct. 23, 1837-Dec. 16, 1837	Rebellions in Canada
Sep. 8, 1810-May, 1812	Astorian Expeditions	Nov. 8, 1837	Mt. Holyoke Seminary Is Founded
Sep. 16, 1810	El Grito de Delores	Jul. 1, 1839	Amistad Slave Revolt
1811	Construction of the National Road	1840's-1850's	"Old" Immigration
Nov. 7, 1811	Battle of Tippecanoe	Dec. 2, 1840	U.S. Election of 1840
Jun. 18, 1812-Dec. 24, 1814	War of 1812	1841	Upper and Lower Canada Unite
Jul. 27, 1813-Aug. 9, 1814	Creek War	Sep. 4, 1841	Preemption Act
Oct. 5, 1813	Battle of the Thames	1842	*Commonwealth v. Hunt*
Spring, 1814-1830	New Harmony and the Communitarian Movement	May, 1842-1854	Frémont's Expeditions
		May 18, 1842	Dorr Rebellion
Dec. 15, 1814-Jan. 5, 1815	Hartford Convention	Aug. 9, 1842	Webster-Ashburton Treaty
1815	Westward Migration	May 6, 1844-Jul. 5, 1844	Anti-Irish Riots
Jan. 8, 1815	Battle of New Orleans	May 24, 1844	First Telegraph Message
Feb. 17, 1815	Treaty of Ghent		

Date	Event	Date	Event
1845-1857	Era of the Clipper Ships	Jul. 1, 1863-Nov. 25, 1863	Battles of Gettysburg, Vicksburg, and Chattanooga
1846	Howe's Sewing Machine		
Feb. 4, 1846-Sep., 1848	Mormon Migration to Utah	Aug., 1863-Sep., 1866	Long Walk of the Navajos
May 13, 1846-Mar. 10, 1848	Mexican War	Dec. 8, 1863-Apr. 24, 1877	Reconstruction
Jun. 15, 1846	Oregon Settlement	Nov. 15, 1864-Apr. 18, 1865	Sherman's March to the Sea
Jun. 30, 1846-Jan. 13, 1847	Occupation of California and the Southwest	Nov. 29, 1864	Sand Creek Massacre
		Mar. 3, 1865	Freedmen's Bureau Is Established
Aug. 6, 1846	Independent Treasury Is Established	Apr. 9 *and* Apr. 14, 1865	Surrender at Appomattox and Assassination of Lincoln
Aug. 10, 1846	Smithsonian Institution Is Founded		
Oct. 16, 1846	Surgical Anesthesia Is Safely Demonstrated	Sep. 26, 1865	Vassar College Is Founded
		Nov. 24, 1865	New Black Codes
Jan. 19, 1847	Taos Rebellion	Dec. 18, 1865	Thirteenth Amendment
Dec. 3, 1847	*The North Star* Begins Publication	1866	Chisholm Trail Opens
Jan. 24, 1848-Sep. 4, 1849	California Gold Rush	1866	Rise of the Ku Klux Klan
Feb. 2, 1848	Treaty of Guadalupe Hidalgo	Apr. 9, 1866	Civil Rights Act of 1866
Jul. 19, 1848-Jul. 20, 1848	Seneca Falls Convention	May *and* July, 1866	Race Riots in the South
1849-1852	Chinese Immigration	May 10, 1866	Suffragists Protest the Fourteenth Amendment
Jan. 29, 1850-Sep. 20, 1850	Compromise of 1850		
May 6, 1850	Bloody Island Massacre	Jun. 13, 1866-Nov. 6, 1868	Bozeman Trail War
Sep. 18, 1850	Second Fugitive Slave Law	Mar. 2, 1867	Office of Education Is Created
1850-1860	Underground Railroad	Mar. 30, 1867	Purchase of Alaska
May 28, 1851-May 29, 1851	Akron Woman's Rights Convention	Jul. 1, 1867	British North America Act
Mar. 2, 1853-1857	Pacific Railroad Surveys	Oct. 21, 1867	Medicine Lodge Creek Treaty
Jul. 6, 1853	National Council of Colored People Is Founded	Dec. 4, 1867	National Grange of the Patrons of Husbandry Forms
Dec. 31, 1853	Gadsden Purchase	Feb. 24, 1868-May 26, 1868	Impeachment of Andrew Johnson
Mar. 31, 1854	Perry Opens Trade with Japan	Jul. 28, 1868	Burlingame Treaty
May 30, 1854	Kansas-Nebraska Act	Jul. 28, 1868	Fourteenth Amendment
Jul. 6, 1854	Birth of the Republican Party	Nov. 27, 1868	Washita River Massacre
May 21, 1856-Aug. 2, 1858	Bleeding Kansas	May, 1869	Rise of Woman Suffrage Associations
Jan. 1, 1857	First African American University	May 10, 1869	Transcontinental Railroad Is Completed
Mar. 6, 1857	*Dred Scott v. Sandford*		
May 12, 1857	New York Infirmary for Indigent Women and Children Opens	Sep. 24, 1869-1877	Scandals of the Grant Administration
		Oct. 11, 1869-Jul. 15, 1870	First Riel Rebellion
Aug., 1857-Dec., 1857	Cart War	Dec., 1869	Western States Grant Woman Suffrage
Spring, 1858	Fraser River Gold Rush	Mar. 3, 1871	Indian Appropriation Act
Jun. 16, 1858-Oct., 1858	Lincoln-Douglas Debates	Apr. 10, 1871	Barnum's Circus Forms
Aug. 4, 1858-Jul. 27, 1866	First Transatlantic Cable	May 8, 1871	Treaty of Washington
Jul., 1859	Last Slave Ship Docks at Mobile	1872-1874	Great American Bison Slaughter
Aug. 27, 1859	First Commercial Oil Well	Nov. 5, 1872	Susan B. Anthony Is Arrested
Oct. 16, 1859-Oct. 18, 1859	John Brown's Raid on Harpers Ferry	Feb. 12, 1873	"Crime of 1873"
Apr. 3, 1860-Oct. 26, 1861	Pony Express	Nov. 5, 1873-Oct. 9, 1878	Mackenzie Era in Canada
Nov. 6, 1860	Lincoln Is Elected President	Jun., 1874-Jun., 1875	Red River War
Dec. 20, 1860	Confederate States Secede from the Union	Oct., 1874	*Minor v. Happersett*
		1875	Supreme Court of Canada Is Established
1861-1865	Stand Watie Fights for the South		
Feb. 6, 1861-Sep. 4, 1886	Apache Wars	Feb. 10, 1875	Page Law
Mar. 4, 1861	Lincoln's Inauguration	1876	Canada's Indian Act
Jul. 21, 1861	First Battle of Bull Run	Mar. 10, 1876	Bell Demonstrates the Telephone
Oct. 24, 1861	Transcontinental Telegraph Is Completed	Jun. 25, 1876	Battle of the Little Bighorn
		Jul. 4, 1876	Declaration of the Rights of Women
Mar. 9, 1862	*Monitor* vs. *Virginia*	Mar. 2, 1877	Hayes Is Elected President
May 20, 1862	Homestead Act	Jun. 15, 1877-Oct. 5, 1877	Nez Perce Exile
Jul. 2, 1862	Morrill Land Grant Act	Sep. 10, 1877-Dec. 17, 1877	Salt Wars
Aug. 17, 1862	Great Sioux War	1878	Macdonald Returns as Canada's Prime Minister
Jan. 1, 1863	Emancipation Proclamation		
Feb. 25, 1863-Jun. 3, 1864	National Bank Acts	1879	Powell's *Report on the Lands of the Arid Region*
Mar. 3, 1863	First National Draft Law		

Date	Event	Date	Event
Oct. 21, 1879	Edison Demonstrates the Incandescent Lamp	May 13, 1908	White House Conservation Conference
Jan. 2, 1882	Standard Oil Trust Is Organized	1909-1913	Dollar Diplomacy
May 9, 1882	Chinese Exclusion Act	Feb. 12, 1909	National Association for the Advancement of Colored People Is Founded
Nov. 12, 1882	Rise of the Chinese Six Companies		
Jan. 16, 1883	Pendleton Act		
May 24, 1883	Brooklyn Bridge Opens	Mar., 1909-1912	Republican Congressional Insurgency
Oct. 15, 1883	Civil Rights Cases	Apr. 6, 1909	Peary and Henson Reach the North Pole
Nov. 4, 1884	U.S. Election of 1884		
Mar. 19, 1885	Second Riel Rebellion	Oct., 1910-Dec. 1, 1920	Mexican Revolution
Dec. 8, 1886	American Federation of Labor Is Founded	1910-1930	Great Northern Migration
		1911-1920	Borden Government in Canada
Feb. 4, 1887	Interstate Commerce Act	Mar. 25, 1911	Triangle Shirtwaist Company Fire
Feb. 8, 1887	General Allotment Act	1912	U.S. Public Health Service Is Established
Sep. 18, 1889	Hull House Opens		
Oct., 1889-Apr., 1890	First Pan-American Congress	Aug. 4, 1912-Nov., 1912	Intervention in Nicaragua
1890	Closing of the Frontier	Nov. 5, 1912	Wilson Is Elected President
Feb. 17, 1890-Feb. 18, 1890	Women's Rights Associations Unite	Feb. 17, 1913	Armory Show
Jul. 20, 1890	Sherman Antitrust Act	Feb. 25, 1913	Sixteenth Amendment
Aug., 1890	Mississippi Disfranchisement Laws	Mar. 1, 1913	Ford Assembly Line Begins Operation
Dec. 29, 1890	Battle of Wounded Knee	May 20, 1913	Alien Land Laws
Jan. 1, 1892-1943	"New" Immigration	Sep., 1913	Anti-Defamation League Is Founded
May 4, 1892	Yellow Peril Campaign	Dec. 23, 1913	Federal Reserve Act
Jul. 4, 1892-Jul. 5, 1892	Birth of the People's Party	1915-1919	National Birth Control League Forms
May 1, 1893-Oct. 30, 1893	World's Columbian Exposition	1916	National Woman's Party Is Founded
Jun. 26, 1894-Jul. 11, 1894	Pullman Strike	Mar. 15, 1916-Feb. 5, 1917	Pershing Expedition
1895-1898	Hearst-Pulitzer Circulation War	Aug. 25, 1916	National Park Service Is Created
May 21, 1895	Chinese American Citizens Alliance Is Founded	Feb. 5, 1917	Immigration Act of 1917
		Mar. 2, 1917	Jones Act
Sep. 18, 1895	Booker T. Washington's Atlanta Exposition Address	Apr. 6, 1917	United States Enters World War I
		Apr. 13, 1917	Propaganda and Civil Liberties in World War I
May 18, 1896	*Plessy v. Ferguson*		
Aug. 17, 1896	Klondike Gold Rush	May, 1917	Universal Negro Improvement Association Is Established
Nov. 3, 1896	McKinley Is Elected President		
1897-Sep. 21, 1911	Laurier Era in Canada	Jun. 15, 1917-May 16, 1918	Espionage and Sedition Acts
Jul. 24, 1897	Dingley Tariff	Jul. 8, 1917	Mobilization for World War I
Nov. 1, 1897	Library of Congress Building Opens	Sep. 20, 1917	Canadian Women Gain the Vote
Mar. 28, 1898	*United States v. Wong Kim Ark*	Sep. 26, 1918-Nov. 11, 1918	Meuse-Argonne Offensive
Apr. 24, 1898-Dec. 10, 1898	Spanish-American War	Nov., 1918-Jun., 1920	Demobilization After World War I
Feb. 4, 1899-Jul. 4, 1902	Philippine Insurrection	Nov. 5, 1918-Nov. 2, 1920	Republican Resurgence
Sep. 6, 1899-Jan. 13, 1905	Hay's "Open Door Notes"	Jan. 18, 1919-Apr. 2, 1921	Treaty of Versailles
1900-1904	Suppression of Yellow Fever	Aug., 1919-May, 1920	Red Scare
1900-1925	Teletype Is Developed	Oct. 1, 1919	Black Sox Scandal
May 27, 1901	Insular Cases	Jan. 16, 1920-Dec. 5, 1933	Prohibition
Sep. 14, 1901	Theodore Roosevelt Becomes President	Feb. 14, 1920	League of Women Voters Is Founded
		Jul. 10, 1920-Sep., 1926	Meighen Era in Canada
May 12, 1902-Oct. 23, 1902	Anthracite Coal Strike	Aug. 20, 1920	Commercial Radio Broadcasting Begins
Jun. 2, 1902-May 31, 1913	Expansion of Direct Democracy		
Jan. 5, 1903	*Lone Wolf v. Hitchcock*	Aug. 26, 1920	U.S. Women Gain the Vote
May 22, 1903	Platt Amendment	1921-1923	Scandals of the Harding Administration
Nov. 18, 1903	Acquisition of the Panama Canal Zone		
Dec. 17, 1903	Wright Brothers' First Flight	1921-1948	King Era in Canada
Jun. 27, 1905	Industrial Workers of the World Is Founded	Nov. 12, 1921-Feb. 6, 1922	Washington Disarmament Conference
		Nov. 23, 1921-Jun. 30, 1929	Sheppard-Towner Act
Jul. 11, 1905	Niagara Movement	Sep. 22, 1922	Cable Act
Apr. 18, 1906	San Francisco Earthquake	Nov. 13, 1922	*Ozawa v. United States*
Jun. 30, 1906	Pure Food and Drug Act	Dec. 10, 1923	Proposal of the Equal Rights Amendment
Mar. 14, 1907	Gentlemen's Agreement		
Feb. 24, 1908	*Muller v. Oregon*	Jun. 2, 1924	Indian Citizenship Act

C

Date	Event	Date	Event
Jul. 1, 1924	Immigration Act of 1924	1941-1945	6.6 Million Women Enter the U.S. Labor Force
Sep. 1, 1924	Dawes Plan		
Oct. 21, 1924	Halibut Treaty	Mar. 11, 1941	Lend-Lease Act
Nov. 4, 1924	Coolidge Is Elected President	Jun. 25, 1941	Executive Order 8802
Jul. 10, 1925-1927	Scopes Trial	Dec. 7, 1941	Bombing of Pearl Harbor
Mar. 16, 1926	Launching of the First Liquid-Fueled Rocket	Dec. 11, 1941	Germany and Italy Declare War on the United States
May 20, 1927	Lindbergh's Transatlantic Flight	Feb. 19, 1942-1945	Censorship and Japanese Internment
Aug. 23, 1927	Sacco and Vanzetti Are Executed	Jun., 1942	Congress of Racial Equality Is Founded
1928	Smith-Hoover Campaign		
Aug. 27, 1928	Kellogg-Briand Pact	Jun. 3, 1942-Jun. 5, 1942	Battle of Midway
Feb. 17, 1929	League of United Latin American Citizens Is Founded	Jun. 17, 1942-Jul. 16, 1945	Manhattan Project
		Aug. 7, 1942-Feb. 9, 1943	Battle of Guadalcanal
Oct. 29, 1929	Stock Market Crash	Sep. 29, 1942-1964	Bracero Program
Oct. 29, 1929-1939	Great Depression	Nov. 7, 1942-Nov. 8, 1942	Invasion of North Africa
1930's	Mass Deportations of Mexicans	Apr. 8, 1943-Jun. 23, 1947	Inflation and Labor Unrest
Summer, 1930	Nation of Islam Is Founded	May, 1943-Aug., 1943	Urban Race Riots
Aug., 1930-1935	Bennett Era in Canada	Jul. 9, 1943-Sep. 19, 1943	Western Allies Invade Italy
Aug. 29, 1930	Japanese American Citizens League Is Founded	Dec. 17, 1943	Magnuson Act
		Apr. 3, 1944	*Smith v. Allwright*
Mar. 25, 1931-Jul., 1937	Scottsboro Trials	Jun. 6, 1944	Operation Overlord
May 1, 1931	Empire State Building Opens	Jun. 15, 1944	Superfortress Bombing of Japan
Dec. 11, 1931	Statute of Westminster	Jun. 22, 1944	G.I. Bill
Jan. 7, 1932	Hoover-Stimson Doctrine	Oct. 23, 1944-Oct. 26, 1944	Battle for Leyte Gulf
Jan. 22, 1932	Reconstruction Finance Corporation Is Created	Dec. 16, 1944-Dec. 26, 1944	Battle of the Bulge
		Feb. 4, 1945-Feb. 11, 1945	Yalta Conference
Jul. 21, 1932-Aug. 21, 1932	Ottawa Agreements	Apr. 25, 1945-Jun. 26, 1945	United Nations Charter Convention
Jul. 28, 1932	Bonus March	May 8, 1945	V-E Day
Nov. 8, 1932	Franklin D. Roosevelt Is Elected President	Jul. 17, 1945-Aug. 2, 1945	Potsdam Conference
		Aug. 6 *and* 9, 1945	Atomic Bombing of Japan
Mar. 4, 1933-1945	Good Neighbor Policy	Dec. 28, 1945	War Brides Act
Mar. 9, 1933-Jun. 16, 1933	The Hundred Days	Feb. 20, 1946	Employment Act
May 18, 1933	Tennessee Valley Authority Is Established	Jan. 1, 1947	Canada's Citizenship Act
		Mar. 12, 1947	Truman Doctrine
Jun. 16, 1933	National Industrial Recovery Act	Jul. 26, 1947	National Security Act
1934-1945	Development of Radar	Dec. 23, 1947	Invention of the Transistor
Mar. 24, 1934	Tydings-McDuffie Act	Mar., 1948-May, 1948	Organization of American States Is Founded
Spring, 1934	The Dust Bowl		
Jun. 18, 1934	Indian Reorganization Act	Mar., 1948-May, 1949	Berlin Blockade
Apr. 8, 1935	Works Progress Administration Is Established	Nov. 2, 1948	Truman Is Elected President
		Nov. 15, 1948	St. Laurent Succeeds King
May 27, 1935	Black Monday	Apr. 4, 1949	North Atlantic Treaty
Jul. 5, 1935	National Labor Relations Act	Jun. 25, 1950-Jul. 27, 1953	Korean War
Aug. 14, 1935	Social Security Act	Oct. 14, 1950-Apr. 11, 1951	Truman-MacArthur Confrontation
Aug. 31, 1935-Nov. 4, 1939	Neutrality Acts	Mar. 21, 1951-Dec., 1954	McCarthy Hearings
Nov. 10, 1935	Congress of Industrial Organizations Is Founded	1952-1956	Development of a Polio Vaccine
		Feb. 28, 1952	Massey Becomes Canada's First Native-Born Governor General
Nov. 11, 1936	Reciprocity Treaty		
Jan. 6, 1937	Embargo on Arms to Spain	Jun. 30, 1952	McCarran-Walter Act
Feb. 5, 1937-Jul. 22, 1937	Supreme Court Packing Fight	Jul. 25, 1952	Puerto Rico Becomes a Commonwealth
Jun., 1938	HUAC Investigations		
Jun. 25, 1938	Fair Labor Standards Act	Nov. 1, 1952	Hydrogen Bomb Is Detonated
Oct. 22, 1938	First Xerographic Photocopy	Nov. 4, 1952	Eisenhower Is Elected President
Apr. 30, 1939	Debut of Commercial Television	Aug. 1, 1953	Termination Resolution
Aug., 1939	Mobilization for World War II	Aug. 7, 1953	Refugee Relief Act
Jun. 14, 1940	United States Builds a Two-Ocean Navy	May 17, 1954	*Brown v. Board of Education*
		Jun. 10, 1954-Jul. 15, 1954	Operation Wetback
Aug. 16, 1940	Ogdensburg Agreement	Jan. 29, 1955	Formosa Resolution
		Dec. 5, 1955	AFL and CIO Merge

Date	Event	Date	Event
Nov. 19, 1985-Nov. 21, 1985	U.S.-Soviet Summit	Jun. 24, 1992	Tailhook Scandal
Jan. 28, 1986	*Challenger* Accident	Oct. 26, 1992	Defeat of the Charlottetown Accord
Nov. 6, 1986	Immigration Reform and Control Act	Nov. 3, 1992	Clinton Is Elected President
Nov. 13, 1986-May 4, 1988	Iran-Contra Scandal	Dec. 9, 1992-Mar. 31, 1994	U.S. Marines Intervene in Somalia
Jun., 1987	Canada's Pay Equity Act	Jan. 3, 1993	Start II Is Signed
Dec. 8, 1987	INF Treaty Is Signed	Feb. 5, 1993	Family and Medical Leave Act
Mar. 22, 1988	Civil Rights Restoration Act	Feb. 26, 1993	World Trade Center Bombing
Oct. 13, 1988	Family Support Act	Apr. 19, 1993	Branch Davidians' Compound Burns
Oct. 17, 1988	Indian Gaming Regulatory Act	Jun. 13, 1993	Campbell Becomes Canada's First Woman Prime Minister
Nov. 8, 1988	Bush Is Elected President		
Mar. 24, 1989	*Exxon Valdez* Oil Spill	Nov. 20, 1993	North American Free Trade Agreement
Apr. 13, 1989	Lincoln Savings and Loan Declares Bankruptcy	Dec. 2, 1993-Dec. 13, 1993	Astronauts Repair the Hubble Space Telescope
Oct. 1, 1989	Human Genome Project Begins	Mar. 1, 1994	Brady Handgun Violence Protection Act
Jun. 22, 1990	Meech Lake Accord Dies		
Jul. 25, 1990	Bloc Québécois Forms	Oct. 21, 1994	U.S.-North Korea Pact
Jul. 26, 1990	Americans with Disabilities Act	Nov. 8, 1994	Republicans Return to Congress
Jan. 17, 1991-Feb. 28, 1991	Persian Gulf War	Dec. 1, 1994	General Agreement on Tariffs and Trade
Sep. 27, 1991	Bush Announces Nuclear Arms Reductions	Apr. 19, 1995	Oklahoma City Federal Building Is Bombed
Nov. 7, 1991	Civil Rights Act of 1991		
Apr. 29, 1992-May 1, 1992	Los Angeles Riots	Jul. 11, 1995	United States Recognizes Vietnam
May 1, 1992	Asian Pacific American Labor Alliance Is Founded	1990's	Rise of the Internet

PERSONAGES INDEX

INDEX